THE ORGANIZATIONAL BEHAVIOR READER

5th Edition

THE ORGANIZATIONAL BEHAVIOR READER

Edited by

David A. Kolb
Case Western Reserve University

Irwin M. Rubin
Temenos, Inc.

Joyce S. Osland
*Instituto Centroamericano
de Administracion de Empresas*

PRENTICE-HALL INTERNATIONAL, INC.

This edition may be sold only in those countries to which
it is consigned by Prentice-Hall International. It is not to
be re-exported and it is not for sale in the U.S.A., Mexico,
or Canada.

 © 1991, 1984, 1979, 1974, 1971 by Prentice-Hall, Inc.
A Division of Simon & Schuster
Englewood Cliffs, New Jersey 07632

Printed in the United States of America

10 9 8 7 6 5 4 3

ISBN 0-13-639980-0

Prentice-Hall of Australia Pty. Limited, *Sydney*
Prentice-Hall Canada Inc., *Toronto*
Prentice-Hall Hispanoamericana, S.A., *Mexico*
Prentice-Hall of India Private Limited, *New Delhi*
Prentice-Hall of Japan, Inc., *Tokyo*
Simon & Schuster Asia Pte. Ltd., *Singapore*
Editora Prentice-Hall do Brasil, Ltda., *Rio de Janeiro*
Prentice-Hall, Inc., *Englewood Cliffs, New Jersey*

Contents

10

Managing
Multi-Group Work   304

11

Managing Diversity   340

PART III: LEADERSHIP AND MANAGEMENT

12

Leadership
and Organizational Culture   369

13

Leadership
and Decision Making   405

Preface

This book is intended as a source of primary material in organizational behavior for the student of management at all three levels—undergraduate, graduate, and in-service. There are represented here the works of scholars and practitioners who have contributed to our understanding of human behavior on the individual, group, and organizational level. In this revised edition we have attempted to portray a balanced view of the field of organizational behavior including basic ideas and concepts, new approaches developed in current research, and emerging perspectives that suggest the future shape of the field.

The articles in this volume fall into one or more of the following categories: (1) classic articles which, though written years ago, are still the best representative of their genre; (2) lucid overviews of the theories about a particular subject matter; (3) descriptions of recently developed theories; and (4) practical guides for managers.

We have tried throughout the volume to provide a balance of research reports and theoretical essays that were readable enough to be understood by the beginning student and at the same time sufficiently weighty to be of help to the active manager who wants an overview of the field. Based on feedback from our students and from colleagues who have used the book, this volume is considerably different from previous editions. Our colleagues, graduates, and doctoral students in the Department of Organizational Behavior at Case Western Reserve University have been particularly helpful in shaping this fifth edition of the book by sharing their views of our field and by their suggestions of readings. In particular we would like to thank Gail Ambuske, Barbara Bird, Gene Bocialetti, Richard Boyatzis, Pamela Johnson, Rebecca Jordan, Karen Locke, Michael Manning, Eric Neilsen, William Pasmore, Asbjorn Osland, Paul Sears, Michael Sokoloff, and Sue Taft for their contributions to this volume. Don McCormick of Antioch College West was especially generous with his suggestions and teaching expertise.

This book is designed to be used with the text/workbook *Organizational Behavior: An Experiential Approach to Organizational Behavior* by the same authors. The articles contained herein form a complete package with the exercises and theory contained in the workbook, allowing the student to go through all the phases of the experiential learning process.

Although designed as a companion volume, this collection of readings stands on its own and should be useful to teachers, managers, and consultants for the breadth of viewpoints and the wealth of data that it provides about the field of organizational behavior.

David A. Kolb
Irwin M. Rubin
Joyce S. Osland

1

The Psychological Contract and Organizational Socialization

THE IMPACT OF CHANGING VALUES ON ORGANIZATIONAL LIFE
Richard E. Boyatzis
Florence R. Skelly

THE PARADOX OF CORPORATE CULTURE:
RECONCILING OURSELVES TO SOCIALIZATION
Richard Pascale

ORGANIZATIONAL SOCIALIZATION AND THE PROFESSION OF MANAGEMENT
Edgar H. Schein

THE IMPACT OF CHANGING VALUES ON ORGANIZATIONAL LIFE[1]

Richard E. Boyatzis
Florence R. Skelly

Decisions as to which organizations to join and our willingness to stay are determined by our values. They will determine how much effort we exert once in a job. An individual's capability, or competencies, will have significant impact on his/her effectiveness in a job, but capability alone will not assure effectiveness. The person must want to be effective and choose to use his/her capability. The willingness to use one's capability can be called commitment. Our values will determine how much commitment we feel toward an organization, or the products and services we offer. Values also affect relationships among people working in an organization. People who grew up in different eras or cultures often must work together and depend on each other. Their differing values, or beliefs on the importance of work, loyalty, entitlements, responsibilities, winning, and life are fertile ground for sowing the seeds of dissension and conflict, as well as those of identity and cooperation.

The compatibility we see between our values and those inherent in the culture of the organization in which we work is the basis for a social or psychological

[1]The authors wish to thank Arthur White and Daniel Yankelovich for their insights, support, and contribution to the research over the years.

contract with the organization. As with a legal contract, our psychological contract with the organization lists what we expect to give and what we expect to get from the organization. It reflects our beliefs, or assumptions, about work and life. Imbedded in the contract are limits to what we will do and descriptions of conditions that we view as fair, exciting and desirable, as well as those we view as unfair, boring, and unpleasant. This contract is seldom written and often not even discussed, but it carries far more than the power of law, it carries the power of our commitment.

The culture of an organization in which we work, as well as the larger societal context within which our organization exists create a climate, or context, for our individual values. This social context will affect development and changes in our personal values. The context may be supportive and encouraging, or hostile and frustrating, or irrelevant and apathetic. Emerson, in his essay *Art* (cf. Schlesinger, 1986) said, "No man can quite emancipate himself from his own age and country, or produce a model in which the education, the religion, the politics, usages, and arts of his time shall have no share."

To explore aspects of our organizational context and the psychological contract, we must first examine the larger societal context in which most of us have grown and entered the workforce. In this paper, current trends will be discussed in light of past values of the workforce of the United States. The excitement, synergy, and conflict that may result from people with diverse values working in the same organization will be discussed.

EMERGING VALUES IN THE UNITED STATES

To understand the values presently expressed in the workforce and the emerging trends, an historical context of the past forty years is important. The following description of the values of the American people are based upon annual, national surveys conducted within the United States over the past thirty years, surveys conducted within numerous organizations,[2] and historical documents. The values of the American people can be described in terms of themes. The dominant values cannot be presumed to reflect every individual but these themes do describe the sentiment of the larger segments, if not the majority of the population.

The Late 1940's to the Early 1960's

As the United States emerged from World War II, the national agenda became the pursuit of economic growth. Government, business, and the public all subscribed to it. Stimulated by government funding of technology and industrial expansion during the war, business moved to continue this expansion.

Upward mobility was the dominant goal in life during this period. It was measured by the acquisition of material possessions. Business provided a wide array

[2]The authors wish to acknowledge the work and contributions of their colleagues at the Daniel Yankelovich Group, Inc., what was then called Yankelovich, Skelly & White, Inc., and McBer and Company, Inc.

2

of new consumer goods, as well as providing well-paying jobs in technology and industry. The government supported growth through housing subsidies to veterans. The resulting expansion of the construction and housing industries provoked growth in the appliance industry and other derivative industries (such as the automotive industry) and development of small businesses in the suburbs. The government supported massive increases in education through the GI Bill. Thus, the government was the initial funding agent of this expansion in many ways.

In the 1950's, the social climate exemplified a commitment to the American dream, realizable by such traditional American values as hard work, sacrifice and allegiance to family. Dedicated to upward mobility—into the middle class—Americans were preoccupied with home ownership, acquisition of cars and other major possessions which signaled middle-class status. Success in achieving this goal was seen to depend on a series of self-denials that are central to the Puritan tradition: stifle one's expressive desires in favor of conformity; deny oneself pleasure in favor of duty and work; deny the present in favor of the future; deny the self in favor of others. This credo of self-denial created a tight social structure which was unidimensional in terms of what the good life and success were all about: a good job with a future, enough money to educate the children and to buy the requisite material possessions for the newly-owned homes. Children flourished in abundance: the 1950's were the heart of the baby boom about which so much has been written. Regardless of one's personal views of husband and wife roles (i.e., in 1950's terms, the man as breadwinner and the woman as superwife, mother and housekeeper), commitment to family and to traditional family roles was seen as a precondition for success.

The mix worked. By the end of the 1950's, the United States had achieved worldwide economic leadership in technology, business theory, and industrial capability. About 70% of the populace formed a true middle class, the largest in the history of the world. This group owned homes, cars, and other trappings of material well-being. The era marked the birth of rock and roll. Many films were musicals. Heroes were military or industrial leaders. The concept of unlimited economic growth was accepted by the public, the government, and business alike. There was a widespread belief that the American dream would never die.

By the end of the 1950's we also were shifting to a "psychology of affluence," the belief that our economic struggles were over and that middle-class status or better was achievable by all. It was in the context of the psychology of affluence that the vast changes in values during the 1960's and 1970's flourished.

The Mid-1960's to Late 1970's

The next era occurred as the national agenda shifted from an economic one to a social agenda, under the psychology of affluence. A major thrust developed to correct the adverse affects of technology and industrialization. The positive contributions of these elements were recognized, but now the negative aspects were of interest and concern. Efforts to clean up and protect the environment (e.g., air, water, waste disposal, land use, etc.) became driving concerns, as well as the focus on the dehumanizing effects of industrial work on people. Worker happiness emerged as an important issue while productivity was more or less assumed. The public began to assert its moral heritage in a new way; a fix-it agenda developed.

Assuming affluence, society moved to expand the middle class and improve the quality of the middle class lifestyle. Target groups were identified for catch-up efforts: minorities, the handicapped, and the elderly. Improvements in education and medical care were sought not only for the target groups, but for everyone.

As part of this egalitarian movement, there was an increasing sense that business was to blame for the inequities. Pressure was applied to make business more accountable to the people. At the same time, corporate ownership was spread over a greater number of stockholders, moving the basic nature of corporate ownership away from family ownership to "public" ownership. Conglomerates emerged as vehicles to stabilize growth in earnings per share and cash flow. This introduced the era of professional management. It also introduced the ultimate power of Wall Street in determining the criteria and assessing the performance of corporations, thereby replacing the customer. Assessments based on financial measures superseded assessments based on product quality or innovation.

A growing concern about the rigidity of values earlier embraced as part of the Protestant Ethic appeared first among up-scale youth, then other youth, then the older wealthy, and eventually the less well-off. The goal became self-fulfillment. Pale versions of hedonism emerged as people searched for the full, rich, high-quality life. The focus on the self replaced the focus on self-denial. People were asked to "turn on and tune out." Flower power and Woodstock were associated with a shift in music. Even the Beatles' music, which coincided with the beginning of the era, started by asking the eternal questions, "Does she love you?" and through the decade changed to describing the ethereal pleasures of being in "Strawberry fields forever."

Pluralism and introspection replaced conformity. The "me" was placed above concern for social units and the future. A sense of entitlements spread quickly. The introspection industry of psychotherapy and personal growth experiences grew from a few hundred million a year to over two billion dollars a year by the middle of this era. Consumer preferences turned to things that were "cold, white, and lite," as seen in the shift from scotch and bourbon to gin and vodka, butter to margarine, beef to chicken, from fullbodied to light beer, and "chilled" anything. The women's movement originally drew its momentum from this agenda. Self-fulfillment and the new focus of self-realization became a driving force for the women's movement of the 1960's and 1970's. It began with upper middle class women who did not want to be constrained by the sex role distinctions of the earlier eras. They found an ideological justification (i.e., egalitarianism) for this quest and the society moved toward blurring of the sexes. The redefinition of the family to include "people living together" by the National Association of Home Economists was further reflection of the changing roles of husband and wife.

New non-institutional elements of the public became the cutting edge in setting the social agenda (i.e., Ralph Nader et al). Their mission was, in their eyes, to identify problems for fixing and to find the warts, not to work out solutions. The methods were assumptive, moralistic, loud, and theatrical. Business became the villain. Government became the major actor, assuming such roles as watch dog and implementor of programs in addition to its funding role via such legislation and agencies as the Occupational Safety and Health Act, Equal Employment Opportunity Commission, Clean Air Act, Coastal Zone Management Act of 1972, Noise Control Act, Federal Insecticide, Fungicide and Rodenticide Act.

The heroes had become anti-heroes, like television's Jim Rockford and Lieutenant Columbo.

Although business and government were no longer as united as they had been in the 1950's, there was still a spirit of optimism and confidence. The activists believed that if we could identify the problems, we as a society had the means to correct them.

The second half of the era of the social, fix-it agenda had a different mood. The remarkable economic success of Japan was a rebuke to American industry, especially in autos and consumer electronics. Now accused of short-sightedness and inadequate commitment to research and development, American business was blamed for a faltering US role in world trade. The OPEC nations made the dependence on foreign powers evident and threatened many assumed aspects of our lives, such as our beliefs that personal automobiles, driving, and use of unlimited amounts of electrical energy were our birthright.

The restoration of the environment had met with some, but only limited, success. The costs were staggering. Inequity still existed. The Great Society did not end poverty, and evidence of racial discrimination persisted. The national debt rose and inflation increased to what were then considered alarming rates. There was a decline in savings and an increase in consumption, fed through the increased use of credit instruments and easier availability of credit cards.

The search for self-fulfillment proved frustrating for many who discovered that the path to happiness still remained hidden. Crime was increasing, as was child abuse, divorce, pornography and such. Many felt these were manifestations of self-expressionism gone too far. Popular music took a demonic shift with groups like the Doors. Science fiction and horror films had changed from non-human, amorphous entities as earlier villains in *The Blob* or plants in *The Day of the Triffids* to decidedly human and violent villains in *Texas Chainsaw Massacre*. In context of the observation that the mood of the country is reflected in the ups and downs of skirt length, further evidence of the depressing mood was the increasing popularity of the maxi-skirt.

New theories of management emerged as popular with an anti-authority tenor, with bottoms-up planning and organizational climate sessions. Communications efforts were seen as a panacea. There was a decrease in personal commitment to organizations and an alarming decrease in respect for managers. Professionalism, and loyalty to one's field, discipline, profession, or self replaced loyalty to the organization. Job hopping became a desirable activity and a sign of being on the "fast track" rather than its earlier interpretation as being a sign of instability or a character flaw.

If the first half of the era (i.e., the mid 1960's to mid 1970's) of the social, fix-it agenda grew out of a reaction to the narrowness of the social outlook under a flowering economy of the 1950's, the second half of the era (i.e., the mid to late 1970's) was a reaction to the breadth and diversity of social commitments in a constricted economy. We had lost the war on poverty declared in the Great Society of President Johnson. We had lost the war in Vietnam. We had lost the war on inflation (remember the Whip Inflation Now program of President Ford). We had lost our trust and respect for the Presidency (i.e., under President Nixon), and the very government that we had viewed as our protector (e.g., President Carter's inability to release Americans in Iran). Fear, followed by disbelief, followed by anger were the reactions to the realities of the late 1970's and our entry into the 1980's. We were treated to the humiliation of America every night on television news and in newspapers and magazines. We were held hostage in Iran, at the gas pump, and in the global marketplace.

The 1980's

The reaction to the anger and sense of growing helplessness of the late 1970's with its increasing complexity resulted in the emergence of a new agenda of "competitive pragmatism." People wanted to win and, in the context of limited opportunities, the mood shifted to a feeling that, "I want mine." There was an acceptance of limits and the notion that we cannot do, be, or have everything. Therefore, the majority of people wanted to be strategic, get competitive, and win. If pragmatism can be considered an American contribution to the field of philosophy, then this agenda of competitive pragmatism can be seen as a practical perspective rather than an ideological one. It was neither the Protestant Ethic of self-denial nor the social, fix-it agenda. People built blended personal agendas, balancing family, financial progress, occupational success, and personal health.

The strategic will to win transcended individuals and emerged in corporations in forms of strategic consolidation, divestments, and a return to the core business. As Peters and Waterman (1982) said, "stick to your knitting." Cost-effectiveness became a god to be worshipped. The reduction of overhead and elimination of costs, especially people that were now being considered "unnecessary," resulted in substantial dislocations of the workforce.

At the same time, within many organizations, competitive pragmatism was converted by individuals into a desire for meritocracy, characterized by compensation and reward systems based on performance rather than longevity or egalitarianism. Organizations were restructured to increase speed and flexibility in decision making. Hierarchies were flattened, and bureaucratic, functional forms of organization structure gave way to decentralization and smaller, strategic business units.

If corporate America could not respond, people were willing to by-pass large organizations that had previously symbolized growth, success, and stability (Kinkead, 1988). Temporary work has become an accepted activity (*Wall Street Journal*, 1987). Entrepreneurship and the excitement of small business was reborn in a workforce that, on the whole, did not remember such earlier eras in America. Even social activists embraced competitive pragmatism and shifted their tactics to taking actions that would result in some accomplishment, even if smaller than desired, instead of taking moralistic stands reminiscent of the 1960's and 1970's.

In the marketplace, consumers became "smart" and turned to quality in an effort to maximize their personal price/performance curve. Self-directed investment vehicles took hold with the by-pass of investment houses and the increase in discount brokerage houses which enabled people to do their own research and make their own investment decisions. Even in pension programs, the IRA, Keough, and 401K became important aspects of a person taking care of himself/herself rather than depending on Social Security and company or union pension programs. As people accepted the necessity of making "trade-offs" and being strategic about things that matter the most, health and physical fitness became a preoccupation. Consciousness about our bodies, the delicate interdependence of our internal physical systems, the effect of nutrition and exercise combined with advances in medical technology and skyrocketing costs to make health a strategic issue. The only way to "beat" increasing costs of health care was to take steps now to prevent illness or anticipate future potential problems.

With competitive pragmatism and the strategic will to win came an increased importance of pride in performance and identification with winning social entities. This emerged as another theme, the importance of belonging to an identifiable group or organization that reflects values in which we believe. If we were to be strategic and competitive and "cheering" for our team, which team was it? We were and are searching for a social context. The marriage to divorce ratio reversed for the first time in many years, reflecting a new popularity of marriage as a desirable form of relationship. Church and temple membership increased. The number of professional, occupational, civic, or interest/hobby centered clubs, associations, and organizations expanded.

In the corporate world, people asked for vision. They wanted their leaders to describe and explain what the organization "stood for" and what beliefs we share. Corporate philosophy statements began appearing in annual reports and image advertisements, while previously they were, if at all, relegated to wall posters inside of organizations or employee newsletters. This theme was occasionally misinterpreted as a hunger for ideology rather than what appeared to be more a case of the search for identity and social context.

At a community level, the development of self-help groups appeared to aid in stemming the increase in crime (i.e., Crime Watch groups), reducing costs (i.e., food buying cooperatives), and volunteerism in helping to clean up neighborhoods, parks, and support community institutions. Even in architecture, what has been called neo-traditional community design appeared to catch public attention (i.e., communities like Seaside in Florida in which the layout of the town incorporates public space for people to congregate and other similar features).

The revival of the importance of the nuclear family is another manifestation of this theme that appeared in the mid 1980's (Miller, 1987). The most popular television shows were family situation shows, like *The Cosby Show* and *Family Ties*. Women who had moved into the labor force eagerly in the 1960's and 1970's began to rethink their roles as superwomen, capable of both a job and the major responsibility for running the home. While not economically able to leave the labor force, many began to think of part time work or of entrepreneurial ventures which they could manage out of their own homes, thereby controlling their hours.

Regional parochialism and nationalism became apparent early in the 1980's as economic, political, and social forces and technology were making the world "smaller" and removing perceived boundaries. This blending of institutional, regional, and national boundaries may have contributed to the speed and strength of this theme. The desire to identify with a relatively local entity (i.e., become increasingly parochial) may be a reaction to greater globalization. If I am increasingly a part of everything, how do I sustain a sense of my identity and difference and uniqueness? Events like the 1984 Olympics and the invasion of Grenada became strong symbols of our success and pride far beyond the impact of similar events in earlier eras. The power of state governments has increased steadily during this era.

Even companies have been demanding cultural compatibility in the services or goods they purchase. For example, parts manufacturers and consultants are asked to provide "customized" rather than generic, off-the-shelf products or services.

Another theme began to emerge in the mid-1980's which is not as clearly tied to competitive pragmatism nor the desire to belong to something in which you can believe; it is the increased importance of formalism and style. There has been an increase in formal weddings, showers, and related events, with the corresponding increase in bridal registrations and purchases of china, crystal, and formal silverware. The "power shower" as an extravagent event is in store for parents to be (*Wall Street Journal*, 1988). Etiquette is again seen as important. At first for young women, then for young men and older people, and now as a practice in corporate America, people are attending etiquette schools and training programs. It is possible that this theme is a manner of distinguishing a person from others, and in that way manifesting a competitive edge in the social arena. That is, "I will use style and form as a way of showing that I am a winner."

The links to the strategic will to win and articulation of belonging to a group that has certain beliefs may be clearer in what appears to be the more recent version of this theme, the growing sense of morality in the United States. The number of embarrassments, scandals, and exposés indicate an increase in moralistic fervor. The Wall Street insider traders were "bad," a number of television evangelists have been exposed as "bad," individuals working in or for the White House have been prosecuted as having been "bad," and of course there is the condemnation of sexual deviations from the norm which is evident in the fear of and reaction to AIDS. If this is a form of "moral" strategic will to win, or moral competitive pragmatism, then we can expect more of it in the years to come.

The era, whose reflective value themes began to appear in the late 1970's but did not attain wide-spread recognition until the early 1980's, can be described as having competitive pragmatism as its agenda. In reaction to the excesses attributed to the self-fulfillment orientation and the relative failures and extreme costs of the social, fix-it agenda, the agenda of the 1980's seems to be a desire to "be smart so I can get my share within a context of limitations." This agenda appears to be shared by the public, business, and government. Because of the very nature of the agenda itself, conflicts emerge. There is all too often an assumption of zero-sum (i.e., "I win, you lose" or "You win, I lose"), and therefore, attempts to be strategically competitive will result in conflicts.

ALTERNATING CYCLES AND THE FUTURE

The approximate fifteen year duration of these eras is supported by the observations and theory of Arthur M. Schlesinger, Jr., in his book, *The Cycles of American History* (1986), in which he reported that he and his father hypothesized that the cycles of intent, or what is called value orientation in this article, appeared to be twelve to sixteen years in duration.

Philosophical Roots

Schlesinger (1986) described the duality of the American tradition as a continual alternating cycle between envisioning our intent as an experiment or destiny. The sense of America being an experiment is rooted in the Calvinist ethos of Providential History. He explained that this belief contends that all secular communities are finite and problematic, therefore they flourish and decay. The "experiment" is a test against the hypothesis of inevitable decay.

From George Washington to Abraham Lincoln, the experiment has been repeatedly proposed. In his first Inaugural Address, President Washington commented on the American opportunity, "The preservation of the sacred fire of liberty and the destiny of the republican model of government are justly considered, perhaps, as deeply, as finally, staked on the experiment intrusted to the hands of the American people." Lincoln, in his first message to Congress asked whether all republics had an inherent and fatal weakness. At Gettysburg, Lincoln asked whether any nation "conceived in liberty and dedicated to the proposition that all men are created equal can long endure?"

According to Schlesinger (1986), the sense of America having a destiny is rooted in the Calvinist ethos via Augustine and the concept of redemptive history. That is, all people were close to God but some were closer. The purpose of life is for the journey of the elect to salvation and beyond the limits of our history. John Winthrop had said to the first New Englanders that they were "as a city upon a hill, with all eyes upon them." With a sacred mission and a sanctified destiny for people yearning to be free, it is not surprising that Americans periodically feel like The Chosen, or at least the recently chosen in the sight of God.

The Duality

The alternation between experiment and destiny, Schlesinger (1986) wrote, is also reflected in alternating cycles of (1) self-critical realism, with its focus on things that need to be changed and (2) ideal-oriented messianism, with its focus on "what might be." The pattern is also reflected in alternating concerns with social and political innovation or individual-rights oriented conservatism, and the alternative attempts to increase plurality and diversity or contain it. He described this as cycles of public purpose and private interest.

Each cycle, he contended, flows out of the conditions and contradictions of the last cycle. Each period of public purpose appeared to be ushered in with a detonating social or political issue. These cycles have remained relatively consistent in theme and duration since 1776 and the founding of the nation.

The first era described earlier in this article, the late 1940's to early 1960's, was a private interest oriented period focused on the economic agenda of growth through materialism. Although this interpretation of the dominant theme, agenda, and duration differs from Schlesinger's (1986) to some degree, the description of this era as a *private interest* oriented period is consistent. The following social, fix-it agenda of the mid 1960's through the late 1970's appeared to be a *public purpose* oriented period in which the attempts were made to experiment with changes in most aspects of life. Following the cycles, the competitive pragmatism agenda of the 1980's appears to be a *private interest* oriented agenda that draws energy from the desire to be fulfilling our destiny.

The duration of the cycles would suggest that this era will not end until the early 1990's. Indications of a shift are beginning to appear: a 1988 survey showed an increase in the number of people who see a positive role for government in our lives. Although the issues that might form the detonating issues for the next cycle are probably present, the periodicity of the cycles suggests that their potency is yet to be realized, at least to the extent that they can shift into the next cycle of the public purpose oriented experiment.

Dominant Values of Each Generation

The dominant values of each generation of Americans appear to be closely related to the agenda and themes of the era in which they grew up. Schlesinger (1986) believed that the thirty year cycle for return to a similar type of dominant concern (i.e., public purpose or private interest) had a relationship to the number of years it takes for people to grow up, enter the workforce, achieve voting age and political consciousness to vote, and to reach positions of power in organizations from which to launch efforts consistent with the personal orientation of the individual. Of course, such generalizations should only be considered when describing and considering behaviors and beliefs of large groups of people. Each person may have their own variations, and certainly entire groups of people will share beliefs and behaviors that are not consistent with nor similar to the majority nor the "dominant trends."

THE IMPACT ON ORGANIZATIONAL LIFE

There appear to be three basic ways in which these value trends have an impact on life in organizations. First, the values a person holds influence his/her desire to join and stay with a particular organization. Second, once in the organization, the degree of value compatibility affects a person's use of discretionary effort, and therefore, determines the extent to which the person uses his/her capability or competencies. Third, since people appear to hold the beliefs consistent with the era in which they grew up (especially through adolescence), there will be inevitable conflicts as managers, subordinates, and colleagues find themselves interacting but having substantially different values about the nature of work and life. These can be considered conflicts among various cultures (i.e., correctly stated it would be sub-cultures) or generation gaps.

Joining and Staying

There are many factors that influence how a person chooses an organization for which to work. During times of high unemployment and for those people in society having a difficult time finding jobs, the more availability or offer of compensated work may be enough to justify joining an organization. For many, the reasons get complicated as the person's sense of efficacy increases. Whether as a result of increasing education, skill development, or higher expectations about the meaning of work, people appear more interested than before in what the organization stands for and aspects of its culture, climate, and values (Kiechel, 1988). This expectation is a result of the value theme of "belonging through believing," of looking for a social, organizational context.

In a study of what members of the workforce viewed as the most important qualities of a job, Yankelovich and Immerwahr (1983) found that 88% felt that "working with people who treat me with respect" and 87% felt that "interesting work" were very important. In addition, 83–84% of the respondents felt that "recognition for good work," "chance to develop skills, abilities, and creativity," "working for people who listen if you have ideas about how to do things," and "having a chance to think for myself rather than just carry out instructions" all rated significantly higher than concerns about job security or financial incentives (i.e., 68% and 64%, respectively). The point is that an increasing number of people feel that they have some choice in what organization to join (or they have the expectation that they should have such a choice) and that the factors influencing the choice are linked to complex forces emphasizing value compatibility more than in previous periods.

People may need more of a sense of belonging to their work organization than previously as a result of certain demographic trends. For example, more Americans are living alone than ever before, a ninety percent increase since 1970 (*Time,* December 12, 1985, page 41). The percentage of one-person households reached 24% of all households in 1986. In part due to people staying single longer (i.e., postponing the age of marriage), increased longevity, increased widowhood and divorces, there is increased pressure on the workplace as a source of context and social meaning.

Some reaction to this trend is expected in living patterns. For example, elderly are sharing homes at an increasing rate rather than living alone. Although some of this is for purposes of safety and economic necessity, social contact and context is also a factor. Given that the number of 20–29 year old men has recently exceeded the number of 18–27 year old women (in 1985), a return to romance, courting, and monogamous concerns expressed through increased marriages is expected in the coming years (*NYT,* June 15, 1988).

The new women's dilemma, reflected in the conclusion that full time work and full time family responsibilities require more than is humanly possible, and the return to the nuclear family lead to new criteria for women in considering joining an organization. Possibilities for flexible work design and creation of meaningful part time work become central in choosing an organization with which to have a career. The organization's policies and practices regarding day care are also an issue to which the test of value compatibility is applied.

The importance of the values of the organization, which is really the values reflected in the culture and climate of the organization, also increases with the diversity of the workforce. With increased pluralism of the workforce, people will continue to find it difficult to assume compatibility with co-workers based on visible similarities. Therefore, people will be forced to look at ideas, values, and products and services.

As people seek to determine their compatibility with the organization, the consistency of an organization's value positions will be under increased scrutiny. Speeches by the CEO emphasizing ethics and conducting ethics training programs will be embarrassments if the newspapers reveal bribery, fraud, or kickback schemes in government contracts. Similarly, an organizational commitment to innovation will be studied to see if it reflects a belief in increased sales, or new markets, or R&D. Consistency will be used as an indication of the veracity of an organization's values.

A longer range problem for the American scene is revealed in the aging of the workforce. As the "baby-bust" generation enters and then dominates the workforce in the years ahead, there will be labor shortages, especially in jobs requiring advanced skills. There are already such shortages appearing in certain regions and specific job markets. As this occurs, organizations will be forced to attract people and compete for employees. The recruiting appeal will take many forms, but it can be expected that one consistent theme will be to "pitch" the values of the organization (i.e., its culture and climate) as a distinguishing feature—making it a better place to work than other organizations.

Giving Your All

Yankelovich (1981) contended that a person's commitment to the organization would be the key factor in determining how much discretionary effort the person used in those jobs that allowed a person to exercise discretion in how he/she performed and acted. In other words, commitment to the organization determined the degree to which a person would use his/her capabilities or competencies. A person's commitment to an organization was, in large part, a function of the degree of value compatibility between the person and the organization. In a survey of about 1,500 managers who were members of the American Management Association, Schmidt and Posner (1983) compared managers who shared their organization's values to a low, moderate, or high degree. They found that managers with highly shared values had: "greater feelings of personal success; stronger feelings of organizational commitment; clearer perspectives on ethical dilemmas; lower levels of work/home stress; better understanding of others' values; greater commitment to organizational goals; higher regard in general for other organizational stakeholders; and different perception of important personal qualities" (Schmidt and Posner, 1983, page 13). These findings are consistent with earlier studies on the consequences of increased commitment and the use of discretionary effort (Yankelovich, 1981; Yaneklovich and Immerwahr, 1983).

A startling and dramatic increase in perceived underutilization of the workforce emerged in the 1985 national survey, entitled *Signal,* by Yankelovich, Skelly, and White Inc. When asked if people could increase the quantity and quality of their job output if conditions were ideal in their organization, 79% and 73% said, "Yes," respectively. Fifty one percent (51%) said they could increase the quantity of their output by more than 20% if conditions were ideal in their organization. This represented a dramatic increase over the 32% answering the same question in the prior year. The perception of underutilization has been reported by other national surveys of the workforce in the mid-1980's by The Opinion Research Corporation and The Hay Group. People reported that they not only have the ability to do more but they even have an idea of how to go about doing it, but conditions in the organization did not induce, encourage, or stimulate them to give their maximum effort.

The values reflected in an organization's culture and climate are conveyed to employees in many ways. The rewards and incentives for performance are a major source of information about values. Given the current trend of competitive pragmatism manifested in the desire for increased meritocracy in organizations, it can be expected that an increasing proportion of today's workforce wants rewards and incentives related to performance, not longevity, equality, or need. Other ways values are conveyed to employees include the method and frequency of communication about the condition of the organization, the visibility and accessibility of top management, the organization structure, the physical condition, attractiveness, and comfort of the work setting, and so forth.

In addition to giving your all to the company (i.e., maximizing discretionary effort), value compatibility between the employees and the organization affects the degree to which people give their all to the product. The recent popularity of quality and customer service concepts are an indication that, as customers or managers, we all want people to give more of themselves to the product or service they offer. Attempts to engage a person's discretionary effort applied to product or service quality will involve similar activities as attempts to stimulate and maintain a person's commitment to the organization.

The competitive pragmatism agenda also appears to increase people's desire to work for those organizations that are "winning." There is a desire to feel proud of the organization. Pride in performance of the organization extends beyond the desire for a context (i.e., belonging through believing) to acknowledged signs of an organization's success.

Conflicting Cultures in the Workplace

If a person's dominant work ethic (i.e., his/her basic orientation to work and its place in life) is shaped during his/her childhood and adolescent years, then inevitable conflicts will arise in work organizations when people from different eras work with and for each other. Managers and leaders set the climate and sometimes the culture of an organization and manage the modifications. This may be explicit or implicit, but it occurs. So what happens when people who embraced or grew to believe in the competitive pragmatism agenda of the 1980s work for managers who embraced or grew to believe in the ethic of self-fulfillment and the social, fix-it agenda of the 1960's and early 1970's, or those who believe in the work ethic of self-denial and the economic growth agenda of the 1950's?

Considering the age distribution of the current workforce, three major value eras are represented. First, the 43–70 year olds who grew up during the era of the economic growth have the ethic of self-denial. They valued and may still value upward mobility. On the whole, they are non-introspective and have a respect for authority. The dominant belief is that people should work hard and have patience, "you will get your turn." This cadre of the workforce can be called prebaby-boomers. They value commitment to a company or organization, have relatively singular views of leadership, and expect obedience and loyalty as repayment for efforts on another's behalf.

Second, the 33–42 year olds grew with the ethic of self-fulfillment during the era of the social, fix-it agenda. They tend to be self-absorbed and do not respond to authority with any automatic respect. This cadre of the workforce has pluralistic models of how to "beat the system." They tend to be more people oriented than older managers and accept concepts like flextime as necessary to respond to varying needs of the workforce. They tend to have a more balanced view of their own life than older managers, including ideas like holistic health and compromising job demands and family demands. They can be called early baby-boomers.

Third, the 23–32 year olds grew with the ethic of self-fulfillment, but in the context of a constricting economy during the latter part of the social, fix-it agenda era. The disappointments and frustration of this era emerge in this group's desire to win. Actually, it appears to be almost an intense desire not to lose. They seek and have self-knowledge. They are cynical of authority, not team players, and willing to by-pass corporate America. This cadre can be called the late baby-boomers. Like the early baby-boomers, they are self- rather than other-oriented, competitive, pluralistic, and rejectors of authority. Unlike their slightly older colleagues, they want the romance of ideology in terms of belonging or identifying with an organization or groups through shared beliefs. This latter group appears willing to commit to a social or organizational context, if he/she feels it is a "winning" or successful organization.

A fourth cadre can be considered "in-process." They are currently in early college, high school, or junior high. They grew up in the era of the competitive pragmatism agenda. Their priorities will most likely be centered on strategic positioning, creating their personal blended agendas—but highly driven to "get their share."

The first source of conflict that appears among these cadres concerns the degree to which a person expects work to be fun and fulfilling versus a blend of obligation and challenge. In most organizations, the higher levels managers believe in the ethic of self-denial (especially in service of the organization's benefit). They have been in the organization longer and tend to have risen to higher levels. When these managers encounter people from the early boomer cadre, they see them as selfish, self-absorbed, and often ungrateful and immature. Meanwhile, the early boomer cadre look upon the pre-boomers as reactionary devotees of the status-quo who are attempting to exploit the people coming along because of archaic notions of paying one's dues and demanding loyalty to the organization.

An odd coalition may occur between the cadres of the workforce we are calling pre-boomers and the later boomers. Both are competitive and feel pressure to not lose. They appreciate the reality that life may not yield pleasant experiences nor fulfilling ones. Although emerging from different value trends, they both have the desire to win. That common agenda may result in a coalition. Of course, this delicate coalition is split apart when and if the organization does not succeed. The late boomer cadre will move out of the organization without looking back while the pre-boomers will stick with the organization through the tough times.

The cadre which appears to be caught in the most conflict are the older pre-boomers. If they have not reached their personal apogees, the path ahead is full of disappointment and battles. Hierarchies are flattened, middle management jobs eliminated, and the sources of authority and material symbols of success that this cadre has worked to attain are being deleted. If people in this position feel defensive and threatened, it is with good reason. The assumptions, based upon their values, with which they labored over the years are being invalidated. The psychological contract with which they joined and entered the organization is broken.

The early boomers appear to be seeking new vehicles for self-fulfillment. As careers have gone stale and organizational mobility is blocked by older managers, they have sought retraining and are returning to educational institutions for advanced degrees. The proliferation of Masters and Doctoral degree programs is, in part, an indication of the thirst of this cadre for continuing self-development.

As this group reaches financial maturity and attains positions of influence in organizations, they can be expected to become advocates for public purpose, social agendas. The projected political conservatism and resistance to change by corporate management will mutate into new forms. Differences in the comfort with and willingness to accept diversity and pluralism of each of these cadres of the workforce will predict future conflict. The conflicts can be expected to shift, sometime in the future, from differences based upon notions of authority or who is right and wrong to differences based upon pragmatic concepts of who can win, or make it, or succeed.

Before concluding this section of the article, several thoughts about individuals who are conspicuously variant from their cadre are necessary. Aspects of a person's ethnoreligious background and family can have a profound effect on shifting him/her into a different value era. For example, children of immigrants who come from ethnoreligious cultures valuing self-reliance and assuming God's blessing on those who succeed, may appear caught in a cusp between the ethic of self-denial and the current notions of competitive pragmatism. In a quite different way, a person may have found emotional and spiritual resonance with a reference group embracing a particular era's dominant values. Maintaining close ties with this reference group over the years, and possibly excluding alternate emergent value trends, may result in a person being "fixed in time." That is, the individual may dedicate himself/herself to a particular set of values with a missionary zeal. If this set of values were not a part of the dominant agenda of the era within which he/she grew up, then this person would appear considerably different from his/her cohort.

CONCLUDING COMMENT

Each of us will inevitably work with others who have different values, having emerged from our formative years with different assumptions about life and work, and a wide variety of expectations concerning desirable conditions in the workplace. Understanding, acceptance, and learning about the diversity is a crucial start. Each of us is both product and producer of our age and social context. To work effectively in organizations with others, the challenge is to be able to hold onto our own beliefs and not feel wimpy or noncommital while at the same time remaining open to the diversity and its possibilities.

REFERENCES

Kinkead, G., "The New Independents," *Fortune,* April 25, 1988, pages 66–80.
Kiechel, W. III, "Love, Don't Lose, The Newly Hired," *Fortune,* June 6, 1988, pages 271–274.
McCarthy, M. J., "On Their Own: In Increasing Numbers, White Collar Workers Leave Steady Positions," *Wall Street Journal,* Vol. 68, No. 25, October 13, 1987.
Miller, T.A.W. (ed.), *The Public Pulse.* New York: The Roper Organization, 1987.
New York Times, June 5, 1988.
Peters, T. J., Waterman, R. H. Jr., *In Search of Excellence: Lessons from America's Best Run Corporations.* New York: Harper & Row, 1982.
Schlesinger, A. M., Jr., *The Cycles of American History.* Boston: Houghton Mifflin, 1986.
Schmidt, W. H., Posner, B. Z., *Managerial Values in Perspective,* American Management Associations Survey Report, New York, 1983.
Time Magazine, December 12, 1985, page 41.
Wall Street Journal, April 28, 1988, page 1.
Wall Street Journal, September 2, 1986, page 27.
Yankelovich, D., Immerwahr, J., *Putting the Work Ethic Back to Work: A Public Agenda Report on Restoring America's Competitive Vitality,* the Public Agenda Foundation, New York, 1983.
Yankelovich, D., *New Rules: Searching for Self-Fulfillment in a World Turned Upside Down,* New York: Random House, 1981.

THE PARADOX OF "CORPORATE CULTURE": RECONCILING OURSELVES TO SOCIALIZATION

Richard Pascale

- An assistant controller at IBM is rehearsed for a stand-up presentation with flip charts—the principal means of formal communication. Each presentation gets

Source: © 1985 by the Regents of the University of California. Reprinted from the *California Management Review, Vol. 27, No. 2. By permission of The Regents.*

"probed"—IBM's secret weapon for training and assessing your professionals. A manager states: "You're so accustomed to being probed you're almost unaware of it. IBM bosses have an uncanny way of pushing, poking, having a follow-up question, always looking for the hidden ball. It's a rigorous kind of self-discipline we impose on ourselves for getting to the heart of problems. It's also management's way of assessing potential and grooming subordinates for the next job. Senior management spends most of its time 'probing.'"[1]

- An MBA joining Bain and Company, the management consulting firm is surprised by the incredible number of meetings he must attend—company meetings, recruiting meetings, officer meetings, office meetings, case team meetings, and near-mandatory participation on sports team and attendance at social events. The objective is to build cohesiveness participation, and close identification with the firm. There are a set of imperatives for working at Bain: "don't compete directly with peers," "make major conceptual contributions without being a prima donna," "demonstrate an ability to build on others' ideas." In aggregate, these features of Bain's culture are viewed as the underpinnings of success—both internally and with clients.[2]

- An applicant for an entry-level position in brand management at Procter and Gamble experiences an exhaustive application and screening process. His or her interviewer is one of an elite cadre who have been selected and trained extensively via lectures, video tapes, films, practice interviews, and role plays. P&G regards this as a crucial task: it predestines the creative and managerial resources on which the institutes' future depends. The applicant is interviewed in depth for such qualities as his or her ability to "turn out high volumes of excellent work," "identify and understand problems," and "reach thoroughly substantiated and well reasoned conclusions that lead to action." The applicant receives two interviews and a general knowledge test, before being flown back to Cincinnati for three more one-on-one interviews and a group interview at lunch. Each encounter seeks corroborating evidence of the traits which P&G believes correlate highly with "what counts" for institutional excellence. Notwithstanding the intensity of this screening process, the recruiting team strives diligently to avoid overselling P&G, revealing both its plusses and minuses. P&G actually *facilitates* an applicant's de-selection, believing that no one knows better than the candidate whether the organization meshes with his or her own objectives and values.[3]

- Morgan Guaranty, a bank so profitable and well run that most other bankers use it as a model, competes fiercely for bright and aggressive talent. Once recruited, an extraordinary amount of institutional energy is invested into molding these strong and talented individuals into the Morgan "collegial" style. All employees go through a one year training program that tests their intellect, endurance, and that *requires teamwork* as an essential factor of survival. Constant evaluation assesses interpersonal skills as well as analytical abilities. "The spirit of camaraderie and togetherness" is an explicit objective of entry level indoctrination. Once on the job, frequent rotations provide cross-training and necessitate building an ever-growing network of relationships. Performance evaluations are based not solely upon one's own boss's opinion but upon inputs from every major department with which one interacts. One learns quickly that to succeed one must succeed through the team. Overt political battles are taboo and conflict is resolved directly but never disagreeably. States one officer: "The Morgan traits provide a basic grammar of understanding that enables divergent elements of our organization to speak a common language."[4]

The common thread of these examples is the systematic means by which firms bring new members into their culture. The technical term is "socializaiton." It encompasses the process of being made a member of a group, learning the ropes, and being taught how one must communicate and interact to get things done. Mention the term "socialization" and a variety of unsavory images come to mind. Some equate it to the teaching of socialism—an incorrect interpretation—but even when correctly understood as the imposition of social conformity, the concept makes most of us cringe. Americans, dedicated by constitution and conviction to the full expression of individuality, regard "socialization" as alien and vaguely sinister. This taboo causes us to undermanage the forces for cohesion in organizations.

The debate between "individuality" and "socialization," like politics or religion, evokes a strong emotional response. Due perhaps to our hypersensitivity to the topic, most corporations avoid the issue. Most American managers know relatively little about the precise process through which strong culture firms "socialize." There is little written on the subject. Business schools give the subject a passing wink. In fact, business schools find themselves in a particular dilemma since, in extolling management as a profession, they foster the view that a cadre of "professional managers" can move from firm to firm with generic skills that enable them to be effective in each. This runs squarely against the requirements of a strong culture. MIT's Edgar Schein states: "I believe that management education, particularly graduate (business schools), are increasingly attempting to train professionals, and in this process are socializing the students to a set of professional values which are, in fact, in a severe and direct conflict with typical organizational values."[5] It is not surprising that many businesses have become disenchanted with MBAs in line management positions because of their tendency to skip from one firm to the next. It is certainly of interest that most strong culture firms, if they hire MBAs at all, insist on starting them from the ground up and promote exclusively from within. There are no significant MBA programs in Japan—and Japanese students earning MBAs in the U.S. are sent primarily for language skills and the cross-cultural experience.[6]

Consider the fad that currently surrounds the subject of "organizational culture." Many adherents lose enthusiasm when brought face-to-face with the stark reality that "creating a strong culture" is a nice way of saying that an organization's members have to be more comprehensively socialized. Most American firms are culturally permissive. We are guided by a philosophy—initially articulated by Locke, Hobbes, and Adam Smith—which holds that individuals who are free to choose make the most efficient decisions. The independence of the parts makes a greater sum. Stemming from this tradition, American organizations allow members to do their own thing to a remarkable degree. Trendy campaigns "to become a strong culture" encounter resistance when a organization's members are asked to give up their idiosyncrasies and some of their individuality for the common good. The end result is usually the status quo.

Of course, some firms do openly worry about their "culture." Many, however, often err on the side of fostering "pseudo-cultures." (There are numerous examples in Silicon Valley.) Issuing "company creeds" or hosting rituals like "Friday night beer busts" may project the aura of corporate culture; but such elements alone do not facilitate organizational effectiveness. Real changes in style cannot prevail without a carefully thought through and interlocking socialization process.

The crux of the dilemma is this: We are intellectually and culturally opposed to the manipulation of individuals for organizational purposes. At the same time, a certain degree of social uniformity enables organizations to work better. The less we rely on informal social controls, the more we must inevitably turn to formal financial controls and bureaucratic procedures. U.S. firms that have perfected and systematized their processes of socialization tend to be a disproportionate majority of the great self-sustaining firms which survive from one generation to the next. Virtually none of these companies discuss "socialization" directly. It occurs as an exercise of the left hand—something that just happens "as the way we do things around here." When we examine any particular aspect (e.g., how the firm recruits, the nature of its entry level training, its reward systems, and so forth), little stands out as unusual. But when the pieces are assembled, what emerges in firms as different at AT&T is from P&G, as Morgan Guaranty is from IBM or Delta Airlines, is an awesome internal consistency which powerfully shapes behavior.

STEPS OF SOCIALIZATION

It is time to take socialization out of the closet. If some degree of socialization is an inescapable necessity for organizational effectiveness, the challenge for managers is to reconcile this with the American insistence upon retaining the latitude for independent action. The solution is neither mind control nor manipulation. It is neither necessary nor desirable to oscillate from extreme individualism to extreme conformity. We can learn from those who have mastered the process. A practical middle road is available. Strong culture firms that have sustained themselves over several generations of management reveal remarkable consistency across seven key steps.

Step One. Careful selection of entry-level candidates. Trained recruiters use standardized procedures and seek specific traits that tie to success in the business. Never oversell a new recruit. Rely heavily on the informed applicant deselecting himself if the organization doesn't fit with his personal style and values.

The earlier Procter and Gamble illustration captures the crucial aspect.[7] Recruitment is the organizational equivalent of "romance." Hiring someone is like marriage—and a broken engagement is preferable to a messy divorce. Recruiters are expected to get deeper than first impressions. Their skill and intuition are developed by intensive training. A great deal of thought is given to articulating precisely and concretely the traits that count. The format for recording these traits is standardized. From the recruit's point of view, the extensive screening sends a signal: "You've got to be special to join." The screening process causes one to reveal oneself and causes most to wonder if they are good enough to get in. This increases receptivity for the second stage.

Step Two. Humility-inducing experiences in the first months on the job precipitate self-questioning of prior behavior, beliefs, and values. A lowering of individual self-comfort and self-complacency promotes openness toward accepting the organization's norms and values.

Most strong culture companies get the new hire's attention by pouring on more work than can possibly be done. IBM and Morgan Guaranty socialize extensively through training where "you work every night until 2:00 a.m. on your own material and then help others."[8] Procter and Gamble achieves the same result via "upending experiences," sometimes requiring a new recruit to color in a sales territory map—a task for which the novitiate is clearly overqualified.[9] These experiences convey a metamessage: "While you're smart in some ways, you're in kindergarten as far as what you know about this organization." One learns to be humble. Humility tends to flourish under certain conditions; especially long hours of intense work that bring you to your limits. When vulnerability is high, one also becomes close to one's colleagues—and cohesiveness is intensified in pressure-cooker environments where little opportunity is given to re-establish social distance and regain one's bearings. At the investment banking firm Morgan Stanley, one is expected to work 12-to-14 hour days and most weekends. Lunches are confined to the firm cafeteria and limited to thirty minutes; trainees are censured for taking lunch outside.[10] Near identical patterns of long hours, exhausting travel schedules, and extensive immersion in case work are true at the major consulting firms and law practices. Socialization is a little like exercise—it's easier to reconcile yourself to it when you're young.

Step Three. In-the-trenches training leads to mastery of one of the core disciplines of the business. Promotion is inescapably tied to a proven track record.

The first phase of socialization aims to attract the right trainees predisposed toward the firm's culture. The second instills enough humility to evoke self-examination; this facilitates "buying" to the firm's values. Increasingly, the organizational culture becomes the relevant universe of experience. Having thus opened one's mind to the company's way of doing business, the task is now to cement this new orientation. The most effective method for doing so is via extensive and carefully reinforced field experience. While IBM hires some MBAs and a few older professionals with prior work experience, almost all go through the same training and start at the same level. It takes six years to grow an IBM marketing representative, twelve years for a controller. McKinsey consultants and Morgan Stanley analysts must likewise earn their way up from the ranks. The gains from such an approach are cumulative. When all trainees understand there is one step by step career path, it reduces politics. There is no quick way to jump ranks and reach the top. Because the evaluation process has a long time horizon, short term behavior is counterproductive. Cutting corners catches up with you. Relationships, staying power and a consistent proven track record are the inescapable requirements of advancement. Those advancing, having been grown from within, understand the business not as financial abstraction but as a hands on reality. Senior managers can communicate with those at the lowest ranks in the "short hand" of shared experience.

Step Four. Meticulous attention is given to systems measuring operational results and rewarding individual performance. Systems are comprehensive, consistent, and triangulate particularly on those aspects of the business that are tied to competitive success and corporate values.

Procter and Gamble measures three "what counts" factors that have been

found to drive brand success. These factors are Building Volume; Building Profit; and Planned Change (defined as changes which simply put, increase effectiveness or otherwise add satisfaction to a job).[11] Operational measures track these factors using Nielsen market share indices as well as traditional financial yardsticks. All performance appraisals are tied to milestones which impact on these factors. Promotions are determined by success against these critiera—plus successful demonstration of management skills.

Another example of comprehensive, consistent, and interlocking systems are those used at IBM to track adherence to its value of "respecting the decency of the individual." This is monitored via climate surveys; "Speak-up!" (a confidential suggestion box); open door procedures; skip-level interviews; and numerous informal contacts between senior-level managers and employees.[12] The Personnel Department moves quickly when any downward changes are noted in the above indices. In addiiton, managers are monitored for percent performance appraisals completed on time and percent of employees missing the required one week a year of training. All first-level managers receive an intensive two-week course in people management and each managerial promotion results in another week-long refresher. These systems provide a near "fail-safe" network of checks and double checks to ensure adherence to IBM's core value of respecting individual dignity.

Included in IBM's mechanisms for respecting the individual is a device known as the "Penalty Box."[13] Often a person sent to the "penalty box" has committed a crime against the culture—for example, harsh handling of a subordinate, over-zealousness against the competition, gaming the reporting system. Most penalty box assignments involve a lateral move to a less desirable location—a branch manager in Chicago might be moved to a nebulous staff position at headquarters. For an outsider, penalty box assignments look like normal assignments, but insiders know they are off the track. Penalty boxes provide a place for people while the mistakes they've made or the hard feelings they've created are gradually forgotten—and while the company looks for a new useful position. The mechanism is one among numerous things IBM does that lend credence to employees' benefits that the firm won't act capriciously and end a career. In the career of strong, effective managers, there are times when one steps on toes. The penalty box is IBM's "half-way house" enabling miscreants to contemplate their errors and play another day. (Don Estridge, maverick pioneer of IBM's success in personal computers and currently head of that division, came from the penalty box.)

Step Five. Careful adherence to the firm's transcendent values. Identification with common values enables employees to reconcile personal sacrifices necessitated by their membership in the organization.[14]

Of all the steps this is perhaps most essential. It is the foundation of trust between organization and individual. Values also serve as the primary safeguard against our great fear that highly socialized organizations will degenerate into an Orwellian nightmare.[15] Much of our resistance to socialization stems from the suspicion that corporations are fundamentally amoral and their members, once socialized, will pursue inappropriate goals. There are, in fact, significant checks and balances in American society against the extremes of social manipulation.

Government, the media, and various other stakeholders such as consumers, environmentalists, and unions become powerfully vocal when corporations cross the line of decorum. And of the great self-sustaining institutions, all over a half century old, little evidence exists of major transgressions despite their strongly socialized cultures. These corporations avoid the undesirable extremes by continually recommitting themselves to shared values that keep them in tune with society.

Placing one's self "at the mercy" of an organization imposes real costs. There are long hours of work, missed weekends, bosses one has to endure, criticism that seems unfair, job assignments and rotations that are inconvenient or undesirable. The countervailing force for commitment under these circumstances is the organization's set of transcedent values which connect *its* purpose with significant higher-order human values—such as serving mankind, providing a first-class product for society, or developing people. Prior to joining Delta Airlines, candidates hear endlessly about the "Delta family feeling." Numerous anecdotes illustrate that Delta's values require sacrifices: management takes pay cuts during lean times; senior flight attendants and pilots voluntarily work fewer hours per week in order to avoid laying off more junior employees.[16] Candidates who accept employment with Delta tend to accept this quid pro quo, believing that the restrictions on individual action comprise a reasonable trade-off. Delta'a family philosophy is deemed worthy enough to make their sacrifices worthwhile. The organization, in turn, needs to honor its values and continually reaffirm their importance. To the outsider, the fuss IBM makes over "respecting the dignity of the individual," the intensity with which Delta Airlines expresses "the Delta family feeling," may seem like overzealousness. But for those within, these values represent a deeply felt mission. Their credibility and constancy is essential to the socialization transaction.

Step Six. Reinforcing folklore provides legends and interpretations of watershed events in the organization's history that validate the firm's culture and its aims. Folklore reinforces a code of conduct for "how we do things around here."

All firms have their stories. The difference among firms that socialize well is that the morals of the stories all tend to "point north." Procter and Gamble fires one of their best brand managers for overstating the features of a product. The moral: ethical claims come ahead of making money. Morgan Stanley canonizes partners with legendary skills at "cutting a deal." One of the richest legacies of folklore was found within the former Bell system where numerous stories and anecdotes extolled employees who made sacrifices to keep the phones working.

The Bell folklore was so powerful and widely shared that when natural disaster struck, all elements of a one million member organization were able to pull together, cut corners, violate procedures, make sacrifices against measurement criteria—all in the interest of restoring phone service. This occurred despite extensive bureaucratic obstacles and illustrates how folklore, when well understood, can legitimize special channels for moving an organization in a hurry.[17]

Step Seven. Consistent role models and consistent traits are associated with those recognized as on the fast track.

Nothing communicates so powerfully to younger professionals within an organization than having peers or superiors who share common qualities and who are formally or informally recognized as winners. Far more can be taught by examples than can ever be conveyed in a classroom. The protégé watches the role model make presentations, handle conflict, write memos—and replicates as closely as possible the traits that seem to work most effectively.

Strong culture firms regard role models as the most powerful ongoing "training program" available. Because other elements of the culture are consistent, those emerging as role models are consistent. Morgan Stanley carefully selects its high-potential cadre for the combination of energy, aggressiveness, and team play that the organization requires.[18] Procter and Gamble exhibits extraordinary consistency among its brand managers across traits such as tough mindedness, motivational skills, enormous energy, and ability to get things done through others.[19]

Unfortunately most firms leave the emergence of role models to chance. Some on the fast track seem to be whizzes at analysis, others are skilled with people, others seem astute at politics: the result for those below is confusion as to what it *really* takes to succeed. The set of companies, formerly parts of the Bell System, have a strong need to become more market oriented and aggressive. Yet the Bell culture continues to discriminate against candidates for the high-potential list who, against the backdrop of the older monopoly culture, are "too aggressive."[20]

The seven dimensions of socialization, while not surprising when examinied individually, tend to be overlooked and undermanaged. Many companies can point to isolated aspects of their organizational practices that follow these patterns but rarely is each of the seven factors managed as a concerted and well-coordinated effort. Rarer yet is the firm where all seven hang together. Indeed, it is *consistency* across all seven elements of socialization process that results in a strong cohesive culture that lasts over time.

THE CASE FOR SOCIALIZATION

All organizations require a certain degree of order and consistency. To achieve this, they either utilize *explicit* procedures and formal controls or *implicit* social controls. Great firms tend to do an artful job of blending both. American firms, in aggregate, tend to rely on formal controls. The result is that management often appears to be over-steering, rigid, and bureaucratic. A United Technologies executive states: "I came from the Bell system. Compared to AT&T, this is a weak culture and there is little socialization. But, of course there is still need for controls. So they put handcuffs on you, shackle you to every nickel, track every item of inventory, monitor every movement in production, and head count. They control you by balance sheet."[21]

An inordinate amount of energy in American companies is invested in fighting "the system." (We often find ourselves playing games to work around it.) When an organization instills a strong, consistent set of implicit understandings, it is effectively establishing a common law to supplement its statutory laws. This enables us to interpret formal systems in the context for which they were designed, to use them as tools rather than straightjackets. An IBM manager states: "Socialization acts as a fine-tuning device: it helps us make sense out of the procedures and quantitative measures. Any number of times I've been faced with a situation where the right thing for the measurement system was 'X' and the right thing for IBM was 'Y'. I've always been counselled to tilt toward what was right for IBM in the long term and what was right for our people. They pay us a lot to do that. Formal controls, without coherent values and culture are too crude a compass to steer by."[22]

Organizations that socialize effectively manage a lot of internal ambiguity. This tends to free up time and energy; more goes toward getting the job done and focusing on external things like the competition and the customer. "At IBM you spend 50% of your time managing the internal context," states a former IBMer, now at ITT, "at most companies it's more like 75%."[23] A marketing manager at Atari states: "You can't imagine how much time and energy around here goes into politics. You've got to determine who's on first base this month in order to figure out how to obtain what you need to get the job done. There are no rules. There are no clear values. Bushnell and Kassar stood for diametrically opposite things. Your bosses are constantly changing. I've had 4 in 18 months. We're spread out over 43 buildings over a 20-mile radius and we're constantly reorganizing. All this means that you never had time to develop a routine way for getting things done at the interface between your job and the next guy's. Without rules for working with one another, a lot of people get hurt, get burned out, are never taught the 'Atari way' of doing things because there isn't an 'Atari way.'"[24]

The absence of cultural rules makes organizational life capricious. This is so because success as middle and senior managers not only requires managing the substance of the business, but increasingly involves managing one's role and relationships. When social roles are unclear, no one is speaking the same language; communication and trust break down. Remember, the power to get things done in corporations seldom depends on formal titles and formal authority alone. In great measure, it depends on a person's track record and reputation, knowledge, and a network of relationships. In effect, the power to implement change and execute effectively relies heavily on one's *social* currency, something a person accumulates over time. Strong culture firms *empower* employees helping them build this social currency by providing continuity and clarity. Organizations which do not facilitate this process incur a cost.

Continuity and clarity also yield great dividends in reducing career anxiety. The ebbs and flows of career fortunes attract close scrutiny in organizations. Mixed signals surrounding such things as rewards, promotions, career paths, criteria for being on the "fast track" or a candidate for termination, inevitably generate a lot of gossip, game playing, and counter productive expenditure of energy. Some might feel that these elements can be entirely resolved by the explicit provisions in the policy manual. Fact is, many of the criteria of success for middle and senior level positions are implicit. It is almost impossible to articulate in writing the nuances and shared understandings that govern the rise or demise of executives. The rules tend to be communicated and enforced via relatively subtle cues. When the socialization process is weak, the cues tend to be poorly or inconsistently communicated.[25]

Look carefully at career patterns in most companies. Ambitious professionals strive to learn the ropes but there are as many "ropes" as there are individuals who have, by one means or another, made their way to the top. So one picks an approach and if by coincidence it coincides with how your superiors do things, you're on the fast track. Far more prevalent, however, the approach that works with one superior is offensive to another. "As a younger manager, I was always taught to touch bases and solicit input before moving ahead," a manager of a Santa Clara electronics firm states, "It always worked. But at a higher level with a different boss, my base touching was equated with 'being political.' Unfortunately, the organization doesn't forewarn you when it changes signals. A lot of good people leave owing to misunderstandings over things of this kind. The human cost in weakly socialized organizations tends to go unrecognized."[26]

What about the cost of conformity? A senior vice-president of IBM states: "Conformity among IBM employees has often been described as stultifying in terms of dress, behavior, and lifestyle. There is, in fact, strong pressure to adhere to certain norms of superficial behavior, and much more intensely to the three tenets of the company philosophy—1) respect for the dignity of the individual, 2) providing first-rate customer service, and 3) excellence. These are the bench marks. Between them there is wide latitude for divergence in opinions and behavior." A Procter and Gamble executive adds: "There is a great deal of consistency around here in how certain things are done and these are rather critical to our sustained success. Beyond that, there are very few hard and fast rules. People on the outside might portray our culture as imposing lock-step uniformity. It doesn't feel rigid when you're inside. It feels like it accommodates you. And best of all, you know the game you're in—you know whether you're playing soccer or football; you can find out very clearly what it takes to succeed and you can bank your career on that."[27]

It is useful to distinguish between norms that are central to the core factors that drive business success and social conventions that signal commitment and belonging. The former set is most essential as it ensures consistency around certain crucial activities that link to a firm's strategy. At IBM, people, customers, and excellence have priority. As noted earlier, IBM's format for stand-up presentations and its style of "probing" are seen as vital to keeping the culture on its toes. Bain, Morgan Guaranty, and Procter & Gamble each imposes variations on this theme.

The second set of norms are, in effect, organizational equivalents of a handshake. They are social conventions that make it easier for people to be comfortable with one another. One need not observe all of them, but as some conventions count more than others, one strives to reassure the organization that one is on the team. The important aspect of this second set of social values is that, like a handshake, they are usually not experienced as oppressive. Partly, this is because adherence is only skin deep. (Most of us don't feel our individualism is compromised by shaking hands.) In addition, these social conventions are usually self-evident to prospective members and self-selection eliminates many whose integrity would be violated by observing them.

MISCONCEPTIONS

The aim of socialization is to establish a base of attitudes, habits, and values that foster cooperation, integrity, and communication. The most frequently advanced objection is that the companies who do so will lose innovativeness over the long haul. The record does not bear this out. Many of the companies who socialize most extensively are the ones that have lasted over many generations—at least prima facie evidence of sufficient innovation to cope with the changing environment. Further consider 3M or Bell Labs. Both socialize extensively and both are highly innovative institutions—and they remain so by fostering social rules that *reward* innovation. Another misconception is that socialization necessarily occurs at the expense of maintaining a desirable amount of internal competition. Again, IBM, P&G, major consulting firms, law practices, and outstanding financial institutions like Morgan Stanley are illustrations of strong culture firms where internal competition tends to be healthy but intense. There is, of course, an ever present danger of strong culture firms becoming incestuous and myopic—the "General Motors syndrome." Most opponents of socialization rally around this argument. But what is learned from the firms that have avoided these pitfalls is that they consciously minimize the downside of socialization by cultivating *obsessions*—not just *any* obsession, but ones that serve to continually wrench attention from internal matters to the world outside. The four most common "obsessions" are quality, competition, customer service, and productivity. Each demands an external focus and serves as a built-in way of maintaining vigilance. Positive examples are McDonald's obsessive concern for quality control. Toyota's for productivity, IBM's for customer service, and Morgan Stanley's for competition. These "obsessions" contribute to a lot of fire drills and are regarded as overkill by some. But they also serve as an organizational equivalent of calisthenics. They maintain organizational alertness and muscle tone for the day when real change is required. It should be noted that organizations which tend to be obsessive over internal matters, such as Delta's with "the family feeling," may be riding for a fall.[28]

The underlying dilemma of socialization is so sensitive to core American values that it is seldom debated. When discussed, it tends toward a polarized debate—especially from members of the media and academics who, as a subset of the U.S. population, tend to be among the most preoccupied with individualism and individual rights. A central premise of this essay is that such polarization generates more heat than light. We will do better if we can advance beyond the extremes of the argument.

Revolutions begin with an assault on awareness. It is time to deal more clear-mindedly with this crucial aspect of organizational effectiveness. Between our *espoused* individualism and the *enacted* reality in most great companies lies a zone where organizational and individual interests overlap, if we can come to grips with our ambivalence about socialization we will undoubtedly make our organizations more effective. Equally important, we can reduce the human costs that arise today as many stumble along ineffectually on careers within companies that lack a sufficient foundation of social rules. This insufficiency is only partly the result of

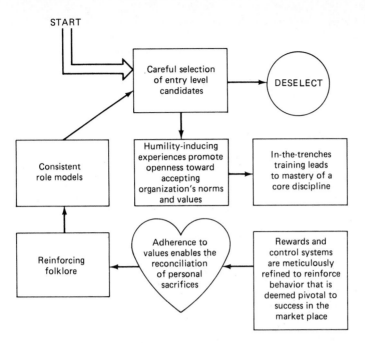

START

Careful selection
of entry level
candidates

DESELECT

Consistent
role models

Humility-inducing
experiences promote
openness toward
accepting
organization's norms
and values

In-the-trenches
training leads
to mastery of a
core discipline

Reinforcing
folklore

Adherence to
values enables the
reconciliation
of personal
sacrifices

Rewards and
control systems
are meticulously
refined to reinforce
behavior that is
deemed pivotal to
success in the
market place

FIGURE 1 Seven Steps of Socialization

ignorance. In equal measure it derives from our instinctive resistance to social controls—even when some measure of them may be in our own best interest.

FIGURE 2 Compute Your "Socialization" Score

Respond to the items below as they apply to the handling of professional employees. Upon completion, compute the total score. For comparison, scores for a number of strong, intermediate, and weak culture firms are to be found below.

	Not true of this company			Very true of this company	
1. Recruiters receive at least one week of intensive training.	1	2	3	4	5
2. Recruitment firms identify several key traits deemed crucial to the firm's success, traits are defined in concrete terms and interviewer records specific evidence of each trait.	1	2	3	4	5
3. Recruits are subjected to at least four in-depth interviews.	1	2	3	4	5
4. Company actively facilitates de-selection during the recruiting process by revealing minuses as well as plusses.	1	2	3	4	5
5. New hires work long hours, are exposed to intensive training of considerable difficulty and/or perform relatively menial tasks in the first months.	1	2	3	4	5
6. The intensity of entry level experience builds cohesivensss among peers in each entering class.	1	2	3	4	5
7. All professional employees in a particular discipline begin in entry level positions regardless of prior experience or advanced degrees.	1	2	3	4	5

8. Reward systems and promotion criteria require mastery of a core discipline as a precondition of advancement. 1 2 3 4 5
9. The career path for professional employees is relatively consistent over the first six to ten years with the company. 1 2 3 4 5
10. Reward systems, performance incentives, promotion criteria and other primary measures of success reflect a high degree of congruence. 1 2 3 4 5
11. Virtually all professional employees can identify and articulate the firm's shared values (i.e., the purpose or mission that ties the firm to society, the customer or its employees). 1 2 3 4 5
12. There are very few instances when actions of management appear to violate the firm's espoused values. 1 2 3 4 5
13. Employees frequently make personal sacrifices for the firm out of commitment to the firm's shared values. 1 2 3 4 5
14. When confronted with trade-offs between systems measuring short-term results and doing what's best for the company in the long term, the firm usually decides in favor of the long-term. 1 2 3 4 5
15. This organization fosters mentor-protégé relationships. 1 2 3 4 5
16. There is considerable similarity among high potential candidates in each particular discipline. 1 2 3 4 5

Compute your score: _____

For comparative purposes:

Scores

Strongly Socialized Firms .... 65–80 ....IBM, P&G, Morgan Guaranty
55–64 ....ATT, Morgan Stanley, Delta Airlines
45–54 ....United Airlines, Coca Cola
35–44 ....General Foods, Pepsi Co.
25–34 ....United Technologies, ITT
Weakly Socialized Firms ....Below 25 ....Atari

REFERENCES

1. Interview with Skip Awalt, Director of Management Development, IBM, Armonk, NY. May 26, 1982.
2. Interviews with Bain Consultants, 1983. Also, see: "Those Who Can't, Consult," *Harpers* (November 1982), pp. 8–17.
3. N. Kaible, Recruitment and Socialization at Procter and Gamble, Stanford Graduate School of Business, Case II S–BP–236, May 1984.
4. Interviews with professional staff, Morgan Guaranty Trust, New York, 1982.
5. Edgar H. Schein, "Organizational Socialization," in Kolb, Rubin, and McIntire, eds. *Organizational Psychology* (Englewood Cliffs, NJ: Prentice Hall, 1974), pp. 1–15.
6. Richard Pascale and Anthony Athos, *The Art of Japanese Management* (New York, NY: Simon & Schuster, 1981).
7. Kaible, op. cit., pp. 2–6.
8. Interview with recent trainees of IBM's sales development program, Palo Alto, CA. May 1982.
9. Kaible, op. cit., p. 10.
10. Interviews with professional staff, Morgan Stanley, New York, March 1983.
11. Kaible, op. cit., p. 16. *See also* "Readiness Criteria for Promotion to Assistant Brand Manager," unpublished P&G internal document #0689A, pp. 1–2.

12. Interview with Skip Awalt, IBM, op. cit. *See also* T. Rohan, "How IBM Stays Non Union," *Industry Week,* November 26, 1979, pp. 85-96.
13. Interviews with IBM managers, Palo Alto, CA, April 13, 1983.
14. See Pascale and Athos, op. cit., Chapter Seven.
15. See for example Zimbardo, "To Control a Mind," *The Stanford Magazine* (Winter 1983), pp. 59-64.
16. J. Guyon, "Family Feeling at Delta Creates Loyal Workers," *Wall Street Journal,* July 17, 1980, p. 13.
17. Interviews with executives of AT&T, Basking Ridge, NJ, February 1982.
18. Interview with professional staff, Morgan Guaranty, Palo Alto, CA, April 1983.
19. Kaible, op. cit., p. 16.
20. Interview with line executives, of Northwestern Bell, Omaha, NE, March 1982.
21. Interview with executives, Pratt & Whitney Division, United Technologies, NY, January 1981.
22. Interview with IBM Marketing and Production managers. Palo Alto, CA, op. cit.
23. Ibid.
24. Interview with product development managers, Atari, Santa Clara, CA, April 1983.
25. Pascale and Athos, op. cit., Chapters 3 & 4.
26. Interview with a production manager of Rolm, Santa Clara, CA, January 1983.
27. Interview with IBM marketing and production managers, Palo Alto, CA. op. cit.
28. M. Loeb, "Staid Delta Air Tries to Stem Losses by Following Other Carriers' Moves." *Wall Street Journal,* July 10, 1983.

2
Theories of Managing People

MASTERING COMPETING VALUES:
AN INTEGRATED APPROACH TO MANAGEMENT
Robert E. Quinn

THE HUMAN SIDE OF ENTERPRISE
Douglas M. McGregor

THE MANAGER'S JOB: FOLKLORE AND FACT
Henry Mintzberg

MASTERING COMPETING VALUES: AN INTEGRATED APPROACH TO MANAGEMENT

Robert E. Quinn

It was awful. Everything was always changing and nothing ever seemed to happen. The people above me would sit around forever and talk about things. The technically right answer didn't matter. They were always making what I thought were wrong decisions, and when I insisted on doing what was right, they got pissed off and would ignore what I was saying. Everything was suddenly political. They would worry about what everyone was going to think about every issue. How you looked, attending cocktail parties—that stuff to me was unreal and unimportant.

I went through five and a half terrible years. I occasionally thought I had reached my level of incompetence, but I refused to give up. In the end, the frustration and pain turned out to be a positive thing because it forced me to consider some alternative perspectives. I eventually learned that there were other realities besides the technical reality.

I discovered perception and long time lines. At higher levels what matters is how people see the world, and everyone sees it a little differently. Technical facts are not as available or as important. Things are changing more rapidly at higher levels, you are no longer buffered from the outside world. Things are more complex, and it takes longer to get people on board. I decided I had to be a lot more receptive and a lot more patient. It was an enormous adjustment, but then things started to change. I think I became a heck of a lot better manager.

Source: Adapted from *Beyond Rational Management* by Robert Quinn, Jossey-Bass, Inc., 1988. With permission of author and publisher.

THE CONCEPT OF MASTERY

If there is such a thing as a master of management, what is it that differentiates the master from others? The answer has to do with how the master of management sees the world.

Most of us learn to think of the concept of organization in a very static way. Particularly at the lower levels, organizations seem to be characterized by relatively stable, predictable patterns of action. They appear to be, or at least we expect them to be, the product of rational-deductive thinking. We think of them as static mechanisms designed to accomplish some single purpose.

One of the most difficult things for most of us to understand is that organizations are dynamic. Particularly as one moves up the organizational ladder, matters become less tangible and less predictable. A primary characteristic of managing, particularly at higher levels, is the confrontation of change, ambiguity, and contradiction. Managers spend much of their time living in fields of perceived tensions. They are constantly forced to make trade-offs, and they often find that there are no right answers. The higher one goes in an organization, the more exaggerated this phenomenon becomes. One-dimensional bromides (care for people, work harder, get control, be innovative) are simply half-truths representing single domains of action. What exists in reality are contradictory pressures, emanating from a variety of domains. This fact is important because much of the time the choice is not between good and bad, but between one good and another or between two unpleasant alternatives. In such cases the need is for complex, intuitive decisions, and many people fail to cope successfully with the resulting tension, stress, and uncertainty. This is well illustrated by the initial failure and frustration of the engineer who was quoted earlier.

The people who come to be masters of management do not see their work environment only in structured, analytic ways. Instead, they also have the capacity to see it as a complex, dynamic system that is constantly evolving. In order to interact effectively with it, they employ a variety of different perspectives or frames. As one set of conditions arises, they focus on certain cues that lead them to apply a very analytic and structured approach. As these cues fade, they focus on new cues of emerging importance and apply another frame, perhaps this time an intuitive and flexible one. At another time they may emphasize the overall task, and at still another they may focus on the welfare of a single individual.

Because of these shifts, masters of management may appear to act in paradoxical ways. They engage the contradictions of organizational life by using paradoxical frames. Viewed from a single point in time, their behaviors may seem illogical and contradictory. Yet these seeming contradictions come together in a fluid whole. Things work out well for these people.

The ability to see the world in a dynamic fashion does not come naturally. It requires a dramatic change in outlook, a redefinition of one's world view. It means transcending the rules of mechanistic logic used for solving well-defined problems and adopting a more comprehensive and flexible kind of logic. It is a logic that comes from experience rather than from textbooks. It requires a change not unlike a religious conversion.

THE EVOLUTION OF MASTERY

Dreyfus, Dreyfus, and Athanasion (1986) provide a five-stage model that describes the evolution from novice to expert.

In the novice stage people learn facts and rules. The rules are learned as absolutes that are never to be violated. For example, in playing chess people learn the names of the pieces, how they are moved, and their value. They are told to exchange pieces of lower value for pieces of higher value. In management, this might be the equivalent of the classroom education of an M.B.A.

In the advanced beginner stage, experience becomes critical. Performance improves somewhat as real situations are encountered. Understanding begins to exceed the stated facts and rules. Observation of certain basic patterns leads to the recognition of factors that were not set forth in the rules. A chess player, for example, begins to recognize certain basic board positions that should be pursued. The M.B.A. discovers the basic norms, values, and culture of the workplace on the first job.

The third stage is competence. Here the individual has begun to appreciate the complexity of the task and now recognizes a much larger set of cues. The person develops the ability to select and concentrate on the most important cues. With this ability competence grows. Here the reliance on absolute rules begins to disappear. People take calculated risks and engage in complex trade-offs. A chess player may, for example, weaken board position in order to attack the opposing king. This plan may or may not follow any rules that the person was ever taught. The M.B.A. may go beyond the technical analysis taught in graduate school as he or she experiments with an innovation of some sort. Flow or excellence may even be experienced in certain specific domains or subareas of management, as in the case of the engineer at the beginning of the article who displayed technical brilliance.

In the proficiency stage, calculation and rational analysis seem to disappear, and unconscious, fluid, and effortless performance begins to emerge. Here no one plan is held sacred. The person learns to unconsciously "read" the evolving situation. Cues are noticed and responded to, and attention shifts to new cues as the importance of the old ones recedes. New plans are triggered as emerging patterns call to mind plans that worked previously. Here there is a holistic and intuitive grasp of the situation. Here we are talking, for example, about the top 1 percent of all chess players, the people with the ability to intuitively recognize and respond to change in board positions. Here the M.B.A. has become an effective, upper-level manager, capable of meeting a wide variety of demands and contradictions.

Experts, those at the fifth stage, do what comes naturally. They do not apply rules but use holistic recognition in a way that allows them to deeply understand the situation. They have maps of the territory programmed into their heads that the rest of us are not aware of. They see and know things intuitively that the rest of us do not know or see (many dimensions). They frame and reframe strategies as they read changing cues (action inquiry). Here the manager has fully transcended personal style. The master manager seems to meet the contradictions of organizational life effortlessly.

THE NEED FOR MORE COMPLEX THEORY

In their popular book, *In Search of Excellence,* Peters and Waterman (1982) seek to discover what differentiates excellent companies from ordinary ones. Embedded in their work is an observation that is quite consistent with our observations. They conclude that managers in excellent companies have an unusual ability to resolve paradox, to translate conflicts and tensions into excitement, high commitment, and superior performance. In reviewing the book, Van de Ven (1983) applauds this insight and notes a grave inadequacy in the theories generated by administrative researchers. He argues that while the managers of excellent companies seem to have a capacity for dealing with paradox, administrative theories are not designed to take this phenomenon into account. In order to be internally consistent, theorists tend to eliminate contradiction. Hence, there is a need for a dynamic theory that can handle both stability and change, that can consider the tensions and conflicts inherent in human systems. Among other things, the theory would view people as complex actors in tension-filled social systems, constantly interacting with a "fast-paced, ever-changing array of forces" (Van de Ven, 1983, p. 624). The theory would center on transforming leadership that focuses on "the ethics and value judgments that are implied when leaders and followers raise one another to higher levels of motivation and morality" (p. 624).

For most of us, discovering the contradictory nature of organizing is not easy. We have biases in how we process information, and we prefer to live in certain kinds of settings. Our biases are further influenced by our organizational experience at both the functional and cultural levels. At the functional level, for example, accountants and marketing people tend to develop very different assumptions about what is "good." At the cultural level, there is often a set of values that conveys "how we do things around here." Because these values tend to be so powerful, it is very difficult to see past them. It is difficult to recognize that there are weaknesses in our own perspective and advantages in opposing perspectives. It is particularly difficult to realize that these various perspectives must be understood, juxtaposed, and blended in a delicate, complex, and dynamic way. It is much more natural to see them as either/or positions in which one must triumph over the other.

A COMPETING VALUES MODEL

In the late seventies and early eighties, many of my colleagues and I became interested in the issue of organizational effectiveness. We were asking the question, What are the characteristics of effective organizations? Many studies were done in which people set out to measure the characteristics of organizations. These measures were then submitted to a technique called factor analysis. It produced lists of variables that characterized effective organizations. The problem was that these variables differed from one study to another. It seemed that the more we learned, the less we knew.

My colleague, John Rohrbaugh, and I therefore tried to reframe the question. Instead of asking what effective organizations looked like, we decided to ask how experts think about effective organizations. This would allow us to get to the assumptions behind the studies and perhaps make sense of what was causing the confusion. In a series of studies (Quinn and Rohrbaugh, 1983), we had organizational theorists and researchers make judgments regarding the similarity or dissimilarity between pairs of effectiveness criteria. The data were analyzed using a technique called multidimensional scaling. Results of the analyses suggested that organizational theorists and researchers share an implicit theoretical framework, or cognitive map (Figure 1).

Note that the two axes in the figure create four quadrants. The vertical axis ranges from flexibility to control, the horizontal axis ranges from an internal to an external focus. Each quadrant of the framework represents one of the four major models in organizational theory. The human relations model, for example, stresses criteria such as those in the upper-left quadrant: cohesion and morale, along with human resource development. The open systems model stresses criteria such as those in the upper-right quadrant. These include flexibility and readiness as well as growth, resource acquisition, and external support. The rational goal model stresses the kind of criteria found in the lower-right quadrant, including planning and goal setting and productivity and efficiency. The internal process model is represented in the lower-left quadrant. It stresses information management and communication, along with stability and control.

FIGURE 1 Competing Values Framework: Effectiveness

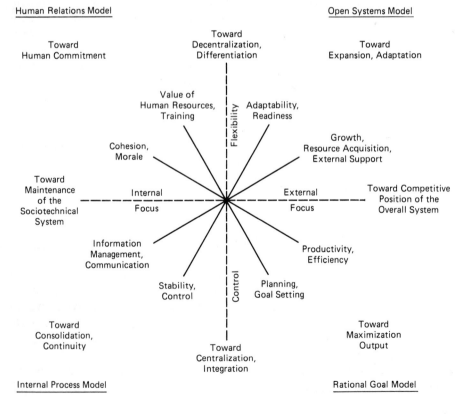

Each model has a polar opposite. The human relations model, which emphasizes flexibility and internal focus, stands in stark contrast to the rational goal model, which stresses control and external focus. The open systems model, which is characterized by flexibility and external focus, runs counter to the internal process model, which emphasizes control and internal focus. Parallels among the models are also important. The human relations and open systems models share an emphasis on flexibility. The open systems and rational goal models have an external focus (responding to outside change and producing in a competitive market). The rational goal and internal process models are rooted in the value of control. Finally, the internal process and human relations models share an internal focus (concern for the human and technical systems inside the organization).

Each model suggests a mode or type of organizing. The two sets of criteria in each quadrant also suggest an implicit means-ends theory that is associated with each mode. Thus, the rational goal model suggests that an organization is a rational economic firm. Here planning and goal setting are viewed as a means of achieving productivity and efficiency. In the open systems model we find the adhocracy, where adaptability and readiness are viewed as a means to growth, resource acquisition, and external support. In the internal process model is the hierarchy, where information management and communication are viewed as a means of arriving at stability and control. In the human relations quadrant we find the team. Here cohesion and morale are viewed as a means of increasing the value of human resources.

This scheme is called the competing values framework because the criteria seem to initially carry a conflictual message. We want our organizations to be adaptable and flexible, but we also want them to be stable and controlled. We want growth, resource acquisition, and external support, but we also want tight information management and formal communication. We want an emphasis on the value of human resources, but we also want an emphasis on planning and goal setting. The model does not suggest that these oppositions cannot mutually exist in a real system. It suggests, rather, that these criteria, values, and assumptions are oppositions in our minds. We tend to think that they are very different from one another, and we sometimes assume them to be mutually exclusive. In order to illustrate this point we will consider how values manifest themselves and, in so doing, consider some applied examples.

HOW VALUES MANIFEST THEMSELVES

In recent years much has been written about culture in organizations. When we think of the manifestation of values in organizations, it is their cultures that we are thinking of. Simply put, culture is the set of values and assumptions that underlie the statement, "This is how we do things around here." Culture at the organizational level, like information processing at the individual level, tends to take on moral overtones. While cultures tend to vary dramatically, they share the common characteristic of providing integration of effort in one direction while often sealing off the possibility of moving in another direction. An illustration may be helpful.

In October 1980 *Business Week* ran an article contrasting the cultures at J. C. Penney and PepsiCo. At Penney's the culture focuses on the values of fairness and long-term loyalty. Indeed, a manager was once chewed out by the president of the company for making too much money! To do so was unfair to the customers, and at Penney's one must never take advantage of the customer. Customers are free to return merchandise with which they are not satisfied. Suppliers know that they can establish stable, long-term relationships with Penney's. Employees know that if their ability to perform a given job begins to deteriorate, they will not find themselves out on the street; rather, an appropriate alternative position will be found for them.

The core of the company's culture is captured in "The Penney Idea." Although it was adopted in 1913, it is a very modern-sounding statement, consisting of seven points: "To serve the public, as nearly as we can, to its complete satisfaction; to expect for the service we render a fair remuneration and not all the profit the traffic will bear; to do all in our power to pack the customer's dollar full of value, quality, and satisfaction; to continue to train ourselves and our associates so that the service we give will be more and more intelligently performed; to improve constantly the human factor in our business; to reward men and women in our organization through participation in what the business produces; to test our every policy, method, and act in this wise: 'Does it square with what is right and just?'"

The culture at PepsiCo is in stark contrast to that at Penney's. After years as a sleepy company that took the back seat to Coca-Cola, PepsiCo underwent a major change by adopting a much more competitive culture. This new culture was manifest both externally and internally. On the outside PepsiCo directly confronted Coca-Cola. In bold ads customers were asked to taste and compare the products of the two companies. Internally, managers knew that their jobs were on the line and that they had to produce results. There was continuous pressure to show improvement in market share, product volume, and profits. Jobs were won or lost over a "tenth of a point" difference in these areas.

Staffs were kept small. Managers were constantly moved from job to job and expected to work long hours. The pressure never let up. During a blizzard, for example, the chief executive officer found a snowmobile and drove it to work. (This story is told regularly at PepsiCo.) Competitive team and individual sports are emphasized, and people are expected to stay in shape. The overall climate is reflected in the often repeated phrase, "We are the marines not the army."

The differences between these two companies could hardly be greater. Reading this account, you have probably concluded that one culture is more attractive than the other, and you would expect others to agree with your choice. But it is very likely that if you visited PepsiCo and spoke of "The Penney Idea," you would be laughed at. If you tried to press it upon PepsiCo employees, they would probably become incensed. Likewise, if you visited Penney's and described or tried to press upon them the values of PepsiCo, they would have the same reaction. You would be violating sacred assumptions.

Interestingly, the major problem at PepsiCo was seen as the absence of loyalty. Coca-Cola's response to the PepsiCo attack, for example, was to hire away some of PepsiCo's best "Tigers," and they were, because of the constant pressure, willing to go. (PepsiCo's rate of tenure is less than one-third of the rate at Penney's.) And what, according to *Business Week,* was the major problem at Penney's? Lack of competitiveness. Despite a reputation as one of the best places to work, and despite intense employee and customer loyalty, Penney's had been rapidly losing market share to KMart. Some critics expressed doubt that Penney's could respond to the challenge.

What is happening here? The surface conclusion is that two opposite cultures exist. Penney's reflects the human relations model in that the company seems to resemble a team, clan, or family. PepsiCo reflects the rational goal model in that it appears to be an instrumental firm. The strength of one is the weakness of the other. While this conclusion is true, there is a deeper insight to be gained. I will later return to this interesting contrast after considering the transformation of values.

INEFFECTIVENESS

The competing values framework consists of juxtaposed sets of organizational effectiveness criteria. Each of these "good" criteria can become overvalued by an individual and pursued in an unidimensional fashion. When this zealous pursuit of a single set of criteria takes place, a strange inversion can result. Good things can mysteriously become bad things. In Figure 2, I show how criteria of effectiveness, when pursued blindly, become criteria of ineffectiveness. These latter criteria are depicted in the negative zone on the outside of the diagram.

The structure of this model parallels the competing values framework of effectiveness. The axes, however, are negatively, rather than positively, labeled. Thus, the vertical dimension ranges from chaos (too much flexibility and spontaneity) to rigidity (too much order and predictability). The horizontal dimension ranges from belligerence and hostility (too much external focus and too much emphasis on competition and engagement) to apathy and indifference (too much internal focus and too much emphasis on maintenance and coordination within the system). Each quadrant represents a negative culture with negative effectiveness criteria. Embedded within these quadrants are eight criteria of ineffectiveness.

In the upper-left quadrant is the irresponsible country club. In this quadrant, human relations criteria are emphasized to the point of encouraging laxity and negligence. Discussion and participation, good in themselves, are carried to inappropriate lengths. Commitment, morale, and human development turn into extreme permissiveness and uncontrolled individualism. Here, administrators are concerned only with employees, to the exclusion of the task.

In the upper-right quadrant is the tumultuous anarchy. In this quadrant, there is so much emphasis on the open systems criteria of effectiveness that disruption and discontinuity result. Emphasis on insight, innovation, and change turn into premature responsiveness and disastrous experimentation. Concern for external support, resource acquisition, and growth turn into political expediency and unprincipled opportunism. Here, administrators are concerned only with

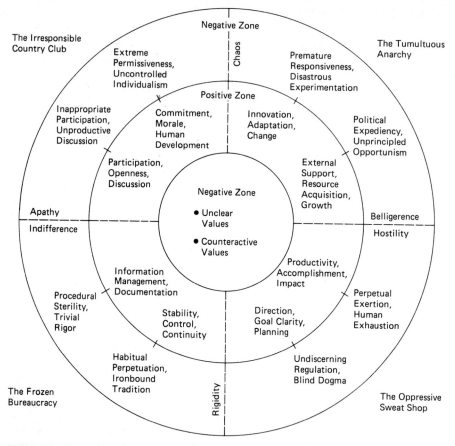

FIGURE 2 The Positive and Negative Zones

having a competitive advantage and show no interest in continuity and control of the work flow.

In the lower-right quadrant is the oppressive sweatshop. In this quadrant, there is too much emphasis on the criteria of effectiveness associated with the rational goal model. Effort, productivity, and emphasis on profit or impact of service turn into perpetual exertion and human exhaustion. Here, we see symptoms of burnout. Concern for goal clarification, authority, and decisiveness turn into an emphasis on strict regulation and blind dogma. There is no room for individual differences; the boss has the final say.

Finally, in the lower-left quadrant is the frozen bureaucracy. Here, there is too much concern with internal processes. The organization becomes atrophied as a result of excessive measurement and documentation; it becomes a system of red tape. Control measures, documentation, and computation turn into procedural sterility and trivial rigor. Everything is "by the book." The emphasis on stability, control, and continuity lead to the blind perpetuation of habits and traditions. Procedures are followed because "we've always done it this way"; there is no room for trying something new.

STRENGTH BECOMING WEAKNESS

Let us return to PepsiCo and J. C. Penney. Earlier I said that introducing the culture of one company into the other would be highly conflictual. Further, I pointed out that each culture had weaknesses. Now we can see that their very strengths put them at risk.

Because of the inability of the PepsiCo culture to tolerate the values in the human resource quadrant, the company is in danger of moving into the negative zone on the right side of Figure 2. Because of the inability of the J. C. Penney culture to more fully absorb the values on the right side of the figure, the company is in danger of moving into the negative zone on the left side of the figure. The more fully that each company pushes a particular set of positive values, without tending to the opposite positive values, the greater the danger to it.

The major point here is that everything in the two outer circles is related. The more that success is pursued around one set of positive values, the greater will be the pressure to take into account the opposite positive values. If these other values are ignored long enough, crisis and catastrophe will result.

STAYING IN THE POSITIVE ZONE: MASTERING PARADOX

Staying in the positive zone requires high levels of complex thought. Consider, for example, the stereotypical entrepreneur, like Steve Jobs of Apple Computer. Entrepreneurs are typically very creative and action oriented. They are usually not very sympathetic to the values in the hierarchy quadrant. When they build a new organization they often try to avoid hierarchy. Unfortunately, if their initial vision is successful, and their new company expands rapidly, the growth (an indicator of success) stimulates a need for hierarchical coordinating mechanisms (often seen as an indication of failure). This phenomenon is often called the formalization crisis. Many successful entrepreneurs are forced, like Steve Jobs, to leave their company because they cannot comprehend the paradox or manage the competing values. For this reason, it is instructive to consider Bill Gates of Microsoft.

Microsoft is the second largest software company in the world. Run by Bill Gates, who is still in his early thirties, Microsoft has been best known for its widely used MS DOS system. But in 1987 Gates was successful in convincing IBM to adopt its newest product, called Windows, for use in IBM's new line of personal computers. Upon completion of the agreement analysts began to predict that within twelve months Microsoft would become the largest software company in the world.

In many ways, Gates is the stereotypical entrepreneur. He is a technical genius with a burning mission. He feels a drive to bring the power of computing to the masses. His company is marked by considerable flexibility and excitement. The median age of the work force is thirty-one. People work long days, with Gates himself setting the example with an early morning to midnight routine. There are frequent picnics, programmers set their own hours, dress is casual, and the turnover rate is less than 10 percent.

The company has grown rapidly. From 1980 to 1981, Gates watched his company go from 80 to 125 employees and saw profits double to $16 million. The market value of the company now exceeds $2 billion. Given our earlier cases, all these indicators would lead us to worry about Gates and his ability to meet the demands for formalization.

In fact, however, Gates has already faced the formalization crisis and has come off well. What were the keys to this success? First, he made a very significant decision to bring in professional managers and to focus his own energies on technology. He seemed to grasp an important paradox that eludes most entrepreneurs: to have power means one must give up power. Maintaining a primary focus on technology, however, does not mean that he has abandoned the tasks of leadership. Instead, he has taken the time to learn the principles of law, marketing, distribution, and accounting and apply them in his work. He also has the paradoxical capacity of simultaneously caring and being tough. For example, dissatisfied with the performance of Microsoft's president, Gates removed him from office after only one year. But not long after, Gates was invited to be the best man at the wedding of the former president.

Perhaps the best summary of Gates and his abilities comes from one of his colleagues: "Bill Gates is very good at evaluating situations as they change." This, of course, is a key characteristic for staying in the positive zone.

Figure 2 has some important implications for management. It suggests that managers need to stay in the positive zone, that is, they need to pursue the seemingly "competing" positive values in the middle circle while also being careful to stay out of the external negative zone. They must maintain a dynamic, creative tension. Over time they must, like Bill Gates, be able to frame and reframe, that is, to move from one set of competing values to another.

SOME IMPLICATIONS FOR MANAGEMENT

The notions of mastery and competing values suggest a more complex and dynamic approach to management. The novice-like "rules" taught in the textbooks are misleading in that they usually represent only one of the competing perspectives or polarities embedded in organizational life. Theory X is not inherently better than theory Y. Change is not inherently better than the status quo. Productivity is not inherently better than cohesion and morale.

The challenge for experienced managers is threefold: the first is far more difficult than it sounds, to recognize and appreciate the positive (and the negative) aspects of all areas of the competing values framework; second, to assess and work on the roles and skills associated with each area (these are identified in Quinn, 1988); third, to analyze the present organizational moment, with all its dilemmas, and trust one's ability to integrate and employ the skills appropriate to that moment. Together these three steps are key points in the process of mastering management.

THE HUMAN SIDE OF ENTERPRISE

Douglas M. McGregor

PREVIEW

A. Theory X is a set of propositions of the conventional view of management's task in harnessing human energy to organizational requirements.
   1. It is management's responsibility to organize the elements of productive enterprise—money, materials, equipment, people—in the interest of economic ends.
   2. To fit the needs of the organization, the behavior of people must be directed, motivated, controlled and modified or else they would be passive.
   3. Additional briefs behind this conventional view show the worker to be indolent by nature, lacking ambition, inherently self-centered, resistant to changes, and gullible.
   4. To accomplish its task, management uses these assumptions as guidelines and ranges its possibilities between "hard" or "strong" and "soft" or "weak" approaches.
   5. Since difficulties exist between the hard and soft approach, the current view is "firm" but "fair."

B. Although social scientists do not deny that the worker's behavior is similar to what the management perceives, they feel that this behavior is not a consequence of the worker's inherent nature, but rather the result of the nature of industrial organizations, of management philosophy, policy, and practice.

C. The subject of motivation is supposedly the best way of indicating the inadequacy of the conventional concepts of management.
   1. At the lowest level in the hierarchy of individual needs are the *physiological needs*.
   2. The next higher level of needs are called *safety needs*.
   3. When the worker's physiological needs and safety needs are satisfied, his other behavior is motivated by *social needs*.
   4. Above the social needs are two kinds of *egoistic needs*; (a) those that relate one's *self-esteem,* and (b) those that relate to one's *reputation*. Unlike the lower needs these are rarely satisfied.
   5. Finally there are needs for *self-fulfillment.*

D. Just as deprivation of physiological needs has behavioral consequences, the same is true for higher level needs.

E. In the carrot-and-stick approach, management can provide or withhold the means for satisfying the worker's physiological and safety needs.
   1. But today the philosophy of management by direction and control is inadequate to motivate, because the human needs under the carrot-and-stick approach are important motivators of behavior.

F. Theory Y is based on more adequate assumptions about human nature and human motivation and therefore has broader dimensions.
   1. Responsibility lies with management for organizing the elements of productive enterprise in the interest of economic ends.

Source: Reprinted by permission of the publisher from *Management Review,* November 1957

2. People have become passive or resistant to organizational needs because of their experience in organizations.
3. Management should enable people to recognize and develop motivational characteristics.
4. By arranging organizational conditions and methods of operation, management's task is to allow people to achieve their own goals by directing their own best efforts towards organizational objectives.
5. Peter Drucker calls this process "management by objectives" in contrast to management by control.

G. The major difference associated with these theories is that Theory X places exclusive reliance upon external control of human behavior, while Theory Y relies heavily on self-control and self-direction.

H. The ideas associated with Theory Y are being applied slowly but with success.
1. Sears Roebuck and Company is an example where decentralization in the organization and delegation of duties is consistent with what the theory proposes.
2. IBM and Detroit Edison are pioneers in job enlargement.
3. The Scanlon Plan illustrates the ideas of participative and consultative management.
4. Most conventional programs of performance appraisal within management ranks reveal consistency with Theory X, although a few companies are taking steps in the direction of Theory Y.

I. Until full implementation of Theory Y is successful, only management that has confidence in human capacities and is itself directed towards organizational objectives rather than towards the preservation of personal power can grasp its implications.

It has become trite to say that industry has the fundamental know-how to utilize physical science and technology for the material benefit of mankind, and that we must now learn how to utilize the social sciences to make our human organizations truly effective.

To a degree, the social sciences today are in a position like that of the physical sciences with respect to atomic energy in the thirties. We know that past conceptions of the nature of man are inadequate and, in many ways, incorrect. We are becoming quite certain that under proper conditions, unimagined resources of creative human energy could become available within the organizational setting.

We cannot tell industrial management how to apply this new knowledge in simple, economic ways. We know it will require years of exploration, much costly development research, and a substantial amount of creative imagination on the part of management to discover how to apply this growing knowledge to the organization of human effort in industry.

MANAGEMENT'S TASK:
THE CONVENTIONAL VIEW

The conventional conception of management's task in harnessing human energy to organizational requirements can be stated broadly in terms of three propositions. In order to avoid the complications introduced by a label, let us call this set of propositions "Theory X":

1. Management is responsible for organizing the elements of productive enterprise—money, materials, equipment, people—in the interest of economic ends.

2. With respect to people, this is a process of directing their efforts, motivating them, controlling their actions, modifying their behavior to fit the needs of the organization.

3. Without this active intervention by management, people would be passive—even resistant—to organizational needs. They must therefore be persuaded, rewarded, punished, controlled—their activities must be directed. This is management's task. We often sum it up by saying that management consists of getting things done through other people.

Behind this conventional theory there are several additional beliefs—less explicit, but widespread:

4. The average man is by nature indolent—he works as little as possible.

5. He lacks ambition, dislikes responsibility, prefers to be led.

6. He is inherently self-centered, indifferent to organizational needs.

7. He is by nature resistant to change.

8. He is gullible, not very bright, the ready dupe of the charlatan and the demagogue.

The human side of economic enterprise today is fashioned from propositions and beliefs such as these. Conventional organization structures and managerial policies, practices; and programs reflect these assumptions.

In accomplishing its task—with these assumptions as guides—management has conceived of a range of possibilities.

At one extreme, management can be "hard" or "strong." The methods for directing behavior involve coercion and threat (usually disguised), close supervision, tight controls over behavior. At the other extreme, management can be "soft" or "weak." The methods for directing behavior involve being permissive, satisfying people's demands, achieving harmony. They they will be tractable, accept direction.

This range has been fairly completely explored during the past half century, and management has learned some things from the exploration. There are difficulties in the "hard" approach. Force breeds counter-forces: restriction of output, antagonism, militant unionism, subtle but effective sabotage of management objectives. This "hard" approach is especially difficult during times of full employment.

There are also difficulties in the "soft" approach. It leads frequently to the abdication of management—to harmony, perhaps, but to indifferent performance. People take advantage of the soft approach. They continually expect more, but they give less and less.

Currently, the popular theme is "firm but fair." This is an attempt to gain the advantages of both the hard and the soft approaches. It is reminiscent of Teddy Roosevelt's "speak softly and carry a big stick."

IS THE CONVENTIONAL VIEW CORRECT?

The findings which are beginning to emerge from the social sciences challenge this whole set of beliefs about man and human nature and about the task of management. The evidence is far from conclusive, certainly, but it is suggestive. It comes from the laboratory, the clinic, the schoolroom, the home, and even to a limited extent from industry itself.

The social scientist does not deny that human behavior in industrial organization today is approximately what management perceives it to be. He has, in fact, observed it and studied it fairly extensively. But he is pretty sure that this behavior is *not* a consequence of man's inherent nature. It is a consequence rather of the nature of industrial organizations, of management philosophy, policy, and practice. The conventional approach of Theory X is based on mistaken notions of what is cause and what is effect.

Perhaps the best way to indicate why the conventional approach of management is inadequate is to consider the subject of motivation.

PHYSIOLOGICAL NEEDS

Man is a wanting animal—as soon as one of his needs is satisfied, another appears in its place. This process is unending. It continues from birth to death.

Man's needs are organized in a series of levels—a hierarchy of importance. At the lowest level, but pre-eminent in importance when they are thwarted, are his *physiological needs.* Man lives for bread alone, when there is no bread. Unless the circumstances are unusual, his needs for love, for status, for recognition are inoperative when his stomach has been empty for a while. But when he eats regularly and adequately, hunger ceases to be an important motivation. The same is true of the other physiological needs of man—for rest, exercise, shelter, protection from the elements.

A *satisfied need is not a motivator of behavior!* This is a fact of profound significance that is regularly ignored in the conventional approach to the management of people. Consider your own need for air: Except as you are deprived of it, it has no appreciable motivating effect upon your behavior.

SAFETY NEEDS

When the physiological needs are reasonably satisfied, needs at the next higher level begin to dominate man's behavior—to motivate him. These are called *safety needs.* They are needs for protection against danger, threat, deprivation. Some people mistakenly refer to these as needs for security. However, unless man is in a dependent relationship where he fears arbitrary deprivation, he does not demand security. The need is for the "fairest possible break." When he is confident of this, he is more than willing to take risks. But when he feels threatened or dependent, his greatest need is for guarantees, for protection, for security.

The fact needs little emphasis that, since every industrial employee in a dependent relationship, safety needs may assume considerable importance. Arbitrary management actions, behavior which arouses uncertainty with respect to continued employment or which reflects favoritism or discrimination, unpredictable administration of policy—these can be powerful motivators of the safety needs in the employment relationship *at every level,* from worker to vice president.

SOCIAL NEEDS

When man's physiological needs are satisfied and he is no longer fearful about his physical welfare, his *social needs* become important motivators of his behavior—needs for belonging, for association, for acceptance by his fellows, for giving and receiving friendship and love.

Management knows today of the existence of these needs, but it often assumes quite wrongly that they represent a threat to the organization. Many studies have demonstrated that the tightly knit, cohesive work group may, under proper conditions, be far more effective than an equal number of separate individuals in achieving organizational goals.

Yet management, fearing group hostility to its own objectives, often goes to considerable lengths to control and direct human efforts in ways that are inimical to the natural "groupiness" of human beings. When man's social needs—and perhaps his safety needs, too—are thus thwarted, he behaves in ways which tend to defeat organizational objectives. He becomes resistant, antagonistic, uncooperative. But this behavior is a consequence, not a cause.

EGO NEEDS

Above the social needs—in the sense that they do not become motivators until lower needs are reasonably satisfied—are the needs of greatest significance to management and to man himself. They are the *egoistic needs,* and they are of two kinds:

1. Those needs that relate to one's self-esteem—needs for self-confidence, for independence, for achievement, for competence, for knowledge.

2. Those needs that relate to one's reputation—needs for status, for recognition, for appreciation, for the deserved respect of one's fellows.

Unlike the lower needs, these are rarely satisfied; man seeks indefinitely for more satisfaction of these needs once they have become important to him. But they do not appear in any significant way until physiological, safety, and social needs are all reasonably satisfied.

The typical industrial organization offers few opportunities for the satisfaction of these egoistic needs to people at lower levels in the hierarchy. The conventional methods of organizing work, particularly in mass-production industries, give little heed to these aspects of human motivation. If the practices of scientific management were deliberately calculated to thwart these needs, they could hardly accomplish this purpose better than they do.

SELF-FULFILLMENT NEEDS

Finally—a capstone, as it were, on the hierarchy of man's needs—there are what we may call the *needs for self-fulfillment.* These are the needs for realizing one's own potentialities, for continued self-development, for being creative in the broadest sense of that term.

It is clear that the conditions of modern life give only limited opportunity for these relatively weak needs to obtain expression. The deprivation most people experience with respect to other lower-level needs diverts their energies into the struggle to satisfy *those* needs, and the needs for self-fulfillment remain dormant.

MANAGEMENT AND MOTIVATION

We recognize readily enough that a man suffering from a severe dietary deficiency is sick. The deprivation of physiological needs has behavioral consequences. The same is true—although less well recognized—of deprivation of higher-level needs. The man whose needs for safety, association, independence, or status are thwarted is sick just as surely as the man who has rickets. And his sickness will have behavioral consequences. We will be mistaken if we attribute his resultant passivity, his hostility, his refusal to accept responsibility to his inherent "human nature." These forms of behavior are *symptoms* of illness—of deprivation of his social and egoistic needs.

The man whose lower-level needs are satisfied is not motivated to satisfy those needs any longer. For practical purposes they exist no longer. Management often asks, "Why aren't people more productive? We pay good wages, provide good working conditions, have excellent fringe benefits and steady employment. Yet people do not seem to be willing to put forth more than minimum effort."

The fact that management has provided for these physiological and safety needs has shifted the motivational emphasis to the social and perhaps to the egoistic needs. Unless there are opportunities at *work* to satisfy these higher-level needs, people will be deprived; and their behavior will reflect this deprivation. Under such conditions, if management continues to focus its attention on physiological needs, its efforts are bound to be ineffective.

People *will* make insistent demands for more money under these conditions. It becomes more important than ever to buy the material goods and services which can provide limited satisfaction of the thwarted needs. Although money has only limited value in satisfying many higher-level needs, it can become the focus of interest if it is the *only* means available.

THE CARROT-AND-STICK APPROACH

The carrot-and-stick theory of motivation (like Newtonian physical theory) works reasonably well under certain circumstances. The *means* for satisfying man's physiological and (within limits) his safety needs can be provided or withheld by management. Employment itself is such a means, and so are wages, working conditions, and benefits. By these means the individual can be controlled so long as he is struggling for subsistence.

But the carrot-and-stick theory does not work at all once man has reached an adequate subsistence level and is motivated primarily by higher needs. Management cannot provide a man with self-respect, or with the respect of his fellows, or with the satisfaction of needs for self-fulfillment. It can create such conditions that he is encouraged and enabled to seek such satisfactions for *himself*, or it can thwart him by failing to create those conditions.

But this creation of conditions is not "control." It is not a good device for directing behavior. And so management finds itself in an odd position. The high standard of living created by our modern technological know-how provides quite adequately for the satisfaction of physiological and safety needs. The only significant exception is where management practices have not created confidence in a "fair break"—and thus where safety needs are thwarted. But by making possible the satisfaction of low-level needs, management has deprived itself of the ability to use as motivators the devices on which conventional theory has taught it to rely—rewards, promises, incentives, or threats and other coercive devices.

The philosophy of management by direction and control—*regardless of whether it is hard or soft*—is inadequate to motivate because the human needs on which this approach relies are today unimportant motivators of behavior. Direction and control are essentially useless in motivating people whose important needs are social and egoistic. Both the hard and the soft approach fail today because they are simply irrelevant to the situation.

People, deprived of opportunities to satisfy at work the needs which are not important to them, behave exactly as we might predict—with indolence, passivity, resistance to change, lack of responsibility, willingness to follow the demagogue, unreasonable demands for economic benefits. It would seem that we are caught in a web of our own weaving.

A NEW THEORY OF MANAGEMENT

For these and many other reasons, we require a different theory of the task of managing people based on more adequate assumptions about human nature and human motivation. I am going to be so bold as to suggest the broad dimensions of such a theory. Call it "Theory Y," if you will.

1. Management is responsible for organizing the elements of productive enterprise—money, materials, equipment, people—in the interest of economic ends.

2. People are *not* by nature passive or resistant to organizational needs. They have become so as a result of experience in organizations.

3. The motivation, the potential for development, the capacity for assuming responsibility, the readiness to direct behavior toward organizational goals are all present in people. Management does not put them there. It is a responsibility of management to make it possible for people to recognize and develop these human characteristics for themselves.

4. The essential task of management is to arrange organizational conditions and methods of operation so that people can achieve their own goals *best* by directing *their own* efforts toward organizational objectives.

This is a process primarily of creating opportunities, releasing potential, removing obstacles, encouraging growth, providing guidance. It is what Peter Drucker has called "management by objectives" in contrast to "management by control." It does *not* involve the abdication of management, the absence of leadership, the lowering of standards, or the other characteristics usually associated with the "soft" approach under Theory X.

SOME DIFFICULTIES

It is no more possible to create an organization today which will be a full, effective application of this theory than it was to build an atomic power plant in 1945. There are many formidable obstacles to overcome.

The conditions imposed by conventional organization theory and by the approach of scientific management for the past half century have tied men to limited jobs which do not utilize their capabilities, have discouraged the acceptance of responsibility, have encouraged passivity, have eliminated meaning from work. Man's habits, attitudes, expectations—his whole conception of membership in an industrial organization—have been conditioned by his experience under these circumstances.

People today are accustomed to being directed, manipulated, controlled in industrial organizations and to finding satisfaction for their social, egoistic, and self-fulfillment needs away from the job. This is true of much of management as well as of workers. Genuine "industrial citizenship"—to borrow again a term from Drucker—is a remote and unrealistic idea, the meaning of which has not even been considered by most members of industrial organizations.

Another way of saying this is that Theory X places exclusive reliance upon external control of human behavior, while Theory Y relies heavily on self-control and self-direction. It is worth noting that this difference is the difference between treating people as children and treating them as mature adults. After generations of the former, we cannot expect to shift to the latter overnight.

STEPS IN THE RIGHT DIRECTION

Before we are overwhelmed by the obstacles, let us remember that the application of theory is always slow. Progress is usually achieved in small steps. Some innovative ideas which are entirely consistent with Theory Y are today being applied with some success.

Decentralization and Delegation

There are ways of freeing people from the too-close control of conventional organization, giving them a degree of freedom to direct their own activities, to assume responsibility, and, importantly, to satisfy their egoistic needs. In this connection, the flat organization of Sears, Roebuck and Company provides an interesting example. It forces "management by objectives," since it enlarges the number of people reporting to a manager until he cannot direct and control them in the conventional manner.

Job Enlargement

This concept, pioneered by I.B.M. and Detroit Edison, is quite consistent with Theory Y. It encourages the acceptance of responsibility at the bottom of the organization; it provides opportunities for satisfying social and egoistic needs. In fact, the reorganization of work at the factory level offers one of the more challenging opportunities for innovation consistent with Theory Y.

Participation and Consultative Management

Under proper conditions, participation and consultative management provide encouragement to people to direct their creative energies toward organizational objectives, give them some voice in decisions that affect them, provide significant opportunities for the satisfaction of social and egoistic needs. The Scanlon Plan is the outstanding embodiment of these ideas in practice.

Performance Appraisal

Even a cursory examination of conventional programs of performance appraisal within the ranks of management will reveal how completely consistent they are with Theory X. In fact, most such programs tend to treat the individual as though he were a product under inspection on the assembly line.

A few companies—among them General Mills, Ansul Chemical, and General Electric—have been experimenting with approaches which involve the individual in setting "targets" or objectives *for himself* and in a *self*-evaluation of performance semiannually or annually. Of course, the superior plays an important leadership role in this process—one, in fact, which demands substantially more competence than the conventional approach. The role is, however, considerabley more congenial to many managers than the role of "judge" or "inspector" which is usually forced upon them. Above all, the individual is encouraged to take a greater responsibility for planning and appraising his own contribution to organizational objectives; and the accompanying effects on egoistic and self-fulfillment needs are substantial.

APPLYING THE IDEAS

The not infrequent failure of such ideas as these to work as well as expected is often attributable to the fact that a management has "bought the idea" but applied it within the framework of Theory X and its assumptions.

Delegation is not an effective way of exercising management by control. Participation becomes a farce when it is applied as a sales gimmick or a device for kidding people into thinking they are important. Only the management that has confidence in human capacities and is itself directed toward organizational objectives rather than toward the preservation of personal power can grasp the implications of this emerging theory. Such management will find and apply successfully other innovative ideas as we move slowly toward the full implementation of a theory like Y.

THE HUMAN SIDE OF ENTERPRISE

It is quite possible for us to realize substantial improvements in the effectiveness of industrial organizations during the next decade or two. The social sciences can contribute much to such developments; we are only beginning to grasp the implications of the growing body of knowledge in these fields. But if this conviction is to become a reality instead of a pious hope, we will need to view the process much as we view the process of releasing the energy of the atom for constructive human ends—as a slow, costly, sometimes discouraging approach toward a goal which would seem to many to be quite unrealistic.

The ingenuity and the perseverance of industrial management in the pursuit of economic ends have changed many scientific and technological dreams into commonplace realities. It is now become clear that the application of these same talents to the human side of enterprise will not only enhance substantially these materialistic achievements, but will bring us one step closer to "the good society."

THE MANAGER'S JOB: FOLKLORE AND FACT

Henry Mintzberg

If you ask a manager what he does, he will most likely tell you that he plans, organizes, coordinates, and controls. Then watch what he does. Don't be surprised if you can't relate what you see to these four words.

When he is called and told that one of his factories has just burned down, and he advises the caller to see whether temporary arrangements can be made to supply customers through a foreign subsidiary, is he planning, organizing, coordinating, or controlling? How about when he presents a gold watch to a retiring employee? Or when he attends a conference to meet people in the trade? Or on returning from that conference, when he tells one of his employees about an interesting product idea he picked up there?

The fact is that these four words, which have dominated management vocabulary since the French industrialist Henri Fayol first introduced them in 1916, tell us little about what managers actually do. At best, they indicate some vague objectives managers have when they work.

The field of management, so devoted to progress and change, has for more than half a century not seriously addressed *the* basic question: What do managers do? Without a proper answer, how can we teach management? How can we design planning or information systems for managers? How can we improve the practice of management at all?

Our ignorance of the nature of managerial work shows up in various ways in the modern organization—in the boast by the successful manager that he never spent a single day in a management training program; in the turnover of corporate planners who never quite understood what it was the manager wanted; in the computer consoles gathering dust in the back room because the managers never used the fancy on-line MIS some analyst thought they needed. Perhaps most important, our ignorance shows up in the inability of our large public organizations to come to grips with some of their most serious policy problems.

Source: Reprinted by permission of *Harvard Business Review.* The Manager's Job: Folklore and Fact by Henry Mintzberg (July-Aug, 1975). Copyright 1975 by the President and Fellows of Harvard College; all rights reserved.

Somehow, in the rush to automate production, to use management science in the functional areas of marketing and finance, and to apply the skills of the

Research on Managerial Work

Considering its central importance to every aspect of management, there has been surprisingly little research on the manager's work, and virtually no systematic building of knowledge from one group of studies to another. In seeking to describe managerial work, I conducted my own research and also scanned the literature widely to integrate the findings of studies from many diverse sources with my own. These studies focused on two very different aspects of managerial work. Some were concerned with the characteristics of the work—how long managers work, where, at what pace and with what interruptions, with whom they work, and through what media they communicate. Other studies were more concerned with the essential content of the work—what activities the managers actually carry out, and why. Thus, after a meeting, one researcher might note that the manager spent 45 minutes with three government officials in their Washington office, while another might record that he presented his company's stand on some proposed legislation in order to change a regulation.

A few of the studies of managerial work are widely known, but most have remained buried as single journal articles or isolated books. Among the more important ones I cite (with full references in the footnotes) are the following:

- Sune Carlson developed the diary method to study the work characteristics of nine Swedish managing directors. Each kept a detailed log of his activities. Carlson's results are reported in his book *Executive Behavior*. A number of British researchers, notably Rosemary Stewart, have subsequently used Carlson's method. In *Managers and Their Jobs*, she describes the study of 160 top and middle managers of British companies during four weeks, with particular attention to the differences in their work.

- Leonard Sayles's book *Managerial Behavior* is another important reference. Using a method he refers to as "anthropological," Sayles studied the work content of middle- and lower-level managers in a large U.S. corporation. Sayles moved freely in the company collecting whatever information struck him as important.

- Perhaps the best-known source is *Presidential Power*, in which Richard Neustadt analyzes the power and managerial behavior of Presidents Roosevelt, Truman, and Eisenhower. Neustadt used secondary sources—documents and interviews with other parties—to generate his data.

- Robert H. Guest, in *Personnel*, reports on a study of the foreman's working day. Fifty-six U.S. foremen were observed and each of their activities recorded during one eight-hour shift.

- Richard C. Hodgson, Daniel J. Levinson, and Abraham Zaleznik studied a team of three top executives of a U.S. hospital. From that study they wrote *The Executive Role Constellation*. (These researchers addressed in particular the way in which work and socio-emotional roles were divided among the three managers.)

- William F. Whyte, from his study of a street gang during the Depression, wrote *Street Corner Society*. His findings about the gang's leadership, which George C. Homans analyzed in *The Human Group*, suggest some interesting similarities of job content between street gang leaders and corporate managers.

My own study invovled five American CEOs of middle- to large-sized organizations—a consulting firm, a technology company, a hospital, a consumer goods company, and a school system. Using a method called "structural observation," during one intensive week of observation for each executive I recorded various aspects of every piece of mail and every verbal contact. My method was designed to capture data on both work characteristics and job content. In all, I analyzed 890 pieces of incoming and outgoing mail and 368 verbal contacts.

behavioral scientist to the problem of worker motivation, the manager—that person in charge of the organization or one of its subunits—has been forgotten.

My intention in this article is simple: to break the reader away from Fayol's words and introduce him to a more supportable, and what I believe to be a more useful, description of managerial work. This description derives from my review and synthesis of the available research on how various managers have spent their time.

In some studies, managers were observed intensively ("shadowed" is the term some of them used); in a number of others, they kept detailed diaries of their activities; in a few studies, their records were analyzed. All kinds of managers were studied—foremen, factory supervisors, staff managers, field sales managers, hospital administrators, presidents of companies and nations, and even street gang leaders. These "managers" worked in the United States, Canada, Sweden, and Great Britain. In the ruled insert on page 51 is a brief review of the major studies that I found most useful in developing this description, including my own study of five American chief executive officers.

A synthesis of these findings paints an interesting picture, one as different from Fayol's classical view as a cubist abstract is from a Renaissance painting. In a sense, this picture will be obvious to anyone who has ever spent a day in a manager's office, either in front of the desk or behind it. Yet, at the same time, this picture may turn out to be revolutionary, in that it throws into doubt so much of the folklore that we have accepted about the manager's work.

I first discuss some of this folklore and contrast it with some of the discoveries of systematic research—the hard facts about how managers spend their time. Then I synthesize these research findings in a description of ten roles that seem to describe the essential content of all managers' jobs. In a concluding section, I discuss a number of implications of this synthesis for those trying to achieve more effective management, both in classrooms and in the business world.

SOME FOLKLORE AND FACTS ABOUT MANAGERIAL WORK

There are four myths about the manager's job that do not bear up under careful scrutiny of the facts.

1. *Folklore.* *The manager is a reflective, systematic planner.* The evidence on this issue is overwhelming, but not a shred of it supports this statement.

Fact. *Study after study has shown that managers work at an unrelenting pace, that their activities are characterized by brevity, variety, and discontinuity, and that they are strongly oriented to action and dislike reflective activities.* Consider this evidence:

- Half the activities engaged in by the five chief executives of my study lasted less than nine minutes, and only 10% exceeded one hour.[1] A study of 56 U.S. foremen found that they averaged 583 activities per eight-hour shift, an average of 1 every 48 seconds.[2] The work pace for both chief executives and foremen was unrelenting. The chief executives met a steady stream of callers and mail from the moment they arrived in the morning until they left in the evening. Coffee breaks and lunches were inevitably work related, and ever-present subordinates seemed to usurp any free moment.

- A diary study of 160 British middle and top managers found that they worked for a half hour or more without interruption only about once every two days.[3]
- Of the verbal contacts of the chief executives in my study, 93% were arranged on an ad hoc basis. Only 1% of the executives' time was spent in open-ended observational tours. Only 1 out of 368 verbal contacts was unrelated to a specific issue and could be called general planning. Another researcher finds that "in *not one single case* did a manager report the obtaining of important external information from a general conversation or other undirected personal communication."[4]
- No study has found important patterns in the way managers schedule their time. They seem to jump from issue to issue, continually responding to the needs of the moment.

Is this the planner that the classical view describes? Hardly. How, then, can we explain this behavior? The manager is simply responding to the pressures of his job. I found that my chief executives terminated many of their own activities, often leaving meetings before the end, and interrupted their desk work to call in subordinates. One president not only placed his desk so that he could look down a long hallway but also left his door open when he was alone—an invitation for subordinates to come in and interrupt him.

Clearly, these managers wanted to encourage the flow of current information. But more significantly, they seemed to be conditioned by their own work loads. They appreciated the opportunity cost of their own time, and they were continually aware of their ever-present obligations—mail to be answered, callers to attend to, and so on. It seems that no matter what he is doing, the manager is plagued by the possibilities of what he might do and what he must do.

When the manager must plan, he seems to do so implicitly in the context of daily actions, not in some abstract process reserved for two weeks in the organization's mountain retreat. The plans of the chief executives I studied seemed to exist only in their heads—as flexible, but often specific intentions. The traditional literature notwithstanding, the job of managing does not breed reflective planners; the manager is a real-time responder to stimuli, an individual who is conditioned by his job to prefer live to delayed action.

2. *Folklore.* *The effective manager has no regular duties to perform.* Managers are constantly being told to spend more time planning and delegating, and less time seeing customers and engaging in negotiations. These are not, after all, the true tasks of the manager. To use the popular analogy the good manager, like the good conductor, carefully orchestrates everything in advance, then sits back to enjoy the fruits of his labor, responding occasionally to an unforeseeable exception.

But here again the pleasant abstraction just does not seem to hold up. We had better take a closer look at those activities managers feel compelled to engage in before we arbitrarily define them away.

Fact.   In addition to handling exceptions, managerial work involved performing a number of regular duties, including ritual and ceremony, negotiations, and processing of soft information that links the organization with its environment. Consider some evidence from the research studies:

- A study of the work of the presidents of small companies found that they engaged in routine activities because their companies could not afford staff specialists and were so thin on operating personnel that a single absence often required the president to substitute.[5]
- One study of field sales managers and another of chief executives suggest that it is a natural part of both jobs to see important customers, assuming the managers wish to keep those customers.[6]
- Someone, only half in jest, once described the manager as that person who sees visitors so that everyone else can get his work done. In my study, I found that certain ceremonial duties—meeting visiting dignitaries, giving out gold watches, presiding at Christmas dinners—were an intrinsic part of the chief executive's job.
- Studies of managers' information flow suggest that managers play a key role in securing "soft" external information (much of it available only to them because of their status) and in passing it along to their subordinates.

3. *Folklore.   The senior manager needs aggregated information, which a formal management information system best provides.* Not too long ago, the words *total information system* were everywhere in the management literature. In keeping with the classical view of the manager as that individual perched on the apex of a regulated, hierarchical system, the literature's manager was to receive all his important information from a giant, comprehensive MIS.

But lately, as it has become increasingly evident that these giant MIS systems are not working—that managers are simply not using them—the enthusiasm has waned. A look at how managers actually process information makes the reason quite clear. Managers have five media at their command—documents, telephone calls, scheduled and unscheduled meetings, and observational tours.

Fact.   Managers strongly favor the verbal media—namely, telephone calls and meetings. The evidence comes from every single study of managerial work. Consider the following:

- In two British studies, managers spent an average of 66% and 80% of their time in verbal (oral) communication.[7] In my study of five American chief executives, the figure was 78%.
- These five chief executives treated mail processing as a burden to be dispensed with. One came in Saturday morning to process 142 pieces of mail in just over three hours, to "get rid of all the stuff." This same manager looked at the first piece of "hard" mail he had received all week, a standard cost report, and put it aside with the comment, "I never look at this."
- These same five chief executives responded immediately to 2 of the 40 routine reports they received during the five weeks of my study and to four items in the 104 periodicals. They skimmed most of these periodicals in seconds, almost ritualistically. In all, these chief executives of good-sized organizations initiated on their own—that is, not in response to something else—a grand total of 25 pieces of mail during the 25 days I observed them.

An analysis of the mail the executives received reveals an interesting picture—only 13% was of specific and immediate use. So now we have another piece in the puzzle: not much of the mail provides live, current information—the action of a competitor, the mood of a government legislator, or the rating of last night's television show. Yet this is the information that drove the managers, interrupting their meetings and rescheduling their workdays.

Consider another interesting finding. Managers seem to cherish "soft" information, especially gossip, hearsay, and speculation. Why? The reason is its timeliness; today's gossip may be tommorow's fact. The manager who is not accessible for the telephone call informing him that his biggest customer was seen golfing with his main competitor may read about a dramatic drop in sales in the next quarterly report. But then it's too late.

To assess the value of historical, aggregated, "hard" MIS information, consider two of the manager's prime uses for his information—to identify problems and opportunities[8] and to build his own mental models of the things around him (e.g., how his organization's budget system works, how his customers buy his product, how changes in the economy affect his organization, and so on! Every bit of evidence suggests that the manager identifies decision situations and builds models not with the aggregated abstractions an MIS provides, but with specific tidbits of data.

Consider the words of Richard Neustadt, who studied the information-collecting habits of Presidents Roosevelt, Truman, and Eisenhower:

> "It is not information of a general sort that helps a President see personal stakes; not summaries, not surveys, not the *bland amalgams.* Rather . . . it is the odds and ends of *tangible detail* that pieced together in his mind illuminate the underside of issues put before him. To help himself he must reach out as widely as he can for every scrap of fact, opinion, gossip, bearing on his interests and relationships as President. He must become his own director of his own central intelligence.[9]

The manager's emphasis on the verbal media raises two important points:

First, verbal information is stored in the brains of people. Only when people write this information down can it be stored in the files of the organization—whether in metal cabinets or on magnetic tape—and managers apparently do not write down much of what they hear. Thus the strategic data bank of the organization is not in the memory of its computers but in the minds of its managers.

Second, the manager's extensive use of verbal media helps to explain why he is reluctant to delegate tasks. When we note that most of the manager's important information comes in verbal form and is stored in his head, we can well appreciate his reluctance. It is not as if he can hand a dossier over to someone; he must take the time to "dump memory"—to tell that someone all he knows about the subject. But this could take so long that the manager may find it easier to do the task himself. Thus the manager is damned by his own information system to a "dilemma of delegation"—to do too much himself or to delegate to his subordinates with inadequate briefing.

4. *Folklore. Management is, or at least is quickly becoming, a science and a profession.* By almost any definitions of *science* and *profession,* this statement

is false. Brief observation of any manager will quickly lay to rest the notion that managers practice a science. A science involves the enaction of systematic, analytically determined procedures or programs. If we do not even know what procedures managers use, how can we prescribe them by scientific analysis? And how can we call management a profession if we cannot specify what managers are to learn? For after all, a profession involves "knowledge of some department of learning or science" (*Random House Dictionary*).[10]

Fact.   The managers' programs—to schedule time, process information, make decisions, and so on—remain locked deep inside their brains. Thus, to describe these programs, we rely on words like *judgment* and *intuition,* seldom stopping to realize that they are merely labels for our ignorance.

I was struck during my study by the fact that the executives I was observing— all very competent by any standard—are fundamentally indistinguishable from their counterparts of a hundred years ago (or a thousand years ago, for that matter). The information they need differs, but they seek it in the same way—by word of mouth. Their decisions concern modern technology, but the procedures they use to make them are the same as the procedures of the nineteenth-century manager. Even the computer, so important for the specialized work of the organization, has apparently had no influence on the work procedures of general managers. In fact, the manager is in a kind of loop, with increasingly heavy work pressures but no aid forthcoming from management science.

Considering the facts about managerial work, we can see that the manager's job is enormously complicated and difficult. The manager is overburdened with obligations, yet he cannot easily delegate his tasks. As a result, he is driven to over-work and is forced to do many tasks superficially. Brevity, fragmentation, and verbal communication characterize his work. Yet these are the very characteristics of managerial work that have impeded scientific attempts to improve it. As a result, the management scientist has concentrated his efforts on the specialized functions of the organization, where he could more easily analyze the procedures and quantify the relevant information.[11]

But the pressures of the manager's job are becoming worse. Where before he needed only to respond to owners and directors, now he finds that subordinates with democratic norms continually reduce his freedom to issue unexplained orders, and a growing number of outside influences (consumer groups, government agencies, and so on) expect his attention. And the manager has had nowhere to turn for help. The first step in providing the manager with some help is to find out what his job really is.

BACK TO BASIC DESCRIPTION OF MANAGERIAL WORK

Now let us try to put some of the pieces of this puzzle together. Earlier, I defined the manager as that person in charge of an organization or one of its subunits. Besides chief executive officers, this definition would include vice presidents, bishops, foremen, hockey coaches, and prime ministers. Can all of these people have anything in common? Indeed they can. For an important starting point, all are vested with formal authority over an organizational unit. From formal authority comes status, which leads to various interpersonal relations, and from these comes access to information. Information, in turn, enables the manager to make decisions and strategies for his unit.

The manager's job can be described in terms of various "roles," or organized sets of behaviors identified with a position. My description, shown in *Exhibit I,* comprises ten roles. As we shall see, formal authority gives rise to the three interpersonal roles, which in turn give rise to the three informational roles; these two sets of roles enable the manager to play the four decisional roles.

Interpersonal Roles

Three of the manager's roles arise directly from his formal authority and involve basic interpersonal relationships.

1. First is the *figurehead* role. By virtue of his position as head of an organizational unit, every manager must perform some duties of a ceremonial nature. The president greets the touring dignitaries, the foreman attends the wedding of a lathe operator, and the sales manager takes an important customer to lunch.

The chief executives of my study spent 12% of their contact time on ceremonial duties; 17% of their incoming mail dealt with acknowledgments and requests related to their status. For example, a letter to a company president requested free merchandise for a crippled schoolchild; diplomas were put on the desk of the school superintendent for his signature.

Duties that involve interpersonal roles may sometimes be routine, involving little serious communication and no important decision making. Nevertheless, they

EXHIBIT I The Manager's Roles

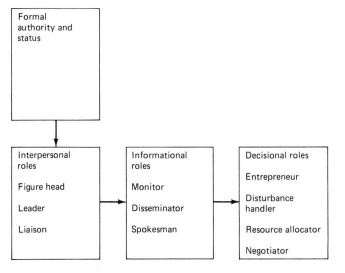

are important to the smooth functioning of an organization and cannot be ignored by the manager.

2. Because he is in charge of an organizatrional unit the manager is responsible for the work of the people of that unit. His actions in this regard constitute the *leader* role. Some of these actions involve leadership directly—for example, in most organizations the manager is normally responsible for hiring and training his own staff.

In addition, there is the indirect exercise of the leader role. Every manager must motivate and encourage his employees, somehow reconciling their individual needs with the goals of the organization. In virtually every contact the manager has with his employees, subordinates seeking leadership clues probe his actions: "Does he approve?" "How would he like the report to turn out?" "Is he more interested in market share than high profits?"

The influence of the manager is most clearly seen in the leader role. Formal authority vests him with great potential power; leadership determines in large part how much of it he will realize.

3. The literature of management has always recognized the leader role, particularly those aspects of it related to motivation. In comparison, until recently it has hardly mentioned the *liaison* role, in which the manager makes contacts outside his vertical chain of command. This is remarkable in light of the finding of virtually every study of managerial work that managers spend as much time with peers and other people outside their units as they do with their own subordinates—and, surprisingly, very little time with their own superiors.

In Rosemary Stewart's diary study, the 160 British middle and top managers spent 47% of their time with peers, 41% of their time with people outside their unit, and only 12% of their time with their superiors. For Robert H. Guest's study of U.S. foremen, the figures were 44%, 46%, and 10%. The chief executives of my study averaged 44% of their contact time with people outside their organizations, 48% with subordinates, and 7% with directors and trustees.

The contacts the five CEOs made were with an incredibly wide range of people: subordinates; clients, business associates, and suppliers; and peers—managers of similar organizations, government and trade organization officials, fellow directors on outside boards, and independents with no relevant organizational affiliations. The chief executives' time with and mail from these groups is shown in *Exhibit II* on page 59. Guest's study of foremen shows, likewise, that their contacts were numerous and wide ranging, seldom involving fewer than 25 individuals, and often more than 50.

As we shall see shortly, the manager cultivates such contacts largely to find information. In effect, the liaison role is devoted to building up the manager's own external information system—informal, private, verbal, but, nevertheless, effective.

Informational Roles

By virtue of his interpersonal contacts, both with his subordinates and with his network of contacts, the manager emerges as the nerve center of his organiza-

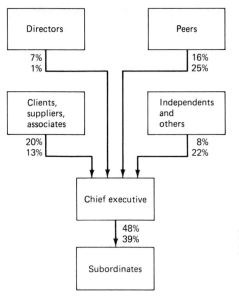

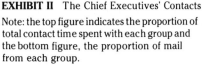

EXHIBIT II The Chief Executives' Contacts

Note: the top figure indicates the proportion of total contact time spent with each group and the bottom figure, the proportion of mail from each group.

tional unit. He may not know everything, but he typically knows more than any member of his staff.

Studies have shown this relationship to hold for all managers, from street gang leaders to U.S. presidents. In *The Human Group,* George C. Homans explains how, because they were at the center of the information flow in their own gangs and were also in close touch with other gang leaders, street gang leaders were better informed than any of their followers.[12] And Richard Neustadt describes the following account from his study of Franklin D. Roosevelt:

> "The essence of Roosevelt's technique for information-gathering was competition. 'He would call you in,' one of his aides once told me, 'and he'd ask you to get the story on some complicated business, and you'd come back after a couple of days of hard labor and present the juicy morsel you'd uncovered under a stone somewhere, and *then* you'd find out he knew all about it, along with something else you *didn't* know. Where he got this information from he wouldn't mention, usually, but after he had done this to you once or twice you got damn careful about *your* information.'"[13]

We can see where Roosevelt "got this information" when we consider the relationship between the interpersonal and informational roles. As leader, the manager has formal and easy access to every member of his staff. Hence, as noted earlier, he tends to know more about his own unit than anyone else does. In addition, his liaison contacts expose the manager to external information to which his subordinates often lack access. Many of these contacts are with other managers of equal status, who are themselves nerve centers in their own organization. In this way, the manager develops a powerful data base of information.

The processing of information is a key part of the manager's job. In my study, the chief executives spent 40% of their contact time on activities devoted exclusively to the transmission of information; 70% of their incoming mail was purely informational (as opposed to request for action). The manager does not leave meetings or hang up the telephone in order to get back to work. In large part, communication *is* his work. Three roles describe these informational aspects of managerial work.

1. As *monitor,* the manager perpetually scans his environment for information, interrogates his liaison contacts and his subordinates, and receives unsolicited information, much of it as a result of the network of personal contacts he has developed. Remember that a good part of the information the manager collects in his monitor role arrives in verbal form, often as gossip, hearsay, and speculation. By virtue of his contacts, the manager has a natural advantage in collecting this soft information for his organization.

2. He must share and distribute much of this information. Information he gleans from outside personal contacts may be needed within his organization. In his *disseminator* role, the manager passes some of his privileged information directly to his subordinates, who would otherwise have no access to it. When his subordinates lack easy contact with one another, the manager will sometimes pass information from one to another.

3. In his *spokesman* role, the manager sends some of his information to people outside his unit—a president makes a speech to lobby for an organization cause, or a foreman suggests a product modification to a supplier. In addition, as part of his role as spokesman, every manager must inform and satisfy the influential people who control his organizational unit. For the foreman, this may simply involve keeping the plant manager informed about the flow of work through the shop.

The president of a large corporation, however, may spend a great amount of his time dealing with a host of influences. Directors and shareholders must be advised about financial performance; consumer groups must be assured that the organization is fulfilling its social responsibilities; and government officials must be satisfied that the organization is abiding by the law.

Decisional Roles

Information is not, of course, an end in itself; it is the basic input to decision making. One thing is clear in the study of managerial work: the manager plays the major role in his unit's decision-making system. As its formal authority, only he can commit the unit to important new courses of action; and as its nerve center, only he has full and current information to make the set of decisions that determines the unit's strategy. Four roles describe the manager as decision-maker.

1. As *entrepreneur,* the manager seeks to improve his unit, to adapt it to changing conditions in the environment. In his monitor role, the president is constantly on the lookout for new ideas. When a good one appears, he initiates a development project that he may supervise himself or delegate to an employee (perhaps with the stipulation that he must approve the final proposal).

There are two interesting features about these development projects at the chief executive level. First, these projects do not involve single decisions or even unified clusters of decisions. Rather, they emerge as a series of small decisions and actions sequenced over time. Apparently, the chief executive prolongs each project so that he can fit it bit by bit into his busy, disjointed schedule and so that he can gradually come to comprehend the issue, if it is a complex one.

Second, the chief executives I studied supervised as many as 50 of these projects at the same time. Some projects entailed new products or processes; others involved public relations campaigns, improvement of the cash position, reorganization of a weak department, resolution of a morale problem in a foreign division, integration of computer operations, various acquisitions at different stages of development, and so on.

The chief executive appears to maintain a kind of inventory of the development projects that he himself supervises—projects that are at various stages of development, some active and some in limbo. Like a juggler, he keeps a number of projects in the air; periodically, one comes down, is given a new burst of energy, and is sent back into orbit. At various intervals, he put new projects on-stream and discards old ones.

2. While the entrepreneur role describes the manager as the voluntary initiator of change, the *disturbance handler* role depicts the manager involuntarily responding to pressures. Here change is beyond the manager's control. He must act because the pressures of the situation are too severe to be ignored: strike looms, a major customer has gone bankrupt, or a supplier reneges on his contract.

It has been fashionable, I noted earlier, to compare the manager to an orchestra conductor, just as Peter F. Drucker wrote in *The Practice of Management:*

> "The manager has the task of creating a true whole that is larger than the sum of its parts, a productive entity that turns out more than the sum of the resources put into it. One analogy is the conductor of a symphony orchestra, through whose effort, vision and leadership individual instrumental parts that are so much noise by themselves become the living whole of music. But the conductor has the composer's score; he is only interpreter. The manager is both composer and conductor."[14]

Now consider the words of Leonard R. Sayles, who has carried out systematic research on the manager's job:

> "[The manager] is like a symphony orchestra conductor, endeavouring to maintain a melodious performance in which the contributions of the various instruments are coordinated and sequenced, patterned and paced, while the orchestra members are having various personal difficulties, stage hands are moving music stands, alternating excessive heat and cold are creating audience and instrument problems, and the sponsor of the concert is insisting on irrational changes in the program."[15]

In effect, every manager must spend a good part of his time responding to high-pressure disturbances. No organization can be so well run, so standardized, that it has considered every contingency in the uncertain environment in advance.

Disturbances arise not only because poor managers ignore situations until they reach crisis proportions, but also because good managers cannot possibly anticipate all the consequences of the actions they take.

3. The third decisional role is that of *resource allocator*. To the manager falls the responsibility of deciding who will get what in his organizational unit. Perhaps the most important resource the manager allocates is his own time. Access to the manager constitutes exposure to the unit's nerve center and decision-maker. The manager is also charged with designing his unit's structure, that pattern of formal relationships that determines how work is to be divided and coordinated.

Also, in his role as resource allocator, the manager authorizes the important decisions of his unit before they are implemented. By retaining this power, the manager can ensure that decisions are interrelated; all must pass through a single brain. To fragment this power is to encourage discontinuous decision making and a disjointed strategy.

There are a number of interesting features about the manager's authorizing others' decisions. First, despite the widespread use of capital budgeting procedures—a means of authorizing various capital expenditures at one time—executives in my study made a great many authorization decisions on an ad hoc basis. Apparently, many projects cannot wait or simply do not have the quantifiable costs and benefits that capital budgeting requires.

Second, I found that the chief executives faced incredibly complex choices. They had to consider the impact of each decision on other decisions and on the organization's strategy. They had to ensure that the decision would be acceptable to those who influence the organization, as well as ensure that resources would not be overextended. They had to understand the various costs and benefits as well as the feasibility of the proposal. They also had to consider questions of timing. All this was necessary for the simple approval of someone else's proposal. At the same time, however, delay could lose time, while quick approval could be ill considered and quick rejection might discourage the subordinate who had spent months developing a pet project.

One common solution to approving projects is to pick the man instead of the proposal. That is, the manager authorizes those projects presented to him by people whose judgment he trusts. But he cannot always use this simple dodge.

4. The final decisional role is that of *negotiator*. Studies of managerial work at all levels indicate that managers spend considerable time in negotiatons: the president of the football team is called in to work out a contract with the holdout superstar; the corporation president leads his company's contingent to negotiate a new strike issue; the foreman argues a grievance problem to its conclusion with the shop steward. As Leonard Sayles puts it, negotiations are a "way of life" for the sophisticated manager.

These negotiations are duties of the manager's job; perhaps routine, they are not to be shirked. They are an integral part of his job, for only he has the authority to commit organizational resources in "real time," and only he has the nerve center information that important negotiations require.

The Integrated Job

It should be clear by now that the ten roles I have been describing are not easily separable. In the terminology of the psychologist, they form a gestalt, an integrated whole. No role can be pulled out of the framework and the job be left intact. For example, a manager without liaison contacts lacks external information. As a result, he can neither disseminate the information his employees need nor make decisions that adequately reflect external conditions. (In fact, this is a problem for the new person in a managerial position, since he cannot make effective decisions until he has built up his network of contacts.)

Here lies a clue to the problems of team management.[16] Two or three people cannot share a single managerial position unless they can act as one entity. This means that they cannot divide up the ten roles unless they can very carefully reintegrate them. The real difficulty lies with the informational roles. Unless there can be full sharing of managerial information—and, as I pointed out earlier, it is primarily verbal—team management breaks down. A single managerial job cannot be arbitrarily split, for example, into internal and external roles, for information from both sources must be brought to bear on the same decisions.

To say that the ten roles form a gestalt is not to say that all managers give equal attention to each role. In fact, I found in my review of the various research studies that

> . . . sales managers seem to spend relatively more of their time in the interpersonal roles, presumably a reflection of the extrovert nature of the marketing activity;
>
> . . . production managers give relatively more attention to the decisional roles, presumably a reflection of their concern with efficient work flow;
>
> . . . staff managers spend the most time in the informational roles, since they are experts who manage departments that advise other parts of the organization.

Nevertheless, in all cases the interpersonal, informational, and decisional roles remain inseparable.

TOWARD MORE EFFECTIVE MANAGEMENT

What are the messages for management in this description? I believe, first and foremost, that this description of managerial work should prove more important to managers than any prescription they might derive from it. That is to say, *the manager's effectiveness is significantly influenced by his insight into his own work.* His performance depends on how well he understands and responds to the pressures and dilemmas of the job. Thus managers who can be introspective about their work are likely to be effective at their jobs. The ruled insert on page 64 offers 14 groups of self-study questions for managers. Some may sound rhetorical; none is meant to be. Even though the questions cannot be answered simply, the manager should address them.

Let us take a look at three specific areas of concern. For the most part, the managerial logjams—the dilemma of delegation, the data base centralized in one

1. Where do I get my information, and how? Can I make greater use of my contacts to get information? Can other people do some of my scanning for me? In what areas is my knowledge weakest, and how can I get others to provide me with the information I need? Do I have powerful enough mental models of those things I must understand within the organization and in its environment?

2. What information do I disseminate in my organization? How important is it that my subordinates get my information? Do I keep too much information to myself because dissemination of it is time-consuming or inconvenient? How can I get more information to others so they can make better decisions?

3. Do I balance information collecting with action taking? Do I tend to act before information is in? Or do I wait so long for all the information that opportunities pass me by and I become a bottleneck in my organization?

4. What pace of change am I asking my organization to tolerate? Is this change balanced so that our operations are neither excessively static nor overly disrupted? Have we sufficiently analyzed the impact of this change on the future of our organization.

5. Am I sufficiently well informed to pass judgment on the proposals that my subordinates make? Is it possible to leave final authorization for more of the proposals with subordinates? Do we have problems of coordination because subordinates in fact now make too many of these decisions independently?

6. What is my vision of direction for this organization? Are these plans primarily in my own mind in loose form? Should I make them explicit in order to guide the decisions of others in the organization better? Or do I need flexibility to change them at will?

7. How do my subordinates react to my managerial style? Am I sufficiently sensitive to the powerful influence my actions have on them? Do I fully understand their reactions to my actions? Do I find an appropriate balance between encouragement and pressure? Do I stiffle their initiative?

8. What kind of external relationships do I maintain, and how? Do I spend too much of my time maintaining these relationships? Are there certain types of people whom I should get to know better?

9. Is there any system to my time scheduling, or am I just reacting to the pressures of the moment? Do I find the appropriate mix of activities, or do I tend to concentrate on one particular function or one type of problem just because I find it interesting? Am I more efficient with particular kinds of work at special times of the day or week? Does my schedule reflect this? Can someone else (in addition to my secretary) take responsibility for much of my scheduling and do it more systematically?

10. Do I overwork? What effect does my work load have on my efficiency? Should I force myself to take breaks or to reduce the pace of my activity?

11. Am I too superficial in what I do? Can I really shift moods as quickly and frequently as my work patterns require? Should I attempt to decrease the amount of fragmentation and interruption in my work?

12. Do I orient myself too much toward current, tangible activities? Am I a slave to the action and excitement of my work, so that I am no longer able to concentrate on issues? Do key problems receive the attention they deserve. Should I spend more time reading and probing deeply into certain issues? Could I be more reflective? Should I be?

13. Do I use the different media appropriately? Do I know how to make the most of written communication? Do I rely excessively on face-to-face communication, thereby putting all but a few of my subordinates at an informational disadvantage? Do I schedule enough of my meetings on a regular basis? Do I spend enough time touring my organization to observe activity at first hand? Am I too detached from the heart of my organization's activities, seeing things only in an abstract way?

14. How do I blend my personal rights and duties? Do my obligations consume all my time? How can I free myself sufficiently from obligations to ensure that I am taking this organization where I want it to go? How can I turn my obligations to my advantage?

brain, the problems of working with the management scientist—revolve around the verbal nature of the manager's information. There are great dangers in centralizing the organization's data bank in the minds of its managers. When they leave, they take their memory with them. And when subordinates are out of convenient verbal reach of the manager, they are at an informational disadvantage.

1. *The manager is challenged to find systematic ways to share his privileged information.* A regular debriefing session with key subordinates, a weekly memory dump on the dictating machine, the maintaining of a diary of important information for limited circulation, or other similar methods may ease the logjam of work considerably. Time spent disseminating this information will be more than regained when decisions must be made. Of course, some will raise the question of confidentiality. But managers would do well to weigh the risks of exposing privileged information against having subordinates who can make effective decisions.

If there is a single theme that runs through this article, it is that the pressures of his job drive the manager to be superficial in his actions—to overload himself with work, encourage interruption, respond quickly to every stimulus, seek the tangible and avoid the abstract, make decisions in small increments, and do everything abruptly.

2. *Here again, the manager is challenged to deal consciously with the pressures of superficiality by giving serious attention to the issues that require it, by stepping back from his tangible bits of information in order to see a broad picture, and by making use of analytical inputs.* Although effective managers have to be adept at responding quickly to numerous and varying problems, the danger in managerial work is that they will respond to every issue equally (and that means abruptly) and that they will never work the tangible bits and pieces of informational input into a comprehensive picture of their world.

As I noted earlier, the manager uses these bits of information to build models of his world. But the manager can also avail himself of the models of the specialists. Economists describe the functioning of markets, operations researchers simulate financial flow processes, and behavioral scientists explain the needs and goals of people. The best of these models can be searched out and learned.

In dealing with complex issues, the senior manager has much to gain from a close relationship with the management scientists of his own organization. They have something important that he lacks—time to probe complex issues. An effective working relationship hinges on the resolution of what a colleague and I have called "the planning dilemma."[17] Managers have the information and the authority; analysts have the time and the technology. A successful working relationship between the two will be effected when the manager learns to share his information and the analyst learns to adapt to the manager's needs. For the analyst, adaptation means worrying less about the elegance of the method and more about its speed and flexibility.

It seems to me that analysts can help the top manager especially to schedule his time, feed in analytical information, monitor projects under his supervision, develop models to aid in making choices, design contingency plans for disturbances that can be anticipated, and conduct "quick-and-dirty" analysis for those that cannot. But there can be no cooperation if the analysts are out of the mainstream of the manager's information flow.

3. *The manager is challenged to gain control of his own time by turning obligations to his advantage and by turning those things he wishes to do in obligations.* The chief executives of my study initiated only 32% of their own contacts (and another 5% by mutual agreement). And yet to a considerable extent they seemed to control their time. There were two key factors that enabled them to do so.

First, the manager has to spend so much time discharging obligations that if he were to view them as just that, he would leave no mark on his organization. The unsuccessful manager blames failure on the obligations; the effective manager turns his obligations to his own advantage. A speech is a chance to lobby for a cause; a meeting is a chance to reorganize a weak department; a visit to an important customer is a chance to extract trade information.

Second, the manager frees some of his time to do those things that he— perhaps no one else—thinks important by turning them into obligations. Free time is made, not found, in the manager's job; it is forced into the schedule. Hoping to leave some time open for contemplation or general planning is tantamount to hoping that the pressures of the job will go away. The manager who wants to innovate initiates a project and obligates others to report back to him; the manager who needs certain environmental information establishes channels that will automatically keep him informed; the manager who has to tour facilities commits himself publicly.

THE EDUCATOR'S JOB

Finally, a word about the training of managers. Our management schools have done an admirable job of training the organization's specialists—management scientists, marketing researchers, accountants, and organizational development specialists. But for the most part they have not trained managers.[18]

Management schools will begin the serious training of managers when skill training takes a serious place next to cognitive learning. Cognitive learning is detached and informational, like reading a book or listening to a lecture. No doubt much important cognitive material must be assimilated by the manager-to-be. But cognitive learning no more makes a manager than it does a swimmer. The latter will drown the first time he jumps into the water if his coach never takes him out of the lecture hall, gets him wet, and gives him feedback on his performance.

In other words, we are taught a skill through practice plus feedback, whether in a real or a simulated situation. Our management schools need to identify the skills managers use, select students who show potential in these skills, put the students into situations where these skills can be practiced, and then give them systematic feedback on their performance.

My description of managerial work suggests a number of important managerial skills—developing peer relationships, carrying out negotiations, motivating subordinates, resolving conflicts, establishing information networks and subsequently disseminating information, making decisions in conditions of extreme ambiguity, and allocating resources. Above all, the manager needs to be introspective about his work so that he may continue to learn on the job.

Many of the manager's skills can, in fact, be practiced, using techniques that range from role playing to videotaping real meetings. And our management schools can enhance the entrepreneurial skills by designing programs that encourage sensible risk taking and innovation.

No job is more vital to our society than that of the manager. It is the manager who determines whether our social institutions serve us well or whether they squander our talents and resources. It is time to strip away the folklore about managerial work, and time to study it realistically so that we can begin the difficult task of making significant improvements in its performance.

1. All the data (from my study can be found in Henry Mintzberg, *The Nature of Managerial Work* (New York: Harper & Row, 1971).

2. Robert H. Guest, "Of Time and the Foreman," *Personnel,* May 1986, p. 478.

3. Rosemary Stewart, *Managers and Their Jobs* (London: Macmillan, 1967); see also Sune Carlson, *Executive Behaviour* (Stockholm: Strombergs, 1951), the first of the diary studies.

4. Francis J. Aguilar: *Scanning the Business Environment:* New York: MacMillan, 1967), p. 102.

5. Unpublished study by Irving Choran, reported in Mintzberg, *The Nature of Managerial Work.*

6. Robert T. Davis, *Performance and Development of Field Sales Managers.* (Boston: Division of Research, Harvard Business School, 1957); George H. Copeman, *The Role of the Managing Director* (London: Business Publications, 1963).

7. Stewart, *Managers and Their Jobs;* Tom Burns, "The Directions of Activity and Communication in a Departmental Executive Group." *Human Relations* 7, no. 1 (1954): 73.

8. H. Edward Wrapp. "Good Managers Don't Make Policy Decisions," HBR September–October 1967, p. 91: Wrapp refers to this as spotting opportunities and relationships in the stream of operating problems and decisions; in his article Wrapp raises a number of excellent points related to this analysis.

9. Richard E. Neustadt, *Presidential Power* (New York: John Wiley, 1960), pp. 153–154: italics added.

10. For a more thorough, though rather different, discussion of this issue, see Kenneth R. Andrews, "Toward Professionalism in Business Management," HBR March–April 1969, p. 49.

11. C. Jackson Grayson, Jr., in "Management Science and Business Practice," HBR July–August 1973, p. 41, explains in similar terms why, as chairman of the Price Commission, he did not use those very techniques that he himself promoted in his earlier career as a management scientist.

12. George C. Homans. *The Human Group* (New York: Harcourt, Brace & World, 1959), based on the study by William F. Whyte entitled *Street Corner Society,* rev. ed. (Chicago: University of Chicago Press, 1955).

13. Neustadt. *Presidential Power,* p. 157.

14. Peter F. Drucker. *The Practice of Management* (New York: Harper & Row, 1954), pp. 341–342.

15. Leonard R. Savles. *Managerial Behavior* (New York: McGraw-Hill, 1964), p. 162.

16. See Richard C. Hodgson, Daniel J. Levinson, and Abraham Zaleznik, *The Executive Role Constellation* (Boston: Division of Research, Harvard Business School, 1965), for a discussion of the sharing of roles.

17. James S. Hekimian and Henry Mintzberg, "The Planning Dilemma." *The Management Review,* May 1968, p. 4.

18. See I. Sterling Livingston, "Myth of the Well-Educated Manager," HBR January–February 1971, p. 79.

3
Individual and Organizational Learning

R&D ORGANIZATIONS AS LEARNING SYSTEMS

Barara Carlsson
Peter Keane
J. Bruce Martin

In comparison with the relatively systematic, logical, and planned process of some organizations, R&D processes often appear to be disorderly and unpredictable—difficult, if not impossible, to manage. However, the hypothesis that the primary output of R&D is *knowledge* (incorporated in formulas and specifications) suggests that its major process is *learning*. We have confirmed that, when R&D activities are viewed as part of a learning process, much of what appears disorderly is seen to have an underlying order. Furthermore, we have determined that this perspective is useful for describing, understanding and improving the R&D process.

Linear models of technical innovation may be useful in describing key steps in the R&D process and in documenting projects after the fact but are not particularly helpful in understanding the process in real time. Linear models can describe what happened but not *how* it happened, and tend to reinforce the belief in a kind of orderliness which does not exist (see Figure 1).[1]

Source: Reprinted by permission of the authors and publisher from *Sloan Management Review,* Spring, 1976.

The authors are indebted to David A. Kolb, whose work has provided the foundation for this paper, and to Richard Beckhard, who introduced us to Kolb and encouraged our work.

[1]This paper is no exception. The relatively orderly description of our research bears little resemblance to the actual cycling and recycling, false starts, definition and redefinition of hypotheses and objectives which occurred. However, Harvard Business School Professor Charles J. Christenson has described God as "using an inelegant method to design the world but cleaning up His approach in the published version." At least we are in good company.

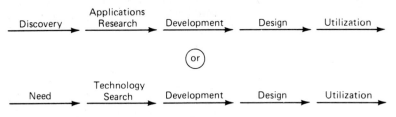

FIGURE 1 Linear Models of Technical Innovation

The model we *have* found to be descriptive of the way learning occurs in R&D organizations is based on D. A. Kolb's work on individual experiential learning.[2] Kolb postulates a four-step repetitive cycle, which provides the framework for the model shown in Figure 2. This cycle is summarized as follows:

> Immediate concrete experience is the basis for observation and reflection. These observations are assimilated into a "theory" from which new implications for action can be deduced. These implications, or hypotheses, then serve as guides in acting to create new experiences.[3]

We have generalized Kolb's work, which focuses on the individual learning process, to the organizational learning process.

FIGURE 2 The Learning Model

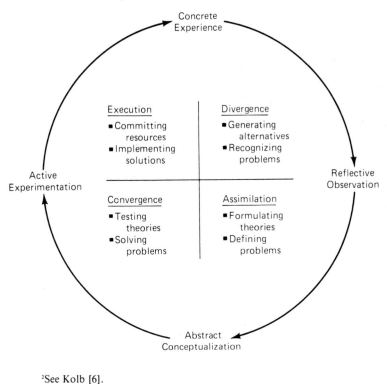

[2]See Kolb [6].
[3]See Kolb [6], p. 2.

Kolb's learning process requires orientations that are polar opposites: active and reflective; concrete and abstract. The shifting orientation results in four kinds of activity, each of which is required at some stage of the learning process.

1. *Divergence* (*concrete* and *reflective*). This kind of activity is required to seek background information and sense opportunities, investigate new patterns, recognize discrepancies and problems, and generate alternatives. Literature Browsing and Brainstorming are techniques which may be used to aid this kind of activity.

2. *Assimilation* (*abstract* and *reflective*). This kind of activity is required to develop theory, compare alternatives, establish criteria, formulate plans and hypotheses, and define problems. Grounded Theory techniques are designed to aid this kind of activity.[4]

3. *Convergence* (*abstract* and *active*). This kind of activity is required to select among alternatives, focus efforts, evaluate plans and programs, test hypotheses, and make decisions. Venture Analysis techniques are designed to aid this kind of activity.

4. *Execution*[5] (*concrete* and *active*). This kind of activity is required to advocate positions or ideas, set objectives, commit to schedules, commit resources, and implement decisions. PERT and Critical Path Scheduling are techniques frequently used to aid this kind of activity.

Organizations differ in their capabilities for performing the tasks associated with each of the stages. There are predictable strengths associated with an appropriate skill level in each stage and there are predictable weaknesses associated with either an excess or a deficiency in any stage. Figure 3 outlines some of these strengths and weaknesses.

EXPERIMENTAL VALIDATION

In a series of experiments, we have demonstrated that the Learning Method provides a useful description of the R&D process in a way which permits strengths and weaknesses to be assessed, identifies bottlenecks, and provides cues to remedial action. We asked R&D managers what factors inhibited innovation in their individual areas. We found that most of their responses fit into the patterns of strengths of weaknesses predicted in Figure 3. The following are a few examples.

Comment	Corresponding Strength or Weakness
"We're not idea poor, but we do need people to push ideas."	Strength in divergence Lack of execution
"Timetables are sometimes too tight to let people explore."	Excessive execution Too little divergence
"We execute well; we need to develop needs."	Sufficient execution Too little divergence

[4]See Glaser and Strauss [3]

[5]We have chosen the term "Execution" rather than "Accommodation," the more precise term used by Kolb, as the label for this stage of the Learning Model. We found that the term "Accommodation" is frequently misunderstood because of its connotations of passivity and compromise.

Comment	Corresponding Strength or Weakness
"We allow ourselves to be diffuse; we need more focus."	Lack of convergence
"We lack conceptualization—fitting at the elements into a full concept."	Lack of assimilation
"We lack good ideas."	Lack of divergence

These data not only suggest that major elements of the R&D process can be expressed in terms of the Learning Model, but also confirm that organizations can develop "flat spots" which may be described in terms of the Learning Model.

In another experiment, we devised a scheme for scoring biweekly progress reports which are written by professional members of our organizations.[6] For each report, this scoring scheme provided a measure of the effort in each stage of the learning process. We applied this scoring scheme to several series of reports

FIGURE 3 Strengths and Weaknesses

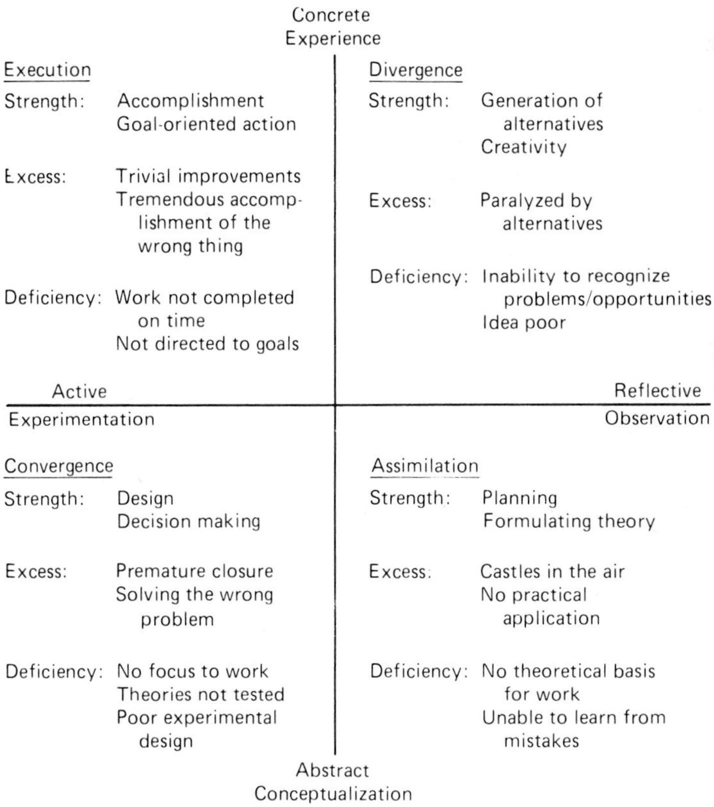

Concrete
Experience

Execution		Divergence	
Strength:	Accomplishment Goal-oriented action	Strength:	Generation of alternatives Creativity
Excess:	Trivial improvements Tremendous accomplishment of the wrong thing	Excess:	Paralyzed by alternatives
Deficiency:	Work not completed on time Not directed to goals	Deficiency:	Inability to recognize problems/opportunities Idea poor

Active — Experimentation / Reflective — Observation

Convergence		Assimilation	
Strength:	Design Decision making	Strength:	Planning Formulating theory
Excess:	Premature closure Solving the wrong problem	Excess:	Castles in the air No practical application
Deficiency:	No focus to work Theories not tested Poor experimental design	Deficiency:	No theoretical basis for work Unable to learn from mistakes

Abstract
Conceptualization

[6]The scoring system was quite complex and specific to the particular reports which were being evaluated. The system consisted essentially of assigning each sentence to a stage of the Learning Model, and totaling the number of sentences in each stage. We are grateful to Sherry Ewald and Paula Miller for their efforts in the sometimes arduous task of scoring the documents.

written by individual staff members. Our findings, which are summarized below, support our hypothesis that the Learning Model is descriptive of the dynamics of R&D projects.

1. Most of the subjects appeared to be following a clockwise sequence through the stages of the Learning Model; that is, a report scoring relatively high in Assimilation was likely to be followed by a report high in Execution, etc.

2. A researcher who had no familiarity with the content of the reports or with the authors could from the scores alone predict with accuracy the strengths and weaknesses of the projects. For example, from a series of scores indicating consistently high levels of Assimilation and Execution, and consistently low levels of Divergence and Convergence, one of the researchers correctly predicted that the project would be suffering from a lack of creativity (Divergence) and lack of focusing and testing of hypotheses (Convergence) prior to execution of new activities, and that these deficiencies could result in executions that failed without adding to understanding.

3. The effect of management interventions could be observed in the scores. For example, late in the project cited above there was a sharp but temporary shift into the Convergence stage. Although we observed the shift, we did not know its cause. Subsequent discussions with the manager revealed that the shift was the result of his probing questions about their research design, and confirmed his fear that the effect of his action had been only temporary.

In a third experiment we collected historical data on the progress of a project and extended the data into real time by periodic interviews with members of the project team. We found that key steps in the progress of the project could be interpreted as representing a clockwise sequence through the Learning Model as shown in Figure 4. A list of the activities involved with the project (corresponding to the numbers on the diagram) and a list of the information inputs which occurred during the project (corresponding to the letters on the diagram) follow Figure 4. Critical examination of this analysis by other project managers and their higher-level R&D managers confirmed that the model represented the realities of the project. The higher-level managers were particularly reassured by the sense of order given to a set of events that had not seemed nearly so orderly at the time.

We have subsequently analyzed other projects in the same manner and found less orderly progression around the model. We found instances of stages being skipped, of project teams "stuck" in a stage, and even instances of reverse (i.e., counterclockwise) movement through the stages. The managers involved generally agreed that the pictures were accurate and that the deviations indicated problems deserving of management attention.

USE OF THE MODEL

We can testify to the usefulness of the Learning Model from our own experience. Our individual strengths are in different stages of the model and our efforts to work together often involved more conflict that the task seemed to warrant. As we learned more about the Learning Model, we each developed an appreciation

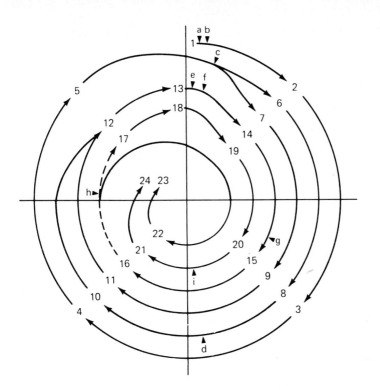

FIGURE 4 Project History in Terms of the Learning Model

List of the Activities for Figure 4

1. Planning activity initiated by a management question: "What businesses should this division be in?"
2. Generation of nine alternatives.
3. Establishment of criteria for selection made jointly with marketing.
4. Evaluation of the nine alternatives against the criteria resulting in the selection of three projects to pursue.
5. Assignment of staff to activate three projects, one of which is the subject of this study.
6. Identifying the options for positioning the product in the market.
7. Identifying the potential process routes to making the product.
8. Establishing the criteria for deciding the competitive targets.
9. Examining standing criteria in the division for choice of processes, and weighting flexibility higher than normal for this project.
10. Deciding on the specific objective for this product.
11. Choosing the process route to be developed.
12. Making the product and placing a consumer test.
13. Obtaining consumer test results that confirmed that the product targets had been met.
14. Generation of alternatives for obtaining a more favorable economic position in the marketplace.
15. Analyzing the alternatives from the standpoint of the user.
16. Selection of the specific target and the attribute to be optimized.
17. Making the product and placing a consumer test. (The path from 16 to 17 is shown as a broken line because the work was incomplete, i.e., the consumer test was placed without having the optimum product.)

18. Obtaining and analyzing consumer test results which were worse than predicted.
19. Generation of alternatives for the project in view of the outcome of the consumer test.
20. Reexamination of criteria.
21. Optimizing product/process variables.
22. Specifying the process details for the test market production and trimming costs to fit within the appropriation. (The path from "h" to 22 is shown as a solid line, because the intervening steps were obviously taken even though they were not specified as activities, e.g., each item of cost was questioned and trimmed if not justified.)
23. Meeting specific requirements for the test market plant.
24. Making product and placing next consumer test.

List of the Information Inputs for Figure 4

a. Management input—desire to capitalize on a new technology and desire to be of service to society.
b. Consumer input—a generally recognized, unmet consumer need.
c. Technical input—temporary transfer in of a scientist familiar with the new technology.
d. Marketing input—desired product target.
e. Economic input—cost estimate for test market plant much higher than expected.
f. Management input—in view of the projected costs, the business opportunity is seen as unattractive.
g. Marketing input—proposal for new product targets.
h. Management input—appropriation for test market (much lower than original estimate).
i. Management input—top management confirmation of overall market staratgy and requirements.

of the contributions of the other members of our group. Our working relationships are greatly improved; now if we find outselves pulling in different directions, we refer to the Model for resolution.

In the course of our experiments, we have exposed the Learning Model to a large number of R&D managers and project team members, and have received responses suggesting that the Model also has been useful to them. Sharing the Learning Model with others in our organization has been most productive when we have communicated the *concept,* and allowed others to discover applications for themselves. Kolb has developed a Learning Style Inventory which we have found very useful in these discussions.[7] The Learning Style Inventory is a brief pencil-and-paper test which gives the subject an indication of his preference for activity in each of the stages of the Learning Model. Members of work teams who shared their individual results have invariably found important differences among themselves, and usually came quickly to understand how these differences in "Learning Style" have influenced their process of working together. Individuals who prefer Execution are likely to be impatient with Assimilation, and Divergers are likely to find Convergers stodgy and stifling of creativity. An understanding of individual differences has generally led to an interest in understanding the

[7]Kolb [5] describes the development of the Learning Style Inventory, which has been published in Kolb, Rubin, and McIntyre [7].

Learning Model, which has in turn led to the kinds of learning and applications reported below.

One project team had been having difficulty in understanding why the character of their interactions with each other shifted sharply from meeting to meeting. In some meetings they found themselves open to new ideas, free to raise questions, and valuing the inputs of other members. In other meetings they found themselves rejecting new ideas, making few significant comments on each other's work, and generally rejecting those ideas which were offered. After being exposed to the Learning Model, they realized that the first condition prevailed when the project was in a Divergence stage, and the latter occurred when the project required Convergence or Execution.

Discussions with the manager of the same project team provided the basis for a new concept of the role of the project manager. Traditional manager's role has been viewed primarily as one of planning, organizing, directing and controlling. When organizations are viewed as learning systems, the manager's role can be viewed as one of providing leadership in the learning process. The following observations developed out of our conversations with the manager of this team.

1. When the development of a product is going smoothly, the manager's role will involve thinking and planning about the next stage, and will be 90^0 to 135^0 ahead of that of the team members. For example, if the team is engaged in Execution, the manager will be thinking about the possible alternatives for the project when the results of Execution are known: if the team is engaged in idea generation, the manager's role will involve thinking about the criteria for solution. By concentrating on what is to come, the manager exerts a useful pull on the project.

2. In time of crisis, when the team is finding it difficult to move through the learning cycle, the role requires the manager to move into the same stage as the project team. For example, the manager may work with the team to develop theories to explain an unexpected result or to help in the pilot plant when there is a critical deadline.

3. The manager must take care that he does not move too far ahead of the project team, thus not only losing sensitivity to their current problems but also confusing them with regard to the path they should take. The manager should avoid pulling the team *across* the Model instead of *around* it.

This same manager used his knowledge of the work team process and his understanding of his role of leadership in the learning process to devise a special plan for supporting the work of one of the team members. The team member had come forward with a proposal to investigate some leads which might result in options which would be alternative or supplemental to those which the team was soon to execute. The manager recognized the merits of the proposal but also recognized that the team member was proposing to involve himself deeply in the Divergence stage of the Model, while the rest of the team was involved in the Convergence of the rest of the team: "I built a fence around the Divergence quadrant and told him to stay in it and the others to stay out." He thus encouraged and supported the team member's independent pursuit of the learning process until it came into phase with the learning process of the rest of the team.

In still another instance, a group of technical information specialists found the model useful in suggesting ways they could increase their effectiveness in providing technical information to project teams. They realized that the information needs of project teams vary according to the stage of the learning process as shown below.[8]

Stage	Activity	Information Need
Divergence	Generation of alternatives	Specific alternatives
	Creativity	Stimulation of the process of generating alternatives (e.g., information about Brainstorming)
	Problem/opportunity sensing	State of the art
		State of the world
Assimilation	Planning	Policy
	Formulating theory	Planning methodology
		Strategy models
	Establishing criteria	Evaluation criteria
Convergence	Interpretation of data	Screening/selection techniques
	Narrowing down alternatives	
	Design of experiments	Experimental design
	Evaluation of outcome	
Execution	Execution of plan	Feedback on results (Monitoring techniques)
	Implementation of decision	
	Goal setting	Information on need

IMPLICATIONS FOR MANAGEMENT OF R&D

The Learning Model provides a basis for several kinds of action which can be taken by management to improve the R&D process.

Staffing decisions can be made in light of the Learning Model. The assignment of individuals with requisite skills in each of the stages of the learning process should result in improving that process. The balance of skills required is likely to shift over the course of a project. In the earliest cycles through the learning process (e.g., during concept and prototype development), skills in the Divergence and Assimilation stages are likely to be most critical. Later (e.g., when the design is fixed and engineering specifications are being prepared) skills in Convergence and Execution become most critical. Shifts in assignment of individuals during the project life may, in *some* instances, not only improve the progress of the project, but also permit individuals to have assignments which match their preferences and abilities.[9]

[8]Thomas J. Allen (private communications) has suggested that the information needs of R&D projects vary with the kind of project (e.g., research, service, engineering) and with the maturity of the project.

[9]We caution against the assumption that the learning preferences of individuals are fixed. It has been our observation that for many individuals learning style preference is highly situational.

Organization policies and reward systems can be used to support an appropriate balance of learning activities. It is our observation (which is supported by research reported by Kolb[10]) that organizations and professional disciplines often develop values which favor activity in one learning stage over the others. When these values are out of balance with the needs of the organization the kinds of problems outlined in Figure 3 can result. Managers can help restore appropriate balance.

Specific problems can be identified and strategies for remedial action suggested by reference to the Learning Model. The most common specific problems, we expect, will arise when an individual or team is either stuck in or deficient in a learning stage. Some of the techniques which can be used in these situations are shown in Figure 5.

IMPLICATIONS BEYOND R&D ORGANIZATIONS

We believe the experience of the technical information specialists can be generalized to many other support organizations. For example, management science groups are sometimes seen as only helpful in decision making (Convergence), and even then only when risks can be quantified and defined.[11] Another view suggests that management science can provide benefits much more broadly.[12] We believe that the ability of management scientists to provide these benefits is dependent upon

FIGURE 5 Intervention Strategies

	Concrete Experience
Execution	Divergence
Critical path scheduling Goal-setting	Brainstorming Synectics Creative problem solving Browsing Literature Visiting General consultants
Active Experimentation	Reflective Observation
Convergence	Assimilation
Decision trees Design of experiments Calculations Methods consultants Experimenting	Thinking Manipulating data **Extracting grounded theory** Game theory Management information "Expert" consultants
	Abstract Conceptualization

[10]See Kolb [6].
[11]For example, see Arcand [1].
[12]For example, see Hammond [4].

their sensitivity to the stage of the learning cycle of the organization (or individuals) they are supporting. The table below relates Hammond's categories of benefits to the corresponding stages of the Learning Model.

Potential Benefits of Management Science*	Corresponding Stage of the Learning Model
1. Provides a structure to a situation which is initially relatively unstructured to the manager.	Assimilation
2. Extends the decision maker's information processing ability.	Divergence
3. Facilitates concept formation.	Assimilation
4. Provides cues to the decision maker.	Assimilation/Convergence
5. Stimulates the collection, organization and utilization of data which might not otherwise be collected.	Divergence
6. Frees from mental set.	Divergence/Assimilation

*The list of benefits is taken directly from Hammond [4], pp. 9–11.

While our research and applications have been almost entirely within R&D systems, we believe the Learning Model has parallel applications in other kinds of systems. The importance of the Model to an organization will be proportionate to the importance of production of new knowledge as an organizational goal. To the extent that technical, social and political turbulance is forcing even the most stable organizations and institutions to adopt a learning orientation if they are to survive, we expect the Learning Model to be increasingly useful.[13]

REFERENCES

1. Arcand, C. G., "Bureaucratic Innovation: The Failure of Rationality," *Chemtech,* 1975, pp. 710–714.
2. Bennis, W. G., and Slater, P. E. *The Temporary Society,* New York: Harper & Row, 1968.
3. Glaser, B. B., and Strauss, A. L. *The Discovery of Grounded Theory: Strategies for Qualitative Research.* Chicago: Aldine Publishing Company, 1967.
4. Hammond, J. S. "The Roles of the Manager and Management Scientist in Successful Implementation." *Sloan Management Review,* Winter 1974, pp. 1–24.
5. Kolb, D. A. *The Learning Style Inventory: Technical Manual,* Boston, Mass.: McBer and Co., 1976.
6. Kolb, D. A., Rubin, I. M., and McIntyre, J. M. *Organization Psychology: An Experiential Approach,* 2nd ed. Englewood Cliffs, N.J.: Prentice-Hall, 1974, pp. 23, 25.
8. Schein, E. H. *Organizational Psychology,* Englewood Cliffs, N.J.: Prentice-Hall, 1965.
9. Schon, D. A. *Beyond the Stable State,* New York: Random House, 1971.

[13]For example, see Bennis and Slater [2], Schon [9], and the discussion of the "adaptive-coping cycle" appearing in Schein [8].

THE EXECUTIVE MIND
AND DOUBLE-LOOP LEARNING

Chris Argyris

Over the past decade, I have been studying the ways executives reason while they are solving difficult human and technical problems. The executive mind seems to work in bewildering ways, a few of which I will discuss in this article. For one thing, I have identified a pattern of three nested paradoxes embedded in executive reasoning.

First, the reasoning executives use to manage people and technical issues leads simultaneously to productive *and* to counterproductive consequences.

Second, they are unaware of this feature because they are disconnected from their own reasoning processes while making tough decisions.

Third, they are disconnected from their reasoning processes because of the skills they have mastered to solve tough problems. The skills that lead to success will also lead to failure.

How can the same reasoning necessarily lead to productive and counterproductive consequences? How can people act and at the same time be disconnected from their reasoning processes? And why is it necessary for them to be disconnected from their reasoning processes in order to solve difficult problems? What impact do these features have on executive problem solving and on the organization?

These nested paradoxes indicate that we are dealing with some deeply embedded features of the human mind. And it is the executive mind that concerns us because executives are most often held responsible for dealing with the difficult issues in organizations and in society at large.

THE EXECUTIVE MIND DEFINED

By "executive mind," I mean the way executives create premises, make inferences, and arrive at conclusions. Surprisingly, executives (or anyone else, for that matter) are usually unaware of their reasoning processes. There are two reasons for this. First, they have great reasoning skill—the activity is second nature to them, and they are rarely aware of it while they are doing it. Indeed, as is true of most skilled behavior, they rarely focus on it unless they make an error. Second, when they do make errors, other people—especially subordinates—may feel it is safest to play down the error, or may ease in the correct information so subtly that the executive will probably not even realize that he did make an error.

These actions at the upper levels are especially detrimental to the organization's capacity to detect and correct errors, to innovate, to take risks, and to know when it is unable to detect and correct error. Such consequences can lead to difficulties in getting the everyday job done correctly. But worse, lack of

Source: Reprinted by permission of publisher, from *Organizational Dynamics,* Autumn 1982.

attention to the underlying policy issues can lead to the organization's losing control of its destiny.

In a previous article I gave an example in which managers at all levels "rounded out" sentences in reports in ways designed to (1) avoid upsetting those at the top too much and, at the same time, (2) permit the subordinates involved to "cover" themselves. The result was a multimillion dollar error that led to the closing of major facilities. The error was known, and the consequences predictable, by managers at the lower levels several years before. the crisis exploded into the open.

Our research indicates that when executives deal with difficult, threatening, underlying issues, they use reasoning processes that, at best, simultaneously lead to immediate success and long-range problems. Often the problems go unsolved, compounding the long-range difficulties. Much of this occurs without executives' realizing it. Or, if they do realize it, many believe that no other outcome is possible. They are correct if they are willing to accept the world as it is, without seeking alternatives. According to the Pentagon Papers, this is what happened at upper levels in the Defense Department as well as in the State Department.

To illustrate how we arrived at these conclusions, I want to present data from a case that concerns one of the most difficult problems executives face—namely, to help fellow executives realize that their performance is deteriorating when they believe otherwise. Later I will show how the results from this case apply to other common but difficult leadership problems. (The reader may wish to try his hand at solving this case and compare his or her response with those of our sample.)

CORRECTING POOR PERFORMANCE: A DIAGNOSTIC CASE

Y, a senior executive, must tell X, an older officer, that his performance during the past five years has fallen below standard. Y knows that the difficulty of his task is compounded by the fact that X believes his performance has topped off because of the way the firm has dealt with him.

We give the executives in a seminar a transcript of several key sentences that Y used in talking with X (Figure 1)—sentences that represent the range of meanings that Y communicated to X during their session.

FIGURE 1   What Y Said to X

1. X, your peformance is not up to standard (and moreover...)
2. You seem to be carrying a chip on your shoulder.
3. It appears to me that this has affected your performance in a number of ways. I have heard words like *lethargy, uncommitted,* and *disinterested* used by others in describing your recent performance.
4. Our senior professionals cannot have those characteristics.
5. Let's discuss your feelings about your performance.
6. X, I know you want to talk about the injustices that you believe have been perpetrated on you in the past. The problem is that I am not discussing something that happened several years ago. Nothing constructive will come from it. It's behind us.
7. I want to talk about you today and about your future in our system.

We then ask the executives to answer three questions:

1. How effective do you believe Y was in dealing with X?
2. What advice would you give Y?
3. Assume that Y asked you for your evaluation of his effectiveness in dealing with X. Write your response, using the following format, for two or three double-spaced pages.

YOUR THOUGHTS AND FEELINGS	WHAT YOU AND Y SAID
(Give in this column any thoughts and feelings you had during the session but which you did not communicate.)	*I:* (Write what you would say) *Y:* (Write what you expect Y's response would be.) *I:* (Write your response to this.) *Y:* (Write Y's response.) *and so forth*

The responses presented below were made by the 15 top senior officers, including the CEO, of a five-billion-dollar corporation. If your answers do not vary significantly from those in our sample, then the consequences that followed for the executives will more than likely occur for you...

THE EXECUTIVES' EVALUATION
OF Y'S EFFECTIVENESS

Figure 2 is a collage of the executives' answers to Question 1. Briefly, the results are as follows:

- The executives evaluated Y as being ineffective in his dealings with X.

By the way, the reader may be interested to know that line executives were as compassionate about X as were governmental executives and organization development professionals. Indeed, the line executives were slightly more concerned than the other two groups that Y was too power-oriented, an "uncaring executioner of company policies."

- The executives organized their responses by inventing what might be called a miniature causal theory of human behavior: *If* Y (or anyone else) communicates meanings of the kind that Y communicated to X, *then* the recipient will feel defensive and learning will be blunted.

If you agree with this explanation, then you are using an explanation that, strictly speaking, doesn't come from the data. For example, why should telling X that his performance is poor and unacceptable make him defensive? "That is obvious," you may respond, "because such statements are probably experienced as punishing and unjust, an attack on the person's competence. Such acts are threatening." To arrive at this conclusion—which is probably correct—you must hold a tacit theory of threat.

FIGURE 2   Analysis of Responses to X and Y Case (by line executives)

Y's Action Strategies

Y's comments have a strong power tone; they smell of conspiratorial knowledge.

Y gives no sign of interest or compassion.

Y set X up to give only the answers Y wants to hear.

Y comes across as a blunt, uncaring executioner of the firm's polilcy decision with regard to X.

Y makes it abundantly clear that he does not want to be bothered with X.

Y is insensitive to X's feelings.

Y waits too long to listen to X.

Y does not give X a chance to respond. He pays lip service to hearing X's side.

Y is too blunt, direct, one-sided.

Y cuts off X.

Y communicates the seriousness of the situation from the company's point of view.

At no time does he appear to communicate that he and the firm genuinely want X to have a second chance.

Impact on X

Makes X feel defensive, rejected.

Makes X defend his past performance aggressively.

X will feel prejudged, as though the "deck" were "loaded."

X is not likely to relax and learn.

X is left with no room for constructive exploration.

X feels totally demoralized and inferior.

X is placed in a no-win situation.

Impact on Learning

Inhibits learning on part of both individuals.

X will probably look for another job.

- Therefore, embedded in the first causal miniature theory is another one, a theory about what makes people defensive.
- All the explanations that the executives produced have a taken-for-granted quality because they have been absorbed and learned in the experience of everyday life. In my jargon, people are socialized to believe this theory of defense because they have been taught from an early age that such an act—telling someone his or her performance is poor—can be counterproductive.

SOME PUZZLES AND SURPRISES

First, two puzzles:

1. If everyone has learned these causal explanations early in life, why have they not also eventually learned *not* to create them? Why, for example, did Y behave the way he did toward X?

2. If Y had asked these executives what they thought of the way he dealt with X, and if the line executives told Y what is in Figure 2, they would be using the same causal theory with Y that they were criticizing Y for using with X. For example, to tell Y that he is insensitive and blunt is to be blunt and insensitive.

When the executives were confronted with the first puzzle, they were quick to reply that either Y was not very competent, or that maybe he was even a bit flustered and tried to cover this up by being directive.

Notice the reasoning. The executives dealt with the first puzzle (of why Y behaved thusly) by saying that Y lacked some skill, or was upset. That places the responsibility on Y. It also means that the executives do not have to question the validity of their diagnoses.

How accurate are their diagnoses? Let us ask Y.

WHEN THE EXECUTIVES SAID THAT Y:	Y COULD HAVE RESPONDED THAT HE:
1. Blamed X completely.	1. Blamed X justly, or only partially.
2. Resisted hearing X's views.	2. Only resisted getting into a past history that was a can of worms.
3. Discounted X's feelings.	3. Understood X's feelings for X's sake, but, he did not want to get mired in them; that he was trying to think positively and look toward the future.

When the executives were confronted with the second puzzle (that they were using the same approach as Y), their initial response was surprise and disbelief. A few tried to prove that this was not an inconsistency on their part, but fellow executives disagreed. When the defensive reactions wore thin, there was a momentary silence. Then someone said:

Yes, you are right; there is the inconsistency. But what you fail to realize is that none of us would say to Y what we have written down.

No, added another with a smile, we're too smart to say what we think.

Note the difference between the executives' reactions to the first and second puzzles. Their response to the first puzzle was to place the blame on Y. In the second, unable to explain away their own inconsistency, they decided that they would not say what they thought. They accepted being surprised about, and unaware of, their impact on Y as natural. But note that they never suggested that Y might have been unaware of his impact on X.

Once the executives had made a diagnosis, they assumed that it was true and countered any questioning of it in ways designed to keep their diagnosis intact.

THE EXECUTIVES' ADVICE TO Y

Recall that the executives tried to evade the second puzzle (that they were using the same causal theory used by Y) by asserting that they would not tell Y their diagnosis.

We collected two kinds of data to test their assertion. First, the executives were asked to write scenarios of a conversation they might have with Y about Y's handling of X. They were at liberty to mold Y's reactions as they wished.

The executives used three basic strategies in their scenarios. The first strategy (used by five executives) was direct. In effect, they told Y their diagnosis. But many who used a direct approach communicated with Y in such a way that they neglected important features of their own advice. For example, most of them were "up front" with Y but were unable to create an "open process," "a receptive mood," a process for the "growth and development" of Y.

Here are examples of how three of these executives began their scenarios, with hypothesized reactions that Y might have had but did not disclose.

Examples of the Direct Approach

EXECUTIVE SAID	ACCORDING TO THE EXECUTIVES, *Y COULD HAVE THOUGHT*
Executive 1: To tell the truth, I don't think you accomplished what you wanted to.	1. He is not only telling me I failed, but that I was blind to that fact.
Executive 2: Some of your comments were bound to hit X pretty hard and force a defensive reaction.	2. I had to be straight with him. Speaking of hitting pretty hard, you're not doing badly yourself!
Executive 3: Well, you started off pretty hard on his performance, his defensive reaction. The poor bastard almost had to defend his record to set you straight.	3. Somebody had to be straight with him. We had been pulling our punches for five years. He didn't have much to defend, and he knew it. I feel I have to set you straight about me!

A more lengthy example from one scenario indicates the flow of conversation and the possible buildup of Y's reactions.

EXECUTIVE SAID	ACCORDING TO WRITER, *Y COULD HAVE THOUGHT*
4. Nobody believes the judgment about their own poor performance is accurate unless they can balance it against a number of successes.	4. If this is true, I really was doomed to failure because this guy has no successes. Are you also thinking the same about me? If so, how about a few successes?
Did you get a defensive reaction from X?	Of course I did, just as you predicted from what you just said.
Well, my only point is that you probably were guaranteed to get some defensiveness.	Just like you are guaranteed to do with me. Let's begin to end this diplomatically. ("Thanks for the advice.")
Don't be afraid to be honest.	I'm not afraid to be honest except with people like you.

To summarize the findings from the scenarios:

THE EXECUTIVES	THE EXECUTIVES ADVISED Y
1. Were in unilateral control.	1. Not to unilaterally control X.

2. Evaluated Y unilaterally and negatively.	2. Not to evaluate X.
3. Failed to hear Y's pent-up feelings.	3. To listen to X's pent-up feelings.
4. Failed to solicit Y's participation.	4. To solicit X's participation.

So a third puzzle was that the executives created the very conditions they advised Y not to create with X, *and* they appeared to be unaware of doing so.

The Easing-in Approach

Another approach we might call an easing-in approach (utilized by ten executives) or a combination of a *beginning* easing-in approach and a *final* direct approach. The easing-in approach basically asked Y questions in order to get him to see his errors.

EXECUTIVE SAID	Y COULD HAVE THOUGHT
1. It's hard to say from just reading your notes. I guess I would like to hear a little about how X reacted.	1. What is he driving at? Why does he want to focus on X's reaction?
2. What do you think he was thinking?	2. How do I know what X was thinking? I told him that X didn't say much. What is he driving at?
3. Do you suppose there might have been a way to let him know you mean it?	3. I did let him know that I meant it. If he didn't believe me, that's more his problem than mine. I think this guy has an agenda.
4. You mean his attitude wasn't any better in the meeting?	4. Couldn't you tell that he was pretty unresponsive? Again, what is he driving at? Does he believe that X's attitude was better?
5. Perhaps if you could persuade him to open up about it, he might get it off his chest.	5. Maybe this is what he is driving at. If so, he is wrong. The last thing I want to do is open up past wounds...oh, these bleeding hearts.

Although the executives asked Y questions, if our interpretations about the impact on Y are valid, they were acting in ways that placed them in control of Y. To summarize:

THE EXECUTIVES	THE EXECUTIVES ADVISED Y
1. Were in unilateral control.	1. Not to unilaterally control X.
2. Evaluated Y as ineffective.	2. Not to prejudge X as being ineffective.
3. Made attributions about Y's motives.	3. Not to make attributions about X's motives.

Again the executives created the very conditions that they advised Y not to create with X, *and* they appeared unaware of having done so.

We conclude that when the executives tried to communciate information that they believed was threatening, they unknowingly created conditions of miscommunication, misunderstanding, and inconsistency. None of them tested their views openly. This led to self-fulfilling prophecies, because every comment made by Y in his defense they saw as validating their diagnosis. This made Y even more defensive, which "proved" to the executives that their diagnosis was correct. Since the executives never publicly tested their views, they did not know that they had created a self-fulfilling prophecy but one that is self-sealing as well!

We have obtained these results with 27 groups, encompassing slightly under 1,000 subjects of varying ages, positions, roles, cultures, and of both sexes. In all cases, we taped the discussions, in which many different views were expressed, as well as feelings of bewilderment and frustration. Analysis of tape recordings of these discussions also illustrate that when the participants disagreed with each other, they did so by using the same counterproductive reasoning and strategies just described.

HOW DO WE EXPLAIN THESE RESULTS?
MODEL I BEHAVIOR

In a previous article, I suggested an explanation for such results. Briefly, people acquire through socialization two kinds of skills and values for dealing with other people. The first are the values and skills that they espouse, the ones of which they are conscious and aware. I call these *espoused* theories of action.

Often when people are dealing with difficult and threatening problems, their behavior is inconsistent with their espoused theories. "Do as I say, not as I do" illustrates the point and at the same time proves that the point is not new.

What is new is the idea that all behavior is designed in accordance with a theory that we actually use. Moreover, we are rarely aware of this type of theory of action because it is ingrained in us from early childhood. I call it the *theory-in-use*. We use it without thinking about it. When we do think about it, we see that the results are often at odds with what we espouse. For example, the executives' espoused theories advocated dealing with Y in such a way that he did not become defensive. Many followed an easing-in approach; the theory-in-use for easing in is to ask Y questions which, if he answers correctly, will enable him to discover what we are hiding. As we have seen, this is a strategy that can be counterproductive and, in fact, the other person may imitate this approach by not saying what he or she really feels.

Although each person varied in what he said when using an easing-in approach, there was almost no variance in people's theory-in-use. We have observed the same theory-in-use among rich and poor, white and black, male and female, young and old, powerful and powerless, and in several different cultures.

We have created a model of the theory and call it *Model I* (Figure 3). It is composed of governing values, or variables, and action strategies and consequences.

Now we can return to the question of why we get such consistent results in the X and Y case.

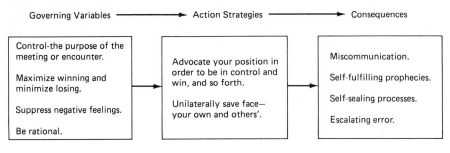

Governing Variables ⟶ Action Strategies ⟶ Consequences

| Control-the purpose of the meeting or encounter. Maximize winning and minimize losing. Suppress negative feelings. Be rational. | Advocate your position in order to be in control and win, and so forth. Unilaterally save face— your own and others'. | Miscommunication. Self-fulfilling prophecies. Self-sealing processes. Escalating error. |

FIGURE 3 Model I Theory-In-Use

Evaluations and attributions the executives made about Y's motives were not self-evident. They required several layers of inference. For example, Y's statement to X, "Your performance is below standard," and so forth, is on the first rung of a ladder of inference. The second rung is the culturally understood meaning of such a sentence: "X, your performance is unacceptable." The third rung up consists of the meanings that the executives imposed. Here is where their theory-in-use came into play. They explained Y's actions by describing him as insensitive, blunt, and not listening.

Why do people use concepts at such a high level of inference (Figure 4)? The environment in which we operate is significantly more complex than what the human mind can process at a given moment. In order for the human mind to deal with reality, we must abstract from the buzzing confusion of everyday life (rung 1) by using more abstract concepts.

There are two key features of these concepts. First, they can be used to cover a lot of different meanings. For example, "blunt" and "insensitive" can apply to many different sentences. A second feature is that they are usually learned at an early age. Hence most of us learn to use the same concepts in similar ways. Soon we take them for granted. They become obvious and concrete, not abstract and questionable. Recall that there was a high degree of consistency and agreement in the way the executives diagnosed Y's actions toward X. It was "obvious" to most of the executives that Y had behaved counterproductively.

But the features of the human mind that make it efficient may also lead to counterproductive consequences. Why? Because, as we have seen, there can be differences between the executives' views and Y's. But so what? Cannot human beings differ in their views? Of course they can. But if they wish to reduce the number of misunderstandings when they do differ, they should test the validity of their reasoning.

FIGURE 4 Ladder of Inference

4	Meanings imposed by the researcher.
3	Meanings imposed by our theories-in-use.
2	Culturally understood meanings.
1	Relatively directly observable data, such as conversations.

Why do people choose not to test the validity of their reasoning? First, because they believe their reasoning is obvious and correct. Second, because they hold a theory of human defensiveness that tells them that the recipient will probably not listen, or will probably become defensive if he does. And it makes little sense for them to test their views with someone who, they believe, will be defensive.

Third, in a Model I world, testing makes the tests vulnerable. They could discover that they are wrong! They could lose unilateral control and they could generate negative feelings, consequences that would violate their Model I governing values.

The same counterproductive reasoning and consequences have been shown to occur when executives deal with technical and organizational problems. The only requirement is that the problems are threatening to some of the key players involved. Once the players diagnose the problem as threatening, they use the same reasoning described in the X-Y case.

Other Examples of the Consequences of Model I Reasoning

People programmed to be in unilateral control and to maximize winning tend to have difficulties in dealing with paradoxes. Paradoxes contain contradictions, and holding contradictory views makes the actor vulnerable to criticisms of being vague or self-contradictory. It is not surprising to learn from Louis B. Barnes's insightful descriptions that the way executives deal with paradoxes may be counterproductive.

BARNES'S OBSERVATIONS	THEORY OF ACTION EXPLANATION
Often we fail to go beyond our initial reactions in order to look at deeper levels of the issue.	Do not run the risk of losing control and making yourself vulnerable—that is, losing.
Issues fall in opposing camps; hard data and facts are better than soft ideas and speculation.	Create win/lose dynamics. Seek hard data to win, to prevent losing. Abhor speculation lest you become vulnerable.

Turning to organizational consequences, recall that people who use Model I tend, as we have seen, to create misunderstanding, self-fulfilling phophecies, self-sealing processes, and escalating error. This drives people to follow Model I behavior even more closely in an attempt to maintain control, to win. It also creates competitive win/lose group and intergroup dynamics with many protective games that are undiscussable. And that undiscussability is itself undiscussable. The Model I world is, as the executives reported to Barnes, "an unsafe place where nice guys finish last."

An excellent illustration of these consequences at the group, intergroup, and interagency level can be found in a recently published story of the interaction among Secretary of Health, Education, and Welfare Joseph A. Califano, Jr., Secretary of Labor Ray Marshall, and President Carter and his aides regarding welfare reform. The players acted toward each other in Model I ways. Califano kept secret for a long time his doubts of genuine welfare reform at zero cost increase. The

President sensed his doubts but apparently never explored them directly with Califano. When Califano said that he was working hard on a plan that Carter might possibly be able to call his own, the President asked Califano for a plan that he would gladly call "the Califano Plan." Califano's policy analysts were frustrated by his actions. They never said so, but they built up strategies to protect themselves. These strategies got them in trouble with Califano and a competing group of analysts in Secretary Marshall's office. This led to interagency warfare, a state in which positions harden and everybody looks out for Number One.

Robert B. Reich's recent article suggests that an entire industry is rising as a result of the self-sealing prophecies, self-sealing processes, and escalating error between private and governmental sectors. The new industry is composed of experts who deal with difficult relationships of private business and government by:

- Seeking to achieve clear controversies in which the client's position can be sharply differentiated from that of its regulatory opponent.
- Exaggerating the danger of the opponent's activities.
- Prolonging and intensifying conflict.
- Keeping business executives and regulatory officials apart.

Remember that regulatory agencies are also administered by Model I reasoning processes. This means that the regulators will probably deal with difficult, threatening issues that are undiscussable by translating them into discussable, non-threatening issues. For example, I have found that if regulators do not trust builders, instead of dealing with that issue they create piles of regulation in an effort to prevent cheating by dishonest builders. But these regulations may drive out the honest builders while stimulating the dishonest ones to new heights of creative dishonesty.

To summarize, holding a Model I theory-in-use makes it highly likely that the reasoning used for any difficult threatening issues, whether technical or personal, whether at the individual, goal, intergroup, organizational, or interorganizational level, will have counterproductive features that lead to self-fulfilling, self-sealing, error-escalating processes.

The reasoning is the same because it is individuals who deal with the human problems; who act as agents for groups, intergroups, organizations, and inter-organizations. Programmed with Model I, they seek to win and not lose, to be in unilateral control, to suppress negative feelings. Thus whether the issue at hand is helping Y realize his error or dealing with a group that the executive believes is recommending the wrong investment strategy, the executives in either case will try to communicate their views in such a way that they cannot be held responsible for upsetting Y or the group members. The executive strives to evade responsibility for the defensiveness of others so that they cannot attack him and ignore the validity of his views. But, as we have seen, the strategies executives used to minimize the potential accusation of making others defensive actually does make others defensive, but in a way that makes it difficult or unlikely for them to say so. We then have the appearance of agreement.

Not only do we find these same consequences at all levels of the organization, we also find that managerial policies and practices are designed to take these consequences into account. For example:

1. To reduce the probabilty that individuals will be able to blame the superior's evaluation of their performance, have them list and sign ahead of time a set of specific goals that are objectively measurable if possible.

2. To reduce the probability of group think, have several competing groups deal with the same problem.

3. To reduce miscommunication about difficult issues, have people send each other detailed position statements, backed up with hard numbers.

4. To reduce possible misunderstanding between regulators and those who are regulated, have the regulators define in detailed, unambiguous terms the standards of acceptable performance.

The first policy requires a technocracy of MBO experts and trainers. The second duplicates efforts. The third requires staff groups that may "pencil and paper an issue to death." The fourth requires mountains of specifications, including specifications on how to understand the specifications.

WHAT CAN BE DONE

What can interested readers do to begin to learn more about the effectiveness of their reasoning processes and their action?

First, may I remind the reader of the two most fundamental findings. They were that the executives' responses were highly automatic and skillful, and that the executives were programmed to be unaware of their faulty reasoning as well as of the counterproductive impact. To change highly skilled action is not easy; to do so hampered by programmed unawareness is difficult indeed. And when the basis for the programmed unawareness is what we have been taught since early childhood, the task becomes formidable.

However, it is by no means an impossible task. The reader is not starting from scratch. We all know how to reason to separate effective from ineffective results, and how to design experiments for learning. Our research suggests that it will take about as long to learn the new reasoning and action skills as it takes to learn to play a good game of tennis or golf. And, in my opinion, that is how it should be. We are talking about changing our reasoning processes, one of our most fundamental human features. The learning should be difficult in order to rule out the gimmick hunters and quick-fix seekers.

Learning new reasoning processes, like learning to play tennis or golf, requires plenty of practice. Herein lies an advantage because most of us are constantly in situations in which we must use reasoning processes. There is plenty of opportunity to practice in everyday life.

The nature of the practice will be different at different stages of learning. During the early stages, you should be able to make errors without a high cost to you or to the organization. Also, you should have plenty of time to get feedback and to redesign your actions. These two features, when combined, suggest that the best kind of learning environment during the early stages is one that allows for slowdown of the action and decomposition of the problem. This in turn means creating a learning environment separate from everyday pressures.

For example, select a double-loop issue that is important to you, one that requires you to deal with others in order to solve it. Using the X-Y case format, write in one paragraph how you define the issue. In a second paragraph, write how you tried to solve it (or might try to solve it if it is a future problem). Next, write an actual scenario of several pages describing the conversation as you can best recall it (or if it is a future problem, what you would expect the conversation to be). Include thoughts and feelings that you might not communicate, for whatever reason.

By the way, do not worry about how accurately you recall the incident, or how well you plan the future dialogue. If our theory is correct, you cannot write down anything except what is consistent with your theory-in-use.

Now put the case away for at least a week. When you reread it, analyze it as if you were trying to help a friend. Here are some of the questions that you can ask yourself about the dialogue.

- Do the sentences indicate advocating a position in order to be in control and to win and not lose? Or is the advocacy of the position combined with encouraging the other person to inquire? Is there an easing-in or forthright strategy? How aware is the writer of the possible interpretations by the receiver?
- Are the evaluations or attributions made with or without illustrations? Are they tested publicly or do they go untested?
- What kind of information is on the left-hand side of the paper (thoughts and feelings)? Does it contain information that would better enable the other person to understand your intentions? If so, what prevented you from communicating this information?
- If the feelings and thoughts in the left-hand column would predictably upset others, what change would be necessary so that they could be effectively communicated?

More important, why does the writer think and feel about other people in ways that are not directly communicable? Sure, it may be that they are S.O.B.s. But is may also be that the writer is unknowingly creating self-fulfilling and self-sealing processes.

The next step would be to try to redesign some part of the dialogue, especially the sentences with which you find it difficult to deal.

- Read the sentence(s) several times and write down the (culturally acceptable) meaning that you infer (rung 2 on the ladder of inference).
- Write down the meaning that you would impose on the cultural meaning (rung 3).
- Invent a possible solution to deal with such meanings.
- Write an actual conversation that produces the invention you just made.

Feel free to make all the changes you wish during the exercise. Every change is a sign of learning and another opportunity for practice. This is not a win/lose competitive situation with yourself or with others.

Again, put your written work away, this time for at least a day, before rereading it. If you prefer not to wait for the week, or the day, show your efforts to someone else. It is best to do this with persons who are also interested in learning about themselves, and who might reciprocate by showing you a case they had written in this format. The set is then one in which both of you are learning.

Another step is to make exercises like those just described part of the firm's executive-development activities. For example, you and your group members could each write a case. One of these could be the subject of discussion during a seminar. (I recommend at least an hour and a half and some trained professional help for each of the early sessions.)

Another possibility is for all individuals to write a case about an organizational problem that plagued, or continues to plague, the organization. It is then possible not only to see how each player conceptualizes the problem, but also how he or she has tried (or would try) to solve it.

During these discussions, the players soon generate a lot of data about the organization, its culture, and the way decisions are made. Grouping the cases provides a new data source for diagnosing organizational features that inhibit or facilitate organizational learning. In a large professional firm, for example, top management realized that if the partners were going to be successful in dealing with mediocre performance, they would have to become much more candid and forthright. They also realized that such candor was countercultural; hence the partners had to learn new skills. They also realized that if the partners learned to confront constructively, and if it worked well with the subordinate professionals, the latter would probably take them up on their challenge and start confronting the partners and the firm's policies.

Top management believed this would lead to constructive dialogue and possibly a new culture. All the top executives agreed with this espoused policy. However, as they examined their scenarios and the self-initiated censorship (what they placed on the left-hand side of their page), they became aware that their theory-in-use was quite different. About half of them were trying to act in ways that were consistent with the new policy. About half were easing-in but denying this was the case. One senior executive then said:

> Let's assume for the moment that our subordination will be watching not only what we espouse but how we act. If that is so, then many of them should be aware of the bipolar nature of our actions. Yet to my knowledge, this is never discussed. They give much lip service to our policies. This means in the name of candor we must be (unknowingly) helping them to identify what is undiscussable, to keep it undiscussable, and to act as if they are not doing so!

The next phase is to use the new skills in everyday situations. In one firm, for example, professionals at all levels went through the X-Y experience. When the officers had to evaluate their professionals in the normal review process, they decided to use the opportunity to practice their new skills. Often they needed practice sessions ahead of time to help them prepare to conduct the review appropriately. The number and length of the preparatory sessions were greatly reduced once the officers felt secure in their new skills.

Since the bewilderment, bafflement, and frustration of the X-Y case were experienced by all, subordinates who came to the review sessions knew how difficult it would be for the officer to behave in line with the new model. It was easy for the officers to say that the evaluation was going to be a learning experience for them as well as for the subordinates. If the subordinate agreed, I participated in the evaluation sessions. The subordinate and the superior often listened to the tape of the session, reporting that doing so was an eye-opener for them.

Another type of intervention is illustrated by the officer who asked his project team to reflect on a recent job they had completed. Although everyone involved evaluated the project as a success, he felt that they could have done better since they were exceptionally talented professionals. In the first session, team members reflected on their experience of the project. They identified ten factors that led the team to be less creative than it could have been. For example, they admitted that, as senior professionals, they had all acted as chiefs, each in his own bailiwick, adding that they had often recognized a lack of coordination and integration throughout the project. Their conclusion was that the team could have gained by stronger leadership.

A second session was held to dig into the reasoning that the team used during the first meeting. I noted, for example, that the team had recognized the lack of coordination early in the project. "Do you recall what prevented you from surfacing these views?" Their replies clustered around (1) the fear that they would step on someone's toes, (2) the fact that they were all very busy, and (3) the assumption that team coordination was the officer's responsibility. The officer mentioned that he had reduced his time with the team because top management had asked him to take on additional and unexpected work. He had agreed to the extra work in part because the team was so senior that he believed they could administer themselves.

I asked what cues or data the members got that led them to believe that they would be stepping on other people's toes. The responses ranged from cues individuals gave each other to informal policies of the firm that made them hesitate to speak out. Their theory-in-use was to cover up their views; to cover up the cover-up in order to get the job done. This deeper analysis pointed to a different change target. If they could change the need for the cover-up, if they could learn to generate more effective cooperative relationships (including being able to make the heretofore undiscussable issues discussable), then the need for a strong leader might be greatly reduced. If so, the firm could use its senior officers more flexibly.

An episode in another firm involved design of a new organizational structure. Sides were taken; subgroups began to view each other as conservatives and liberals. In X-Y case terminology, each side held untested and often unillustrated attributions that led to divisive intergroup dynamics. Instead of reenacting their history of intergroup warfare, several executives pointed out the connection between the reasoning they were currently using. A meeting was held with the key players on both sides present. In presenting their analysis of the situation, several executives asked, "If this makes sense to you, would you all be willing to join us in reflecting on what we are doing?" Most agreed spontaneously; a few agreed but were concerned—As one commented, "This could lead to blows." Well, it never did. They were able to map the attributions and evaluations people were making and not testing, the games that were being played, and the possible negative consequences of all this on their final decisions and on the firm. The result was a jointly developed plan on how to reduce counterproductive factors. The participants agreed that the result was a greater degree of internal commitment to make the new design work, as evidenced by their willingness to monitor it actively and to design and implement changes that would make it more effective.

One of the other important consequences of the exercise was not learned until several months later. Many of the executives at the middle and near-top level—especially those who tended to play it safe—were baffled by the degree of commitment, and especially by the near absence of undiscussable issues, on the part of the top people. Many had predicted that it would take years to implement the plan. They told their subordinates not to become too anxious because top management would probably be changed before the new scheme had an important impact on their levels. This led middle-level executives to reduce their vigilance and concern about implementation. However, unlike previous occasions, the implementation not only moved faster but greatly reduced the space for hiding. This taught the middle and lower levels a more vivid lesson about the change in the firm than could have occurred in the usual information and exhortation exchanges.

MODEL II THEORY-IN-USE

Embedded in the advice above is a different theory-in-use that we shall call Model II (Figure 5). Its governing variables are valid information, free and informed choice, and an internal commitment to that choice in order to monitor the effectiveness of the implementation of the action. Model II is a theory of action that combines learning and inquiry with advocating one's views. It is not a nondirective model (such a model would simply be the opposite of Model I). Model II action strategies are to combine advocacy with inquiry, to minimize face saving, and to encourage the acceptance of personal responsibility.

Let us now consider the X-Y case with a view to redesigning it along lines more consistent with Model II. Recall that the meanings the executives produced were high up on the ladder of inference, unillustrated, and untested; that executives believed their evaluations and attributions were *low* on the ladder of inference—that is, they were concrete and obvious inferences—and that it was therefore unnecessary to test them.

An outstanding feature of the participants' evaluations of Y was their negativeness. The most probable explanation for this negativeness was that Y's actions *were* negative. What is ineffective about communicating negative judgments if they are valid? The answer, from this perspective, is "Nothing." The problem is that negative evaluations should not be communicated by using the same features

FIGURE 5 Model II Theory-In-Use

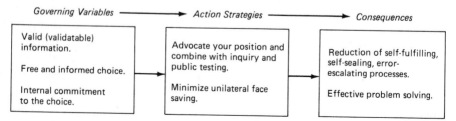

that the actors believe it is ineffective for someone else to use. To the extent that meanings are communicated in a way that follows the same causal theory the sender has told the recipient is counterproductive, the sender will be experienced by the recipient as behaving inconsistently and unjustly.

The participants' attributions had two major features. First, they explained Y's actions by attributing motives "in" Y. For example, Y was protecting himself, was seeking to frighten X, intended to intimidate X, and was insecure. Second, the attributions stated that the cause was in the role or the position that Y held. For example, Y was acting like a company man, like an authoritarian boss, like a superior identifying with the hierarchy.

Not only do the attributions contain negative evaluations—they imply that Y intended to make X defensive in order to protect himself or the organization.

If we combine the features of the evaluations and attributions just described, and if we keep in mind that the receiver is also programmed with Model I, then we have the basis for the predictions of self-fulfilling prophecies, self-sealing processes, and escalating error that were illustrated.

To invent and produce a different way of dealing with X, let us first identify the key features of an intervention that contains negative or threatening meanings even through the intention is to facilitate learning.

Messages should be designed so that they are experienced as credible by the recipients. Recipients must have access to the data and to the reasoning used by the sender to arrive at his or her evaluation or attribution. Hence the evaluations or attributions should be illustrated and the reasoning made explicit.

The message should be communicated in ways that will minimize individuals' automatic response to defend themselves. This means that senders should state their messages in such a way as to encourage inquiry into or confrontation of their reasoning and meanings.

From the preceding, it is possible to infer rules for producing such messages:

1. Provide the (relatively) directly observable data (first rung on the ladder) that you use to infer your evaluations or attributions, and check to see whether the recipient agrees with your data.
2. Make explicit the cultural meanings that you inferred from the data and seek confirmation from the other person.
3. Make explicit your judgments and opinions in ways that permit you to show why the consequences of the actors's action were inevitable, but without implying intentions to produce such consequences.
4. Encourage others to express feelings or ideas that they may have about the process.

The reader might ask, "How efficient can such rules be? Can we get anything done under real-time constraints?" First, recall that these rules are for dealing with double-loop issues. Second, how much is actually accomplished in the present modes of communication? Research suggests that present modes actually take longer and, worse, that they generate a social pollution of misunderstanding and mistrust that gives people a sense of helpless hopelessness. As our world becomes saturated with this pollution, even a small incremental error can touch off a breakdown of our natural defenses against it. As we shall see, the process of designing and implementing meanings in accordance with Model II does not take much longer. When we have clocked Model I and Model II roleplay, we have discovered that Model II (when produced by actors who are moderately competent) usually requires the same amount of time as the Model I roleplay, or even less.

We now turn to an illustration of how the interventionist might deal with Y. Remember the ladder of inference and Y's statement that led us to infer the meaning "X, your performance is unacceptable." Remember, too, that inferences are subject to error and hence should be put to public test. Every move up or down the ladder necessarily means that inferences are made; the higher up the ladder of inference and the more abstract the ideas, the greater the chance of error and therefore the greater the importance of public testing. Whatever theory one uses, it should make public testing as easy as possible.

To test an inference with someone else, it is necessary to make explicit both the premise and the conclusions drawn from the premise. The inference "Your performance is unacceptable" in the X-Y case is based on the premise of Y's words to X.

One can test the inference by asking Y: "When you said, 'X, your performance is not up to standard,' did you mean that his performance was unacceptable," or "When you said 'You seem to be carrying a chip on your shoulder,' did you intend to attribute to him unacceptable attitudes?" If Y responds yes, then the meanings have been affirmed and it is possible to proceed to the next rung on the ladder.

If a participant in an X-Y seminar wanted to reveal his diagnostic frame, it is at this point that he would have to say something like "Well, I infer from these data that you prejudged X," or "You were too blunt," or "You were insensitive." Such a response is likely to produce defensiveness in Y for several reasons. First, you may not agree with the evaluations/attributions. Y may believe that he had to be blunt or insensitive in order to get through to X. Or he may believe that he did not prejudge X, that X generated years of data that led to the present judgment. Second, the evaluations not only attribute errors to Y, but imply that he intended to be blunt, insensitive and so on. Since no one knowingly produces error, if Y knew what he was doing, then he knew that he was being blunt and insensitive. An explicit negative evaluation is coupled with an implicit attribution that Y intended the encounter with X to produce these negative consequences.

Under these conditions, the interventionist's testing is more of a trick than a helpful strategy. He or she may have tested the first two levels of inference only in order to nail Y with his or her third-level evaluations and attributions, themselves difficult to test. Indeed, in our experience it is difficult both for the interventionist and for the participants to see and agree with the logic of inference between successive levels of inference. Recall how often in the transcripts the participants either were unable to illustrate their inferences or illustrated them with further inferences. If inferences are to be tested, then no matter how high on the ladder of inference they occur it should be possible to proceed down the ladder and explicitly connect them with the first and second levels.

To summarize: Whatever concepts ar being used, one should be able to order them on a ladder of inference, advancing from relatively directly observable data to the culturally acceptable meaning and then up to the concepts used to organize the previous two rungs into a problem. It is at this point that interventionists are introducing their own (usually tacit) theory of help.

Let's return to the interventionist's two questions to Y. Recall that Y confirmed the meanings. But let us assume that Y said *yes* but was showing signs of impatience: "Of course I meant the performance is unacceptable!" or "Naturally I think X's attitudes are wrong! What are you driving at?" At this point the interventionist, using our theory of action, could say:

> I'll be glad to tell you what I am driving at. First, though, I want to make sure that I understood you correctly.
>
> I have a way of understanding the effectiveness of the kinds of comments that you made to X. Your first comment (repeats it) I call an "unillustrated evaluation." It tells the person he is wrong, but it does not include the data and logic of how you arrived at that conclusion.
>
> People tend to react to these unillustrated evaluations and attributions by feeling bewildered and/or misunderstood. Depending on how free they feel, they may confront you or they may imitate your style and make their own unillustrated evaluations and attributions about you. If they do the latter, it upsets the receiver, just as X was upset by your comments. Now, if X reacted on inferences that he is keeping secret, you would probably sense that secrecy because you would not see clearly the reasoning he used to come to his stated conclusions.
>
> Let's stop for a moment. What is your reaction? Does this make sense? (or) Am I communicating?

Several features of this response should be highlighted. First, not only do the concepts of "unillustrated evaluation" and "unillustrated attribution" provide insight into a problem, but the insight is in the form of a causal theory. *If someone produces unillustrated evaluations, whoever receives the evaluations or attributions will not know the basis of them unless they are illustrated. The receiver will feel bewildered and misunderstood. He may therefore react defensively (unless he is afraid or prefers to be dependent on you).*

The causal theory in these propositions is true for anyone, not simply for Y. Therefore, framing it as we do gives Y a degree of distancing from the problem that may help him or her to understand it better. We are not saying "Y, *you* are wrong." We are saying that anyone who behaves as Y did will produce the unintended consequences described above.

When individuals observe the redesign of what they could have said to Y, they are often impressed with its simplicity and obviousness. Many report that they expected the answer to be more surprising. The redesign may not be surprising because the ideas behind it are self-evident and not new. Another reason is that many individuals report that they had considered some of these intervention ideas but did not know how to design responses that made sense.

Both of these reasons show how crucial is the distinction between being aware of a possible action and being able to produce that action. In our terms the roleplay may not seem surprising, because it fits many individuals' espoused theories. But the difficulty is evident when people try to produce such redesign and find themselves unable to do so. They are surprised that they have difficulty redesigning their own interventions. The reason for their difficulty is that they *still hold* a Model I theory-in-use. When they are listening or advising, individuals use their espoused Model II theories. When they try to produce action, their Model I theory-in-use is activated.

The governing values of the theory are especially important. It is possible to make Model II statements to Y and yet fail because the actor still holds, and subtly conveys, Model I governing values such as "Win, don't lose," or "Maintain unilateral control." Indeed, some people initially react to the Model II redesign as if they were utilizing a new and more subtle form of Model I. Their disguised Model I approach usually shows when they try to defend their views.

To close, the skills and competencies that executives learn for dealing with an X-Y type of problem can be used for dealing with any double-loop problem. The key is to learn the new skills *and* to acquire a new set of governing values. If executives learn the new skills—such as advocating their position and encouraging inquiry—but use them to maintain unilateral control and to maximize winning, they would be using their new skills in the service of Model I values. They remain within a Model I mode; they hide their views about the gimmickiness of the new behavior, yet act as if they are not hiding anything. As a result, others may interpret their newly acquired skills as gimmicks or as new ways to manipulate people.

Luckily, people judge the credibility of human skills by evaluating what values they serve. This means that those who learn the new skills as gimmicks and tricks will be discovered. It means further that those who wish to gain credibility not only must learn the new skills, but also must internalize a new set of values.

SELECTED BIBLIOGRAPHY

The ideas in this paper come from the author's *Reasoning, Learning and Action: Individual and Organizational* (Jossey-Bass, 1982). Also relevant is a study of a group of presidents learning Model II, *Increasing Leadership Effectiveness* (Wiley-Interscience, 1976). Shorter versions of the theory behind the research may be found in the author's previous *Organizational Dynamics* article, "Leadership, Learning, and Changing the Status Quo" (Winter, 1976).

Two studies in government policy making and regulation are Laurence E. Lynn and David de F. Whitman's *The President as Policymaker: Jimmy Carter and Welfare Reform* (Temple University Press, 1981) and Robert B. Reich's "Regulation by Confrontation or Negotiation" (*Harvard Business Review,* May–June 1981).

The research on managing paradoxes can be found in Louis B. Barnes's "Managing the Paradox of Organizational Trust" (*Harvard Business Review,* March–April 1981).

4

Individual Motivation and Organizational Behavior

MOTIVATION: A DIAGNOSTIC APPROACH
David A. Nadler
Edward E. Lawler III

THAT URGE TO ACHIEVE
David C. McClelland

THE NEED FOR CLOSE RELATIONSHIPS AND THE MANAGER'S JOB
Richard E. Boyatzis

GOOD GUYS MAKE BUM BOSSES
David C. McClelland
David H. Burnham

MOTIVATION: A DIAGNOSTIC APPROACH

David A. Nadler
Edward E. Lawler III

- What makes some people work hard while others do as little as possible?
- How can I, as a manager, influence the performance of people who work for me?
- Why do people turn over, show up late to work, and miss work entirely?

These important questions about employees' behavior can only be answered by managers who have a grasp of what motivates people. Specifically, a good understanding of motivation can serve as a valuable tool for *understanding* the causes of behavior in organizations, for *predicting* the effects of any managerial action, and for *directing* behavior so that organizational and individual goals can be achieved.

Source: J. R. Hackman and E. E. Lawler, *Perspectives on Behavior in Organizations.* New York: McGraw-Hill, 1977.

EXISTING APPROACHES

During the past twenty years, managers have been bombarded with a number of different approaches to motivation. The terms associated with these approaches are well known—"human relations," "scientific management," "job enrichment," "need hierarchy," "self-actualization," etc. Each of these approaches has something to offer. On the other hand, each of these different approaches also has its problems in both theory and practice. Running through almost all of the approaches with which managers are familiar are a series of implicit but clearly erroneous assumptions.

Assumption 1: All employees are alike. Different theory present different ways of looking at people, but each of them assumes that all employees are basically similar in their makeup. Employees all want economic gains, or all want a pleasant climate, or all aspire to be self-actualizing, etc.

Assumption 2: All situations are alike. Most theories assume that all managerial situations are alike, and that the managerial course of action for motivation (for example, participation, job enlargement, etc.) is applicable in all situations.

Assumption 3: One best way. Out of the other two assumptions there emerges a basic principle that there is "one best way" to motivate employees.

When these "one best way" approaches are tried in the "correct" situation they will work. However, all of them are bound to fail in some situations. They are therefore not adequate managerial tools.

A NEW APPROACH

During the past ten years, a great deal of research has been done on a new approach to looking at motivation. This approach, frequently called "expectancy theory," still needs further testing, refining, and extending. However, enough is known that many behavioral scientists have concluded that it represents the most comprehensive, valid, and useful approach to understanding motivation. Further, it is apparent that it is a very useful tool for understanding motivation in organizations.

The theory is based on a number of specific assumptions about the causes of behavior in organizations.

Assumption 1: Behavior is determined by a combination of forces in the individual and forces in the environment. Neither the individual nor the environment alone determines behavior. Individuals come into organizations with certain "psychological baggage." They have past experiences and a developmental history which has given them unique sets of needs, ways of looking at the world, and expectations about how organizations will treat them. These all influence how individuals respond to their work environment. The work environment provides structures (such as a pay system or a supervisor) which influence the behavior of people. Different environments tend to produce different behavior in similar people just as dissimilar people tend to behave differently in similar environments.

Assumption 2: People make decisions about their own behavior in organizations. While there are many constraints on the behavior of individuals in organizations, most of the behavior that is observed is the result of individuals' conscious decisions. These decisions usually fall into two categories. First, individuals make decisions about *membership behavior*—coming to work, staying at work, and in other ways being a member of the organization. Second, individuals make decisions about the amount of *effort* they will direct *towards performing their jobs*. This includes decisions about how hard to work, how much to produce, at what quality, etc.

Assumption 3: Different people have different types of needs, desires, and goals. Individuals differ on what kinds of outcomes (or rewards) they desire. These differences are not random; they can be examined systematically by an understanding of the differences in the strength of individuals' needs.

Assumption 4: People make decisions among alternative plans of behavior based on their perceptions (expectancies) of the degree to which a given behavior will lead to desired outcomes. In simple terms, people tend to do those things which they see as leading to outcomes (which can also be called "rewards") they desire and avoid doing those things they see as leading to outcomes that are never desired.

In general, the approach used here views people as having their own needs and mental maps of what the world is like. They use these maps to make decisions about how they will behave, behaving in those ways which their mental maps indicate will lead to outcomes that will satisfy their needs. Therefore, they are inherently neither motivated nor unmotivated; motivation depends on the situation they are in, and how it fits their needs.

THE THEORY

Based on these general assumptions, expectancy theory states a number of propositions about the process by which people make decisions about their own behavior in organizational settings. While the theory is complex at first view, it is in fact made of a series of fairly straightforward observations about behavior. (The theory is presented in more technical terms in Appendix A.) Three concepts serve as the key building blocks of the theory:

Performance-outcome expectancy. Every behavior has associated with it, in an individual's mind, certain outcomes (rewards or punishments). In other words, the individual believes or expects that if he or she behaves in a certain way, he or she will get certain things.

Examples of expectancies can easily be described. An individual may have an expectancy that if he produces ten units he will receive his normal hourly rate while if he produces fifteen units he will receive his hourly pay rate plus a bonus. Similarly an individual may believe that certain levels of performance will lead to approval or disapproval from members of her work group or from her supervisor. Each performance can be seen as leading to a number of different kinds of outcomes and outcomes can differ in their types.

Valence. Each outcome has a "valence" (value, worth, attractiveness) to a specific individual. Outcomes have different valences for different individuals. This comes about because valences result from individual needs and perceptions, which differ because they in turn reflect other factors in the individual's life.

For example, some individuals may value an opportunity for promotion or advancement because of their needs for achievement or power, while others may not want to be promoted and leave their current work group because of needs for affiliation with others. Similarly, a fringe benefit such as a pension plan may have great valence for an older worker but little valence for a young employee on his first job.

Effort-performance expectancy. Each behavior also has associated with it in the individual's mind a certain expectancy or probability of success. This expectancy represents the individual's perception of how hard it will be to achieve such behavior and the probability of his or her successful achievement of that behavior.

For example, you may have a strong expectancy that if you put forth the effort, you can produce ten units an hour, but that you have only a fifty-fifty chance of producing fifteen units an hour if you try.

Putting these concepts together, it is possible to make a basic statement about motivation. In general, the motivation to attempt to behave in a certain way is greatest when:

a. The individual believes that the behavior will lead to outcomes (performance-outcome expectancy).
b. The individual believes that these outcomes have positive value for him or her (valence).
c. The individual believes that he or she is able to perform at the desired level (effort-performance expectancy).

Given a number of alternative levels of behavior (ten, fifteen, and twenty units of production per hour, for example) the individual will choose that level of performance which has the greatest motivational force associated with it, as indicated by the expectancies, outcomes, and valences.

In other words, when faced with choices about behavior, the individual goes through a process of considering questions such as, "Can I perform at that level if I try?" "If I perform at that level, what will happen?" "How do I feel about those things that will happen?" The individual then decides to behave in that way which seems to have the best chance of producing positive, desired outcomes.

A General Model

On the basis of these concepts, it is possible to construct a general model of behavior in organizational settings (see Figure 1). Working from left to right in the model, motivation is seen as the force on the individual to expend effort. Motivation leads to an observed level of effort by the individual. Effort, alone, however, is not enough. Performance results from a combination of the effort that an individual puts forth *and* the level of ability which he or she has (reflecting skills, training, information, etc.). Effort thus combines with ability to produce a given level of performance. As a result of performance, the individual attains certain outcomes. The model indicates this relationship in a dotted line, reflecting the fact that sometimes people perform but do not get desired outcomes. As this process of performance-reward occurs, time after time, the actual events serve to provide information which influences the individual's perceptions (particularly expectancies) and thus influences motivation in the future.

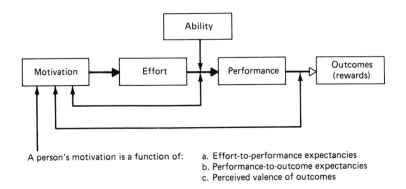

A person's motivation is a function of: a. Effort-to-performance expectancies
b. Performance-to-outcome expectancies
c. Perceived valence of outcomes

FIGURE 1 The Basic Motivation-Behavior Sequence

Outcomes, or rewards, fall into two major categories. First, the individual obtains outcomes from the environment. When an individual performs at a given level he or she can receive positive or negative outcomes from supervisors, co-workers, the organization's rewards systems, or other sources. These environmental rewards are thus one source of outcomes for the individual. A second source of outcomes is the individual. These include outcomes which occur purely from the peformance of the task itself (feelings of accomplishment, personal worth, achieve-ment, etc.). In a sense, the individual gives these rewards to himself or herself. The environment cannot give them or take them away directly; it can only make them possible.

Supporting Evidence

Over fifty studies have been done to test the validity of the expectancy-theory approach to predicting employee behavior.[1] Almost without exception, the studies have confirmed the predictions of the theory. As the theory predicts, the best per-formers in organizations tend to see a strong relationship between performing their jobs well and receiving rewards they value. In addition they have clear performance goals and feel they can perform well. Similarly, studies using the expectancy theory to predict how people choose jobs also show that individuals tend to interview for and actually take those jobs which they feel will provide the rewards they value. One study, for example, was able to correctly predict for 80 percent of the people studied which of several jobs they would take.[2] Finally, the theory correctly predicts that beliefs about the outcomes associated with performance (expectancies) will be better predictors of performance than will feelings of job satisfaction since expectancies are the critical causes of performance and satisfaction is not.

Questions about the Model

Although the results so far have been encouraging, they also indicate some problems with the model. These problems do not critically affect the managerial implications of the model, but they should be noted. The model is based on the assumption that individuals make very rational decisions after a thorough explora-tion of all the available alternatives and on weighing the possible outcomes of all these alternatives. When we talk to or observe individuals, however, we find that their decision processes are frequently less thorough. People often stop considering alternative behavior plans when they find one that is at least moderately satisfying, even though more rewarding plans remain to be examined.

People are also limited, in the amount of information they can handle at one time, and therefore the model may indicate a process that is much more complex than the one that actually takes place. On the other hand, the model does provide enough information and is consistent enough with reality to present some clear implications for managers who are concerned with the question of how to motivate the people who work for them.

Implications for Managers

The first set of implications is directed toward the individual manager who has a group of people working for him or her and is concerned with how to motivate good performance. Since behavior is a result of forces both in the person and in the environment, you as manager need to look at and diagnose both the person and the environment. Specifically, you need to do the following:

Figure out what outcomes each employee values. As a first step, it is important to determine what kinds of outcomes or rewards have valence for your employees. For each employee you need to determine "what turns him or her on." There are various ways of finding this out, including (a) finding out employees' desires through some structured method of data collection, such as a questionnaire, (b) observing the employees' reactions to different situations or rewards, or (c) the fairly simple act of asking them what kinds of rewards they want, what kind of career goals they have, or "what's in it for them." It is important to stress here that it is very difficult to change what people want, but fairly easy to find out what they want. Thus, the skillful manager emphasizes diagnosis of needs, not changing the individuals themselves.

Determine what kinds of behavior you desire. Managers frequently talk about "good performance" without really defining what good performance is. An important step in motivating is for you yourself to figure out what kinds of performances are required and what are adequate measures or indicators of performance (quantity, quality, etc.). There is also a need to be able to define those performances in fairly specific terms so that observable and measurable behavior can be defined and subordinates can understand what is desired of them (e.g., produce ten products of a certain quality standard—rather than only produce at a high rate).

Make sure desired levels of performance are reachable. The model states that motivation is determined not only by the performance-to-outcome expectancy, but also by the effort-to-performance expectancy. The implication of this is that the levels of performance which are set as the points at which individuals receive desired outcomes must be reachable or attainable by these individuals. If the employees feel that the level of performance required to get a reward is higher than they can reasonably achieve, then their motivation to perform well will be relatively low.

Link desired outcomes to desired performances. The next step is to directly, clearly, and explicitly link those outcomes desired by employees to the specific performances desired by you. If your employee values external rewards, then the emphasis should be on the rewards systems concerned with promotion, pay, and approval. While the linking of these rewards can be initiated through your making statements to your employees, it is extremely important that employees see a clear example of the reward process working in a fairly short period of time if the motivating "expectancies" are to be created in the employees' minds. The linking must be done by some concrete public acts, in addition to statements of intent.

If your employee values internal rewards (e.g., achievement), then you should concentrate on changing the nature of the person's job, for he or she is likely to respond well to such things as increased autonomy, feedback, and challenge, because these things will lead to a situation where good job performance is inherently rewarding. The best way to check on the adequacy of the internal and external reward system is to ask people what their perceptions of the situation are. Remember it is the perceptions of people that determine their motivation, not reality. It doesn't matter for example whether you feel a subordinate's pay is related to his or her motivation. Motivation will be present only if the subordinate sees the relationship. Many managers are misled about the behavior of their subordinates because they rely on their own perceptions of the situation and forget to find out what their subordinates feel. There is only one way to do this: ask. Questionnaires can be used here, as can personal interviews. . . .

Analyze the total situation for conflicting expectancies. Having set up positive expectancies for employees, you then need to look at the entire situation to see if other factors (informal work groups, other managers, the organization's reward systems) have to set up conflicting expectancies in the minds of the employees. Motivation will only be high when people see a number of rewards associated with good performance and few negative outcomes. Again, you can often gather this kind of information by asking your subordinates. If there are major conflicts, you need to make adjustments, either in your own performance and reward structure, or in the other sources of rewards or punishments in the environment.

Make sure changes in outcomes are large enough. In examining the motivational system, it is important to make sure that changes in outcomes or rewards are large enough to motivate significant behavior. Trivial rewards will result in trivial amounts of effort and thus trivial improvements in performance. Rewards must be large enough to motivate individuals to put forth the effort required to bring about significant changes in performance.

Check the system for its equity. The model is based on the idea that individuals are different and therefore different rewards will need to be used to motivate different individuals. On the other hand, for a motivational system to work it must be a fair one—one that has equity (not equality). Good performers should see that they get more desired rewards than do poor performers, and others in the system should see that also. Equity should not be confused with a system of equality where all are rewarded equally, with no regard to their performance. A system of equality is guaranteed to produce low motivation.

Implications for Organizations

Expectancy theory has some clear messages for those who run large organizations. It suggests how organizational structures can be designed so that they increase rather than decrease levels of motivation or organization members. While there are many different implications, a few of the major ones are as follows:

Implication 1: The design of pay and reward systems. Organizations usually get what they reward, not what they want. This can be seen in many situations, and pay systems are a good example.[3] Frequently, organizations reward people for membership (through pay tied to seniority, for example) rather than for performance. Little wonder that what the organization gets is behavior oriented towards "safe," secure employment rather than effort directed at performing well. In addition, even where organizations do pay for performance as a motivational device, they frequently negate the motivational value of the system by keeping pay secret, therefore preventing people from observing the pay-to-performance relationship that would serve to create positive, clear, and strong performance-to-reward expectancies. The implication is that organizations should put more effort into rewarding people (through pay, promotion, better job opportunities, etc.) for the performances which are desired, and that to keep these rewards secret is clearly self-defeating. In addition, it underscores the importance of the frequently ignored performance evaluation or appraisal process and the need to evaluate people based on how they perform clearly defined specific behaviors, rather than on how they score on ratings of general traits such as "honesty," "cleanliness," and other, similar terms which frequently appear as part of the performance appraisal form.

Implication 2: The design of tasks, jobs, and roles. One source of desired outcomes is the work itself. The expectancy-theory model supports much of the job enrichment literature, in saying that by designing jobs which enable people to get their needs fulfilled, organizations can bring about higher levels of motivation.[4] The major difference between the traditional approaches to job enlargement or enrichment and the expectancy-theory approach is the recognition by expectancy theory that different people have different needs and, therefore, some people may not want enlarged or enriched jobs. Thus, while the design of tasks that have more autonomy, variety, feedback, meaningfulness, etc., will lead to higher motivation in some, the organization needs to build in the opportunity for individuals to make choices about the kind of work they will do so that not everyone is forced to experience job enrichment.

Implication 3: The importance of group structures. Groups, both formal and informal, are powerful and potent sources of desired outcomes for individuals. Groups can provide or withhold acceptance, approval, affection, skill training, needed information, assistance, etc. They are a powerful force in the total motivational environment of individuals. Several implications emerge from the importance of groups, First, organizations should consider the structuring of at least a portion of rewards around group performance rather than individual performance. This is particularly important where group members have to cooperate with each other to produce a group product or service, and where the individual's contribution is often hard to determine. Second, the organization needs to train managers to be aware of how groups can influence individual behavior and to be sensitive to the kinds of expectancies which informal groups set up and their conflict or consistency with the expectancies that the organization attempts to create.

Implication 4: The supervisor's role. The immediate supervisor has an important role in creating, monitoring, and maintaining the expectancies and reward structures which will lead to good performance. The supervisor's role in the motivation process becomes one of defining clear goals, setting clear reward expectancies, and providing the right rewards for different people (which could include both organizational rewards and personal rewards such as recognition, approval, or support from the supervisor). Thus, organizations need to provide supervisors with an awareness of the nature of motivation as well as the tools (control over organizational rewards, skill in administering those rewards) to create positive motivation.

Implication 5: Measuring motivation. If things like expectancies, the nature of the job, supervisor-controlled outcomes, satisfaction, etc., are important in understanding how well people are being motivated, then organizations need to monitor employee perceptions along these lines. One relatively cheap and reliable method of doing this is through standardized employee questionnaires. A number of organizations already use such techniques, surveying employees' perceptions and attitudes at regular intervals (ranging from once a month to once every year-and-a-half) using either standardized surveys or surveys developed specifically for the organization. Such information is useful both to the individual manager and to top management in assessing the state of human resources and the effectiveness of the organization's motivational systems. . . .[5]

Implication 6: Individualizing organizations. Expectancy theory leads to a final general implication about a possible future direction for the design of organizations. Because different people have different needs and therefore have different valences, effective motivation must come through the recognition that not all employees are alike and that organizations need to be flexible in order to accommodate individual differences. This implies the "building in" of choice for employees in many areas, such as reward systems, fringe benefits, job assignments, etc., where employees previously have had little say. A successful example of the building in of such choice can be seen in the experiments at TRW and the Educational Testing Service with "cafeteria fringe-benefits plans" which allow employees to choose the fringe benefits they want, rather than taking the expensive and often unwanted benefits which the company frequently provides to everyone.[6]

SUMMARY

Expectancy theory provides a more complex model of man for managers to work with. At the same time, it is a model which holds promise for the more effective motivation of individuals and the more effective design of organizational systems. It implies, however, the need for more exacting and thorough diagnosis by the manager to determine (a) the relevant forces in the individual, and (b) the relevant forces in the environment, both of which combine to motivate different kinds of behavior. Following diagnosis, the model implies a need to act—to develop a system of pay, promotion, job assignments, group structures, supervision, etc.—to bring about effective motivation by providing different outcomes for different individuals.

Performance of individuals is a critical issue in making organizations work effectively. If a manager is to influence work behavior and performance, he or she must have an understanding of motivation and the factors which influence an individual's motivation to come to work, to work hard, and to work well. While simple models offer easy answers, it is the more complex models which seem to offer more promise. Managers can use models (like expectancy theory) to understand the nature of behavior and build more effective organizations.

APPENDIX A: THE EXPECTANCY THEORY
MODEL IN MORE TECHNICAL TERMS

A person's motivation to exert effort towards a specific level of performance is based on his or her perceptions of associations between actions and outcomes. The critical perceptions which contribute to motivation are graphically presented in Figure 2. These perceptions can be defined as follows:

a. The effort-to-performance expectancy $(E \rightarrow P)$: This refers to the person's subjective probability about the likelihood that he or she can perform at a given level, or that effort on his or her part will lead to successful performance. This term can be thought of as varying from 0 to 1. In general, the less likely a person feels that he or she can perform at a given level, the less likely he or she will be to try to perform at that level. A person's $E \rightarrow P$ probabilities are also strongly influenced by each situation and by previous experience in that and similar situations.

b. The performance-to-outcomes expectancy $(P \rightarrow O)$ and valence (V): This refers to a combination of a number of beliefs about what the outcomes of successful performance will be and the value or attractiveness of these outcomes to the individual. Valence is considered to vary from $+1$ (very desirable) to -1 (very undesirable) and the performance-to-outcomes probabilities vary from $+1$ (performance sure to lead to outcome) to 0 (performance not related to outcome). In general, the more

FIGURE 2 Major Terms in Expectancy Theory

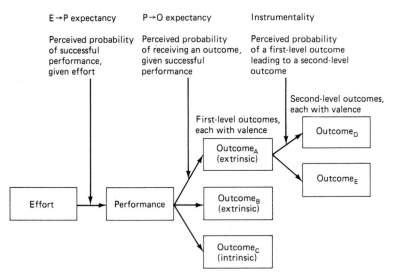

Motivation is expressed as follows: $M \cdot [E \rightarrow P] \times \geq [(P \cdot O)(V)]$

likely a person feels that performance will lead to valent outcomes, the more likely he or she will be to try to perform at the required level.

c. Instrumentally: As Figure 2 indicates, a single level of performance can be associated with a number of different outcomes, each having a certain degree of valence. Some outcomes are valent because they have direct value or attractiveness. Some outcomes, however, have valence because they are seen as leading to (or being "instrumental" for) the attainment of other "second level" outcomes which have direct value or attractiveness.

d. Intrinsic and extrinsic outcomes: Some outcomes are seen as occurring directly as a result of performing the task itself and are outcomes which the individual thus gives to himself (i.e., feelings of accomplishment, creativity, etc.). These are called "intrinsic" outcomes. Other outcomes that are associated with performance are provided or mediated by external factors (the organization, the supervisor, the work group, etc.). These outcomes are called "extrinsic" outcomes.

Along with the graphic representation of these terms presented in Figure 2, there is a simplified formula for combining these perceptions to arrive at a term expressing the relative level of motivation to exert effort towards performance at a given level. The formula expresses these relationships:

a. The person's motivation to perform is determined by the P→O expectancy multiplied by the valence (V) of the outcome. The valence of the first order outcome subsumes the instrumentalities and valences of second order outcomes. The relationship is multiplicative since there is no motivation to perform if either of the terms is zero.

b. Since a level of performance has multiple outcomes associated with it, the products of all probability-times-valence combinations are added together for all the outcomes that are seen as related to the specific performance.

c. This term (the summed P→O expectancies times valences) is then multiplied by the E→P expectancy. Again the multiplicative relationship indicates that if either term is zero, motivation is zero.

d. In summary, the strength of a person's motivation to perform effectively is influenced by (1) the person's belief that effort can be converted into performance, and (2) the net attractiveness of the events that are perceived to stem from good performance.

So far, all the terms have referred to the individual's perceptions which result in motivation and thus an intention to behave in a certain way. Figure 3 is a sim-

FIGURE 3 Simplified Expectancy-Theory Model of Behavior

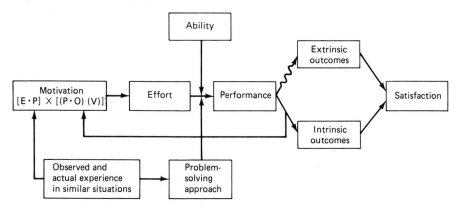

plified representation of the total model, showing how these intentions get translated into actual behavior.[7] The model envisions the following sequence of events:

a. First, the strength of a person's motivation to perform correctly is most directly reflected in his or her effort—how hard he or she works. This effort expenditure may or may not result in good performance, since at least two factors must be right if effort is to be converted into performance. First, the person must possess the necessary abilities in order to perform the job well. Unless both ability and effort are high, there cannot be good performance. A second factor is the person's perception of how his or her effort can best be converted into performance. It is assumed that this perception is learned by the individual on the basis of previous experience in similar situations. This "how to do it" perception can obviously vary widely in accuracy, and—where erroneous perceptions exist—performance is low even though effort or motivation may be high.

b. Second, when performance occurs, certain amounts of outcomes are obtained by the individual. Intrinsic outcomes, not being mediated by outside forces, tend to occur regularly as a result of performance, while extrinsic outcomes may or may not accrue to the individual (indicated by the wavy line in the model).

c. Third, as a result of the obtaining of outcomes and the perceptions of the relative value of the outcomes obtained, the individual has a positive or negative affective response (a level of satisfaction or dissatisfaction).

d. Fourth, the model indicates that events which occur influence future behavior by altering the $E \rightarrow P$, $P \rightarrow O$, and V perceptions. This process is represented by the feedback loops running from actual behavior back to motivation.

REFERENCES

1. For reviews of the expectancy theory research see Mitchell, T. R. Expectancy models of job satisfaction, occupational preference and effort. A theoretical methodological, and empirical appraisal, *Psychological Bulletin,* 1974, 81, 1053–1077. For a more general discussion of expectancy theory and other approaches to motivation see Lawler, E. E. *Motivation in work organizations,* Belmont Calif.: Brooks/Cole, 1973.
2. Lawler, E. E., Kuleck, W. J., Rhode, J. G., & Sorenson, J. F. Job choice and post-decision dissonance. *Organizational Behavior and Human Performance,* 1975, 13, 133–145.
3. For a detailed discussion of the implications of expectancy theory for pay and reward systems, see Lawler, E. E. *Pay and organizational effectiveness: A psychological view.* New York: McGraw-Hill, 1971.
4. A good discussion of job design with an expectancy theory perspective is in Hackman, J. R., Oldham, G. R., Janson, R., & Purdy, K. A new strategy for job enrichment. *California Management Review.* Summer, 1975, p. 57.
5. The use of questionnaires for understanding and changing organizational behavior is discussed in Nadler, D. A. *Feedback and organizational development: Using data-based methods.* Reading, Mass.: Addison-Wesley, 1977.
6. The whole issue of individualizing organizations is examined in Lawler, E. E. The individualized organization: Problems and promise. *California Management Review,* 1974, 17(2), 31–39.
7. For a more detailed statement of the model see Lawler, E. E. Job attitudes and employee motivation: Theory, research and practice. *Personnel Psychology,* 1970, 23, 223–237.

THAT URGE TO ACHIEVE

David C. McClelland

Most people in this world, psychologically, can be divided into two broad groups. There is that minority which is challenged by opportunity and willing to work hard to achieve something, and the majority which really does not care all that much.

For nearly twenty years now, psychologists have tried to penetrate the mystery of this curious dichotomy. Is the need to achieve (or the absence of it) an accident, is it hereditary, or is it the result of environment? Is it a single, isolatable human motive, or a combination of motives—the desire to accumulate wealth, power, fame? Most important of all, is there some technique that could give this will to achieve to people, even whole societies, who do not now have it?

While we do not yet have complete answers for any of these questions, years of work have given us partial answers to most of them and insights into all of them. There is a distinct human motive, distinguishable from others. It can be found, in fact tested for, in any group.

Let me give you one example. Several years ago, a careful study was made of 450 workers who had been thrown out of work by a plant shutdown in Erie, Pennsylvania. Most of the unemployed workers stayed home for a while and then checked back with the United States Employment Service to see if their old jobs or similar ones were available. But a small minority among them behaved differently: the day they were laid off, they started job-hunting.

They checked both the United States and the Pennsylvania Employment Office: they studied the "Help Wanted" sections of the papers; they checked through their union, their church, and various fraternal organizations; they looked into training courses to learn a new skill; they even left town to look for work, while the majority when questioned said they would not under any circumstances move away from Erie to obtain a job. Obviously the members of that active minority were differently motivated. All the men were more or less in the same situation objectively: they needed work, money, food, shelter, job security. Yet only a minority showed initiative and enterprise in finding what they needed. Why? Psychologists, after years of research, now believe they can answer that question. They have demonstrated that these men possessed in greater degree a specific type of human motivation. For the moment let us refer to this personality characteristic as "Motive A" and review some of the other characteristics of the persons who have more of the motive than other persons.

Suppose they are confronted by a work situation in which they can set their own goals as to how difficult a task they will undertake. In the psychological laboratory, such a situation is very simply created by asking them to throw rings over a peg from any distance they may choose. Most persons throw more or less randomly, standing now close, now far away, but those with Motive A seem to calculate carefully where they are most likely to get a sense of mastery. They stand

Source: Reprinted by permission from *THINK Magazine,* published by IBM, © 1966 by International Business Machines Corporation, and from the author.

nearly always at moderate distances, not so close as to make the task ridiculously easy, nor so far away as to make it impossible. They set moderately difficult, but potentially achievable goals for themselves, where they objectively have only about a 1-in-3 chance of succeeding. In other words, they are always setting challenges for themselves, tasks to make them stretch themselves a little.

But they behave like this only if *they* can influence the outcome by performing the work themselves. They prefer not to gamble at all. Say they are given a choice between rolling dice with one in three chances of winning and working on a problem with a one-in-three chance of solving in the time alloted, they choose to work on the problem even though rolling the dice is obviously less work and the odds of winning are the same. They prefer to work at a problem rather than leave the outcome to chance or to others.

Obviously they are concerned with personal achievement rather than with the rewards of success *per se,* since they stand just as much chance of getting those rewards by throwing the dice. This leads to another characteristic the Motive A persons show—namely, a strong preference for work situations in which they get concrete feedback on how well they are doing, as one does, say in playing golf, or in being a salesman, but as one does not in teaching, or in personnel counseling. A golfer always knows his score and can compare how well he is doing with par or with his own performance yesterday or last week. A teacher has no such concrete feedback on how well he is doing in "getting across" to his students.

THE *n* ACH PERSON

But why do certain persons behave like this? At one level the reply is simple: because they habitually spend their time thinking about doing things better. In fact, psychologists typically measure the strength of Motive A by taking samples of a person's spontaneous thoughts (such as making up a story about a picture they have been shown) and counting the frequency with which he mentions doing things better. The count is objective and can even be made these days with the help of a computer program for content analysis. It yields what is referred to technically as an individual's *n* Ach score (for "need for Achievement"). It is not difficult to understand why people who think constantly about "doing better" are more apt to do better at job-hunting, to set moderate achievable goals for themselves, to dislike gambling (because they get no achievement satisfaction from success), and to prefer work situations where they can tell easily whether they are improving or not. But why some people and not others come to think this way is another question. The evidence suggests it is not because they are born that way, but because of special training they get in the home from parents who set moderately high achievement goals but who are warm, encouraging and nonauthoritarian in helping their children reach these goals.

Such detailed knowledge about one motive helps correct a lot of common sense ideas about human motivation. For example, much public policy (and much business policy) is based on the simpleminded notion that people will work harder "if they have to." As a first approximation, the idea isn't totally wrong, but it is only a half-truth. The majority of unemployed workers in Erie "had to" find work as much as those with higher n Ach, but they certainly didn't work as hard at it. Or again, it is frequently assumed that *any* strong motive will lead to doing things better. Wouldn't it be fair to say that most of the Erie workers were just "unmotivated"? But our detailed knowledge of various human motives shows that each one leads a person to behave in *different ways.* The contrast is not between being "motivated" or "unmotivated" but between being motivated toward A or toward B or C, etc.

A simple experiment makes the point nicely: subjects were told that they could choose as a working partner either a close friend or a stranger who was known to be an expert on the problem to be solved. Those with higher n Ach (more "need to achieve") chose the experts over their friends, whereas those with more n Aff (the "need to affiliate with others") chose friends over experts. The latter were not "unmotivated"; their desire to be with someone they liked was simply a stronger motive than their desire to excel at the task. Other such needs have been studied by psychologists. For instance, the need for Power is often confused with the need for Achievement because both may lead to "outstanding" activities. There is a distinct difference. People with a strong need for Power want to command attention, get recognition, and control others. They are more active in political life and tend to busy themselves primarily with controlling the channels of communication both up to the top and down to the people so that they are more "in charge." Those with high n Power are not as concerned with improving their work performance daily as those with high n Ach.

It follows, from what we have been able to learn, that not all "great achievers" score high in n Ach. Many generals, outstanding politicians, great research scientists do not, for instance, because their work requires other personality characteristics, other motives. A general or a politician must be more concerned with power relationships, a research scientist must be able to go for long periods without the immediate feedback the person with high n Ach requires, etc. On the other hand, business executives, particularly if they are in positions of real responsibility or if they are salesmen, tend to score high in n Ach. This is true even in a Communist country like Poland: apparently there, as well as in a private enterprise economy, a manager succeeds if he is concerned about improving all the time, setting moderate goals, keeping track of his or the company's performance, etc.

MOTIVATION AND HALF-TRUTHS

Since careful study has shown that common sense notions about motivation are at best half-truths, it also follows that you cannot trust what people tell you about their motives. After all, they often get their ideas about their own motives from common sense. Thus a general may say he is interested in achievement (because he has obviously achieved), or a businessman that he is interested only in making money (because he has made money), or one of the majority of unemployed in Erie that he desperately wants a job (because he knows he needs one); but a careful check of what each one thinks about and how he spends his time may show that each is concerned about quite different things. It requires special measurement techniques to identify the presence of n Ach and other such motives. Thus what people say and believe is not very closely related to these "hidden" motives which seem to affect a person's "style of life" more than his political, religious or social attitudes. Thus n Ach produces enterprising men among labor leaders or managers, Republicans or Democrats, Catholics or Protestants, capitalists or Communists.

Wherever people begin to think often in n Ach terms, things begin to move. Men with higher n Ach get more raises and are promoted more rapidly, because they keep actively seeking ways to do a better job. Companies with many such men grow faster. In one comparison of two firms in Mexico, it was discovered that all but one of the top executives of a fast growing firm had higher n Ach scores than the highest scoring executive in an equally large but slow-growing firm. Countries with many such rapidly growing firms tend to show above-average rates of economic growth. This appears to be the reason why correlations have regularly been found between the n Ach content in popular literature (such as popular songs or stories in children's textbooks) and subsequent rates of national economic growth. A nation which is thinking about doing better all the time (as shown in its popular literature) actually does do better economically speaking. Careful quantitative studies have shown this to be true in Ancient Greece, in Spain in the Middle Ages, in England from 1400–1800, as well as among contemporary nations, whether capitalist or Communist, developed or underdeveloped.

Contrast these two stories for example. Which one contains more n Ach? Which one reflects a state of mind which ought to lead to harder striving to improve the way things are?

Excerpt from story A (4th grade reader): "Don't Ever Owe a Man—The world is an illusion. Wife, children, horses and cows are all just ties of fate. They are ephemeral. Each after fulfilling his part in life disappears. So we should not clamour after riches which are not permanent. As long as we live it is wise not to have any attachments and just think of God. We have to spend our lives without trouble, for is it not time that there is an end to grievances? So it is better to live knowing the real state of affairs. Don't get entangled in the meshes of family life."

Excerpt from story B (4th grade reader): "How I Do Like to Learn—I was sent to an accelerated technical high school. I was so happy I cried. Learning is not very easy. In the beginning I couldn't understand what the teacher taught us. I always got a red cross mark on my papers. The boy sitting next to me was very enthusiastic and also an outstanding student. When he found I could not do the problems he offered to show me how he had done them. I could not copy his work. I must learn through my own reasoning. I gave his paper back and explained I had to do it myself. Sometimes I worked on a problem until midnight. If I couldn't finish, I started early in the morning. The red cross marks on my work were getting less common. I conquered my difficulties. My marks rose. I graduated and went on to college."

Most readers would agree, without any special knowledge of the n Ach coding system, that the second story shows more concern with improvement than the first, which comes from a contemporary reader used in Indian public schools. In fact the latter has a certain Horatio Alger quality that is reminiscent of our own

McGuffey readers of several generations ago. It appears today in textbooks of Communist China. It should not, therefore, come as a surprise that a nation like Communist China, obsessed as it is with improvement, tended in the long run to outproduce a nation like India, which appears to be more fatalistic.

The n Ach level is obviously important for statesmen to watch and in many instances to try to do something about, particularly if a nation's economy is lagging. Take Britain, for example. A generation ago (around 1925) it ranked fifth among 25 countries where children's readers were scored for n Ach—and its economy was doing well. By 1950 the n Ach level had dropped to 27th out of 39 countries—well below the world average—and today, its leaders are feeling the severe economic effects of this loss in the spirit of enterprise.

ECONOMICS AND n ACH

If psychologists can detect n Ach levels in individuals or nations, particularly before their effects are widespread, can't the knowledge somehow be put to use to foster economic development? Obviously detection or diagnosis is not enough. What good is it to tell Britain (or India for that matter) that it needs more n Ach, a greater spirit of enterprise? In most such cases, informed observers of the local scene know very well that such a need exists, though they may be slower to discover it than the psychologist hovering over n Ach scores. What is needed is some method of developing n Ach in individuals or nations.

Since about 1960, psychologists in my research group at Harvard have been experimenting with techniques designed to accomplish this goal, chiefly among business executives whose work requires the action characteristics of people with high n Ach. Initially, we had real doubts as to whether we could succeed, partly because like most American psychologists we have been strongly influenced by the psychoanalytic view that basic motives are laid down in childhood and cannot really be changed later, and partly because many studies of intensive psychotherapy and counseling have shown minor if any long-term personality effects. On the other hand we were encouraged by the nonprofessionals: those enthusiasts like Dale Carnegie, the Communist ideologue or the Church missionary, who felt they could change adults and in fact seemed to be doing so. At any rate we ran some brief (7 to 10 days) "total push" training courses for businessmen, designed to increase their n Ach.

FOUR MAIN GOALS

In broad outline the courses had four main goals: (1) They were designed to teach the participants how to think, talk and act like a person with high n Ach, based on our knowledge of such people gained through 17 years of research. For instance, individuals learned how to make up stories that would code high in n Ach (i.e., how to think in n Ach terms), how to set moderate goals for themselves in the ring toss game (and in life). (2) The courses stimulated the participants to set higher but carefully planned and realistic work goals for themselves over the next two years. Then we checked back with them every six months to see how well they were doing in terms of their own objectives. (3) The courses also utilized techniques for giving the participants knowledge about themselves. For instance, in playing the ring toss game, they could observe that they behaved differently from others—perhaps in refusing to adjust a goal downward after failure. This would then become a matter for group discussion and the man would have to explain what he had in mind in setting such unrealistic goals. Discussion could then lead on to what a person's ultimate goals in life were, how much he cared about actually improving performance v. making a good impression or having many friends. In this way the participants would be freer to realize their achievement goals without being blocked by old habits and attitudes. (4) The courses also usually created a group *esprit de corps* from learning about each other's hopes and fears, successes and failures, and from going through an emotional experience together, away from everyday life, in a retreat setting. This membership in a new group helps a person achieve his goals, partly because he knows he has their sympathy and support and partly because he knows they will be watching to see how well he does. The same effect has been noted in other therapy groups like Alcoholics Anonymous. We are not sure which of these course "inputs" is really absolutely essential—that remains a research question—but we are taking no chances at the outset in view of the general pessimism about such efforts, and we wanted to include any and all techniques that were thought to change people.

The courses have been given: to executives in a large American firm, and in several Mexican firms; to underachieving high school boys; and to businessmen in India from Bombay and from a small city—Kakinada in the state of Andhra Pradesh. In every instance save one (the Mexican case), it was possible to demonstrate statistically, some two years later, that the men who took the course had done better (made more money, got promoted faster, expanded their businesses faster) than comparable individuals who did not take the course or who took some other management course.

Consider the Kakinada results, for example. In the two years preceding the course 9 men, 18 percent of the 52 participants, had shown "unusual" enterprise in their businesses. In the 18 months following the course 25 of the individuals, in other words nearly 50 percent, were unusually active. And this was not due to a general upturn of business in India. Data from a control city, some forty-five miles away, show the same base rate of "unusually active" men as in Kakinada before the course—namely, about 20 percent. Something clearly happened in Kakinada: the owner of a small radio shop started a chemical plant; a banker was so successful in making commercial loans in an enterprising way that he was promoted to a much larger branch of his bank in Calcutta; the local political leader accomplished his goal (it was set in the course) to get the federal government to deepen the harbor and make it into an all-weather port; plans are far along for establishing a steel rolling mill, etc. All this took place without any substantial capital input from the outside. In fact, the only costs were for four 10-day courses plus some brief follow-up visits every six months. The men are raising their own capital and using their own resources for getting business and industry moving in a city that had been considered stagnant and unenterprising.

The promise of such a method of developing achievement motivation seems very great. It has obvious applications in helping underdeveloped countries, or "pockets of poverty" in the United States, to move faster economically. It has great potential for businesses that need to "turn around" and take a more enterprising approach toward their growth and development. It may even be helpful in developing more n Ach among low-income groups. For instance, data show that lower-class Negro Americans have a very low level of n Ach. This is not surprising. Society has systematically discouraged and blocked their achievement striving. But as the barriers to upward mobility are broken down, it will be necessary to help stimulate the motivation that will lead them to take advantage of new opportunities opening up.

EXTREME REACTIONS

But a word of caution: Whenever I speak of this research and its great potential, audience reaction tends to go to opposite extremes. Either people remain skeptical and argue that motives can't really be changed, that all we are doing is dressing Dale Carnegie up in fancy "psychologese," or they become converts and want instant course descriptions by return mail to solve their local motivational problems. Either response is unjustified. What I have described here in a few pages has taken 20 years of patient research effort, and hundreds of thousands of dollars in basic research costs. What remains to be done will involve even larger sums and more time for development to turn a promising idea into something of wide practical utility.

ENCOURAGEMENT NEEDED

To take only one example, we have not yet learned how to develop n Ach really well among low-income groups. In our first effort—a summer course for bright underachieving 14-year-olds—we found that boys from the middle class improved steadily in grades in school over a two-year period, but boys from the lower class showed an improvement after the first year followed by a drop back to their beginning low grade average (see the accompanying chart). Why? We speculated that it was because they moved back into an environment in which neither parents nor friends encouraged achievement or upward mobility. In other words, it isn't enough to change a man's motivation if the environment in which he lives doesn't support at least to some degree his new efforts. Negroes striving to rise out of the ghetto frequently confront this problem: they are often faced by skepticism at home and suspicion on the job, so that even if their n Ach is raised, it can be lowered again by the heavy odds against their success. We must learn not only to raise n Ach but also to find methods of instructing people in how to manage it, to create a favorable environment in which it can flourish.

Many of these training techniques are now only in the pilot testing stage. It will take time and money to perfect them, but society should be willing to invest heavily in them in view of their tremendous potential for contributions to human betterment.

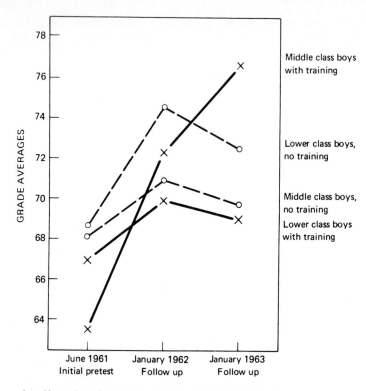

In a Harvard study, a group of underachieving 14-year-olds was given a six-week course designed to help them do better in school.

Some of the boys were also given training in achievement motivation, or *n* Ach (solid lines). As graph reveals, the only boys who continued to improve after a two-year period were the middle-class boys with the special *n* Ach training.

Psychologists suspect the lower-class boys dropped back, even with *n* Ach training, because they returned to an environment in which neither parents nor friends encouraged achievement.

THE NEED FOR CLOSE RELATIONSHIPS AND THE MANAGER'S JOB

Richard E. Boyatzis

The results of research on the affiliative motive are somewhat contradictory although they tend to relate high levels of this motive with poor performance as a manager. Boyatzis (1972) proposed a new theory of affiliation motivation in which he claimed there are two forms of the motive: one is called *affiliative*

Source: By permission of the author.

assurance and the other *affiliative interest*. With these types of affiliation motivation in mind, prior findings are reconciled into clear patterns of behavior: one would lead to effective performance of a manager's job, and the other would not.

THE MANAGER AND HIS SUBORDINATE

Past research on the affiliation motive has shown that a person with a high level of that motive would act in some ways which are necessary to a manager's job, such as communicating with others and understanding their feelings. Such a person may also exhibit behavior which inhibits the manager in effectively performing his job, such as seeking the approval of subordinates.

A corporate unit or "spin-off" (research and development organizations, in particular) headed by a manager with a high need for affiliation does not do as well as do other similar organizations (Harris, 1969; Wainer and Rubin, 1969). Such a manager prefers to work in collaboratively structured groups and in a relaxed atmosphere (deCharms, 1957; French, 1955). Both of these situational factors are often difficult to establish because of economic pressures and requirements of the marketplace.

A manager with a high need for affiliation would strive for approval from his subordinates and superiors (Byrne, 1961), we would be sensitive to others' facial expressions and their feelings (Atkinson and Walker, 1956), and if the manager and his subordinate were to disagree, the manager would change his attitude to one which was more acceptable to the subordinate's, especially if the manager likes the subordinates (Burdick and Burnes, 1958; Byrne, 1961).

If this manager with a high need for affiliation were given a choice as to which of his subordinates he would like to work with on a task, he would choose the subordinate with whom he has a close, friendly relationship—even if this person were less competent to perform the task than another subordinate (French, 1956). He would also choose a subordinate less likely to reject his offer, rather than choose a more qualified subordinate (Rosenfeld, 1964).

The manager with the high need for affiliation is so concerned about his relationships that performance objectives of his job become confused. The goal of building and maintaining friendly relations supersedes a concern over the effectiveness of his organizational unit's performance toward corporate objectives. But, he sincerely believes that friendly relations are *necessary* to healthy corporate performance.

In contrast to these findings, several studies have shown that a person with affiliation motivation demonstrates behavior which contributes to the effectiveness of corporate performance. Lawrence and Lorsch (1967) report that effective "integrators" (managers whose function is to integrate the work of various people or units) rank higher in the need for affiliation than their less effective peers.

Kolb and Boyatzis (1970) showed that people who were effective at helping others change their behavior were higher in the need for affiliation than their less effective counterparts. This is relevant because one of the manager's functions is to "help" his subordinate develop their behavioral skills to more effectively perform their present job, as well as to aid the subordinate in planning his career development.

After several days with this effective affiliation motivated manager, you would noitice that he spent more time communicating with subordinates (Noujaim, 1968) and writing, calling, and visiting friends (Lansing and Heyns, 1959) than would other managers you know. The disposition to communicate with others is a critical aspect of the manager's job. Without that communication, it is very difficult to integrate people's efforts in a manner which builds their commitment to their work.

The evidence is somewhat contradictory. On the one hand, managers with high affiliation motivation exhibit behavior which interferes with their job and the poor performance of their organizational units show it. On the other hand, aspects of a manager's job require some of the behavior demonstrated by a person with affiliation motivation. Is it a matter of degree—i.e., do managers who show ineffective behavior stemming from affiliative concerns have levels of affiliation motivation which are too high? Or is it a function of the way in which they experience and express their affiliation motive?

GRASPING OR CONCERN?

A manager may have a low, moderate, or high concern about close relationships relative to his other concerns, such as concerns about having impact on others, prestige or reputation, attempting to do better against a standard of excellence, or doing something unique, to mention a few.

Affiliative concerns which are moderate or high with respect to other concerns may lead a manager to increase the performance of his unit and develop commitment in his subordinates, or it may cause him to act in a way which interferes with his job. The difference in the effects of a person's affiliative motive is determined by the *type* of affiliation motive.

As a result of methodological and conceptual difficulties, I contend that the research on the need for affiliation taps primarily the *affiliative assurance* form of the motive. The early experiments performed in an attempt to develop a method of measuring the need for affiliation based their research on a definition of affiliation motive as a striving for close relationships in the sense of security needs (Shipley and Veroff, 1952; Atkinson, Heyns, and Veroff, 1954). The arousal of the motive in these studies consisted of having individual members of fraternities stand, while others in his group described them on an adjective checklist (used in two studies), or using people adversely affected by being rejected from a fraternity during a rush period (used in one study). Both techniques bias the measuring system in a way which causes the measure of affiliation motivation to tap the person's concerns about being evaluated, being accepted or rejected more than his unanxious concerns about being a part of close relations. The component of anxiety about being rejected or negatively evaluated by friends was probably present in people who participated in the studies.

A preliminary attempt to separate the affiliative assurance motive from the affiliative interest motive demonstrated support for the theory, but lacked enough substantial results to consider it a definitive theoretical and methodological solution to the problem of measuring affiliation motives (Boyatzis, 1972). The support found did confirm the basic notion that the two forms exist, and they do determine different forms of interpersonal behavior.

A manager with a high affiliative assurance motive will basically be concerned about obtaining assurance as to the security and strength of his close relations. He will be anxious about not being rejected. This concern leads him to look for "proof" of others' commitments to him and to avoid issues or conflict which may threaten the stability of the relationship. He would tend to be jealous or possessive of his subordinates (and possibly of his superior), search for communications which support the closeness of the relationship, and look for signs of approval from the others around him. He would avoid conflict situations by smoothing things over, or abdicating his role in intervening to resolve the conflict. *It is this assurance form of affiliation motivation which would interfere with a person's work as a manager.* It would be his "grasping" onto close relationships which would drain his energy and absorb his time. He would spend time seeking approval and security, rather than doing his job.

The manager with an assurance motive would be concerned about the subordinate's feelings toward him and the job. He would be looking for acceptance and approval from the subordinate. This manager would equate the subordinate's happiness in the job with acceptance of the manager as a person, and would not feel comfortable confronting the subordinate with negative feedback on job performance. He might even ignore this type of information to avoid the interpersonal situation of telling the subordinate. The rules of behavior in his relationship to his subordinates would include much concern but little openness—for example, the subordinate would not be allowed to disagree with the manager or give him negative feedback because it would threaten the relationship.

The manager would not look forward to a transfer or promotion of him or his subordinates, but, instead would like to keep them all in the family. The objectives of this manager's organizational unit would be ambiguous to his subordinates. Although corporate objectives would be evident, the manager would actually be spending time working on the relationships, and at times, at the expense of performance objectives.

The manager with predominantly an affiliative interest motive would want the subordinate to feel a part of a human organization. The rules of behavior in his relationships would include interpersonal concern and openness, and because the relationship was in the context of the whole organization, there would be a sense of closeness evolved from working together toward performance objectives. This would not threaten, or diminish, the manager's feelings of closeness to his subordinates.

This type of manager could evaluate a subordinate's piece of work, give him negative or positive feedback, and not communicate a positive or negative overall evaluation of the subordinate as a person. As a result of the openness and concern over the subordinate's welfare, a climate of trust would be established which would encourage the subordinate to make his motives or concerns clear to the manager. This would enable the manager to direct the subordinate's work more effectively, designing his subordinate's job in a manner which responded to his motives or concerns.

Such a manager would be enthusiastic about the transfer or promotion of one of his subordinates, not feeling the separation as a loss and would look forward to establishing a close relationship with a new subordinate.

It is the affiliative interest form of the motive which would lead to increased managerial effectiveness. Such a person's show of "concern" would not occur at the expense of goal-oriented behavior.

Most organizational theorists emphasize the importance of personnel feeling as a part of an organization. The manager with an affiliative interest motive can stimulate those feelings on a human level by making it clear that the subordinate's thoughts and feelings are important to him. The manager with an assurance motive has a tendency to confuse his subordinates. They are not sure whether the quality of interpersonal relationships is the most important factor on the job, or if it is performance toward organizational objectives. The objectives of this manager's performance are often toward building and maintaining a set of close relationships.

In his relationship to his superior, the manager with an assurance motive would be looking for approval and acceptance. He would exaggerate in his mind the relevance of positive feedback and would tend to ignore negative feedback. With some negative feedback, he might assume that the superior did not like him as a person and he would not utilize the information to improve performance, but begin to withdraw from the job.

He would do things which would please the superior and make him notice. Constantly seeking more personal contact, such a manager would not take moderate risks in job assignments and would prefer to stay away from challenging tasks which might result in failure. He might also do the opposite, which is to accept task assignments which are high-risk (challenging, but hardly attainable) in the hope that if he succeeds, his superior would appreciate him greatly.

The manager with an affiliative interest motive would be able to separate interpersonal relationships and job performance issues. Feedback to him, or from him to his superior, could be related to a task and not have implications for the future quality of their relationship. Informal meetings with the interest-type manager and his superior would be more relaxed than such encounters with an assurance-type manager.

The reader should remember that the affiliation motive is but one of many motives of the individual. The character of the person's affiliative motive will interact with his other motives in a variety of ways. Providing a person who has either type of affiliative motive with a warm, interpersonal environment in which to work will stimulate him. In particular, a person with an assurance motive will not be able to devote energy to objectives other than maintaining relationships if he does not feel like an accepted part of the organizational unit. A manager with such a motive may find it difficult to stimulate goal-oriented thinking and behavior in his subordinates because of his needs.

TOWARD A GENUINE CONCERN

Managers with relatively low concerns about close relationships compared to other concerns will find the performance of their organizational unit increasing and turnover decreasing if they develop the ability to demonstrate genuine concern toward others around them.

Managers with high affiliative assurance motives would find the performance of their units increasing if they could realize that people around them do not necessarily want to reject them. Their relationships are a part of a work organization whose main objectives are performance toward corporate objectives. The concerns for assurance are this manager's needs, not his subordinates' or superior's needs.

A healthy and productive organization is a humane effort toward corporate performance objectives. By increasing the behavior which would appear to emanate from an affiliative interest motive, a manager will create a climate of interpersonal concern and trust which builds the capability of the organization to reach its objectives and grow.

REFERENCES

J. W. Atkinson, R. W. Heyns, and J. Veroff, "The Effect of Experimental Arousal of the Affiliation Motive on Thematic Apperception," *Journal of Abnormal and Social Psychology,* 1954, *49,* 405–410.

J. W. Atkinson and Walker, "The Affiliation Motive and Perceptual Sensitivity to Faces," *Journal of Abnormal and Social Psychology,* 1956, *53,* 38–41.

R. E. Boyatzis, "A Two-Factor Theory of Affiliation Motivation" (unpublished doctoral dissertation, Harvard University, 1972).

H. A. Burdick and A. J. Burnes, "A Test of 'Strain Toward Symmetry' Theories," *Journal of Abnormal and Social Psychology,* 1958, *57,* 367–370.

D. Byrne, "Anxiety and the Experimental Arousal of the Affiliation Need," *Journal of Abnormal and Social Psychology,* 1961, *63,* 660–662.

D. Byrne, "Interpersonal Attraction as a Function of Affiliation Need and Attitude Similarity," *Human Relations,* 1961, *14,* 283–289.

R. deCharms, "Affiliation Motivation and Productivity in Small Groups," *Journal of Abnormal and Social Psychology,* 1957, *55,* 222–226.

E. G. French, "Some Characteristics of Achievement Motivation," *Journal of Experimental Psychology,* 1955, *50,* 232–236.

E. G. French, "Motivation as a Variable in Work Partner Selection," *Journal of Abnormal and Social Psychology,* 1956, *53,* 96–99.

H. Harris, "An Experimental Model of the Effectiveness of Project Management Offices" (unpublished Master's dissertation. Massachusetts Institute of Technology, 1969).

D. A. Kolb and R. E. Boyatzis, "On the Dynamics of the Helping Relationship," *Journal of Applied Behavioral Sciences,* 1970.

J. B. Lansing and R. W. Heyns, "Need for Affiliation and Four Types of Communication," *Journal of Abnormal and Social Psychology,* 1959, *58,* 365–372.

P. R. Lawrence and J. W. Lorsch, "New Management Job: The Integrator," *Harvard Business Review,* 1967, *45,* 142–151.

K. Noujaim, "Some Motivational Determinants of Effort Allocation and Performance" (unpublished doctoral dissertation. Massachusetts Institute of Technology, 1968).

H. Rosenfeld, "Social Choice Conceived as a Level of Aspiration," *Journal of Abnormal and Social Psychology,* 1964, *3,* 491–499.

T. E. Shipley and J. Veroff, "A Projective Measure of Need for Affiliation," *Journal of Experimental Psychology,* 1952, *43,* 349–356.

H. A. Wainer and I. M. Rubin, "Motivation of Research and Development Entrepreneurs," *Journal of Applied Psychology,* 1969, *53,* 178–184.

GOOD GUYS MAKE BUM BOSSES

David C. McClelland
David H. Burnham

Fred and Paul are two managers in the same large corporation. Fred is a friendly sort of guy. He spends lots of time rapping with his subordinates, and prides himself on being warm and sympathetic. If an employee were to ask for time off to take care of a personal problem, Fred would worry about the rules but probably give in.

Paul, on the other hand, loves to be a boss and spends his time nudging subordinates to do their jobs. Although his manner is amiable, it is distinctly less personal and warm than Fred's. His primary loyalty is to the organization. If an employee asked him for time off because of a personal problem, Paul would suggest that he use up some vacation days or take an unpaid leave of absence.

Who is the better manager? Many people would quickly choose generous, friendly Fred. He is humane, egalitarian and understanding. But our research shows that nice guys like Fred often make bum bosses. Compared to Paul, he gets less work out of his people and creates lower morale.

In our search for the key to executive personality, we have found that effective managers share a striking characteristic—the need for power. This motive, a basic desire to influence and lead others, drives able executives in many different lines of work. Like Paul, most go by the rule book.

POWER AND AFFILIATION

We began one recent experiment by testing the managers of 49 departments in a large American corporation. The tests showed whether each executive was concerned primarily with achievement, with power, or with affiliation (having friendly relations with others). We knew from 20 years of research that entrepreneurs, the innovators who start new businesses, have a high need for achievement. But only in the last five years have we gone beyond those who start new organizations to study the people who later move into the chains of command.

Power and affiliation, not achievement, turned out to be the important scores among the 49 line managers. They divided into two basic types, the power-motivated managers like Paul and the affiliative managers like Fred.

We worked first with sales departments, dividing them evenly between those with above-average and those with below-average sales. Only 20 percent of the better half were run by managers with a higher need for affiliation than for power. But 90 percent of the poorer ones were run by affiliatives. So power managers ran 80 percent of the best, only 10 percent of the worst. (The characteristics of women managers are somewhat different. All the managers in this study were male.)

In other departments (design, development, production) we found the same link between the manager's drive and the department's performance. Affiliative managers ran only 27 percent of the better departments, but 78 percent of the weaker half. On the other hand, power managers ran 73 percent of the good ones, only 22 percent of the weak ones.

WISHY-WASHY DECISIONS

We had previously asked the employees in each department to fill out a detailed questionnaire about their morale and how their bosses ran things. These reports provided clear insight into the connection between the manager's personality and the department's success or failure.

The affiliative manager has a greater need for fellowship than for power and influence. His desire to be liked leads him into wishy-washy decisions. Because he wants to stay on good terms with anyone he works with, he cares more about the happiness of particular individuals than the well-being of the whole working group. By making many exceptions to company rules, he violated one of bureaucracy's first principles—fairness.

When a manager bends the rules for particular individuals, he often alienates other workers. His failure to treat people equally destroys the worker's faith in the corporate reward system. His inconsistent decisions may also make his subordinates feel powerless to control events by their behavior. Whether they do well or badly, they don't know what to expect next.

Because the need for power takes two different forms, power managers tend to fall into two groups: the personal-power group and the social- or institutional-power group. In previous research, we had found that these two forms of the power motive even affect the way people drive cars or drink whiskey (see "The Power of Positive Drinking," *pt.* January 1971). Men with a strong need for personal power use their cars like weapons and make mean drunks, but the ones who use power for the benefit of others are safer drivers and are convivial, social drinkers.

This same split shows in a manager's style. The personal-power type strives for dominance. He is the impulsive tough guy. He may be rude, fight with others, boast of sexual conquest, and try to exploit women. Such men tend to reject institutional responsibility, and hate to join organizations. In history, they have been the conquistadors and feudal chieftains.

Such an executive is the business equivalent of a tank commander. Like General George Patton, he can inspire the troops to heroic performance. His underlings feel a sense of responsibility and team spirit. He fails, however, to draw clear lines of organization. Our studies suggest that the personal-power manager does not want his subordinates to be responsible to the organization, only to him personally. As long as he is there to lead them, they do well, but when he leaves, morale plummets and the organization falls apart. His employees are loyal to him, not to the company or unit.

The institutionalized-power manager is too inhibited for such antics. Here, the model is the German civil servant in the Bismarck tradition. In fact, we have compared German and American responses to the power-motive test and found that the Germans use more than five times as many negative statements in ways that reflect a strong inhibition against the use of personal power. They are very correct managers of organization.

The institutionalized-power manager is more successful at creating a good climate for regular work. His subordinates have both a sense of responsibility and a clear knowledge of the organization. They stick to the work rules, not because they are hit over the head, but because they become loyal to the institution.

On the surface, our findings seem to fly in the face of the case against authoritarian management made by the majority of organizational psychologists. Proponents of this view urge managers to be more people oriented and less concerned about power. But where productivity and morale are primary goals, the power-driven manager does the job best.

And he pays a price. Nearly 24 years ago we ran power-motive tests on a group of Harvard graduates who had finished school about 12 years earlier and were then in their early 30s. We are now completing a follow-up study on this group of men. Of those who scored high in institutionalized-power with its strong inhibitions, 58 percent now either have high blood pressure or are dead of heart failure.

MARCHING OVER GRANDMOTHER

But nobody is a captive of his own character. Whatever motive drives him, a manager can adopt any one of several different styles to control those who work for him. He may play dictator or be the helpful coach, who suggests, encourages and is acutely aware of his employees' limitations and abilities. We found that 63 percent of the best managers preferred the helping hand to the authoritarian order. Only 22 percent of the worst managers acted like coaches. Since the better managers were also those who had a strong power need, we assume they expressed it noncoercively.

One young executive we met, George P., had a high need for power and a low need for affiliation, plus the inhibitions of the institutionalized manager. He had more concern for his company than for his personal ambitions. But he also had a reputation of being ready to march over his grandmother if she stood between him and advancement. He tried to direct others on the job by ordering them to do what he said—or else.

At one of our workshops, we explained to George that his way of dealing with people was likely to defeat his own objectives. He began to realize that his job was not to force others to perform, but to help them figure out ways of getting their tasks done.

126

George soon began to act more like a coach and less like a drill sergeant. His reputation changed dramatically, and he became known as a man who cared about people. But he did not turn into an affiliative manager. His aim was not to buddy up to subordinates, but to help them hit the company goals.

Since Americans view any lust for power with deep suspicion, our finding that effective corporate executives have a need for power may confirm some of the political stereotypes. But since this motive works best through a coaching style, as George P. discovered, a fear of submitting to more and more autocratic bureaucracies is not justified. Worry about power executives would be better placed in a broader social context of our general concerns about efficient companies driven by able, expansion-minded executives. Such fears are hardly new.

One final characteristic of institutionalized-power managers needs to be grasped. They gain maturity. They are less defensive and more willing when they need it, to seek expert advice in personal matters. They collect fewer status symbols. They seem older and wiser, and appear to be less worried about their personal futures.

Some American businessmen fear this kind of maturity in themselves. They think it means becoming less aggressive. Our research, however, can allay their fears. An overriding sense of personal importance is not necessary for high performance. Indeed, the institutionalized-power manager is often willing to sacrifice his own immediate self-interest for the welfare of the organization. He does not see self-sacrifice for the company benefit as self-defeating because he sees his own power as deriving from the company.

Such a manager does not make himself a weak boss, as the affililative one does, out of his need to be liked. He feels confident that if a man works hard, he will get his just rewards. What's good for the company, he honestly feels, is good for him.

5
Personal Growth and Career Development

THE INDIVIDUAL, THE ORGANIZATION AND THE CAREER:
A CONCEPTUAL SCHEME
Edgar H. Schein

CAREER DEVELOPMENT, PERSONAL GROWTH
AND EXPERIENTIAL LEARNING
Donald M. Wolfe
David A. Kolb

ON THE REALIZATION OF HUMAN POTENTIAL:
A PATH WITH A HEART
Herbert A. Shepard

THE INDIVIDUAL, THE ORGANIZATION, AND THE CAREER, A CONCEPTUAL SCHEME

Edgar H. Schein

INTRODUCTION

The purpose of this paper is to present a conceptual scheme and a set of variables which make possible the description and analysis of an indivdual's movement through an organization. We usually think of this set of events in terms of the word "career," but we do not have readily available concepts for describing the multitude of separate experiences and adventures which the individual encounters during the life of his organizational career. We also need concepts which can articulate the relationship between (1) the career seen as a set of attributes and experiences of the *individual* who joins, moves through, and finally leaves an organization, and (2) the career as defined by the *organization*—a set of expectations held by individuals inside the organization which guide their decisions about whom to move, when, how, and at what "speed." It is in the different perspectives which are held

Source: The ideas in this paper derive from research conducted from 1958–1964 with funds from the Office of Naval Research, Contract NONR 1841 (83) and subsequently with funds from the Sloan Research Fund, M.I.T. Reprinted from Sloan School of Management, M.I.T., Working Paper No. 326–68, with permission of Edgar H. Schein.

toward careers by those who act them out and those who make decisions about them, that one may find some of the richest data for understanding the relationship between individuals and organizations.

The ensuing discussion will focus first on structural variables, those features of the organization, the individual, and the career which are the more or less stable elements. Then we will consider a number of "process" variables which will attempt to describe the dynamic interplay between parts of the organization and parts of the individual in the context of his ongoing career. Basically there are two kinds of processes to consider: 1) the influence of the organization on the individual, which can be thought of as a type of *acculturation* or *adult socialization;* and 2) the influence of the individual on the organization, which can be thought of as a process of *innovation* (Schein, 1968).

Both socialization and innovation involve the relationship between the individual and the organization. They differ in that the former is initiated by the organization and reflects the relatively greater power of the social system to induce change in the individual, whereas the latter is initiated by the individual and reflects his power to change the social system. Ordinarily these two processes are discussed as if they were mutually exclusive of each other and as if they reflected *properties* of the organization or the individual. Thus certain organizations are alleged to produce conformity in virtually all of their members, while certain individuals are alleged to have personal strengths which make them innovators wherever they may find themselves. By using the concept of career as a process over time which embodies many different kinds of relationships between an organization and its members, I hope it can be shown that typically the same person is both influenced (socialized) and in turn influences (innovates), and that both processes coexist (though at different points in the life or a career) within any given organization.

I. THE STRUCTURE OF THE ORGANIZATION

Organizations such as industrial concerns, government agencies, schools, fraternities, hospitals, and military establishments which have a continuity beyond the individual careers of their members can be characterized structurally in many different ways. The particular conceptual model one chooses will depend on the purposes which the model is to fulfill. The structural model which I would like to propose for the analysis of careers is not intended to be a general organizational model; rather, it is designed to elucidate that side of the organization which involves the movement of people through it.

My basic proposition is that the organization should be conceived of as a three-dimensional space like a cone or cylinder in which the external vertical surface is essentially round and in which a core or inner center can be identified. What we traditionally draw as a pyramidal organization on organization charts should really be drawn as a cone in which the various boxes of the traditional chart would represent adjacent sectors of the cone but where movement would be possible within each sector toward or away from the center axis of the cone. Figure 1 shows a redrawing of a typical organization chart according to the present formulation.

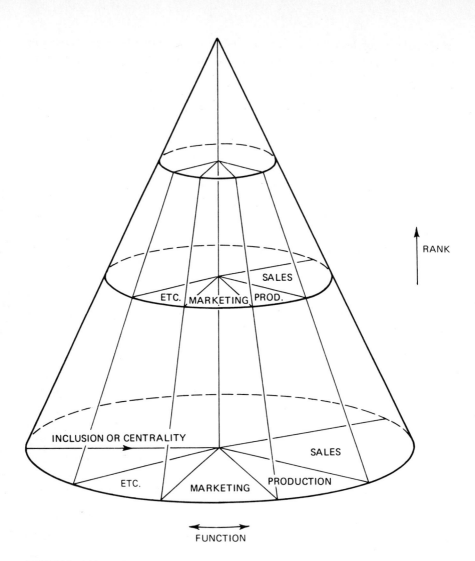

FIGURE 1 A Three Dimensional Model of an Organization

Movement within the organization can then occur along three conceptually distinguishable dimensions:

1. *Vertically*—corresponding roughly to the notation of increasing or decreasing one's *rank* or *level* in the organization;
2. *Radically*—corresponding roughy to the notion of increasing or decreasing one's *centrality* in the organization, one's degree of being more or less "on the inside";
3. *Circumferentially*—corresponding roughly to the notion of changing one's function or one's division of the organization.

Whether movement along one of these dimensions is ever independent of movement along another one is basically an empirical matter. For present purposes it is enough to establish that it would be, in principle, possible for an individual to move along any one of the dimensions without changing his position on either of the other ones.

Corresponding to the three types of movement one can identify three types of *boundaries* which characterize the internal structure of the organization:

1. *Hierarchical boundaries*—which separate the hierarchical levels from each other;
2. *Inclusion boundaries*—which separate individuals or groups who differ in the degree of the centrality;[1]
3. *Functional or departmental boundaries*—which separate departments, divisions, or different functional groupings from each other.

Boundaries can vary in (1) *number,* (2) *degree of permeability,* and (3) type of *filtering properties* they possess. For example, in the military there are a great many functional boundaries separating the different line and staff activities, but the overall policy of rotation and keeping all officers highly flexible makes these boundaries highly permeable in the sense that people move a great deal from function to function. On the other hand, a university would also have many functional boundaries corresponding to the different academic departments, but these would be highly impermeable in the sense that no one would seriously consider the movement of an English professor to a Chemistry department, or vice versa. A small family-run business, to take a third example, is an organization with very few functional boundaries in that any manager performs all of the various functions.

Similarly, with respect to hierarchical or inclusion boundaries one can find examples of organizations in which there are many or few levels, many or few degrees of "being in," with the boundaries separating the levels or inner regions being more or less permeable. The external inclusion boundary is, of course, of particular significance, in that its permeability defined the ease or difficulty of initial entry into the organization. Those companies or schools which take in virtually anyone but keep only a small percentage of high performers can be described as having a highly permeable external inclusion boundary, but a relatively impermeable inclusion boundary fairly close to the exterior. On the other hand, the company or school which uses elaborate selection procedures to take in only very few candidates, expects those taken in to succeed, and supports them accordingly, can be described as having a relatively impermeable external inclusion boundary but no other impermeable boundaries close to the exterior.

Further refinement can be achieved in this model if one considers the particular types of filters which characterize different boundaries, i.e., which specify the process or set of rules by which one passes through the boundary. Thus hierarchical boundaries filter individuals in terms of attributes such as seniority, merit, personal characteristics, types of attitudes held, who is sponsoring them, and so on. Functional boundaries filter much more in terms of the specific competencies of the individual, or his "needs" for broader experience in some scheme of training and development (the latter would certainly not be considered in reference to

[1]The organization as a multi-layered system corresponds to Lewin's concept of the personality as a multi-layered system like an onion (Lewin, 1948).

a hierarchical boundary). Inclusion boundaries are probably the most difficult to characterize in terms of their filtering system in that the system may change as one gets closer to the inner core of the organization. Competence may be critical in permeating the external boundary, but factors such as personality, seniority, and willingness to play a certain kind of political game may be critical in becoming a member of the "inner circle."[2] Filter properties may be formally stated requirements for admission or may be highly informal norms shared by the group to be entered.

With reference to individual careers, organizations can be analyzed and described on the basis of (1) number of boundaries of each type, (2) the boundary permeability of the different boundaries, and (3) the filtering system which characterizes them. For example, most universities have two hierarchical boundaries (between the ranks of assistant, associate, and full professor), two inclusion boundaries (for initial entry and tenure), and as many functional boundaries as there are departments and schools. Filters for promotion and tenure may or may not be the same depending on the university, but will generally involve some combination of scholarly or research publication, teaching ability, and "service" to the institution. Organizations like industrial ones which do not have a tenure system will be harder to diagnose as far as inclusion filters go, but the inclusion boundaries are just as much a part of their system. The variables identified thus far are basically intended as a set of categories in terms of which to describe and compare different types of organizations in respect to the career paths they generate.

A final variable which needs to be considered is the *shape* of the three-dimensional space which characterizes the organization. The traditional pyramidal organization would presumably become in this scheme a cone. An organization with very many levels could be thought of as a very steep cone, while one with few levels could be thought of as a flat cone. The drawing of the organization as a cone implies, however, that the highest level person is also the most central which is, of course, not necessarily the case. If the top of the organization is a management team, one might think of a truncated cone; if there is a powerful board of directors who represent a higher level but a wider range of centrality one might think of an inverted cone, the point of which touches the apex of the main cone and which sits on top of the main one. In universities where the number of full professors is as large as the number of assistant professors, one might think of the organization more as a cylinder with a small cone on top of it representing the administration.

I am not stating any requirements that the shape of the organization be summetrical. If a certain department is very large but very peripheral, it might best be thought of as a large bulge on an otherwise round shape. If one considers internal inclusion boundaries one may have some departments which are in their entirety very central and thus reach the vertical axis (core), while other departments do not contain anyone who is very central in the organization and thus do not reach the core at all. The shape of the inner core is also highly variable. It may be an

<hr>

[2]One of the best descriptions of such filters in an organization can be found in Dalton's (1959) discussion of career advancement in the companies to be studied.

inverted cone which would imply that the number of central people *increases* with rank. Or it might be a cylinder which would imply that there are equal numbers of central people at all ranks. Or it might be some highly asymmetrical shape reflecting the reality that the number of central people varies with length of service, department, political connections with higher ranks, access to critical company informations, etc.[3]

Some Problems of Measuring Organizational Structure

The problem of measurement varies greatly as a function of the degree to which boundaries and their filtering characteristics are explicitly acknowledged by a given organization and by wider society. Thus, hierarchical boundaries which separate levels are a widely accepted fact of organizational life and the rules for permeating them tend to be fairly explicit. To the extent that implicit informal factors do operate it becomes more difficult to measure the filtering properties of the hierarchical boundaries in any given organization.

Functional boundaries are generally the easiest to identify because our typical analysis of organizations emphasizes different functions and departments. Similarly, the rules of entry to a function or department tend to be fairly explicit.

The inclusion boundaries are the hardest to identify and measure because to a considerable extent their very existence usually remains implicit. While it may be clear to everyone in a company that there is an inner circle (which may cut across many rank levels), this fact may be denied when an outsider probes for the data. The filtering mechanism may be even more difficult to identify because even the willing informant, including members of the inner circle, may be unclear about the actual mechanisms by which people move toward the center. Even the *concept* of centrality is unclear in that it does not discriminate between (1) an individual person's *feeling* of being central or peripheral, and (2) some *objective criterion* of his actual position in the organization's social structure.

In the discussion thus far I have meant by the term "centrality" the person's objective position as measured by the degree to which company secrets are entrusted to him, by ratings of others of his position, and by his power. His subjective rating of himself might correlate highly with these other measures and thus might prove to be a simpler measuring device, but it does not basically define centrality because a person may misperceive his own position.

It may be argued that I have over-stated the assumption that the organization is an integrated unified entity. It may after all be only a group of individual people or sub-groups coordinating their activities to some degree but operating from quite different premises. Therefore there are no "organizational" boundaries, only individual approaches to the movement and promotion of their subordinates.

There is ample evidence for the assertion that people who associate with each other around a common task for any length of time *do* develop group boundaries of various sorts and a set of norms which define their probability and filtering

[3]Dalton (1959) has identified what he calls "vertical cliques" which cover different ranks as well as departments of an industrial organization.

properties (e.g., Homans, 1950). But it is quite possible that several such groups co-exist within a larger social system and develop different norms. In applying the concepts which I am outlining in this paper it is therefore necessary to identify as the "organization" a group which has interacted for a sufficient length of time to have developed some common norms. Later, in analyzing the progress of a career, it will of course be necessary to consider the difficulties which are created for the individual as he moves from a group with one set of norms about boundaries to another group with a different set of norms about boundaries, even though both groups are part of the same larger organization.

II. THE STRUCTURE OF THE INDIVIDUAL

Any given individual can be thought of as a more or less integrated set of social selves organized around a basic image or concept of self. His basic temperament, intellectual equipment, learned patterns of feeling expression, and psychological defenses underlie and partially determine this self-image and the kinds of social selves which the individual constructs for himself to deal with his environment. But our focus is on the constructed selves which make it possible for the individual to fulfill various role expectations in his environment, not on the more enduring underlying qualities.

I am using the concept of a constructed social self in the sense of Mead (1934) and more recently Becker (1961) and Goffman (1955, 1957, 1959), as a set of assumptions about, perceptions of, and claims on a given social situation in which role expectations may be more or less well defined. The basic rules of conduct and interaction in terms of which the person orients himself to any social situation are largely culturally determined, but these basic rules still leave each individual a wide latitude in how he will choose to present himself in any given situation (the "line" he will take), and how much social value or status he will claim for himself (his "face").

This conception of the individual places primary emphasis on those aspects of his total being which are the most immediate product of socialization, which most immediately engage other persons in daily life, and which are most dependent on the reinforcement or confirmation of others. For example, at a *basic* level, a person may be temperamentally easily frustrated, may have developed a character structure around the repression of strong aggressive impulses, and may rely heavily on denial and reaction-formation as defense mechanisms. These characteristics describe his basic underlying personality structure but they tell us practically nothing of how he presents himself to others, what his self-image is, how he takes characteristic occupational or social roles, how much value he places on himself, and what kind of interaction patterns he engages in with others.

Focusing on his constructed selves, on the other hand, might show us that this person presents himself to others as very even tempered and mild mannered, that in group situations he takes a role of harmonizing any incipient fights which develop between others, that he tries to appear as the logical voice of reason in discussions and is made uneasy by emotions, that he prefers to analyze problems

134

and advise others rather than getting into action situations (i.e., he prefers some kind of "staff" position), and that he does not get too close to people or depend too heavily upon them. None of the latter characteristics are inconsistent with the basic structure. Persons with the same kind of underlying character structure might enter similar interactive situations quite differently. In other words, I am asserting that it is not sufficient to describe a person in terms of basic personality structure, but they could not have been specifically predicted from the basic structure, if we are to understand his relationship to organizations. Furthermore, it is possible to analyze the person's functioning at the social self level and this level of analysis is most likely to be productive for the understanding of career patterns and the reciprocal influence process between individual and organization.

Each of us learns to construct somewhat different selves for the different kinds of situations in which we are called on to perform, and for the different kinds of roles we are expected to take. Thus, I am a somewhat different person at work than at home; I present myself somewhat differently to my superior than to my subordinate, to my wife than to my children, to my doctor than to a salesman, when I am at a party than when I am at work, and so on. The long and complex process of socialization teaches us the various norms, rules of conduct, values and attitudes, and desirable role behaviors through which one's obligations in situations and roles can be fulfilled. All of these patterns become part of us so that to a large extent we are not conscious of the almost instantaneous choices we make among possible patterns as we "compose ourselves" for entry into a new social situation. Yet these patterns can be immediately brought to consciousness if the presented self chosen is one which does not fit the situation, that is, fails to get confirmation from others.

Failure to get confirmation of a self which involves a certain claimed value is felt by the actor as a threat to his face; he finds himself in a situation in which he is about to lose face if he and the others do not take action to reequilibrate the situation (Goffman, 1955). A simple example of this process can be seen if a person presents himself to others as a humorous fellow who can tell a good joke, tries telling a joke which turns out not to be seen as funny, and "recoups" or avoids the loss of face which is threatened by the silence of others by humorously derogating his own joke telling ability, thereby signalling to the others that he is now claiming a different and somewhat less "valuable" (i.e., more humble) self. The others may signal their acceptance of the latter self by various reassurances, but all parties know very well the unmistakable meaning of the silence following the first joke.

The various selves which we bring to situations and from which we choose as we present ourselves to others, overlap in varying degrees in that many of the attributes possessed by the person are relevant to several of his selves. Thus, emotional sensitivity may be just as relevant when a person is dealing with a customer in a sales relationship as it is with his wife and children in a family relationship. The person's attributes and underlying character structure thus provide some of the common threads which run through the various social selves he constructs, and provide one basis for seeking order and consistency among them.

Another basis for such order and consistency is to be found in the role demands the person faces. That is, with respect to each role which the person takes or to which he aspires, one can distinguish certain central expectations, certain essential attributes which the person must have or certain behaviors he must be willing to engage in, in order to fulfill the role minimally (pivotal attributes or norms). Other attributes and behaviors are desirable and relevant though not necessary (*relevant* attributes or norms), while still another set can be identified as irrelevant with respect to the role under analysis, though this other set may define various "latent" role capacities the person may have (*peripheral* attributes or norms).[4] The pivotal, relevant, and peripheral attributes of a role will define to some degree the filters which operate at the boundary guarding access to that role.

These changes which occur in a person during the course of his career, as a result of adult socialization or acculturation, are changes in the nature and integration of his social selves. It is highly unlikely that he will change substantially in his basic character structure and his pattern of psychological defenses, but he may change drastically in his social selves in the sense of developing new attitudes and values, new competencies, new images of himself, and new ways of entering and conducting himself in social situations. As he faces new roles which bring new demands, it is from his repertory of attributes and skills that he constructs or reconstructs himself to meet these demands.

A final point concerns the problem of locating what we ordinarily term as the person's beliefs, attitudes, and values at an appropriate level of his total personality. It has been adequately demonstrated (e.g., Adorno *et al.*, 1950; Smith, Bruner, and White, 1956; Katz, 1960) that beliefs, attitudes, and values are intimately related to basic character structure and psychological defenses. But this relationship differs in different people according to the functions which beliefs, attitudes, and values serve for them. Smith *et al.* distinguish three such functions: (1) *reality testing*—where beliefs and attitudes are used by the person to discover and test the basic reality around him; (2) *social adjustment*—where beliefs and attitudes are used by the person to enable him to relate comfortably to others, express his membership in groups, and his social selves; and (3) *externalization*—where beliefs and attitudes are used to express personal conflicts, conscious and unconscious motives, and feelings.

The kind of function which beliefs and attitudes serve for the individual and the kind of flexibility he has in adapting available social selves to varying role demands will define for each individual some of his strengths and weaknesses with respect to organizational demands and the particular pattern of socialization and innovation which one might expect in his career.

For example, a given individual might well have a number of highly labile social selves in which his beliefs and attitudes serve only a social adjustment function. At the same time, he might have one or more other highly stable selves in which he shows great rigidity of belief and attitude. The process of socialization might then involve extensive adaptation and change on the part of the person in his "labile" social selves without touching other more stable parts of him. He might show evidence of having been strongly influenced by the organization, but only

---

[4]This analysis is based on the distinction made by Nadel (1957) and utilized in a study of outpatient nurses by Bennis *et al* (1959).

in certain areas.[5] Whether this same person would be capable of innovating during his career would depend on whether his job would at any time call on his more stable social selves. The activation of such stable selves might occur only with promotion, the acquisition of increasing responsibility, or acceptance into a more central region of the organization.

When we think of organizations infringing on the private lives of their members we think of a more extensive socialization process which involves stable social selves. Clearly it is possible for such "deeper" influence to occur, but in assessing depth of influence in any given individual—organizational relationship we must be careful not to overlook adaptational patterns which look like deep influence but are only the activation of and changes in relatively more labile social selves.

Some Problems of Measuring Individual Structure

I do not know of any well worked out techniques for studying a person's repertory of social selves, their availability, lability, and associated beliefs and attitudes. Something like rating behavior during role-playing or socio-drama would be a possible method but it is difficult to produce in full force the situational and role demands which elicit from us the social selves with which we play for keeps. Assessment techniques which involve observing the person in actual ongoing situations are more promising but more expensive. It is possible that a well motivated person would find it possible to provide accurate data through self-description, i.e., tell accurately how he behaves in situations that he typically faces.

If observation and interview both are impractical, it may be possible to obtain written self-descriptions or adjective check-list data (where the adjectives are specifically descriptive of interactional or social behavior) in response to hypothetical problem situations which are posed for the individual. The major difficulty with this technique would be that it is highly likely that much of the taking of a social self is an unconscious process which even a well motivated subject could not reconstruct accurately. Hence his data would be limited to his conscious self-perceptions. Such conscious self-perceptions could, of course, be supplemented by similar descriptions of the subject made by others.

III. THE STRUCTURE OF THE CAREER

The career can be looked at from a number of points of view. The individual moving through an organization builds certain pespectives having to do with advancement, personal success, nature of the work, and so on (Becker *et al.,* 1961). Those individuals in the organization who take the "organizational" point of view, build perspectives in terms of the development of human resources, allocation of the right people to the right slots, optimum rates of movement through departments

---

[5]For a relevant analysis of areas which the organization is perceived to be entitled to influence, see Schein and Ott (1962) and Schein and Lippitt (1965).

and levels, and so on. A third possible perspective which one can take toward the career is that of the outside observer of the whole process, in which case one is struck by certain basic similarities between organizational careers and other transitional processes which occur in society such as socialization, education, and acculturation of immigrants, initiation into groups, etc. If one takes this observer perspective one can describe the structure and process of the career in terms of a set of basic *stages* which create transitional and terminal *statuses* or *positions,* and involve certain psychological and organizational processes (see Table 1).

In the first column of Table 1, I have placed the basic stages as well as the key transitional events which characterize movement from one stage to another. The terminology chosen deliberately reflects events in organizations such as schools, religious orders, or fraternities where the stages are well articulated. These same

TABLE 1   Basic Stages, Positions, and Processes Involved in a Career

Basic Stages and Transitions	Statuses or Positions	Psychological and Organizational Processes: Transactions between Individual and Organization
1. Pre-entry	Aspirant, applicant, rushee	Preparation, education, anticipatory socialization
Entry (trans.)	Entrant, postulant, recruit	Recruitment, rushing, testing, screening, selection, acceptance ("hiring"); passage through external inclusion boundary; rites of entry; induction and orientation
2. Basic training, novitiate	Trainee, novice, pledge	Training, indoctrination, socialization, testing of the man by the organization, tentative acceptance into group
Initiation, first vows (trans.)	Initiate, graduate	Passage through first inner inclusion boundary, acceptance as member and conferring of organizational status, rite of passage and acceptance.
3. First regular assignment	New member	First testing by the person of his or her own capacity to function; granting of real responsibility (playing for keeps); passage through functional boundary with assignment to specific job or department
Sub-stages 3a. Learning the job 3b. Maximum performance 3c. Becoming obsolete 3d. Learning new skills, etc.		Indoctrination and testing of person by immediate work group leading to acceptance or rejection, if accepted further education and socialization (learning the ropes); preparation for higher status through coaching, seeking visibility, finding sponsors, etc.
Promotion of leveling off (trans.)		Preparation, testing, passage through hierarchical boundary, rite of passage; may involve passage through functional boundary as well (rotation)
4. Second assignment	Legitimate member (fully accepted)	Processes under no. 3 repeat
5. Granting of tenure	Permanent member	Passage through another inner conclusion boundary
Termination and exit (trans.)	Old timer, senior citizen	Preparation for exit, cooling the mark out, rites of exit (testimonial dinners, etc.)
6. Post-exit	Alumnus emeritus, retired	Granting of peripheral status

stages and events are assumed to exist and operate in industrial, governmental, and other kinds of organizations even though they are not as clearly defined or labelled. Where a stage does not exist of a given organization, we can ask what the functional equivalent of that stage is. For example, the granting of tenure and the stage of permanent membership is not clearly identified in American business or industrial concerns, yet there are powerful norms operating in most such organizations to retain employees who have reached a certain level and/or have had a certain number of years of service. These norms lead to personnel policies which on the average guarantee the employee a job and thus function as equivalents to a more formal tenure system.

It should be noted that the kind of stages and terminology chosen also reflects the assumption that career movement is basically a process of learning or socialization (during which organizational influence is at a maximum), followed by a process of performance (during which individual influence on the organization is at a maximum), followed by a process of either becoming obsolete or learning new skills which lead to further movement. These are relatively broad categories which are not fully refined in the table. For example, in the case of becoming obsolete a further set of alternative stages may be provided by the organizational structure— (1) retraining for new career; (2) lateral transfer and permanent leveling off with respect to rank, but not necessarily with respect to inclusion; (3) early forced exit (early "retirement"); (4) retention in the given stage in spite of marginal performance (retaining "dead wood" in the organization).

In the second column of the table are found the kinds of terms which we use to characterize the statuses or positions which reflect the different stages of the career. In the third column I have tried to list the kinds of interactional processes which occur between the individual and the organization. These processes can be thought of as reflecting preparation of the incumbent for boundary transition, preparation of the group for his arrival, actual transition processes, such as tests, rites of passage, status conferring ceremonies, and post transition processes prior to preparation for new transitions.[6]

Basically the dynamics of the career can be thought of as a *sequence of boundary passages*. The person can move up, around, and in, and every career is some sequence of moves along these three paths. Thus, it is possible to move primarily inward without moving upward or around as in the case of the janitor who has remained a janitor all of his career but, because of association with others who have risen in the hierarchy, enjoys their confidences and a certain amount of power through his opportunities to coach newcomers.

It is also possible to move primarily upward without moving inward or around, as in the case of the scarce highly trained technical specialist who must be elevated in order to be held by the organization but who is given little administrative power or confidential information outside of his immediate area. Such careers are frequently found in universities where certain scholars can become full professors without ever taking the slightest interest in the university as an organization and where they are not seen as being very central to its functioning.

[6]See Strauss (1959) for an excellent description of some of these processes.

The problem of the professional scientist or engineer in industry hinges precisely on this issue, in that the scientist often feels excluded in spite of "parallel ladders," high salaries, frequent promotions, and fancy titles. Moving in or toward the center of an organization implies increase in power and access to information which enables the person to influence his own destiny. The "parallel ladder" provides rank but often deprives the professional in industry of the kind of power and sense of influence which is associated with centrality.

Finally, movement around without movement in or up is perhaps most clearly exemplified in the perpetual student, or the person who tries some new skill or work area as soon as he has reasonably mastered what he had been doing. Such circumferential or lateral movement is also a way in which organizations handle those whom they are unwilling to promote to get rid of. Thus, they get transferred from one job to another, often with the polite fiction that the transfers constitute promotions of a sort.

In most cases, the career will be some combination of movement in all three dimensions—the person will have been moved up, will have had experience in several departments, and will have moved into a more central position in the organization. Whether any given final position results from smooth or even movement or represents a zig-zagging course is another aspect to consider. Because sub-cultures always tend to exist within a large organization, one may assume that any promotion or transfer results in some *temporary* loss of centrality, in that the person will not immediately be accepted by the new group into which he has been moved. In fact, one of the critical skills of getting ahead may be the person's capacity to regain a central position in any new group into which he is placed.[7] In the military service, whether a person is ultimately accepted as a good leader or not may depend upon his capacity to take a known difficult assignment in which he temporarily loses acceptance and centrality and to success in spite of this in gaining high productivity and allegiance from the men.

The attempt to describe the career in terms of sequential steps or stages introduces some possible distortions. For example, various of the stages may be collapsed in certain situations into a single major event. A young man may report for work and be given as his first assignment a highly responsible job, may be expected to learn as he actually performs, and is indoctrinated by his experiences at the same time that he is using them as a test of his self. The whole assignment may serve the function of an elaborate initiation rite during which the organization tests the man as well. The stages outlined in the chart all occur in one way or another, but they may occur simultaneously and thus be difficult to differentiate.

Another distortion is the implication in the chart that boundaries are crossed in certain set sequences. In reality it may be the case that the person enters a given department on a provisional basis before he has achieved any basic acceptance by the organization so that the functional boundary passage precedes inclusion boundary passage. On the other hand, it may be more appropriate to think of

---

[7]In a fascinating experiment with children, Merei, 1941, showed that a strong group could resist the impact of a strong leader child and force the leader child to conform to group norms, but that the skillful leader child first accepted the norms, gained acceptance and centrality, and then began to influence the group toward his own goals.

the person as being located in a kind of organizational limbo during his basic training, an image which certainly fits well those training programs which rotate the trainee through all of the departments of the organization without allowing him to do any real work in any of them.

A further complexity arises from the fact that each department, echelon, and power clique is a sub-organization with a sub-culture which superimposes on the major career pattern a set of, in effect, sub-careers within each of the sub-organizations. The socialization which occurs in sub-units creates difficulties or opportunities for the person to the degree that the sub-culture is well integrated with the larger organizational culture. If conficts exist, the person must make a complex analysis of the major organizational boundaries to attempt to discover whether subsequent passage through a hierarchical boundary (promotion) for example, is more closely tied to acceptance or rejection of subcultural norms (i.e., does the filter operate more in terms of the person's capacity to show loyalty even in the face of frustration or in terms of disloyalty for the sake of larger organizational goals even though this entails larger personal risks?).

IV. IMPLICATIONS AND HYPOTHESES

Thus far I have tried to develop a set of concepts and a kind of model of the organization, the individual, and the career. The kinds of concepts chosen were intended to be useful in identifying the interactions between the individual and the organization as he pursues his career within the organization. We need concepts of this sort to make it possible to compare organizations with respect to the kinds of career paths they generate, and to make it possible to describe the vicissitudes of the career itself. Perhaps the most important function of the concepts, however, is to provide an analytical frame of reference which will make it possible to generate some hypotheses about the crucial process of organizational influences on the individual (socialization) and individual influences on the organization (innovation). Using the concepts defined above, I would now like to try to state some hypotheses as a first step toward building a genuinely sociopsychological theory of career development.

Hypothesis 1.   Organizational *socialization will occur primarily in connection with the passage through hierarchical and inclusion boundaries; efforts at education* and *training* will occur primarily in connection with the passage through functional boundaries. In both instances, the amount of effort at socialization and/or training will be at a maximum just prior to boundary passage, but will continue for some time after boundary passage.

The underlying assumption behind this hypothesis is that 1) the organization is most concerned about correct values and attitudes at the point where it is granting a member more authority and/or centrality, and 2) the individual is most vulnerable to socialization pressures just before and after boundary passage. He is vulnerable before because of the likelihood that he is anxious to move up or in and is therefore motivated to learn organizational norms and values; he is vulnerable after boundary passage because of the new role demands and his needs to reciprocate with correct attitudes and values for having been passed. It is a commonly observed organizational fact that a griping employee often becomes a devoted, loyal follower once he has been promoted and has acquired responsibility for the socialization of other employees.[8]

Hypothesis 2. *Innovation,* or the individual's influence on the organization, will occur *in the middle* of a given stage of the career, at a maximum distance from boundary passage.

The person must be far enough from the earlier boundary passage to have learned the requirements of the new position and to have earned centrality in the new sub-culture, yet must be far enough from his next boundary passage to be fully involved in the present job without being concerned about preparing himself for the future. Also, his power to induce change is lower if he is perceived as about to leave (the lame duck phenomenon). Attempts to innovate closer to boundary passage either will meet resistance or will produce only temporary change.

Hypothesis 3. In general, the process of socialization will be more prevalent in the early stages of a career and the process of innovation late in the career, *but both processes occur at all stages.*

Figure 2 attempts to diagram the relationships discussed above. The boundaries that are most relevant to these influence processes are the hierarchical ones

FIGURE 2 Socialization and Innovation During the Stages of the Career

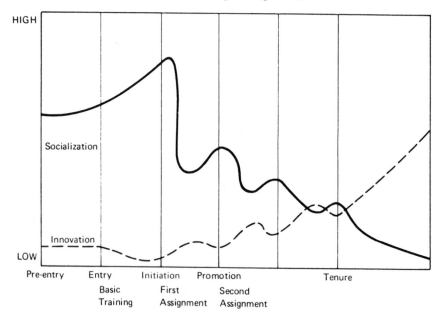

[8]See also Lieberman (1956) for an excellent research study demonstrating attitude change after promotion.

142

in that the power of the organization to socialize is most intimately tied to the status rewards it can offer. One cannot ignore, however, the crucial role which inclusion boundaries and centrality may play in affecting the amount of socialization or innovation. If it is a correct assumption that genuinely creative innovative behavior can occur only when the person is reasonably secure in his position, this is tantamount to saying that he has to have a certain amount of acceptance and centrality to innovate. On the other hand, if the acceptance and centrality involves a sub-culture which is itself hostile to certain organizational goals, it becomes more difficult for the person to innovate (except in reference to sub-cultural norms). This is the case of the men in the production shop with fancy rigs and working routines which permit them to get the job done faster and more comfortably (thus innovating in the service of sub-group norms), yet which are guarded from management eyes and used only to make life easier for the men themselves. One thing which keeps these processes from being shared is the sub-group pressure on the individual and his knowledge that his acceptance by the sub-group hinges on his adherence to its norms. Innovation by individuals will always occur to some degree, but it does not necessarily lead to any new ideas or processes which are functional for the total organization.

Whether or not organizational innovation occurs, then becomes more a function of the degree to which sub-group norms are integrated with the norms and goals of the total organization. In complex organizations there are many forces acting which tend to make group defensive and competitive, thus increasing the likelihood of their developing conflicting norms (Schein, 1965). Where this happens the process of innovation can still be stimulated through something akin to the "heroic cycle" by which societies revitalize themselves. Campbell shows how the myth of the hero in many cultures is essentially similar (Campbell, 1956). Some respected member of the total organization or society is sent away (freed from the sub-group norms) to find a magic gift which he must bring back to revitalize the organization. By temporarily stepping outside the organization the person can bring back new ideas and methods without directly violating sub-group norms and thus protect his own position as well as the face of the other group members.

Hypothesis 4. Socialization or influence will involve primarily the more labile social selves of the individual, while innovation will involve primarily the more stable social selves of the individual, provided the individual is not held captive in the organization.

I am assuming that if socialization forces encounter a stable part of the person which he is unable or unwilling to change, he will leave the organization if he can. On the other hand, if a given way of operating which flows from a stable portion of the individual is incompatible with other organizational procedures or norms, i.e., if innovation is impossible, the individual will also leave. The only condition under which neither of these statements would hold is the condition in which the individual is physically or psychologically unable to leave.

Hypothesis 5. A change in the more stable social selves as a result of socialization will occur only under conditions of coercive persuasion, i.e., where the individual cannot or does not psychologically feel free to leave the organization.

Conditions under which coercive persuasion would operate can be produced by a variety of factors: a tight labor market in which movement to other organizations is constrained; an employment contract which involves a legal or moral obligation to remain with the organization; a reward system which subtly but firmly entraps the individual through stock options, pension plans, deferred compensation plans and the like.

If conditions such as those mentioned above do operate to entrap the individual and, if he in turn begins to conform to organizational norms even in terms of the more stable parts of his self, he will indeed become unable to innovate. It is this pattern which has been identified by Merton as operating in bureaucratic frameworks and which writers like W. H. Whyte have decried with the label of "organizational man." It should be noted, however, that this pattern occurs only under certain conditions; it should not be confused with normal processes of socialization, those involving the more labile parts of the person's self and the more pivotal role requirements or norms of the organization.

An important corollary of this hypothesis is that if organizations wish to insure a high rate of innovation, they must also insure highly permeable external boundaries, i.e., must insure that employees feel free to leave the organization. The less permeable the exit boundary, the greater the pressures for total conformity.

SUMMARY

In this paper I have tried to present a set of concepts about the nature of the organization, the nature of the individual, and the nature of the career—the set of events which tie the individual and the organization together. My purpose has been to provide a frame of reference and a set of concepts which would make it possible to think in more empirical terms about a variable like "career," yet which would relate this variable both to organizational and psychological variables. Using concepts such as "organizational boundaries," labile and stable "social selves," career stages and transitional processes, I have tried to identify some hypotheses about organizational influences on the individual (socialization) and individual influences on the organization (innovation).

REFERENCES

Adorno, T. W. *The authoritarian personality*. New York: Harper, 1950.
Becker, H. S. *et al., Boys in white*. Chicago: University of Chicago Press, 1961.
Bennis, W. G. *et al.,* The role of the nurse in the OPD. Boston University Research Rept. No. 39, 1959.
Campbell, J. *The hero with a thousand faces*. New York: Meridian, 1956.
Dalton, M. *Men who manage*. New York: Wiley, 1959.
Goffman, E. On face work, *Psychiatry*, 1955, 18, 213–231.
Goffman, E. Alienation from interaction *Human Relations*, 1957, 10, 47–60.
Goffman, E. *The presentation of self in everyday life*. Garden City, N.Y.: Doubleday Anchor, 1959.

Homans, G. C. *The human group.* New York: Harcourt Brace, 1950.

Katz, D. (ed.) Attitude change, *Public Opinion Quarterly,* 1960, 24, 163–365.

Lewin, K. *Resolving social conflicts.* New York: Harper, 1948.

Lieberman, S. The effects of changes in roles on the attitudes of role occupants. *Human Relations,* 1956, 9, 385–402.

Mead, G. H. *Mind, self, and society.* Chicago: University of Chicago Press, 1934.

Merei, F. Group leadership and institutionalization. *Human Relations,* 1941, 2, 23–39.

Nadel, F. *The theory of social structure.* Glencoe, Ill.: Free Press, 1957.

Schein, E. H. & Ott, J. S. The legitimacy of organizational influence. *American Journal of Sociology,* 1962, 6, 682–689.

Schein, E. H. *Organizational psychology.* Englewood Cliffs, N.J.: Prentice-Hall, 1965.

Schein, E. H. & Lippitt, G. L. Supervisory attitudes toward the legitimacy of influencing subordinates. *Journal of Applied Behavioral Science,* 1966, 2, 199–209.

Schein, E. H. Organizational socialization. *Industrial Management Review* (M.I.T.), 1968.

Smith, M. B., Bruner, J. S., and White, R. W. *Opinions and personality,* New York: Wiley, 1956.

Strauss, A. *Mirrors and masks.* Glencoe, Ill.: Free Press, 1959.

White, R. W. Motivation reconsidered: The concept of competence, *Psychological Review,* 1959, Vol. 66, 297–333.

Wolpe, J. *Psychotherapy by reciprocal inhibition.* Stanford: Stanford University Press, 1958.

Zachs, J. Collaborative therapy for smokers. Unpublished manuscript, Harvard University, 1965.

CAREER DEVELOPMENT, PERSONAL GROWTH, AND EXPERIENTIAL LEARNING

Donald M. Wolfe
David A. Kolb

Career development involves one's whole life, not just occupation. As such, it concerns the whole person—needs and wants, capacities and potentials, excitements and anxieties, insights and blindspots, warts and all. More than that, it concerns him/her in the every-changing contexts of his/her life. The environmental pressures and constraints, the bonds that tie him/her to significant others, responsibilities to children and aging parents, the total structure of one's circumstances are also factors that must be understood and reckoned with. In these terms, career development and personal development converge. Self and circumstance—evolving, changing, unfolding in mutual interaction—constitute the focus and the drama of career development.

I. CURRENT PERSPECTIVES ON LEARNING AND ADULT DEVELOPMENT

The overwhelming bulk of the theory and research on personality development has focused on childhood stages and processes. Since the time of Freud's early work on psychosexual development, the emphasis even among researchers with quite different theoretical orientations (e.g., Piaget) has been on the impact of early experiences and maturational factors on the structure of adult personality, which is presumably quite stable, past adolescence. This is in keeping with our general cultural orientation, which treats the first 20 plus years as formative, after which one is, or should be, "mature." The predominant structures of both family life and our educational system are geared to these assumptions.

Primary and secondary education and much of college are aimed toward the acquisition of broad areas of knowledge and skills which can be applied to many fields of work; specialized training through trade or professional schools or apprenticeships for a specific career is, in educational terms, the last formative step toward becoming a full adult. The implicit assumption is that one can learn by the mid-twenties those things one needs to know to pursue a successful life career, in spite of our common knowledge that job changes are frequent and often necessary later in life.

In recent years there has been a growing interest in more differentiated views of career development, recognizing that "success" often leads to promotions which require new knowledge and competencies and that "failures" may require a new start in a different field. In any event, the earlier assumptions are oversimplified and distressingly off-target—people can and do learn and develop throughout their life spans, and there are many significant turns in the road which require new learning for many, if not all, career paths. Maturity in life and career is more appropriately viewed as a continuing process of unfolding than as a status achieved once and for all.

The scientific study of personality development, in spite of its major emphasis on the childhood years, has in recent years begun to address the processes of growth throughout the life cycle. In 1950 Erikson published the first of several seminal works on his epigenetic eight-stage model of psychosocial development throughout the life cycle, building on Freud's theory of psychosexual development. This work, in particular, has stimulated the current generation of work on the adult stages of development [cf. Levinson et al. (1974, 1977), Gould (1972), Nuegarten (1968), and Havighurst (1972)—popularized by Sheehy (1976)]. In Erikson's model (and in others as well) the stages are precipitated by the convergence of internal and environmental forces which require a new kind of adaptation and from which one undertakes the development of new capacities and strengths. In childhood, the internal forces emerge primarily from biological maturation (e.g., the sexual awakening at puberty), and even in later life, biological changes (acute illness, physical deterioration) may impose new adaptive responses. But for the most part, the inner forces for change in adults derive from psychological needs.

Environmental forces are similarly more predictable in the early years—mothers no longer tolerate giving constant attention to the post-infancy child, with increasing mobility of the two- to three-year-old, parents must put the brakes on at least the more destructive and intrusive behavior; and so on. In the adult stages the environmental forces vary more widely from one career path to another (career defined quite broadly to incorporate both occupational roles and other major walks of life, e.g., childbearing). Nonetheless, for the adult as for the child, significant external events (e.g., the birth of a first child, taking on new major work assignments, becoming responsible for aging parents, being blocked from long-dreamed-of achievements), whether planned or haphazard, produce changes in the environmental press to which one must adapt. In any case, the emerging centrality of new developmental tasks, marking entry to a new stage, is always a joint function of personal and situational factors. Research on adult development must also have this dual focus.

The Phases and Developmental Tasks of Adult Life

While there are minor disagreements among the authors mentioned above, a general model is emerging from their collective research efforts. The essential features of this model are:

1. Personality development throughout the life cycle occurs through a succession of relatively predictable phases.
2. Within each phase there is a cycle of intensity and quiescence—a disruption to the quasi-stationary equilibrium (in Lewin's terms) of one's former pattern of adaptation, leading to intense coping efforts and heightened activity (often involving significant changes in orientation and situational arrangements), followed by establishment of a new equilibrium.
3. The disequilibrium is generated, in each phase, by the emergence of a new focal conflict or dilemma created by new internal forces, environmental pressures and demands, or both.
4. One can cope with the focal conflict in defensive, or developmental ways (i.e., the consequences may be positive or negative, growthful or regressive).
5. Growth involves the active engagement in a set of "developmental tasks" appropriate to resolving the focal conficts and satisfying personal needs and social responsibilities.

Havighurst (1977) defines a developmental task as one that "arises at or about a certain period in the life of the individual, successful achievement of which leads to his happiness and to success with later tasks, while failure leads to unhappiness in the individual, disapproval by the society, and difficulty with later tasks." He sees the young adult (20 to 35) as faced with two basic tasks: "He wants to explore possibilities, before making some permanent choices, especially about his occupational career. At the same time he wants to get himself established in a life structure which offers continuity and growth." The specific developmental tasks of this period are (1) selecting a mate, (2) starting a family, (3) rearing children, (4) managing a home, (5) getting started in an occupation, and (6) taking on civil responsibility. The major striving during this period (according to Neugarten, 1963) is toward establishing mastery over the outer world. Hence, one's orientation is largely other-directed, in keeping with his concerns about where and how he "fits" in society. Major preoccupations are achievement and recognition.

Toward the end of this period, many people begin to reexamine their purposes, drives, and life-style. They take stock of their accomplishments and resources and begin to question what they should do with the rest of their lives. That is to say, they enter the (often disconcerting) *midlife transition*.

In middle adulthood the frenetic turning inward of the midlife transition mellows to a more quiet preoccupation with the inner life, associated with an acceptance of the limited time left in life and with increased confidence in oneself and what one can do. The developmental tasks of middle adulthood, according to Havighurst, are (1) achieving mature social and civil responsibility, (2) assisting teenaged children to become responsible and happy adults, (3) reaching and maintaining satisfactory performance in one's occupational career, (4) developing adult leisure-time activities, (5) accepting and adjusting to the physiological changes of middle age, and (6) adapting to aging parents.

The life cycle thus can be conceived as spanning these broad phases: the formative years up to age 18 to 20, early adulthood to age 35 to 40, and middle-late adulthood. Each of these can be further subdivided for special purposes; in fact, many people experience a much larger number of phases as the conditions of their lives change. We distinguish these three because they typically involve quite different stances toward life, each with its special developmental dissection. In childhood and adolescence, the focus is on *acquisition* of those interest, values, propensities, and competencies that make one a unique person ready to live in the adult world.

The next 15 to 20 years or so constitute a period of differentiation and specialization during which the person finds his place in that world and learns how to function more or less effectively within it. Generally, during this period one's focus is outward, attending to environmental possibilities and constraints and what one needs to do to adapt to and master living in one's life structure (the pattern of roles, groups, and organizations which we have included under the umbrella term circumstances).

Sometime in midlife there tends to be a (not always deliberate or articulated) questioning and reexamination of one's life and turning inward of focus aimed toward a more effective and comfortable *integration* of the whole self and life circumstances. There is, of course, nothing magical about age per se; the shift from one phase to another, while fairly predictable, varies considerably from person to person, depending both on her/his psychological condition and on how s/he is viewed and treated by others.

We think it is also important to differentiate life phases from developmental stage or level. The phases Sheehy identifies, for example, reflect age-related conditions and challenges of life. Developmental tasks are set before one. These may or may not be faced and worked through in developmental ways. Consequently, personal growth or increased maturity may or may not accrue from them. Growth in terms of enhancement of self-insight, wisdom, competence, ego strength, adaptability, or personal integrity (while perhaps correlated with the movement through life phases) clearly reflects a different conceptual dimension. Changing circumstances and adjustments to them do not automatically imply personality development, although they often provide the conditions and stimulus for growth to occur.

Changing Life Structures

The transition from one life phase to another is often marked by some significant circumstantial change (e.g., marriage, divorce, moving to a new community, taking a new job) or internal changes in meanings, attitude, or purpose, calling for a rearrangement of one's relationship to the structures in his/her environment. Levinson refers to such changes as "marker events."

Much about one's circumstances is influenced by forces outside oneself. Some changes (e.g., death of a loved one) are imposed upon the person—s/he is a victim of her/his circumstances. S/he has no choice. Nevertheless, people generally have a great deal of choice in life structure. Even in situations totally defined and structured by others, it is the person, more often than not, who chooses whether to involve himself/herself in that situation.

To a considerable extent, once in a situation, much can be done to alter one's environment—to restructure conditions and relationships in ways that make them more fitting and fulfilling for the person. For example, a manager may not have full choice in what responsibilities fall within his/her purview or which subordinates will be assigned to his/her area, but s/he often has considerable latitude in determining how tasks will be approached and in style of management (e.g., participative, or group-centered vs. unilateral or one-on-one supervision). Similarly, family members can often renegotiate responsibilities for various household tasks.

In these terms, adaptation is a two-way street; one can alter the situation to fit himself/herself as well as adjusting herself/himself to fit the situation. One is active agent as well as sometimes pawn in the flux of changing life structures. Choice in entering, altering, and leaving various environmental structures is ultimately what gives one at least some mastery over circumstances. A consequence of this is that, just as people can create or find living arrangements that give some modicum of comfort, security, and gratification, they can seek out and build new life structures that provide conditions and experiences for further personal development.

Learning as the Core Process of Development

Movement through life's phases may occur with dramatic or only minor changes in circumstantial structure. Similarly, it may coincide with substantial or with little or no personal growth and development. One may adapt to new circumstances or new life demands in old ways and, in spite of modification in behavior, remain essentially unchanged by the experience. Yet the changing pressures, conditions, and opportunities are often the ground for new spurts in personal growth.

The difference between mere readjustment and development is a function of the learning that occurs through the experience. Personal development involved increasing self-insight and recognition and acceptance of one's complex, ever-changing dynamics. It also involves increased understanding of one's world and how it works. It involves increased capacity for taking responsibiilty for oneself, coupled with increased competence in pursuing one's ends in personally fulfilling and socially beneficial ways. All of these increases come about through a variety of learning processes—processes that can occur in any setting and continue throughout one's life.

II. THE THEORY OF EXPERIENTIAL LEARNING

Experiential learning theory provides a model of learning and adaptation processes consistent with the structure of human cognition and the stages of human growth and development. It conceptualizes the learning process in such a way that differences in individual learning styles and corresponding learning environments can be identified. The core of the model, shown in Figure 1, is a simple description of the learning cycle; of how experience is translated into concepts which, in turn, are used as guides in the choice of new experiences.

FIGURE 1   The Experiential Learning Model

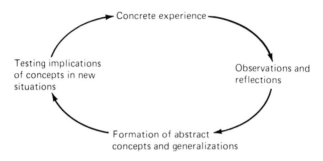

Concrete experience

Observations and reflections

Formation of abstract concepts and generalizations

Testing implications of concepts in new situations

Learning is conceived of as a four-stage cycle. Immediate concrete experience is the basis for observation and reflection. These observations are assimilated into a "theory" from which new implications for action can be deduced. These implications or hypotheses then serve as guides in acting to create new experiences. The learner, if s/he is to be effective, needs four different kinds of generic adaptive abilities: *concrete experience* abilities (CE), *reflective observation* (RO) abilities, *abstract conceptualization* (AC) abilities, and *active experimentation* (AE) abilities. That is, s/he must be able to involve herself/himself fully, openly, and without bias in new experiences (CE); s/he must be able to observe and reflect on these experiences from many perspectives (RO); s/he must be able to create concepts that integrate her/his observations into logically sound theories (AC); and s/he must be able to use these theories to make decisions and solve problems (AE). Yet this ideal is difficult to achieve. Can anyone become highly skilled in all these abilities, or are they necessarily in conflict? How can one be concrete and immediate and still be theoretical?

A closer examination of the four-stage learning model would suggest that learning requires abilities that are polar opposites and that the learner, as a result, must continually choose which set of learning abilities s/he will bring to bear in a specific learning situation. More specifically, there are two primary dimensions to the learning process. The first dimension represents the concrete experiencing of events at one end and abstract conceptualization at the other. The other dimension has active experimentation at one extreme and reflective observation at the other. Thus, in the process of learning, one moves in varying degrees from actor to observer, from specific involvement to general analytic detachment.

These two dimensions represent the major direction of cognitive development identified by Piaget. In his view, the course of individual cognitive development from birth to adolescence moves from a phenomenolistic (concrete) view of the world to a constructivist (abstract) view and from an egocentric (active) view to a reflective internalized model of knowing. Piaget also maintains that these have also been the major directions of development in scientific knowledge (Piaget, 1970).

Many other cognitive psychologists (e.g., Bruner, 1960, 1966; Harvey, Hunt, and Shroeder, 1961) have identified the concrete/abstract dimension as a primary dimension on which cognitive growth and learning occurs. Goldstein and Scheerer suggest that greater abstractness results in the development of the following abilities:

1. To detach one's ego from the outer world or from inner experience.
2. To assume a mental set.
3. To account for acts to oneself; to verbalize the account.
4. To shift reflectively from one aspect of the situation to another.
5. To hold in mind simultaneously various aspects.
6. To grasp the essential of a given whole: to break up a given into parts to isolate and to synthesize them.
7. To abstract common properties reflectively; to form hierarchic concepts.
8. To plan ahead ideationally, to assume an attitude toward the more possible, and to think or perform symbolically (1941, p. 4).

Concreteness, on the other hand, represents, according to these theorists, the absence of these abilities, the immersion in and domination by one's immediate experiences. Yet the circular, dialectic model of the learning process would imply that abstractness is not exclusively good and concreteness exclusively bad. Witkin's (1962, 1973) extensive research on the related cognitive styles of global vs. analytic functioning has shown that both extremes of functioning have their costs and benefits; the analytic style includes competence in analytical functioning combined with an impersonal orientation, while the global style reflects less competence in analytic functioning combined with greater social orientation and social skill. Similarly, when we consider the highest form of learning—creativity—we see a requirement that one be able to experience anew, freed somewhat from the constraints of previous abstract concepts. In psychoanalytic theory this need for a concrete childlike perspective in the creative process is referred to as regression in service of the ego (Kris, 1952). Bruner (1966), in his essay on the conditions for creativity, emphasizes the dialectic tension between abstract and concrete involvement. For him the creative act is a project of detachment and commitment, of passion and decorum, and of a freedom to be dominated by the object of one's injury.

The active/reflective dimension is the other major dimension of cognitive growth and learning. As growth occurs, thought becomes more reflective and internalized, based more on the manipulation of symbols and images than overt actions. The modes of active experimentation and reflection, like abstractness/concreteness, stand in opposition to one another. Kagan's (Kagan and Kogan, 1970) research on the cognitive-style dimension of reflection-impulsivity suggests that extremes of functioning on this continuum represent opposing definitions of competence and strategies for achieving. The impulsive strategy is based on seeking reward for active accomplishment, while the reflective strategy is based on seeking reward through the avoidance of error. Reflection tends to inhibit action, and vice versa. For example, Singer (1968) has found that children who have active internal fantasy lives are more capable of inhibiting action for long periods of time than are children with little internal fantasy life. Kagan et al. (1964) have found on the other hand, that very active orientations toward learning situations inhibit reflection and thereby preclude the development of analytic concepts. Herein lies the second major dialectic in the learning process—the tension between actively testing the implications of one's hypotheses and reflectively interpreting data already collected.

Individual Learning Styles

Over time, accentuation forces operate on individuals in such a way that the dialectic tensions between these dimensions are consistently resolved in a characteristic fashion. As a result of our hereditary equipment, our particular past life experience, and the demands of our present environment, most people develop learning styles that emphasize some learning abilities over others. Through socialization experiences in family, school, and work, we come to resolve the conflicts between being active and reflective and between being immediate and analytical in characteristic ways. Some people develop minds that excel as assimilating disparate facts into coherent theories, yet these same people are incapable of, or uninterested in, deducing hypotheses from the theory. Others are logical geniuses but find it impossible to involve and surrender themselves to an experience. And so on. A mathematician may come to place great emphasis on abstract concepts, while a poet may value concrete experience more highly. A manager may be primarily concerned with the active application of ideas, while a naturalist may develop his/her observational skills highly. Each of us in a unique way develops a learning style that has some weak and strong points.

We have developed a brief self-descriptive inventory called the Learning Style Inventory (LSI) to measure differences in learning styles along the two basic dimensions of abstract/concrete and action/reflection (Kolb, 1976). While the individuals tested on the LSI show many different patterns of scores, we have identified four statistically prevalent types of learning styles. We have called these four styles the converger, the diverger, the assimilator, and the accommodator. The following is a summary of the characteristics of these types based both on our research and on clinical observation of these patterns of LSI scores.

The *converger's* dominant learning abilities are abstract conceptualization (AC) and active experimentation (AE). His/her greatest strength lies in the practical application of ideas. We have called this learning style the "converger" because a person with this style seems to do best in those situations, such as conventional intelligence tests, where there is a single correct answer or solution to a question or problem (Torrealba, 1972). His/her knowledge is organized in such a way that, through hypothetical-deductive reasoning, s/he can focus it on specific problems. Liam Hudson's (1966) research in this style of learning (using different measures than the LSI) shows that convergers are relatively unemotional, preferring to deal with things rather than people. They tend to have narrow interests, and often choose to specialize in the physical sciences. Our research shows that this learning style is characteristic of many engineers (Kolb, 1976).

The *diverger* has the opposite learning strengths of the converger. S/he is best at concrete experience (CE) and reflective observation (RO). His/her greatest strength lies in his/her imaginative ability. S/he excels in the ability to view concrete situations from many perspectives and to organize many relationships into a meaningful "gestalt." We have labeled this style "diverger" because a person of this type performs better in situations that call for the generation of ideas, such as in a "brainstorming" idea session. Divergers are interested in people and tend to be imaginative and emotional. They have broad cultural interests and tend to specialize in the arts. Our research shows that this style is characteristic of persons with humanities and liberal arts backgrounds. Counselors, organization development consultants, and personnel managers often have this learning style.

The *assimilator's* dominant learning abilities are abstract conceptualization (AC) and reflective observation (RO). His/her greatest strength lies in his/her ability to create theoretical models. S/he excels in inductive reasoning; in assimilating disparate observations into an integrated explanation (Grochow, 1973). S/he, like the converger, is less interested in people and more concerned about abstract concepts, but s/he is less concerned with the practical use of theories. For him/her it is more important that the theory be logically sound and precise. As a result, this learning style is more characteristic of the basic sciences and mathematics rather than the applied sciences. In organizations, this learning style is found most often in the research and planning departments (Kolb, 1976; Strasmore, 1973).

The *accommodator* has the opposite strengths of the assimilator. S/he is best at concrete experience (CE) and active experimentation (AE). His/her greatest strength lies in doing things; in carrying out plans and experiments and involving himself/herself in new experiences. S/he tends to be more of a risk taker than people with the other three learning styles. We have labeled this style "accommodator" because s/he tends to excel in those situations where s/he must adapt himself/herself to specific immediate circumstances. In situations where the theory or plans do not fit the facts, s/he will most likely discard the plan or theory. (The opposite type, the assimilator, would be more likely to disregard or reexamine the facts.) S/he tends to solve problems in an intuitive, trial-and-error manner (Grochow, 1973), relying heavily on other people for information rather than his/her own analytic ability (Stabell, 1973). The accommodator is at ease with people but is sometimes seen as impatient and "pushy." His/her educational background is often in technical or practical fields such as business. In organizations, people with this learning style are found in "action-oriented" jobs, often in marketing or sales.

Developmental Stages: An Experiential Learning Perspective

In addition to providing a framework for conceptualizing individual differences in style of adaptation to the world, the experiential learning model suggests more normative directions for human growth and development. As we have seen in the previous section, individual learning styles affect how people learn, not only in the limited educational sense, but also in the broader aspects of adaptation to life, such as decision making, problem solving, and life-style in general. Experiential learning is not a molecular educational concept, but a molar concept describing the central process of human adaptation to the social and physical environment. It, like Jungian theory (Jung, 1923), is a holistic concept that seeks to describe the emergence of basic life orientations as a function of dialectic tensions between basic modes of relating to the world. As such, it encompasses other more limited adaptive concepts, such as creativity, problem solving, decision making, and attitude change, that focus heavily on one or another of the basic aspects of adaptation. Thus, creativity research has tended to focus on the divergent (concrete and reflective) factors in adaptation, such as tolerance for ambiguity, metaphorical thinking and flexibility, while research on decision making has emphasized more convergent (abstract and active) adaptive factors, such as the rational evaluation of solution alternatives.

From this broader perspective, learning becomes a central life task, and how one learns becomes a major determinant of the course of his/her personal development. The experiential learning model provides a means of mapping these different developmental paths and a normative adaptive ideal—a learning process wherein the individual has highly developed abilities to experience, observe, conceptualize, and experiment.

The human growth process is divided into three broad developmental stages. The first stage, *acquisition,* extends from birth to adolescence and marks the acquisition of basic learning abilities and cognitive structures. The second stage, *specialization,* extends through formal education and/or career training and the early experiences of adulthood in work and personal life. In this stage, development primarily follows paths that accentuate a particular learning style. Individuals shaped by social, educational, and organizational socialization forces develop increased competence in a specialized mode of adaptation that enables them to master the particular life tasks they encounter in their chosen career (in the broadest sense of that word). This stage, in our thinking, terminates at midcareer, although the specific chronology of the transition to stage 3 will vary widely from person to person and from one career path to another. The third stage, *integration,* is marked by the reassertion and expression of the nondominant adaptive modes or learning styles. Means of adapting to the world that have been suppressed in favor of the development of the more highly rewarded dominant learning style now find expressions in the form of new career interests, changes in life-styles, and/or innovation and creativity in one's chosen career.

Through these three stages, development is marked by increasing complexity and relativism in dealing with the world and one's experiences, and by higher-level integrations of the dialectic conflicts between the four primary genotypic adaptive modes—concrete experience, reflective observation, abstract conceptualization, and active experimentation. With each of these four modes, a major dimension of personal growth is associated. Development in the concrete experience adaptive mode is characterized by increases in *affective complexity.* Development in the reflective observation mode is characterized by increases in *perceptual complexity.* Development in the abstract conceptualization and active experimentation modes are characterized by increases in *symbolic complexity* and *behavioral complexity,* respectively.

154

In the early stages of development, progress along one of these four dimensions can occur with relative independence from the others. The child and young adult, for example, can develop highly sophisticated symbolic proficiencies and remain naive emotionally. At the highest stages of development, however, the adaptive commitment to learning and creativity produces a strong need for integration of the four adaptive modes. Development in one mode precipitates development in the others. Increases in symbolic complexity, for example, redefine and sharpen both perceptual and behavioral possibilities. Thus, complexity and the integration of dialectic conflicts among the adaptive modes are the hallmarks of true creativity and growth.

Figure 2 graphically illustrates the experiential learning model of growth and development as it has been outlined thus far. The four dimensions of growth are depicted in the shape of a cone, the base of which represents the lower stages of development and the apex of which represents the peak of development— representing the fact that the four dimensions become more highly integrated at higher stages of development. Any individual learning style would be represented on this cone by four data points on the four vertical dimensions of development. Thus, a converger in developmental stage 2 (specialization) would be characterized by high complexity in the affective and perceptual modes. As s/he moved into stage 3 of development, her/his complexity scores in the affective and perceptual modes would increase.

While we have depicted the stages of the growth process in the form of a simple three-layer cone, the actual process of growth in any single individual life history probably proceeds through successive oscillations from one stage to another. Thus, a person may move from stage 2 to 3 in several separate subphases of integrative advances followed by consolidation or regression into specialization. (For a more detailed description of this development model, see Kolb and Fry, 1975.)

III. LEARNING PRESS OF DISCIPLINES
AND CAREERS

Situations differ in the adaptational demands they place on the person in two major ways. First, they differ in degree of complexity: some situations are simple, familiar, predictable, and consequently easy to understand and deal with, while others are complex, turbulent, and highly taxing of one's coping resources.

Second, they differ in the kinds of adaptive response that tends to be effective. For example, many interpersonal situations call for a heightened sensitivity to emotional dynamics and nuances. Active listening and tuning in to others through skills in concrete experiencing is more effective than, for example, withdrawing into reflection or categorizing others in abstract terms. Other problems are more readily dealt with through creation and application of abstract analytic schemes. Consequently, it is important in examining career possibilities, to differentiate the kind as well as the degree of complexity within which one must function.

The concept of environmental learning press is based on differential complexity inherent in the situation—on the kind of learning process that facilitates adaptation. But learning press implies more than that. It also reflects the fact that

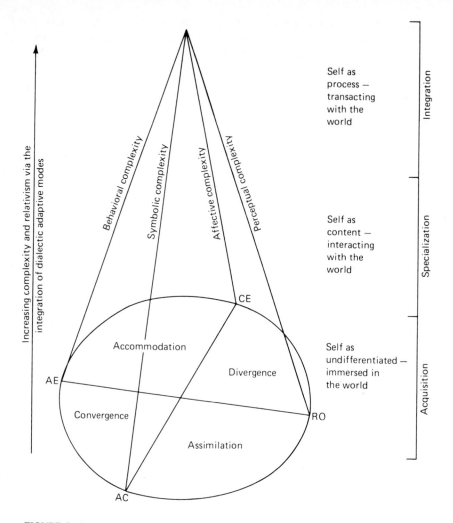

FIGURE 2 The Experiential Learning Theory of Growth and Development

practice in dealing with a particular kind of complexity stretches the person's capacity for dealing with it more readily. A situation that demands experimenting with behavioral alternatives enhances and reinforces active experimentation, to the extent that the person engages in this process. One expands his/her learning and adaptive processes through exercising them. Hence, a particular environment may be a fertile field for enriching one or another generic adaptive competence. Thus, given an appropriate methodology, environments can be assessed for the extent to which they require and thereby stimulate development on each of the four basic learning modalities.

We do not mean to imply that a press toward a particular style of learning necessarily results in that kind of learning. Just as one acquires through childhood and adolescence some capacity to engage in learning modes, one also acquires a variety of ways of coping with overwhelming or intolerable complexity. Complex situations can be defended against as well as engaged in. Among the ways one can deal defensively with complex situations are selective inattention, polarizing (black-white thinking), stereotyping, intellectualizing, withdrawing, impulsive action, and routinization.

A mismatch of style and press is more apt to lead to a defensive response and to an artificial simplication of situational complexity. Divergers are apt to turn aside the challenge and tedium of abstract analysis in favor of pursuing new excitements, or to resist and delay making the decisions required for taking action when that is called for. Convergers, on the other hand, are apt to ignore or stereotype others in favor of applying abstract principles to problem solving. The former often defends against symbolic and behavioral complexity, while the latter defends against the affective and perceptual. Accommodators and assimilators likewise have their ways of reducing and defending against kinds of complexity with which they are ill-equipped to deal.

Differential Learning Press
Across Academic Disciplines

Let us turn now to the question of whether different fields involve characteristic kinds of complexity and therefore press toward particular adaptive competencies. More particularly, we are concerned with whether the two-dimensional learning style grid might accurately portray the similarities, differences, and interrelations among fields. To explore this question, we examined data collected in the 1969 Carnegie Commission on Higher Education study of representative American colleges and university. These data consisted of 32,963 questionnaires from graduate students in 158 institutions and 60,028 questionnaires from faculty in 303 institutions. Using tabulations of these data reported in Feldman (1974), *ad hoc* indices were created of the abstract/concrete and active/reflective dimensions for the 45 academic fields identified in the study. The abstract/concrete index was based on graduate-student responses to two questions asking how important an undergraduate background in mathematics and humanities were for their fields. The mathematics and humanities questions were highly negatively correlated ($-.78$). The index was computed using the percentage of graduate-student respondents who strongly agreed that either humanities or mathematics were very important:

$$\frac{\% \text{ math important } + (100 - \% \text{ humanities important})}{2}$$

Thus, high index scores indicated a field where a mathematics background was important and humanities was not important.

The active/reflective index used faculty data on the percent of faculty in a given field who were engaged in paid consultation to business, government, and so on. This seemed to be the best indicator on the questionnaire of the active, applied orientation of the field. As Feldman observed, "Consulting may be looked upon not only as a source of added income but also as an indirect measure of the 'power' of a discipline, that is, as a chance to exert the influence and knowledge of a discipline outside the academic setting'' (1974, p. 52). The groupings of academic fields based on these indices are shown in Figure 3.

The indices produce a pattern of relationships among academic fields that is highly consistent with other studies (see Biglan, 1973) and with the learning style data (reported in a later section). The results support the widely shared view that cultural variation in academic fields divide the academic community into two camps, the scientific and the artistic (e.g., Snow, 1963; Hudson, 1966). They also suggest that this is usefully enriched by the addition of a second dimension of action/reflection or applied/basic. When academic fields are mapped on this two-dimensional

FIGURE 3   Concrete/Abstract and Active/Reflective Orientations of Academic Fields Derived from the Carnegie Commission Study of American Colleges and Universities

space, a fourfold typology of disciplines emerges. The *natural sciences and mathematics,* calling for assimilitative adaptive skills, are appropriately clustered in the abstract/reflective quadrant, while the abstract/active quadrant incorporates the *science-based professions,* most notably the engineering fields, reflecting their requirements for skills in convergence around applied problems. The *social professions* (such as education, social work, and law) press for accommodative competencies and are found in the concrete/active quadrant. The concrete/reflective quadrant encompasses the *arts, humanities, and social sciences,* all of which tend to be enriched by divergent mentalities.

Some fields seem to include within their boundaries considerable variation on these two dimensions of learning style. Several of the professions (particularly management, medicine, and architecture) are themselves multidisciplinary, including specialities that emphasize different learning styles. Medicine requires both a concern for human service and scientific knowledge. Architecture has requirements for artistic and engineering excellence. Management involves skill at both quantitative and qualitative analysis: dealing with things and dealing with people. Several of the social sciences, particularly psychology, sociology, and economics, can vary greatly in their basic inquiry paradigm. Clinical psychology emphasizes divergent learning skills, while experimental psychology emphasizes convergent skills; industrial and educational psychology emphasize practical accommodative skills. Sociology can be highly abstract and theoretical (as in Parsonian structural functionalism) or concrete and active (as in phenomenology or ethnomethodology). Some economics departments may be very convergent, emphasizing the use of econometric models in public policy, while others are divergent, emphasizing economic history and philosophy.

Indeed, every field will show variation on these dimensions within a given department, between departments, from undergraduate to graduate levels, and so on. The purpose of this analysis is not to "pigeonhole" fields but to identify useful dimensions for describing variations in the learning/inquiry process that characterize different career paths.

The Structure of Knowledge. When one examines fields in the four major groupings we have identified—the social professions, the science-based professions, humanities/social science, and natural science/mathematics—it becomes apparent that what constitutes valid knowledge in these four groupings differs widely. This is easily observed in differences in how knowledge is reported (e.g., numerical or logical symbols, words, or images), in inquiry methods (e.g., case studies, experiments, logical analysis), or in criteria for evaluation (e.g., practical vs. statistical significance). In this typology the professions are predominately discrete in their inquiry strategy, seeking to understand particular events or phenomena, while the basic disciplines are integrated in their inquiry strategies, seeking structures or processes that apply universally. The scientific professions and basic disciplines are predominately analytic, seeking to understand wholes by identifying their component parts, while the social/humanistic fields tend to be synthetic, believing that the whole can never be explained solely by its component parts.

Learning Press in Professional Education

The data presented above deal with learning press as a generalized direction of a field—the dominant "style" of the field, analogous to the learning style of a person. But if we are to understand how learning press reinforces and enhances development of adaptive competencies, we must take a more microscopic look. What are the specific conditions, events, and social psychological processes through which the environmental press impacts the person?

In educational settings, a major focal point for learning press is the immediate learning environment, determined primarily by teachers and the course designs. For example, we have found correlations between the learning styles of students and the learning styles of teachers they found influential, as well as correlations between student learning styles and preference for educational methods, such as lectures, small-group discussions, and so on (Kolb, 1976). Fry (1977) has developed a reliable assessment procedure for determing the extent to which a given learning environment stimulates development on the four basic learning style modes: affective complexity, perceptual complexity, symbolic complexity, and behavioral complexity. His technique examines five areas of a learning environment: (1) objectives, (2) principal focus and source of information, (3) nature of feedback and rewards, (4) the learner's role, and (5) the teacher's role.

Table 1 identifies characteristics of the four "pure" types of learning environments. In each case, practice in and reinforcement of the associated learning mode is required and supported. Formal lectures, textbook reading, and test taking exemplify symbolically complex situations intended to expand one's capacity for abstract conceptionalization. Most graduate seminars and paper writing assignments are both perceptually and symbolically complex, field placements in social work or

TABLE 1 Characteristics of Educational Environment Which Press toward and Reinforce Basic Learning Modes

---

1. Affectively complex environments are characterized by:
   a. Focus on here-and-now experiences.
   b. Legitimization of expression of feelings and emotions.
   c. Situations structured to allow ambiguity.
   d. High degree of personalization.

2. Perceptually complex environments are characterized by:
   a. Opportunities to view subject matter from different perspectives.
   b. Time to reflect and roles (e.g., listener, observer) that allow reflection.
   c. Complexity and multiplicity of observational frameworks.

3. Symbolically complex environments are characterized by:
   a. Emphasis on recall of concepts.
   b. Thinking or acting governed by rules of logic and inference.
   c. Situations structured to maximize certainty.
   d. Authorities respected as caretakers of knowledge.

4. Behaviorally complex environments are characterized by:
   a. Responsibility for setting own learning goals.
   b. Opportunities for real risk taking.
   c. Environmental responses contingent upon self-initiated action.

---

clinical fields involve both concrete experiencing and active experimenting, stretching one's competence in dealing with affective and behavioral complexity.

From Fry's analysis it becomes clear that enhancement of those generic adaptive competencies most relevant to a particular career field is a function not just of *what* is learned, but also of *how* it is learned and under what immediate conditions in the educational context. Pedagogical strategies and teaching styles can be congruent or incongruent not only with the subject matter, but also with the adaptive competencies required for success in the field. Initial socialization into a career occurs perhaps most forcefully through these processes.

The Learning Press of Work Roles
and Environments

Adaptation and learning are called for in every context throughout life. In most work settings, one is interdependent with a variety of others who have a stake in how the assigned role is performed. These others (colleagues, clients, supervisors, subordinates, and others with whom s/he interacts) each hold expectations about what s/he should and should not do, how problems should be handled, and how relationships should be maintained. In some fields the issues are restricted to task behaviors, but in many the expectations go beyond this to what one should believe and how one should think and feel.

When these role expectations are communicated, through word or action, they become *role pressures.* They are most apt to be expressed, of course, when one's behavior violates expectations or when other conditions call for a change in behavior. It is through these sometimes distinct, but often subtle and indirect pressures that one learns, day by day, how to be in his/her career.

Four functions are involved in virtually every endeavor: perceiving, thinking, acting, and feeling, and any of these may be the target of role expectations. Consequently, we think of expectations being in the perceptual domain if they deal with what the person becomes aware of, recognizes, and attends to. At the group or organizational level, this has to do with a shared sense of reality. In highly stable situations where simple, routine tasks are to be performed, a common sense of reality is readily maintained with little active communication of role expectations. Turbulent situations or those which require simultaneous attention to many facets and issues are more apt to involve role pressures having to do with the person's awareness or observational capacities. Thus, we can assess roles (and career lines) in terms of their relative perceptual complexity.

Roles that involve complex analysis, synthesis, and problem solving tend to be rich in symbolic complexity. People in such roles (e.g., researchers, educators) tend to be evaluated in terms of the depth and quality of their thought processes and their ability to integrate complex issues through abstract reasoning. Role pressures on this dimension tend to deal with logic, comprehensiveness, keeping abreast of knowledge development, potential applications, and the like.

In other fields, the emphasis is on action—on decision making and generating useful results. Managers, engineers, physicians, nurses, and many trades deal with high degrees of behavioral complexity. Role pressures tend to focus on the quality of decisions taken and solutions achieved. How one deals with the facts in the situation to produce valued outcomes is the major concern of role senders.

Affective complexity is central to certain roles (e.g., psychiatrist, personnel manager, social worker, minister, actor) and is generally highly valued in the humanities and arts. Role pressures in the affective domain are apt to focus on having an appropriate value system and using it with empathy and understanding.

At any given time, whatever one's career, one may be subjected to role pressures in any of these domains—perceptual, symbolic, behavioral, or affective—but clearly those roles which center on one or another tend to reinforce specialization in a corresponding learning style. Early in one's career the press is often specialized, only to be broadened in later phases. For example, engineers generally experience the strongest role press in the symbolic and behavioral domains, but with advancement to management positions, there is increasing pressure to attend also to the affective and perceptual. Thus, changing roles may generate conflict for the person, but may also be the stimulus for increased integration.

Role Constellations and Life-Styles

Most of us occupy several roles during any given phase of life. That is, one is not only a butcher but also a parent/spouse, a neighbor, a member of the committee on social problems at church, a volunteer fireman, and an umpire for the Little League. Each of these roles involve relationships and expectations. Each holds its potential for learning, fulfillment, and stress. They may all contribute to specialization in learning and adaptive style or toward complementarity of different styles.

Role constellations vary along several dimensions that may have important consequences for adult development. They range from simple to complex, depending on the number of separate roles and contexts one engages in. They vary in the extent to which one role dominates the others (e.g., for many housewives, being a mother is central at all times and colors engagement in every other role). They vary in unity vs. disjointedness: some people manage to keep their various roles and role relationships quite isolated from one another—working in the city with one set of colleagues but never taking work or colleagues to their homes in the suburbs.

The pattern of one's role constellation may yield a unified sense of self; that is, one carries the same identity, interests, and adaptive style into all roles. It is equally possible, depending on the constellation, for one to be a "different person" in each role (e.g., to be strong and domineering at work, passive and dependent at home, aloof in community relations, and a "tiger" with a hidden lover). One's life-style, in this sense, may promote learning and stretching one's capacities in some areas while retarding development in others. It may contribute to specialization as well as balancing toward integration.

IV. CAREER CHOICE AND SPECIALIZATION IN EARLY ADULTHOOD

The transition from adolescence to early adulthood involves a great many changes in one's life structure. The provisional selection of a career and one's first job as an adult are marker events in the resolution of adolescent identity confusion. Entering the adult world begins the elaboration and confirmation of one's newly formed identity. This involves the actualization of one's personal dreams of adult accomplishment, entering a career that holds promise of implementing those dreams, and arranging a new life structure that supports adult–adult relationships, personal fulfillment, and opportunity for the future. Interpersonal issues take on new significance as the person works through the departure from family of origin toward independent life and reaches toward intimacy in selecting a mate and starting a family.

During this early adult transition, one is torn between the need to make career and marital choices which will establish structure, direction, and stability and the desire to keep open the options and possibilities for further development. For some, college offers an extended opportunity to explore various fields, try out relationships with potential partners, and get to know themselves better before making the critical and seemingly irreversible life decisions. In any event, one strives to make choices that yield a good match between personal aspirations and dispositions, on the one hand, and environmental demands, opportunities and resources, on the other. One seeks not just any nitch in the adult world, but one that fits oneself and one's adaptive style.

In the experiential learning theory of career development, stability and change in career paths is seen as resulting from the interaction between internal personality dynamics and external social forces in a manner much like that described by Super and co-workers (1963). The most powerful development dynamic that emerges from this interaction is the tendency for there to be a closer and closer match between self characteristics and environmental demands. This match comes about in two ways: (1) environments tend to change personal characteristics to fit them (i.e., socialization), and (2) individuals tend to select themselves into environments that are consistent with their personal characteristics. Thus, career development in general tends to follow a path toward accentuation of personal characteristics and skills (Feldman and Newcombe, 1969; Kolb, 1973b), in that development is a product of the interaction between choices and socialization experiences that match these dispositions, and the resulting experiences further reinforce the same choice disposition for later experience. Many adult life paths follow a cycle of job, education, and life-style choices that build upon the experiences resulting from similar previous choices. Indeed, the common stereotype of the successful career is a graded ladder of similar experiences on which one climbs to success and fulfillment.

Learning Styles and Career Choice

To illustrate this process, let us first examine the relationship between individuals' learning styles and their career choice. If we examine the undergraduate major of the individuals in a sample of 800 practicing managers and graduate students in management, a correspondence can be seen between their Learning Style Inventory (LSI) scores and their initial career interests (Kolb, 1976). This is done by plotting the average LSI scores for managers in the sample who reported their undergraduate college major (see Figure 4); only those managers with more than 10 people responding are included.

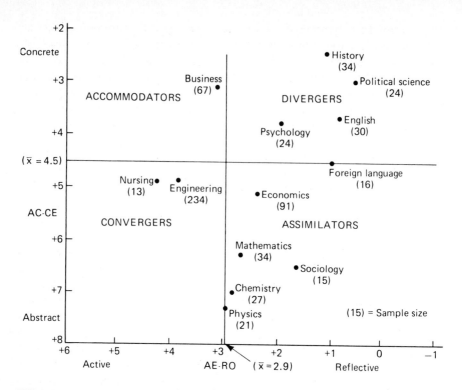

FIGURE 4 Average LSI Scores on Active/Reflective (AE–RO) and Abstract/Concrete (AC–CE) by Undergraduate College Major

The distribution of undergraduate majors on the learning style grid is quite consistent with theory. Undergraduate business majors tend to have accommodative learning styles, while engineers on the average fall in the convergent quadrant. History, english, political science, and psychology majors all have divergent learning styles. Mathematics and chemistry majors have assimilative learnings styles along with economics and sociology. Physics majors are very abstract, falling between convergent and assimilative quadrant. Subsequent studies have consistently replicated this basic pattern of relationship between undergraduate majors and learning styles (Kolb, 1976), a pattern that directly corresponds to the typology of career fields presented earlier (see Figure 3). What these studies show is that undergraduate education is a major factor in the development of learning style. Whether this is because individuals are shaped by the fields they enter or because of selection/evaluation processes that put people into and out of disciplines is an open question at this point. Most probably both factors are operating—people choose fields that are consistent with their learning styles and are further shaped to fit the learning norms of their field once they are in it. When there is a mismatch between the field's learning norms and the individuals's learning style, people will either change or leave the field.

Although the data above are suggestive of some general correspondence between learning styles and careers, they do not offer evidence for the accentuation process. In a first attempt to examine the details of this process, Plovnick (1971) studied a major university department using the concepts of convergence and divergence defined by Hudson (1966). He concluded that the major emphasis in physics education was on convergent learning. He predicted that physics students who had divergent learning styles would be more uncertain of physics as a career and would take more courses outside the physics department than their convergent colleagues. His predictions were confirmed. Those students who were not fitted for the convergent learning style required in physics tended to turn away from physics as a profession, while those physics students having a convergent style continued to specialize in physics, both in their course choice and their career choices.

In another study of MIT seniors (Kolb, 1973b), we further examined the consequences of matches and mismatches between student learning style and discipline demands. Several criteria were used to choose four departments whose learning style demands matched the four dominant learning styles. To study the career choices of the students in the four departments, each student's LSI scores were used to position him/her in the LSI grid with a notation of the career field s/he had chosen to pursue after graduation. If the student was planning to attend graduate school, his/her career field was circled. If the accentuation process were operating in the career choices of the students, we should find that those students who fall in the same quadrant as the norm of their academic major should be more likely to pursue graduate training and careers related to that major, while students with learning styles that differ from their discipline norms should be more inclined to pursue other careers and not attend graduate school in their discipline. We can illustrate this pattern by examining students in the mathematics department (Figure 5). Ten of the 13 mathematics student (77 percent) whose learning styles are congruent with departmental norms choose careers and graduate training in mathematics. Only two of the 13 students (15 percent) whose learning styles are not congruent plan both careers and graduate training in mathematics (these differences are significant using the Fisher exact test $p < .01$). Similar patterns occurred in the other three departments.

To further test the accentuation process in the four departments, we examined whether the student's choice/experience career development cycle indeed operated as an accentuating positive feedback loop. If this were so, those students whose learning style dispositions matched and were reinforced by their discipline demands should show a greater commitment to their choice of future career field than those whose learning styles were not reinforced by their experiences in their discipline. As part of a questionnaire, students were asked to rate how important it was for them to pursue their chosen career field. In all four departments, the average importance rating was higher for the students with a match between learning style and discipline norms (the differences being statistically significant in the mechanical engineering and economics departments). Thus, it seems that learning experiences that reinforce learning style dispositions tend to produce greater commitment in career choices than those learning experiences that do not reinforce learning style dispositions.

To examine if this correspondence between learning styles and career field continued in the jobs individuals held in midcareer, we studied about 20 managers

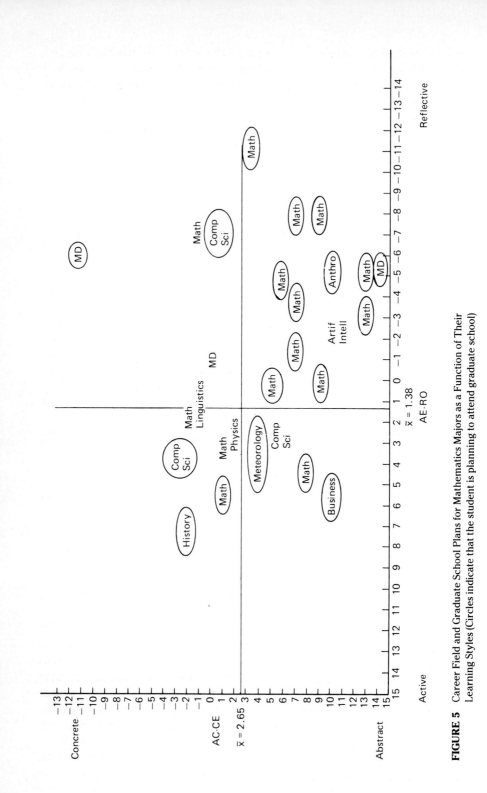

FIGURE 5 Career Field and Graduate School Plans for Mathematics Majors as a Function of Their Learning Styles (Circles indicate that the student is planning to attend graduate school)

from each of five functional groups in a midwestern division of a large American industrial corporation. The five functional groups are described below, followed by our hypothesis about the learning style that should characterize each group given the nature of their work.

1. Marketing ($n = 20$). This group is made up primarily of former salespersons. They have a nonquantitative "intuitive" approach to their work. Because of their practical sales orientation in meeting customer demand, they should have accommodative learning styles (i.e., concrete and active).

2. Research ($n = 22$). The work of this group is split about 50/50 between pioneer research and applied research projects. The emphasis is on basic research. Researchers should be the most assimilative group (i.e., abstract and reflective), a style fitted to the world of knowledge and ideas.

3. Personnel/Labor relations ($n = 20$). In this company, people from this department serve two primary functions, interpreting personnel policy and promoting interaction among groups to reduce conflict and disagreement. Because of their "people orientation," these workers should be predominantly divergers, concrete and reflective.

4. Engineering ($n = 18$). This group is made up primarily of design engineers who are quite production-oriented. They should be the most convergent subgroup (i.e., abstract and active), although they should be less abstract than the research group. They represent a bridge between thought and action.

5. Finance ($n = 20$). This group has a strong computer, information-system bias. Financial workers, given their orientation toward the mathematical task of information system design, should be highly abstract. Their crucial role in organizational survival should produce an active orientation. Thus, finance group members should have convergent learning styles.

Figure 6 shows the average scores on the active/reflective (AE–RO) and abstract/concrete (AC–CE) learning dimensions for the five functional groups. These results are consistent with the predictions above, with the exception of the finance group, whose score is less active than predicted (it fell between the assimilative and the convergent quadrants). The LSI clearly differentiates the learning styles that characterize managers following different career paths within a single company.

We draw two main conclusions from this research. First, the experiential learning typology seems to provide a useful grid for mapping individual differences in learning style and for mapping corresponding differences in the environmental demands of different career paths. As such, it is a potentially powerful tool for describing the differentiated paths of career development. Second, the research data present enticing, if not definitive, evidence that early career choices tend to follow a path toward accentuation of one's learning style. Learning experiences congruent with learning styles tend to positively influence the choice of future learning and work experiences that reinforce that particular learning style. On the other hand, those who find a learning or work environment incongruent with their learning style tend to move away from that kind of environment in future learning and work choices. The research to date suggests that accentuation is a powerful force in early career development. Correspondingly, the major cause of change or devia-

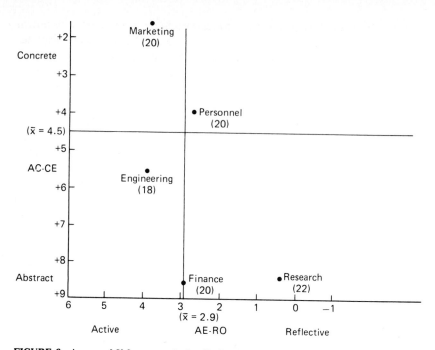

FIGURE 6 Average LSI Scores on Active/Reflective (AE–RO) and Abstract/Concrete (AC–CE) by Organizational Functions

tion from accentuation in the early career results from individual choice errors in choosing a career environment that matches the individual style. The primary reason for the strength of the accentuation forces in early career seems to stem from identity pressures to choose a specialized job and career. Integrative fulfillment needs seem to have second priority at this time.

V. MIDCAREER TRANSITION AND THE MOVE TOWARD INTEGRATION

The developmental model of experiential learning theory holds that specialization of learning style typifies early adulthood and that the role demands of career and family are likely to reinforce specialization. We expect, however, that this pattern changes in midcareer. Specifically, we expect that as individuals mature, accentuation forces play a smaller role. On the contrary, the approach of the middle years brings with it a questioning of one's purposes and aspirations, a reassessment of life structure and direction. For many, choices made earlier have led down pathways no longer rewarding, and some kind of change is needed. At this point many finally face up to the fact that they will never realize their youthful dreams and that new, more realistic goals must be found if life is to have purpose. Others, even if successful in their earlier pursuits, discover that they have purchased success in career at the expense of other responsibilities (e.g., to spouse and children) or other kinds of human fulfillment.

Erikson identifies this as the crisis of generativity vs. stagnation. Continued accentuation of an overspecialized version of oneself eventually becomes stultifying—one begin to feel stuck, static, in a rut. The vitality of earlier challenges too easily is replaced by routinized application of well-established solutions. In the absence of new and fresh challenges, creativity gives way to merely coping and going through the motions. Many careers plateau at this time and one faces the prospect of drying up and stretching out the remaining years in tedium. Finding new directions for generativity is essential.

There is considerable agreement among adult development scholars that growth occurs through processes of differentiation and hierarchic integration and that the highest stages of development are characterized by personal integration. From the perspective of experiential learning theory this goal is attained through a dialectic process of adaptation to the world. Fulfillment, or individuation as Jung calls it, is accomplished by expression of nondominant modes of dealing with the world and their higher-level integration with specialized functions. For many, the needs of modern society are seen to be in direct conflict with these individual needs for fulfillment. Jung puts this case as follows:

> The favoritism of the superior function is just as serviceable to society as it is prejudicial to the individuality. This prejudicial effect has reached such a pitch that the great organizations of our present day civilization actually strive for the complete disintegration of the individual, since their very existence depends upon a mechanical application of the preferred individual functions of men. It is not man that counts but his one differentiated function. Man no longer appears as man in collective civilization; he is merely represented by a function—nay, further, he is even exclusively identified with this function and denied any responsible membership to the other inferior functions. Thus, the modern individual sinks to the level of a mere function because it is this that represents a collective value and alone affords a possibility of livelihood. But as Schiller clearly discerns, differentiation of function could have come about in no other way: "There was not other means to develop man's manifold capacities than to set them one against the other. This antagonism of human qualities is the great instrument of culture; it is only the instrument, however, for so long as it endures, man is only upon the way to culture" (Jung, 1923).

Yet the implication of Schiller's observation is that while human beings are the instrument of culture in their specialized adaptation, they are creators of culture through integrative fulfillment. This can be illustrated by comparing the development of scientific knowledge and the personal career paths of scientists. As Piaget (1970) and others (e.g., Kuhn, 1962) have documented, the historical development of scientific knowledge has been increasingly specialized moving from egocentrism to reflection and from phenomenalism to constructivism—in experiential learning terms from active to reflective and concrete to abstract. Yet the careers of highly successful scientists follow a different path. These individuals make their specialized abstract/reflective contributions often quite early in their careers. With recognition of their achievements, comes a new set of tasks with active and concrete demands. The Nobel prize winner must help to shape social policy and to articulate the ethical and value implications of his/her discoveries. The researcher becomes department chairperson and must manage the nurturance of the younger generation. So in this career, and most others as well, the higher levels of responsibility require an integrative perspective that can help shape cultural responses to emergent issues. In fact, there are integrative developmental challenges at all occupational levels. Many first line supervisors for example, have created personal job definitions that transcend the specialized boundaries of their trade to include the development of younger workers and the building of meaningful community and family relationships.

There is little argument that integrative development is important for both personal fulfillment and cultural development. Yet little research has been done on the integrative phase of adult development. The only study to date on learning styles in later phases of adult development was conducted by Clark et al. (1977). Their study compared cross-sectional samples of accountant and marketing students and professionals at various career stages. The learning styles of marketing and accounting MBA's were similar, being fairly balanced on the four learning modes. Lower-level accountants had convergent learning styles, and this convergent emphasis was even more pronounced in middle-level accountants, reflecting a highly technical emphasis in the early and middle stages of accounting careers. The senior-level accountants, however, were accommodative in their learning style, reflecting a greater concern with client relations and administration than with technical functions. Marketing professionals at the lower level also were convergent in learning style but became highly concrete at middle-level responsibilities, reflecting a shift from technical to creative concerns. The senior marketing personnel had accommodative learning styles similar to those of senior accountants, probably reflecting the same client and management concerns.

These results indicate that progression to new challenges, even within a given career path, calls for giving up excessive reliance on a specialized style in favor of integrating nondominant (and thus underdeveloped) functions. Thus, many forces—both internal and environmental—generate this period of reexamination and transition to middle adulthood.

The Experience of Crisis in Midlife Transition

Within each of life's major stages, the person maintains a relative balance of personal and situational factors. That is not to say, *static,* for one can be quite active in the pursuit of relevant developmental tasks, not to mention in the management of the vagaries of day-to-day life. The equilibrium is reflected, rather, in the patterning of living arrangements (e.g., role relationships in family, school, work tend to persist), and there is general continuity of meaning and purpose. The transitions from one stage to the next, although not always dramatic, tend to be experienced as discontinuities, as disruptions in the flow of life, involving some break with past orientations and arrangements to make room for new developmental tasks.

At times, as often happens in the transition from juvenile to adolescent, the transition is a major upheaval, frought with a loss of orientation and purpose. Conditions and events lose their old meanings and are not yet understandable in new terms. Old perspectives no longer quite handle the significant realities and possibilities one senses only dimly. One enters a period of confusion, restlessness, and uncertainty.

Some degree of reorientation is in order for everyone at this stage, requiring a giving up or breaking from some of the old patterns and frameworks. However, many hold doggedly to those things that have provided security, comfort, acceptance from others, or satisfaction. In the face of uncertainty about what comes in their place, the breaking of old patterns is disorienting and anxiety-producing. Consequently, some respond to the middle years with stubborn resistance to change.

When the change is abrupt and pervasive, as in divorce or being fired from a job held over many years, the tension and disorientation reach crisis proportions. Confusion, acute anxiety, depression, anger, resentment, and a sense of helplessness, hopelessness, or worthlessness are not uncommon emotional reactions at such times. The transition, even if growthful in the long run, may be very painful and debilitating for a time.

For a great many people, the transition is difficult and prolonged—the term "midlife crisis" is most apt. As we currently conceive it, a midlife crisis is distinguished from a more evolutionary developmental transition by a number of interrelated characteristics:

1. It is unanticipated or at least unplanned.
2. There is a loss of self-direction and control; the person feels as though events are happening to him/her.
3. Changes are not bounded but expand to encompass the person's whole life space (e.g., a divorce leads to abandoning friends, changing job, moving away, and so on).
4. It creates acute stress and anxiety, influencing the person's day-to-day coping behavior (e.g., inability to concentrate, labile emotions, accident-proneness).
5. Attempts to cope with the crisis are rigid and stereotyped, dominated by black-white thinking. They create more problems than they resolve, producing a vicious downward spiral.

The plaguing dilemma, if the transition involves crisis of any real intensity, is that usual modes of coping interfere with both learning and environmental manipulation. Anxiety, rigidification, and loss of focus undermine those very learning processes that would resolve the crisis and facilitate new growth. Similarly, typical responses to environmental stress—withdrawal, avoidance, attack are seldom effective in setting to right those conditions which create the stress. In the short run, those natural human reactions to crisis are of service to immediate self-maintenance, but they also tend to prolong the crisis without the understanding and help of others or the good fortune of being able to lay low without the rest of one's world going to hell.

Learning and Change in the Transition Process

Whatever the content of the issues and concerns one faces in midlife, there are two process agendas to be addressed if the transition is to be productive in terms of growth and development: changing environmental conditions and investments in personal learning.

To the extent that the transition is precipitated by significant environmental events (e.g., loss of job, divorce) or by internal changes that make one's circumstances untenable or dissatisfying, the transition is likely to call for some kinds of environmental change. For some, this means a rather massive pulling up of roots and moving to a new job in a new location. Others may find that relatively small scale modifications in certain key work or family roles are sufficient.

Role expectations and demands tend to dominate one's life space in early adulthood. One lives by the oughts and shoulds associated with many roles. At some level, one is driven by both career and family role requirements, whether those demands are expressed by others or by the power of the situation (e.g., the needs of a newborn child). One *is* what one's role calls for, in the extreme, especially if the rewards for specialization are ample.

For many individuals, however, withdrawal of reward for accentuation may be a precondition for the emergence of fulfillment concerns. Our notion here is that rewards for accentuation are often so powerful and overwhelming that the individual develops what we call a role-encapsulated ego. That is, rewards for specialized role performance tend to prevent the emergence of nondominant fulfillment needs. Thus, in many cases, withdrawal of these rewards may have to precede the awareness of fulfillment needs.

People as they approach midlife are seldom content to have their lives totally defined from the outside. The other-directedness of early adulthood must give way to a greater sense of being one's own person. This shift alone usually requires some renegotiation of roles, even when the content of one's role-related activities remains the same. Relationships with colleagues, boss, spouse, and children undergo subtle, if not dramatic change. Especially during the transition itself, the role-boundedness of many people's lives must be relieved to make room for the exploration of new possibilities.

The transition from early to middle adulthood involves a breaking from the authority of role expectations toward a centering in oneself as the course of purpose, meaning, and action. Instead of being driven, the mature person becomes the driver. This is not to say that with the transition, one no longer performs his/her roles or cares about the expectations of others. Rather, it means that one begins to recognize the role (and the social structure within which it is embedded) as a platform from which s/he can accomplish purposes s/he owns. The role belongs to her/him, not s/he to the role.

As one become autonomous from the excessive demands of role expectations, s/he becomes her/his own person—a nonrole person. Among other things, this is essential preparation for the time when, through retirement, increasing independence of one's children and the like, one begins a full disengagement from roles altogether, to live out his/her life with integrity. Increasing personal autonomy and centeredness is part and parcel of the integration of adaptive styles.

A growthful transition inevitably involves the person in new learning ventures, directed both inward and outward. It is a time for giving up some of the illusions and pretenses associated with early adult adaption. A successful resolution requires more accurate and comprehensive self-knowledge—hence, the turn to introspection and the questioning of one's ambition, drives, wants, and capacities. Thus, learning, especially during critical transitions, is highly personal.

If there is any significant change of scene, one also moves into an active phase of learning about new environmental realities and how they can be understood in terms relevant to one's new purpose. Moreover, a change of career or even taking on new responsibilities in the community is apt to require the development of new competencies or the refinement of underutilized ones. Gaining new knowledge and skills often makes the difference between stagnation and development.

The developmental challenge of the midlife transition is to face up to and move toward those personal and situational changes that show promise of growth and authenticity without causing undue pain or disruption to oneself or others.

Not everyone, of course, faces up to that challenge. Many do not find or recognize the need; life seems to be tolerable in its current plan. Others, fearing the stress and turmoil, retreat not only from change but even from every deep questioning. Still others find it genuinely fulfilling and recommit to present structures and directions.

Generally, we see the midlife transition as a constructive move toward human fulfillment, toward becoming a whole person and rounding out a life worth living. As in other developmental transitions, the internal psychological work and resultant behavioral and situational changes are the mechanisms through which one corrects the excesses and deficiencies of one's former adaptations. Under favorable conditions, the midlife transition involves minor recalibration on many issues and reorientation toward investing time and energy in those things one cares most about. The move is toward living more authentically, creatively, and harmoniously.

REFERENCES

Biglan, A., "The Characteristics of Subject Matter in Different Academic Areas," *Journal of Applied Psychology,* 57, (1973), 195–203.

Bruner, Jerome S., *On Knowing: Essays for the Left Hand.* (New York: Atheneum, 1966).

Bruner, Jerome S., *The Process of Education.* (Cambridge, Mass.: Harvard University Press, 1960).

Clark, Diana, et. al., "A Study of the Adequacy of the Learning Environment for Business Students in Hawaii in the Fields of Accounting and Marketing," a Working Paper, (University of Hawaii School of Management, 1977).

Feldman, Kenneth, and Theodore Newcombe, *The Impact of College on Students,* Vols. I and II, (San Francisco: Jossey-Bass, Inc., 1969).

Feldman, Saul D. (ed.), *Escape from the Doll's House.* (New York: McGraw-Hill, 1974).

Fry, R., "Diagnosing Professional Learning Environments: An Observational Framework for Matching Learner Styles with Types of Situational Complexity," Ph.D. Dissertation, (Cambridge, Mass.: Massachusetts Institute of Technology, Sloan School of Management, 1977).

Goldstein, K., and M. Scheerer, "Abstract and Concrete Behavior: An Experimental Study with Special Tests." *Psychological Monographs,* 53, (1941).

Gould, Robert, "The Phases of Adult Life: A Study in Developmental Psychology," *American Journal of Psychiatry,* 129, (1972), 521–531.

Grochow, Jerrold, "Cognitive Style as a Factor in the Design of Interactive Decision-Support Systems," an unpublished Doctoral Dissertation, (Cambridge, Mass.: Massachusetts Institute of Technology, Sloan School of Management, 1973).

Harvey, O. J., D. Hunt, and H. Schroeder, *Conceptual Systems and Personality Organization.* (New York: John Wiley & Sons, Inc., 1961).

Havighurst, Robert, "The Life Cycle," *The Future American College.* Edited by A. Chickering. (San Francisco: Jossey-Bass, Inc. In press. 1979).

Hudson, Liam, *Contrary Imaginations.* (Middlesex, England: Penguin Books, 1966).

Jung, C. G., *Psychological Types.* (London: Pantheon Books, Inc., 1923).

Kagan, J. and N. Kogan, "Individual Variations in Cognitive Processes," *Carmichael's Manual of Child Psychology,* (3rd ed.), Vol. 1. Edited by P. H. Mussen, (New York: John Wiley & Sons, 1970).

Kagan, Jerome, Bernice L. Rosman, Deborah Day, Joseph Albert, and William Phillips, "Information Processing in the Child: Significance of Analytic and Reflective Attitudes," *Psychological Monographs,* 78(1), (1964).

Kolb, David, *The Learning Style Inventory: Technical Manual.* (Boston, Mass.: McBer and Co., 1976).

Kolb, David, "Toward a Typology of Learning Styles and Learning Environments: An Investigation of the Impact of Learning Styles and Discipline Demands on the Academic Performance, Social Adaption and Career Choices of M.I.T. Seniors," a Working Paper, No. 688–73, (Cambridge, Mass.: Massachusetts Institute of Technology, Sloan School of Management, 1973).

Kolb, David, and Ronald Fry, "Toward an Applied Theory of Experiental Learning," *Theories of Group Processes.* Edited by Cary L. Cooper. (New York: John Wiley & Sons, Inc., 1975).

Kris, Ernst, *Psychoanalytic Explorations in Art.* (New York: International Universities Press, 1962).

Kuhn, Thojmas, *The Structure of Scientific Revolutions* (2nd ed.). (Chicago: University of Chicago Press, 1970).

Levinson, Daniel, "The Mid-Life Transition: A Period in Adult Psycho-Social Development," *Psychiatry,* (May 1977).

Neugarten, Bernice L. (editor), *Middle Age and Aging.* (Chicago: University of Chicago Press, 1968).

Piaget, Jean, *The Place of the Sciences of Man in the System of Sciences.* (New York: Harper & Row, Inc., 1974).

Plovnick, Mark S., "Primary Care Career Choices and Medical Student Learning Styles," *Journal of Medical Education,* 50, (1975), 849–855.

Sheehy, Gail, *Passages.* (New York: E. P. Dutton & Co., Inc., 1976).

Singer, Jerome, "The Importance of Daydreaming." *Psychology Today,* 1(11), (1968), 18–26.

Snow, Charles P., *The Two Cultures: And a Second Look.* (New York: Cambridge University Press, 1970).

Softer, Cyril, *Men in Mid-Career.* (New York: Cambridge University Press, 1970).

Stabell, C., "The Impact of a Conversational Computer System on Human Development Perspective," Master's Thesis, (Cambridge, Mass.: Massachusetts Institute of Technology, Sloan School of Management, 1973).

Strasmore, M., "The Strategic Function Reevaluated from the Organization Development Perspective," Master's Thesis, (Cambridge, Mass.: Massachusetts Institute of Technology, Sloan School of Management, 1973).

Super, D., et. al., *Career Development Self Concept Theory.* (Princeton, N.J.: Princeton College Entrance Exam Board, 1963).

Torrealba, D., "Convergent and Divergent Learning Styles," Master's Thesis, (Cambridge, Mass.: Massachusetts Institute of Technology, Sloan School of Management, 1972).

Witkin, H. A., "The Role of Cognitive Style on Academic Performance and in Teacher/Student Relationships," *Research Bulletin,* 73(11). (Princeton, N.J.: Educational Testing Service, 1973).

Witkin, H. A., et. al. *Psychological Differentiation.* (New York: The Halsted Press Division of John Wiley & Sons, Inc., 1974).

ON THE REALIZATION OF HUMAN POTENTIAL: A PATH WITH A HEART

Herbert A. Shepard

A VISION UNFULFILLED

The central issue is a life fully worth living. The test is how you feel each day as you anticipate that day's experience. The same test is the best predictor of health and longevity. It is simple.

If it's simple, why doesn't everyone know it? The answer to that question is simple, too. We have been brought up to live by rules that mostly have nothing to do with making our lives worth living; some of them in fact are guaranteed not to. Many of our institutions and traditions introduce cultural distortions into our vision, provide us with beliefs and definitions that don't work, distract us from the task of building lives that are fully worth living, and persuade us that other things are more important.

The human infant is a life-loving bundle of energy with a marvelous array of potentialities, and many vulnerabilities. It is readily molded. If it is given a supportive environment, it will flourish and continue to love its own life and the lives of others. It will grow to express its own gifts and uniqueness, and to find joy in the opportunity for doing so. It will extend these talents to the world and feel gratified from the genuine appreciation of others. In turn, it will appreciate the talents of others and encourage them, too, to realize their own potential and to express their separate uniqueness.

But if a child is starved of a supportive environment, it will spend the rest of its life trying to compensate for that starvation. It becomes hungry for what it has been denied, and compulsively seeks to satisfy perceived deficiencies. In turn, these perceived deficiencies become the basis for measuring and relating to others. As Maslow pointed out, such deficiency motivation does not end with childhood (Maslow, 1962; Maslow and Chang, 1969). Rather, the struggle makes a person continually dependent on and controllable by any source that promises to remove the deficiencies.

Deficiency Motivation in Operation

Frequently we refer to deficiency motivation in terms of needs: needs for approval, recognition, power, control, status; needs to prove one's masculinity, or smartness, or successfulness in other's eyes—and in one's own eyes, which have been programmed to see the world in terms of one's deficiencies. An emphasis on such needs can lead to a denial of individual uniqueness and may make us vulnerable to exploitation. In either case, the outcome for the individual can be devastating, and the rich promise of human potential remains unfulfilled.

Source: Working With Careers by Michael B. Arthur, Lotte Barilyn, Daniel J. Levinson, Herbert A. Shepard. Columbia University School of Business, 1984.

Denial of Uniqueness. The way this process takes place can be illustrated by a fable, "The School for Animals":

> Once upon a time the animals got together and decided to found a school. There would be a core curriculum of six subjects: swimming, crawling, running, jumping, climbing and flying. At first the duck was the best swimmer, but it wore out the webs of its feet in running class, and then couldn't swim as well as before. And at first the dog was the best runner, but it crash landed twice in flying class and injured a leg. The rabbit started out as the best jumper, but it fell in climbing class and hurt its back. At the end of the school year, the class valedictorian was an eel, who could do a little bit of everything, but nothing very well.

The school for animals, of course, is much like our schools for people. And the notion of a common, unindividualized curriculum has permeated the whole fabric of our society, bringing with it associated judgments about our worth as human beings. It is all too easy for uniqueness to go unrecognized, and to spend a lifetime trying to become an eel.

Exploitation of Uniqueness. A second, perhaps subtler way that deficiency motivation can operate is illustrated by the story of the cormorant. Dr. Ralph Siu, when asked what wisdom the ancient oriental philosophers could contribute to modern man in modern orgnaizations on how to preserve his mental health, developed a list of "advices." One of them was as follows:

> Observe the cormorant in the fishing fleet. You know how cormorants are used for fishing. The technique involves a man in a rowboat with about half a dozen or so cormorants, each with a ring around the neck. As the bird spots a fish, it will dive into the water and unerringly come up with it. Because of the ring, the larger fish are not swallowed but held in the throat. The fisherman picks up the bird and squeezes out the fish through the mouth. The bird then dives for another, and the cycle repeats itself.
>
> Observe the cormorant...Why is it that of all the different vertebrates the cormorant has been chosen to slave away day and night for the fisherman? Were the bird not greedy for fish, or not efficient in catching it, or not readily trained, would society have created an industry to exploit the bird? Would the ingenious device of a ring around its neck, and the simple procedure of squeezing the bird's neck to force it to regurgitate the fish have been devised? Of course not (Siu, 1971).

The neo-Taoist alerts us to how the cormorant's uniqueness is exploited by the fisherman for his own selfish use. Similarly, human motives can get directed to making others prosper, but not always in a way that benefits the person providing the talent. Human life can too easily parallel that of the captive cormorant.

Institutions and Deficiency Motivation

Let us stay with Dr. Siu's cormorant story a little longer. His advice continues:

> Greed, talent, and capacity for learning, then, are the basis of exploitation. The more you are able to moderate and/or hide them from society, the greater will be your chances of escaping the fate of the cormorant...It is necessary to remember

that the institutions of society are geared to making society prosper, not necessarily to minimize suffering on your part. It is for this reason, among others, that the schools tend to drum into your mind the high desirability of those characteristics that tend to make society prosper—namely, ambition, progress, and success. These in turn are valued in terms of society's objectives. All of them gradually but surely increase your greed and make a cormorant out of you (Siu, 1971).

The further point here is even more far-reaching: that the institutions and organizations in which we spend our lives collude with one another in causing denials, deflections, or distortions of human potential. In particular, three sets of institutions—parents, schools and organizations—demand consideration.

Parents. First, parents, sincerely concerned for their children's ability to survive in the world, unwittingly ignore their individuality and measure their offspring's progress by a a simple set of common standards. What parents are not delighted to be able to say that their children are ambitious, talented, and have a great capacity for learning? It is something to boast about, rather than something to hide. Outside confirmation of achievement earns love and recognition, its absence draws disapproval. Any evidence of "A" student behavior is immediately rewarded. Lesser performance calls for added effort so that deficiencies can be corrected. Much of this parental energy is targeted toward helping children qualify for an occupational future that will in no way reflect their true interests and abilities. The expression or suppression of talent is externally defined, and parents stand as the most immediate custodians of society's standards and its dogma.

Schools. In our schools, the ideal is the "Straight A" student. It is this student who is most sought after, either at the next stage of institutional learning, or by employers from the world of work. What "Straight A" means is that the student has learned to do a number of things at a marketable level of performance, regardless of whether the student has any interest in or innate talent for the activity, and regardless of whether it brings pain, joy, or boredom. The reward is in the grade, not the activity. On the one hand, schools collaborate with parents to reinforce this concern over grades as ends in themselves. On the other, as Dr. Siu points out, the school's objectives are to serve the needs of society, not necessarily those of the student. Once more, a person's uniqueness is not valued for its own sake. Schools are selective about the talents they identify, and represent outside interests in the talents that they choose to develop.

Organizations. Lastly, in organizations, the continued external denial or manipulation of talent has its direct career consequences. Organizations have implicit ways of teaching about careers, regardless of whether they have explicit career planning and development programs. Reward systems are geared to common deficiencies—needs for status, approval, power—and a career consists of doing the right things to move up the ladder. A vice president of one company counselled his subordinates: "The work day is for doing your job; your overtime is for your promotion."

In many companies the message about careers is very clear: not only is your career more important than the rest of your life, it is more important than your life. In one large corporation, great emphasis was placed on moving young professionals and managers through many company functions as their preparation for general management responsibility. The career plan was well understood: "When you're rotated, don't ask if it's up, down or sideways; the time to worry is when you stop rotating." In such companies, successful careers are based on working hard at any job you are given whether you like it or not, and on conforming to the organization's unwritten rules and to the expectations of your superiors in such matters as office manners, dress, presentation style, language, and prejudices.

Do these paths have "heart"? Do they provide for the expression of human potential and facilitate individual growth? For some, as much through good luck as good management, they do. But perhaps a greater number ultimately lose their way, and get labeled as suffering from "burnout" or "retiring on the job."

In one company that recruits only top graduates, that devotes a great deal of managerial time to tracking their performance, that moves each one along at what is judged to be an appropriate pace into jobs that are judged to be suited to his or her talents and potentials, the amount of burn-out observed in mid-career management ranks became a matter of concern. As a result, the company offered career planning workshops to mid-career managers, the main objective of which was, according to one executive: "...to revitalize them by reminding them that in an ultimate sense each of them is in business for himself!"

For deficiency-motivated people, moving up the hierarchy of management is likely to be such a compelling need that they may desert careers that did have some heart for them. In an informal survey of industrial research scientists conducted by the author some years ago, it was possible to identify the ones for whom their career path had a heart, by their response to the question: "What is your main goal over the next two or three years?" Some responded in such terms as: "Some equipment I've tried to get for three years has finally made it into this year's budget. With it, I can pursue some very promising leads." Others responded in such terms as: "I hope to become a department head." But the second group seemed to have lost its zest. Many of them enjoyed their work and had no real desire to leave it in order to direct the work of others. They were just singing the preferred organizational song.

Don Juan, in teaching Carlos Casteneda about careers, asserted that to *have* a path of knowledge, a path with a *heart,* made for a joyful journey and was the only conceivable way to live. But he emphasized the importance of thinking carefully about our paths before we set out on them. For by the time a man discovers that his path "has no heart," the path is ready to kill him. At that point, he cautions, very few men stop to deliberate, and leave that path (Castaneda, 1968). For example, in a life/career planning workshop for the staff of a mid-west military research laboratory, a 29-year-old engineer confessed that he was bored to death with the laboratory work, but his eyes lit up at the prospect of teaching physical education and coaching athletic teams at the high school level. He emerged with a career plan to do just that, and to do it in his favorite part of the country, northern New England. He resolved to do it immediately upon retirement from his civil service job as an engineer—at age 65, a mere 36 years away!

Thus, all these institutions—parents, schools, and organizations—are suspect when they attempt to give career guidance. Suspect if, like the school for animals, they discourage uniqueness and enforce conformity. Suspect if, like the fisherman with his cormorant, they harness talent only to serve their vested interests. Suspect if they address only the development of a career, so that the rest of life becomes an un-anticipated consequence of the career choice. Suspect if they stress only the how-to's of a career and not its meaning in your life. And suspect, too, if they describe a career as a way to make a living, and fail to point out that the wrong career choice may be fatal. In sum, suspect because they are not concerned with whether a life is fully worth living.

A FRAMEWORK FOR UNDERSTANDING HUMAN POTENTIAL

An outcome of people's experience with society and its institutions is that many adults cannot remember, if they ever knew, what their unique talents and interests were. They cannot remember what areas of learning and doing were fulfilling for them, what paths had heart. These have to be discovered and rediscovered.

For many, the relationship between formal schooling and subsequent occupation needs to be re-examined. In adult life/career planning workshops, the author has found that of the things participants actually enjoy doing, less than 5% are things they learned in school as part of formal classroom work. A related outcome is that adults distinguish between work and play. Work is something you have to be "compensated" for, because it robs you of living. Play is something you usually have to pay for, because your play is often someone else's work. Children have to be taught these distinctions carefully, for they make no sense to anyone whose life is fully worth living. As one philosopher put it:

> A master in the art of living draws no sharp distinction between his work and his play, his labor and his leisure, his mind and his body, his education and his recreation. He scarcely knows which is which. *He simply pursues his vision of excellence* through whatever he is doing and leaves others to determine whether he is working or playing. To himself he always seems to be doing both.

But pursuing a vision of excellence is not always simple. What does "vision of excellence" mean? How do you acquire your own? We can be reasonably sure that it has little to do with getting A's, excelling against others in competition, or living up to someone else's standards. It is one's own unique vision. It will not emerge in school, if each person must be comparable to every other person so that grades and rank can be assigned. Such a system defines individuality as differences in degree, not in kind. Consider, too, the word "genius." To most of us it means a person with a high IQ. But differences in IQ are differences of degree, whereas the notion of "unique" makes it impossible to rank and compare.

In the search for your own unique vision, you need a different definition of "genius," one closer to the dictionary definition as "the unique and identifying spirit of a person or place.'' By this definition, your genius consists of those of your talents that you love to develop and use. These are the things that you can now or potentially could do with excellence, which are fulfilling in the doing of them; so fulfilling that if you also get paid to do them, it feels not like compensation, but like a gift.

Discovering Genius and Developing Autonomy

Discovering your genius may be easy or difficult. At some level of your being you already know it; you are fortunate if it is in your conscious awareness. If not, there are several routes to discovery, and many sources of pertinent information.

The first source is *play*. Make a list of the things you enjoy doing and find the common themes. Observe what you do when you are not obliged to do anything. What activities are you likely to engage in? What catches your eye when you thumb through a magazine? When you are in an unfamiliar environment, what interests you, what catches your attention? What are the contents of your fantasies and daydreams? What do you wish you were doing? Your sleep-dreams are also important. Record them, for some of them contain important wishes that you may want to turn into plans.

The second source is your own *life history*. Record in some detail the times in your past when you were doing something very well and enjoying it very much. What themes or patterns of strength, skill, and activity pervade most of those times? What were the sources of satisfaction in them?

The third source is *feedback* from others. What do those who know you have to say about your strengths and talents? As they see it, what seems to excite you, give you pleasure, engage you? And if you can find people who knew you when you were a child, can they recall what used to capture your attention and curiosity, what activities you enjoyed, what special promise and talents you displayed?

The fourth source is *psychological instruments,* which provide a variety of ways of helping you to organize and interpret your experience. There are many such instruments that can provide you with clues to your interests, strengths, and sources of satisfaction. Perhaps the most valuable is the Myers-Briggs Type Indicator, which is based on the insights of the psychologist Carl Jung. A recent book, based on these ideas, identifies four basic temperaments, four quite different ways of approaching life (Keirsey and Bats, 1978). One of these is oriented to tradition and stability in the world, and devoted to making systems work and to the maintenance of order. The second type loves action, freedom, excitement, and the mastery of skills. The third type is oriented to the future and to mastery of the unknown. The fourth loves to work in the service of humanity and bring about a better world. One can learn to perform competently in activities that do not fit one's temperament, and to some extent one must, but it always feels like ''work.'' In contrast, if the activities are in accord with one's temperament, it feels more like ''play.'' It follows that your temperament is one of the important components of your genius.

As you take these four routes, you may find the same messages about yourself over and over again—and you may also find a few surprises and contradictions.

In general, the truth strategy you employ is the one enunciated in *Alice in Wonderland:* "What I tell you three times is true." You may emerge from the search with some hunches to explore further; you may emerge with certainty about a new direction to take; or you may simply affirm what you already knew—confirming or disconfirming the life and career choices you have already made. This discovery or affirmation of your genius is a first step. but it needs also to be nourished and developed, and you need to learn how to create the conditions that will support you in practicing it. The second step then, is to acquire the resources you need in order to build a world for yourself that supports you in the pursuit and practice of your genius. The process of acquiring these resources can be called the *development of autonomy*—learning the skills needed to build that world.

Consider the following case:

Jerome Kirk, a well-known sculptor, discovered his genius through play, though not until his late twenties. Alone on an island off the Maine coast for a week, he amused himself by fashioning sculptures out of driftwood. It was a dazzling experience. But his education had prepared him for work in the field of personnel administration. For the following twenty years he developed his skill as a sculptor, while "earning a living" as a personnel administrator—and he was quite successful in this profession. After twenty years, his sculptures matched his own vision of excellence, he was a recognized artist, and the income from his art was sufficient to enable him to devote all his time to it. It was the realization of a dream. His comment: "I was good in the personnel field, but I never really enjoyed it. It wasn't me. And now I'm utterly convinced that if a person really loves something, and focuses his energy there, there's just no way he can fail to fulfill his 'vision of excellence.'"

The point of this story is not to idealize the creative arts. For others, discovery of genius would take them in a different direction, perhaps toward greater interaction with people rather than away from it. But the story does illustrate the qualities that get released when a person discovers his or her genius. Passion, energy, and focus all came as a natural by-product of Kirk's discovery. These were the qualities needed to develop the autonomy that ultimately allowed Kirk to realize his dream. They were inspired by the knowledge of his genius that he carried within him. The same qualities will be evident in any person who has discovered his or her genius, whether it is in sculpture or in the leadership of organizations (Vaill, 1982).

Living Out Your Potential

You began your life as a bundle of life-loving energy with a marvelous array of potentialities. As you grew up you learned to do many things and not to do other things. Some of these things were good for you, some bad for you, some good for others, some bad for others. Out of the things you learned, you fashioned an identity, a self-image. Thus, your self-image is a cultural product, and the distortion it contains may prevent you from recognizing yourself anymore as a bundle of life-loving energy with a marvelous array of potentialities. Acquiring a renewed identity, an identification with what is truly wonderful about yourself and therefore worth nourishing and loving, is not an easy task. It requires a lot of unlearning and letting go, as well as new learning and risk-taking.

How can you tell when you have achieved this goal? What can you feel from communion with others that confirms your own life as fully worth living? What should living out your potential mean in relationship to the outer world? Three qualities are critical indications that you have achieved a life fully worth living. They can be called tone, resonance, and perspective. Tone refers to feeling good about yourself, resonance to feeling good about your relationships, and perspective to feeling good about the choices in your life. To experience these qualities consistently is to know that you are living life well. Once again, though, our society interferes with and disguises the messages that we receive. Therefore, it is necessary not only to grasp the essence of these qualities, but also to recognize and to separate oneself from the distortions of them that our culture imposes.

Tone. Tone refers to your aliveness as an organism. When you think of good muscle tone, you think of a relaxed alertness, a readiness to respond. As used here, the term tone refers to your entire being, your mental and emotional life as well as your muscle and organ life. Hence anxiety is as much the enemy of tone as drugs or being overweight. Lowen expressed this idea as follows:

> A person experiences the reality of the world only through his body... If the body is relatively unalive, a person's impressions and responses are diminished. The more alive the body is, the more vividly does he perceive reality and the more actively does he respond to it. We have all experienced the fact that when we feel particularly good and alive, we perceive the world more sharply... The aliveness of the body denotes its capacity for feeling. In the absence of feeling, the body goes 'dead' insofar as its ability to be impressed by or respond to situations is concerned... It is the body that melts with love, freezes with fear, trembles in anger, and reaches for warmth and contact. Apart from the body these words are poetic images. Experienced in the body, they have a reality that gives meaning to existence (Lowen, 1967).

But the self-images we forge on our journey through society's institutions often deprive us of our ability to maintain tone. We are no longer in touch with our bodies or with our genuine feelings, and our self-images have been distorted.

One of the most common distortions is to comprise your self-image out of some role or roles you play in society. Great actors and actresses use their capacity for total identification with another human being as a basis for a great performance, but their self-image is not that of a person portrayed. That costume is removed at the end of each performance. Cornelia Otis Skinner declared that the first law of the theater is to love your audience. She meant, of course, that the actor or actress, rather than the character portrayed, must love the audience. You cannot love the audience unless you love yourself, and yourself is not a role. Thus, it is vitally important to recognize your roles as costumes you wear for particular purposes, and not to let them get stuck to you. Your prospects at retirement from your profession or organization will otherwise be for a very short life.

A second common distortion is to make your head (your brain) your self-image, and the rest of you part of your environment. Cutting your body into two segments places enormous stress on it, and your tone will suffer severely. "You don't exist within your body. Your body is a person." (Lowen, 1967). A third distortion is to make your gender your self-image. The sexual-reproductive aspects of people are among their most wonderful potentialities, but to identify with your gender leads you to spend the first years of your life learning some bad habits that you spend the rest of your life trying to liberate yourself from.

Other common distortions include being the public relations representative of your family (often forced on boys and girls), being an underdog, a clown, or a representative of superior values. All such distortions will exact their price by robbing you of tone: by causing you to eat too much or drink too much or worry too much or keep your body in continuous stress, and miss the joy of being alive.

Resonance. The second quality for living out your genius is your capacity for resonance. This involves an enhanced, stimulated, and yet relaxed vitality that you can experience in interaction with particular others and particular environments. Discovering those others and those environments that are able to provide resonance can be one of the most fulfilling aspects of the journey through a life fully worth living. The word resonance is chosen rather than the word love, with which it has much in common, because the very meaning of love has become distorted in our society. It has become a commodity in short supply, a marketable item, a weapon used to control others; it is difficult to distinguish love from exploitation or imprisonment.

The term resonance is chosen for other reasons as well. It conveys the notion of being "in tune" with other people and environments; it suggests the synergy and expansion of tone when your energy has joined with the energy of others. It also implies harmony. Harmony is a beautiful arrangement of different sounds, in contrast to mere noise, which is an ugly arrangement. Resonance, as used here, implies people's capacity to use their differences in ways that are beautiful rather than ugly.

The world you build that supports you in the pursuit of your genius is not worth living in if it lacks resonance. But once again, your capacity to build and maintain resonant relationships, and to transform dead or noisy relationships into resonant ones, may have been damaged. To regain that capacity first requires that you become aware of the cultural forces that have damaged it, and robbed you of the potential resonance in your life.

Perhaps the greatest distortion to resonance that we face comes from our intensely adversarial society. Almost everything is perceived in competitive, win-lose, success-failure terms. "Winning isn't everything. It's the *only* thing!" We have been encouraged to believe that the world is our enemy. One must be either on the defensive or offensive, or both at once. One must conquer, control, exploit, or be conquered, controlled, exploited. One must fight or run away. As a result one experiences others and is experienced by them either as hostile, aggressive, aloof, or as frightened, shy, withdrawn. Under these circumstances, resonance is hard to come by and short-lived. For many people, win-lose competitiveness does not dominate all aspects of their lives, but is induced by particular kinds of situations—and destroys the potential resonance and synergy of those situations. For example, many seminars and staff meetings bring in thoughts of winning or losing, succeeding or failing, proving oneself or making points. These displace the potential resonance and synergy that can evolve when a group works creatively together, building on one another's thoughts, stimulating each other's ideas, and mixing work and laughter.

Three further cultural themes that can cripple the capacity for resonance are materialism, sexism, and violence. Materialism is defined as the tendency to measure one's self-worth by the number and kinds of possessions one has, and the tendency to turn experiences into things so that they can be possessions. Collectibles are a way of "life." Sexism is defined as the tendency to turn sexual relationships and partners into materials, and to use sexual labels to sum oneself and others up— gay, macho, or liberated. Morality and fidelity have lost all but their sexual meanings. Lastly, "Violence is as American as apple pie." We have more guns than people. Our folk heroes were violent men.

Various combinations of adversarial, materialistic, sexist, and violent themes are commonly destructive of resonance in intimate relationships, such as marriage. Jealousy, possessiveness, and feelings of being exploited can dominate the relationship and the partners become each other's prisoners and jailers. But if they are able to free themselves of these distortions, the relationship can be transformed and resonance restored. If you think of any intimate relationships as consisting of three creatures: yourself, the other person, and the couple, you can see that the phrase "a life fully worth living" applies to each. It follows that you would reserve for the couple only those things that are growthful and fulfilling for it. In pursuing the other aspects of your life, your partner can be a resource to you, and you a resource to your partner. Rather than being each other's jailers, you become the supporters of each other's freedom—and this will enhance your resonance. An application of this principle is not difficult for most parents to grasp; your delight in seeing your child leading a fulfilling life as a result of the support you provided. Cultural distortions make it more difficult to understand that the principle applies equally to intimate relationships among adults.

Perspective. The third important quality of a worthwhile life is the perspective necessary to guide choices and to inform experience. If you have only one way of looking at the situation you are in, you have no freedom of choice about what to do. And if you have only one framework for understanding your experience, all of your experiences will reinforce that framework. If your outlook is adversarial, you will interpret whatever happens as evidence that the world is hostile, and your choices will be limited to fighting or running away. If you fight, it will confirm your belief that the world is hostile. If you run away, you will know that you were wise to do so. If your perspective is differentiated—if you can see, for example, the potential of a new relationship to be either collaborative or adversarial—you enlarge your range of choices. Thus, if you are aware of "the multiple potential of the moment," you will usually be able to make a choice that will make the next moment better for you and for the others in the situation.

The cultural distortions that lock you into a limited undifferentiated perspective, which lead you to make self-destructive choices, are the same ones that interfere with your tone and self-image, or your capacity for resonance. The messages of adversarialism, materialism, and sexism seek to dictate to you how you should see the world. And your life roles, as defined by other people, are an all too convenient set of prescriptions for your behavior. Take heed of your own feelings, ask what may be causing them, and whether cultural forces are at work. That such distortions are blocking your access to a useful perspective is evidenced whenever you find yourself humorless. The essence of humor is a sudden shift in point of view. To be without humor is to be dying, and laughter is one of the most valuable sources of health and well-being on the journey called a life fully worth living (Cousins, 1979).

Thus tone, resonance, and perspective are the signs that you have discovered your genius and have developed the autonomy to live by it, rather than by society's dictates.

PROSPECTS FOR CHANGE

The foregoing pages have offered a framework for understanding human potential, parts of which may be familiar, parts of which may be new. In some ways the categories of genius, autonomy, tone, resonance, and perspective are arbitrary, and they should only be used when they fit your purposes. And, clearly, these aspects of life are not separable. The expression of genius needs autonomy. Poor tone, low resonance, and limited perspective almost always have a confirming effect upon one another, and serve to limit autonomy. The essential point is to work in a direction that will begin to free human potential, and to rid it of its cultural fetters.

A Role for Institutions

The view presented here is critical of the way society's institutions impose cultural distortions on people, and prevent them from finding a path with a heart. Does this mean that, for the well-being of all of us, our institutions should refrain from showing any interest in careers? Does it mean that there can be no institution with a vested interest in people having a life that is fully worth living?

I believe the answer to both questions is no. Two concurrent forces are operating to change the culture quite rapidly. One of these is the dawning realization in many American organizations that the theories of management and organization on which our society has operated in the past have failed us, and will not serve us in the future. They have failed because they have regarded human beings as part of a social machine and have treated as irrelevant individual spirit and well-being. Nor have these theories capitalized on individuals' needs and capacities to work harmoniously with each other. This realization of past failure is bringing about a transformation in industrial organizations, and non-industrial organizations will eventually catch up. The second force for change is technological progress, especially the rapid development of electronic communications and computers. The more that routine operations are performed by machines, the more demand there is that the non-routine operations be performed with excellence. This kind of excellence in human performance can only be attained by persons who are fully alive and operating in the area of their genius. Only if the path has a heart will it sustain excellence.

When the aerospace industry was in its infancy, the technical challenge, and hence the need for creativity and teamwork, was immense. One of the most successful companies recognized this fully in its organizational structure and culture. It invented new organizational forms that were suited to its mission and the capacities of its members to work together creatively. In the process, it created most of the principles and processes that are in use today in what has come to be called organization development. Among other things, it offered its members Life and Career Planning workshops, to help them identify their talents and interests. The approach was somewhat different from the one outlined in this paper, but its intent was the same. The spirit of these workshops was summed up in the way the company introduced them: "What you do with your life and career is your responsibility. But because you are a member of this company, the company shares some of that responsibility with you. Perhaps it's 80% yours, 20% the company's. This workshop is the company's effort to contribute towards its 20%." In a similar spirit, another company offers workshops based on their version of Dalton and Thompson's career-stages model, to help employees identify their position on the path, understand their potential more clearly, and find ways of fulfilling it (Dalton, Thompson, and Price, 1977).

These companies have a vested interest in having their members rediscover their genius. Our hope for changing the order of things is that more and more organizations will follow their example. But we must insist that their interventions are explicitly on their members' behalf. And their processes must seek to liberate people from their cultural surroundings—including organizational cultures—rather than to reaffirm their dependencies. Then their example can be picked up by the schools, who can help others much earlier in their lives. Parents, in turn, will come to appreciate the freedom of spirit that they can encourage in their own children. The path with a heart is also the path to improving our institutions. Let our teaching about careers stand for nothing less.

6

Interpersonal Communication

ACTIVE LISTENING
Carl R. Rogers
Richard E. Farson

COMMUNICATION: THE USE OF TIME, SPACE AND THINGS
Anthony G. Athos

DEFENSIVE COMMUNICATION
Jack R. Gibb

ACTIVE LISTENING

Carl R. Rogers
Richard E. Farson

THE MEANING OF ACTIVE LISTENING

One basic responsibility of the supervisor or manager is the development, adjustment, and integration of individual employees. He tries to develop employee potential, delegate responsibility, and achieve cooperation. To do so, he must have, among other abilities, the ability to listen intelligently and carefully to those with whom he works.

There are, however, many kinds of listening skills. The lawyer, for example, when questioning a witness, listens for contradictions, irrelevancies, errors, and weaknesses. But this is not the kind of listening skill we are concerned with. The lawyer usually is not listening in order to help the witness adjust, cooperate, or produce. Our emphasis will be on listening skills of the supervisor or manager that will help employees gain a clearer understanding of their situations, take responsibility, and cooperate with each other.

Source: Reprinted by special permission of the Industrial Relations Center of the University of Chicago and the authors.

Two Examples

The kind of listening we have in mind is called "active listening." It is called "active" because the listener has a very definite responsibility. He does not passively absorb words which are spoken to him. He actively tries to grasp the facts and the feelings in what he hears, and he tries, by his listening, to help the speaker work out his own problems.

To get a clearer picture of what active listening means, let us consider two different approaches to the same work problem. The example is set in the printing industry, but the behavior of the men could surface in any organization.

EXAMPLE NO. 1:

FOREMAN: Hey, Al, I don't get this rush order. We can't handle any 50,000 run today. What do they think we are?

SUPERVISOR: But that's the order. So get it out as soon as you can. We're under terrific pressure this week.

F: Don't they know we're behind schedule already because of that press breakdown?

S: Look, Kelly, I don't decide what goes on upstairs. I just have to see that the work gets out and that's what I'm gonna do.

F: The guys aren't gonna like this.

S: That's something you'll have to work out with them, not me.

EXAMPLE NO. 2

F: Hey, Ross, I don't get this rush order. We can't handle any run of 50,000 today. What do they think we are?

S: They're pushing you pretty hard aren't they Kelly?

F: They sure are and I'm getting sore. We were just about back to schedule after the press breakdown. Now this comes along.

S: As if you didn't have enough work to do, huh?

F: Yeah. I don't know how I'm going to tell the pressman about this.

S: Hate to face him with a rush order now, is that it?

F: I really do. Joe is under a real strain today. Seems like everything we do around here is rush, rush, rush!

S: I guess you feel it's unfair to load anything more on him today.

F: Well, yeah. I know there must be plenty of pressure on everybody to get the work out, but—well, Joe doesn't deserve all the rush orders. But, if that's the way it is—I guess I'd better get the word to him and see how I can rearrange the work flow.

There are obviously many differences between these two examples. The main one, however, is that Ross, the supervisor in the second example is using the active-listening approach. He is listening and responding in a way that makes it clear that he appreciates both the meaning and the feeling behind what Kelly is saying.

Active listening does not necessarily mean long sessions spent listening to grievances, personal or otherwise. It is simply a way of approaching those problems which arise out of the usual day-to-day events of any job.

To be effective, active listening must be firmly grounded in the basic attitudes of the user. We cannot employ it as a technique if our fundamental attitudes are in conflict with its basic concepts. If we try, our behavior will be empty and sterile, and our associates will be quick to recognize such behavior. Until we can demonstrate a spirit which genuinely respects the potential worth of the individual, which considers his rights and trusts his capacity for self-direction, we cannot begin to be effective listeners.

What We Achieve by Listening

Active listening is an important way to bring about changes in people. Despite the popular notion that listening is a passive approach, clinical and research evidence clearly shows that sensitive listening is a most effective agent for individual personality change and group development. Listening brings about changes in people's attitudes toward themselves and others, and also brings about changes in their basic values and personal philosophy. People who have been listened to in this new and special way become more emotionally mature, more open to their experiences, less defensive, more democratic, and less authoritarian.

When people are listened to sensitively, they tend to listen to themselves with more care and make clear exactly what they are feeling and thinking. Group members tend to listen more to each other, become less argumentative, more ready to incorporate other points of view. Because listening reduces the threat of having one's ideas criticized, the person is better able to see them for what they are and is more likely to feel that his contributions are worthwhile.

Not the least important result of listening is the change that takes place within the listener himself. Besides the fact that listening provides more information about people than any other activity, it builds deep, positive relationships and tends to alter constructively the attitudes of the listener. Listening is a growth experience.

HOW TO LISTEN

The goal of active listening is to bring about changes in people. To achieve this end, it relies upon definite techniques—things to do and things to avoid doing. Before discussing these techniques, however, we should first understand why they are effective. To do so, we must understand how the individual personality develops.

The Growth of the Individual

Through all of our lives, from early childhood on, we have learned to think of ourselves in certain, very definite ways. We have built up pictures of ourselves. Sometimes these self-pictures are pretty realistic but at other times they are not. For example, an average, overweight lady may fancy herself a youthful, ravishing siren, or an awkward teenager regard himself as a star athlete.

All of us have experiences which fit the way we need to think about ourselves. These we accept. But it is much harder to accept experiences which don't fit. And sometimes, if it is very important for us to hang on to this self-picture, we don't accept or admit these experiences at all.

These self-pictures are not necessarily attractive. A man, for example, may regard himself as incompetent and worthless. He may feel that he is doing his job poorly in spite of favorable appraisals by the organization. As long as he has these feelings about himself he must deny any experiences which would seem not to fit this self-picture, in this case any that might indicate to him that he is competent. It is so necessary for him to maintain this self-picture that he is threatened by anything which would tend to change it. Thus, when the organization raises his salary, it may seem to him only additional proof that he is a fraud. He must hold onto this self-picture, because, bad or good, it's the ony thing he has by which he can identify himself.

This is why direct attempts to change this individual or change his self-picture are particularly threatening. He is forced to defend himself or to completely deny the experience. This denial of experience and defense of the self-picture tend to bring on rigidity of behavior and create difficulties in personal adjustment.

The active-listening approach, on the other hand, does not present a threat to the individual's self-picture. He does not have to defend it. He is able to explore it, see it for what it is, and make his own decision as to how realistic it is. He is then in a position to change.

If I want to help a man or woman reduce defensiveness and become more adaptive, I must try to remove the threat of myself as a potential changer. As long as the atmosphere is threatening, there can be no effective communication. So I must create a climate which is neither critical, evaluative, nor moralizing. The climate must foster equality and freedom, trust and understanding, acceptance and warmth. In this climate and in this climate only does the individual feel safe enough to incorporate new experiences and new values into his concept of himself. Active listening helps to create this climate.

What to Avoid

When we encounter a person with a problem, our usual response is to try to change his way of looking at things—to get him to see his situation the way we see it, or would like him to see it. We plead, reason, scold, encourage, insult, prod—anything to bring about a change in the desired direction, that is, in the direction we want him to travel. What we seldom realize, however, is that under these circumstances we are usually responding to *our own* needs to see the world in certain ways. It is always difficult for us to tolerate and understand actions which are different from the ways in which *we* believe *we* should act. If, however, we can free ourselves from the need to influence and direct others in our own paths, we enable ourselves to listen with understanding, and thereby employ the most potent available agent of change.

One problem the listener faces is that of responding to demands for decisions, judgments, and evaluations. He is constantly called upon to agree or disagree with someone or something. Yet, as he well knows, the question or challenge frequently is a masked expression of feelings or needs which the speaker is far more anxious to communicate than he is to have the surface questions answered. Because he cannot speak these feelings openly, the speaker must disguise them to himself and to others in an acceptable form. To illustrate, let us examine some typical questions and the type of answers that might best elicit the feeling beneath it.

Employee's Question	Listener's Answer
Just who is responsible for getting this job done?	Do you feel that you don't have enough authority?
Don't you think talent should count more than seniority in promotions?	What do you think are the reasons for your opinion?
What does the boss expect us to do about those broken-down machines?	You're tired of working with worn-out equipment, aren't you?
Don't you think my performance has improved since the last review?	Sounds as if you feel your work has picked up over these last few months?

These responses recognize the questions but leave the way open for the employee to say what is really bothering him. They allow the listener to participate in the problem or situation without shouldering all responsibility for decision-making or actions. This is a process of thinking *with* people instead of *for* or *about* them.

Passing judgment, whether critical or favorable, makes free expression difficult. Similarly, advice and information are almost always seen as efforts to change a person and thus serve as barriers to his self-expression and the development of a creative relationship. Moreover, advice is seldom taken and information hardly ever utilized. The eager young trainee probably will not become patient just because he is advised that, "The road to success is a long, difficult one, and you must be patient." And it is no more helpful for him to learn that "only one out of a hundred trainees reach top management positions."

Interestingly, it is a difficult lesson to learn that *positive evaluations* are sometimes as blocking as negative ones. It is almost as destructive to the freedom of a relationship to tell a person that he is good or capable or right, as to tell him otherwise. To evaluate him positively may make it more difficult for him to tell of the faults that distress him or the ways in which he believes he is not competent.

Encouragement also may be seen as an attempt to motivate the speaker in certain directions or hold him off rather than as support. "I'm sure everything will work out O.K." is not a helpful response to the person who is deeply discouraged about a problem.

In other words, most of the techniques and devices common to human relationships are found to be of little use in establishing the type of relationship we are seeking here.

What to Do

Just what does active listening entail, then? Basically, it requires that we get inside the speaker, that we grasp, *from his point of view,* just what it is he is communicating to us. More than that, we must convey to the speaker that we are seeing things from his point of view. To listen actively, then, means that there are several things we must do.

Listen for Total Meaning. Any message a person tries to get across usually has two components: the *content* of the message and the *feeling* or attitude underlying this content. Both are important, both give the message *meaning*. It is this total meaning of the message that we must try to understand. For example, a secretary comes to her boss and says: "I've finished that report." This message has obvious factual content and perhaps calls upon the boss for another work assignment. Suppose, on the other hand, that the secretary says: "Well! I'm finally finished with your damn report!" The factual content is the same, but the total meaning of the message has changed—and changed in an important way for both supervisor and worker. Here sensitive listening can facilitate the work relationship in this office. If the boss were to respond by simply giving his secretary some letters to type, would the secretary feel that she had gotten her total message across? Would she feel free to talk to her boss about the difficulty of her work? Would she feel better about the job, more anxious to do good work on her next assignment?

Now, on the other hand, suppose the supervisor were to respond, "Glad to get that over with, huh?" or "That was a rough one, wasn't it?" or "Guess you don't want another one like that again," or anything that tells the worker that he heard and understands. It doesn't necessarily mean that her next work assignment need be changed or that he must spend an hour listening to the worker complain about the problems she encountered. He may do a number of things differently in the light of the new information he has from the worker—but not necessarily. It's just that extra sensitivity on the part of the supervisor that can transform an average working climate into a good one.

Respond to Feelings. In some instances the content is far less important than the feeling which underlies it. To catch the full flavor or meaning of the message one must respond particularly to the feeling component. If, for instance, our secretary had said, "I'd like to pile up all those carbons and make a bonfire out of them!" responding to content would be obviously absurd. But to respond to her disgust or anger in trying to work with the report recognizes the meaning of this message. There are various shadings of these components in the meaning of any message. Each time the listener must try to remain sensitive to the total meaning the message has to the speaker. What is she trying to tell me? What does this mean to her? How does she see this situation?

Note All Cues. Not all communication is verbal. The speaker's words alone don't tell us everything he is communicating. And hence, truly sensitive listening requires that we become aware of several kinds of communication besides verbal. The way in which a speaker hesitates in his speech can tell us much about his feelings. So too can the inflection of his voice. He may stress certain points loudly and clearly, and he may mumble others. We should also note such things as the person's facial expressions, body posture, hand movements, eye movements, and breathing. All of these help to convey his total message.

What We Communicatee by Listening

The first reaction of most people when they consider listening as a possible method for dealing with human beings is that listening cannot be sufficient in itself. Because it is passive, they feel, listening does not communicate anything to the speaker. Actually, nothing could be farther from the truth.

By consistently listening to a speaker you are conveying the idea that: "I'm interested in you as a person, and I think that what you feel is important. I respect your thoughts, and even if I don't agree with them, I know that they are valid for you. I feel sure that you have a contribution to make. I'm not trying to change you or evaluate you. I just want to understand you. I think you're worth listening to, and I want you to know that I'm the kind of person you can talk to."

The subtle but most important aspect of this is that it is the *demonstration* of the message that works. Although it is most difficult to convince someone that you respect him by *telling* him so, you are much more likely to get this message across by really *behaving* that way—by actually *having* and *demonstrating* respect for this person. Listening does this most effectively.

Like other behavior, listening behavior is contagious. This has implications for all communications problems, whether between two people, or within a large organization. To insure good communication between associates up and down the line, one must first take the responsibility for setting a pattern of listening. Just as one learns that anger is usually met with anger, argument with argument, and deception with deception, one can learn that listening can be met with listening. Every person who feels responsibility in a situation can set the tone of the interaction, and the important lesson in this is that any behavior exhibited by one person will eventually be responded to with similar behavior in the other person.

It is far more difficult to stimulate constructive behavior in another person but far more valuable. Listening is one of these constructive behaviors, but if one's attitude is to "wait out" the speaker rather than really listen to him, it will fail. The one who consistently listens with understanding, however, is the one who eventually is most likely to be listened to. If you really want to be heard and understood by another, you can develop him as a potential listener, ready for new ideas, provided you can first develop yourself in these ways and sincerely listen with understanding and respect.

Testing for Understanding

Because understanding another person is actually far more difficult than it at first seems, it is important to test constantly your ability to see the world in the way the speaker sees it. You can do this by reflecting in your own words what the speaker seems to mean by his words and actions. His response to this will tell you whether or not he feels understood. A good rule of thumb is to assume that one never really understands until he can communicate this understanding to the other's satisfaction.

Here is an experiment to test your skill in listening. The next time you become involved in a lively or controversial discussion with another person, stop for a moment and suggest that you adopt this ground rule for continued discussion. Before either participant in the discussion can make a point or express an opinion of his own, he must first restate aloud the previous point or position of the other person. This restatement must be in his own words (merely parroting the words of another does not prove that one has understood, but only that he has heard the words). The restatement must be accurate enough to satisfy the speaker before the listener can be allowed to speak for himself.

You might find this procedure useful in a meeting where feelings run high and people express themselves on topics of emotional concern to the group. Before another member of the group expresses his own feelings and thought, he must rephrease the *meaning* expressed by the previous speaker to that person's satisfaction. All the members in the group should be alert to the changes in the emotional climate and the quality of the discussion when this approach is used.

PROBLEMS IN ACTIVE LISTENING

Active listening is not an easy skill to acquire, it demands practice. Perhaps more important, it may require changes in our own basic attitudes. These changes come slowly and sometimes with considerable difficulty. Let us look at some of the major problems in active listening and what can be done to overcome them.

The Personal Risk

To be effective in active listening, one must have a sincere interest in the speaker. We all live in glass houses as far as our attitudes are concerned. They always show through. And if we are only making a pretense of interest in the speaker, he will quickly pick this up, either consciously or subconsciously. And once he does, he will no longer express himself freely.

Active listening carries a strong element of personal risk. If we manage to accomplish what we are describing here—to sense the feelings of another person, to understand the meaning his experiences have for him, to see the world as he sees it we risk being changed ourselves. For example, if we permit ourselves to listen our way into the life of a person we do not know or approve of—to get the meaning that life has for him we risk coming to see the world as he sees it. We are threatened when we give up, even momentarily, what we believe and start thinking in someone else's terms. It takes a great deal of inner security and courage to be able to risk one's self in understanding another.

For the manager, the courage to take another's point of view generally means that he must see *himself* through another's eyes—he must be able to see himself as others see him. To do this may sometimes be unpleasant, but it is far more *difficult* than unpleasant. We are so accustomed to viewing ourselves in certain ways—to seeing and hearing only what we want to see and hear—that it is extremely difficult for a person to free himself from the need to see things his way.

Developing an attitude of sincere interest in the speaker is thus no easy task. It can be developed only by being willing to risk seeing the world from the speaker's point of view. If we have a number of such experiences, however, they will shape an attitude which will allow us to be truly genuine in our interest in the speaker.

Hostile Expressions

The listener will often hear negative, hostile expressions directed at himself. Such expressions are always hard to listen to. No one likes to hear hostile words or experience hostility which is directed against them. And it is not easy to get to the point where one is strong enough to permit these attacks without finding it necessary to defend himself or retaliate.

Because we all fear that people will crumble under the attack of genuine negative feelings, we tend to perpetuate an attitude of pseudo-peace. It is as if we cannot tolerate conflict at all for fear of the damage it could do to us, to the situation, to the others involved. But of course the real damage is done by the denial and suppression of negative feelings.

Out-of-Place Expressions

Expressions dealing with behavior that is not usually acceptable in our society also pose problems for the listener. These out-of-place expressions can take the extreme forms that psychotherapists hear—such as homicidal fantasies or expressions of sexual perversity. The listener often blocks out such expressions because of their obvious threatening quality. At less extreme levels, we all find unnatural or inappropriate behavior difficult to handle. Behavior that brings on a problem situation may be anything from telling an "off-color" story in mixed company to seeing a man cry.

In any face-to-face situation, we will find instances of this type which will momentarily, if not permanently, block any communication. In any organization, expressions of weakness or incompetency will generally be regarded as unacceptable and therefore will block good two-way communication. For example, it is difficult to listen to a manager tell of his feelings of failure in being able to "take charge" of a situation in his department because *all* administrators are supposed to be able to "take charge."

Accepting Positive Feelings

It is both interesting and perplexing to note that negative or hostile feelings or expressions are much easier to deal with in any face-to-face relationship than are positive feelings. This is especially true for the manager because the culture expects him to be independent, bold, clever, and aggressive and manifest no feelings of warmth, gentleness, and intimacy. He therefore comes to regard these feelings as soft and inappropriate. But no matter how they are regarded, they remain a human need. The denial of these feelings in himself and his associates does not get the manager out of a problem of dealing with them. The feelings simply become veiled and confused. If recognized they would work for the total effort; unrecognized, they work against it.

Emotional Danger Signals

The listener's own emotions are sometimes a barrier to active listening. When emotions are at their height, when listening is most necessary, it is most difficult to set aside one's own concerns and be understanding. Our emotions are often our own worst enemies when we try to become listeners. The more involved and invested we are in a particular situation or problem, the less we are likely to be willing or able to listen to the feelings and attitudes of others. That is, the more we find it necessary to respond to our own needs, the less we are able to respond to the needs of another. Let us look at some of the main danger signals that warn us that our emotions may be interfering with our listening.

Defensiveness. The points about which one is most vocal and dogmatic, the points which one is most anxious to impose on others—these are always the points one is trying to talk oneself into believing. So one danger signal becomes apparent when you find yourself stressing a point or trying to convince another. It is at these times that you are likely to be less secure and consequently less able to listen.

Resentment of Opposition. It is always easier to listen to an idea which is similar to one of your own than to an opposing view. Sometimes, in order to clear the air, it is helpful to pause for a moment when you feel your ideas and position being challenged, reflect on the situation, and express your concern to the speaker.

Clash of Personalities. Here again, our experience has consistently shown us that the genuine expression of feelings on the part of the listener will be more helpful in developing a sound relationship than the suppression of them. This is so whether the feelings be resentment, hostility, threat, or admiration. A basically honest relationship, whatever the nature of it, is the most productive of all. The other party becomes secure when he learns that the listener can express his feelings honestly and openly to him. We should keep this in mind when we begin to fear a clash of personalities in the listening relationship. Otherwise, fear of our own emotions will choke off full expression of feelings.

Listening to Ourselves

To listen to oneself is a prerequisite to listening to others. And it is often an effective means of dealing with the problems we have outlined above. When we are most aroused, excited, and demanding, we are least able to understand our own feelings and attitudes. Yet, in dealing with the problems of others, it becomes most important to be sure of one's own position, values, and needs.

The ability to recognize and understand the meaning which a particular episode has for you, with all the feelings which it stimulates in you, and the ability to express this meaning when you find it getting in the way of active listening, will clear the air and enable you once again to be free to listen. That is, if some person or situation touches off feelings within you which tend to block your attempts to listen with undetstanding, begin listening to yourself. It is much more helpful in developing effective relationships to avoid suppressing these feelings. Speak them out as clearly as you can, and try to enlist the other person as a listener to your feelings. A person's listening ability is limited by his ability to listen to himself.

ACTIVE LISTENING
AND ORGANIZATION GOALS

"How can listening improve productivity?"

"We're in business, and it is a rugged, fast, competitive affair. How are we going to find time to counsel our employees?"

"We have to concern ourselves with organizational problems first."

"We can't afford to spend all day listening when there is work to do."

"What's morale got to do with service to the public?"

"Sometimes we have to sacrifice an individual for the good of the rest of the people in the organization."

Those of us who are trying to advance the listening approach in organizations hear these comments frequently. And because they are so honest and legitimate, they pose a real problem. Unfortunately, the answers are not so clear-cut as the questions.

Individual Importance

One answer is based on an assumption that is central to the listening approach. That assumption is: the kind of behavior which helps the individual will eventually be the best thing that could be done for the work group. Or saying it anohter way: the things that are best for the individual are best for the organization. This is a conviction of ours, based on our experience in psychology and education. The research evidence from organizations is still coming in. We find that putting the group first, at the expense of the individual, besides being an uncomfortable individual experience, does *not* unify the group. In fact, it tends to make the group less a group. The members become anxious and suspicious.

We are not at all sure in just what ways the group does benefit from a concern demonstrated for an individual, but we have several strong leads. One is that the group feels more secure when an individual member is being listened to and provided for with concern and sensitivity. And we assume that a secure group will ultimately be a better group. When each individual feels that he need not fear exposing himself to the group, he is likely to contribute more freely and spontaneously. When the leader of a group responds to the individual, puts the individual first, the other members of the group will follow suit, and the group comes to act as a unit in recognizing and responding to the needs of a particular member. This positive, constructive action seems to be a much more satisfying experience for a group than the experience of dispensing with a member.

Listening and Productivity

As to whether or not listening or any other activity designed to better human relations in an organization actually makes the organization more productive—whether morale has a definite relationship to performance is not known for sure. There are some who frankly hold that there is no relationship to be expected between morale and productivity—that productivity often depends upon the social misfit, the eccentric, or the isolate. And there are some who simply choose to work in a climate of cooperation and harmony, in a high-morale group, quite aside from the question of achievement or productivity.

A report from the survey Research Center at the University of Michigan on research conducted at the Prudential Life Insurance Company lists seven findings related to production and morale. First-line supervisors in high-production work groups were found to differ from those in low-production groups in that they:

1. Are under less close supervision from their own supervisors.
2. Place less direct emphasis upon production as the goal.
3. Encourage employee participation in the making of decisions.
4. Are more employee-centered.
5. Spend more of their time in supervision and less in straight production work.
6. Have a greater feeling of confidence in their supervisory roles.
7. Feel that they know where they stand with the company.

After mentioning that other dimensions of morale, such as identification with the company, intrinsic job satisfaction, and satisfaction with job status, were not found significantly related to productivity, the report goes on to suggest the following psychological interpretation:

> People are more effectively motivated when they are given some degree of freedom in the way in which they do their work when every action is prescribed in advance. They do better when some degree of decision-making about their jobs is possible than when all decisions are made for them. They respond more adequately when they are treated as personalities than as cogs in a machine. In short if the ego motivation of self-determination, of self-expression, of a sense of personal worth can be tapped, the individual can be more effectively energized. The use of external sanctions, or pressuring for production may work to some degree, but not to the extent that the more internalized motives do. When the individual comes to identify himself with his job and with the work of his group, human resources are much more fully utilized in the production process.

The survey Research Center has also conducted studies among workers in other industries. In discussing the results of these studies, Robert L. Kahn writes:

> In the studies of clerical workers, railroad workers, and workers in heavy industry, the supervisors with the better production records gave a larger proportion of their time to supervisory functions, especially to the interpersonal aspects of their jobs. The supervisors of the lower-producing sections were more likely to spend their time in tasks which the men themselves were performing, or in the paper-work aspects of their jobs.

Maximum Creativeness

There may never be enough research evidence to satisfy everyone on this question. But speaking from an organizational point of view, in terms of the problem of developing resources for productivity, the maximum creativeness and productive effort of the human beings in the organization are the richest untapped source of power available. The difference between the maximum productive capacity of people and that output which the organization is now realizing is immense. We simply suggest that this maximum capacity might be closer to realization if we sought to release the motivation that already exists within people rather than try to stimulate them externally.

This releasing of the individual is made possible first of all by listening, with respect and understanding. Listening is a beginning toward making the individual feel himself worthy of making contributions, and this could result in a very dynamic and productive organization. Profit making organizations are never too rugged or too busy to take time to procure the most efficient technological advances or to develop rich sources of raw materials. But technology and materials are but paltry resources in comparison with the resources that are already within the people in the organization.

G. L. Clements, of Jewel Tea Co., Inc., in talking about the collaborative approach to management says:

> We feel that this type of approach recognizes that there is a secret ballot going on at all times among the people in any business. They vote for or against their supervisors. A favorable vote for the supervisor shows up in the cooperation, teamwork, understanding, and production of the group. To win this secret ballot, each supervisor must share the problems of his group and work for them.

The decision to spend time listening to employees is a decision each supervisor or manager has to make for himself. Managers increasingly must deal with people and their relationships rather than turning out goods and services. The minute we take a man from work and make him a supervisor he is removed from the basic production of goods or services and now must begin relating to men and women instead of nuts and bolts. People are different from things and our supervisor is called upon for a different line of skills completely. These new tasks call for a special kind of person. The development of the supervisor as a listener is a first step in becoming this special person.

COMMUNICATION: THE USE OF TIME, SPACE, AND THINGS[1]

Anthony G. Athos

It was amazing to me to discover how many ways we have of talking about time. We have time, keep time, buy time, and save time; we mark it, spend it, sell it, and waste it; we kill time, pass time, give time, take time, and make time. With

Source: Reprinted by permission of the author and publisher from A. G. Athos and J. Gabarro, *Interpersonal Behavior* (Englewood Cliffs, N.J.: Prentice-Hall, Inc., 1978).

[1]Some of the ideas in this chapter were developed in a lecture given by Anthony G. Athos which was first published in *Behavior in Organizations: A Multidimensional View,* by A. G. Athos and R. E. Coffey, Prentice-Hall, Englewood Cliffs, N.J., 1968. The author is greatly indebted to the stimulation of Edward T. Hall's *The Silent Language* (Premier paperback, 1961) and *The Hidden Dimension* (Doubleday, 1966). Hall's work is much recommended to those who find that this brief discursive introduction stimulates further interest in a different and more systematic approach.

so many ways of dealing with time in the English language, we must be as sensitive to it as Eskimos are to snow, for which they have many words and no small respect.

Our American[2] concepts of time are that it is continuous, irreversible, and one-dimensional. Recent movies that shuffle the sequence of events so that they do not proceed in the same order as they "do" in "real" time, including flashaheads as well as the old standard flashbacks, are effective in disturbing us into powerful experiencing precisely because they deny our long-standing assumptions about time. We often seem to experience tomorrow as spatially in front of us and yesterday as almost literally behind us. With some effort we might be able to think of today as the space we were just in and the space we will very soon be in as we walk in a straight line. "Now" is even harder for many Americans, and it seems we experience it as the space filled by our bodies.

Perhaps that is why such interesting variations exist in different parts of the United States in orientations toward time. My personal experience in New England leads me to see people here as more oriented toward the past and the future than toward the present. Southern Californians seem more present- and future-oriented, with some important emphasis upon now (and thus greater familiarity with their bodies). The Latin Americans I know seem more past- and future-oriented. My point here is that we differ in our experiencing of time (as contrasted with our ways of thinking about it), focusing upon different aspects of it. Yet there is a tendency for us to assume that it is linear "in" space: i.e., as a "straight line" from the past through the present into the future.

Of course, those who live more in touch with nature, say, farmers or resort operators, might also see time as cyclical. The earth makes its daily round of the sun; the seasons, like circles, "each mark to the instant their ordained end" and cycle again. And many of us, on an island vacation, for example, "unwind" like a corkscrew from what we left behind, slowly lose our concerns for tomorrow, and relax into letting days happen so that each merges with the one before and into the one after as an experienced, continuous present. The loosening delight of such vacations is in contrast with our more usual patterns, wherein our concerns about time can easily become compulsive.

Accuracy

I can recall being in Athens, Greece, and asking my Greek cousin "How long does it take to walk from here to the library?" I was staying with her family and I wanted to spend the afternoon at the library and leave there in time to get back home for a 6 P.M. appointment with an American friend. She said, "Not long." I replied with some irritation "No. I need to know, so I can stay there as long as possible. How long does it take?" She shrugged and said "It's a short walk." I said with a frown "Come on. I want to know exactly. How long?" With great exasperation she finally dismissed me with "A cigarette!" Well, I feel a bit defeated, if a little amused, for to her a 10- or even 20-minute error in estimate would have been simply irrelevant. Any greater precision would confine her. Yet

---

[2]"United States" and "America" refer here to the whole country, ignoring the considerable differences in the "cultures" of Hawaii, Alaska, Texas, and other parts of the whole.

we want to know *exactly*. Our concern for accuracy is enormous. Where else but in the Western industrialized world would watches get advertised as not being off more than a few seconds a month? Where else would people literally have time-pieces strapped to their bodies so they can be sure they "keep on time"? Because of our concern for accuracy, the way we use time in our culture "talks" to other people.

Many men can remember the first time they ever drove to pick up someone for a date. It's not surprising that many of us got there a bit early and drove around the block a while so as not to communicate our anxiety or eagerness too openly. To arrive at 7:00 for a 7:30 date is to "tell" the other about these feelings and may result in "seeming" naive, unless the boy can explain it away. To arrive at 8:00 for a 7:30 date "says" you feel somwhat indifferent, and a decent explanation is required if the evening is to make any sense at all. Similarly, it is not uncommon for professors to assume that a student who is frequently late for class "doesn't care." Most get angry as a result. Students tend to assume that professors who are late to class also don't care very much. Time thus often "tells" caring, whether accurately or not.

We also use time to tell how we feel and see others in terms of relative status and power. If the President of the United States called you to Washington to talk with him next Tuesday at 3 P.M., it is unlikely that you would arrange your flight to arrive at National Airport at 2 P.M. You would most likely want very much to be sure you were at the White House no later than 3 P.M., and might very well get to Washington on Monday to be certain nothing would go wrong. Because of the great difference between the status of the President and the rest of us, we would likely feel that any inconvenience in waiting ought to be ours.

The same can be true in companies. If the president of a large organization calls a young salesman to his office for a 3 P.M. meeting, the chances are awfully good that the salesman will arrive before 3 P.M., even if he walks around the block for an hour, so as not to arrive "too early."

Imagine two men who are executives in the same large company, whose respective status is virtually the same but who are very competitive in many ways. One calls the other on the phone, and asks him to come to his office for a meeting at 1 P.M. that afternoon. (Notice that one is initiating, which generally indicates higher status; that he is specifying the place and the time, which diminishes the other's influence on those decisions; and that the "invitation" comes only a few hours before the intended meeting, which may imply that the other has nothing more important to do.) The chances are good that the second man will not arrive before or even at 1 P.M. for the meeting, unless his compulsiveness about time in general is so great that it overcomes his feelings about being "put down" (in which case he has lost a round in the competition and may be searching for a "victory" during the meeting). He might well arrive late, perhaps 5 minutes, which is enough to irritate but not openly insult, and then offer either no apology or only a very casual one. The way he handles time in this setting will communicate to the first executive, and so he may plan his response as carefully as a choreographer plans a ballet. Yet little of the process may be fully conscious for him. As Hall says in the title of his book, these are often truly silent languages for many of us.

The longer people are kept waiting, the worse they feel. If the young salesman who was invited to his company president's office for a 3 P.M. meeting arrives at a "respectful" 2:50 and is told by the secretary to have a seat, he remains relatively comfortable until 3 P.M. If the secretary waits until 3:10 to phone the president and remind him the salesman is there, she may communicate (i.e., the salesman may "hear") that she thinks a 10-minute wait is about all she can handle without feeling that the salesman will be feeling the first pangs of being unwanted. If she hangs up the phone and says "He'll be right with you" and the clock continues to tick until 3:25, she might feel impelled to say something about how busy the president is today (i.e., "Don't feel bad. It's nothing personal."). By 3:45 the salesman is likely to be somewhat angry, since he is likely to assume that the president doesn't really care about seeing him. If the president comes out of his office (note this use of space) to get the salesman and apologizes for being late and explains why (especially if the explanation includes information about "the top" that the salesman is not usually aware of), the salesman may "forgive" his boss ("That's all right. I don't mind at all. Your time is more important than mine.") and all can go well. If the president buzzes his secretary and tells her to send the salesmen in, and then proceeds directly to the business at hand, the salesman is likely to be torn between the anger he feels and the fear of expressing it, which may affect their meeting without either knowing why. In short, then, the longer a person is kept waiting, the more "social stroking" is required to smooth ruffled feathers. Awareness of the process can reduce its power to discomfort when you are on the receiving end, and can increase your skills at helping others to realize when you were not deliberately, with intent, trying to "put them down." Being "thoughtless" and thus "hurting other's feelings" is all too often just what we call it: thoughtless. Thinking about our uses of time can, after an awkward self-consciousness, lead to an increase in intuitive, out-of-awareness skill in dealing with self and others.

Using time to manipulate or control others is common, even if we who do so are unaware of it. I once hired a gardener on a monthly contract to care for my yard. When we were discussing the arrangements, I felt somewhat uncertain that he would do all I wanted done or do it to my satisfaction. My feelings of mistrust were expressed by focusing upon time. I wanted to know precisely what day of the week he would come and how many hours he would stay. He seemed to understand and said "Thursday. Four hours."

Well, he actually did come on Thursday once in a while, but he also came on every other day of the week except Sunday and Monday. He never to my knowledge stayed four hours even when I happened to be home. I was sure I was being "taken" until it occurred to me the yard had never looked so good and everything really needing to be done was done.

The gardener apparently thought in terms of planting and cutting and fertilizing cycles. He felt his duty was to the yard, not to me. He sent me bills about every three or four months and then he often had to ask me what I owed him. He trusted me completely to pay him what he deserved. He worked in terms of seasons of the year, and I was trying to pin him down to an hourly basis. My attempt to replace my mistrust with the brittle satisfaction of controlling another person, in time, would eventually have led him to quit or me to fire him. I was lucky to see what was happening, and I left him alone. We got along fine.

Time is viewed as both precious and personal, and when we allow someone to structure our time, it is usually in deference to his or her greater status or power. This is especially true when we would rather be doing something else, as is the case with some employees in many organizations who "put in their time" from nine to five. Many people today are looking for an opportunity to "do their own thing" (when they can figure out what that is) and their reluctance to be controlled vis-à-vis a dimension as personal as time is reflected in such questions as "How much of your time is yours?", "Did you take time to smell the flowers?", and "Do you own your life?" "Private time" (such as weekends) is often "intruded upon" by work, with the notable exception of the Pacific Northwest, where it is generally regarded more strongly as "non-work" time.

The use of time to define relationships can also be seen in most marriages. How many Americans do you know who work through the dinner hour or into the night without calling their spouses? By contrast, people in other cultures often handle the time of their arrival home differently. In Greece I found that dinner was served at my uncle's house whenever he came home—and that might be anywhere from 6 to 9 P.M. This variation in the use of time, as well as my dealing with the gardener, introduces still another major notion about time.

Scarcity

We seem to see time as a limited resource for each person, so we think that what they choose to do with what time they have is a signal about how they feel about us. You are already experienced with the application of this notion. We all have feelings about how frequently we "ought" to see certain persons in order to express a "suitable" amount of affection. Take visits home to see your parents. Some students go home every weekend, some only on vacations, some only on holidays, some every few years, and some never. But almost all parents are pleased, assuming they like their children, to find their offspring choose to visit them rather than do something else. There is a mutual exclusivity operating here. If you go home to see your parents, they know you did so at the expense of some other option. If your other options were attractive, they hear you care enough about your relationship with them to forego some other pleasure. Simply choosing to "spend your time" with them is thus a gift of sorts and a signal about your sentiments. the same is true with other people, of course, especially subordinates in an organization.

Even when the choice of how or with whom we spend our time is not really our own, others may "hear" a communication about our feelings. If you and two other persons begin to meet after class once a week for a beer and then you take a part-time job that forces you to go directly from class to work, your absence in the pub will be "understood" as out of your control (given the choice you made to work). But the loss of interaction must be made up elsewhere or your friends will probably feel that you "withdrew."

Some people are really tough on this one. You may have three final exams to study and a broken leg, and like most professors some friends will insist you come to the appointed meeting and bring your leg with you. And yet there need be no unreasonable demands involved for misunderstandings to occur. Perfectly reasonable people can think we don't care for them because we do something else rather than see them. They can misjudge the importance to us of the something else and be ignorant of the conditions that made it important. A supervisor who spends more time per day with one subordinate because the tasks being done temporarily require closer supervision may communicate to other subordinates, especially if time with them is temporarily reduced, that the supervisor "cares" more about what the one subordinate is doing, and perhaps will come to care more about that person than them. There may be more than a little truth in this. Sociologists have noted that it is not uncommon for positive sentiment to increase as the frequency of interaction increases, albeit with several important exceptions (including the problem of formal authority).

We sometimes experience with new friends an increase in frequency of interaction that accelerates beyond a point of equilibrium, given the importance the relationship comes to have for one or both persons. Then, if one person begins to withdraw a bit in order to adjust the frequency of contact to the kind and amount of sentiment, the other person—especially if s/he is desirous of more frequent interaction—tends to feel hurt. This hurt can lead them to react by further reducing or demanding increases in the frequency of contact, and until someone says openly what they are feeling, the cycle can proceed to the destruction of the relationship.

The scarcity of time for a person at a given moment is also his/her "cost" of time. When two people "spend" time together in any activity, communication will be strained and difficult unless the time being spent has approximately the same value for each participant. This is obvious when we by chance meet a friend in the street or hallway; if one begins to chat and the other is in a hurry, the encounter is bound to be a little awkward even if the person "short of time" explains why.

Our notion that time is scarce fits most Americans' feelings that things should be ordered, and that earlier is better than later. First born, first position, number two man, fourteenth in a class of 655, top 10 percent all assume meaning because of their position.

Early promotions in business or an advanced degree in two years instead of three are seen as praiseworthy, even if some run right by what they are trying to catch. These notions of time sequence are not inborn; they are culturally conditioned. Edward Hall reports that it takes the average child a little more than twelve years to master time and the concepts of order. I am constantly reminded of this by my young daughter, who recently asked: "But how long away is Friday?"

The point of this is, again, that time is seen as scarce, and thus whom you choose to "give your time to" is a way of measuring your sentiments. Just being more aware of this can help you recognize the usefulness of simply saying, out loud, what the meaning of your choice is for you. And, of course, such awareness also helps prevent you from assuming (without awareness of the assumption) the meanings of other persons without checking their intent.

Repetition

Finally, time has meaning for us in terms of repetition of activities. Some of our personal rhythms are so intimate and familiar to us that we are unaware of them. Most of us eat three meals a day, for example, not two, not five. The culture assumes that lunch is at noon for the most part, and this was probably defined originally in response to what people experienced in terms of hunger. But the convention also becomes a structure to which we adapt and with which we become familiar. When we experience an interruption of our pattern, we often become irritated. I can recall, for example, that I found it difficult to adjust to a change in schedule on my first teaching job. For several years as a doctoral candidate, I had had coffee at 10 o'clock with a group of congenial colleagues. The coffee hour became one of the central social functions of my day, in addition to a means of getting some caffeine into my reluctantly awakening body. When I began teaching I had a 9 o'clock and a 10 o'clock class three days a week, and I was troubled by the 10 o'clock class and adjusted by bringing a cup of coffee into class with me. The pattern was so well developed and so valued within me that I was willing to "break a norm" (and, in fact, a rule) against food in the classrooms in order to have my 10 o'clock coffee. It sounds like a small matter, and in one sense it is, but it makes my point even if it is a trivial example. There are daily cycles we are used to, and while there are many we share, there are others relatively unique to each of us. The closer to the body any repetitions of activity come, the more important they are to us.

Take seasons of the year, for example. In areas that have weather rather than climate, say, New England rather than southern California, the use of time varies from season to season as activities change. People in Boston not only put away their silver and use their stainless steel in August, but they give different kinds of parties with different time rules than they do in winter. In general, the rules are relaxed, more variety is "allowed," and time is less carefully measured for meaning.

Our rhythms are also influenced by our feasts and holidays and rituals. Christmas, Easter, Rosh Hashonah, Chanukah, Father's Day, Thanksgiving, Memorial Day, and the like, all have their "time" in the year. It has been hypothesized that Christ was really born in August, and the December celebration of his birth came about because the people in northern Europe had long had a pagan winter festival which they were used to. In any event, we are accustomed to certain activities and feelings in connection with each "special day."

Take Christmas, for example. Most businesspeople know there will be less work done just prior to and after Christmas than is usual. People experience a need for closeness, for family, for ritual, for the nostalgia of past Christmases, for gift giving and midnight services. They eat more and drink more and even get fond of their old Aunt Minny. It is a time set aside for warmth, affection, children, family, friends, and ritual.

The Greeks, however, celebrate their Easter much as we do our Christmas, and mark their Christmas almost as casually as we do our Easter. If you were to spend Christmas in Athens, you would likely sense something was missing. If you were there on Easter, you would get a "bonus." If you were in the United States working on a job that peaked in volume between December 20 and January 3, say in a post office, and you had to work long hours, the chances are you would feel quite resentful. The rhythms of our days, our weeks, our months, our years are all deeply familiar to us even if we are unaware of them. Any serious disruption of any of them is felt as deprivation. Just being aware of this can help you in many ways—planning changes, for example. Can you see why major changes in work design or location or personnel are particularly resented during the Christmas holidays?

Then, for students (and nowadays nearly everyone in the country spends at least twelve years as one, and more are spending sixteen or even eighteen), certain rhythms that matter are established. Where else in our culture do people get promoted every year for anything better than dreadful work? Where else can people choose their bosses (professors) so as to avoid certain ones, and where else can they drop one of them with no penalty after several weeks work? If you look at the assumptions students naturally take with them to work from school, you can see why the yearly immigration of graduates into business is such a trauma for both students and companies. Subculture shock is what it is.

A subsummary may help here. Basically, all I am saying is that time is important to us in many ways, that *when* you do what you do says things to others about what you feel, and that the "rules" about time vary from setting to setting. If you will just watch for one day what is going on in your life vis-à-vis time, I think you will see some interesting things. How you and others use time to communicate would make a terrific din if "talking" with time made noise.

SPACE

Space is a language just as expressive as time. Indeed, as hinted above, it is hard to separate it from the language of time, but it is useful to try.

More Is Better Than Less

The chances are good that you have seen various business organizations. The chances are even better that you found the size of offices related to the status of people there. It is rare indeed to find a company president occupying a smaller office than his subordinates, and it is not uncommon to find the top person ensconced in a suite of rooms. One of the ways we "tell" about the importance of people is by the amount of space we assign to them. Space, like time, is a scarce and limited resource.

I recall a distinguished senior professor returning to school after a long and nearly fatal illness. He was being moved from his old office to a new one in an air-conditioned new building, largely because the dean of his school believed the air conditioning would be of help to him. The professor may have thought he "heard" something else, for as I passed his office one day I found him on his hands and knees measuring his new office with a 12-inch ruler. It was a good deal smaller than his prior office, and from how he behaved later I think he was "learning" that his illness had diminished his importance to the school, so that he was reduced to a small office. It would be amusing if it were not so painful.

Another time I was being toured through a new and beautiful office building of a large corporation. The president's office was handsome indeed, but when I was taken next door to the executive vice president's office, I realized that the VP had a larger and recognizably more stunning space in which to work. I later asked my guide, an officer of the company, if the president and executive vice president had been vying for power. He looked surprised and defensively asked "Why do you ask?" I told him what I saw in the use of space. He laughed and said "Another theory bites the dust! The VP's office is better because he has charge of sales in this district and his office is our best example of what we can do for customers."

A year later the VP and president came into open conflict in seeking the support of the board of directors, and the VP left the organization. Of course, the offices were not "the" cause. But they were a signal that something was off. There are few organizations that can accept incongruence in the use of space when it communicates so clearly to hundreds of employees. In the company mentioned, I heard later, a frequent question in the executive ranks prior to the VP's departure was: "Who is running this place?"

Of course, we observe this in everyday life. We want larger houses on more land. We want lots with a view. (Although I notice few people with a picture window looking out at the view. What we want, I suspect, is mostly the illusion of an enlargement of our space.) Yet other people are more comfortable in smaller spaces. Latin people love to be awed by cathedrals and vistas in parks, but they seem to enjoy being "hugged" by smaller rooms at home and at work. The smaller space apparently is associated with warmth and touch and intimacy, while larger spaces are associated with status and power and importance. Perhaps this is why entering a huge office intimidates many of us. We almost physically inflate the person who occupies it. In any event there is a strong tendency in organizational subcultures to relate the amount of space assigned to individuals to their formal status or organizational height. Check this out around school or in any business. When the pattern does not hold, something interesting may be going on.

Private Is Better Than Public

As a doctoral candidate I was first given a desk in a large room with many other desks, then was "upgraded" to a cubicle with 6-foot walls and an open top, then to a private office. It was minuscule, but I could close it and be alone or private within it. When I began working as a professor, I shared an office with two others, then I shared it with one other, and now once again I have my own private office, roughly twice as big as my last one. Sequence and size are what matter here. It is "better" to have your own space than to share it, and it is "better" if it can be closed off for privacy than if it is open to the sight or hearing of others. And each "advantage" was distributed by rank, and by seniority within rank.

We use much the same thinking about country clubs or pools or university clubs. By excluding some others, on whatever criteria, we make it feel more private to us. And we apparently like that. The very process of exclusion marks the boundaries of our space both physically and socially, and, of course, psychologically. When we say that a person is "closed," we mean that we are excluded from him/her and vice versa. Thus, the process of defining the extent to which our various spaces are private is complex. As we set our boundaries we also exclude. And we need our own space, as we also at times need to be "open." Yet in organizations, it is clearly the rule that private offices are better than public ones. To go from a large but public office to a smaller but private one is a mixed blessing, but often the balance is favorable. For we are not like Miss Garbo who wants to be alone, but we do want to be able to be alone or private when we wish.

A powerful illustration of the value we place on privacy took place in the 1920s. A coal company in West Virginia owned the houses in which its miners lived. When the miners struck, the company took the doors off the houses. It is not hard to imagine the wrath of the miners. Another example is the automobile company that took the doors off the men's room stalls in the 1950s to discourage workers for long toilet breaks. The response in this instance was also very strong, and understandably so. When a space is designed for activity that is close to our body, we value its privacy all the more. Our free-flowing modern houses almost always have doors on at least two rooms, the bedroom and the bathroom. Perhaps that infamous "key to the executive men's room" is of more utility than arbitrary status.

Given the importance we attach to privacy, the way we use the space we have "talks" to others. If we have a private office and shut its door to speak with someone, we announce a message to that person and to those outside. We are saying "This conversation is important and not to be overheard or casually interrupted." Neither the person nor those outside know whether the news is good or bad, but they do know that you care about it and they may make unwarranted assumptions. For we close off our space for more private or personal behavior. Whether it is angry or loving, we intend to focus importantly.

Higher Is Better Than Lower

A few years ago I watched my three-year-old daughter playing "I'm the king of the castle" with friends. They laughingly fought each other for position at the top of a small steep hill. Each wanted to be on top, to be higher up than the others—in this instance, quite literally, in space. When they grow up, I fell to musing, they'll jockey for height with less laughter and more discomfort.

Perhaps our desire to be higher rather than lower is inherited from our primitive ancestors or perhaps it comes from such childlike games, or rather from the important business of being little for so long, and thus less powerful than we might wish. In any event, houses higher on the hill, from Hong Kong to Corning, are "better" (and usually more expensive) than those below. The view is often cited as the reason, but I doubt it. It's more likely a residue of our childhood that probably reaches back in evolution far beyond the Greeks, who built the Acropolis on a sharp-rising rock for protection as much as grandeur. Much as dogs still circle about before they lie to sleep (a still visible link to their wild forebears, who circled to crush tall grass into a kind of nest), we seek height for reasons in large part lost to us.

We move up in organizations, or "climb the ladder." We go up to the head office and down to the shop. We call the wealthiest people the upper classes and the poorest the lower classes. Much of our imagery for what we value is in terms of up and down. People from Boston go "down" to Maine, although it is north of Boston. Allegedly this is because early travelers were referring to tides, but it also fits the notion of some Bostonians that Boston is the apex from which one can only go down.

On a more concrete level, the ground-floor walk-in legal aid centers that have opened their doors in deprived neighborhoods are less frightening to prospective clients partly because of their ground-level location. Here again space speaks. To be higher than you is to be better than you.

Near Is Better Than Far

Really, this one can be just the reverse of what it says. It depends upon whether sentiments are positive or negative. Near is better if the sentiments are positive. Far is better if the sentiments are negative.

In a business organization, it is not uncommon for the offices near the boss to be more highly valued than those farther away. If the chief executive officer is on the third floor, the others on that floor are also assumed to be privileged. They are closer to the top person and thus have more opportunities for informal inter-action, as well as the formal designation of spatial assignment near the boss's space.

The same principle holds at formal dinner parties, where nearness to the host is valued. The farther down the table one is placed, the lower one's status at the dinner. In branch organizations that cover large territories a common problem is that each branch develops internal loyalties greater than the loyalty to the head office. The distance from the center of the organization impedes communication.

Thus when the sentiments are positive, being near is better than being far away. As I mentioned, the reverse can also be true. People prefer to increase distance when their sentiments are negative.

In Is Better Than Out

We seem to assume that people who work inside are better than those who work outside, perhaps because of the respective associations with mental and manual work. Baseball teams prefer to be in their own field, their most familiar space. Often when we are uneasy or anxious we move to our own space. In it we feel more secure.

The basic difference between in-out and near-far is that the former works from a specific point while the latter is a matter of degree. But they are closely related. For example, a few years ago a wedding was to take place in the side chapel off the main seating area of a church. The number of guests exceeded the number of seats in the chapel. So decisions needed to be made about who sat in the chapel and who sat outside it. There were thus created two "classes" of guests: those sitting inside and those sitting outside, yet within each class there was a sliding scale at work. How close to the front of your class were you seated? I can tell you those who sat at the back of the school class felt like relative "outsiders." Certainly, they were not among the "in" group.

Naturally these five dimensions of space are related. An office that is smaller but private and near an important executive may be highly desirable in spite of its size. When you consider the impact of space, you must look at the possible influence of each of the five dimensions and how they can balance each other in specific settings, as well as how they influence the use of time as a language.

Interpersonal Space

On a more personal level we have another silent language related to space. We have the general notion that we own the space around us, much like an invisible bubble. Others are to stay outside the bubble except when powerful feelings—of intimacy or anger—are being expressed. Touch is especially to be avoided in our culture, with the same exceptions. How many times have you sat next to a stranger in a movie theater and jockeyed for the single armrest? Since touching is out, it often ends up under the arm of the bolder person, who risks touch.

I recall an amusing yet painful incident at a recent cocktail party. A woman, newly arrived from Israel, was talking with an American male of Swedish descent. Her conception of the proper distance from her face to his was about half the distance he apparently felt comfortable with. She would step in, he would step back. She virtually chased him across the room before they both gave up. She dismissed him as "cold." He saw her as "pushy." Each had a different notion of the appropriateness of distance given their relationship, and neither could feel comfortable with the other's behavior.

When someone with a different notion of the use of interpersonal space steps into our bubble we feel either uncomfortable and crowded, aggressed upon and threatened, or expectant of affection. Getting that close in the United States is for many a hit-or-kiss affair.

In addition, in our mouthwashed, deodorant-using culture the idea of smelling another's body or breath is often thought to be repugnant. The experience is avoided except in lovemaking, and even there many perfume away all traces of personal odor. Yet some people enjoy being close enough to others in public settings to feel their body warmth and smell their natural odors, and they touch others more often that we do. When we meet such people we have a terrible time because they "say" things, in the way they use space, that we do not appreciate or understand. They, in turn find us as difficult as we find them.

Yet within this huge country there are many subgroups with variations in their use of interpersonal space. Men walking down the street in the Italian district of Boston often do so arm-in-arm, something one would seldom, if ever, see around most universities in the Boston area. And in any large business organization, you can see the effects of variations in the use of space complicating relationships. A warm, expressive executive who feels comfortable touching the arm or shoulder of a subordinate may make him exceedingly uncomfortable if he is the nontouch, keep-your-distance type. You can watch your own behavior here to see how you use your own space and how you react to others who behave differently. Just being aware of it helps a great deal.

Since the American experience of small, body warmth, and touch is so poorly developed, most of what we say to each other using these media does not take place in our awareness. But it does take place. Communication by smell, largely a chemical process, is far more extensive than we think. Edward Hall reports that in discussing olfactory messages with a psychoanalyst, a skillful therapist with an unusual record of success, he learned that the therapist could clearly distinguish the smell of anger in patients at a distance of 6 feet or more. Schizophrenic patients are reputed to have a characteristic odor and Dr. Kathleen Smith of St. Louis has demonstrated that rats readily distinguish between the smell of a schizophrenic and a nonschizophrenic. If chemical messages are this powerful, one wonders how many of what we consider to be well-hidden feelings are being "telegraphed" by the smells we are unable to disguise.

If smell as a communicator is out of awareness, how much more so is the skin as a major sense organ. Yet the skin has remarkable thermal characteristics and apparently has an extraordinary capacity both to emit and detect infrared heat. Under stress or strong emotion, we can send out thermal messages which can be "read" by perceptive individuals (usually spouses, lovers, or children) who can get within 2 feet. Getting "red in the face" in anger or embarrassment or sexual arousal is so common we hardly think about it. Yet the coloration of skin talks, too.

In summary, remember that people use space to say things they are often unaware of, but highly responsive to. To the extent that you can become more aware of your own behavior and that of others, you can be more skillful at "saying" what you mean to others and "hearing" what they mean. It is a fascinating exploration.

THINGS

This aspect of communication is so easily grasped that I will just briefly present 10 rather obvious generalizations. Each points to what I see as a major assumption operating in our culture. Each naturally has exceptions, and each interacts with the others much as the various dimensions of space modify outcomes, and relate to time.

1. *Bigger is better than smaller.* Until recently, the automobile has been a good example in the United States. Except for small sports cars, bigger cars (which, see below, are often more expensive) were generally regarded as better than smaller.
2. *More is better than fewer.* Two cars, houses, etc., are better than one.
3. *Clean is better than dirty.* The American fetish under attack.
4. *Neat and orderly is better than messy and disorderly.* A clean desk may communicate efficiency, while a messy one may "say" you are disorganized in many settings.
5. *Expensive is better than cheap.* Original works of art are "better" than reproductions.
6. *Unique is better than common.* Ditto.
7. *Beautiful is better than ugly.* Ditto.
8. *Accurate is better than inaccurate.* Back to Acutron.
9. *Very old or very new is better than recent.* Victorian furnishings are now becoming "old" enough to be of increasing value after 60 years of being "recent."
10. *Personal is better than public.* One's own object, say, chair or desk, is valued as a possession. In offices, as in homes, the boss or host often has "his" chair and others usually stay out of it. The news photo of a student sitting in the chair of the president of Columbia University during the 1969 uprising was used so often because it showed someone breaking this "rule."

SUMMARY

Just as the various aspects of space are interrelated (remember the small but private office near the boss?) and influence the uses of time as language, so, too, do both overlap with our use of things. If that same office near the boss has an expensive, one-of-a-kind Persian rug and antique furniture, it can become even more valued, even though it is small.

The way we and others use time and space and things talks. If you are deaf to the messages, you miss much of the richness of what is being said by you and others. If you start "listening" consciously, you can begin to appreciate more of the subtle languages that are in use and thus gradually increase your personal intuitive skill in being with other persons in and out of organizations.

REFERENCES

Hall, Edward, J. *The Silent Dimension*. New York: Premier Paperback, 1961.
Hall, Edward J. *The Hidden Dimension*. New York: Doubleday, 1966.
Sommer, Robert. *Personal Space: The Behavioral Basis of Design*. Englewood Cliffs, N.J.: Prentice-Hall, 1966.,
Steele, Fred I. *Physical Settings and Organization Development*. Reading, Mass.: Addison-Wesley, 1973.

DEFENSIVE COMMUNICATION

Jack R. Gibb

One way to understand communication is to view it as a people process rather than as a language process. If one is to make fundamental improvement in communication, he must make changes in interpersonal relationships. One possible type of alteration—and the one with which this paper is concerned—is that of reducing the degree of defensiveness.

DEFINITION AND SIGNIFICANCE

"Defensive behavior" is behavior which occurs when an individual perceives threat or anticipates threat in the group. The person who behaves defensively, even though he also gives some attention to the common task, devotes an appreciable portion of his energy to defending himself. Besides talking about the topic, he thinks about how he appears to others, how he may be seen more favorably, how he may win, dominate, impress or escape punishment, and/or how he may avoid or mitigate a perceived or anticipated attack.

Source: Reprinted from the *Journal of Communication,* XI, No. 3 (September 1961), 141–48, by permission of the author and the publisher.

Such inner feelings and outward acts tend to create similarly defensive postures in others; and, if unchecked, the ensuing circular response becomes increasingly destructive. Defensive behavior, in short, engenders defensive listening, and this in turn produces postural, facial, and verbal cues which raise the defense level of the original communicator.

Defensive arousal prevents the listener from concentrating upon the message. Not only do defensive communicators send off multiple value, motive, and affect cues, but also defensive recipients distort what they receive. As a person becomes more and more defensive, he becomes less and less able to perceive accurately the motives, the values, and the emotions of the sender. The writer's analyses of tape recorded discussions revealed that increases in defensive behavior were correlated positively with losses in efficiency in communication.[1] Specifically, distortions became greater when defensive states existed in the groups.

The converse also is true. The more "supportive" or defense reductive the climate the less the receiver reads into the communication distorted loadings which arise from projections of his own anxieties, motives, and concerns. As defenses are reduced, the receivers become better able to concentrate upon the structure, the content, and the cognitive meanings of the message.

CATEGORIES OF DEFENSIVE AND SUPPORTIVE COMMUNICATION

In working over an eight-year period with recordings of discussions occurring in varied settings, the writer developed the six pairs of defensive and supportive categories presented in Table 1. Behavior which a listener perceives as possessing any of the characteristics listed in the left-hand column arouses defensiveness, whereas that which he interprets as having any of the qualities designated as supportive reduces defensive feelings. The degree to which these reactions occur depend upon the personal level of defensiveness and upon the general climate in the group at the time.[2]

TABLE 1 Categories of Behavior Characteristic of Supportive and Defensive Climates in Small Groups

Defensive Climates	Supportive Climates
1. Evaluation	1. Description
2. Control	2. Problem orientation
3. Strategy	3. Spontaneity
4. Neutrality	4. Empathy
5. Superiority	5. Equality
6. Certainty	6. Provisionalism

[1] J. R. Gibb, "Defense Level and Influence in Small Groups," in *Leadership and Interpersonal Behavior,* ed. L. Petrullo and B. M. Bass (New York: Holt, Rinehart & Winston, 1961), pp. 66–81.

[2] J. R. Gibb, "Sociopsychological Processes of Group Instruction," in *The Dynamics of Instructional Groups,* ed. N. B. Henry (Fifty-ninth Yearbook of the National Society for the Study of Education, Part II, 1960), pp. 115–35.

Evaluation and Description

Speech or other behavior which appears evaluative increases defensiveness. If by expression, manner of speech, tone of voice, or verbal content of the sender seems to be evaluating or judging the listener, then the receiver goes on guard. Of course, other factors may inhibit the reaction. If the listener thinks that the speaker regards him as an equal and is being open and spontaneous, for example, the evaluativeness in a message will be neutralized and perhaps not even perceived. This same principle applies equally to the other five categories of potentially defense-producing climates. The six sets are interactive.

Because our attitudes toward other persons are frequently, and often necessarily, evaluative, expressions which the defensive person will regard as non-judgmental are hard to frame. Even the simplest question usually conveys the answer that the sender wishes or implies the response that would fit into his value system. A mother, for example, immediately following an earth tremor that shook the house, sought for her small son with the quesion: "Bobby, where are you?" The timid and plaintive "Mommy, I didn't do it" indicated how Bobby's chronic mild defensiveness predisposed him to react with a projection of his own guilt and in the context of his chronic assumption that questions are full of accusation.

Anyone who has attempted to train professionals to use information-seeking speech with neutral affect appreciates how difficult it is to teach a person to say even the simple "Who did that?" without being seen as accusing. Speech is so frequently judgmental that there is a reality base for the defensive interpretations which are so common.

When insecure, group members are particularly likely to place blame, to see others as fitting into categories of good or bad, to make moral judgments of their colleagues, and to question the value, motive, and affect loadings of the speech which they hear. Since value loadings imply a judgment of others, a belief that the standards of the speaker differ from his own causes the listener to become defensive.

Descriptive speech, in contrast to that which is evaluative, tends to arouse a minimum of uneasiness. Speech acts which the listener perceives as genuine requests for information or as material with neutral loadings is descriptive. Specifically, presentations of feelings, events, perceptions, or processes which do not ask or imply that the receiver change behavior or attitude are minimally defense-producing. The difficulty in avoiding overtone is illustrated by the problems of news reporters in writing stories about unions, Communists, Negroes, and religious activities without tipping off the "party" line of the newspaper. One can often tell from the opening words in a news article which side the newspaper's editorial policy favors.

Control and Problem Orientation

Speech which is used to control the listener evokes resistance. In most of our social intercourse someone is trying to do something to someone else—to change an attitude, to influence behavior, or to restrict the field of activity. The degree to which attempts to control produce defensiveness depends upon the openness of the effort, for a suspicion that hidden motives exist heightens resistance. For this reason attempts of non-directive therapists and progressive educators to refrain from imposing a set of values, a point of view, or a problem solution upon the receivers meet with many barriers. Since the norm is control, non-controllers must earn the perceptions that their efforts have no hidden motives. A bombardment of persuasive "messages" in the fields of politics, education, special causes, advertising, religion, medicine, industrial relations, and guidance has bred cynical and paranoidal responses in listeners.

Implicit in all attempts to alter another person is the assumption by the change agent that the person to be altered is inadequate. That the speaker secretly views the listener as ignorant, unable to make his own decisions, uninformed, immature, unwise, or possessed of wrong or inadequate attitudes is a subconscious perception which gives the latter a valid base for defensive reactions.

Methods of control are many and varied. Legalistic insistence on detail, restrictive regulations and policies, conformity norms, and all laws are among the methods. Gestures, facial expressions, other forms of non-verbal communication, and even such simple acts as holding a door open in a particular manner are means of imposing one's will upon another and hence are potential sources of resistance.

Problem orientation, on the other hand, is the antithesis of persuasion. When the sender communicates a desire to collaborate in defining a mutual problem and in seeking its solution, he tends to create the same problem orientation in the listener; and, of greater importance, he implies that he has no predetermined solution, attitude, or method to impose. Such behavior is permissive in that it allows the receiver to set his own goals, make his own decisions, and evaluate his own progress—or to share with the sender in doing so. The exact methods of attaining permissiveness are not known, but they must involve a constellation of cues, and they certainly go beyond mere verbal assurances that the communicator has no hidden desires to exercise control.

Strategy and Spontaneity

When the sender is perceived as engaged in a strategem involving ambiguous and multiple motivations, the receiver becomes defensive. No one wishes to be a guinea pig, a role player, or an impressed actor, and no one likes to be the victim of some hidden motivation. That which is concealed, also, may appear larger than it really is, with the degree of defensiveness of the listener determining the perceived size of the suppressed element. The intense reaction of the reading audience to the material in the *Hidden Persuaders* indicates the prevalence of defensive reactions to multiple motivations behind strategy. Group members who are seen as "taking a role," as feigning emotion, as toying with their colleagues, as withholding information, or as having special sources of data are especially resented. One participant once complained that another was "using a listening technique" on him!

A large part of the adverse reaction to much of the so-called human relations training is a feeling against what are perceived as gimmicks and tricks to fool or to "involve" people, to make a person think he is making his own decision, or to make the listener feel that the sender is genuinely interested in him as a person. Particularly violent reactions occur when it appears that someone is trying to make a stratagem appear spontaneous. One person has reported a boss who incurred resentment by habitually using the gimmick of "spontaneously" looking at his watch and saying. "My gosh, look at the time—I must run to an appointment." The belief was that the boss would create less irritation by honestly asking to be excused.

Similarly, the deliberate assumption of guilelessness and natural simplicity is especially resented. Monitoring the tapes of feedback and evaluation sessions in training groups indicates the surprising extent to which members perceive the strategies of their colleagues. This perceptual clarity may be quite shocking to the strategist, who usually feels that he has cleverly hidden the motivational aura around the "gimmick."

This aversion to deceit may account for one's resistance to politicians who are suspected of behind-the-scenes planning to get his vote; to psychologists whose listening apparently is motivated by more than the manifest or content-level interest in his behavior, or to the sophisticated, smooth, or clever person whose "oneupmanship" is marked with guile. In training groups the role-flexible person frequently is resented because his changes in behavior are perceived as strategic maneuvers.

Conversely, behavior which appears to be spontaneous and free of deception is defense reductive. If the communicator is seen as having a clean id, as having uncomplicated motivations, as being straightforward and honest, and as behaving spontaneously in response to the situation, he is likely to arouse minimal defense.

Neutrality and Empathy

When neutrality in speech appears to the listener to indicate a lack of concern for his welfare, he becomes defensive. Group members usually desire to be perceived as valued persons, as individuals of special worth, and as objects of concern and affection. The clinical, detached, person-is-an-object-of-study attitude on the part of many psychologist-trainers is resented by group members. Speech with low affect that communicates little warmth or caring is in such contrast with the affect-laden speech in social situations that it sometimes communicates rejection.

Communication that conveys empathy for the feelings and respect for the worth of the listener, is partiuclarly supportive and defense reductive. Reassurance results when a message indicates that the speaker identifies himself with the listener's problems, shares his feelings, and accepts his emotional reactions at face value. Abortive efforts to deny the legitimacy of the receiver's emotions by assuring the receiver that he need not feel bad, that he should not feel rejected, or that he is overly anxious, though often intended as support giving, may impress the listener as lack of acceptance. The combination of understanding and empathizing with the other person's emotions with no accompanying effort to change him apparently is supportive at a high level.

The importance of gestural behavior cues in communicating empathy should be mentioned. Apparaently spontaneous facial and bodily evidences of concern are often interpreted as especially valid evidence of deep-level acceptance.

Superiority and Equality

When a person communicates to another that he feels superior in position, power, wealth, intellectual ability, physical characteristics, or other ways, he arouses defensiveness. Here, as with the other sources of disturbance, whatever arouses feelings of inadequacy causes the listener to center upon the affect loading of the statement rather than upon the cognitive elements. The receiver then reacts by not hearing the message, by forgetting it, by competing with the sender, or by becoming jealous of him.

The person who is perceived as feeling superior communiates that he is not willing to enter into a shared problem-solving relationship, that he probably does not desire feedback, that he does not require help, and/or that he will be likely to try to reduce the power, the status, or the worth of the receiver.

Many ways exist for creating the atmosphere that the sender feels himself equal to the listener. Defenses are reduced when one perceives the sender as being willing to enter into participative planning with mutual trust and respect. Differences in talent, ability, worth, appearance, status, and power often exist, but the low defense communicator seems to attach little importance to these distinctions.

Certainty and Provisionalism

The effects of dogmatism in producing defensiveness are well known. Those who seem to know the answers, to require no additional data, and to regard themselves as teachers rather than as co-workers tend to put others on guard. Moreover, in the writer's experiment, listeners often perceived manifest expressions of certainty as connoting inward feelings of inferiority. They saw the dogmatic individual as needing to be right, as wanting to win an argument rather than solve a problem, and as seeing his ideas as truths to be defended. This kind of behavior often was associated with acts which others regarded as attempts to exercise control. People who were right seemed to have low tolerance for members who were "wrong"—i.e., who did not agree with the sender.

One reduces the defensiveness of the listener when he communicates that he is willing to experiment with his own behavior, attitudes, and ideas. The person who appears to be taking provisional attitudes, to be investigating issues rather than taking sides on them, to be problem solving rather than debating, and to be willing to experiment and explore tends to communiate that the listener may have some control over the shared quest or the investigation of the ideas. If a person is genuinely searching for information and data, he does not resent help or company along the way.

CONCLUSION

The implications of the above material for the parent, the teacher, the manager, the administrator, or the therapist are fairly obvious. Arousing defensiveness interferes with communication and thus makes it difficult—and sometimes impossible—for anyone to convey ideas clearly and to move effectively toward the solution of therapeutic, educational, or managerial problems.

7
Interpersonal Perception

COMMUNICATION REVISITED
Jay Hall

PERCEPTION: IMPLICATIONS FOR ADMINISTRATION
Sheldon S. Zalkind
Timothy W. Costello

COMMUNICATION REVISITED

Jay Hall

High on the diagnostic checklist of corporate health is communication; and the prognosis is less than encouraging. In a recent cross-cultural study,[1] roughly 74 percent of the managers sampled from companies in Japan, Great Britain, and the United States cited communication breakdown as the single greatest barrier to corporate excellence.

Just what constitutes a problem of communication is not easily agreed upon. Some theorists approach the issue from the vantage point of information bits comprising a message; others speak in terms of organizational roles and positions of centrality or peripherality; still others emphasize the directional flows of corporate data. The result is that more and more people are communicating about communication, while the achievement of clarity, understanding, commitment, and creativity—the goals of communication—becomes more and more limited.

More often than not, the communication dilemmas cited by people are not communication problems at all. They are instead *symptoms of* difficulties at more basic and fundamental levels of corporate life. From a dynamic standpoint, prob-

Source: ©1973 by the Regents of the University of California. Reprinted from the *California Management Review,* Vol. 15, No. 3. By permission of The Regents.

lems of communication in organizations frequently reflect dysfunctions at the level of *corporate climate.* The feelings people have about where or with whom they work—feelings of impotence, distrust, resentment, insecurity, social inconsequence, and all the other very human emotions—not only define the climate which prevails but the manner in which communciations will be managed. R. R. Blake and Jane S. Mouton[2] have commented upon an oddity of organizational life: when management is effective and relationships are sound, problems of communciation tend not to occur. It is only when relationships among members of the organization are unsound and fraught with unarticulated tensions that one hears complaints of communication breakdown. Thus, the quality of relationships in an organiza- tion may dictate to a great extent the level of communication effectiveness achieved.

INTERPERSONAL STYLES
AND THE QUALITY OF RELATIONSHIPS

The critical factor underlying relationship quality in organizations is in need of review. Reduced to its lowest common denominator, the most significant deter- minant of the quality of relationships is the interpersonal style of the parties to a relationship. The learned, characteristic, and apparently preferred manner in which individuals relate to others in the building of relationships—the manner in which they monitor, control, filter, divert, give and seek the information germane to a given relationship—will dictate over time the quality of relationships which exist among people, the emotional climate which will characterize their interactions, and whether or not there will be problems of communication. In the final analysis, individuals are the human links in the corporate network, and the styles they employ interpersonally are the ultimate determinants of what information goes where and whether it will be distortion-free or masked by interpersonal constraints.

The concept of interpersonal style is not an easy one to define; yet, if it is to serve as the central mechanism underlying the quality of relationships, the nature of corporate climate, managerial effectiveness, and the level of corporate excellence attainable, it is worthy of analysis. Fortunately, Joseph Luft[3] and Harry Ingham— two behavioral scientists with special interests in interpersonal and group processes—have developed a model of social interaction which affords a way of thinking about interpersonal functioning, while handling much of the data encountered in everyday living. The Johari Window, as their model is called, iden- tifies several interpersonal styles, their salient features and consequences, and suggests a basis for interpreting the significance of style for the quality of relation- ships. An overview of the Johari model should help to sharpen the perception of interpersonal practices among managers and lend credence to the contention of Blake and Mouton that there are few communication problems as such, only un- sound relationships. At the same time, a normative statement regarding effective interpersonal functioning and, by extension, the foundations of corporate excellence may be found in the model as well. Finally, the major tenets of the model are testable under practical conditions, and the latter portion of this discussion will be devoted to research on the managerial profile in interpersonal encounters. The author has taken a number of interpretive liberties with the basic provisions of the Johari Awareness model. While it is anticipated that none of these violate the integrity of the model as originally described by Luft, it should be emphasized that many of the inferences and conclusions discussed are those of the author, and Dr. Luft should not be held accountable for any lapses of logic or misapplications of the model in this paper.

THE JOHARI WINDOW: A GRAPHIC
MODEL OF INTERPERSONAL PROCESSES

As treated here, the Johari Window is essentially an information processing model; interpersonal style and individual effectiveness are assessed in terms of information processing tendencies and the performance consequences thought to be associated with such practices. The model employs a four celled figure as its format and reflects the interaction of two interpersonal sources of information—Self and Others—and the behavioral processes required for utilizing that information. The model, depicted in Figure 1, may be thought of as representing the various kinds of data available for use in the establishment of interpersonal relationships. The squared field, in effect, represents a personal space. This in turn is partitioned into four regions, with each representing a particular combination or mix of relevant information and having special significance for the quality of relationships. To fully appreciate the implications that each informational region has for interpersonal effectiveness, one must consider not only the size and shape of each region but also the reasons for its presence in the interpersonal space. In an attempt to "personalize" the model, it is helpful to think of oneself as the *Self* in the relationship for, as will be seen presently, it is what the Self does interpersonally that has the most direct impact on the quality of resulting relationships. In organizational

FIGURE 1 The Johari Window: A Model of Interpersonal Processes

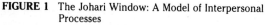

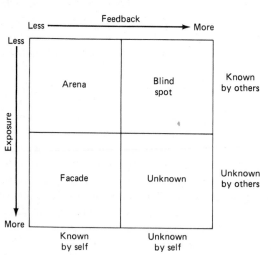

terms, it is how the management-Self behaves that is critical to the quality of corporate relationships.

Figure 1 reveals that the two informational sources, Self and Others, have information which is pertinent to the relationship and, at the same time, each lacks information that is equally germane. Thus, there is relevant and necessary information which is *Known by the Self, Unknown by the Self, Known by Others* and *Unknown by Others.* The Self/Other combinations of known and unknown information make up the four regions within the interpersonal space and, again, characterize the various types and qualities of relationships possible within the Johari framework.

Region I, for example, constitutes that portion of the total interpersonal space which is devoted to mutually held information. This Known by Self-Known by Others facet of the interpersonal space is thought to be the part of the relationship which, because of its shared data characteristics and implied likelihood of mutual understanding, controls interpersonal productivity. That is, the working assumption is that productivity and interpersonal effectiveness are directly related to the amount of mutually held information in a relationship. Therefore, the larger Region I becomes, the more rewarding, effective, and productive the relationship. As the informational context for interpersonal functioning, Region I is called the "Arena."

Region II, using the double classification approach just described, is that portion of the interpersonal space which holds information Known by Others but Unknown by the Self. Thus, this array of data constitutes an interpersonal handicap for the Self, since one can hardly understand the behaviors, decisions, or potentials of others if he doesn't have the data upon which these are based. Others have the advantage of knowing their own reactions, feelings, perceptions, and the like while the Self is unaware of these. Region II, an area of hidden unperceived information, is called the "Blindspot." The Blindspot is, of course, a limiting factor with respect to the size of Region I and may be thought of, therefore, as inhibiting interpersonal effectiveness.

Region III may also be considered to inhibit interpersonal effectiveness, but it is due to an imbalance of information which would seem to favor the Self; as the portion of the relationship which is characterized by information Known by the Self but Unknown by Others, Region III constitutes a protective feature of the relationship for the Self. Data which one perceives as potentially prejudicial to a relationship or which he keeps to himself out of fear, desire for power, or whatever, make up the "Facade." This protective front, in turn, serves a defensive function for the Self. The question is not one of whether a Facade is necessary but rather how much Facade is required realistically; this raises the question of how much conscious defensiveness can be tolerated before the Arena becomes too inhibited and interpersonal effectiveness begins to diminish.

Finally, Region IV constitutes that portion of the relationship which is devoted to material neither known by the self nor by other parties to the relationship. The information in this Unknown by Self-Unknown by Others area is thought to reflect psychodynamic data, hidden potential, unconscious idiosyncrasies, and the database of creativity. Thus, Region IV is the "Unknown" area which may become known as interpersonal effectiveness increases.

Summarily, it should be said that the information within all regions can be of any type—feeling data, factual information, assumptions, task skill data, and prejudices—which are relevant to the relationship at hand. Irrelevant data are not the focus of the Johari Window concept: just those pieces of information which have a bearing on the quality and productivity of the relationship should be considered as appropriate targets for the information processing practices prescribed by the model. At the same time, it should be borne in mind that the individuals involved in a relationship, particularly the Self, control what and how information will be processed. Because of this implicit personal control aspect, the model should be viewed as an open system which is *dynamic* and amendable to change as personal decisions regarding interpersonal functioning change.

BASIC INTERPERSONAL PROCESSES: EXPOSURE AND FEEDBACK

The dynamic character of the model is critical; for it is the movement capability of the horizontal and vertical lines which partition the interpersonal space into regions which gives individuals control over what their relationships will become. The Self can significantly influence the size of his Arena in relating to others by the behavioral processes he employs in establishing relationships. To the extent that one takes the steps necessary to apprise others of relevant information which he has and they do not, he is enlarging his Arena in a downward direction. Within the framework of the model, this enlargement occurs in concert with a reduction of one's Facade. Thus, if one behaves in a non-defensive, trusting, and possibly risk taking manner with others, he may be thought of as contributing to increased mutual awareness and sharing of data. The process one employs toward this end has been called the "Exposure" process. It entails the open and candid disclosure of one's feelings, factual knowledge, wild guesses, and the like in a conscious attempt to share. Frothy, intentionally untrue, diversionary sharing does not constitute exposure; and, as personal experience will attest, it does nothing to help mutual understanding. The Exposure process is under the direct control of the Self and may be used as a mechanism for building trust and for legitimizing mutual exposures.

The need for mutual exposures becomes apparent when one considers the behavioral process required for enlarging the Arena laterally. As a behavior designed to gain reduction in one's Blindspot, the Feedback process entails an active solicitation by the Self of the information he feels others might have which he does not. The active, initiative-taking aspect of this solicitation behavior should be stressed, for again the Self takes the primary role in setting interpersonal norms and in legitimizing certain acts within the relationship. Since the extent to which the Self will actually receive the Feedback he solicits is contingent upon the willingness of others to expose their data, the need for a climate of mutual exposures becomes apparent. Control by the Self of the success of his Feedback-seeking behaviors is less direct therefore than in the case of self-exposure. He will achieve a reduction of his Blindspot only with the cooperation of others; and his own prior willingness to deal openly and candidly may well dictate what level of cooperative and trusting behavior will prevail on the part of other parties to the relationship.

Thus, one can theoretically establish interpersonal relationships characterized by mutual understanding and increased effectiveness (by a dominant Arena) if he will engage in exposing and feedback soliciting behaviors to an optimal degree. This places the determination of productivity and amount of interpersonal reward—and the quality of relationships—directly in the hands of the Self. In theory, this amounts to an issue of interpersonal competence; in practice, it amounts to the conscious and sensitive management of interpersonal processes.

INTERPERSONAL STYLES
AND MANAGERIAL IMPACTS

While one can theoretically employ Exposure and Feedback processes not only to a great but to a similar degree as well, individuals typically fail to achieve such an optimal practice. Indeed, they usually display a significant preference for one or the other of the two processes and tend to overuse one while neglecting the other. This tendency promotes a state of imbalance in interpersonal relationships which, in turn, creates disruptive tensions capable of retarding productivity. Figure 2 presents several commonly used approaches to the employment of Exposure and Feedback processes. Each of these may be thought of as reflecting a basic interpersonal style—that is, fairly consistent and preferred ways of behaving interpersonally. As might be expected, each style has associated with it some fairly predictable consequences

FIGURE 2 Interpersonal Styles as Functions of Exposure Use and Feedback Solicitation

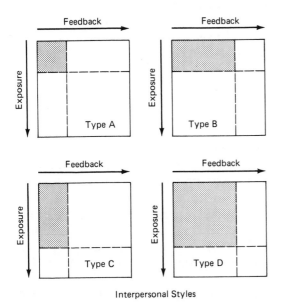

Interpersonal Styles

Type A. This interpersonal style reflects a minimal use of both Exposure and Feedback processes; it is a fairly impersonal approach to interpersonal relationships. The Unknown region dominates under this style; and unrealized potential, untapped creativity, and personal psychodynamics prevail as the salient influences. Such a style would seem to indicate withdrawal and an aversion to risk-taking on the part of its user; interpersonal anxiety and safety-seeking are likely to be prime sources of personal motivation. Persons who characteristically use this style appear to be detached, mechanical, and uncommunicative. They may often be found in bureaucratic highly structured organizations of some type where it is possible, and perhaps profitable, to avoid personal disclosure or involvement. People using this style are likely to be reacted to with more than average hostility, since other parties to the relationship will tend to interpret the lack of Exposure and Feedback solicitation largely according to their own needs and how this interpersonal lack affects need fulfillment.

Subordinates whose manager employs such a style, for example, will often feel that his behavior is consciously aimed at frustrating them in their work. The person in need of support and encouragement will often view a Type A manager as aloof, cold, and indifferent. Another individual in need of firm directions and plenty of order in his work may view the same manager as indecisive and administratively impotent. Yet another person requiring freedom and opportunities to be innovative may see the Type A interpersonal style as hopelessly tradition-bound and as symptomatic of fear and an overriding need for security. The user of Type A behaviors on a large scale in an organization reveals something about the climate and fundamental health of that organization. In many respects, interpersonal relationships founded on Type A uses of exposure and feedback constitute the kind of organizational ennui about which Chris Argyris[4] has written so eloquently. Such practices are, in his opinion, likely to be learned ways of behaving under oppressive policies of the sort which encourage people to act in a submissive and dependent fashion. Organizationally, of course, the result is lack of communication and a loss of human potentials; the Unknown becomes the dominant feature of corporate relationships, and the implications for organizational creativity and growth are obvious.

Type B. Under this approach, there is also an aversion to Exposure, but aversion is coupled with a desire for relationships not found in Type A. Thus, Feedback is the only process left in promoting relationships and it is much overused. An aversion to the use of Exposure may typically be interpreted as a sign of basic mistrust of self and others, and it is therefore not surprising that the Facade is the dominant feature of relationships resulting from neglected Exposure coupled with overused Feedback. The style appears to be a probing supportive interpersonal ploy and, once the Facade becomes apparent, it is likely to result in a reciprocal withdrawal of trust by other parties. This may promote feelings of suspicion on the part of others: such feelings may lead to the manager being treated as a rather superficial person without real substance or as a devious sort with many hidden agenda.

Preference for this interpersonal style among managers seems to be of two types. Some managers committed to a quasi-permissive management may employ Type B behaviors in an attempt to avoid appearing directive. Such an approach results in the manager's personal resources never being fully revealed or his opinions being expressed. In contrast—but subject to many of the same inadequacies—is the use of Type B behaviors in an attempt to gain or maintain one's personal power in relationships. Many managers build a facade to maintain personal control and an outward appearance of confidence. As the Johari model would suggest, however, persons who employ such practices tend to become isolated from their subordinates and colleagues alike. Lack of trust predominates and consolidation of power and promotion of an image of confidence may be the least likely results of Type B use in organizations. Very likely, the seeds of distrust and conditions for covert competitiveness—with all the implications for organizational teamwork—will follow from widespread use of Type B interpersonal practices.

Type C. Based on a overuse of Exposure to the neglect of Feedback, this interpersonal style may reflect ego-striving and/or distrust of others' competence. The person who uses this style usually feels quite confident of his own opinions and is likely to value compliance from others. The fact that he is often unaware of his impact or of the potential of others' contributions is reflected in the dominant Blindspot which results from this style. Others are likely to feel disenfranchised by one who uses this style; they often feel that he has little use for their contributions or concern for their feelings. As a result, this style often triggers feelings of hostility, insecurity, and resentment on the part of others. Frequently, others will learn to perpetuate the manager's Blindspot by witholding important information or giving only selected feedback; as such, this is a reflection of the passive-aggressiveness and unarticulated hostility which this style can cause. Labor-management relations frequently reflect such Blindspot dynamics.

The Type C interpersonal style is probably what has prompted so much interest in "listening" programs around the country. As the Johari model makes apparent, however, the Type C over-use of Exposure and neglect of Feedback is just one of several interpersonal tendencies that may disrupt communications. While hierarchical organizational structure or centrality in communication nets and the like may certainly facilitate the use of individual Type C behaviors, so can fear of failure, authoritarianism, need for control, and over-confidence in one's own opinions; such traits vary from person to person and limit the utility of communication panaceas. Managers who rely on this style often do so to demonstrate competence; many corporate cultures require that the manager be *the* planner, director, and controller and many managers behave accordingly to protect their corporate images. Many others are simply trying to be helpful in a paternalistic kind of way; others are, of course, purely dictatorial. Whatever the reasons, those who employ the Type C style have one thing in common: their relationships will be dominated by Blindspots and they are destined for surprise whenever people get enough and decide to force feedback on them, solicited or not.

Type D. Balanced Exposure and Feedback processes are used to a great extent in this style; candor, openness, and a sensitivity to others' needs to participate are the salent features of the style. The Arena is the dominant characteristic, and productivity increases. In initial stages, this style may promote some defensiveness on the part of others who are not familiar with honest and trusting relationships; but perserverance will tend to promote a norm of reciprocal candor over time in which creative potential can be realized.

Among managers, Type D practices constitute an ideal state from the standpoint of organizational effectiveness. Healthy and creative climates result from its widespread use, and the conditions for growth and corporate excellence may be created through the use of constructive Exposure and Feedback exchanges. Type D practices do not give license to "clobber," as some detractors might claim; and, for optimal results, the data explored should be germane to the relationships and problems at hand, rather than random intimacies designed to overcome self-consciousness. Trust is slowly built, and managers who experiment with Type D processes should be prepared to be patient and flexible in their relationships. Some managers, as they tentatively try out Type D strategies, encounter reluctance and distrust on the part of others, with the result that they frequently give up too soon, assuming that the style doesn't work. The reluctance of others should be assessed against the backdrop of previous management practices and the level of prior trust which characterizes the culture. Other managers may try candor only to discover that they have opened a Pandora's box from which a barrage of hostility and complaints emerges. The temptation of the naive manager is to put the lid back on quickly; but the more enlightened manager knows that when communications are opened up after having been closed for a long time, the most emotionally laden issues—ones which have been the greatest sources of frustration, anger, or fear—will be the first to be discussed. If management can resist cutting the dialogue short, the diatribe will run its course as the emotion underlying it is drained off, and exchanges will become more problem centered and future oriented. Management intent will have been tested and found worthy of trust, and creative unrestrained interchanges will occur. Organizations built on such practices are those headed for corporate climates and resource utilization of the type necessary for true corporate excellence. The manager's interpersonal style may well be the catalyst for this reaction to occur.

Summarily, the Johari Window model of interpersonal processes suggests that much more is needed to understand communication in an organization than information about its structure or one's position in a network. People make very critical decisions about what information will be processed, irrespective of structural and network considerations. People bring with them to organizational settings propensities for behaving in certain ways interpersonally. They prefer certain interpersonal styles, sharpened and honed by corporate cultures, which significantly influence—if not dictate entirely—the flow of information in organizations. As such, individuals and their preferred styles of relating one to another amount to the synapses in the corporate network which control and coordinate the human system. Central to an understanding of communication in organizations, therefore, is an appreciation of the complexities of those human interfaces which comprise organizations. The work of Luft and Ingham, when brought to bear on management practices and corporate cultures, may lend much needed insight into the constraints unique to organizational life which either hinder or facilitate the processing of corporate data.

RESEARCH ON THE MANAGERIAL PROFILE:
THE PERSONNEL RELATIONS SURVEY

As treated here, one of the major tenets of the Johari Window model is that one's use of Exposure and Feedback soliciting processes is a matter of personal decision. Whether consciously or unconsciously, when one employs either process or fails to do so he has decided that such practices somehow serve the goals he has set for himself. Rationales for particular behavior are likely to be as varied as the goals people seek; they may be in the best sense of honest intent or they may simply represent evasive logic or systems of self-deception. The *purposeful* nature of interpersonal styles remains nevertheless. A manager's style of relating to other members of the organization is never simply a collection of random, unconsidered acts. Whether he realizes it or not, or admits it or denies it, his interpersonal style *has purpose* and is thought to serve either a personal or interpersonal goal in his relationships.

Because of the element of decision and purposeful intent inherent in one's interpersonal style, the individual's inclination to employ Exposure and Feedback processes may be assessed. That is, his decisions to engage in open and candid behaviors or to actively seek out the information that others are thought to have may be sampled, and his Exposure and Feedback tendencies thus measured. Measurements obtained may be used in determining the manager's or the organization's Johari Window configuration and the particular array of interpersonal predilections which underlie it. Thus, the Luft-Ingham model not only provides a way of conceptualizing what is going on interpersonally, but it affords a rationale for actually assessing practices which may, in turn, be coordinated to practical climate and cultural issues.

Hall and Williams have designed a paper-and-pencil instrument for use with managers which reveals their preferences for Exposure and Feedback in their relationships with subordinates, colleagues, and superiors. The *Personnel Regulations Survey*,[5] as the instrument is entitled, has been used extensively by industry as a training aid for providing personal feedback of a type which "personalizes" otherwise didactic theory sessions on the Johari, on one hand, and as a catalyst to evaluation and critique of ongoing relationships, on the other hand. In addition to its essentially training oriented use, however, the *Personnel Relations Survey* has been a basic research tool for assessing current practices among managers. The results obtained from two pieces of research are of particular interest from the standpoint of their implications for corporate climates and managerial styles.

Authority Relationships and Interpersonal Style Preferences. Using the *Personnel Relations Survey,* data were collected from 1000 managers. These managers represent a cross-section of those found in organizations today; levels of management ranging from company president to just above first-line supervisor were sampled from all over the United States. Major manufacturers and petroleum and food producers contributed to the research, as well as a major airline, state and federal governmental agencies, and nonprofit service organizations.

Since the *Personnel Relations Survey* addresses the manner in which Exposure and Feedback processes are employed in one's relationships with his subordinates, colleagues, and superiors, the data from the 1000 managers sampled reveal some patterns which prevail in organizations in terms of downward, horizontal, and upward communications. In addition, the shifting and changing of interpersonal tactics as one moves from one authority relationship to another is noteworthy from the standpoint of power dynamics underlying organizational life. A summary of the average tendencies obtained from managers is presented graphically in Figure 3.

Of perhaps the greatest significance for organizational climates is the finding regarding the typical manager's use of Exposure. As Figure 3 indicates, one's tendency to deal openly and candidly with others is directly influenced by the amount of power he possesses relative to other parties to the relationship. Moving from relationships with subordinates in which the manager obviously enjoys greater formal authority, through colleague relationships characterized by equal authority positions, to relationships with superiors in which the manager is least powerful, the plots of Exposure use steadily decline. Indeed, a straight linear relationship is suggested between amount of authority possessed by the average manager and his use of candor in relationships.

While there are obvious exceptions to this depiction, the average managerial profile on Exposure reveals the most commonly found practices in organizations which, when taken diagnostically, suggest that the average manager in today's organizations has a number of "hang-ups" around authority issues which seriously curtail his interpersonal effectiveness. Consistent with other findings from communication research, these data point to power differences among parties to relationships

FIGURE 3   Score Plots on Exposure and Feedback
for the "Average" Manager from a Sample
of 1000 Managers in the United States

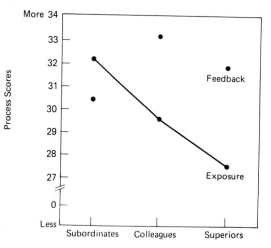

as a major disruptive influence on the flow of information in organizations. A more accurate interpretation, however, seems to be that it is not power differences as such which impede communication, but the way people *feel* about these differences and begin to monitor, filter, and control their contributions in response to their own feelings and apprehensions.

Implications for overall corporate climate may become more obvious when the data from the Exposure process are considered with those reflecting the average manager's reliance on Feedback acquisition. As Figure 3 reveals, Feedback solicitation proceeds differently. As might be expected, there is less use of the Feedback process in relationships with subordinates than there is of the Exposure process. This variation on the Type C interpersonal style, reflecting an overuse of Exposure to some neglect of Feedback, very likely contributes to subordinate feelings of resentment, lack of social worth, and frustration. These feelings—which are certain to manifest themselves in the *quality* of subordinate performance if not in production quantity—will likely remain as hidden facets of corporate climate, for a major feature of downward communication revealed in Figure 3 is that of managerial Blindspot.

Relationships at the colleague level appear to be of a different sort with a set of dynamics all their own. As reference to the score plots in Figure 3 will show, the typical manager reports a significant preference for Feedback seeking behaviors over Exposure in his relationships with his fellow managers. A quick interpretation of the data obtained would be that, at the colleague level, everyone is seeking information but very few are willing to expose any. These findings may bear on a unique feature of organizational life—one which has serious implications for climate among corporate peers. Most research on power and authority relationships suggests that there is the greatest openness of equal power. Since colleague relationships might best be considered to reflect equal if not shared distributions of power, maximum openness coupled with maximum solicitation of others' information might be expected to characterize relationships among management co-workers. The fact that a fairly pure Type B interpersonal style prevails suggests noise in the system. The dominant Facade which results from reported practices with colleagues signifies a lack of trust of the sort which could seriously limit the success of collaborative or cooperative ventures among colleagues. The climate implications of mistrust are obvious, and the present data may shed some light on teamwork difficulties as well as problems of horizontal communication so often encountered during inter-departmental or inter-group contacts.

Interviews with a number of managers revealed that their tendencies to become closed in encounters with colleagues could be traced to a competitive ethic which prevailed in their organizations. The fact was a simple one: "You don't confide in your 'buddies' because they are bucking for the same job you are! Any worthwhile information you've got, you keep to yourself until a time when it might come in handy." To the extent that this climate prevails in organizations, it is to be expected that more effort goes into facade building and maintenance than is expended on the projects at hand where colleague relationships are concerned.

Superiors are the targets of practices yielding the smallest, and therefore least productive, Arena of the three relationships assessed in the survey. The average manager reports a significant reluctance to deal openly and candidly with his superior while favoring the Feedback process as his major interpersonal gambit; even the use of Feedback, however, is subdued relative to that employed with colleagues. The view from high in organizations is very likely colored by the interpersonal styles addressed to them; and, based on the data obtained, it would not be surprising if many members of top management felt that lower level management was submissive, in need of direction, and had few creative suggestions of their own. Quite aside from the obvious effect such an expectation might have on performance reviews, a characteristic reaction to the essentially Type B style directed at superiors is, on their part, to invoke Type C behaviors. Thus, the data obtained call attention to what may be the seeds of a self-reinforcing cycle of authority-obedience-authority. The long-range consequences of such a cycle, in terms of relationship quality and interpersonal style, has been found to be corporatewide adoption of Type A behaviors which serve to depersonalize work and diminish an organization's human resources.

Thus, based on the present research at least, a number of interpersonal practices seem to characterize organizational life which limit not only the effectiveness of communication within, but the attainment of realistic levels of corporate excellence without. As we will see, which style will prevail very much depends upon the individual manager.

Interpersonal Practices and Managerial Styles. In commenting upon the first of their two major concerns in programs of organization development, Blake and Mouton[6] have stated: "The underlying causes of communication difficulties are to be found in the character of supervision. . . . The solution to the problem of communication is for men to manage by achieving production and excellence through sound utilization of people." To the extent that management style is an important ingredient in the communication process, a second piece of research employing the Johari Window and Managerial grid models in tandem may be of some interest to those concerned with corporate excellence.

Of the 1000 managers sampled in the *Personnel Relations Survey,* 384 also completed a second instrument, the *Styles of Management Inventory,*[7] based on the Managerial Grid (a two-dimensional model of management styles).[8] Five "anchor" styles are identified relative to one's concern for production vis-à-vis people, and these are expressed in grid notation as follows: 9,9 reflects a high people concern; 5,5 reflects a moderate concern for each; 9,1 denotes high production coupled with low people concerns, while 1,9 denotes the opposite orientation; 1,1 reflects a minimal concern for both dimensions. In an attempt to discover the significance of one's interpersonal practices for his overall approach to management, the forty individuals scoring highest on each style of management were selected for an analysis of their interpersonal styles. Thus, 200 managers—forty each who were identified as having dominant managerial styles either 9,9; 5,5; 9,1; 1,9; or 1,1—were studied relative to their tendencies to employ Exposure and Feedback Processes in relationships with their subordinates. The research question addressed was: How do individuals who prefer a given managerial style differ in terms of their interpersonal orientations from other individuals preferring other managerial approaches?

The data were subjected to a discriminant function analysis and statistically significant differences were revealed in terms of the manner in which managers employing a given dominant managerial style also employed the Exposure and Feedback processes. The results of the research findings are presented graphically in Figure 4. As a bar graph of Exposure and Feedback scores reveals, those managers identified by a dominant management style of 9,9 displayed the strongest tendencies to employ both Exposure and Feedback in their relationships with subordinates. In addition, the Arena which would result from a Johari plotting of their scores would be in a fairly good state of balance, reflecting about as much use of one process as of the other. The data suggest that the 9,9 style of management—typically described as one which achieves effective production through the sound utilization of people—also entails the sound utilization of personal resources in establishing relationships. The Type D interpersonal style which seems to be associated with the 9,9 management style is fully consistent with the open and unobstructed communciation which Blake and Mouton view as essential to the creative resolution of differences and sound relationships.

The 5,5 style of management appears, from the standpoint of Exposure and Feedback employment, to be a truncated version of the 9,9 approach. While the reported scores for both processes hover around the fiftieth percentile, there is a noteworthy preference for Exposure over Feedback. Although a Johari plotting of these scores might also approach a Type D profile, the Arena is less balanced and accounts for only 25 percent of the data available for use in a relationship. Again, such an interpersonal style seems consistent with a managerial approach based on expediency and a search for the middle ground.

As might be expected, the 9,1 managers in the study displayed a marked preference for Exposure over Feedback in their relationships with subordinates. This suggests that managers who are maximally concerned with production issues also are given to an overuse of Exposure—albeit not maximum Exposure—and

FIGURE 4 A Comparison of Exposure and Feedback Use among Managers with Different Dominant Managerial Styles

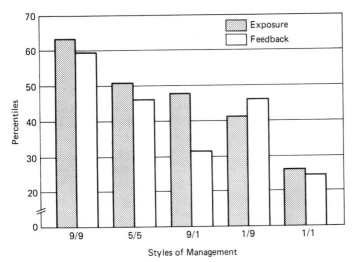

this is very likely to maintain personal control. In general, a Type C interpersonal style seems to underlie the 9,1 approach to management; and it is important that such managerial practices may be sustained by enlarged Blindspots.

Considering the opposing dominant concerns of the 1,9 manager as compared to the 9,1, it is not too surprising to find that the major interpersonal process of these managers is Feedback solicitation. As with the 9,1 style, the resulting Arena for 1,9 managers is not balanced; but the resulting tension likely stems from less than desired Exposure, leading to relationships in which the managerial Facade is the dominant feature. The Type B interpersonal style may be said to characterize the 1,9 approach to management, with its attendant effects on corporate climate.

Finally, the use of Exposure and Feedback processes reported by those managers identified as dominantly 1,1 is minimal. A mechanical impersonal approach to interpersonal relationships which is consistent with the low profile approach to management depicted under 1,1 is suggested. The Unknown region apparently dominates relationships, and hidden potential and untapped resources prevail. The consequences of such practices for the quality of relationships, climates, and communication effectiveness have already been described in the discussion of Type A interpersonal behaviors.

In summary, it appears that one's interpersonal style is a critical ingredient in his approach to management. While the uses of Exposure and Feedback reported by managers identified according to management style seem to be quite consistent with what one might expect, it is worthy to mention that the test items comprising the *Personnel Relations Survey* have very little, if anything, to do with production versus people concerns. Rather, one's willingness to engage in risk-taking disclosures of feelings, impressions, and observations coupled with his sensitivity to others' participative needs and a felt responsibility to help them become involved via Feedback solicitation were assessed. The fact that such purposive behaviors coincide with one's treatment of more specific context-bound issues like production and people would seem to raise the question: Which comes first, interpersonal or managerial style? The question is researchable, and management practices and information flow might both be enhanced by the results obtained.

CORPORATE CLIMATE
AND PERSONAL DECISION

The major thesis of this article has been that interpersonal styles are at the core of a number of corporate dilemmas: communication breakdowns, emotional climates, the quality of relationships, and even managerial practices have been linked to some fairly simple dynamics between people. The fact that the dynamics are simple should not be taken to mean that their management is easy—far from it. But, at the same time, the fact that individuals can and do change their interpersonal style—and thereby set in motion a whole chain of events with corporate significance—should be emphasized. A mere description of one's interpersonal practices has only limited utility, if that is as far as it goes. The value of the Johari Window model lies not so much with its utility for assessing what is but, rather, in its inherent statement of what might be.

Although most people select their interpersonal styles as a *reaction* to what they anticipate from other parties, the key to effective relationships lies in "pro-action"; each manager can be a norm setter in his relationships if he will but honestly review his own interpersonal goals and undertake the risks necessary to their attainment. Organizations can criticize their policies—both formal and unwritten—in search for provisions which serve to punish candor and reward evasiveness while equating solicitation of data from others with personal weakness. In short, the culture of an organization and the personal and corporate philosophies which underlie it may be thought of as little more than a *decision product* of the human system. The quality of this decision will directly reflect the quality of the relationships existing among those who fashion it.

If the model and its derivations make sense, then corporate relationships and managerial practices based on candor and trust, openness and spontaneity, and optimal utilization of interpersonal resources are available options to every member of an organizational family. As we have seen, power distributions among people may adversely influence their interpersonal choices. Management styles apparently constrain individuals, but the choice is still there. Type A practices require breaking away from the corporate womb into which one has retreated; personal experiments with greater Exposure and Feedback, however anxiety producing, may be found in the long-run to be their own greatest reward. For the manager locked into Type B behaviors, the task is more simple; he already solicits Feedback to an excellent degree. Needed is enough additional trust in others—whether genuine or forced—to allow a few experiences with Exposure. Others may be found to be less fragile or reactionary than one imagined. Learning to listen is but part of the task confronting managers inclined toward Type C styles; they must learn to seek out and encourage the exposures of others. This new attention to the Feedback process should not be at the expense of Exposure, however. Revamping Type C does not mean adopting Type B. These are all forms of low-risk high-potential-yield personal experiments. Whether they will ever be undertaken and their effects on corporate excellence determined depends upon the individual; the matter is one of personal decision.

REFERENCES

1. R. R. Blake and Jane S. Mouton, *Corporate Excellence Through Grid Organization Development* (Houston, Texas: Gulf Publishing Co., 1968), p. 4.
2. *Ibid.,* pp. 3–5.
3. Joseph Luft, *Of Human Interaction* (Palo Alto, California: National Press Books, 1969), *passim.*
4. C. Argyris, *Interpersonal Competence and Organizational Effectiveness* (Homewood, Illinois: Dorsey, 1962), *passim.*
5. J. Hall and Martha S. Williams, *Personnel Relations Survey* (Conroe, Texas: Teleometrics International, 1967).
6. R. R. Blake and Jane S. Mouton, *op. cit.,* p. 5.
7. J. Hall, J. B. Harvey, and Martha S. Williams, *Styles of Management Inventory* (Conroe, Texas: Teleometrics International, 1963).
8. R. R. Blake and Jane S. Mouton, *The Managerial Grid* (Houston, Texas: Gulf Publishing Co., 1964), *passim.*

PERCEPTION:
IMPLICATIONS FOR ADMINISTRATION

Sheldon S. Zalkind
Timothy W. Costello

Management practice is being increasingly influenced by behavioral science research in the areas of group dynamics, problem solving and decision making, and motivation. One aspect of behavior which has not been fully or consistently emphasized is the process of perception, particularly the recent work on person perception.

In this paper we shall summarize some of the findings on perception as developed through both laboratory and organizational research and point out some of the administrative and managerial implications. We discuss first some basic factors in the nature of the perceptual process including need and set; second, some research on forming impressions; third, the characteristics of the perceiver and the perceived; fourth, situational and organizational influences on perception; and finally, perceptual influences on interpersonal adjustment.

NATURE OF THE PERCEPTUAL PROCESS

What are some of the factors influencing perception? In answering the question it is well to begin by putting aside the attitude of naive realism, which suggests that our perceptions simply register accurately what is "out there." It is necessary rather to consider what influences distort one's perceptions and judgments of the outside world. Some of the considerations identified in the literature up to the time of Johnson's 1944 review of the research on object perception (where distortion may be even less extreme than in person perception) led him to suggest the following about the perceiver[1]:

1. He may be influenced by considerations that he may not be able to identify, responding to cues that are below the threshold of his awareness. For example, a judgment as to the size of an object may be influenced by its color even though the perceiver may not be attending to color.
2. When required to form difficult perceptual judgments, he may respond to irrelevant cues to arrive at a judgment. For example, in trying to assess honesty, it has been shown that the other person's smiling or not smiling is used as a cue to judge his honesty.
3. In making abstract or intellectual judgments, he may be influenced by emotional factors—what is liked is perceived as correct.

Source: Reprinted from *Administrative Science Quarterly,* VII (September 1962), 218-35, by permission of the authors and the publisher. Portions of this article were originally presented at the Eighth Annual International Meeting of The Institute of Management Sciences in Brussels, August 1961.

[1]D. M. Johnson, "A Systematic Treatement of Judgment," *Psychological Bulletin,* XLII (1945), 193-224.

4. He will weigh perceptual evidence coming from respected (or favored) sources more heavily than that coming from other sources.

5. He may not be able to identify all the factors on which his judgments are based. Even if he is aware of these factors he is not likely to realize how much weight he gives to them.

These considerations do not imply that we respond only to the subtle or irrelevant cues or to emotional factors. We often perceive on the basis of the obvious, but we are quite likely to be responding as well to the less obvious or less objective.

In 1958, Bruner, citing a series of researches, described what he called the "New Look" in perception as one in which personal determinants of the perceptual process were being stressed.[2] Bruner summarized earlier work and showed the importance of such subjective influences as needs, values, cultural background, and interests on the perceptual process. In his concept of a "perceptual readiness" he described the importance of the framework or category system that the perceiver himself brings to the perceiving process.

Tapping a different vein of research, Cantril described perceiving as a "transaction" between the perceiver and the perceived, a process of negotiation in which the perceptual end product is a result both of influences within the perceiver and of characteristics of the perceived.[3]

One of the most important of the subjective factors that influence the way we perceive identified by Bruner and others, is *set*. A study by Kelley illustrated the point.[4] He found that those who were previously led to expect to meet a "warm" person, not only made different judgments about him, but also behaved differently toward him, than those who were expecting a "cold" one. The fact was that they simultaneously were observing the same person in the same situaiton. Similarly, Strickland indicated the influence of set in determining how closely supervisors feel they must supervise their subordinates.[5] Because of prior expectation one person was trusted more than another and was thought to require less supervision than another, even though performance records were identical.

FORMING IMPRESSIONS OF OTHERS

The data on forming impressions is of particular importance in administration. An administrator is confronted many times with the task of forming an impression of another person—a new employee at his desk, a visiting member from the home office, a staff member he has not personally met before. His own values, needs, and expectations will play a part in the impression he forms. Are there other

[2]J. S. Bruner, "Social Psychology and Perception," in *Readings in Social Psychology,* ed. E. Maccoby, T. Newcomb, and E. Hartley (3rd ed.; New York, 1958), pp. 85–94.

[3]H. Cantril, "Perception and Interpersonal Relations," *American Journal of Psychiatry,* CXIV (1957), 119–26.

[4]H. H. Kelley, "The Warm-Cold Variable in First Impressions of Persons," *Journal of Personality,* XVIII (1950), 431–39.

[5]L. H. Strickland, "Surveillance and Trust," *Journal of Personality,* XXVI (1958), 200–215.

factors that typically operate in this area of administrative life? One of the more obvious influences is the physical appearance of the person being perceived. In a study of this point Mason was able to demonstrate that people agree on what a leader should look like and that there is no relationship between the facial characteristics agreed upon and those possessed by actual leaders.[6] In effect, we have ideas about what leaders look like and we can give examples, but we ignore the many exceptions that statistically cancel out the examples.

In the sometimes casual, always transitory situations in which one must form impressions of others it is a most natural tendency to jump to conclusions and form impressions without adequate evidence. Unfortunately, as Daily showed, unless such impressions are based on important and relevant data, they are not likely to be accurate.[7] Too often in forming impressions the perceiver does not know what is relevant, important, or predictive of later behavior. Dailey's research furthermore supports the cliche that, accurate or not, first impressions are lasting.

Generalizing from other research in the field, Soskin described four limitations on the ability to form accurate impressions of others.[8] First, the impression is likely to be disproportionately affected by the type of situation or surroundings in which the impression is made and influenced too little by the person perceived. Thus the plush luncheon club in which one first meets a man will dominate the impression of the man himself. Second, although impressions are frequently based on a limited sample of the perceived person's behavior, the generalization that the perceiver makes will be sweeping. A third limitation is that the situation may not provide an opportunity for the person perceived to show behavior relevant to the traits about which impressions are formed. Casual conversation or questions, for example, provide few opportunities to demonstrate intelligence or work characteristics, yet the perceiver often draws conclusions about these from an interview. Finally, Soskin agrees with Bruner and Cantril that the impression of the person perceived may be distorted by some highly individualized reaction of the perceiver.

But the pitfalls are not yet all spelled out; it is possible to identify some other distorting influences on the process of forming impressions. Research has brought into sharp focus some typical errors, the more important being stereotyping, halo effect, projection, and perceptual defense.

Stereotyping

The word "stereotyping" was first used by Walter Lippmann in 1922 to describe bias in perceiving people. He wrote of "pictures in people's heads," called stereotypes, which guided (distorted) their perception of others. The term has long been used to describe judgments made about people on the basis of their ethnic group membership. For example, some say, "Herman Schmidt [being German] is industrious." Stereotyping also predisposes judgments in many other areas of interpersonal

[6] D. J. Mason, "Judgments of Leadership Based on Physiognomic Cues," *Journal of Abnormal and Social Psychology,* LVI (1957), 273–74.

[7] C. A. Dailey, "The Effects of Premature Conclusion upon the Acquisition of Understanding of a Person," *Journal of Psychology,* XXIII (1952), 133–52.

[8] W. E. Soskin, "Influence of Information on Bias in Social Perception," *Journal of Personality,* XXII (1953), 118–27.

relations. Stereotypes have developed about many types of groups, and they help to prejudice many of our perceptions about their members. Examples of stereotypes of groups other than those based on ethnic identification are bankers, supervisors, union members, poor people, rich people, and administrators. Many unverified qualitites are assigned to people principally because of such group memberships.

In a research demonstration of stereotyping, Haire found that labeling a photograph as that of a management representative caused an impression to be formed of the person, different from that formed when it was labeled as that of a union leader.[9] Management and labor formed different impressions, each seeing his opposite as less dependable than his own group. In addition, each side saw his own group as being better able than the opposite group to understand a point of view different from its own. For example, managers felt that other managers were better able to appreciate labor's point of view than labor was able to appreciate management's point of view. Each had similar stereotypes of his opposite and considered the thinking, emotional characteristics, and interpersonal relations of his opposite as inferior to his own. As Stagner pointed out, "It is plain that unionists perceiving company officials in a stereotyped way are less efficient than would be desirable. Similarly, company executives who see all labor unions as identical are not showing good judgment or discrimination."[10]

One of the troublesome aspects of stereotypes is that they are so widespread. Finding the same stereotypes to be widely held should not tempt one to accept their accuracy. It may only mean that many people are making the same mistake. Allport has demonstrated that there need not be a "kernel of truth" in a widely held stereotype.[11] He has shown that while a prevalent stereotype of Armenians labeled them as dishonest, a credit reporting association gave them credit ratings as good as those given other ethnic groups.

Bruner and Perlmutter found that there is an international stereotype for "businessmen" and "teachers."[12] They indicated that the more widespread one's experience with diverse members of a group, the less their group membership will affect the impression formed.

An additional illustration of stereotyping is provided by Luft.[13] His research suggests that perception of personality adjustment may be influenced by stereotypes, associating adjustment with high income and maladjustment with low income.

Halo Effect

The term "halo effect" was first used in 1920 to describe a process in which a general impression which is favorable or unfavorable is used by judges to evaluate several traits. The "halo" in such case serves as a screen keeping the perceiver

[9] M. Haire, "Role Perceptions in Labor-Management Relations: An Experimental Approach," *Industrial Labor Relations Review,* VIII (1955), 204–16.

[10] R. Stagner, *Psychology of Industrial Conflict* (New York, 1956), p. 35.

[11] G. Allport, *Nature of Prejudice* (Cambridge, Mass., 1954).

[12] J. S. Bruner and H. V. Perlmutter, "Compatriot and Foreigner: A Study of Impression Formation in Three Countries," *Journal of Abnormal and Social Psychology,* LV (1957), 253–60.

[13] J. Luft, "Monetary Value and the Perception of Persons," *Journal of Social Psychology,* XLVI, 245–51.

from actually seeing the trait he is judging. It has received the most attention because of its effect on rating employee performance. In the rating situation, a supervisor may single out one trait, either good or bad, and use this as the basis for his judgment of all other traits. For example, an excellent attendance record causes judgments of productivity, high quality of work, and so forth. One study in the U.S. Army showed that officers who were liked were judged more intelligent than those who were disliked, even though they had the same scores on intelligence tests.

We examine halo effect here because of its general effect on forming impressions. Bruner and Taguiri suggest that it is likely to be most extreme when we are forming impressions of traits that provide minimal cues in the individual's behavior, when the traits have moral overtones, or when the perceiver must judge traits with which he has had little experience.[14] A rather disturbing conclusion is suggested by Symonds that halo effect is more marked the more we know the acquaintance.[15]

A somewhat different aspect of the halo effect is suggested by the research of Grove and Kerr.[16] They found that knowledge that the company was in receivership caused employees to devalue the higher pay and otherwise superior working conditions of their company as compared to those in a financially secure firm.

Psychologists have noted a tendency in perceivers to link certain traits. They assume, for example, that when a person is aggressive he will also have high energy or that when a person is "warm" he will also be generous and have a good sense of humor. This logical error, as it has been called, is a special form of the halo effect and is best illustrated in the research of Asch.[17] In his study the addition of one trait to a list of traits produced a major change in the impression formed. Knowing that a person was intelligent, skillful, industrious, determined, practical, cautious, and warm led a group to judge him to be also wise, humorous, popular, and imaginative. When warm was replaced by cold, a radically different impression (beyond the difference between warm and cold) was formed. Kelley's research illustrated the same type of error.[18] This tendency is not indiscriminate; with the pair "polite–blunt," less change was found than with the more central traits of "warm–cold."

In evaluating the effect of halo on perceptual distortion, we may take comfort from the work of Wishner, which showed that those traits that correlate more highly with each other are more likely to lead to a halo effect than those that are unrelated.[19]

Projection

A defense mechanism available to everyone is projection, in which one relieves one's feelings of guilt or failure by projecting blame onto someone else. Over the

J. S. Bruner and A. Taguiri, "The Perception of People," in *Handbook of Social Psychology*, ed. G. Lindzey (Cambridge, Mass., 1954), chap. xvii.

[15]P. M. Symonds, "Notes on Rating," *Journal of Applied Psychology*, VII (1925), 188–95.

[16]A. Grove and W. A. Kerr, "Specific Evidence on Origin of Halo Effect in Measurement of Morale," *Journal of Social Psychology*, XXXIV (1951), 165–70.

[17]S. Asch, "Forming Impressions of Persons," *Journal of Abnormal and Social Psychology*, LX (1946), 258–90.

[18]Kelley, *op. cit.*

[19]J. Wishner, "Reanalysis of 'Impressions of Personality,'" *Psychological Review*, LXVII (1960), 96–112.

years the projection mechanism has been assigned various meanings. The original use of the term was concerned with the mechanism to defend oneself from unacceptable feelings. There has since been a tendency for the term to be used more broadly, meaning to ascribe or attribute any of one's own characteristics to other people. The projection mechanism concerns us here because it influences the perceptual process. An early study by Murray illustrates its effect.[20] After playing a dramatic game, "Murder," his subjects attributed much more maliciousness to people whose photographs were judged than did a control group which had not played the game. The current emotional state of the perceiver tended to influence his perceptions of others; i.e., frightened perceivers judged people to be frightening. More recently, Feshback and Singer revealed further dynamics of the process.[21] In their study, subjects who had been made fearful judged a stimulus person (presented in a moving picture) as both more fearful and more aggressive than did non-fearful perceivers. The authors were able to demonstrate further that the projection mechanism at work here was reduced when their subjects were encouraged to admit and talk about their fears.

Sears provides an illustration of a somewhat different type of projection and its effects on perception.[22] In his study projection is seeing our own undesirable personality characteristics in other people. He demonstrated that people high in such traits as stinginess, obstinacy, and disorderliness, tended to rate others much higher on these traits than did those who were low in these undesirable characteristics. The tendency to project was particularly marked among subjects who had the least insight into their own personalities.

Research thus suggests that our perceptions may characteristically be distorted by emotions we are experiencing or traits that we possess. Placed in the administrative settings, the research would suggest, for example, that a manager frightened by rumored organizational changes might not only judge others to be more frightened than they were, but also assess various policy decisions as more frightening than they were. Or a general foreman lacking insight into his own incapacity to delegate might be oversensitive to this trait in his superiors.

Perceptual Defense

Another distorting influence, which has been called perceptual defense, has also been demonstrated by Haire and Grunes to be a source of error.[23] In their research they ask, in effect, "Do we put blinders on to defend ourselves from seeing those events which might disturb us?" The concept of perceptual defense offers an excellent description of perceptual distortion at work and demonstrates that when confronted with a fact inconsistent with a stereotype already held by a person,

[20]H. A. Murray, "The Effect of Fear upon Estimates of the Maliciousness of Other Personalities," *Journal of Social Psychology,* IV (1933), 310–29.

[21]S. Feshback and S. D. Singer, "The Effects of Fear Arousal upon Social Perception," *Journal of Abnormal and Social Psychology,* LV (1957), 283–88.

[22]R. R. Sears, "Experimental Studies of Perception. I. Attribution of Traits," *Journal of Social Psychology,* VII (1936), 151–63.

[23]M. Haire and W. F. Grunes, "Perceptual Defenses: Processes Protecting an Original Perception of Another Personality," *Human Relations,* III (1958), 403–12.

the perceiver is able to distort the data in such a way as to eliminate the inconsistency. Thus, by perceiving inaccurately, he defends himself from having to change his stereotypes.

CHARACTERISTICS OF PERCEIVER AND PERCEIVED

We have thus far been talking largely about influences on the perceptual process without specific regard to the perceiver and his characteristics. Much recent research has tried to identify some characteristics of the perceiver and their influence on the perception of other people.

The Perceiver

A thread that would seem to tie together many current findings is the tendency to use oneself as the norm or standard by which one perceives or judges others. If we examine current research, certain conclusions are suggested:

1. *Knowing oneself makes it easier to see others accurately.* Norman showed that when one is aware of what his own personal characteristics are, he makes fewer errors in perceiving others.[24] Weingarten has shown that people with insight are less likely to view the world in black-and-white terms and to give extreme judgments about others.[25]

2. *One's own characteristics affect the characteristics he is likely to see in others.* Secure people (compared to insecure) tend to see others as warm rather than cold, as was shown by Bossom and Maslow.[26] The extent of one's own sociability influences the degree of importance one gives to the sociability of other people when one forms impressions of them.[27] The person with "authoritarian" tendencies is more likely to view others in terms of power and is less sensitive to the psychological or personality characteristics of other people than is a non-authoritarian.[28] The relatively few categories one uses in describing other people tend to be those ones uses in describing oneself.[29] Thus traits which are important to the perceiver will be used more when he forms impressions of others. He has

[24]R. D. Norman, "The Interrelationships among Acceptance-Rejection, Self-Other, Insight into Self, and Realistic Perception of Others," *Journal of Social Psychology,* XXXVII (1953), 205–35.

[25]E. Weingarten, "A Study of Selective Perception in Clinical Judgment," *Journal of Personality,* XVII (1949), 369–400.

[26]J. Bossom and A. H. Maslow, "Security of Judges as a Factor in Impression of Warmth in Others," *Journal of Abnormal and Social Psychology,* LV (1957), 147–48.

[27]D. T. Benedetti and J. G. Hill, "A Determiner of the Centrality of a Trait in Impression Formation," *Journal of Abnormal and Social Psychology,* LX (1960), 278–79.

[28]E. E. Jones, "Authoritarianism as a Determinant of First-Impressions Formation," *Journal of Personality,* XXIII (1954), 107–27.

[29]A. H. Hastorf, S. A. Richardson, and S. M. Dombusch, "The Problem of Relevance in the Study of Person Perception," in *Person Perception and Interpersonal Behavior,* ed. R. Taguiri and L. Petrullo (Stanford, Calif., 1958).

certain constant tendencies, both with regard to using certain categories in judging others and to the amount of weight given to these categories.[30]

3. *The person who accepts himself is more likely to be able to see favorable aspects of other people.*[31] This relates in part to the accuracy of his perceptions. If the perceiver accepts himself as he is, he widens his range of vision in seeing others; he can look at them and be less likely to be very negative or critical. In those areas in which he is more insecure, he sees more problems in other people.[32] We are more likely to like others who have traits we accept in ourselves and reject those who have the traits which we do not like in ourselves.[33]

4. *Accuracy in perceiving others is not a single skill.* While there have been some variations in the findings, as Gage has shown, some consistent results do occur.[34] The perceiver tends to interpret the feelings others have about him in terms of his feeling toward them.[35] One's ability to perceive others accurately may depend on how sensitive one is to differences between people and also to the norms (outside of oneself) for judging them.[36] Thus, as Taft has shown, the ability to judge others does not seem to be a single skill.[37]

Possibly the results in these four aspects of person perception can be viewed most constructively in connection with earlier points on the process of perception. The administrator (or any other individual) who wishes to perceive someone else accurately must look at the other person, not at himself. The things that he looks at in someone else are influenced by his own traits. But if he knows his own traits, he can be aware that they provide a frame of reference for him. His own traits help to furnish the categories that he will use in perceiving others. His characteristics, needs, and values can partly limit his vision and his awareness of the differences between others. The question one could ask when viewing another is: "Am I looking at him, and forming my impression of his behavior in the situation, or am I just comparing him with myself?"

There is the added problem of being set to observe the personality traits in another which the perceiver does not accept in himself, e.g., being somewhat autocratic. At the same time he may make undue allowances in others for those of his own deficiencies which do not disturb him but might concern some people, e.g., not following prescribed procedures.

[30]L. J. Cronbach, "Processes Affecting Scores on 'Understanding of Others' and 'Assumed Similarity,' " *Psychology Bulletin,* LII (1955), 173–93.

[31]K. T. Omwake, "The Relation between Acceptance of Self and Acceptance of Others Shown by Three Personality Inventories," *Journal of Consulting Psychology,* XVIII (1954), 443–46.

[32]Weingarten, *op. cit.*

[33]R. M. Lundy *et al.,* "Self Acceptability and Descriptions of Sociometric Choices," *Journal of Abnormal and Social Psychology,* LI (1955), 260–62.

[34]N. L. Gage, "Accuracy of Social Perception and Effectiveness in Interpersonal Relationships," *Journal of Personality,* XXII (1953), 128–41.

[35]R. Taguiri, J. S. Bruner, and R. Blake, "On the Relation between Feelings and Perceptions of Feelings among Members of Small Groups," in *Readings in Social Psychology.*

[36]U. Bronfenbrenner, J. Harding, and M. Gallway, "The Measurement of Skill in Social Perception," in *Talent and Society,* ed. McClalland *et al.* (Princeton, N.J., 1958), pp. 29–111.

[37]R. Taft, "The Ability to Judge People, *Psychological Bulletin,* LII (1955), 1–21.

The Perceived

Lest we leave the impression that it is only the characteristics of the perceiver that stand between him and others in his efforts to know them, we turn now to some characteristics of the person being perceived which raise problems in perception. It is possible to demonstrate, for example, that the status of the person perceived is a variable influencing judgments about his behavior. Thibaut and Riecken have shown that even though two people behave in identical fashion, status differences between them cause a perceiver to assign different motivations for the behavior.[38] Concerning co-operativeness, they found that high status persons are judged as wanting to co-operate and low status persons as having to co-operate. In turn, more liking is shown for the person of high status than for the person of low status. Presumably, more credit is given when the boss says, "Good morning," to us than when a subordinate says the same thing.

Bruner indicated that we use categories to simplify our perceptual activities. In the administrative situation, status is one type of category, and the role provides another. Thus the remarks of Mr. Jones in the sales department are perceived differently from those of Smith in the purchasing department, although both may say the same thing. Also, one who knows Jones's role in the organization will perceive his behavior differently from one who does not know Jones's role. The process of categorizing on the basis of roles is similar to, if not identical with, the stereotyping process described earlier.

Visibility of the traits judged is also an important variable influencing the accuracy of perception.[39] Visibility will depend, for example, on how free the other person feels to express the trait. It has been demonstrated that we are more accurate in judging people who like us than people who dislike us. The explanation suggested is that most people in our society feel constraint in showing their dislike, and therefore the cues are less visible.

Some traits are not visible simply because they provide few external cues for their presence. Loyalty, for example, as opposed to level of energy, provides few early signs for observation. Even honesty cannot be seen in the situations in which most impressions are formed. As obvious as these comments might be, in forming impressions many of us nevertheless continue to judge the presence of traits which are not really visible. Frequently the practical situation demands judgments, but we should recognize the frail reeds upon which we are leaning and be prepared to observe further and revise our judgments with time and closer acquaintance.

SITUATIONAL INFLUENCES ON PERCEPTION

Some recent research clearly points to the conclusion that the whole process of interpersonal perception is, at least in part, a function of the *group* (or interpersonal)

---

[38]J. W. Thibaut and H. W. Riecken, "Some Determinants and Consequences of the Perception of Social Causality," *Journal of Personality,* XXIV (1955), 113–33.

[39]Bruner and Taguiri, *op cit.*

context in which the perception occurs. Much of the research has important theoretical implications for a psychology of interpersonal relations. In addition, there are some suggestions of value for administrators. It is possible to identify several characteristics of the interpersonal climate which have direct effect on perceptual accuracy. As will be noted, these are characteristics which can be known, and in some cases controlled, in administrative settings.

Bieri provides data for the suggestion that when people are given an opportunity to interact in a friendly situation, they tend to see others as similar to themselves.[40] Applying his suggestion to the administrative situation, we can rationalize as follows: Some difficulties of administrative practice grow out of beliefs that different interest groups in the organization are made up of different types of people. Obviously once we believe that people in other groups are different, we will be predisposed to see the differences. We can thus find, from Bieri's and from Rosenbaum's work, an administrative approach for attacking the problem.[41] If we can produce an interacting situation which is cooperative rather than competitive, the likelihood of seeing other people as similar to ourselves is increased.

Exline's study adds some other characteristics of the social context which may influence perception.[42] Paraphrasing his conclusions to adapt them to the administrative scene, we can suggest that when a committee group is made up of congenial members who are willing to continue work in the same group, their perceptions of the goal-directed behavior of fellow committee members will be more accurate, although observations of purely personal behavior (as distinguished from goal-directed behavior) may be less accurate.[43] The implications for setting up committees and presumably other interacting work groups seem clear: Do not place together those with a past history of major personal clashes. If they must be on the same committee, each must be helped to see that the other is working toward the same goal.

An interesting variation in this area of research is the suggestion from Ex's work that perceptions will be more influenced or swayed by relatively unfamiliar people in the group than by those who are intimates.[44] The concept needs further research, but it provides the interesting suggestion that we may give more credit to strangers for having knowledge, since we do not really know them, than we do to our intimates, whose backgrounds and limitations we feel we do know.

The *organization,* and one's place in it, may also be viewed as the context in which perceptions take place. A study by Dearborn and Simon illustrates this point.[45] Their data support the hypothesis that the administrator's perceptions will

[40]J. Bieri, "Change in Interpersonal Perception Following Interaction," *Journal of Abnormal and Social Psychology,* XLVII (1953), 61–66.

[41]M. E. Rosenbaum, "Social Perception and the Motivational Structure of Interpersonal Relations," *Journal of Abnormal and Social Psychology,* LIX (1959), 130–33.

[42]R. V. Exline, "Interrelations among Two Dimensions of Sociometric Status, Group Congeniality and Accuracy of Social Perception," *Sociometry,* XXIII (1960), 85–101.

[43]R. V. Exline, "Group Climate as a Factor in the Relevance and Accuracy of Social Perception," *Journal of Abnormal and Social Psychology,* LV (1957), 382–88.

[44]J. Ex, "The Nature of the Relation between Two Persons and the Degree of Their Influence on Each Other," *Acta Psychologica,* XVII (1960), 39–54.

[45]D. C. Dearborn and H. A. Simon, "Selective Perception: A Note on the Departmental Identifications of Executives," *Sociometry,* XXI (1958), 140–44.

often be limited to those aspects of a situation which relate specifically to his own department, despite an attempt to influence him away from such selectivity.

Perception of self among populations at different levels in the hierarchy also offers an opportunity to judge the influence of organizational context on perceptual activity. Porter's study of the self-descriptions of managers and line workers indicated that both groups saw themselves in different terms, which corresponded to their positions in the organization's hierarchy.[46] He stated that managers used leadership-type traits (e.g., inventive) to describe themselves, while line workers used follower-type terms (e.g., cooperative). The question of which comes first must be asked: Does the manager see himself this way because of his current position in the organization? Or is this self-picture an expression of a more enduring personal characteristic that helped bring the manager to his present position? This study does not answer that question, but it does suggest to an administrator the need to be aware of the possibly critical relationship between one's hierarchical role and self-perception.

PERCEPTUAL INFLUENCES
ON INTERPERSONAL ADJUSTMENT

Throughout this paper, we have examined a variety of influences on the perceptual process. There has been at least the inference that the operations of such influences on perception whould in turn affect behavior that would follow. Common-sense judgment suggests that being able to judge other people accurately facilitates smooth and effective interpersonal adjustments. Nevertheless, the relationship between perception and consequent behavior is itself in need of direct analysis. Two aspects may be identified: (1) the effect of accuracy of perception on subsequent behavior and (2) the effect of the duration of the relationship and the opportunity for experiencing additional cues.

First then, from the applied point of view, we can ask a crucial question: Is there a relationship between accuracy of social perception and adjustment to others? While the question might suggest a quick affirmative answer, research findings are inconsistent. Steiner attempted to resolve some of these inconsistencies by stating that accuracy may have an effect on interaction under the following conditions: when the interacting persons are co-operatively motivated, when the behavior which is accurately perceived is relevant to the activities of these persons, and when members are free to alter their behavior on the basis of their perceptions.[47]

Where the relationship provides opportunity only to form an impression, a large number of subjective factors, i.e., set, stereotypes, projections, etc., operate to create an early impression, which is frequently erroneous. In more enduring relationships a more balanced appraisal may result, since increased interaction provides additional cues for judgment. In his study of the acquaintance process,

[46]L. W. Porter, "Differential Self-Perceptions of Management Personnel and Line Workers," *Journal of Applied Psychology,* XLII (1958), 105–9.

[47]I. Steiner, "Interpersonal Behavior As Influenced by Accuracy of Social Perception," *Psychological Review,* LXII (1955), 268–75.

Newcomb showed that while early perception of favorable traits caused attraction to the perceived person, over a four-month period the early cues for judging favorable traits became less influential.[48] With time, a much broader basis was used which included comparisons with others with whom one had established relationships. Such findings suggest that the warning about perceptual inaccuracies implicit in the earlier sections of this paper apply with more force to the short-term process of impression forming than to relatively extended acquaintance-building relationships. One would thus hope that rating an employee after a year of service would be a more objective performance than appraising him in a selection interview—a hope that would be fulfilled only when the rater had provided himself with opportunities for broadening the cues he used in forming his first impressions.

SUMMARY

Two principal suggestions which increase the probability of more effective administrative action emerge from the research data. One suggestion is that the administrator be continuously aware of the intricacies of the perceptual process and thus be warned to avoid arbitrary and categorical judgments and to seek reliable evidence before judgments are made. A second suggestion grows out of the first: increased accuracy in one's self-perception can make possible the flexibility to seek evidence and to shift position as time provides additional evidence.

Nevertheless, not every effort designed to improve perceptual accuracy will bring about such accuracy. The dangers of too complete reliance on formal training for perceptual accuracy are suggested in a study by Crow.[49] He found that a group of senior medical students were somewhat less accurate in their perceptions of others after a period of training in physician-patient relationships than were an untrained control group. The danger is that a little learning encourages the perceiver to respond with increased sensitivity to individual differences without making it possible for him to gauge the real meaning of the differences he has seen.

Without vigilance to perceive accurately and to minimize as far as possible the subjective approach in perceiving others, effective administration is handicapped. On the other hand research would not support the conclusion that perceptual distortions will not occur simply because the administrator says he will try to be objective. The administrator or manager will have to work hard to avoid seeing only what he wants to see and to guard against fitting everything into what he is set to see.

We are not yet sure of the ways in which training for perceptual accuracy can best be accomplished, but such training cannot be ignored. In fact, one can say that one of the important tasks of administrative science is to design research to test various training procedures for increasing perceptual accuracy.

[48]T. M. Newcomb, "The Perception of Interpersonal Attraction," *American Psychologist,* XI (1956), 575–86.

[49]W. J. Crow, "Effect of Training on Interpersonal Perception," *Journal of Abnormal and Social Psychology,* LV (1957), 355–59.

8

Group Dynamics

THE NATURE OF HIGHLY EFFECTIVE GROUPS

Rensis Likert

We concluded in Chapter 8 that the form of organization which will make the greatest use of human capacity consists of highly effective work groups linked together in an overlapping pattern by other similarly effective groups. The highly effective work group is, consequently, an important component of the newer theory of management. It will be important to understand both its nature and its performance characteristics. We shall examine these in this chapter, but first a few words about groups in general.

Although we have stressed the great potential power of the group for building effective organizations, it is important to emphasize that this does *not* say that all groups and all committees are highly effective or are committed to desirable goals. Groups as groups can vary from poor to excellent. They can have desirable values and goals, or their objectives can be most destructive. They can accomplish much that is good, or they can do great harm. There is nothing *implicitly* good or bad, weak or strong, about a group.

Source: New Patterns of Management by Rensis Likert. Copyright © 1961 by McGraw-Hill, Inc., used by permission of McGraw-Hill Book Company.

The nature of the group determines the character of its impact upon the development of its members. The values of the group, the stability of these values, the group atmosphere, and the nature of the conformity demanded by the group determine whether a group is likely to have a positive or negative impact upon the growth and behavior of its members. If the values of the group are seen by the society as having merit, if the group is warm, supportive, and full of understanding, the group's influence on the development of its members will be positive. A hostile atmosphere and socially undesirable or unstable values produce a negative impact upon the members' growth and behavior.

Loyalty to a group produces pressures toward conformity. A group may demand conformity to the idea of supporting, encouraging, and giving recognition for individual creativity, or it may value rigidity of behavior, with seriously narrowing and dwarfing consequences. This latter kind of pressure for conformity keeps the members from growing and robs the group of original ideas. Many writers have pointed to these deleterious effects of conformity. They often overlook the capacity of groups to stimulate individual creativeness by placing a high value on imaginative and original contributions by their members. As Pelz's findings, reported in Chapter 2, demonstrate, groups can contribute significantly to creativity by providing the stimulation of diverse points of view within a supportive atmosphere which encourages each individual member to pursue new and unorthodox concepts.

Some business executives are highly critical of groups—or committees—and the inability of committees to accomplish a great deal. Their criticisms are often well warranted. In many instances, committees are wasteful of time and unable to reach decisions. Sometimes the decisions, when reached, are mediocre. Moreover, some members of management at various hierarchical levels use committees as escape mechanisms—as a way to avoid the responsibility for a decision.

The surprising thing about committees is not that many or most are ineffective, but that they accomplish as much as they do when, relatively speaking, we know so little about how to use them. There has been a lack of systematic study of ways to make committees effective. Far more is known about time-and-motion study, cost accounting and similar aspects of management than is known about groups and group processes. Moreover, in spite of the demonstrated potentiality of groups, far less research is being devoted to learning the role of groups and group processes and how to make the most effective use of them in an organization than to most management practices. We know appreciably less about how to make groups and committees effective than we know about most matters of managing.

We do know that groups can be powerful. The newer theory takes this into account and tries to make constructive use of the group's potential strength for developing and mobilizing human resources.

In this and other chapters the use of the term "group" may give the impression that groups have the capacity to behave in ways other than through the behavior of their members. Thus, such expressions appear as the "group's goals," "the group decides," or the "group motivates." In many instances, these expressions are used to avoid endless repetition of the words, "the members of the group." In other instances, something more is meant. Thus, in speaking of "group values," the intent is to refer to those values which have been established by the group through a group-decision process involving consensus. Once a decision has been reached by consensus, there are strong motivational forces, developed within each individual as a result of his membership in the group and his relationship to the other members, to be guided by that decision. In this sense, the group has goals and values and makes decisions. It has properties which may not be present, as such, in any one individual. A group may be divided in opinion, for example, although this may not be true of any one member. Dorwin Cartwright puts it this way: "The relation between the individual members and the group is analogous to the distinction made in mathematics between the properties of a set of elements and the properties of the elements within a set. Every set is composed of elements, but sets have properties which are not identical with the properties of the elements of the set."

THE HIGHLY EFFECTIVE WORK GROUP

Much of the discussion of groups in this chapter will be in terms of an ideal organizational model which the work groups in an organization can approach as they develop skill in group processes. This model group, of course, is always part of a large organization. The description of its nature and performance characteristics is based on evidence from variety of sources. Particularly important are the observational and experimental studies of small groups such as those conducted by the Research Center for Group Dynamics (Cartwright & Zander, 1960; Hare et al., 1955; Institute for Social Research, 1956; Institute for Social Research, 1960; Thibaut & Kelly, 1959). Extensive use is made of data from studies of large-scale organizations. Another important source is the material from the National Training Laboratories (Foundation for Research on Human Behavior, 1960d; National Training Laboratories, 1953; National Training Laboratories, 1960; Stock & Thelen, 1958). The NTL has focused on training in sensitivity to the reactions of others and in skills to perform the leadership and membership roles in groups.

In addition to drawing upon the above sources, the description of the ideal model is derived from theory. Some of the statements about the model for which there is little or limited experimental or observational data have been derived directly from the basic drive to achieve and maintain a sense of importance and personal worth. At several points in this chapter the author has gone appreciably beyond available specific research findings. The author feels, however, that the generalizations which are emerging based on research in organizations and on small groups, youth, and family life, personality development, consumer behavior, human motivation, and related fields lend strong support to the general theory and the derivations contained in this book.

It has been necessary to go beyond the data in order to spell out at this time in some detail the general pattern of the more complex but more effective form of organization being created by the higher-producing managers. The author hopes that the theory and model proposed will stimulate a substantial increase in basic and developmental research and that they will be tested and sharpened by that research.

The body of knowledge about small groups, while sufficiently large to make possible this description of the ideal model, is still relatively limited. Without question, as the importance of the work group as the basic building block of organizations becomes recognized, there will be a great increase in the research on groups and our knowledge about them. The over-all pattern of the model described here will be improved and clarified by such research. Our understanding of how to develop and use groups effectively will also be greatly advanced.

The following description of the ideal model defines what we mean by *a highly effective group*. The definition involves reference to several different variables. Each of them can be thought of as a continuum, i.e., as a characteristic which can vary from low to high, from unfavorable to favorable. For example, a group can vary from one in which there is hostility among the members to one in which the attitudes are warm and friendly. The ideal model is at the favorable end of each variable.

THE NATURE OF HIGHLY EFFECTIVE WORK GROUPS

The highly effective group, as we shall define it, is always conceived as being a part of a larger organization. A substantial proportion of persons in a company are members of more than one work group, especially when both line and staff are considered. As a consequence, in such groups there are always linking functions to be performed and relationships to other groups to be maintained. Our highly effective group is not an isolated entity.

All the persons in a company also belong to groups and organizations outside of the company. For most persons, membership in several groups both within and outside the company is the rule rather than the exception. This means, of course, that no single group, even the highly effective work group, dominates the life of any member. Each member of the organization feels pressures from membership in several different groups and is not influenced solely by loyalty to any one group.

Since the different groups to which a person belongs are apt to have somewhat different and often inconsistent goals and values, corresponding conflicts and pressures are created within him. To minimize these conflicts and tensions, the individual seeks to influence the values and goals of each of the different groups to which he belongs and which are important to him so as to minimize the inconsistencies and conflicts in values and goals. In striving for this reconciliation, he is likely to press for the acceptance of those values most important to him.

The properties and performance characteristics of the ideal highly effective group are as follows:

1. The members are skilled in all the various leadership and membership roles and functions required for interaction between leaders and members and between members and other members.

2. The group has been in existence sufficiently long to have developed a well-established, relaxed working relationship among all its members.

3. The members of the group are attracted to it and are loyal to its members, including the leader.

4. The members and leaders have a high degree of confidence and trust in each other.

5. The values and goals of the group are a satisfactory integration and expression of the relevant values and needs of its members. They have helped shape these values and goals and are satisfied with them.

6. In so far as members of the group are performing linking functions, they endeavor to have the values and goals of the groups which they link in harmony, one with the other.

7. The more important a value seems to the group, the greater the likelihood that the individual member will accept it.

8. The members of the group are highly motivated to abide by the major values and to achieve the important goals of the group. Each member will do all that he reasonably can—and at times all in his power—to help the group achieve its central objectives. He expects every other member to do the same. This high motivation springs, in part, from the basic motive to achieve and maintain a sense of personal worth and importance. Being valued by a group whose values he shares, and deriving a sense of significance and importance from this relationship, leads each member to do his best. He is eager not to let the other members down. He strives to do what he believes is expected of him.

9. All the interaction, problem-solving, decision-making activities of the group occur in a supportive atmosphere. Suggestions, comments, ideas, information, criticisms are all offered with a helpful orientation. Similarly, these contributions are received in the same spirit. Respect is shown for the point of view of others both in the way contributions are made and in the way they are received.

There are real and important differences of opinion, but the focus is on arriving at sound solutions and not on exacerbating and aggravating the conflict. Ego forces deriving from the desire to achieve and maintain a sense of personal worth and importance are channeled into constructive efforts. Care is taken not to let these ego forces disrupt important group tasks, such as problem-solving. Thus, for example, a statement of the problem, a condition which any solution must meet, a suggested solution, or an item of relevant fact are all treated as from the group as a whole. Care is taken so that one statement of the problem is not John's and another Bill's. A suggested solution is not referred to as Tom's and another as Dick's. All the material contributed is treated as *ours:* "One of our proposed solutions is *A,* another is *B.*" In all situations involving actual or potential differences or conflict among the members of the group, procedures are used to separate the ego of each member from his contribution. In this way, ego forces do not stimulate conflict between members. Instead, they are channeled into supporting the activities and efforts of the group.

The group atmosphere is sufficiently supportive for the members to be able to accept readily any criticism which is offered and to make the most constructive use of it. The criticisms may deal with any relevant topic such as operational problems, decisions, supervisory problems, interpersonal relationships, or group processes, but whatever their content, the member feels sufficiently secure in the supportive atmosphere of the group to be able to accept, test, examine, and benefit from the criticism offered. Also, he is able to be frank and candid, irrespective of the content of the discussion: technical, managerial, factual, cognitive, or emotional. The supportive atmosphere of the group with the feeling of security it provides, contributes to a cooperative relationship between the members. And this cooperation itself contributes to and reinforces the supportive atmosphere.

10. The superior of each work group exerts a major influence in establishing the tone and atmosphere of that work group by his leadership principles and practices. In the highly effective group, consequently, the leader adheres to those principles of leadership which create a supportive atmosphere in the group and a cooperative rather than a competitive relationshp among the members. For example, he shares information fully with the group and creates an atmosphere where the members are stimulated to behave similarly.

11. The group is eager to help each member develop to his full potential. It sees, for example, that relevant technical knowledge and training in interpersonal and group skills are made available to each member.

12. Each member accepts willingly and without resentment the goals and expectations that he and his group establish for themselves. The anxieties, fears, and emotional stresses produced by direct pressure for high performance from a boss in a hierarchical situation are not present. Groups seem capable of setting high performance goals for the group as a whole and for each member. These goals are high enough to stimulate each member to do his best, but not so high as to create anxieties or fear of failure. In an effective group, each person can exert sufficient infuence on the decisions of the group to prevent the group from setting unattainable goals for any member while setting high goals for all. The goals are adapted to the member's capability to perform.

13. The leader and the members believe that each group member can accomplish "the impossible." These expectations stretch each member to the maximum and accelerate his growth. When necessary, the group tempers the expectation level so that the member is not broken by a feeling of failure or rejection.

14. When necessary or advisable, other members of the group will give a member the help he needs to accomplish successfully the goals set for him. Mutual help is a characteristic of highly effective groups.

15. The supportive atmosphere of the highly effective group stimulates creativity. The group does not demand narrow conformity as do the work groups under authoritarian leaders. No one has to "yes the boss," nor is he rewarded for such an attempt. The group attaches high value to new, creative approaches and solutions to its problems and to the problems of the organization of which it is a part. The motivation to be creative is high when one's work group prizes creativity.

16. The group knows the value of "constructive" conformity and knows when to use it and for what purposes. Although it does not permit conformity to affect adversely the creative efforts of its members, it does expect conformity on mechanical and administrative matters to save the time of members and to facilitate the group's activities. The group agrees, for example, on administrative forms and procedures, and once they have been established, it expects its members to abide by them until there is good reason to change them.

17. There is strong motivation on the part of each member to communicate fully and frankly to the group all the information which is relevant and of value

to the group's activity. This stems directly from the members' desire to be valued by the group and to get the job done. The more important to the group a member feels an item of information to be, the greater is his motivation to communicate it.

18. There is high motivation in the group to use the communication process so that it best serves the interests and goals of the group. Every item which a member feels is important, but which for some reason is being ignored, will be repeated until it receives the attention that it deserves. Members strive also to avoid communicating unimportant information so as not to waste the group's time.

19. Just as there is high motivation to communicate, there is correspondingly strong motivation to receive communications. Each member is genuinely interested in any information on any relevant matter that any member of the group can provide. This information is welcomed and trusted as being honestly and sincerely given. Members do not look "behind" the information item and attempt to interpret it in ways opposite to its purported intent. This interest of group members in information items and treatment of such items as valid reinforces the motivation to communicate.

20. In the highly effective group, there are strong motivations to try to influence other members as well as to be receptive to influence by them. This applies to all the group's activities: technical matters, methods, organizational problems, interpersonal relationships, and group processes.

21. The group processes of the highly effective group enable the members to exert more influence on the leader and to communicate far more information to him, including suggestions as to what needs to be done and how he could do his job better, than is possible in a man-to-man relationship. By "tossing the ball" back and forth among its members, a group can communicate information to the leader which no single person on a man-to-man basis dare do. As a consequence, the boss receives all the information that the group possesses to help him perform his job effectively.

22. The ability of the members of a group to influence each other contributes to the flexibility and adaptability of the group. Ideas, goals, and attitudes do not become frozen if members are able to influence each other continuously.

Although the group is eager to examine any new ideas and methods which will help it do its job better and is willing to be influenced by its members, it is not easily shifted or swayed. Any change is undertaken only after rigorous examination of the evidence. This stability in the group's activities is due to the steadying influence of the common goals and values held by the group members.

23. In the highly effective group, individual members feel secure in making decisions which seem appropriate to them because the goals and philosophy of operation are clearly understood by each member and provide him with a solid base for his decisions. This unleashes initiative and pushes decisions down while still maintaining a coordinated and directed effort.

24. The leader of a highly effective group is selected carefully. His leadership ability is so evident that he would probably emerge as a leader in any unstructured situation. To increase the likelihood that persons of high leadership competence are selected, the organization is likely to use peer nominations and related methods in selecting group leaders.

An important aspect of the highly effective group is its extensive use of the principle of supportive relationships. An examination of the above material reveals that virtually every statement involves an application of this principle.

LEADERSHIP FUNCTIONS

Several different characteristics of highly effective groups have been briefly examined. The role of the leader in these groups is, as we have suggested, particularly important. Certain leadership functions can be shared with group members; others can be performed only by the designated leader. In any organization, for example, the leader of a unit is the person who has primary responsibility for linking his work group to the rest of the organization. Other members of the group may help perform the linking function by serving as linking pins in overlapping groups other than that provided by the line organization, but the major linking is necessarily through the line organization. The leader has full responsibility for the group's performance and for seeing that his group meets the demands and expectations placed upon it by the rest of the organization of which it is a part. Other members of the group may share this responsibility at times, but the leader can never avoid full responsibility for the adequate performance of his group.

Although the leader has full responsibility, he does not try to make all the decisions. He develops his group into a unit which, with his participation, makes better decisions than he can make alone. He helps the group develop efficient communciation and influence processes which provide it with better information, more technical knowledge, more facts, and more experience for decision-making purposes than the leader alone can marshal.

Through group decision-making each member feels fully identified with each decision and highly motivated to execute it fully. The over-all performance of the group, as a consequence, is even better than the excellent quality of the decisions.

The leader knows that at times decisions must be made rapidly and cannot wait for group processes. He anticipates these emergencies and establishes procedures with his group for handling them so that action can be taken rapidly with group support.

The leader feels primarily responsible for establishing and maintaining at all times a thoroughly supportive atmosphere in the group. He encourages other members to share this responsibility, but never loses sight of the fact that as the leader of a work group which is part of a larger organization his behavior is likely to set the tone.

Although the leader accepts the responsibility associated with his role of leader of a group which is part of a larger organization, he seeks to minimize the influence of his hierarchical position. He is aware that tyrying to get results by "pulling rank" affects adversely the effectiveness of his group and his relationship to it. Thus, he endeavors to deemphasize status. He does this in a variety of ways that fit his personality and methods of leading, as for example by:

1. Listening well and patiently.
2. Not being impatient with the progress being made by the group, particularly on difficult problems.
3. Accepting more blame than may be warranted for any failure or mistake.
4. Giving the group members ample opportunity to express their thoughts without being constrained by the leader pressing his own views.
5. Being careful never to impose a decision upon the group.
6. Putting his contributions often in the form of questions or stating them speculatively.
7. Arranging for others to help perform leadership functions which enhance their status.

The leader strengthens the group and group processes by seeing that all problems *which involve the group* are dealt with by the group. He never handles such problems outside of the group nor with individual members of the group. While the leader is careful to see that all matters which involve and affect the whole group are handled by the whole group, he is equally alert not to undertake in a group-meeting agenda items or tasks which do not concern the group. Matters concerning one individual member and only that member are, of course, handled individually. Matters involving only a subgroup are handled by that subgroup. The total group is kept informed, however, of any subgroup action.

The leader fully reflects and effectively represents the views, goals, values, and decisions of his group in those other groups where he is performing the function of linking his group to the rest of the organization. He brings to the group of which he is the leader the views, goals, and decisions of those other groups. In this way, he provides a linkage whereby communication and the exercise of influence can be performed in both directions.

The leader has adequate competence to handle the technical problems faced by his group, or he sees that access to this technical knowledge is fully provided. This may involve bringing in, as needed, technical or resource persons. Or he may arrange to have technical training given to one or more members of his group so that the group can have available the necessary technical know-how when the group discusses a probelm and arrives at a decision.

The leader is what might be called "group-centered," in a sense comparable with the "employee-centered" supervisor described. He endeavors to build and maintain in his group a keen sense of responsibility for achieving its own goals and meeting its obligations to the larger organization.

The leader helps to provide the group with the stimulation arising from a restless dissatisfaction. He discourages complacency and passive acceptance of the present. He helps the members to become aware of new possibilities, more important values, and more significant goals.

The leader is an important source of enthusiasm for the significance of the mission and goals of the group. He sees that the tasks of the group are important and significant and difficult enough to be challenging.

As an over-all guide to his leadership behavior, the leader understands and uses with sensitivity and skill the principle of supportive relationships.

Many of these leadership functions, such as the linking function, can be performed only by the designated leader. This makes clear the great importance of selecting competent persons for leadership positions.

ROLES OF MEMBERSHIP AND LEADERSHIP

In the highly effective group, many functions are performed either by the leader or by the members, depending upon the situation or the requirements of the moment. The leader and members, as part of their roles in the group, establish and maintain an atmosphere and relationships which enable the communication, influence, decision-making, and similar processes of the group to be performed effectively. This means not only creating positive conditions, such as a supportive atmosphere, but also eliminating any negative or blocking factors. Thus, for example, groups sometimes have to deal with members who are insensitive, who are hostile, who talk too much, or who otherwise behave in ways adversely affecting the capacity of the group to function. In handling such a problem, the group makes the member aware of his deficiency, but does this in a sensitive and considerate manner and in a way to assist the member to function more effectively in the group. The members of most ordinary groups stop listening to a member who expresses himself in a fuzzy or confused manner. In a highly effective group, the members feed back their reaction to the person involved with suggestions and assistance on how to make his contributions clear, important, and of the kind to which all will want to listen. Friendly assistance and coaching can help a member overcome excessive talking or help him to learn to think and express himself more clearly.

Benne and Sheats (1948) have prepared a description of the different roles played in well-functioning groups. These roles may at times be performed by one or more group members, at other times by the leader. The list, while prepared on the basis of roles in discussion and problem-solving groups, is useful in considering the functions to be performed in any work group which is part of a larger organization.

The following material is taken from the Benne and Sheats article (pp. 42–45) with slight modifications. Group roles are classified into two broad categories:

1. *Group task roles*. These roles are related to the task which the group is deciding to undertake or has undertaken. They are directly concerned with the group effort in the selection and definition of a common problem and in the solution of that problem.
2. *Group building and maintenance roles*. These roles concern the functioning of the group as a group. They deal with the group's efforts to strengthen, regulate, and perpetuate the group as a group.

Group Task Roles

The following analysis assumes that the task of the group is to select, define, and solve common problems. The roles are identified in relation to functions of facilitation and coordination of group problem-solving activities. Each member may, of course, enact more than one role in any given unit of participation and a wide range of roles in successive participations. Any or all of these roles may be performed, at times, by the group "leader" as well as by various members.

1. *Initiating-contributing:* suggesting or proposing to the group new ideas or a changed way of regarding the group problem or goal. The novelty proposed may take the form of suggestions of a new group goal or a new definition of the problem. It may take the form of a suggested solution or some way of handling a difficulty that the

group has encountered. Or it may take the form of a proposed new procedure for the group, a new way of organizing the group for the task ahead.

2. *Information seeking:* asking for clarification of suggestions made in terms of their factual adequacy, for authoritative information and facts pertinent to the problems being discussed.

3. *Opinion seeking:* seeking information not primarily on the facts of the case, but for a clarification of the values pertinent to what the group is undertaking or of values involved in a suggestion made or in alternative suggestions.

4. *Information giving:* offering facts or generalizations which are "authoritative" or involve presenting an experience pertinent to the group problem.

5. *Opinion giving:* stating beliefs or opinions pertinent to a suggestion made or to alternative suggestions. The emphasis is on the proposal of what should become the group's view of pertinent values, not primarily upon relevant facts or information.

6. *Elaborating:* spelling out suggestions in terms of examples or developed meanings, offering a rationale for suggestions previously made, and trying to deduce how an idea or suggestion would work out if adopted by the group.

7. *Coordinating:* showing or clarifying the relationships among various ideas and suggestions, trying to pull ideas and suggestions together or trying to coordinate the activities of various members or sub-groups.

8. *Orienting:* defining the position of the group with respect to its goals by summarizing what has occurred, departures from agreed upon directions or goals are pointed to, or questions are raised about the direction the group discussion is taking.

9. *Evaluating:* subjecting the accomplishment of the group to some standard or set of standards of group functioning in the context of the group task. Thus, it may involve evaluating or questioning the "practicality," the "logic," or the "procedure" of a suggestion or of some unit of group discussion.

10. *Energizing:* prodding the group to action or decision, attempting to stimulate or arouse the group to "greater" activity or to activity of a "higher quality."

11. *Assisting on procedure:* expediting group movement by doing things for the group— performing routine tasks, e.g., distributing materials, or manipulating objects for the group, e.g., rearranging the seating or running the recording machine, etc.

12. *Recording:* writing down suggestions, making a record of group decisions, or writing down the product of discussion. The recorder role is the "group memory."

Group Building and Maintenance Roles

Here the analysis of member-functions is oriented to those activities which build group loyalty and increase the motivation and capacity of the group for candid and effective interaction and problem-solving. One or more members or the leader may perform each of these roles.

1. *Encouraging:* praising, showing interest in, agreeing with, and accepting the contributions of others; indicating warmth and solidarity in one's attitudes toward other group members, listening attentively and seriously to the contributions of group members, giving these contributions full and adequate consideration even though one may not fully agree with them; conveying to the others a feeling that—"that which you are about to say is of importance to me."

2. *Harmonizing:* mediating the differences between other members, attempting to reconcile disagreements, relieving tension in conflict situations through jesting, or pouring oil on troubled waters, etc.

3. *Compromising:* operating from within a conflict in which one's ideas or position is involved. In this role one may offer a compromise by yielding status, admitting error, by disciplining oneself to maintain group harmony, or by "coming half-way" in moving along with the group.

4. *Gate-keeping and expediting:* attempting to keep communication channels open by encouraging or facilitating the participation of others or by proposing regulation of the flow of communication.

5. *Setting standards or ideals:* expressing standards for the group or applying standards in evaluating the quality of group processes.

6. *Observing:* keeping records of various aspects of group process and feeding such data with proposed interpretation into the group's evaluation of its own procedures. The contribution of the person performing this role is usually best received or most fittingly received by the group when this particular role has been performed by this person at the request of the group and when the report to the group avoids expressing value judgments, approval, or disapproval.

7. *Following:* going along with the group, more or less passively accepting the ideas of others, serving as an audience in group discussion and decision.

The *group task roles* all deal with the intellectual aspects of the group's work. These roles are performed by members of the group during the problem-solving process, which usually involves such steps as:

1. Defining the problem.
2. Listing the conditions or criteria which any satisfactory solution to the problem should meet.
3. Listing possible alternative solutions.
4. Obtaining the facts which bear on each possible solution.
5. Evaluating the suggested solutions in terms of the conditions which a satisfactory solution should meet.
6. Eliminating undesirable solutions and selecting the most desirable solution.

The *group building and maintenance roles* are, as the label suggests, concerned with the emotional life of the group. These roles deal with the group's attractiveness to its members, its warmth and supportiveness, its motivation and capacity to handle intellectual problems without bias and emotion, and its capacity to function as a "mature" group.

The membership roles proposed by Benne and Sheats, while they are not definitive or complete, nevertheless point to the many complex functions performed in groups and dealt with by leader and members. The members of a highly effective group handle these roles with sensitivity and skill, and they see that the emotional life of the group contributes to the performance of the group's tasks rather than interfering with them.[1]

The highly effective group does not hesitate, for example, to look at and deal with friction between its members. By openly putting such problems on the table and sincerely examining them, they can be dealt with constructively. An effective group does not have values which frown upon criticism or which prevent bringing friction between members into the open. As a consequence, it does not put the lid on these emotional pressures, causing them to simmer below the surface and be a constant source of disruption to the performance of group tasks. The

---

[1]Although the Benne and Sheats list does not define each category unambiguously, it is useful in helping a group analyze and improve its processes. Another list has been prepared by Bales (1950) which has relatively precise definitions. The Bales list will be of interest to those who wish to do research on group processes or who wish to observe and analyze them systematically.

intellectual functions of any group can be performed without bias and disruption only when the internal emotional tensions and conflicts have been removed from the life of the group. Differences in ideas are stimulating and contribute to creativity, but emotional conflict immobilizes a group.

Group building and maintenance functions and group task functions are interdependent processes. In order to tackle difficult problems, to solve them creatively, and to achieve higher performance, a group must be at a high level of group maintenance. Success in task processes, fortunately, also contributes to the maintenance of the group and to its emotional life, including its attraction to members and its supportive atmosphere.

In the midst of struggling with a very difficult task, a group occasionally may be faced with group maintenance problems. At such times, it may be necessary for the group to stop its intellectual activity and in one way or another to look at and deal with the disruptive emotional stresses. After this has been done, the group can then go forward with greater unity and will be more likely to solve its group task constructively.

The leader and the members in the highly effective group know that the building and maintenance of the group as well as the carrying out of tasks need to be done well. They are highly skilled in performing each of the different membership and leadership roles required. Each member feels responsible for assuming whatever role is necessary to keep the group operating in an efficient manner. In performing these required roles, the member may carry them out by himself or in cooperation with other group members. Each exercises initiative as called for by the situation. The group has a high capacity to mobilize fully all the skills and abilities of its members and focus these resources efficiently on the jobs to be done.

The larger the work group, the greater the difficulty in building it into a highly effective group. Seashore (1954) found that group cohesiveness, i.e., attraction of the members to the group, decreased steadily as work groups increased in size. This finding is supported by other data (Indik, 1961; Revans, 1957).

To facilitate building work groups to high levels of effectiveness it will be desirable, consequently, to keep the groups as small as possible. This requirement, however, must be balanced against other demands on the organization, such as keeping the number of organizational levels to a minimum. This suggests the desirability of running tests and computing the relative efficiencies and costs of different-sized work groups. It is probable also that the optimum size for a group will vary with the kind of work the group is doing.

The highly effective group as described in this chapter, it will be recalled, is an "ideal model." It may sound completely unattainable. This does not appear to be the case. There is impressive evidence supporting the view that this ideal can be approximated, if not fully reached, in actual operations in any organization. This evidence is provided by the highest-producing managers and supervisors in American industry and government. If the measurements of their work groups and reports of their work-group members are at all accurate, some of these managers have built and are operating work groups strikingly similar to our ideal model.

This chapter started by observing that groups can have constructive or destructive goals and can achieve these goals fully or partially, that there is nothing inherently good or bad about groups. If we reflect on the nature and functional characteristics of the highly effective group, however, some qualification of our initial comments may be warranted. In the highly effective group, the members can and do exercise substantial amounts of influence on the group's values and goals. As a consequence, these goals reflect the long-range as well as the short-range needs, desires, and values of its members. If we assume that the long-range desires and values will reflect, on the average, some of the more important long-range values and goals of the total society, we can draw some inferences about the highly effective group. These groups will, in terms of probability, reflect the constructive values and goals of their society. They are likely to be strong groups seeking "good" goals.

GROUP THINK

Irving L. Janis

"How could we have been so stupid?" President John F. Kennedy asked after he and a close group of advisers had blundered into the Bay of Pigs invasion. For the last two years I have been studying that question, as it applies not only to the Bay of Pigs decision-makers but also to those who led the United States into such other major fiascos as the failure to be prepared for the attack on Pearl Harbor, the Korean War stalemate and the escalation of the Vietnam War.

Stupidity certainly is not the explanation. The men who participated in making the Bay of Pigs decision, for instance, comprised one of the greatest arrays of intellectual talent in the history of American Government—Dean Rusk, Robert McNamara, Douglas Dillon, Robert Kennedy, McGeorge Bundy, Arthur Schlesinger Jr., Allen Dulles and others.

It also seemed to me that explanations were incomplete if they concentrated only on disturbances in the behavior of each individual within a decision-making body: temporary emotional states of elation, fear, or anger that reduce a man's mental efficiency, for example, or chronic blind spots arising from a man's social prejudices or idiosyncratic biases.

I preferred to broaden the picture by looking at the fiascos from the standpoint of group dynamics as it has been explored over the past three decades, first by the great social psychologist Kurt Lewin and later in many experimental situations by myself and other behavioral scientists. My conclusion after pouring over hundreds of relevant documents—historical reports about formal group meetings and informal conversations among the members—is that the groups that committed the fiascos were victims of what I call "group think."

Source: Psychology Today, November 1971. Copyright © 1971 Ziff-Davis Publishing Company. Reprinted by permission of *Psychology Today* magazine and the author.

"GROUPY"

In each case study, I was surprised to discover the extent to which each group displayed the typical phenomena of social conformity that are regularly encountered in studies of group dynamics among ordinary citizens. For example, some of the phenomena appear to be completely in line with findings from social-psychological experiments showing that powerful social pressures are brought to bear by the members of a cohesive group whenever a dissident begins to voice his objections to a group consensus. Other phenomena are reminiscent of the shared illusions observed in encounter groups and friendship cliques when the members simultaneously reach a peak of "groupy" feelings.

Above all, there are numerous indications pointing to the development of group norms that bolster morale at the expense of critical thinking. One of the most common norms appears to be that of remaining loyal to the group by sticking with the policies to which the group has already committed itself, even when those policies are obviously working out badly and have unintended consequences that disturb the conscience of each member. This is one of the key characteristics of groupthink.

1984

I use the term groupthink as a quick and easy way to refer to the mode of thinking that persons engage in when *concurrence-seeking* becomes so dominant in a cohesive ingroup that it tends to override realistic appraisal of alternative courses of action. Groupthink is a term of the same order as the words in the newspeak vocabulary George Orwell used in his dismaying world of *1984*. In that context, groupthink takes on an invidious connotation. Exactly such a connotation is intended, since the term refers to a deterioration in mental efficiency, reality testing and moral judgments as a result of group pressures.

The symptoms of groupthink arise when the members of decision-making groups become motivated to avoid being too harsh in their judgments of the leaders' or their colleagues' ideas. They adopt a soft line of criticism, even in their own thinking. At their meetings, all the members are amiable and seek complete concurrence on every important issue, with no bickering or conflict to spoil the cozy, "we-feeling" atmosphere.

KILL

Paradoxically, soft-headed groups are often hard-hearted when it comes to dealing with outgroups or enemies. They find it relatively easy to resort to dehumanizing solutions—they will readily authorize bombing attacks that kill large numbers of civilians in the name of the noble cause of persuading an unfriendly government to negotiate at the peace table. They are unlikely to pursue the more difficult and controversial issues that arise when alternatives to a harsh military solution come up for discussion. Nor are they inclined to raise ethical issues that carry the implication that *this fine group of ours, with its humanitarianism and its high-minded principles, might be capable of adopting a course of action that is inhumane and immoral.*

NORMS

There is evidence from a number of social-psychological studies that as the members of a group feel more accepted by the others, which is a central feature of increased group cohesiveness, they display less overt conformity to group norms. Thus we would expect that the more cohesive a group becomes, the less the members will feel constrained to censor what they say out of fear of being socially punished for antagonizing the leader or any of their fellow members.

In contrast, the groupthink type of conformity tends to increase as group cohesiveness increases. Groupthink involves nondeliberate suppression of critical thoughts as a result of internalization of the group's norm's, which is quite different from deliberate suppression on the basis of external threats of social punishment. The more cohesive the group, the greater the inner compulsion on the part of each member to avoid creating disunity, which inclines him to believe in the soundness of whatever proposals are promoted by the leader or by a majority of the group's members.

In a cohesive group, the danger is not so much that each individual will fail to reveal his objections to what the others propose but that he will think the proposal is a good one, without attempting to carry out a careful, critical scrutiny of the pros and cons of the alternatives. When groupthink becomes dominant, there also is considerable suppression of deviant thoughts, but it takes the form of each person's deciding that his misgivings are not relevant and should be set aside, that the benefit of the doubt regarding any lingering uncertainties should be given to the group concensus.

STRESS

I do not mean to imply that all cohesive groups necessarily suffer from groupthink. All ingroups may have a mild tendency toward groupthink, displaying one or another of the symptoms from time to time, but it need not be so dominant as to influence the quality of the group's final decision. Neither do I mean to imply that there is anything necessarily inefficient or harmful about group decisions in general. On the contrary, a group whose members have properly defined roles, with traditions, concerning the procedures to follow in pursuing a critical inquiry, probably is capable of making better decisions than any individual group member working alone.

The problem is that the advantages of having decisions made by groups are often lost because of powerful psychological pressures that arise when the members work closely together, share the same set of values and, above all, face a crisis situation that puts everyone under intense stress.

The main principle of groupthink, which I offer in the spirit of Parkinson's Law, is this:

> *The more amiability and esprit de corps there is among the members of a policy-making ingroup, the greater the danger that independent critical thinking will be replaced by groupthink, which is likely to result in irrational and dehumanizing actions directed against outgroups.*

SYMPTOMS

In my studies of high-level governmental decision-makers, both civilian and military, I have found eight main symptoms of groupthink.

1 Invulnerability

Most or all of the members of the ingroup share an *illusion* of invulnerability that provides for them some degree of reassurance about obvious dangers and leads them to become overoptimistic and willing to take extraordinary risks. It also causes them to fail to respond to clear warnings of danger.

The Kennedy ingroup, which uncritically accepted the Central Intelligence Agency's disastrous Bay of Pigs plan, operated on the false assumption that they could keep secret the fact that the United States was responsible for the invasion of Cuba. Even after news of the plan began to leak out, their belief remained unshaken. They failed even to consider the danger that awaited them: a world-wide revulsion against the U.S.

A similar attitude appeared among the members of President Lyndon B. Johnson's ingroup, the "Tuesday Cabinet," which kept escalating the Vietnam War despite repeated setbacks and failures. "There was a belief," Bill Moyers commented after he resigned, "that if we indicated a willingness to use our power, they [the North Vietnamese] would get the message and back away from an all-out confrontation. . . . There was a confidence—it was never bragged about, it was just there—that when the chips were really down, the other people would fold."

A most poignant example of an illusion of invulnerability involves the ingroup around Admiral H. E. Kimmel, which failed to prepare for the possibility of a Japanese attack on Pearl Harbor despite repeated warnings. Informed by his intelligence chief that radio contact with Japanese aircraft carriers had been lost, Kimmel joked about it: "What, you don't know where the carriers are? Do you mean to say that they could be rounding Diamond Head (at Honolulu) and you wouldn't know it?" The carriers were in fact moving fullsteam toward Kimmel's command post at the time. Laughing together about a danger signal, which labels it as a purely laughing matter, is a characteristic manifestation of groupthink.

2 Rationale

As we see, victims of groupthink ignore warnings: they also collectively construct rationalizations in order to discount warnings and other forms of negative feedback that, taken seriously, might lead the group members to reconsider their assumptions each time they recommit themselves to past decisions. Why did the Johnson ingroup avoid reconsidering its escalation policy when time and again the expectations on which they based their decisions turned out to be wrong? James C. Thompson Jr., a Harvard historian who spent five years as an observing participant in both the State Department and the White House, tells us that the policymakers avoided critical discussion of their prior decisions and continually invented new rationalizations so that they could sincerely recommit themselves to defeating the North Vietnamese.

In the fall of 1964, before the bombing of North Vietnam began, some of the policymakers predicted that six weeks of air strikes would induce the North Vietnamese to seek peace talks. When someone asked, "What if they don't?" the answer was that another four weeks certainly would do the trick.

Later, after each setback, the ingroup agreed that by investing just a bit more effort (by stepping up the bomb tonnage a bit, for instance), their course of action would prove to be right. *The Pentagon Papers* bear out these observations.

In *The Limits of Intervention*, Townsend Hoopes, who was acting Secretary of the Air Force under Johnson, says that Walt W. Rostow in particular showed a remarkable capacity for what has been called "instant rationalization." According to Hoopes, Rostow buttressed the group's optimism about being on the road to victory by culling selected scraps of evidence from news reports or, if necessary, by inventing "plausible" forecasts that had no basis in evidence at all.

Admiral Kimmel's group rationalized away their warnings, too. Right up to December 7, 1941, they convinced themselves that the Japanese would never dare attempt a full-scale surprise assault against Hawaii because Japan's leaders would realize that it would precipitate an all-out war which the United States would surely win. They made no attempt to look at the situation through the eyes of the Japanese leaders—another manifestation of groupthink.

3 Morality

Victims of groupthink believe unquestioningly in the inherent morality of their ingroup; this belief inclines the members to ignore the ethical or moral consequences of their decisions.

Evidence that this symptom is at work usually is of a negative kind—the things that are left unsaid in group meetings. At least two influential persons had doubts about the morality of the Bay of Pigs adventure. One of them, Arthur Schlesinger Jr., presented his strong objections in a memorandum to President Kennedy and Secretary of State Rusk but suppressed them when he attended meetings of the Kennedy team. The other, Senator J. William Fulbright, was not a member of the group, but the President invited him to express his misgivings in a speech to the policymakers. However, when Fulbright finished speaking the President moved on to other agenda items without asking for reactions of the group.

David Kraslow and Stuart H. Loory, in *The Secret Search for Peace in Vietnam*, report that during 1966 President Johnson's ingroup was concerned primarily with selecting bomb targets in North Vietnam. They based their selections on four factors—the military advantage, the risk to American aircraft and pilots, the danger of forcing other countries into the fighting, and the danger of heavy civilian casualties. At their regular Tuesday luncheons, they weighed these factors the way school teachers grade examination papers, averaging them out. Though evidence on this point is scant, I suspect that the group's ritualistic adherence to a standardized procedure induced the members to feel morally justified in their destructive way of dealing with the Vietnamese people—after all, the danger of heavy civilian casualties from U.S. air strikes was taken into account on their checklists.

4 Stereotypes

Victims of groupthink hold stereotyped views of the leaders of enemy groups: they are so evil that genuine attempts at negotiating differences with them are unwarranted, or they are too weak or too stupid to deal effectively with whatever attempts the ingroup makes to defeat their purposes, no matter how risky the attempts are.

Kennedy's groupthinkers believed that Premier Fidel Castro's air force was so ineffectual that obsolete B-26s could knock it out completely in a surprise attack before the invasion began. They also believed that Castro's army was so weak that a small Cuban-exile brigade could establish a well-protected beachhead at the Bay of Pigs. In addition, they believed that Castro was not smart enough to put down any possible internal uprisings in support of the exiles. They were wrong on all three assumptions. Though much of the blame was attributable to faulty intelligence, the point is that none of Kennedy's advisers even questioned the CIA planners about these assumptions.

The Johnson advisers' sloganistic thinking about "the Communist apparatus" that was "working all around the world" (as Dean Rusk put it) led them to overlook the powerful nationalistic strivings of the North Vietnamese government and its efforts to ward off Chinese domination. The crudest of all stereotypes used by Johnson's inner circle to justify their policies was the domino theory ("if we don't stop the Reds in South Vietnam, tomorrow they will be in Hawaii and next week they will be in San Francisco," Johnson once said). The group so firmly accepted this stereotype that it became almost impossible for any adviser to introduce a more sophisticated viewpoint.

In the documents on Pearl Harbor, it is clear to see that the Navy commanders stationed in Hawaii had a naive image of Japan as a midget that would not dare to strike a blow against a powerful giant.

5 Pressure

Victims of groupthink apply direct pressure to any individual who momentarily expresses doubts about any of the group's shared illusions or who questions the validity of the arguments supporting a policy alternative favored by the majority. This gambit reinforces the concurrence-seeking norm that loyal members are expected to maintain.

President Kennedy probably was more active than anyone else in raising skeptical questions during the Bay of Pigs meetings, and yet he seems to have encouraged the group's docile, uncritical acceptance of defective arguments in favor of the CIA's plan. At every meeting, he allowed the CIA representatives to dominate the discussion. He permitted them to give their immediate refutations in response to each tentative doubt that one of the others expressed, instead of asking whether anyone shared the doubt or wanted to pursue the implications of the new worrisome issue that had just been raised. And at the most crucial meeting, when he was calling on each member to give his vote for or against the plan he did not call on Arthur Schlesinger, the one man there who was known by the President to have serious misgivings.

Historian Thompson informs us that whenever a member of Johnson's in-group began to express doubts, the group used subtle social pressures to "domesticate" him. To start with, the dissenter was made to feel at home, provided that he lived up to two restrictions: 1) that he did not voice his doubts to outsiders, which would play into the hands of the opposition: and 2) that he kept his criticisms within the bounds of acceptable deviation, which meant not challenging any of the fundamental assumptions that went into the group's prior commitments. One such "domesticated dissenter" was Bill Moyers. When Moyers arrived at a meeting, Thompson tells us, the President greeted him with, "Well, here comes Mr. Stop-the-Bombing."

6 Self-Censorship

Victims of groupthink avoid deviating from what appears to be group consensus; they keep silent about their misgivings and even minimize to themselves the importance of their doubts.

As we have seen, Schlesinger was not at all hesitant about presenting his strong objections to the Bay of Pigs plan in a memorandum to the President and the Secretary of State. But he became keenly aware of his tendency to suppress objections at the White House meetings. "In the months after the Bay of Pigs I bitterly reproached myself for having kept so silent during those crucial discussions in the cabinet room," Schlesinger writes in *A Thousand Days*. "I can only explain my failure to do more than raise a few timid questions by reporting that one's impulse to blow the whistle on this nonsense was simply undone by the circumstances of the discussion."

7 Unanimity

Victims of groupthink share an *illusion* with unanimity within the group concerning almost all judgments expressed by members who speak in favor of the majority view. This symptom results partly from the preceding one, whose effects are augmented by the false assumption that any individual who remains silent during any part of the discussion is in full accord with what the others are saying.

When a group of persons who respect each other's opinions arrives at a unanimous view, each member is likely to feel that the belief must be true. This reliance on consensual validation within the group tends to replace individual critical thinking and reality testing, unless there are clear-cut disagreements among the members. In contemplating a course of action such as the invasion of Cuba, it is painful for the members to confront disagreements within their group, particularly if it becomes apparent that there are widely divergent views about whether the preferred course of action is too risky to undertake at all. Such disagreements are likely to arouse anxieties about making a serious error. Once the sense of unanimity is shattered, the members no longer can feel complacently confident about the decision they are inclined to make. Each man must then face the annoying realization that there are troublesome uncertainties and he must diligently seek out the best information he can get in order to decide for himself exactly how serious the risks might be. This is one of the unpleasant consequences of being in a group of hardheaded, critical thinkers.

To avoid such an unpleasant state, the members often become inclined, without quite realizing it, to prevent latent disagreements from surfacing when they are about to initiate a risky course of action. The group leader and the members support each other in playing up the areas of convergence in their thinking, at the expense of fully exploring divergencies that might reveal unsettled issues.

"Our meetings took place in a curious atmosphere of assumed consensus," Schlesinger writes. His additional comments clearly show that, curiously, the consensus was an illusion—an illusion that could be maintained only because the major participants did not reveal their own reasoning or discuss their idiosyncratic assumptions and vague reservations. Evidence from several sources makes it clear that even the three principals—President Kennedy, Rusk and McNamara—had widely differing assumptions about the invasion plan.

8 Mindguards

Victims of groupthink sometimes appoint themselves as mindguards to protect the leader and fellow members from adverse information that might break the complacency they shared about the effectiveness and morality of past decisions. At a large birthday party for his wife, Attorney General Robert F. Kennedy, who had been constantly informed about the Cuban invasion plan, took Schlesinger aside and asked him why he was opposed. Kennedy listened coldly and said, "You may be right or you may be wrong, but the President has made his mind up. Don't push it any further. Now is the time for everyone to help him all they can."

Rusk also functioned as a highly effective mindguard by failing to transmit to the group the strong objections of three "outsiders" who had learned of the invasion plan—Undersecretary of State Chester Bowles, USIA Director Edward R. Murrow, and Rusk's intelligence chief, Roger Hilsman. Had Rusk done so, their warnings might have reinforced Schlesinger's memorandum and jolted some of Kennedy's ingroup, if not the President himself, into reconsidering the decision.

PRODUCTS

When a group of executives frequently displays most or all of these interrelated symptoms, a detailed study of their deliberations is likely to reveal a number of immediate consequences. These consequences are, in effect, products of poor decision-making practices because they lead to inadequate solutions to the problems being dealt with.

First, the group limits its discussions to a few alternative courses of action (often only two) without an initial survey of all the alternatives that might be worthy of consideration.

Second, the group fails to reexamine the course of action initially preferred by the majority after they learn of risks and drawbacks they had not considered originally.

Third, the members spend little or no time discussing whether there are non-obvious gains they may have overlooked or ways of reducing the seemingly prohibitive costs that made rejected alternatives appear undesirable to them.

Fourth, members make little or no attempt to obtain information from experts within their own organizations who might be able to supply more precise estimates of potential losses and gains.

Fifth, members show positive interest in facts and opinions that support their preferred policy; they tend to ignore facts and opinions that do not.

Sixth, members spend little time deliberating about how the chosen policy might be hindered by bureaucratic inertia, sabotaged by political opponents, or temporarily derailed by common accidents. Consequently, they fail to work out contingency plans to cope with foreseeable setbacks that could endanger the overall success of their chosen course.

SUPPORT

The search for an explanation of why groupthink occurs had led me through a quagmire of complicated theoretical issues in the murky area of human motivation. My belief, based on recent social psychological research, is that we can best understand the various symptoms of groupthink as a mutual effort among the group members to maintain self-esteem and emotional equanimity by providing social support to each other, especially at times when they share responsibility for making vital decisions.

Even when no important decision is pending, the typical administrator will begin to doubt the wisdom and morality of his past decisions each time he receives information about setbacks, particularly if the information is accompanied by negative feedback from prominent men who originally had been his supporters. It should not be surprising, therefore, to find that individual members strive to develop unanimity and esprit de corps that will help bolster each other's morale, to create an optimistic outlook about the success of pending decisions, and to reaffirm the positive value of past policies to which all of them are committed.

PRIDE

Shared illusions of invulnerability, for example, can reduce anxiety about taking risks. Rationalizations help members believe that the risks are really not so bad after all. The assumption of inherent morality helps the members to avoid feelings of shame or guilt. Negative stereotypes function as stress-reducing devices to enhance a sense of moral righteousness as well as pride in a lofty mission.

The mutual enhancement of self-esteem and morale may have functional value in enabling the members to maintain their capacity to take action, but it has maladaptive consequences insofar as concurrence-seeking tendencies interfere with crucial, rational capacities and lead to serious errors of judgment.

While I have limited my study to decision-making bodies in Government, groupthink symptoms appear in business, industry and any other field where small, cohesive groups make the decisions. It is vital, then for all sorts of people—and especially group leaders—to know what steps they can take to prevent groupthink.

REMEDIES

To counterpoint my case studies of the major fiascos, I have also investigated two highly successful group enterprises, the formulation of the Marshall Plan in the Truman Administration and the handling of the Cuban missile crisis by President Kennedy and his advisers. I have found it instructive to examine the steps Kennedy took to change his group's decision-making processes. These changes ensured that the mistakes made by his Bay of Pigs ingroup were not repeated by the missile-crisis ingroup, even though the membership of both groups was essentially the same.

The following recommendations for preventing groupthink incorporate many of the good practices I discovered to be characteristic of the Marshall Plan and missile-crisis groups:

1. The leader of a policy-forming group should assign the role of critical evaluator to each member, encouraging the group to give high priority to open airing of objections and doubts. This practice needs to be reinforced by the leader's acceptance of criticism of his own judgments in order to discourage members from soft-pedaling their disagreements and from allowing their striving for concurrence to inhibit criticism.

2. When the key members of a hierarchy assign a policy-planning mission to any group within their own organization, they should adopt an impartial stance instead of stating preferences and expectations at the beginning. This will encourage open inquiry and impartial probing of a wide range of policy alternatives.

3. The organization routinely should set up several outside policy-planning and evaluation groups to work on the same policy questions, each deliberating under a different leader. This can prevent the insulation of an ingroup.

4. At intervals before the group reaches a final consensus, the leader should require each member to discuss the group's deliberations with associates in his own unit of the organization—assuming that those associates can be trusted to adhere to the same security regulations that govern the policy-makers—and then to report back their reactions to the group.

5. The group should invite one or more outside experts to each meeting on a staggered basis and encourage the experts to challenge the views of the core members.

6. At every general meeting of the group, whenever the agenda calls for an evaluation of policy alternatives, at least one member should play devil's advocate, functioning as a good lawyer in challenging the testimony of those who advocate the majority position.

7. Whenever the policy issue involves relations with a rival nation or organization, the group should devote a sizable block of time, perhaps an entire session, to a survey of all warning signals from the rivals and should write alternative scenarios on the rivals' intentions.

8. When the group is surveying policy alternatives for feasibility and effectiveness, it should from time to time divide into two or more subgroups to meet separately, under different chairmen, and then come back together to hammer out differences.

9. After reaching a preliminary consensus about what seems to be the best policy, the group should hold a "second-chance" meeting at which every member expresses as vividly as he can all his residual doubts, and rethinks the entire issue before making a definitive choice.

HOW

These recommendations have their disadvantages. To encourage the open airing of objections, for instance, might lead to prolonged and costly debates when a rapidly growing crisis requires immediate solution. It also could cause rejection, depression and anger. A leader's failure to set a norm might create cleavage between leader and members that could develop into a disruptive power struggle if the leader looks on the emerging consensus as anathema. Setting up outside evaluation groups might increase the risk of security leakage. Still, inventive executives who know their way around the organizational maze probably can figure out how to apply one or another of the prescriptions successfully, without harmful side effects.

They also could benefit from the advice of outside experts in the administrative and behavioral sciences. Though these experts have much to offer, they have had few chances to work on policy-making machinery within large organizations. As matters now stand, executives innovate only when they need new procedures to avoid repeating serious errors that have deflated their self-images.

In this era of atomic warheads, urban disorganization and ecocatastrophes, it seems to me that policymakers should collaborate with behavioral scientists and give top priority to preventing groupthink and its attendant fiascos.

9
Problem Management

CREATIVITY IN THE EVERYDAY BUSINESS OF MANAGING
Robert E. Kaplan

OF BOXES, BUBBLES, AND EFFECTIVE MANAGEMENT
David K. Hurst

LEADERSHIP PRINCIPLES FOR PROBLEM SOLVING CONFERENCES
Norman R. F. Maier

CREATIVITY IN THE EVERYDAY
BUSINESS OF MANAGING

Robert E. Kaplan

Asked to list different types of creative professions, the participants in Creativity Week V mentioned writers, scientists, artists, engineers, architects, inventors, musicians, poets, psychologists, creativity specialists, and entrepreneurs. No one mentioned managers. But managers—at least the good ones—are creative all the time. They have to be to meet the confusing, fast-changing procession of demands on their intelligence, adaptability, and people-handling skill.

Creativity is evident in the *process* of management—the moment-to-moment and day-to-day flow of events in the manager's worklife. Claiming that management texts have ignored the management process, Leonard Sayles (1979) described it as:

> ...the actual day-to-day behavior and fragmented give-and-take, and the art of coping and negotiating with the unanticipated, the ambiguous, and the contradictory.
> First-rate manager...seek to orchestrate...the behavior of aggregations of personnel, some motivated, but many obtuse and recalcitrant. The nimble and com-

Source: Reprinted by permission from *Issues and Observations.* Copyright 1983. Center for Creative Leadership, Greensboro, NC.

plex behavior patterns of these superb managers is a delight to behold as they move to motivate, integrate, and modify the structure and personnel that surround them. Yet few texts capture the spirit of excitement and challenge (Sayles might also have said creativity) inherent in these tasks.

Sayles used language that evokes images of management process as an art form. Although often overlooked, the artistic qualities of the effective manager deserve their share of appreciation.

CREATING RHYTHMS IN THE MANAGER'S WORKDAY

Managers are busy, beseiged, harrassed, in demand, and verging out of control. A manager's day is a miscellany of activities: scheduled meetings, impromptu conversations, reading, writing, making presentations, going on tours. Managers jump from one thing to another, from one person or group to another. To fashion order from this potential chaos is a creative act.

What managers create are rhythms, or alternations between giving in to the swirl of events and getting out of the swirl. Three of these rhythms are the alternation between accessibility and inaccessiblity, the alternation between activity and reflection, and the alternation between work and leisure.

RHYTHM: ACCESSIBILITY AND INACCESSIBILITY

Interruptions pose a dilemma because, although they are the bane of the manager's existence, they are also the lifeline to fresh and necessary information. Managers can afford neither a truly open-door policy, which would rip their workdays to shreds, nor can they afford to close themselves off entirely and miss important news while alienating the very people upon whom they themselves rely for ready accessibility and instant responsiveness.

Effective managers create an ebb and flow; they regulate their boundaries, making them more and then less permeable, admitting intrusions and then resisting or deferring them. The boundaries become more or less permeable depending on the competing pressures—the individual's need to focus on the task at hand versus the pressure to respond to people and events impinging from outside the bounds of the task at hand. Robert Townsend (1970) former president of Avis Rent-A-Car, handled incoming phone calls by having them taken by a secretary until 11:00 A.M., when he returned the calls and accepted additional calls. He used the same method in the afternoon, having calls taken for him from noon to 4:00 P.M., then answering them for the next hour. His was a highly structured way of achieving a rhythm of accessibility and inaccessibility. Other, more flexible methods can be equally effective.

RHYTHM: ACTIVITY AND REFLECTION

For managers, the time for reflection is hard to come by. Barbara Tuchman (1980), writing about working for the government, observed:

> Given schedules broken down into 15 minute appointments and staffs numbering in the hundreds and briefing memos of never less than 30 pages, policy makers never have time to *think*.

For some managaers, the only respite from the swift currents of activity comes when they are away from the office—at home, traveling between home and work, on trips. But those who manage their days creatively find havens from activity while at the office. President Nixon had a knack for this (Webber, 1982). He would escape from the White House to a hide-away office across the street in the Executive Office Building where, with his yellow legal pads in front of him, he would concentrate on the larger issues.

As Warren Bennis discovered while he was president of the University of Cincinnati, routine work commonly drives out nonroutine work; only creative managers avoid having the larger issues banished by the details (Bennis, 1976).

Nevertheless, the bustle of the manager's day is not entirely to blame. While sheer activity can overwhelm managers, so can it tempt them. Managers may allow themselves to be seduced by mere activity when the alternative is the anxiety-provoking challenge of reflection and creativity (Ashkenas & Schaffer, 1982). Effective managers find the time to reflect despite being busy and despite the temptation to stay that way.

Alternating rhythmically between action and reflection is partly a matter of making dexterous transitions from one to the ohter. Managers struggle, after a long bout of activity, to face the unsettling quiet of contemplative work. But activity need not inhibit reflection afterwards, if the period of activity is short. A short burst of activity to start the day can build the momentum needed to glide into reflection later on (Webber, 1982). The key is keeping activity in proportion.

RHYTHM: WORK AND LEISURE

Managers work long and hard; "brute persistence" is important to their success (Peters, 1980). Even so, all work and no play can dull a manager's wits and dampen creativity. According to a board chariman:

> When I hear a man talk about how hard he works, and how he hadn't taken a vacation in 5 years, and how seldom he sees his family, I am almost certain that this man will not succeed in the creative aspects of the business, and most of the important things that have to be done are the result of creative acts. (Mackenzie, 1975, p. 8)

When managers proclaim proudly that they haven't taken a vacation in years, the implication is that they are highly committed to their work and uncommonly loyal to their corporation—qualities that are indeed necessary to career advancement in large organizations (Kanter, 1977). But what does a single-minded devotion to the job sacrifice in the long run? Vaillant (1977) studied 100 men from their college years into their 50's and found that success (in career and family) was associated with, among other things, taking interesting vacations. May (1975) called this pattern the "alternation of the marketplace and the mountain" (p. 65).

Sticking tenaciously to the task can be counterproductive, one can't always attack problems frontally. That may be why Einstein was prompted to ask, "Why is it I get my best ideas in the morning while I'm shaving?" Perhaps because "the mind needs the relaxation of inner controls—needs to be freed in reverie or daydreaming—for the unaccustomed ideas to emerge" (May, 1975, p. 67).

Creative managers achieve this rhythmic interplay between work and diversion in fashioning their workdays and their worklives. If work is fight and diversion is flight, then the diversion considered here is what John Glidewell called constructive flight—not escapism, but a renewal through involvement in other spheres of activity or inactivity.

With these three rhythms, managers attempt to exercise a modicum of creative control over forces that would control them. The rhythms constitute an order that managers with a talent for orchestrating workday and worklife create out of the disorder of their jobs.

GIVING SHAPE TO PROBLEMS

Despite the play given in the management literature to the solving of problems, managers are equally challenged to find, in the first place, the problems in need of solving. (I mean here, problems as situations to resolve *or* exploit, difficulties *or* opportunities.) "Problem finding is no less important a task than problem solving" (Livingston, 1971). This is not to suggest that all of the items in a manager's short- and long-range docket are there because the manager sought them out. Certainly, a sizeable proportion of a manager's work comes already defined. But, to varying degrees, managers are responsible for ferreting out problems—for being attuned to the cues that indicate trouble or opportunity, and for developing a sense of what the cues mean and what action is indicated.

Finding and defining problems is a creative act with similarities to the visual arts. The manager gives form to a problem in the way a potter sees and then shapes the possibilities in a lump of clay. The difference is that managers practice their craft using an intangible medium—information.

Whether they are employed in an organization that manufactures goods or offers services, managers are more or less removed from the reality of making the product or service. Managers function in a social-informational milieu, in which reality is *constructed.* In other words, managers often decide what is real and what is not. John F. Kennedy and his cabinet interacted in such a way that they came to believe, wrongly, that an invasion of Cuba at the Bay of Pigs would meet with no significant opposition (Janis, 1972). When reality has an indisputable physical basis, there is less room for argument—or construction—although social psychologists have shown that, in a certain percentage of cases, a group can lead an individual to deny the evidence of his or her senses (Asch, 1956). By contrast, social reality is up for grabs. Was the meeting we just attended a productive one or a waste of time? Is morale high, medium or low in this organization? Are women and minorities treated fairly or unfairly in this organization? Does the future of this organization look rosy or bleak? To questions like these, which are the substance of the managear's job, answers are developed—reality is constructed—by a complex mental, emotional, interactive, political process; ultimately, by a creative process.

One way in which managers construct reality is by setting agendas. The notion of agenda setting as a major task of management was developed in an intensive study by Kotter (1982) of 15 general managers. Kotter found that these high-level managers all entered their new positions with only a half-formed idea of what needed to be done. It was in the first 6 to 12 months on the job that these managers developed a firm sense of their short- and long-range goals and the projects that would serve as vehicles to achieve those goals.

The GM's formed their agendas through an elaborate, continuous, and incremental process in which they aggressively collected information—primarily from people not documents, and to a large extent, from people with whom they already had relationships. In addition they sought information constantly and certainly did not limit their quest to formal planning meetings. Finally, they shaped plans using a combination of analysis and intuition. Out of this searching, sifting, and shaping came a loose and largely unwritten configuration of goals, plans, and projects (Kotter, 1982). In this way the GM's created their sense of what the reality of their organization was and should be.

John DeLorean, whose recent fall from grace should not erase his earlier accomplishments, provides an example of how a GM goes about creating such an agenda (Wright, 1979). Upon taking over the reins as general manager of General Motors' Chevrolet Division in 1969, DeLorean knew the division was in trouble but he didn't know why. Profits were dropping, budgets were being overspent, departments were not coordinating well. To discover the causes of the problem and to give direction to his executive strategy, DeLorean set out on a three-month personal inquiry into the Chevy situation.

What distinguished his search was its inclusiveness. By no means did he limit himself to the people in the immediate organizational vicinity. Instead he visited plants and talked to managers and employees alike; he met with Chevy dealers; he sought out disgruntled employees, even those who had left the division; he consulted with competitors and other informed individuals in and outside of the automobile industry. He neither sat is his office responding to day-to-day problems, nor did he attempt to assess the state of the organization by reading reports. He approached a variety of people and so gave shape to the sources of the division's problems and to a strategy for dealing with those problems.

The urge of managers to make sense of their complex, fast-changing world can be described as a "passion for form" (May, 1975). Fundamentally, it is a wordly version of the artistic instinct that enabled Michelangelo to see and sculpt the statue of David out of Carrera marble.

o work revamping it. Creativity has value to the extent that it is directed to
ul purposes. One participant in the Looking Glass simulation, overwhelmed
he material and feeling out of his element, adjusted to his plight by putting
show of playing his role. Stumped by a question at one point, he excused
elf from the meeting and went back to his office to consult his calendar about
he to meet the next day (there was no next day). Observing this, I admired
ngenuity but regretted this manager's response to his ignorance, which was
est ways to save face. The manager demonstrated creativity, but it was put
service not of job performance but of defensiveness.
Effective managers regularly perform unrecognized creative acts. But to
p this underrated talent in the art of managing, and to harness the talent
eful purposes, is no mean feat. Like any artist, the manager puts in years
ctice honing skills to a fine edge, but few managers performing their every-
t get the acclaim accorded artists in other fields.

RENCES

. E. "Studies of Independence of Conformity. A Minority of One Against a
Unanimous Majority." *Psychological Monographs* 70(9), 1956, Whole No. 416.
as, R. N., and R. H. Schaffer. "Managers Can Avoid Wasting Time." *Harvard
usiness Review* 60(3), 1982, pp. 84–104.
W. *The Unconscious Conspiracy: Why Leaders Can't Lead*. New York:
MACOM, 1976.
J. K., J. M. Power, and C.J.L. Yewett. *Public Planning: The Intercorporate
imension*. London: Tavistock, 1974.,
h, J. R. "Designing the Innovating Organization." *Organizational Dynamics,*
inter 1982, pp. 5–25.
L. *Victims of Groupthink*. Boston: Houghton Mifflin, 1972.
R. M. "The Middle Manager as Innovator." *Harvard Business Review,* July–
gust 1982, pp. 95–105.
R. M. *Men and Women of the Corporation*. New York: Basic Books. 1977.
R. E., and M. S. Mazique. *Trade routes: The Manager's Network of Relation-
ps* (Technical Report 22). Greensboro, N.C.: Center for Creative Leadership,
bruary 1983.
P. *The General Managers*. New York: The Free Press, 1982.
n, J. S. "Myth of the Well-educated Manager." *Harvard Business Review* 49(1),
l, pp. 78–89.
, R. A. *The Time Trap*. New York: AMACOM, 1975.
he Courage to Create. New York: Norton, 1975.
J. "A Style for All Seasons." *The Executive*. Summer, 1980.
Leadership. New York: McGraw-Hill, 1979.
B. "An Inquiry into the Persistence of Unwisdom in Government." *Esquire
*), 1980, pp. 25–31.
. E. *Adaptation to Life*. Boston: Little, Brown, 1977.
. A. "The Art of Construction Procrastination (Manager's Journal)." *The
Street Journal,* August, 13, 1982.
P. *On a Clear Day You Can See General Motors*. New York: Avon, 1979.

CREATING SOCIAL ARRANGEMENTS

When we consider the *products* of creative endeavor, we tend to think of *things*—physical objects like industrial products or works of art, or mental objects like ideas. We don't often think of an arrangement as being the creative product itself.

But good managers regularly create social arrangements. Although organizational structure is an obvious example of social creativity, it is a semipermanent structure that becomes an object. More to the point here are the temporary arrangements of people around a task. These arrangements vary from a task force that exists for months, to a group that meets one time on an issue of common concern, to the sequence of people that a manager calls upon during the course of a day to solve a problem.

Creating relationships is a basic form of social creativity, upon which the rest of the manager's work is built. There is no alternative to the developing of relationships; managers depend on a whole host of others without whom they can't perform their jobs at any level of effectiveness (Kaplan & Mazique, 1983). Making up the networks of job-relevant others of the general managers Kotter (1982) studied were hundreds and sometimes thousands of people in and outside of the organization.

Relationships are not bestowed upon a manager, they are developed as a product of individual roles and personalities. A good relationship exists when a manager can depend on another person for a cooperative response. The other person will tend to resepond cooperatively when the manager has something to offer. In other words, relationships are based on exchange, whether of tangible or intangible commodities. Effective relationships are reciprocal.

An appreciation of the need to develop reciprocal relationships is shown by an executive who several years ago faced the challenge of introducing computers to the several divisions of his corporation. He headed a new staff function and none of the division heads reported to him. "I spent a lot of time on the opposing forces trying to build credibility—my own and my group's. It was a slam-dunk operation, not loved. I saw us as a change agent, and my approach was to teach a need, induce a need. I tried to build relationships when we weren't in a fight so that when a burning issue came up, you've got money in the bank. When fires broke out, we fought them with face-to-face meetings with our antagonists." This executive had a knack for building relationships under adversity. He gained influence with the division heads by making them aware of how the new function could meet their needs, built trust by interacting when there wasn't conflict, dealt with conflict by sitting down face to face.

Creating contact is what the manager must do to build or to call upon relationships. The episodes in which a manager and others come together can be likened to a dance. Sayles wrote vividly about how the parties to an effective interaction coordinate their movements. They simultaneously move and respond to the other's movement. As he puts it, "These verbal strokings, this mutual adaptation, appeal to the basic animal nature that calls for rhythmical give-and-take" (1979, p. 67).

Just as managers can synchronize their interactions, can dance together, they can also be out-of-step. Managers show a clumsiness on the dance floor of interactions when they only talk and rarely listen, when they only listen and hardly talk, when they can't hold anything but long drawn-out conversations, or when they can only converse on the run.

If contact is dance, then part of creating contact is choosing a suitable stage on which to perform the dance. A plant manager tells the story of how, when he first took over the plant, his predecessor brought him along to a meeting with the union bargaining committee. The adversarial relationship between union and management was demonstrated by the haranguing between the old plant manager and the union president from opposite ends of a long conference table. After his predecessor had left for good, the new man went to the next union-management meeting and sat down immediately beside the union president, who began as usual to shout and gesture dramatically. But, because it is difficult to yell at a person sitting next to you, the union president moderated his tone and approach, and the relationship between union and management eventually became more cooperative. Thus, by his choice of seating, the manager created a contact with his opposite number that signalled the relationship he wanted. Although his predecessor sought to usher him into the hostile tradition, the new manager saw a choice where others might have thought none existed.

Activating relationships is another dimension of creating social arrangements. With relationships at their disposal, managers get work done by mobilizing these relationships at particular times, in particular ways (some of which have to do with creating contact), around particular tasks.

If contact is dance, then activating relationships is choreography. To begin a project, managers must decide whom to bring on stage to work on which piece of the larger task, in what combinations actors are to be brought together, in what sequence these subgroups are to be convened, and what mode of contact (telephone, written communication, scheduled meeting, impromptu conversation) is to be used among the manager and the others. The manager as choreographer, however, has nothing like a set script to follow, but must improvise the arrangements as he or she goes along.

Something of the quality of the social choreography managers perform is evident in the observation by Bennis (1976):

> To function properly, the leader must have an "executive constellation" [which works] through temporary systems of assembling task forces for a particular assignment, then reassembling others for a different task. (p. 135)

Friend, et al. (1974) also recognize this choreographic talent:

> Knowing how to make effective use of a network is...the mobilization of decision networks in an intelligently selective way, which depends on the capacity to understand both the structure of a problem and the structure of organizational and political relations that surround them. (p. 364)

The choreographic art lies in activating relationships in light of the structure of the problem being attacked. Rosebeth Kanter (1982), writing from research on 165 innovative middle managers from five corporations, shows how the success of a project hinges upon the manager's ability to activate r up the commitment of key players over the long course of middle managers make use of briefings, assignments, mee informal), team-building, praise, new structural arrangemer by high-level supporters, and the careful management of the ups (Kanter, 1982). When to resort to which of these and othe mechanisms is part of the skill of activating relationship

Thus, managers who are creative in the social spher call microsocial structure—small scale and often epher people—designed in such a way as to enlist the help of ot of the bits and pieces of larger tasks.

THE MANAGER AS ARTIST

Managers exhibit creativity in the way they arrange a disperse information, ideas, tasks and people. Managers departures, and sometimes radical departures, from w their talents, energies and history, they make up their they go along. Like the jazz musician, effective mana a larger thematic framework; they improvise in dealing Ineffective managers replay the same tune, use the s a narrow band mentally and interpersonally. Versatility the ineffective manager.

But let's not romanticize creativity. It takes *en* than it does to follow routines. Creative challenges als takes a pure form in artists like Giacometti who su despairing of capturing on canvas his vision of the will become completely empty: then what will becom quoted in May, 1975, p. 93). Managers may not ag but they do worry about the tough issues that ma Anxiety in the face of creative tasks can tempt ma paced routines of their job.

No joyride for the manager, creativity often tive element. Picasso observed that "every act of destruction" (May, 1975, p. 63). For this reason, to make the next technological advance. The man did not invent the electric typewriter, and the man did not invent the word processor. The huge ca nology works as a disincentive to develop truly n The next technological breakthrough is, in this managers destroy an old idea when they adopt when they choose another for a desirable assi

We can avoid making a fetish of creati creativity for creativity's sake. Executives with harm than good if they take over a stable, effec

REFE

Asch,

Ashken

Bennis,

Friend,

Galbrai

Janis, I.
Kanter,

Kanter,
Kaplan,
    shi

Kotter, J
Livingsto
    197
Mackenzi
May, R.
Peters, T.
Sayles, L.
Tuchman,
    93(5
Vaillant,
Webber, R
    Wal
Wright, J.

OF BOXES, BUBBLES,
AND EFFECTIVE MANAGEMENT

David K. Hurst

Harvard Buisness Review
Soldiers Field Road
Boston, Massachusetts 02163

Dear Editors:

We are writing to tell you how events from 1979 on have forced us, a team of four general managers indistinguishable from thousands of others, to change our view of what managers should do. In 1979 we were working for Hugh Russel Inc., the fiftieth largest public company in Canada. Hugh Russel was an industrial distributor with some $535 million in sales and a net income of $14 million. The organization structure was conventional: 16 divisions in four groups, each with a group president reporting to the corporate office. Three volumes of corporate policy manuals spelled out detailed aspects of corporate life, including our corporate philosophy. In short, in 1979 our corporation was like thousands of other businesses in North America.

During 1980, however, through a series of unlikely runs, that situation changed drastically. Hugh Russel found itself acquired in a 100% leveraged buyout and then merged with a large, unprofitable (that's being kind!) steel fabricator, York Steel Construction, Ltd. The resulting entity was York Russel Inc., a privately held company except for the existence of some publicly owned preferred stock which obliged us to report to the public.

As members of the acquired company's corporate office, we waited nervously for the ax to fall. Nothing happened. Finally, after about six weeks, Wayne (now our president) asked the new owner if we could do anything to help the deal along. The new chairman was delighted and gave us complete access to information about the acquirer.

It soon became apparent that the acquiring organization had little management strength. The business had been run in an entrepreneurial style with hundreds of people reporting to a single autocrat. The business had, therefore, no comprehensive plan and, worse still, no money. The deal had been desperately conceived to shelter our profits from taxes and use the resulting cash flow to fund the excessive debt of the steel fabrication business.

Our first job was to hastily assemble a task force to put together a $300 million bank loan application and a credible turnaround plan. Our four-member management team (plus six others who formed a task force) did it in only six weeks. The merged business, York Russel, ended up with $10 million of equity and $275 million of debt on the eve of a recession that turned out to be the worst Canada had experienced since the Great Depression. It was our job then to save the new company, somehow.

Conceptual frameworks are important roads to managers' perceptions, and every team should have a member who can build them. Before the acquisition, the framework implicit in our organization was a "hard," rational model rather like those Thomas Peters and Robert Waterman describe.[1] Jay Galbraith's elaborate model is one of the purest examples of the structure-follows-strategy school.[2] The model clearly defines all elements and their relationships to each other, presumably so that they can be measured (see the *Exhibit*).

EXHIBIT 1   The hard and soft model and how they work together

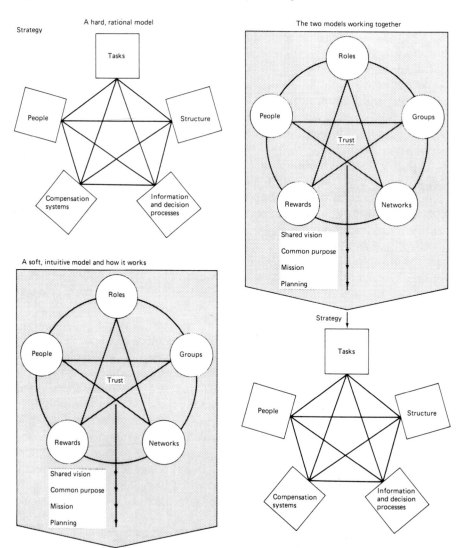

Because circumstances changed after the acquisition, our framework fell apart almost immediately. Overnight we went from working for a growth company to working for one whose only objective was survival. Our old decentralized organization was cumbersome and expensive; our new organization needed cash, not profits. Bankers and suppliers swarmed all over us, and the quiet life of a management-controlled public company was gone.

Compounding our difficulties, the recession quickly revealed all sorts of problems in businesses that up to that time had given us no trouble. Even the core nuggets offered up only meager profits, while merest rates of up to 25% quickly destroyed what was left of the balance sheet.

In the heat of the crisis, the management team jelled quickly. At first each member muddled in his own way, but as time went by, we started to plan a new understanding of how to be effective. Even now we do not completely understand the conceptual framework that has evolved, and maybe we never will. What follows is our best attempt to describe to you and our readers what guides us today.

Yours truly,

The management team

TWO MODELS ARE BETTER THAN ONE

The hard, rational model isn't wrong; it just isn't enough. There is something more. As it turns out, there is a great deal more.

At York Russel we have had to develop a "soft," intuitive framework that offers a counterpart to every element in the hard, rational framework. As the exhibit shows and the following sections discuss, in the soft model, roles are the counterparts of tasks, groups replace structure, networks operate instead of information systems, the rewards are soft as opposed to hard, and people are viewed as social animals rather than as rational beings.

That may not sound very new. But we found that the key to effective management of not only our crisis but also the routine is to know whether we are in a hard "box" or a soft "bubble" context. By recognizing the dichotomy between the two, we can choose the appropriate framework.

☐ **TASKS** ... & ...	○ **ROLES**
☐ Static	○ Fluid
☐ Clarity	○ Ambiguity
☐ Content	○ Process
☐ Fact	○ Perception
☐ Science	○ Art

These are some of our favorite words for contrasting these two aspects of management. Here's how we discovered them.

The merger changed our agenda completely. We had new shareholders, a new bank, a new business (the steel fabrication operations consisted of nine divisions), and a new relationship with the managers of our subsidiaries, who were used to being left alone to grow. The recession and high interest rates rendered the corporation insolvent. Bankruptcy loomed large. Further, our previously static way of operating became very fluid.

In general, few of us had clear tasks, and for the most part we saw the future as ambiguous and fearful. We found ourselves describing what we had to do as roles rather than as tasks. At first our descriptions were crude. We talked of having an "inside man" who deals with administration, lawyers, and bankers versus an "outside man" who deals with operations, customers, and suppliers. Some of us were "readers," others "writers," some "talkers," and others "listeners." As the readers studied the work of behavioral science researchers and talked to the listeners, we found more useful classifications. Henry Mintzberg's description of managers' work in terms of three roles—interpersonal (figurehead, leaders, liaison), information (monitor, disseminator, spokesperson), and decisional—helped us see the variety of the job.[3] Edgar Schein's analysis of group roles helped us concentrate on the process of communication as well as on what was communicated.[4]

The most useful framework we used was the one Ichak Adize developed for decision-making roles.[5] In his view, a successful management team needs to play four distinct parts. The first is that of producer of results. A *producer* is action oriented and knowledgeable in his or her field; he or she helps compile plans with an eye to their implementability. The *administrator* supervises the system and manages the detail. The *entrepreneur* is a creative risk taker who initiates action, comes up with new ideas, and challenges existing policies. And the *integrator* brings people together socially and their ideas intellectually, and interprets the significance of events. The integrator gives the team a sense of direction and shared experience.

According to Adize, each member must have some appreciation of the others' roles (by having some facility in those areas), and it is essential that they get along socially. At York Russel the producers (who typically come out of operations) and administrators (usually accountants) tend to be hard box players, while the entrepreneurs tend to live in the soft bubble. Integrators (friendly, unusually humble MBAs) move between the hard and the soft, and we've found a sense of humor is essential to being able to do that well.

The key to a functioning harmonious group, however, has been for members to understand that they might disagree with each other because they are in two different contexts. Different conceptual frameworks may lead people to different conclusions based on the same facts. Of the words describiing tasks and roles, our favorite pair is "fact" versus "perception." People in different boxes will argue with each other over facts, for facts in boxes are compelling—they seem so tangible. Only from the bubble can one see them for what they are: abstractions based on the logical frameworks, or boxes, being used.

☐ **STRUCTURE**	... & ...	○ **GROUPS**
☐ Cool		○ Warm
☐ Formal		○ Informal
☐ Closed		○ Open
☐ Obedience		○ Trust
☐ Independence		○ Autonomy

Our premerger corporation was a pretty cold place to work. Senior management kept control in a tight inner circle and then played hardball (in a hard box, of course) with the group presidents. Managers negotiated budgets and plans on a win-lose basis: action plans almost exclusively controlled what was done in the organization. Top managers kept a lot of information to themselves. People didn't trust each other very much.

The crises that struck the corporation in 1980 were so serious that we could not have concealed them even if we had wanted to. We were forced to put together a multitude of task forces consisting of people from all parts of the organization to address these urgent issues, and in the process, we had to reveal everything we knew, whether it was confidential or not.

We were amazed at the task forces' responses: instead of resigning en masse (the hard box players had said that people would leave the company when they found out that it was insolvent), the teams tackled their projects with passion. Warmth, a sense of belonging, and trust characterized the groups; the more we let them know what was going on, the more we received from them. Confidentiality is the enemy of trust. In the old days strategic plans were stamped "confidential." Now we know that paper plans mean nothing if they are not in the minds of the managers.

Division managers at first resented our intrusion into their formal, closed world. "What happened to independence?" they demanded. We described the soft counterpart—autonomy—to them. Unlike independence, autonomy cannot be granted once and for all. In our earlier life, division personnel told the corporate office what they thought it wanted to hear. "You've got to keep those guys at arm's length" was a typical division belief. An autonomous relationship depends on trust for its nourishment. "The more you level with us," we said, "the more we'll leave you alone." That took some getting use to.

But in the end autonomy worked. We gave division managers confidential information, shared our hopes and fears, and incorporated their views in our bubble. They needed to be helped out of their boxes, not to abandon them altogether but to gain a deeper appreciation of and insight into how they were running their businesses. Few could resist when we walked around showing a genuine interest in their views. Because easy access to each other and opportunities for communication determine how groups form and work together, we encouraged managers to keep their doors open. We called this creation of opportunities for communication by making senior management accessible "management by walking around." Chance encounters should not be left to chance.

Although the primary objective of all this communication is to produce trust among group members, an important by-product is that the integrators among us have started to "see" the communication process.[6] In other words, they are beginning to understand why people say what they say. This ability to "see" communication is elusive at times, but when it is present, it enables us to "jump out of the box"—that is, to talk about the frameworks supporting conclusions rather than the conclusions themselves. We have defused many potential confrontations and struck many deals by changing the context of the debate rather than the debate itself.[7]

Perhaps the best example of this process was our changing relationship with our lead banker. As the corporation's financial position deteriorated, our relationship with the bank became increasingly adversarial. The responsibility for our account rose steadily up the bank's hierarchy (we had eight different account managers in 18 months), and we received tougher and tougher "banker's speeches" from successively more senior executives. Although we worried a great deal that the bank might call the loan, the real risk was that our good businesses would be choked by overzealous efforts on the part of individual bankers to "hold the line."

Key to our ability to change the relationship was to understand why individuals were taking the position they were. To achieve that understanding we had to rely on a network of contacts both inside and outside the bank. We found that the bank had as many views as there were people we talked to. Fortunately, the severity of the recession and the proliferation of corporate loan problems had already blown everyone out of the old policy "boxes." It remained for us to gain the confidence of our contacts, exchange candid views of our positions, and present options that addressed the corporation's problems in the bank's context and dealt with the bank's interests.

The "hard" vehicle for this was the renegotiation of our main financing agreements. During the more than six month negotiating process, our relationship with the bank swung 180 degrees from confrontation to collaboration. The corporation's problem became a joint bank-corporation problem. We had used the bubble to find a new box in which both the corporation and the bank could live.

☐ **INFORMATION PROCESSES** ... & ... ○ **NETWORKS**

☐ Hard	○ Soft
☐ Written	○ Oral
☐ Know	○ Feel
☐ Control	○ Influence
☐ Decision	○ Implementation

Over the years our corporation has developed some excellent information systems. Our EDP facility is second to none in our industry. Before the acquisition and merger, when people talked about or requested information, they meant hard, quantitative data and written reports that would be used for control and decision making. The crisis required that we make significant changes to these systems. Because, for example, we became more interested in cash flow than earnings per share, data had to be aggregated and presented in a new way.

The pivotal change, however, was our need to communicate with a slew of new audiences over which we had little control. For instance, although we still have preferred stock quoted in the public market, our principal new shareholders were family members with little experience in professional management of public companies. Our new bankers were in organizational turmoil themselves and took 18 months to realize the horror of what they had financed. Our suppliers, hitherto benign, faced a stream of bad financial news about us and other members of the industry. The rumor mill had us in receivership on a weekly basis.

Our plant closures and cutbacks across North America brought us into a new relationship with government, unions, and the press. And we had a new internal audience: our employees, who were understandably nervous about the "imminent" bankruptcy.

We had always had some relationship with these audiences, but now we saw what important sources of information they were and expanded these networks vastly.[8] Just as we had informed the division managers at the outset, we decided not to conceal from these other groups the fact that the corporation was insolvent but worthy of support. We made oral presentations supported by formal written material to cover the most important bases.

To our surprise, this candid approach totally disarmed potential antagonists. For instance, major suppliers could not understand why we had told them we were in trouble before the numbers revealed the fact. By the time the entire war story was news, there was no doubt that our suppliers' top managers, who tended not to live in the hard accounting box, were on our side. When their financial specialists concluded that we were insolvent, top management blithely responded, "We've known that for six months."

Sharing our view of the world with constituencies external to the corporation led to other unexpected benefits, such as working in each other's interests. Our reassurance to customers that we would be around to deliver on contracts strengthened the relationship. Adversity truly is opportunity!

Management by walking around was the key to communicating with employees in all parts of the company. As a result of the continual open communication, all employees appreciated the corporation's position. Their support has been most gratifying. One of our best talker-listeners (our president) tells of a meeting with a very nervous group of employees at one facility. After he had spent several hours explaining the company's situation, one blue-collar worker who had been with the company for years took him aside and told him that a group of employees would be prepared to take heavy pay cuts if it would save the business. It turns out that when others hear this story it reinforces *their* belief in the organization.

We have found that sharing our views and incorporating the views of others as appropriate has a curious effect on the making and the implementing of decisions. As we've said, in our previous existence the decisions we made were always backed up by hard information; management was decisive, and that was good. Unfortunately, too few of these "good" decisions ever got implemented. The simple process of making the decision the way we did often set up resistance down the line. As the decision was handed down to consecutive organizational levels, it lost impetus until eventually it was unclear whether the decision was right in the first place.

Now we worry a good deal less about making decisions; they arise as fairly obvious conclusions drawn from a mass of shared assumptions. It's the assumptions that we spend our time working on. One of our "producers" (an executive vice president) calls it "conditioning" and indeed it is. Of course, making decisions this way requires that senior management build networks with people many layers down in the organization. This kind of communication is directly at odds with the communication policy laid down in the premerger corporation, which emphasized direct-line reporting.

A consequence of this network information process is that we often have to wait for the right time to make a decision. We call the wait a "creative stall."

In the old organization it would have been called procrastination, but what we're doing is waiting for some important players to come "on-side" before making an announcement.[9] In our terms, you "prepare in the box and wait in the bubble."

Once the time is right, however, implementation is rapid. Everyone is totally involved and has given thought to what has to be done. Not only is the time it takes for the decision to be made and implemented shorter than in the past but also the whole process strengthens the organization rather than weakening it through bitterness about how the decision was made.

☐ **PEOPLE** ... & ...	○ **PEOPLE**
☐ Rational	○ Social
☐ Produce	○ Create
☐ Think	○ Imagine
☐ Tell	○ Inspire
☐ Work	○ Play

In the old, premerger days, it was convenient to regard employees as rational, welfare-maximizing beings; it made motivating them so much easier and planning less messy.

But because the crisis made it necessary to close many operations and terminate thousands of employees, we had to deal with people's social nature. We could prepare people intellectually by sharing our opinions and, to some extent, protect them physically with severance packages, but we struggled with how to handle the emotional aspects. Especially for long service employees, severing the bond with the company was the emotional equivalent of death.

Humor is what rescued us. Laughter allows people to jump out of their emotional boxes or rigid belief structures. None of us can remember having laughed as much as we have over the past three years. Although much of the humor has inevitably been of the gallows variety, it has been an important ingredient in releasing tension and building trust.

Now everyone knows that people are social as well as rational animals. Indeed, we knew it back in the premerger days, but somehow back then we never came to grips with the social aspect, maybe because the rational view of people has an appealing simplicity and clarity. Lombard's Law applied to us—routine, structured tasks drove out nonroutine, unstructured activities.[10]

☐ **COMPENSATION SYSTEMS** ... & ...	○ **REWARDS**
☐ Direct	○ Indirect
☐ Objective	○ Subjective
☐ Profit	○ Fun
☐ Failure	○ Mistake
☐ Hygiene	○ Motivator
☐ Managing	○ Caring

In our premerger organization, the "total compensation policy" meant you could take your money any way you liked—salary, loans, fringes, and so forth. Management thought this policy catered to individual needs and was, therefore, motivating. Similarly, the "Personnel Development Program" required managers to make formal annual reviews of their employees' performances. For some reason, management thought that this also had something to do with motivation. The annual reviews, however, had become a meaningless routine, with managers constrained to be nice to the review subject because they had to work with him or her the next day.

The 1981 recession put a stop to all this by spurring us to freeze all direct compensation. Profit-based compensation disappeared; morale went up.

The management team discussed this decision for hours. As the savings from the freeze would pay for a few weeks' interest only; the numbers made no sense at all. Some of us prophesied doom. "We will lose the best people," we argued. Instead, the symbolic freeze brought the crisis home to everyone. We had all made a sacrifice, a contribution that senior management could recognize at a future time.

Even though the academics say they aren't scientifically valid, we still like Frederick Herzberg's definition of motivations (our interpretations of them are in parentheses):[11]

Achievement (what you believe you did).
Recognition (what others think you did).
Work itself (what you really do).
Responsibility (what you help others do).
Advancement (what you think you can do).
Growth (what you believe you might do).

THE NEW FRAMEWORK AT WORK

The diagram of the soft model in the exhibit shows our view of how our management process seems to work. When the motivating rewards are applied to people playing the necessary roles and working together in groups that are characterized by open communication and are linked to networks throughout the organization, the immediate product is a high degree of mutual trust. This trust allows groups to develop a shared vision that in turn enhances a sense of common purpose. From this process people develop a feeling of having a mission of their own. The mission is spiritual in the sense of being an important effort much larger than oneself. This kind of involvement is highly motivating. Mission is the soft counterpart of strategy.

☐ STRATEGY ... & ...	○ MISSION
☐ Objectives	○ Values
☐ Policies	○ Norms
☐ Forecast	○ Vision
☐ Clockworks	○ Frameworks
☐ Right	○ Useful
☐ Target	○ Direction
☐ Precise	○ Vague
☐ Necessary	○ Sufficient

Listed are some of our favorite words for contrasting these two polarities. We find them useful for understanding why clear definition of objectives is not essential for motivating people. Hard box planners advocate the hard box elements and tend to be overinvested in using their various models, or "clockworks" as we call them. Whether it's a Boston Consulting Group matrix or an Arthur D. Little life-cycling curve, too often planners wind them up and managers act according to what they dictate without looking at the assumptions, many of which may be invalid, implicit in the frameworks.

We use the models only as take-off points for discussion. They do not have to be right, only useful. If they don't yield genuine insights we put them aside. The hard box cannot be dispensed with. On the contrary, it is essential—but not sufficient.

The key element in developing a shared purpose is mutual trust. Without trust, people will engage in all kinds of self-centered behavior to assert their own identities and influence coworkers to their own ends. Under these circumstances, they just won't hear others, and efforts to develop a shared vision are doomed. Nothing destroys trust faster than hard box attitudes toward problems that don't require such treatment.

Trust is self-reproductive. When trust is present in a situation, chain reactions occur as people share frameworks and exchange unshielded views. The closer and more tightly knit the group is, the more likely it is that these reactions will spread, generating a shared vision and common purpose.

Once the sense of common purpose and mission is established, the managing group is ready to enter the hard box of strategy (see the right-hand side of the exhibit). Now the specifics of task, structure, information, and decision processes are no longer likely to be controversial or threatening. Implementation becomes astonishingly simple. Action plans are necessary to control hard box implementation, but once the participants in the soft bubble share the picture, things seem to happen by themselves as team members play their roles and fill the gaps as they see them. Since efforts to seize control of bubble activity are likely to prove disastrous, it is most fortunate that people act spontaneously without being "organized." Paradoxically, one can achieve control in the bubble only by letting go—which gets right back to trust.

In the hard box, the leadership model is that of the general who gives crisp, precise instructions as to who is to do what and when. In the soft bubble, the leadership model is that of the shepherd,who follows his flock watchfully as it meanders along the natural contours of the land. He carries the weak and collects the strays, for they all have a contribution to make. This style may be inefficient, but it is effective. The whole flock reaches its destination at more or less the same time.[12]

☐ BOXES	... & ...	○ BUBBLES
☐ Solve		○ Dissolve
☐ Sequential		○ Lateral
☐ Left brain		○ Right brain
☐ Serious		○ Humorous
☐ Explain		○ Explore
☐ Rational		○ Intuitive

☐ Conscious	◯ Unconscious
☐ Learn	◯ Remember
☐ Knowledge	◯ Wisdom
☐ Lens	◯ Mirror
☐ Full	◯ Empty
☐ Words	◯ Pictures
☐ Objects	◯ Symbols
☐ Description	◯ Parable

Thought and language are keys to changing perceptions. Boxes and bubbles describe the hard and soft thought structures, respectively. Boxes have rigid, opaque sides; walls have to be broken down to join boxes, although if the lid is off one can jump out. Bubbles have flexible, transparent sides that can easily expand and join with other bubbles. Bubbles float but can easily burst. In boxes problems are to be solved; in bubbles they are dissolved. The trick is to change the context of the problem, that is, to jump out of the box. This technique has many applications.

We have noticed a number of articles in your publication that concern values and ethics in business, and some people have suggested that business students be required to attend classes in ethics. From our view of the world, sending students to specific courses is a hard box solution and would be ineffective. Ethical behavior is absent from some businesses not because the managers have no ethics (or have the wrong ones) but because the hard "strategy box" does not emphasize them as being valuable. The hard box deals in objectives, and anyone who raises value issues in that context will not survive long.

In contrast, in the "mission bubble" people feel free to talk about values and ethics because there is trust. The problem of the lack of ethical behavior is dissolved.

We have found bubble thinking to be the intellectual equivalent of judo; a person does not resist an attacker but goes with the flow, thereby adding his strength to the other's momentum. Thus when suppliers demanded that their financial exposure to our lack of creditworthiness be reduced, we agreed and suggested that they protect themselves by supplying goods to us on consignment. After all, their own financial analysis showed we couldn't pay them any money! In some cases we actually got consignment deals, and where we didn't the scheme failed because of nervous lawyers (also hard box players) rather than reluctance on the part of the supplier.

Bubble thought structures are characterized by what Edward de Bono calls lateral thinking.[13] The sequential or vertical thought structure is logical and rational; it proceeds through logical stages and depends on a yes-no test at each step. De Bono suggests that in lateral thinking the yes-no test must be suspended, for the purpose is to explore not explain, to test assumptions not conclusions.

We do the same kind of questioning when we do what we call "humming a lot." When confronted with what initially appears to be an unpalatable idea, an effective manager will say "hmm" and wait until the idea has been developed and its implications considered. Quite often, even when an initial idea is out of the question, the fact that we have considered it seriously will lead to a different, innovative solution.

We have found it useful to think of the action opposite to the one we intend taking. When selling businesses we found it helpful to think about acquiring purchasers. This led to deeper research into purchasers' backgrounds and motives and to a more effective packaging and presentation of the businesses to be sold. This approach encourages novel ideas and makes the people who generate them (the entrepreneurs) feel that their ideas, however "dumb," will not be rejected out of hand.

In hard box thought structures, one tends to use conceptual frameworks as lenses, to sit on one side and examine an object on the other. In bubble structures, the frameworks are mirrors reflecting one's own nature and its effect on one's perceptions; object and subject are on the same side. In the hard box, knowledge is facts, from learning; in the bubble knowledge is wisdom, from experience.

Bubble thought structures are not easily described in words. Language itself is a box reflecting our cultural heritage and emphasizing some features of reality at the expense of others. Part of our struggle during the past three years has been to unlearn many scientific management concepts and develop a new vocabulary. We have come up with some new phases and words: management by walking around, creative stall, asking dumb questions, jumping out of the box, creating a crisis, humming a lot, and muddling. We have also attached new meanings to old words such as fact and perception, independence and autonomy, hard and soft, solve and dissolve, and so forth.

THREE YEARS LATER

What we have told you about works in a crisis. And we can well understand your asking whether this approach can work when the business is stable and people lapse back into boxes. We have developed two methods of preventing this lapse.

1. If there isn't a crisis, we create one.   One way to stir things up is familiar to anyone who has ever worked in a hard box organization. Intimidation, terror, and the use of raw power will produce all the stress you need. But eventually people run out of adrenalin and the organization is drained, not invigorated.

In a bubble organization, managers dig for opportunities in a much more relaxed manner. During the last three years, for instance, many of our divisions that were profitable and liquid were still in need of strategic overhaul. During the course of walking around, we unearthed many important issues by asking dumb questions.

The more important of the issues that surface this way offer an opportunity to put a champion (someone who believes in the importance of the issue) in charge of a team of people who can play all the roles required to handle the issue. The champion then sets out with his or her group to go through the incremental development process—developing trust, building both a hard box picture and a shared vision, and, finally, establishing strategy. By the time the strategy is arrived at, the task force disciples have such zeal and sense of mission that they are ready to take the issue to larger groups, using the same process.

Two by-products of asking dumb questions deserve mention. First, when senior management talks to people at all levels, people at all levels start talking to each other. Second, things tend to get fixed before they break. In answering a senior manager's casual question, a welder on the shop floor of a steel fabrication plant revealed that some critical welds had failed quality tests and the customer's inspector was threatening to reject an entire bridge. A small ad hoc task force, which included the inspector (with the customer's permission), got everyone off the hook and alerted top management to a potential weakness in the quality control function.

Applying the principles in other areas takes years to bear fruit. We are now using the process to listen to customers and suppliers. We never knew how to do this before. Now it is clear that it is necessary to create an excuse (crisis) for going to see them, share "secrets," build trust, share a vision, and capture them in your bubble. It's very simple, and early results have been excellent. We call it a soft revolution.

2. Infuse activities that some might think prosaic with real significance. The focus should be on people first, and always on caring rather than managing. The following approach works in good times as well as bad:

> Use a graphic vocabulary that describes what you do.
>
> Share confidential information, personal hopes and fears to create a common vision and promote trust.
>
> Seize every opportunity (open doors, management by walking around, networks) to make a point, emphasize a value, disseminate information, share an experience, express interest, and show you care.
>
> Recognize performance and contribution of as many people as possible. Rituals and ceremonies—retirements, promotions, birthdays—present great opportunities.
>
> Use incentive programs whose main objective is not compensation but recognition.

We have tried to approach things this way, and for us the results have been significant. Now, we are a very different organization. Of our 25 divisions, we have closed 7 and sold 16. Five of the latter were bought by Federal Industries, Ltd. of Winnipeg. Some 860 employees including us, the four members of the management team, have gone to Federal. These divisions are healthy and raring to go. Two divisions remain at York Russel, which has changed its name to YRI-YORK, Ltd.

Now we face new questions, such as how one recruits into a management team. We know that we have to help people grow into the team, and fortunately we find that they flourish in our warm climate. But trust takes time to develop, and the bubble is fragile. The risk is greatest when we have to transplant a senior person from outside, because time pressures may not allow us to be sure we are compatible. The danger is not only to the team itself but also to the person joining it.

Our new framework has given us a much deeper appreciation of the management process and the roles effective general managers play. For example, it is clear that while managers can delegate tasks in the hard box rather easily—perhaps because they can define them—it's impossible to delegate soft bubble activities. The latter are difficult to isolate from each other because their integration takes place in one brain.

Similarly, the hard box general management roles of producer and administrator can be formally taught, and business schools do a fine job of it. The soft roles of entrepreneur and integrator can probably not be taught formally. Instead, managers must learn from mentors. Over time they will adopt behavior patterns that allow them to play the required roles. It would seem, however, that natural ability and an individual's upbringing probably play a much larger part in determining effectiveness in the soft roles than in the hard roles; it is easier to teach a soft bubble player the hard box roles than it is to teach the soft roles to a hard box player.

In the three-year period when we had to do things so differently, we created our own culture, with its own language, symbols, norms, and customs. As with other groups, the acculturation process began when people got together in groups and trusted and cared about each other.[14]

In contrast with our premerger culture, the new culture is much more sympathetic toward and supportive of the use of teams and consensus decision making. In this respect, it would seem to be similar to oriental ways of thinking that place a premium on the same processes. Taoists, for instance, would have no trouble recognizing the polarities of the hard box and the soft bubble and the need to keep a balance between the two.[15]

☐ **HEAVEN**	... & ...	○ **EARTH**
☐ Yang		○ Yin
☐ Father		○ Mother
☐ Man		○ Woman

These symbols are instructive. After all, most of us grew up with two bosses: father usually played the hard box parts, while mother played the soft, intuitive, and entrepreneurial roles. The family is the original team, formed to handle the most complex management task ever faced. Of late, we seem to have fired too many of its members—a mistake we can learn from.

TOWARD A MANAGERIAL THEORY OF RELATIVITY

The traditional hard box view of management, like the traditional orientation of physics, is valid (and very useful) only within a narrow range of phenomena. Once one gets outside the range, one needs new principles. In physics, cosmologists at the macro level as well as students of subatomic particles at the micro level use Einstein's theory of relativity as an explanatory principle and set Newton's physics aside.[16] For us, the theory in the bubble is our managerial theory of relativity. At the macro level it reminds us that how management phenomena appear depends on one's perspective and biases. At the micro level we remember that all jobs have both hard and soft components.

This latter point is of particular importance to people like us in the service industry. The steel we distribute is indistinguishable from anyone else's We insist on rigid standards regarding how steel is handled, what reporting systems are used, and so forth. But hard box standards alone wouldn't be enough to set us apart from our competitors. That takes service, a soft concept. And everyone has to be involved. Switchboard operators are in the front line; every contact is an opportunity to share the bubble. Truck drivers and warehouse workers make their own special contribution—by taking pride in the cleanliness of their equipment or by keeping the inventory neat and accessible.

With the box and bubble concept, managers can unlock many of the paradoxes of management and handle the inherent ambiguities. You don't do one or the other absolutely; you do what is appropriate. For instance, the other day in one of our operations the biweekly payroll run deducted what appeared to be random amounts from the sales representatives' pay packets. The branch affected was in an uproar. After taking some hard box steps to remedy the situation, our vice president of human resources seized the opportunity to go out to the branch and talk to the sales team. He was delighted with the response. The sales force saw that he understood the situation and cared about them, and he got to meet them all, which will make future contacts easier. But neither the hard box nor soft bubble approach on its own would have been appropriate. We need both. As one team member put it, "You have to find the bubble in the box and put the box in the bubble." Exactly.

The amazing thing is that the process works so well. The spirit of cooperation among senior managers is intense, and we seem to be getting "luckier" as we go along. When a "magic" event takes place it means that somehow we got the timing just right.[17] And there is great joy in that.

REFERENCES

1. Thomas I. Peters and Robert H. Waterman, *In Search of Excellence* (New York: Harper and Row, 1981), p. 29.
2. For the best of the hard box models we have come across, see Jay R. Galbraith, *Organization Design* (Reading, Mass.: Addison-Wesley, 1977).
3. Henry Mintzberg, "The Manager's Job: Folklore and Fact." HBR July–August, 1975, p. 49.
4. Edgar H. Schein, *Process Consultation: Its Role in Organization Development* (Reading, Mass.: Addison-Wesley, 1969).
5. Ichak Adize, *How to Solve the Mismanagement Crisis* (Los Angeles, MDOR Institute, 1979).
6. Edgar H. Schein's *Process Consultation,* p. 10, was very helpful in showing us how the process differs from the content.
7. Getting consensus among a group of managers poses the same challenge as negotiating a deal. *Getting to Yes* by Robert Fisher and William Ury (Boston: Houghton Mifflin, 1981) is a most helpful book for understanding the process.
8. For discussion of the importance or networks, see John P. Kotter. "What Effective General Managers Really Do." HBR November–December 1982, p. 156.
9. For discussion of a "creative stall" being applied in practice, see Stratford P. Sherman. "Muddling to Victory at Geico." *Fortune* September 5, 1983, p. 66.
10. Louis B. Barnes. "Managing the Paradox of Organizational Trust." HBR March–April 1981, p. 107.
11. In "One More Time: How Do You Motivate Employees?" HBR January–February 1968, p. 53.
12. For another view of the shepherd role, see the poem by Nancy Esposito. "The Good Shepherd." HBR July–August 1983, p. 121.

13. See Edward de Bono. *The Use of Lateral Thinking* (London: Jonathan Cape, 1967) and *Beyond Yes and No* (New York: Simon and Schuster, 1972).
14. To explore the current concern with creating strong organizational cultures in North American corporations, see Terrence E. Deal and Alan A. Kennedy *Corporate Cultures* Reading, Mass.: Addison-Wesley, 1982).
15. For discusison of Tao and some applications, we highly recommend Benjamin Hoff, *The Tao of Pooh* (New York: E. P. Dutton, 1982), p. 67; also Allen Watts, *Tao: The Watercourse Way* (New York: Pantheon Books, 1975).
16. Frityof Capra, *The Tao of Physics* (London: Fontana Paperbacks, 1963).
17. Carl Jung developed the concept of synchronicity to explain such events. See, for example, Ira Progoff. *Jung Synchronicity and Human Destiny—Non-Causal Dimensions of Human Experience* (New York: Julian Press, 1973). For an excellent discussion of Jung's work and its relevance to our times, see Laurens van de Post, *Jung and the Story of Our Time* (New York: Random House, 1975).

LEADERSHIP PRINCIPLES
FOR PROBLEM SOLVING CONFERENCES

Norman R. F. Maier

It is possible for a discussion leader to increase the ability of a group of people to solve problems by means of the application of certain principles. No claim is made that the nine principles described below constitute a complete list, and it is also possible that the number eventually may be reduced to fewer and more fundamental principles. The reader may find that some of the principles overlap in certain respects. Nevertheless, the principles stated below are adequate in their present form to serve as a guide to the discussion leader.

PRINCIPLE 1

Success in problem solving requires that effort be directed toward overcoming SURMOUNTABLE *obstacles.* If we think of a problem situation as one in which obstacles block us from reaching a goal, it follows that some of these obstacles will be more readily overcome than others. As a matter of fact, a problem will be insoluble if attempts are made to reach a goal over an insurmountable obstacle. This means that persistent attempts to overcome some obstacles might be doomed to failure. Success in problem solving, therefore, depends on locating obstacles that can more readily be overcome.[1]

It is the common tendency to persist in following an initial approach to a problem. In other words, a particular obstacle is selected and pursued despite the fact that it cannot be overcome. Usually this obstacle is the most obvious or is

Source: Reprinted with permission of the publisher from Norman Maier, *Problem Solving and Creativity,* (Monterey, Calif.: Brooks/Cole Publishing Company, 1970).

[1] N. R. F. Maier, "An Aspect of Human Reasoning," *Brit, J. Psychol.,* 1933, 24, 144–155.

one that previous experience has suggested. For example, medical research reveals that the innoculation of a serum to create immunity has been a successful approach for dealing with some diseases so it tends to be followed for others. In business it is not uncommon to approach new problems with approaches previously found successful. Yet difficult problems require new and unusual approaches; if they did not, they would not be difficult problems.

A common tendency that frequently leads to a failure is associated with the attempt to solve a problem by locating a person or group that is at fault. For example, a solution to international problems that require another nation to behave differently may meet with failure because the problem solvers cannot control the action they recommend. Lacking such control, when it is essential to the solution, represents an insurmountable obstacle. A solution that cannot be effectuated falls short of solving the problem and hence leads us only to the insurmountable obstacles. Successful solutions must be workable.

PRINCIPLE 2

Available facts should be used even when they are inadequate. A solution that was effective in one situation becomes favored and is used in new situations even when the similarity between the old and new situation is superficial. The assumption that the situations are the same tends to detract from a careful examination of the facts that are available.

When a good deal of information is available, problem solvers are more prone to work with the evidence. There is then enough information given to permit them to reject some solutions. However, in the absence of adequate information, it becomes more difficult to be selective and as a consequence imagination and biases dominate the problem solving.[2]

PRINCIPLE 3

The starting point of a problem is richest in solution possibilities. The solution of a problem may be envisaged as a route from the starting point to the goal. The process of thinking about a solution is like proceeding along a particular route. Once one starts in a particular direction one moves away from certain alternatives and thus reduces the number of possible alternative directions that may be pursued.

Each route may confront one with obstacles. As discussion of a problem proceeds, successive obstacles present themselves. A group may have successfully by-passed two obstacles along the way and then find difficulty with others that face them at their advanced stage of progress. Because of this partial success in moving forward, it is difficult for them to revert and start all over again, yet a new start is the only way to increase the variety of solution possibilities. For example,

[2]N. R. F. Maier, "Screening Solutions To Upgrade Quality: A New Approach to Problem Solving Under Conditions of Uncertainty," *J. Psychol.,* 1960, 49, 217–231.

a great deal of progress was made with propeller-driven planes; however, they had limitations. They were not able to fly above a certain height because of the lack of atmosphere. Increasing their power and design could raise the flying ceiling somewhat; nevertheless, the need for atmosphere limited the ceiling for propeller-driven craft. A plane with an entirely different power plant—the jet engine— represented a fresh start in aviation.

In the usual problem-situation a person develops certain ideas about solutions. This means he moves from the starting point in a particular direction toward the goal. Thus the supervisor who wishes to improve phone-answering services in his office by eliminating or reducing personal calls finds it difficult to think of approaches that do not limit personal calls. Rather he thinks of different approaches for *limiting* personal calls and loses sight of the original goal of improving phone-answering service. The solution reached now becomes confused with the problem. This is why statements of problems frequently contain suggestions of solutions. Obviously such statements of problems are so near the goal that they limit other solution possibilities. Such suggested solutions may be unacceptable and unimaginative.

In order to get a better appreciation of the starting point of a problem, a discussion leader should ask himself why he wishes or favors a certain solution. What purpose does my solution serve? Such a question may suggest the nature of the starting point of the problem. Spending time with the group to explain the prime objective, therefore, represents a procedure for finding the starting point.

All solutions represent methods for reaching a goal, but frequently sight is lost of the starting point. Rather the goal becomes an ideal toward which to strive. Practical consideration, however, requires that we reach a goal from the point at which we find ourselves. It may be unrealistic to get to an ideal goal from certain points. If one could start over again, more problems could be solved, or more ideal goals could be reached, but this is not realistic problem solving. A solution is a path *from* the starting point *to* a goal, and sight of this starting point should not be lost.

PRINCIPLE 4

Problem-mindedness should be increased while solution-mindedness is delayed. By nature people progress too rapidly toward a solution. This is what is meant by solution-mindedness. This tendency is similar to the phenomenon known as the Zeigarnik[3] effect. Once a task is begun psychological forces are set up to push the task to completion. The reader will understand how he himself resists being interrupted while engaged in a task and how he worries over unfinished activities. It is only natural, therefore, that since the goal of a problem is to find a solution, energy and activity toward accomplishing this end are set in motion.

This means that in almost any discussion the responses of various persons

[3]B. Zeigarnik, "Ueber das Behalten von erledigten und unerledigten Handlungen." *Psychol. Forsch.*, 1927, 9, 1–85. M. Ovsiankina, "Die Wiederaufnahme unterbrochener Handlungen." *Psychol. Forsch.* 1928, 11, 302–379.

tend to interrupt the thinking process of one another, and this is often disturbing. It is only natural for a dominant person to push through his ideas, and when he happens to be the leader, the value of group participation is lost.

Experimental evidence supporting the value of delaying the reaching of a solution and spending more time focusing on the problem is available.[4] Common experience also may be cited.

It is not uncommon to find that people who disagree about solutions later find that they have not even agreed on the problem. The first prerequisite to reaching agreement on a solution would seem to be one of reaching agreement on the problem. The reader also will recall that when he asks his friends for help on a problem, they offer suggestions before he has finished his statement of the problem.

It is apparent that a discussion leader can cause a group to be more problem-minded. Usually he is a strong force in encouraging solution-mindedness. He must not only inhibit this tendency, but encourage problem-mindedness in his group in the process of improving his discussion leadership.

PRINCIPLE 5

Disagreement can lead either to hard feelings or to innovation, depending on the discussion leadership. Two strong forces make for conformity: fear of the leader's unfavorable judgment and fear of unfavorable responses from the group to which one belongs. These factors unfortunately operate only too frequently in group discussion so that the leader must be prepared to deal with both of them. Experimental evidence in support of this conclusion is to be found in several of our recent studies.[5]

Almost everyone has learned that he can get into more trouble by disagreeing with his boss than by agreeing with him. This is the kind of learning that develops "yes-men." In most organizations, conferees need a great deal of encouragement to feel free to disagree with the boss. This does not mean that disagreeing is a virtue. Rather the subordinate must feel free to disagree if he is to contribute the best of his thinking. The leader takes the first steps in reducing conformity by withholding judgment, entertaining criticism, and trying to understand strange ideas.

The dangers of disagreeing with the majority members of one's own group or with society in general is less readily learned. The dissenter and the innovator sometimes find themselves popular and sometimes unpopular. For this reason, any hard feelings created by disagreement are not too apparent. However, an additional factor also operates. This is the security gained in "going along with the crowd." When people are unsure of themselves they are particularly prone to follow group opinion rather than risk a deviant opinion.[6] Conformity to group standards

[4]N. R. F. Maier and A. R. Solem, "Improving Solutions by Turning Choice Situations into Problems." *Pers. Psychol.* 1962, 15, 151–157.

[5]N. R. F. Maier and J. J. Hayes, *Creative Management,* New York, John Wiley & Sons, Inc., 1962.

[6]E. L. Walker and R. W. Heyns, *An Anatomy for Conformity,* Englewood Cliffs, N.J., Prentice-Hall, 1962.

becomes unfortunate when it inhibits free expression or when the group rejects the person who innovates without examining or understanding his contributions. A majority does not have to prove or justify itself because it does not have to change minds, but a minority can be laughed down and hence is denied the opportunity to prove itself. Original ideas are new so the original person frequently finds himself in the minority. This means that he may not only be a lonely person, but will have to justify many of his views.

When one person disagrees with another, the latter is inclined to feel that he has been attacked. As a consequence he feels hurt, defends himself, or becomes angry and counter-attacks. Such emotional reactions lead to interpersonal conflict and this type of interaction tends to worsen. As a result, some people avoid hurting others. "Good" group members, therefore, tend to be sensitive to group opinion and become careful in expressing their views. As a matter of fact, they may find that the easiest way to be careful is to avoid disagreeing. People who get along with other participants by conforming may be good group members, but they also become poor problem solvers.[7] Members cannot learn from one another by agreeing. They can avoid generating hard feelings but eventually they may become bored. Satisfaction in group problem solving should come from task accomplishment, otherwise the group activity is primarily social.

We therefore are confronted with the fact that because disagreeing with others frequently leads to injured pride and interpersonal conflict, it is considered to be poor manners. In attempts to avoid trouble, people learn to refrain from disagreeing and hence move toward conformity. However, that alternative also is undesirable. The resolution of this dilemma is not only to prevent the suppression of disagreement but to encourage a respect for disagreement and thereby turn it into a stimulant for new ideas. How is this to be done?

First of all, each individual can learn to be less defensive himself, even if he cannot expect this tolerance from others. This is not much of a gain but it can be a personal one. A group leader, however, can accomplish a good deal in this respect. The leader of a group discussion can create a climate where disagreement is encouraged, he can use his position in the group to protect minority individuals, and he can turn disagreements among group members into situational problems. This is a second of the important skill areas for reducing the undesirable aspects of conformity, and in addition this skill in group leadership makes for innovation by using disagreement constructively.

Group thinking has a potential advantage over individual thinking in that the resources making for disagreement are greater in a group. Group thinking also has a potential disadvantage in that the dominant thinking may be that of the majority. The leader's responsibility is to capitalize on the advantages and avoid the disadvantages of group processes.

While organizations search for creative talent and attempt to develop it, the creative talent already present in the organization is being depressed at all levels.

[7]L. R. Hoffman, "Homogeneity of Member Personality and Its Effect on Group Problem-Solving," *J. Abn. Soc. Psychol.,* 1959, 58, 27–32. L. R. Hoffman and N. R. F. Maier, "Quality and Acceptance of Problem Solutions by Members of Homogeneous and Heterogeneous Groups," *J. Abn. Soc. Psychol.,* 1961, 62, 401–407.

In a recent study[8] the solution of four person groups taken from four populations differing in organizational orientation were compared. The problem used involved an industrial situation in which the need for a change in work procedure was raised.

The results showed that the least creative solutions came from management groups, better solutions came from students in the school of business administration, still better ones from students in a college course on industrial psychology, while the greatest number of innovative solutions came from students in Liberal Arts courses. It appears that the farther the problem solvers were removed from organizational experience, the more innovative were their solutions. Unless something is done to prevent it, awareness of organization structure suppresses innovation. The key factor seems to be the perception of the role of the boss in introducing and gaining acceptance of change.

PRINCIPLE 6

The "idea-getting" process should be separated from the "idea-evaluation" process because the latter inhibits the former. "Idea-evaluation" involves the testing and the comparison of solutions in the light of what is known, their probability for succeeding, and other practical considerations. It is the practical side of problem solving and is the phase of problem solving when judgment is passed on solutions. "Idea-getting" requires a willingness to break away from past experience. It is this process that requires an escape from the bonds of learning and demands that we search for unusual approaches and entertain new and untried ideas.

Robert Ingersoll once said "Colleges polish the pebbles and dim the diamonds." This may be an overstatement, but it points up the dual aspect of learning. It is the creative potentials that are inhibited by knowledge. Insofar as education teaches us what is known, it develops us and permits us to meet situations that have been previously met. In this way our problem solving is enhanced— our knowledge can generalize—and this is polish. However, in order to escape from the search into the past, new combinations of elements must be generated. The process of learning is to build associative bonds between elements of experience that are found and observed in conjunction with one another. Thus we learn names of things, we relate causes with effects, and we compare and see likenesses and differences. Creativity, however, requires the combination of elements and events that have never been experienced together—the generation of a new route from the starting point to the goal, made up of parts of old routes.

In other words, creativity requires the ability to fragment past experience to permit the formation of new spontaneous combinations. In contrast, learning requires the ability to combine or connect elements that have been contiguous to each other in our experience. Since these two abilities are basically different, they do not necessarily go together. One person may possess an unusual learning ability and be uncreative, another may be unusually creative but not be outstanding in learning ability. Both the abilities to learn and to fragment experience are necessary

[8]N. R. F. Maier, "Organization and Creative Problem Solving," *J. Appl. Psychol.* 1961, 45, 277–280.

for good problem solving. However, the second of these has been largely overlooked because of our emphasis on the study of learning.[9]

In order to illustrate the difference between learning and fragmenting, let us turn to the string problem which we have used widely in our research. This problem requires that the ends of two strings hanging from the ceiling be tied together. They are spaced so that a person cannot reach one while holding the other. With the aid of strings or sticks one could readily solve this problem. However, the only tool available is a pair of pliers, so the obvious solutions are excluded. Past experience has associated this tool with certain functional uses and as a consequence it becomes less likely to be seen as a weight than would an ordinary piece of metal. The creative solution requires that a pendulum be constructed by using the pair of pliers as a pendulum weight. Thus the distant string can be made to swing within reach. To find this solution the old associate bonds must be broken in order to permit the pliers to become a pendulum bob. When this new connection is made (pliers fastened to the string) and the pendulum is discovered, there is a sharp change in functional meanings. It is this change in meaning that causes the experience of insight. Sudden insights are associated with creative discoveries because the new meaning is not gradually built up through experience, but comes suddenly as a result of a spontaneous new combination.[10]

The acquisition of knowledge, such as college training, actually may give an individual a mental set that reduces his creativity in certain respects, even though such knowledge is valuable in other ways. This is because the educated person may attempt to solve a problem by applying what he knows, and although this would be a successful approach on some occasions, it would not be a creative solution. This set prevents him from making up unique solutions and thereby developing a combination of parts that cannot be found in his past. Thus a potentially creative person (a diamond) might be dimmed (in Ingersoll's sense) by a knowledge of standard or known approaches to a problem.

Past learning, practical consideration, and evaluation all tend to depress flights of imagination—the forward leap that is based on a hunch (insufficient evidence). Creative thinking is a radical rather than a conservative look at a problem situation and requires encouragement if it is to be nurtured. To demand proof of new ideas at a time of their inception is to discourage the creative process.

However, creative ideas and insane ideas sometimes are difficult to distinguish. Both represent a departure from the common and traditional ways of thinking; both are new and unique to the person. But there is also a difference. The creative idea has a basis in objective reality, even though the evidence to convince others is inadequate; in contrast, the product of the insane mind is made up of elements derived largely from internal stimulation, such as hallucinations and imagined events.

The discussion leader can delay a group's criticism of an idea by asking for alternative contributions and he can encourage variety in thinking by encouraging the search for something different—something new. Turning ideas upside down,

[9]N. R. F. Maier. "Selector-Integrator Mechanisms in Behavior." In: *Perspectives in Psychological Theory* (Ed. by B. Kaplan and S. Wapner). New York: International Universities Press, 1960.

[10]N. R. F. Maier, "Reasoning in Humans, II. The Solutions of a Problem and its Appearance in Consciousness," *J. Comp. Psychol.,* 1931, 12, 181-194.

backwards, trying out different combinations of old ideas all represent ways to encourage the expression and generation of new ideas.

PRINCIPLE 7

Choice-situations should be turned into problem-situations. The characteristic of a choice-situation is one of being confronted with two or more alternatives. As a consequence, behavior is blocked until one of the alternatives is selected. The characteristic of a problem-situation, on the other hand, is one of being confronted with an obstacle that prevents the reaching of a goal. Behavior is blocked until the obstacle can be removed or surmounted. Creative alternatives tend to be overlooked in choice-situations because a choice is made between the obvious alternatives. The fact that such alternatives exist directs the energy toward making a choice and thus detracts from the search for additional alternatives.

Creative or unusual alternatives, not being among the obvious ones, are unlikely to characterize behavior in choice-situations because activity is directed toward a choice between existing alternatives. Something must be done to delay this choice until the possibility of additional alternatives is explored. This is something the discussion leader can do. Since the unusual alternatives are not readily apparent it is necessary to encourage considerable searching.[11]

The discovery or creation of solutions is inherent in the nature of problem solving. This means that the discussion leader should approach each choice-situation as one in which the possibility of additional alternatives exists. When he encourages this searching behavior in group discussion, he is turning a choice-situation into a problem-situation. Only after other alternatives are found or invented should the process of making a choice be undertaken.

PRINCIPLE 8

Problem-situations should be turned into choice-situations. Because problem-situations block behavior, the natural reaction for people is to act on the first solution that is obtained. The objective in problem-situations is to remove or get around an obstacle. As a consequence, the discovery of the first successful possibility tends to terminate the search. The fact that one solution is found does not preclude the possibility that there may be others, yet people frequently behave as though this were the case.

If the leader accepts the first solution as a possibility, he may then ask the group to see if they can find another solution. If a second and even more solutions are obtained, the problem-situation will have been turned into a choice-situation. The opportunity to make a choice must necessarily improve the final decision because a choice between alternatives is permitted and the better one can win.

A recent study from our laboratory reveals that a second solution to a prob-

---

[11]N. R. F. Maier, *The Appraisal Interview,* New York: John Wiley & Sons, Inc., 1958.

lem actually tends to be superior in quality to the first. This is not surprising when one realizes that a second solution requires further searching. Continued searching tends to lead to less obvious discoveries and these are likely to be the more innovative possibilities. Other factors may also favor the superior quality of the second solution. A dominant leader or certain vocal members may have pushed their ideas because of their inability to dominate, thereby discouraging the development of disagreement in the groups. Hoffman[12] in reviewing a number of studies, believes that balanced conflict, in which opposing members are equally strong, favors creative solutions. Such conflict requires an innovative solution, he believes, because one point of view cannot dominate over another. Both alternatives are likely to be obvious alternatives for conflicting parties and hence each might be overlooking something.

Turning problem situations into choice situations thus has two advantages. It leads to more unusual solutions, which would tend to be the more creative; and it permits the opportunity to select the best of the alternatives.

Decision-making requires both choice behavior and problem-solving behavior. To identify decision-making either with choice behavior or with problem solving is to restrict its function. Both activities go on in decision making, and since the two processes differ, it is desirable to make capital of the difference and thereby upgrade each.

PRINCIPLE 9

Solutions suggested by the leader are improperly evaluated and tend either to be accepted or rejected. When the discussion leader conducts a discussion with his subordinates he is in a position of power so that his ideas receive a different reception than those coming from participants. This point is basic to the group decision process. In this connection an experiment by Solem[13] nicely illustrates the principle. He found that discussion leaders acting as superiors had more successful conferences when they did not have a chance to study a problem beforehand. When they studied a problem and reached a decision before the discussion, they tended to express their ideas. As a result, the discussion was diverted into a reaction to their ideas so that alternatives were not generated. The tendency of members was either to show acceptance or rejection reactions to the leader's ideas. Thus the leader's previous study of a problem caused the group to reach less acceptable and poorer decisions.

Even when the discussion leader has no formal authority over the group his position is seen as one of power. Actually such a leader exerts considerable power by merely approving or disapproving of ideas that are expressed. Thus a leader's suggestions are either blindly followed or resented rather than weighed.

The best way to avoid these two undesirable reactions is for the leader to refrain from introducing his views or passing judgment on the ideas expressed by

[12]L. R. Hoffman, "Conditions for Creative Problem Solving," *J. Psychol.,* 1961, 52, 429–444.
[13]A. R. Solem, "An Evaluation of Two Attitudinal Approaches to Delegation." *J. Appl. Psychol.,* 1958, 22, 36–39.

participants. His job is to conduct the discussion and show his proficiency in this regard. In applying these principles his position becomes analogous to that of a symphony orchestra conductor. He plays no instrument but makes use of the instruments of the participants. Similarly the discussion leader uses the minds of conferees and is interested in the best end results. At this point the analogy breaks down because the orchestra conductor has a particular outcome in mind, while the discussion leader strives for acceptable and high quality solutions, not his particular one.

CONCLUSION

Quality and acceptance are essential dimensions in decision-making.[14] The quality dimension refers to the objective features of a decision—in other words, how does it square with the objective facts? The acceptance dimension refers to the degree to which the group that must execute the decision accepts it—in other words, how does the group feel about the decision? High quality and high acceptance are both needed for effective decisions. This means that group discussion must effectively deal with both facts and feelings.

A major problem is raised because the methods for dealing with facts are quite different from those for dealing with feelings. The skilled conference leader must recognize when he is dealing with facts and ideas and when he is confronted with feelings and biases. The difference is not always too apparent because feelings are often couched behind made-up reasons or rationalizations. Diagnostic skill therefore is one of his leadership requirements.

Once he is able to make diagnostic judgments his next step is to deal effectively with each. The skills for removing conference obstacles in the form of feelings and in the form of ideas are quite different, and each set of skills has its place.

The problem-solving principles discussed in this paper are primarily relevant to handling the intellectual aspects of discussion. In dealing with emotional aspects the leader performs a more permissive function and serves more in the role of a group counselor.

The skill requirements in conference leadership are not difficult to learn. The problem lies more with the interference causes by old habits. Once one can break away from these and get a fresh start, the battle is half won. The first step is to recognize the existence of qualitative distinction. No one skill is best for all purposes. If the basic distinctions are made, progress in each area becomes relatively easy.

[14]N. R. F. Maier and J. J. Hayes, *Creative Management, op. cit.*

10
Managing Multi-Group Work

MANAGING GROUP CONFLICT
L. David Brown

TACTICS OF LATERAL RELATIONSHIP: THE PURCHASING AGENT
George Strauss

INGROUP AND INTERGROUP RELATIONS: EXPERIMENTAL ANALYSIS
Musafer Sherif
Carolyn W. Sherif

MANAGING CONFLICT AMONG GROUPS

L. Dave Brown

Conflict among groups is extremely common in organizations, although it often goes unrecognized. Managing conflict among groups is a crucial skill for those who would lead modern organizations. To illustrate:

> Maintenance workers brought in to repair a production facility critize production workers for overworking the machinery and neglecting routine maintenance tasks. The production workers countercharge that the last maintenance work was improperly done and caused the present breakdown. The argument results in little cooperation between the two groups to repair the breakdown, and the resulting delays and misunderstandings ultimately inflate organization-wide production costs.
>
> A large manufacturing concern has unsuccessful negotiations with a small independent union, culminating in a bitter strike characterized by fights, bombings, and sabotage. The angry workers, aware that the independent union has too few resources to back a protracted battle with management, vote in a powerful international union for the next round of negotiations. Management prepares for an even worse strike, but comparatively peaceful and productive negotiations ensue.
>
> Top management of a large bank in a racially mixed urban area commits the organization to system-wide integration. Recruiters find several superbly qualified

Source: Prepared specifically for this volume.

young black managers, after a long and highly competitive search, to join the bank's prestigious but all-white trust division and yet, subsequently, several leave the organization. Since virtually all the managers in the trust division are explicitly willing to integrate, top management is mystified by the total failure of the integration effort.

These cases are all examples of conflict or potential conflict among organizational groups that influence the performance and goal attainment of the organization as a whole. The cases differ in two important ways.

First, the extent to which the potential conflict among groups is *overt* varies across cases: conflict is all too obvious in the labor-management situation; it is subtle but still evident in the production-maintenance relations; it is never explicit in the attempt to integrate the bank's trust division. It is clear that *too much* conflict can be destructive, and much attention has been paid to strategies and tactics for reducing escalated conflict. Much less attention has been paid to situations in which organizational performance suffers because of *too little* conflict, or strategies and tactics for making potential conflicts more overt.

Second, the cases also differ in the *defining characteristics* of the parties: the production and maintenance groups are functionally defined; the distribution of power is critical to the labor and management conflict; the society's history of race relations is important to the black-white relations in the bank. Although there has been much examination of organizational conflict among groups defined by function, there has been comparatively little attention to organizational conflicts among groups defined by *power differences* (e.g., headquarters-branch relations, some labor-management relations) or by *societal history* (e.g., religious group relations, black-white relations, male-female relations).

It is increasingly clear that effective management of modern organizations calls for dealing with various forms of intergroup conflict: too little as well as too much conflict, and history-based and power-based as well as function-based conflicts. This paper offers a framework for understanding conflict among groups in the next section, and suggests strategies and tactics for diagnosing and managing different conflict situations.

CONFLICT AND INTERGROUP RELATIONS

Conflict: Too Much or Too Little?

Conflict is a form of interaction among parties that differ in interests, perceptions, and preferences. Overt conflict involves adversarial interaction that ranges from mild disagreements through various degrees of fighting. But it is also possible for parties with substantial differences to act as if those differences did not exist, and so keep potential conflict from becoming overt.

It is only too clear that it is possible to have *too much* conflict between or among groups. Too much conflict produces strong negative feelings, blindness to interdependencies, and uncontrolled escalation of aggressive action and counteraction. The obvious costs of uncontrolled conflict have sparked a good deal of interest in strategies for conflict reduction and resolution.

It is less obvious (but increasingly clear) that it is possible to have *too little* conflict. Complex and novel decisions, for example, may require pulling together perspectives and information from many different groups. If group representatives are unwilling to present and argue for their perspectives, the resulting decision may not take into account all the available information. The Bay of Pigs disaster during the Kennedy Administration may have been a consequence of too little conflict in the National Security Council, where critical information possessed by representatives of different agencies was suppressed to preserve harmonious relations among them (Janis, 1972).

In short, moderate levels of conflict—in which differences are recognized and extensively argued—are often associated with high levels of energy and involvement, high degrees of information exchange, and better decisions (Robbins, 1974). Managers should be concerned, in this view, with achieving levels of conflict that are *appropriate* to the task before them, rather than concerned about preventing or resolving immediately all intergroup disagreements.

Conflict among Groups

Conflict in organizations takes many forms. A disagreement between two individuals, for example, may be related to their personal differences, their job definitions, their group memberships, or all three. One of the most common ways that managers misunderstand organizational conflict, for example, is to attribute difficulties to "personality" factors, when it is, in fact, rooted in group memberships and organizational structures. Attributing conflict between production and maintenance workers to their personalities, for example, implies that the conflict can be reduced by replacing the individuals. But if the conflict is, in fact, related to the differing goals of the two groups, *any* individual will be under pressure to fight with members of the other group, regardless of their personal preferences. Replacing individuals in such situations without taking account of intergroup differences will *not* improve relations.

Groups are defined in organizations for a variety of reasons. Most organizations are differentiated horizontally, for example, into functional departments or product divisions for task purposes. Most organizations also are differentiated vertically into levels or into headquarters and plant groups. Many organizations also incorporate in some degree group definitions significant in the larger society, such as racial and religious distinctions.

A good deal of attention has been paid to the relations among groups of relatively equal power, such as functional departments in organizations. Much less is known about effective management of relations between groups of unequal power or those having different societal histories. But many of the most perplexing intergroup conflicts in organizations include all three elements—functional differences, power differences, and historical differences. Effective management of the differences between a white executive from marketing and a black hourly worker from production is difficult indeed, because so many issues are likely to contribute to the problem.

Intergroup relations, left to themselves, tend to have a regenerative, self-fulfilling quality that makes them extremely susceptible to rapid escalation. The dynamics of escalating conflict, for example, have impacts within and between the groups involved. *Within* a group (i.e., within the small circles in Figure 1), conflict with another group tends to increase cohesion and conformity to group norms (Sherif, 1966; Coser, 1956) and to encourage a world view that favors "us" over "them" (Janis, 1972; Deutsch, 1973). Simultaneously, *between-groups* (i.e., the relations between the circles in Figure 1) conflict promotes negative stereotyping and distrust (Sherif, 1966), increased emphasis on differences (Deutsch, 1973), decreased communications (Sherif, 1966), and increased distortion of communications that do take place (Blake and Mouton, 1961). The *combination* of negative stereotypes, distrust, internal militance, and aggressive action creates a vicious cycle: "defensive" aggression by one group validates suspicion and "defensive" counteraggression by the other, and the conflict escalates (Deutsch, 1973) unless it is counteracted by external factors. A less well understood pattern, in which positive stereotypes, trust, and cooperative action generates a benevolent cycle of increasing cooperation may also exist (Deutsch, 1973).

To return to one of the initial examples, both the maintenance concern with keeping the machines clean and the production concern with maximizing output were organizationally desirable. But those concerns promoted a negative maintenance stereotype of production ("too lazy to clear the machines") and a production stereotype of maintenance ("want us to polish the machine, not use it") that encouraged them to fight. Part A of Figure 1 illustrated the overt but not escalated conflict between the parties.

Introducing power differences into intergroup relations further suppresses communications among the groups. The low-power group is vulnerable, and so must censor communication—such as dissatisfaction—that might elicit retaliation from the high-power group. In consequence, the high-power group remains ignorant of information considered sensitive by the low-power group. The long-term consequences of this mutually reinforcing fear and ignorance can be either escalating oppression—a peculiarly destructive form of too little conflict—or sporadic eruptions of intense and unexpected fighting (Brown, 1978).

The fight between the small independent union and the large corporation described at the outset illustrates the potential for outbursts of violent conflict when the parties are separated by large differences in power. The small union felt unable to influence the corporation at the bargaining table, and so used violence and guerilla tactics to express its frustration and to influence management without exposing the union to retaliation. Part B of Figure 1 illustrates the positions of the parties and the quality of their conflict.

Conflicts among groups that involve societal differences may be even more complicated. Differences rooted in societal history are likely to be expressed in a network of mutually reinforcing social mechanisms—political, economic, geographic, educational—that serve to *institutionalize* the differences. Societal differences do not necessarily imply power differences between the groups, but very frequently the effect of institutionalization is to enshrine the dominance of one party over another. Relations among such groups within organizations are strongly influenced by the larger society. Organizational tensions may be the result of environmental developments that the organization cannot control. In addition,

FIGURE 1 Varieties of Intergroup Conflict

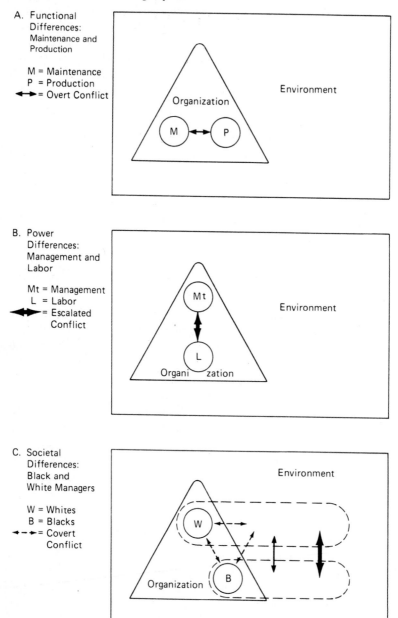

A. Functional
   Differences:
   Maintenance and
   Production

   M = Maintenance
   P = Production
   ◄─► = Overt Conflict

   Organization

   M ◄─► P

   Environment

B. Power
   Differences:
   Management and
   Labor

   Mt = Management
   L = Labor
   ◄─► = Escalated
         Conflict

   Mt

   L

   Organi   zation

   Environment

C. Societal
   Differences:
   Black and
   White Managers

   W = Whites
   B = Blacks
   ◄-► = Covert
         Conflict

   Environment

   W

   B

   Organization

differences associated with histories of discrimination or oppression may involve strong feelings and entrenched stereotypes that can lead to explosive conflict. Societal differences in organizations call for careful management that permits enough overt conflict so the differences are understood, but not so much that they are exacerbated.

The failure to integrate the trust division illustrates the problem of managing institutionalized racism. The black recruits had all the technical skills for success, but they could not join the all-white clubs or buy a house in the all-white suburbs where their colleagues lived, played, and learned the social ropes of the trust business. Nor could they challenge top-level decisions to keep them away from the oldest (and richest) clients ("who might be racist and so take their business elsewhere"). But the failure to face the potential conflicts—among members of the organization and between the organization and its clients—in essence made it impossible for the black managers to become full members. This situation is diagrammed in Part C of Figure 1.

MANAGING CONFLICT AMONG GROUPS

Diagnosing the Conflict

Diagnosis is a crucially important and often-neglected phase of conflict management. Since conflict problems are often not recognized until after they have become acute, the need for immediate relief may be intense. But intervention in a poorly understood situation is not likely to produce instant successes. On the contrary, it may make the situation worse.

The manager of conflict should at the outset answer three questions about the situation:

1. At what level or levels is the conflict rooted (e.g., personal, interpersonal, intergroup, etc.)?
2. What role does s/he play in the relations among the parties?
3. What is a desirable state of relations among the parties?

A conflict may be the result of an individual, an interpersonal relationship, an intergroup relationship, or a combination of the three. If the manager understands the contributions of different levels, s/he can respond appropriately. It is generally worthwhile to examine the conflict from *each* of these perspectives early in the diagnosis.

The position of the manager vis-à-vis the parties is also important. Managers who are themselves parties to the dispute are likely to be biased, and almost certainly will be perceived by their opponents as biased. Actual bias requires that the manager be suspicious of his/her own perceptions and strive to empathize with the other party; perceived bias may limit the manager's ability to intervene credibly with the other party until the perception is dealt with. Conflict managers who are organizationally superior to the parties may not be biased in favor of either, but they are likely to have poor access to information about the conflict. For such persons special effort to understand the parties' positions may be necessary. Third parties that are respected and seen as neutral by both sides are in perhaps the best position to intervene, but they are a rare luxury for most situations. In any case, awareness of one's position vis-à-vis the parties can help the manager avoid pitfalls.

Finally, a conflict manager needs to develop a sense of what is too much and what is too little conflict among the parties—when is intervention merited, and should it increase or decrease the level of conflict? Relations among groups may be diagnosed in terms of attitudes, behavior, and structure, and each of those categories have characteristic patterns associated with too much and too little conflict.

Attitudes include the orientations of groups and group members to their own and other groups—the extent to which they are aware of group interdependencies, the sophistication of group representatives about intergroup relations, and the quality of feelings and stereotypes within groups. Too much conflict is characterized by blindness to interdependencies, naiveté about the dynamics and costs of conflict, and strong negative feelings and stereotypes. Too little conflict, in contrast, is marked by blindness to conflicts of interests, naiveté about the dynamics and costs of collusion, and little awareness of group differences.

Behaviors include the ways in which groups and their members act—levels

TABLE 1 Diagnosing Conflict among Groups

Area of Concern	General Issue	Symptoms of Too Much Conflict	Symptoms of Too Little Conflict
Attitudes	Awarenesss of similarities and differences	Blind to interdependence	Blind to conflicts of interest
	Sophistication about intergroup relations	Unaware of dynamics and costs of conflict	Unaware of dynamics and costs of collusion
	Feelings and perceptions of own and other group	Elaborated stereotypes favorable to own and unfavorable to other group	Lack of consciousness of own group and differences from other group
Behavior	Behavior within groups	High cohesion and conformity; high mobilization	Fragmentization; mobilization
	Conflict management style of groups	Overcompetitive style	Overcooperative style
	Behavior between groups	Aggressive, exploitative behavior; preemptive attack	Avoidance of conflict; appeasement
Structure	Nature of larger system	Separate or underdefined common larger system	Shared larger system that discourages conflict
	Regulatory context for interaction	Few rules to limit escalation	Many rules that stifle differences
	Relevant structural mechanisms	No inhibiting third parties available	No third parties to press differences
	Definition of groups and their goals	Impermeably bounded groups obsessed with own interests	Unbounded groups aware of own interests

of cohesion and conformity within groups, the action strategies of group representatives, the extent to which interaction between the groups is marked by escalating conflict or cooperation. Too much conflict often involves monolithically conforming groups, rigidly competitive action strategies, and escalating aggression among the groups. Too little conflict is associated with undefined or fragmented groups, unswervingly cooperative action strategies, and collusive harmony and agreement in place of examination of differences.

Structures are underlying factors that influence interaction in the long term—the larger systems in which parties are embedded, structural mechanisms that connect the parties, group boundaries and long-term interests, and regulatory contexts that influence interaction. Too much conflict is promoted by undefined or differentiated larger systems, lack of integrative mechanisms that link the groups, clearly defined and conflicting group interests and identities, and few rules or regulations to limit conflict. Too little conflict is encouraged by a shared larger system that suppresses conflict, no mechanisms to promote examination of differences, vague definitions of conflicting group interests and identities, and regulations that discourage overt conflict.

These diagnostic categories and the earmarks of too much and too little conflict are summarized in Table 1. Attitudinal, behavioral, and structural aspects of intergroup relations tend to interact with and support one another. The result is a tendency to escalate either the conflict or the collusion until some external force exerts a moderating effect. Thus, intergroup relations are volatile and capable of rapid escalatory cycles, but they also offer a variety of leverage points at which their self-fulfilling cycles may be interrupted by perceptive managers.

Intervention

Intervention to promote constructive conflict may involve *reducing* conflict in relations with too much or *inducing* conflict in relations with too little. In both cases, intervention involves efforts to disrupt a cyclical process produced by the interaction of attitudes, behavior, and structure. Interventions may start with any aspect of the groups' interaction, although long-term change will probably involve effects in all of them. More work has been done on the problem of reducing conflict than on inducing it—but conflict-reduction strategies often have the seeds of conflict induction within them.

Changing *attitudes* involves influencing the ways in which the parties construe events. Thus *altering group perceptions of their differences or similarities* may influence their interaction. Sherif (1966), for example, reports reduction in intergroup conflicts as a consequence of introducing superordinate goals that both groups desired but whose achievement required cooperation; emphasizing interdependencies may reduce escalated conflict. On the other hand, inducing conflict may require deemphasizing interdependencies and emphasizing conflicts of interest. Attitudes may also be changed by *changing the parties' understanding of their relations.* Increased understanding of the dynamics of intergroup conflict and its costs, for example, may help participants reduce their unintentional contributions to escalation (e.g., Burton, 1969). By the same token, increased understanding may help parties control the development of collusion (Janis, 1972). *Feelings and stereotypes may also be changed* by appropriate interventions. Sharing discrepant perceptions of each other has helped depolarize negative stereotypes and reduce conflict in a number of intergroup conflicts (e.g., Blake, Shepard, and Mouton, 1964), and consciousness raising to clarify self and other perceptions may help to increase conflict in situations where there is too little. Attitude-change interventions, in short, operate on the ways in which the parties understand and interpret the relations among the groups.

Changing *behaviors* requires modifying ways in which group members act. *Altering within-group behavior,* for example, may have a substantial impact on the ways in which the groups deal with each other. When members of a highly cohesive group confront explicitly differences that exist *within* the group, their enthusiasm for fighting with outside groups may be reduced. Similarly, an internally fragmented group that becomes more cohesive may develop an increased appetite for conflict with other groups (Brown, 1977). A second behavior-changing strategy is to *train group representatives to manage conflict more effectively.* Where too much conflict exists, representatives can be trained in conflict-reduction strategies, such as cooperation induction (Deutsch, 1973) or problem solving (Filley, 1975). Where the problem is too little conflict, the parties might benefit from training in assertiveness or bargaining skills. A third alternative is to *monitor between-group behavior,* and so influence escalations. Third parties trusted by both sides can control escalative tendencies or lend credibility to reduction initiatives by the parties that might otherwise be distrusted (Walton, 1969). Similarly, conflict induction may be an outcome of third-party "process consultation" that raises questions about collusion (Schein, 1969). Behavior-change strategies, in summary, focus on present activities as an influence on levels of conflict, and seek to move those actions into more constructive patterns.

Changing structures involve altering the underlying factors that influence long-term relations among groups. A common alternative is to *invoke larger system interventions.* Conflict between groups in the same larger system is often reduced through referring the question at issue to a higher hierarchical level (Galbraith, 1971). A similar press for conflict induction may be created when too little conflict results in lowered performance that catches the attention of higher levels. A related strategy for managing conflict is to *develop regulatory contexts* that specify appropriate behaviors. Such regulatory structures can limit conflict by imposing rules on potential fights, as collective bargaining legislation does on labor-management relations. Changes in regulatory structures can also loosen rules that stifle desirable conflict. A third strategy is the *development of new interface mechanisms* that mediate intergroup relations. Integrative roles and departments may help to reduce conflict among organizational departments (Galbraith, 1971), while the creation of ombudsmen or "devil's advocates" can help surface conflict that might otherwise not become explicit (Janis, 1972). Another possibility is *redefinition of group boundaries and goals,* so the nature of the parties themselves is reorganized. Redesigning organizations into a matrix structure, for example, in effect locates the conflicted interface within an individual to ensure that effective management efforts are made (Galbraith, 1971). Alternatively, too little conflict may call for clarifying group boundaries and goals so the differences among them become more apparent and more likely to produce conflict. Structural interventions typically demand heavier initial investments of time and energy, and they may take longer to bear fruit than attitudinal and behavioral interventions. But they are also more likely to produce long-term changes.

These strategies for intervention are summarized in Table 2. This sample of strategies is not exhaustive, but it is intended to be representative of interventions that have worked with groups that are relatively equal in power and whose differences are primarily related to the organization's task. The introduction of power differences and societal differences raises other issues.

TABLE 2 Intervening in Conflict among Groups

Area of Concern	General Issue	Strategies for Too Much Conflict	Strategies for Too Little Conflict
Attitudes	Clarify differences and similarities	Emphasize interdependencies	Emphasize conflict of interest
	Increased sophistication about intergroup relations	Clarify dynamics and costs of escalation	Clarify costs and dynamics of collusion
	Change feelings and perceptions	Share perceptions to depolarize stereotypes	Consciousness raising about group and others
Behavior	Modify within-group behavior	Increase expression of within-group differences	Increase within-group cohesion and consensus
	Train group representatives to be more effective	Expand skills to include cooperative strategies	Expand skills to include assertive, confrontive strategies
	Monitor between-group behavior	Third party peacemaking	Third-party process consultation
Structure	Invoke larger system interventions	Refer to common hierarchy	Hierarchical pressure for better performance
	Develop regulatory contexts	Impose rules on interaction that limit conflict	Deemphasize rules that stifle conflict
	Create new interface mechanisms	Develop intergrating roles of groups	Create "devil's advocates" or ombudsmen
	Redefine group boundaries and goals	Redesign organization to emphasize task	Clarify group boundaries and goals to increase differentiation

Power Differences

Relations between high-power and low-power groups are worth special examination because of their potential for extremely negative outcomes. The poor communications that result from fear on the part of the low-power group and ignorance on the part of the high-power group can result in either extreme oppression (too little conflict) or unexpected explosions of violence (too much).

It is understandable that high-power groups prefer too little conflict to too much, and that low-power groups are anxious about the risks of provoking conflict with a more powerful adversary. But organizations that in the short run have too little conflict often have too much in the long term. Inattention to the problems

313

of low-power groups requires that they adopt highly intrusive influence strategies in order to be heard (e.g., Swingle, 1976). So the comfort of avoiding conflict between high- and low-power groups may have high costs in the long run.

Managing conflict between high- and low-power groups requires dealing in some fashion with their power differences, since those differences drastically affect the flow of information and influence among the parties. A prerequisite to conflict management interventions may well be *evening the psychological odds,* so that both groups feel able to discuss the situation without too much risk. Evening the odds does not necessarily mean power equalization, but it does require trustworthy protection (to reduce the fear of low-power groups) and effective education (to reduce the ignorance of high-power groups). Given psychological equality, interventions related to attitudes, behavior, and structure that have already been discussed may be employed to promote constructive levels of conflict (e.g., Brown, 1977). It should be noted that for different powerful groups the boundary between too much and too little conflict is easily crossed. Managers may find themselves oscillating rapidly between interventions to induce and interventions to reduce conflict between such groups.

To return once again to an initial example, the history of fighting and violence between the small union and the corporation led the latter's managers to expect even worse conflict when faced by the international union. But voting in the international in effect evened the odds between labor and management. Violent tactics considered necessary by the small union were not necessary for the international, and the regulatory structure of collective bargaining proved adequate to manage the conflict subsequently.

Societal Differences

Organizations are increasingly forced to grapple with societal differences. These differences are typically not entirely task-related; rather, they are a result of systemic discrimination in the larger society. Group members enter the organization with sets toward each other with which the organization must cope to achieve its goals. Societal differences are most problematic when they involve histories of exploitation (e.g., blacks by whites, women by men), and successful conflict management of such differences requires more than good intentions.

Managing societal differences in organizations may call for evening the odds, as in managing power differences, since societal differences so often include an element of power asymmetry. But coping with societal differences may also require more, since the effect of institutionalization is to ensure that the differences are preserved. *Invoking pressures from the environment* may be required even to get members of some groups into the organization at all. External forces such as federal pressure for "equal opportunity" and expanding educational opportunities for minorities can be used to press for more attention to societally based conflicts within organizations. Organizations may also develop *internal counterinstitutions* that act as checks and balances to systemic discrimination. A carefully designed and protected "communications group," which includes members from many groups and levels, can operate as an early warning system and as a respected third party for managing societal intergroup tensions in an organization (Alderfer, 1977).

314

The bank's failure to integrate the trust department turned largely on institutionalized racism. The decision to hire black managers was made partly in response to environmental pressure, and so overcame the initial barrier to letting blacks into the division at all. But once into the division, no mechanisms existed to press for overt discussion of differences. Without that discussion, no ways could be developed for the black managers to scale the insurmountable barriers facing them. The bank colluded with its supposedly racist clients by protecting them from contact with the new recruits. Although the first step—recruiting the black managers—was promising, trust division managers were unable to make the differences discussable or to develop the mechanisms required for effective management of the black-white differences in the division.

CONCLUSION

It may be helpful to the reader to summarize the major points of this argument and their implications. It has been argued that relations among groups in organizations can be characterized by too much or too little conflict, depending on their task, the nature of their differences, and the degree to which they are interdependent. This proposition suggests that *conflict managers should strive to maintain some appropriate level of conflict,* rather than automatically trying to reduce or resolve all disagreements. Effective management of intergroup conflict requires both understanding and appropriate action. Understanding intergroup conflict involves diagnosis of attitudes, behaviors, structures, and their interaction. *Effective intervention to increase or decrease conflict requires action to influence attitudes, behaviors, and structures grounded in accurate diagnosis.*

Power differences between groups promote fear and ignorance that result in reduced exchange of information between groups and the potential for either explosive outbursts of escalated conflict or escalating oppression. evening the odds, at least in psychological terms, may be a prerequisite to effective intervention in such situations. *Managers must cope with fear, ignorance, and their consequences to effectively manage conflicts between unequally powerful groups.*

Societal differences institutionalized in the larger society may further complicate relations among groups in organizations by introducing environmental events and long histories of tension. Managing such differences may require invocation of environmental pressures and the development of counterinstitutions that help the organization deal with the effects of systemic discrimination in the larger society. *Environmental developments produce the seeds for organizational conflicts, but they also offer clues to their management.*

The importance of effective conflict management in organizations is increasing, and that development is symptomatic of global changes. We live in a rapidly shrinking, enormously heterogeneous, increasingly interdependent world. The number of interfaces at which conflict may occur is increasing astronomically, and so are the stakes of too much or too little conflict at those points. If we are to survive—let alone prosper—in our onrushing future, we desperately need skilled managers of conflict among groups.

REFERENCES

Alderfer, C. P. Improving Organizational Communication Through Long-Term Intergroup Intervention. *Journal of Applied Behavioral Science, 13,* 1977, 193–210.

Blake, R. R., and Mouton, J. S. Reactions to Intergroup Competition Under Win-Lose Conditions. *Management Science, 4,* 1961.

Blake, R. R., Shepard, H. A., and Mouton, J. S. *Managing Intergroup Conflict in Industry,* Ann Arbor, Mich.: Foundation for Research on Human Behavior, 1964.

Brown, L. D. Can Haves and Have-Nots Cooperate? Two Efforts to Bridge a Social Gap. *Journal of Applied Behavioral Science, 13,* 1977, 211–224.

Brown, L. D. Toward a Theory of Power and Intergroup Relations, in *Advances in Experiential Social Process,* edited by C. A. Cooper and C. P. Alderfer. London: Wiley, 1978.

Burton, J. W. *Conflict and Communication: The Use of Controlled Communication in International Relations,* London: Macmillan, 1969.

Coser, L. A. *The Functions of Social Conflict.* New York: Free Press, 1973.

Deutsch, M. *The Resolution of Conflict.* New Haven, Conn.: Yale University Press, 1973.

Filley, A. C. *Interpersonal Conflict Resolution.* Glenview, Ill.: Scott, Foresman, 1975.

Galbraith, J. R. *Designing Complex Organizations.* Reading, Mass.: Addison-Wesley, 1971.

Janis, I. *Victims of Groupthink.* Boston: Houghton-Mifflin, 1972.

Lawrence, P. R., and Lorsch, J. W. *Organization and Environment.* Boston: Harvard Business School, 1967.

Robbins, S. P. *Managing OrganizationaL Conflict.* Englewood Cliffs, N.J.: Prentice-Hall, 1974.

Schein, E. G. *Process Consultation.* Reading, Mass.: Addison-Wesley, 1969.

Sherif, M. *In Common Predicament.* Boston: Houghton-Mifflin, 1966.

Swingle, P. G. *The Management of Power.* Hillsdale, N.J.: Erlbaum Associates, 1976.

Walton, R. *Interpersonal Peacemaking.* Reading, Mass.: Addison-Wesley, 1969.

TACTICS OF LATERAL RELATIONSHIP: THE PURCHASING AGENT

George Strauss

This is a study of the tactics used by one functional group in an organization—purchasing—to influence the behavior of other functional departments of relatively equal status. It deals in part with "office politics" and "bureaucratic gamesmanship."

Most studies of human relations in management have dealt with *vertical* relations between superiors and subordinates or between line and staff.[1] Yet the pur-

Source: Reprinted from *Administrative Science Quarterly,* 7, No. 2 (1962), 161–186. Used by permission of Administrative Science Quarterly and George Strauss.

[1]There have been many studies of lateral relations within or among primary work groups, but such studies have been concerned primarily with rank-and-file workers, not management. Three notable studies of horizontal relations within management are Melville Dalton, *Men Who Manage* (New York, 1959); Elliot R. Chapple and Leonard Sayles, *The Measure of Management* (New York, 1961); and Henry A. Landsberger, "The Horizontal Dimension in a Bureaucracy," *Administrative Science Quarterly,* 6, (1961), 298–332.

chasing agent's[2] internal relationships (as opposed to his external relationships with salesmen) are almost entirely *lateral*; they are with other functional departments of about the same rank in the organizational hierarchy—departments such as production scheduling, quality control, engineering, and the like. Most agents receive relatively little attention from their superiors; they must act on their own, with support being given by higher management only in exceptional cases. They are given broad freedom to define their own roles and are "controlled" chiefly by the client departments with which they deal.

Although purchasing is technically a staff department, its relations with other departments can best be analyzed in terms of work flow rather than according to the typical staff-line concept. At the beginning of the typical work flow the sales department receives an order; on the basis of this the engineering department prepares a blueprint; next the production scheduling department initiates a work order for manufacturing and a requisition for purchasing; with this requisition the purchasing department buys the needed parts.

But this process does not always work smoothly. Each department has its specialized point of view which it seeks to impose on others, and each department is struggling for greater authority and status. The purpose of this exploratory study is to illustrate the range of tactics available in the interdepartmental conflict which almost always results.

RESEARCH METHOD

The research methodology included a considerable number of informal contacts with agents, observation of them at work for periods of up to one week, twenty-five formal interviews, a written questionnaire, a review of purchasing journals, and an analysis of how agents, both individually and in groups, handled specially prepared case problems.[3] In the selection of firms to be studied there was a strong bias in favor of those with large engineering staffs, since agents in these firms face the most complex problems.

The discussion which follows will be largely impressionistic and will deal with broad aspects of tactics used by purchasing agents, since their problems vary greatly and various means are used to solve them. It should also be noted that the examples illustrate extreme cases, which, being extreme, illustrate some of the basic dilemmas which most agents face, though often in an attenuated form. This study is primarily concerned with the agent himself, the man who heads the purchasing office. It does not directly concern the buyers and expediters under him or the

[2]Henceforth, I shall refer to the purchasing agent as the "agent."

[3]I am indebted for assistance to the Buffalo and Northern California Association of Purchasing Agents and to the chairmen of their respective Committees for Professional Development, Messrs. Roger Josslyn and M. J. McMahon. Helpful criticism was provided by Profs. Delbert Duncan, E. T. Malm, and Lyman Porter at the Unviersity of California, Berkeley; Prof. John Gullahorn of Michigan State College; Prof. Leonard Sayles at Columbia University; and Dean Arthur Butler and Prof. Perry Bliss at the University of Buffalo. Part of the research was done while the author was a research associate at the Institute of Industrial Relations, University of California, Berkeley.

added complications that occur when division or plant agents have a staff relationship with a corporation-wide purchasing office.

CAUSES OF FRICTION

The agent originally had two primary functions: (1) to negotiate and place orders at the best possible terms—but only in accordance with specifications set by others—and (2) to expedite orders, that is, to check with suppliers to make sure that deliveries are made on time. This arrangement gave the agent broad power in dealing with salesmen but made him little more than an order clerk in terms of power or status within the company.

The ambitious agent feels that placing orders and expediting deliveries are but the bare bones of his responsibilities. He looks upon his most important function as that of keeping management posted about market developments: new materials, new sources of supply, price trends, and so forth. And to make this information more useful, he seeks to be consulted before the requisition is drawn up, while the product is still in the planning stage. He feels that his technical knowledge of the market should be accorded recognition equal to the technical knowledge of the engineer and accountant.

Specifically, the ambitious agent would like to suggest (1) alternative materials or parts to use, (2) changes in specifications or redesign of components which will save money or result in higher quality or quicker delivery, and (3) more economical lot sizes, and to influence (4) "make or buy" decisions. The agent calls these functions "value analysis."

One way of looking at the agent's desire to expand his influence is in terms of interaction. Normally orders flow in one direction only, from engineering through scheduling to purchasing. But the agent is dissatisfied with being at the end of the line and seeks to reverse the flow. Value analysis permits him to initiate for others. Such behavior may, however, result in ill feeling on the part of other departments, particularly engineering and production scheduling.

Conflicts with Engineering

Engineers write up the *specifications* for the products which the agents buy. If the specifications are too tight or, what is worse, if they call for one brand only, agents have little or no freedom to choose among suppliers, thus reducing their social status internally and their economic bargaining power externally. Yet engineers find it much easier to write down a well-known brand name than to draw up a lengthy functional specification which lists all the characteristics of the desired item. Disagreements also arise because, by training and job function, engineers look first for quality and reliability and thus, agents charge, are indifferent to low cost and quick delivery, qualitites of primary interest to purchasing.

All these problems are aggravated by the "completion barrier." Usually the agent seeks to change specifications only after the engineer has already committed his plans to blueprints and feels he has completed his work—in fact, he may be starting another project; the agent's interference inevitably threatens the engineer's feeling of accomplishment and completion. In any case engineers are jealous of their professional status and often resent the efforts of the agent to suggest new techniques or materials. These are areas in which the engineer feels that he is uniquely competent. Finally, agents are particularly anxious to prevent "backdoor selling" which occurs when a salesman bypasses them and seeks to influence someone else in the organization (usually an engineer) to requisition the salesman's product by name or—more subtly—to list specifications which only this product can meet. Backdoor selling threatens the agent's status in two ways: (1) it encourages specification by brand and (2) it makes both salesmen and engineers less dependent on him.

Conflicts with Production Scheduling

The size of the order and the date on which it is to be delivered are typically determined by production scheduling. The agent's chief complaint against scheduling is that delivery is often requested on excessively short notice—that scheduler's engage in sloppy planning or "cry wolf" by claiming they need orders earlier than they really do—and thus force the agent to choose from a limited number of suppliers, to pay premium prices, and to ask favors of salesmen (thus creating obligations which the agent must later repay). Schedulers, on the other hand, claim that "short lead times" are not their fault, but the fault of the departments farther up the line, such as engineering (which delays its blueprints) or sales (which accepts rush orders). In addition agents claim that schedulers order in uneconomic lot sizes and fail to consider inventory costs of the savings from quantity discounts. In some instances, as we shall see, the purchasing agent seeks to solve these problems through combining production scheduling, inventory control, and purchasing into one "materials handling" department, which he hopes he will head.

TECHNIQUES FOR DEALING WITH OTHER DEPARTMENTS

Normally the agent attempts to fill requisitions as instructed. The majority of interdepartmental contacts are handled routinely and without friction in accordance with standard operating procedures. Yet many difficult problems cannot be easily programmed. Other departments are constantly placing pressures on the agent, who must take countermeasures, if only to preserve the *status quo*. And if the purchasing agent wishes to expand his power aggressively, as many do, he will inevitably run into conflict.

Understandably, then, successful agents have developed a variety of techniques for dealing with other departments, particularly when they wish to influence the terms of the requisitions received. These techniques will first be summarized briefly under five general headings and then be discussed in greater detail.

1. *Rule oriented tactics*
   a. Appeal to some common authority to direct that the requisition be revised or withdrawn.

      b. Refer to some rule (assuming one exists) which provides for longer lead times.
      c. Require the scheduling department to state in writing why quick delivery is required.
      d. Require the requisitioning department to consent to having its budget charged with the extra cost (such as air freight) required to get quick delivery.
2. *Rule-evading tactics*
      a. Go through the motions of complying with the request, but with no expectations of getting delivery on time.
      b. Exceed formal authority and ignore the requisitions altogether.
3. *Personal-political tactics*
      a. Rely on friendships to induce the scheduling department to modify the requisition.
      b. Rely on favors, past and future, to accomplish the same result.
      c. Work through political allies in other departments.
4. *Educational tactics*
      a. Use direct persuasion, that is, try to persuade scheduling that its requisition is unreasonable.
      b. Use what might be called indirect persuasion to help scheduling see the problem from the purchasing department's point of view (in this case it might ask the scheduler to sit in and observe the agent's difficulty in trying to get the vendor to agree to quick delivery).
5. *Organizational-interactional tactics*
      a. Seek to change the interaction pattern, for example, have the scheduling department check with the purchasing department as to the possibility of getting quick delivery *before* it makes a requisition.
      b. Seek to take over other departments, for example, to subordinate scheduling to purchasing in an integrated materials department.

     Note that neither the over-all categories nor the tactics listed under them are all-exclusive and that there is a great deal of over-lapping. They are proposed not as comprehensive tools of analysis, but merely as fairly common examples of bureaucratic gamesmanship.

     Each agent interviewed in the study was evaluated in terms of his reported success (in terms of specific accomplishments) in getting other departments to accept a wider role for purchasing. Although this measure was crude and subjective,[4] there seemed to be quite clear differences between the tactics used by those who looked upon their job description as a defensive bastion and those who sought to expand their power beyond it. (Note that success is measured here in terms of expansion of power, rather than money saved for the company.)

RULE-ORIENTED TACTICS

The tactics listed below are rule-oriented in the sense that the agent's approach is perfectly legitimate under the formal rules of the organization. Agents who emphasize these tactics seem to fit into Melville Dalton's category of "systemizers."

---

    [4]*Reported* success obviously involves a fair amount of wishful thinking—aspiration rather than accomplishment—but for the general character of this study this limitation was not too serious. It should be emphasized, however, that whether an agent was a successful expansionist depended not only on his own personality and his choice of techniques but also on the institutional characteristics of the organization in which he worked.

According to the Boss

According to traditional organizational theory, whenever two executives on about the same level cannot agree, they should take the problem to their common superior for solution. Yet, most agents looked upon this as a drastic step to be taken only when other means failed.

Only five of the agents interviewed mentioned appealing to their superior as a reasonably common means of dealing with interdepartmental problems. In three cases low status seemed to be largely responsible for their inability to handle problems on their own.

Two of these agents were new to the job. For example, one was a man in his early twenties, who had only a few months' experience and who commented that his chief problems were his age and his inability to understand what engineers were talking about. This man met daily to review his problems with his boss and commented that his boss ran interference for him, at least in big problems.

The purchasing agent of a large scientific laboratory was very successful in extending his authority. In dealing with research departments, however, he used the laboratory manager "as a buffer between me and the department heads." But in regard to equipment-maintenance departments, whose heads had much lower status than did the scientists, he commented that "if there were differences, I would discuss them with them. If we didn't agree, the laboratory manager would have to arbitrate. But this has never happened here." Significantly, this agent did not have a college degree, while many of the scientists were Ph.D.'s.

The other two agents who frequently worked through their superiors came from branch plants of nation-wide firms, which placed strong emphasis on individual responsibility to live within rigid rules.

The more expansionist agents rarely relied on their superiors to help them in interdepartmental disputes (in part because they had little success in doing this). They often explained that they would take problems to a man's superior if necessary but that they rarely found it necessary. Many repeated versions of the following:

> We have a policy against engineers having lunch with salesmen. Since the engineer is on my level I couldn't *tell* him to stop it. But in a nice way I could talk to him. If this didn't work, I'd see the plant manager.

> *Q.* Have you ever done this [appealed to the boss]?
> *A.* No.

The general feeling, particularly among stronger agents, was that too frequent reference to the superior would weaken their relations both with the superior and with their fellow employees. ("After all, you've got to live with them.") To bring in top management too often would, in effect, be an admission that the agent could not handle his own problems. Moreover there is a myth in many corporations of being "one great big happy family," and, as a consequence, it is difficult to bring conflicts out in the open. Furthermore, since the agent is usually the aggressor, in the sense that he is seeking to expand his power beyond its formal limits, he is unlikely to go to the boss unless his case is unusually good.

On the other hand, the threat of going to the boss loses its effectiveness as a weapon if the threat is *never* carried out. The following quotation summarizes a common position:

> It depends on how much fuss you want to make. If it is really important, you can tell him you will discuss it with his boss. But, I don't want you to get the wrong impression. If you have to resort to this, you are probably falling down on the job. By and large, we have a good relationship with our engineers. However, there are times when you have to take a tough position. You aren't doing your job if you always go along with them in a wishy-washy fashion."

One agent explained how he "educated" engineers to accept substitute products instead of insisting on one brand.

> We prepared our evidence and we were all set to take it to the top—and then, at the last minute, we backed down and told them it was too late in the game. But we indicated that in the future we would take similar issues to the top and they knew we would. So there has been much more understanding. . . . You have to risk making a few enemies once in a while.

Use of Rules

A second traditional bureaucratic means of dealing with other departments is to cite applicable rules or to rely on a formal statement of authority (such as a job description). For instance, an agent may circumvent pressure to place an order with a given company by referring to company rules requiring competitive bidding on all purchases in excess of $10,000. Most agents agreed, in theory, that rules of this sort are useful weapons, but they varied greatly in the extent to which they relied upon them in practice.

Some agents went very much "by the book," day in and day out. In general, these were men without college training, and they worked for larger, rule-oriented companies that were not changing rapidly. In answer to questions, these men often said, "This matter is governed by corporate policy" or made references to manuals and procedures. They also had a tendency to draw the lines of responsibility quite tightly, so that there were few areas of joint decision making; for example, "Engineering has the final word as far as specs are concerned. But we decide from whom to buy, provided they meet the specs." On the other hand, many agents operated very effectively without any formal written statement of their authority; their authority was understood by everybody in the organization and there was no need to put it in writing.

The evidence suggests that the most successful expansionists preferred to operate informally until there was an open conflict with another department. When this happened, they were very glad to refer to rules to bolster their position. Thus, paradoxically, we found strong agents who worked hard to introduce purchasing manuals and then paid relatively no attention to them in daily practice. In effect these agents take the position of "speak softly and carry a big stick." Indeed, the use of rules involves an implicit threat to appeal to higher management if the rules are not obeyed. ("When everyone in the organization knows what your responsibility is—and that you are backed up—then there is no need to mention it constantly.")

If flexibly used, procedure manuals provide the agent with an added bargaining weapon in dealing with other departments. Even though he may permit rules in the manual to be ignored most of the time, he can always do this as a favor in return for which he may ask favors. And the rules put a legal stamp on his efforts whenever he decides to ensnarl another department in a mass of red tape. But the expansionist agent must be careful not to become too rule-oriented. After all, his goal is to expand his influence beyond the areas over which rules give him definite authority—not to retreat behind them.

Requiring Written Acceptance
of Responsibility

Another bureaucratic technique used by many agents is to require others to justify their decisions in writing. For example, if a production scheduler orders a part for delivery with very short lead time, the agent can ask him to explain in writing why there is such a rush. He hopes the scheduler will be embarrassed unless he has a good excuse—and in any case, the effort will make him reluctant to make such last-minute requests in the future. Certainly this helps expose the scheduler who constantly cries "wolf."

Agents may ask for written explanations to clear themselves. Just as often, however, this is done to make others hesitate or to have evidence against them later. In insisting that such reports be written, the purchasing agent can refer to company rules or to possible audits. Thus in asking for such a statement, agents often say, "I need it to document my records."

Again, it is the weaker, noncollege agent who makes the most persistent use of such tactics. Many seem to feel that an approach of this sort is cowardly and defeatist. As one put it, "If you are trying to get a man to say 'yes,' I don't see any value in forcing him to put his 'no' in writing. Then he will never move." And another said, "I suppose you do punish an engineer by forcing him to give you a long written explanation, but that's hardly the way to win friends or advance your point of view." Furthermore, "You can always ask an engineer to give you a formal test result, but if he wishes he can always make the test fail."

Financial Charges

Cost-accounting procedures may also be used as a lever. A number of agents made comments like this:

> Whenever I get a request for a rush delivery, I ask the department which wants it whether they are willing to authorize overtime[5] or air freight. Since this gets charged against their budget, they usually hesitate a bit. If they go along I know they really need it. And if they have too many extra charges the auditor starts asking questions.

This tactic resembles the one previously discussed, particularly when the agent enters a statement into his records that the product would have been cheaper had the requisition been received on time. (Some companies charge inbound freight

---

[5]That is, the vendor is authorized to make an extra charge for having his men work overtime.

to the budget of the purchasing or traffic department; in such cases purchasing's leverage is somewhat less effective.)

Some companies have what is often called an efficiency (or profit) improvement plan. According to such a plan each department (and sometimes each executive) receives credit[6] for the cost savings which can be attributed to the department's activities. Agents in two companies reported that engineers showed little enthusiasm for value analysis because the purchasing department got all the credit, even though part of the work was done by the engineering department. The situation greatly improved in one of these companies when "primary" credit was transferred to engineering, with purchasing retaining "participating" credit.

RULE-EVADING TACTICS

Literal Compliance

In dealing with pressures from other departments the agent can always adopt a policy of passive resistance—that is, he can go through the motions in hopes of satisfying the demands. This tactic of feigned acceptance[7] is often used with production scheduling. For instance, after completing a lengthy phone call in which he half-heartedly tried to persuade a vendor to make a very quick delivery, an agent commented, "My buyer tried already and I knew that they just weren't going to be able to deliver that soon. Still production scheduling was screaming and they threatened to go to the plant manager. So I tried to handle it in such a way as not to hurt my relations with the vendor. They knew why I had to call."

This game of passive resistance can be skillfully played in such a way as to set a trap for the other department.

Example. One agent told how he dealt with an engineer who had placed a requisition for one company's products after having been lavishly entertained by its salesman. The agent wrote a long memo explaining why he felt this to be a poor choice and presented it to the engineer in a fashion which he knew the engineer would reject. The agent then placed the order. As he had predicted, the products arrived late and were totally inappropriate. The subsequent investigation led both to this engineer's transfer and demotion and to other engineers having greater respect for the agent's advice.[8]

It should be noted, however, that these tactics were reported by only a minority of agents. In almost every case the agent was "weak" (in terms of expansionism) or worked in large companies where there was considerable emphasis on following formal rule books. Instead of passively seeming to accept unreasonable requests, the stronger agents actively oppose them.

---

[6]Though there is no direct pay-off, performance under the plan is often taken into account in determining bonuses or promotions.

[7]Dalton, *op cit.*, p. 232.

[8]A tactic like this can always backfire. The agent himself may be blamed for the failure.

Exceeding Authority

Occasionally agents may revise the terms of requisitions on their own initiative, even though they have no formal authority to do so. For instance, an agent may extend a lead time if he knows the production scheduler has set the delivery date much earlier than is really required. Where a requisition calls for a given brand, he may purchase a substitute which he feels sure is an equivalent. Or, he may buy a larger quantity than requested in order to take advantage of quantity discounts.

When an agent revises requisitions in this manner, he may or may not tell the requisitioning department what he is doing. In either case he is exceeding his formal authority. In effect, he is daring the requisitioning department to make an issue of it. This requires considerable courage. No sensible agent will expose himself in this way unless (1) his over-all political position is secure and (2) he feels the terms of the original requisition were clearly so unreasonable that the requisitioning department will hesitate to raise the issue and expose its mistake.

Most agents were reluctant to use this tactic. Even if they could safely change orders in a given case, continual flouting of the requisitioning department's desires would create too much antagonism in the long run.

PERSONAL–POLITICAL TACTICS

Friendships and exchange of favors are used in almost every organization to get things done and to oil the wheels of formal bureaucracy. The agent is no exception to this rule; yet the author found to his surprise that informal relations played a less important role than he had expected. Agents, on the whole, seemed oriented to doing things "through channels."

None of the tactics which follow are contemplated by the company's formal scheme; all involve the use of personal relations. It would seem that Dalton's "adapters" would make greatest use of these tactics.

Friendships

Most agents prefer to deal with friends. Friendships help reduce the kinds of tensions to which agents are commonly subject. Even where friendship is not involved, it is easier to deal with people when you know their idiosyncracies and special interests. Not surprisingly, comments like this were common: "[In handling problems] friendships count a lot. Many people here started when I did twenty-five years ago. We are all at about the same level and most of them are pretty good friends of mine. A lot is a matter of trust and confidence."

Agents seem to rely on friendship contacts as a means of communication and of getting quick acceptances of proposals that could be justified on their merits in any case. Rarely do agents rely on friendship alone. As one put it, "You can accomplish some things on the basis of friendship, but you can't do too much or you will strain your friendship."

Exchange of Favors

To some extent agents operate on the principle of "reward your friends, punish your enemies," and are involved in a network of exchange of favors—and sometimes even reprisals. Favors of various sorts may be given. Most agents are under pressure to make personal purchases, for example, to help someone in management buy a set of tires at wholesale rates. Since there are usually no formal rules as to such extracurricular purchasing, the agent has a strong incentive to help those who help him most. Similarly an agent is in a position to suggest to a salesman that it might be strategic to take a "cooperative" engineer to lunch. And there are always people in management who would like him to do a favor for a friend or relative who is a salesman or who owns a small business.

Other favors are more work-related. An agent may expedite delivery for a production scheduler who normally gives plenty of lead time for his orders but who now has a real emergency on his hands. Or he may rush parts for an engineer who is building a prototype model. "If a man is reasonable with me," one agent commented, "I'll kill myself to get him what he wants." The agent is less likely to exert himself for the man who has been uncooperative in the past. Yet, in general, agents seem to play down the exchange of favors, perhaps because they have relatively few favors to offer, other than trivial ones such as personal purchases or lunches for salesmen.[9]

The use of reprisals can be seen most clearly in dealing with salesmen. As one agent put it, "I play ball with those who play ball with me. If a salesman operates behind my back, he's going to have a hell of a time getting me to give him an order." Reprisals are more risky in dealing with management.

Example. One assistant agent, for example, told me how he "delayed" getting catalogues for "uncooperative" engineers and gave "slow service" to engineers who habitually cried wolf. However, both this man's supervisor and his personnel director expressed concern over his poor human relations and his tendency to antagonize others.

The typical agent, however, seemed to feel that if he used such techniques he ran the risk of permanently impairing his relations with others. Furthermore, these techniques might always backfire; for example, if production were delayed because components were delivered late, he would be blamed.

Interdepartmental Politics

In addition to their personal relations with people, agents inevitably get involved in interdepartmental power struggles. Indeed, as the following quotations suggests, the agent is often a man in the middle, subject to conflicting pressures from all sides.

Production scheduling wants quick delivery, engineering wants quality, manufacturing wants something easy-to-make, accounting wants to save money,

---

[9]Reciprocity in the broader sense, as suggested by Gouldner and others, is, of course, inherent in the entire framework of relations discussed here. Cf. Alvin W. Gouldner, "The Norm of Reciprocity: A Preliminary Statement," *American Sociological Review,* 25 (1960), 161–177.

quality control has their own interests. And then you've got to deal with the supplier—and present the supplier's position back to your own organization (sometimes you think you are wearing two hats, you represent both the supplier and the company). Everybody has his own point of view and only the agent sees the over-all picture.

Much of the agent's time is spent seeking informal resolution of such problems[10]—and in these meetings he often acts as a mediator. The following is a common situation:

Example. Production scheduling has been pushing hard to get early delivery of a particular component (perhaps because the sales department has been pressing for increased production). In response to this pressure the vendor puts new, inexperienced men on the job. But when the components are delivered, quality control declares the work is sloppy, rejects it *in toto,* and wants to disqualify the vendor from doing further work for the company. Production scheduling and vendor are naturally upset; the vendor insists that the defects are trivial and can be easily remedied; and purchasing is placed in the difficult position of trying to mediate the issue.

If the agent is not careful in situations like this, he may become a scapegoat; everyone may turn on him and blame him for the unhappy turn of events. On the other hand, the successful agent is able to play one pressure off against another and free himself—or he may enlist the support of a powerful department to back him. If he is shrewd, he can get both sides to appeal to him to make the final decision and thus gain prestige as well as bestow favors which he may later ask returned.

Like it or not, agents of necessity engage in power politics. In doing this, they necessarily develop allies and opponents. Each department presents a special problem.

1. *Engineering.* Unless the relationship with engineering is handled with great tact, engineering tends to become an opponent, since value analysis invades an area which engineers feel is exclusively their own. Purchasing is at a disadvantage here. Engineers have the prestige of being college-trained experts, and engineering is much more strongly represented than purchasing in the ranks of higher management.

2. *Manufacturing.* There is often a tug of war between purchasing and manufacturing over who should have the greatest influence with production scheduling. These struggles are particularly sharp where purchasing is trying to absorb either inventory control or all of production scheduling.

3. *Comptroller.* The comptroller is rarely involved in the day-to-day struggles over specifications or delivery dates. But when purchasing seeks to introduce an organizational change which will increase its power—for example, absorbing inventory control—then the comptroller can be a most effective ally. But the agent must present evidence that the proposed innovation will save money.

4. *Sales.* Sales normally has great political power, and purchasing is anxious to maintain good relations with it. Sales is interested above all in being able to

---

[10]Dalton (*op cit.,* pp. 227–228) points out the function of meetings in short-circuiting formal means of handling problems.

make fast delivery and shows less concern with cost, quality, or manufacturing ease. In general, it supports or opposes purchasing in accordance with these criteria. But sales is also interested in reciprocity—in persuading purchasing "to buy them from those firms which buy from us."

5. *Production scheduling.* Relations with production scheduling are often complex. Purchasing normally has closer relations with production scheduling than any other department, and conflicts are quite common. Yet these departments are jointly responsible for having parts available when needed and, in several companies at least, they presented a common front to the outside world. Unfortunately, however, production scheduling has little political influence, particularly when it reports relatively low down in the administrative hierarchy.

The shrewd agent knows how to use departmental interests for his own ends. Two quotations illustrate this:

> Engineering says we can't use these parts. But I've asked manufacturing to test a sample under actual operating conditions—they are easy to use. Even if engineering won't accept manufacturing's data, I can go to the boss with manufacturing backing me. On something like this, manufacturing is tremendously powerful.

> [To get acceptance of new products] I may use methods and standards. Or I might go to engineering first and then to methods and standards if engineering shows no interest. If I go to methods and standards I got to emphasize the cost-saving aspect [as contrasted to engineering's interest in quality].

EDUCATIONAL TACTICS

Next we come to a set of tactics designed to persuade others to think in purchasing terms.

Direct Persuasion

Direct persuasion—the frank attempts to sell a point of view—is, of course, the agent's typical means of influencing others. Successful persuasion means "knowing your products backwards and forwards...building your case so that it can't be answered...knowing what you are talking about."

Most agents feel it essential that they have complete command of the facts, particularly if they are to bridge the status gap and meet engineers on equal terms. As one of them said, "The engineer thinks he is the expert; the only way you can impress him is to know more than he does." Thus many agents go to considerable lengths to acquire expertise; they spend a great deal of time learning production processes or reading technical journals.

Yet some of the stronger agents pointed out that too much expertise can be dangerous in that it threatens the other man's status. "Never put a man in a corner. Never prove that he is wrong. This is a fundamental in value analysis. It doesn't pay to be a know-it-all." Thus some agents look upon themselves primarily as catalysts who try to educate others to think in purchasing terms:

Actually it is an asset not to be an engineer. Not having the [engineering] ability myself, I've had to work backwards. I can't tell them what to do but I can ask questions. They know that I'm not trying to design their instrument. . . . You have to give the engineer recognition. The less formal you are in dealing with them the better. It doesn't get their dander up.

Indirect Persuasion

Recognizing the danger of the frontal approach, agents often try forms of indirection—manipulation, if you like—which are designed to induce the other departments to arrive at conclusions similar to those of the agent but seemingly on their own. For example:

We were paying $45.50 a unit, but I found a vendor who was producing a unit for $30 which I felt would meet our needs just as well. There was a lot of reluctance in engineering to accept it, but I knew the engineer in charge of the test was susceptible to flattery. So I wrote a letter for general distribution telling what a good job of investigating he was doing and how much money we'd save if his investigation was successful. . . . That gave him the motivation to figure out how it *could* work rather than how it *could not* work.

Indirect persuasion often involves presenting the facts and then letting the other person draw his own conclusions. The agent may ask the engineer to run a test on a product or even simply attach a sample of the product to an interoffice buck slip, asking, "Can we use this?" Similarly, choosing which salesmen may see engineers, he can indirectly influence the specifications process. (In fact, once an agent decides that a product should be introduced, he and the salesman will often co-ordinate their strategies closely in order to get it accepted by others in management.)

Most agents feel engineers should have no part in negotiating prices; they feel this would be encroaching on purchasing's jurisdiction. But one successful agent encourages engineers to help out in the bargaining because "that's the best way I know to make these engineers cost conscious." Another arranges to have foreman and production schedulers sit in while he negotiates delivery dates with salesmen. "In that way they will know what I'm up against when they give me lead times which are too short for normal delivery."

ORGANIZATIONAL–INTERACTIONAL TACTICS

Organizational factors play an important part in determining (1) whether the agent's relations with other departments will be formal or informal (for exmaple, whether most contacts will be face-to-face, by phone, or in writing), (2) whether it will be easy or hard for other departments to initiate for purchasing, and (3) whether purchasing can make its point of view felt while decisions are being considered—or can intervene only after other departments have already taken a position. All these involve interaction patterns. We shall consider here only two types of organizational changes: informal measures which make it easier for other departments to initiate change in the usual flow of orders and formal changes involving grants of additional authority.

Inducing Others to Initiate Action

In most of the examples discussed here, the agent seeks to initiate change in the behavior of other departments. He is the one who is trying to change the engineer's specifications, the production scheduler's delivery schedules, and so forth. The other departments are always at the receiving (or resisting) end of these initiations. As might be expected, hard feelings are likely to develop if the initiations move only one way.[11]

Recognizing this, many of the stronger agents seem to be trying to rearrange their relations with other departments so that others might initiate changes in the usual work flow more often for them. Specifically they hope to induce the other departments to turn instinctively to purchasing for help whenever they have a problem—and at the earliest possible stage. Thus one agent explained that his chief reason for attending production planning meetings, where new products were laid out, was to make it easier for others to ask him questions. He hoped to encourage engineers, for example, to inquire about available components before they drew up their blueprints. Another agent commented, "I try to get production scheduling to ask us what the lead times for the various products are. That's a lot easier than our telling them that their lead times are unreasonable after they have made commitments based on these."

Some purchasing departments send out what are, in effect, ambassadors to other departments. They may appoint purchase engineers, men with engineering background (perhaps from the company's own engineering group) who report administratively to purchasing but spend most of their time in the engineering department. Their job is to be instantly available to provide information to engineers whenever they need help in choosing components. They assist in writing specifications (thus making them more realistic and readable) and help expedite delivery of laboratory supplies and material for prototype models. Through making themselves useful, purchase engineers acquire influence and are able to introduce the purchasing point of view before the "completion barrier" makes this difficult. Similar approaches may be used for quality control.

Work assignments with purchasing are normally arranged so that each buyer can become an expert on one group of commodities bought. Under this arrangement the buyer deals with a relatively small number of salesmen, but with a relatively large number of "client" departments within the organization. A few agents have experimented with assigning men on the basis of the departments with which they work rather than on the basis of the products they buy. In one case work assignments

---

[11]Actually, of course, initiations do occur in both directions. The production schedulers initiate for the agent when they file requisitions and the engineers initiate when they determine specifications. This normal form of programmed, routine initiation is felt to be quite different from the agent's abnormal attempts to introduce innovation. This distinction is quite important.

in both purchasing and scheduling were so rearranged that each production scheduler had an exact counterpart in purchasing and dealt only with him. In this way closer personal relations developed than would have occurred if the scheduler had no specific individual in purchasing to contact.

Even the physical location of the agent's office makes a difference. It is much easier for the agent to have informal daily contacts with other departments if his office is conveniently located. Some companies place their agents away from the main office, to make it easier for salesmen to see them. Although this facilitates the agents' external communications, it makes their internal communications more difficult. Of course, those companies that have centralized purchasing offices and a widespread network of plants experience this problem in an exaggerated form. Centralized purchasing offers many economic advantages, but the agent must tour the plants if he is not to lose all contact with his client departments.

Value analysis techniques sharply highlight the agent's organizational philosophy. Some agents feel that value analysis should be handled as part of the buyer's everyday activities. If he comes across a new product which might be profitably substituted for one currently used, he should initiate engineering feasibility studies and promote the idea ("nag it" in one agent's words) until it is accepted. Presumably purchasing then gets the credit for the savings, but resistance from other departments may be high. Other agents, particularly those with college training, reject this approach as unnecessarily divisive; they prefer to operate through committees, usually consisting of engineers, purchasing men, and production men. Though committees are time consuming, communications are facilitated, more people are involved, more ideas are forthcoming—and, in addition, the purchasing department no longer has the sole responsibility for value analysis.

To the extent that he allows others to take the initiative the agent himself must take a passive role. Not all agents are emotionally prepared to do this.[12] Some feel that it smacks too much of the "order clerk." A number commented, in effect, "I don't want to be everyone's door mat." Many asked questions like, "How far do you go in cost estimating, in getting quotes for hypothetical orders?... What do you do if a man throws a label at you and says get me some of this? After all, our time is limited."

Formal Organizational Change

The final approach is for the agent to seek to expand the formal grant of authority given his department (which might mean a larger budget too), as, for example, to place other functions such as traffic, stores, or even inventory control and production scheduling in one combined materials department. Agents who exert their energies in this direction generally reject the "human relations" or "participative" approach to management. They like to resolve problems through memoranda ("it helps keep emotions down") and are not particularly optimistic about the possibilities of converting other departments to think in purchasing terms

---

[12]After all, a certain type of active, initiating sort of personality is required if the agent is to bargain successfully with suppliers; it is hard for the same individual to adopt a passive role within the organization.

("after all every department has its own point of view—that's natural"). They spend considerable time developing statistical means of measuring their own efficiency and that of their subordinates, and they are more likely to be in companies that have similar philosophies. For example, one agent explained why value analysis in his organization was concentrated in the purchasing department, "[Our company] doesn't believe in joint assignments or committees. If a man isn't competent to do the job himself, then we find another man. We don't want weak sisters." And another argued, "The responsibility must be concentrated in one department or another. It can't fall between two stools."[13]

CHOICE OF TECHNIQUES

The foregoing list of tactics is presented not as a formal typology but merely to illustrate the *range* of techniques available to the agent. Most agents use all of these techniques at one time or another, depending on the problem. A different technique might well be used in introducing a major policy change than in handling routine orders. In trying to promote changes, one agent observed:

> You have to choose your weapons. I vary them on purpose. . . . I ask myself, who has the final decision? How does the Chief Engineer operate? What does he delegate? What does he keep for himself? It all involves psychological warfare. Who are the people to be sold? Who will have the final say?

And even in dealing with one problem, a mixture of tactics will generally be used. Nevertheless, the over-all strategies used by various agents seem to vary greatly in terms of which tactics receive the greatest emphasis.

1. Some agents seek formal grants of power (for example, to get inventory placed under purchasing); others merely seek influence (for example, to persuade inventory control to order in more economic lot sizes).

2. Some agents want to influence decisions *before* they are made (for example, through encouraging engineers to turn instinctively to purchasing for help whenever they are even considering the use of a new component); others *after* (for example, through having their decisions upheld often enough for engineering to hesitate to make an issue of a request whenever purchasing questions a specification).

3. Some agents think in terms of their long-run position and thus seek to improve procedures; whereas others are interested chiefly in exerting their influence in each conflict as it comes along.

We have already noted a difference between successful expansionists and those content with their roles as they are. On the whole, expansionists seemed to be more likely to choose informal tactics such as indirect persuasion, inducing others to make changes in the work flow, and interdepartmental politics. They had long-run strategies and sought to influence decisions before they were made. Those who

---

[13]Yet it could be argued that the committee system does not itself divide responsibility; it merely recognizes the fact that responsibility for value analysis is of necessity divided among departments.

were successful in achieving more formal power were also well aware of the value of informal influence; those who merely *talked* about formal power seemed to be relatively unsuccessful even in informal influence. In fact, one of the most noticeable characteristics of successful expansionists was their flexibility. Most were equally adept at using both formal and informal tactics and were not averse to turning the formal organization against itself.

Differences in success in expansionism seem to be due to a number of factors:

1. *Technology.* Obviously the agent cannot expand very much in a service industry or one where only raw materials are bought. He has his greatest chance for power in companies which make goods to order and in which there is a great deal of subcontracting.

2. *Management philosophy.* Where lines of authority are sharply drawn, the agent has little chance to extend his influence—except through direct seizure of another department's power, which is not easy. Note the comments of one agent in a highly rule-oriented company:

> We are a service department. . . We must see that parts are here at the proper time. . . . I usually let engineering pretty much make its own decisions. I may try to persuade an engineer to accept a new product. But if he says "no" all I can do is wait till he gets transferred and try to persuade his successor.

Of the agents interviewed, the most successful was one in a company which had just introduced a new management and in which all relationshps were in flux.

3. *Education.* Purchasing agents who were college graduates seemed to be more expansionist than those who were not. This may be due to their higher level of aspiration. Moreover, any company that appoints a college graduate may well expect to grant him greater influence. The college-trained man may feel more as an equal of the engineer and therefore more willing to come into conflict with him.

Furthermore, the more educated men (and particularly those with a business school background) seemed more prone to rely on techniques that were informal and not rule-oriented. Specifically, they were less likely to rely on formal statements of authority, to require others to take formal responsibilities for decisions, or to insist that an agent should "yell loudly whenever his rights are violated"; and they were more willing to work through committees.[14]

CONCLUSION

Traditional organization theory emphasizes authority and responsibility; it deals largely with two types of relationships: (1) those between superiors and subordinates, which it conceives as being primarily authoritarian (though perhaps

---

[14]These conclusions are consistent with the findings of the questionnaire sample ($N = 142$). The results are in the direction indicated for both degree of education and business school background (each taken separately) although only three out of eight relationships are significant at the .05 level. The questionnaire data are somewhat suspect, however, since the values which agents report are not always consistent with their observed behavior: in answering questionnaires many agents seem to place greater emphasis on formal techniques than they do in practice.

modifiable by participation, general supervision, and the like) and (2) those of staff and line, which are nonauthoritarian. Though the purchasing department is traditionally classified as a staff department, my own feeling is that the staff-line dichotomy in this case (as perhaps for most other purposes) tends to obscure more problems than it illuminates. As we have seen, the purchasing department's relations with other departments cannot be explained by any one simple phrase, such as "areas of responsibility," "exchange of favors," "advice," "control," or the like. Instead the skillful agent blends all these approaches and makes use of authoritarian and persuasive tactics as the situation requires. His effectiveness is largely dependent on the political power he is able to develop.

Recent authors have suggested that the study of organization should begin first with "the work to be done and resources and techniques available to do it."[15] The emphasis is on the technology of the job ("technology" being defined broadly to include marketing problems and the like as well as external environment) and the relationships between people which this technology demands. "Organizations should be constructed from the *bottom up,* rather than from the *top down.* In establishing work-group boundaries and supervisory units, management should start with the actual work to be performed, an awareness of who must co-ordinate his job with whom, when, and where."[16]

Some of us who are interested in this area are groping toward a concept of *work flow,* meaning the communications or interactions required by the job and including the flow of raw materials and products on the assembly line, the flow of paper work when a requisition moves through engineering, scheduling, and purchasing, as well as the flow of instruction, which may move down the chain of command from president to janitor.

This has been an exploratory study of the interrelationship between power struggles and lateral work flow. Of particular interest in this study, are: (1) the agent's strong desire for increased status, which upsets the stability of his relationship with other departments, (2) his attempts to raise his status through influencing the terms of the requisitions he receives and thus make interactions flow both ways, (3) the relatively limited interference on the part of higher management, which makes the lateral relationship especially important for the agent, (4) the "completion barrier," which requires the agent to contact an engineer before a blueprint is finished if the agent is to be successful in influencing the terms of the requisition, and (5) the differing vested interests or terms of reference of the various departments, which make agreement more difficult.

Finer mapping and more intensive research into interdepartmental relations is required; interactions should be precisely counted[17] and work should be done with specialties other than purchasing.

---

[15]Wilfred Brown, *Exploration in Management* (London, 1960), p. 18. See Chapple and Sayles, *op. cit.;* William F. Whyte, *Men at Work* (Homewood, Ill., 1961).

[16]George Strauss and Leonard R. Sayles, *Personnel: The Human Problems of Management* (Englewood Cliffs, N.J., 1960), p. 392. The sentence is Sayles's.

[17]Albert H. Ruberstein of Northwestern University has completed an unpublished quantitative study of communications within a purchasing department.

INGROUP AND INTERGROUP RELATIONS: EXPERIMENTAL ANALYSIS

Musafer Sherif
Carolyn W. Sherif

The development and effects of ingroup and outgroup delineation in a situation that fostered rivalry were examined in an experimental study of boys in a summer camp setting. By structuring the boys' activities the experiments were able to observe the effects of intergroup competitive tournaments and frustrating events on intergroup hostility. Hostile clashes were observed, but despite the high level of intergroup aggression, procedures were found that had the effect of reducing the level of conflict.

When individuals who have established relationships are brought together to interact in group activities with common goals, they produce a group structure that contains hierarchical statuses and roles.

If two ingroups thus formed are brought into functional relationships in conditions of competition and group frustration, attitudes and appropriate hostile actions in relation to the outgroup and its members will arise and will be standardized and shared in varying degrees by group members.

To test these motions three separate experiments were conducted in the natural setting of a boys' summer camp. The subjects were 11- to 12-year-old boys who had similar family backgrounds but had no previous acquaintance with the other boys in the camp.

The specific hypotheses tested during the three-week camp sessions in the three experiments were as follows.

Group Formation

Hypothesis 1. When individuals participate in group formation, their initially formed friendship choices will be switched to favor members of their new group.

Hypothesis 2. When a collectivity of individuals, unknown to one another, interact together in activities that have a common goal and appeal and require their concerted effort, over time a group will form and will be evidenced by (1) differntial roles and statuses and (2) norms regulating group behavior.

Intergroup Conflict

Hypothesis 3. When two established groups participate in competitive activities that only one may win, over time friendly competition will turn into intergroup hostility.

Hypothesis 4. During competitive activities unfavorable attitudes and conceptions (stereotypes) of the outgroup will form, resulting in lack of communication or contact between groups.

Source: Abstracted from *Social Psychology,* chap. 11 (New York: Harper & Row, 1969).

Hypothesis 5. Conflict between the groups serves to increase ingroup unity.

Hypothesis 6. Ingroup unity and pride is shown by the members' overestimation of the ingroup's achievement and lower estimates of outgroup performance.

Hypothesis 7. Interaction between groups (i.e., conflict) will produce changes in the ingroup's organization and practices.

Conflict Reduction

Hypothesis 8. Activities that both groups' members participate in as individuals and that require no interdependency do not reduce intergroup conflict.

Hypothesis 9. When groups must work together toward a goal that is highly appealing to each group but cannot be attained by one group alone, they will cooperate.

Hypothesis 10. Cooperation between the groups toward a series of superordinate goals serves to reduce the social distance and negative impressions of the outgroup and thus reduces intergroup conflict.

In all three experiments the data were collected by trained observers who acted in roles of camp leaders and made daily ratings on the developing relationships among the boys in terms of the amount of effective initiative each boy showed (a measure of status). Informal interview notes also determined whom the boys considered to be their current best friends (sociometric measure). The camp leaders did not initiate or guide camp activities, and gave advice only when directly asked by the boys. Every effort was made to keep the boys naive about the experimental nature of the camp.

At the beginning of camp the boys were free to choose companions in the camp activities. Following the formation of these small friendship circles, the boys in the first two experiments (1949 and 1953) were split into two groups in such a way that in each group two-thirds of the best friends were in different groups. In the 1954 study this stage of group formation began when *Ss* were divided into two groups according to the matched size and skills of the individual boys. During the week the groups in all three experiments had little contact with each other and separately engaged in appealing and cooperative activities (i.e., cooking, transporting canoes). At the end of the week (1949 and 1953 experiments) the boys were asked who their best friends were. As shown in Figure 1, Hypothesis 1 was confirmed—the boys switched their friendship choices to group members.

Gradually, as expected in Hypothesis 2, the experiments' two groups formed into a definite group organization involving differentiated roles according to the boys' individual talents and status positions. The highest status boy showed effective initiative in many activities and assumed a leadership position. Also, as predicted, each group developed norms peculiar to the group. For example, in the 1954 study one group developed a norm of toughness to such an extent that members refused to report any injury to camp leaders. The other group, however, created a norm that emphasized the importance of being good (no swearing, praying before meals). Gradually, as the groups formed, nicknames were given to individual members, and each group developed a little culture consisting of secrets, private jokes and vocabulary, and secret hiding places. Further, each group developed ways of punishing those members who violated group norms. The groups

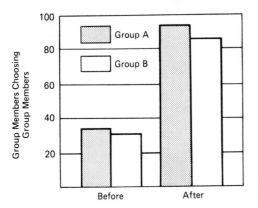

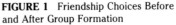
FIGURE 1 Friendship Choices Before and After Group Formation

then named themselves in order to be distinguished from the other groups—the Red Devils and the Bull Dogs (1949), Panthers and Pythons (1953), and Rattlers and Eagles (1954). Thus the criteria for group formation as described in Hypothesis 2 seem to be satisfied.

In order to begin to examine *inter*group relations in the three experiments, it was arranged for the two groups to compete in a tournament of games. Prizes were to be given to the victorious group and indiviudal prizes to the winning group's members. The tournament in each experiment began with a spirit of friendly competition. However, as the games progressed, the sense of good sportsmanship vanished. For example, after the Red Devils (1949) had experienced a losing streak they began accusing the proud Bull Dogs of playing dirty.

After the tournament the camp leaders planned a purposely frustrating situation that appeared to have been devised by one group. A party was held for both groups in order to bury the hatchet. Through the camp leaders' careful timing (not suspected by the boys), the Red Devils arrived at the party before the Bull Dogs and were thus able to enjoy the best of the assorted refreshments. On arrival the Bull Dogs realized that they had been left the less delectable food and immediately started to insult and taunt the Red Devils.

A series of hostile clashes followed, including food wars, sneak raids on each other's cabins and hate posters displayed around camp. Gradually the hostility on both sides took on quite a premeditated and scheming character (i.e., collecting and hiding caches of green apples for ammunition). Thus, as predicted (Hypotheses 3 and 4), out of the competitive nature of the tournament rose intergroup hostility. Further, as evidenced by the posters and name calling, derogatory images and stereotypes of the outgroup (the beginning of prejudice) were formed and led to great social distance between groups. Also, boys described ingroup members in favorable terms (brave and tough) but rated outgroup members unfavorably (sneaky, smart alecks).

In order to test the predictions about a group's achievement estimation, a game of bean toss was arranged and a prize was offered to the group that not only collected the most beans but also judged the game's outcome most accurately. Figure 2 indicates judgment errors in the boys' estimates of the amount collected by ingroup and outgroup members. As expected (Hypothesis 6), the members of

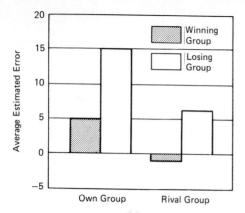

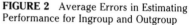

FIGURE 2 Average Errors in Estimating Performance for Ingroup and Outgroup

one group tended to overestimate their group's achievement and underestimate the performance of the other group. Winners tended to make larger errors.

Sociometric measures taken after the tournament further supported Hypothesis 5. The conflict between the groups tended to increase group unity, and friendship choices were made almost exclusively within the ingroup. The hostility also served to produce the expected organizational changes within the groups (Hypothesis 7). In the Eagles the leader role changes hands from peacetime (group formation) to this period of conflict. In another group a low status bully found himself in the leadership role when the intergroup conflict began. To an outside observer these intelligent, well adjusted, middle class boys would probably be described as violent, disturbed, or delinquent.

Now, to the constructive phase of these experiments. How can we reduce the intergroup conflict? As expected (Hypothesis 8), activities such as moviegoing or shooting firecrackers that had appeal but no need for cooperation between groups did not reduce hostility. Therefore, superordinate goals were created (i.e., goals that are important to both groups but cannot be attained by only one group), such as finding a fault in a water supply line and pooling money to see a desired movie. After a series of these cooperative activities, the amount of intergroup conflict was reduced (Hypothesis 10) and members began to act friendlier. Interviews reflected this change in attitudes. Many friendship choices were now made from the outgroup, and negative ideas about outgroup members rapidly dissipated (Figure 3).

Can we dismiss these findings as being true only among children and not applicable in the sphere of adults? Current research (Blake, Shepard & Mouton, 1964) suggests that we most definitely cannot. Adults in human relations workshops were divided into two groups, given problems, and asked to find better solutions than the other group could devise. The events that occurred faithfully replicated the Sherifs' findings. The competitive activities engendered hostility between groups, but cooperative activities dissipated the hostility. Perhaps nations can coexist peacefully if they develop goals that are mutually meaningful and beneficial and can be realized only if the nations jointly cooperate.

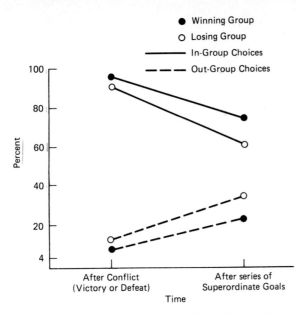

FIGURE 3   Friendship Choices Before and After Series of Subordinate Goals. Figure 11.21b (p. 263) in *Social Psychology* by Muzafer Sherif and Carolyn W. Sherif (Harper & Row, 1969).

REFERENCE

Blake, R. R.; Shepard, H. A.; and Mouton, Jane S. 1964. *Managing intergroup conflict in industry.* Houston, Texas: Gulf Publishing.

11
Managing Diversity

THE JOB MAKES THE PERSON
Rosabeth Moss Kanter

MOTIVATION, LEADERSHIP, AND ORGANIZATION:
DO AMERICAN THEORIES APPLY ABROAD?
Geert Hofstede

THE JOB MAKES THE PERSON

Rosabeth Moss Kanter

"I'd never work for a woman," a woman draftsman told me." "They are too mean and petty."

Research on female workers has for years looked for sex differences on the job. Women, the surveys show, have lower job aspirations than men, less commitment to work, and more concern with friendships than with the work itself. And many people assume that women make poor leaders because their personalities do not allow them to be assertive. Women who do make it to management positions are presumed to fit the mold of the dictatorial, bitchy boss.

To explain why more women don't seek or find career success, many people concentrate on supposed personality differences between the sexes: women's "motive to avoid success" or incapacity to handle power. Or they look at childhood training and educational training: how women learn to limit their ambitions and hide their accomplishments. Because women learn that high achievement means a loss of traditional femininity, they choose to preserve the latter and sacrifice the former.

Source: Reprinted with permission from *Psychology Today* magazine, copyright © 1976 (PT Partners, L.P.).

When I began to study women in work organizations three years ago, I also was looking for sex-related individual differences that would explain women's absence from high-status, powerful jobs. If women were ever going to make it in a man's world, the conventional wisdom said, we would have to get them when they're young and make sure they don't pick up any motives to avoid success or other bad habits. When I looked more closely at how real people in organizations behave, however, the picture changed. I could find nothing about women in my own research and that of others that was not equally true of men in some situations. For example, some women do have low job aspirations, but so do men who are in positions of blocked opportunity. Some women managers are too interfering and coercive, but so are men who have limited power and responsibility in their organizations. Some women in professional careers behave in stereotyped ways and tend to regard others of their sex with disdain, but so do men who are tokens— the only member of their group at work.

So I dropped my search for sex differences, and I concentrated instead on three aspects of a business organization that do the most to explain the conventional wisdom about women: opportunity, power and tokenism.

OPPORTUNITY

Are women less ambitious and committed to work than men? According to one large corporation I investigated, they are. This company has surveyed 111 hourly employees in white-collar jobs about their attitudes toward promotion. Sure enough, the men showed greater motivation to advance in rank than the women, and the mean had higher self-esteem, considering themselves more competent in the skills that would win them promotions. The women seemed much less interested in advancement, sometimes saying that they cared more about their families.

Yet in this company, like many, there were dramatic differences in the actual opportunities for promotion that men and women had. Men made up only a small proportion of white-collar workers; most were clustered in professional roles with steps toward management positions. Over two thirds of the women were secretaries or clerks in dead-end jobs. They could hope to advance two or three steps up to executive secretary, and there they would stop. Only rarely had a secretary moved up into professional or managerial ranks. No wonder the women found promotion a far-fetched idea.

If the company had looked at women in high-ranking jobs, the apparent sex difference in work attitudes would have vanished utterly. In my interviews, I found that ambition, self-esteem, and career commitment were all flourishing among women in sales jobs, which are well-paid and on the way to top management. Indeed, one successful young woman in the sales force told me she hoped someday to run the company.

Lack of opportunity to succeed, not a personality style that shuns success, is often what separates the unambitious from the climbers—and the women from the men. The great majority of women hold jobs that have short, discouraging career ladders—secretarial, clerical, factory work. When the jobs include opportunities for advancement, women want to advance. But jobs without such opportunities depress a person's ambition and self-esteem, for men as well as women.

The early research that first specified the circumstances under which workers are not highly committed to work or hungry for promotion was all focused on men. Social scientists Eli Chinov (who studied auto workers), Harry Purcell (meat-packers), and Robert Dublin (factory workers) concluded that the men in these routine jobs behaved just like the typical woman, they defined their jobs as temporary and dreamed of leaving. They claimed to have little interest in climbing to a higher-status job, preferring, they said, "easy work." And they placed a higher value on family life than on their careers. In effect, they adopted values that rationalized the reality of their roles.

GOSSIP AT THE DEAD END

Opportunity also determines what kinds of relationships a person forms on the job. Workers who have few prospects of moving up and out compensate by making close friends. The very limitations of the job insure that those friends will be around for a while, and one better make sure that at least the social side of an unchallenging job is pleasurable. Being well-liked becomes another meaning of success to people in dead-end work, and if you've got the best stories to offer the office, you can add a bit of excitement to mundane work. So it often looks as if women are "talk-oriented," not "task-oriented," in their jobs. Some employers point to the gossipy office coffee klatch as a direct result of women's natural concern with people, rather than with achievement. Instead, I think it is more accurate to say that female socializing reflects the jobs they have.

Highly mobile jobs demand that a person be most concerned with the work. Such jobs make close friendships with co-workers less likely. The corporate world requires its participants to be willing to relocate, to surpass rivals without hesitation, to use other people to advance in status. The aggressive, striving junior executive is as much a creation of his place in the organization hierarchy as is the talkative, unambitious secretary.

A laboratory study by Arthur Cohen clearly showed what happens to young men when their opportunity for advancement is varied. He set up some groups to be highly mobile, with a strong potential for individual promotions, and he set up other groups to believe they had no such potential. The highly mobile groups quickly became more involved with the task they had to do. They dropped irrelevant chatter, and reported later that they cared more about the high-power people who were supervising them than about each other. The nonmobile group members, by contrast, concentrated on each other. They virtually ignored the powerful supervisors, because they had nothing to gain from them anyway. They were more openly critical and resentful of people with power.

THE FRUSTRATED FOX

People who are placed in dead-end jobs set a self-fulfilling prophecy in motion. Such workers cope with career limitations by giving up hope; like the frustrated fox, they decide they don't want the grapes after all. Instead they create peer groups that give them moral support for not seeking advancement, and develop a hostility to outsiders and power figures. Peer groups make a bad job endurable or even fun, but they also put pressure on an individual to stay put. To leave would be a sign of disloyalty. For this reason, the rare man who is offered a promotion out of a dead-end factory slot feels the same ambivalence as the rare secretary who gets a chance at management.

When workers lower their aspirations, their employers logically conclude that they don't have the right attitudes for promotion. The organization decides to invest less of its resources in developing people who seem uninterested, and this decision reinforces the workers' perceptions of blocked opportunity. The vicious circle is complete.

POWER

One of the reasons given to explain why so few women have organizational authority is that people don't like female bosses. In a 1965 *Harvard Business Review* survey of almost 2,000 executives, few respondents of either sex said that they or others would feel comfortable about working for a woman, although the women were more ready to do so than the men. Over half of the men felt that women were "tempermentally unfit" for management, echoing the stereotype of the ineffective lady boss who substitutes pickiness about rules for leadership.

In fact, there is no solid evidence of lasting differences in the leadership styles of men and women. Nor is there evidence that people who work for women have lower morale. Research points in the other direction: those who have worked for a woman boss are much more likely to be favorably disposed toward female leaders.

One clear factor distinguishes good leaders from bad, effective from ineffective, liked from disliked. It is not sex, but power. It is not a matter of personality, but of clout.

Just because people have been given formal authority by virtue of position and title, they do not necessarily have equal access to power in the organization. It is not enough to be the most skillful handler of people in the world. One also needs system-granted power to back up one's demands and decisions and to ensure the confidence and loyalty of subordinates.

System power comes from having influence in the upper echelons of the organization, through membership in informal inner circles and by having high status. As a number of social-psychological studies have shown, people who bring such signs of status and influence into a group tend to be better liked—not resented—and to get their way more often. Organization members, as my interviews revealed, prove to be very knowledgeable about who is in and who is out, and when I asked them to describe desirable bosses, they decidedly preferred those with power to those with style or expertise.

That preference carries real as well as symbolic payoffs. Powerful leaders get more rewards and resources to dispense, and their own mobility promises advancement for the subordinates they bring along. Powerful leaders on the move also pick up a few practices that make them admired. As sociologist Bernard

Levenson suggests, promotable supervisors generally adopt a participatory style in which they share information with employees, delegate responsibility, train successors, and are flexible about rules and regulations. They also want to show that they are not indispensable in their current jobs, and they seek to fill the vacancy created by their own advancements with one of their own lieutenants. Since highly mobile people also want to please those above them more than nonmobile people do, they effectively build the relationships that ensure system power.

PUNITIVE, PETTY TYRANTS

Now consider again the stereotype of the bossy woman boss, who is supposedly rigid, petty, controlling, and likely to poke her nose into the personal affairs of employees. This image is the perfect picture of the powerless. Powerless leaders, men and women alike, often become punitive, petty tyrants. Psychologically, they expect resistance from subordinates. And because they have fewer organizational rewards to trade for compliance, they try to coerce employees into supporting them. Blocked from exercising power in the larger hierarchy, they substitute the satisfaction of lording it over subordinates. Unable to move ahead, they hold everyone back, and praise conformity to rules rather than talent and innovation.

Burleigh Gardner, a human-relations consultant, reviewed the experiences of women who took over supervisory jobs from men during World War II. He concluded: "Any new supervisor who feels unsure of himself, who feels that his boss is watching him critically, is likely to demand perfect behavior and performance from his people, to be critical of minor mistakes, and to try too hard to please his boss. A woman supervisor, responding to the insecurity and uncertainty of her position as a woman, knowing that she is being watched both critically and doubtfully, feels obliged to try even harder. And for doing this she is said to be 'acting just like a woman.' " In truth, she is acting just as any insecure person would.

We again come full circle. Those who have a favorable place in the power structure are more likely to become effective leaders, to be liked, and thus to gain more power. Sponsorship, for example, is a typical road to the top for many men. The protégé system, whether in academia, politics, or business, is a tough and informal way of keeping outsiders out, and making sure the best insiders keep on the fastest track. For this reason, it has been almost impossible for a woman to succeed in business without sponsorship or membership in the company's ruling family. But when women do get real power, whether in politics like Indira Gandhi or in business like advertising executive Mary Wells, they behave just as well—or badly—as men do.

TOKENISM

I studied what happens to women when they do manage to get closer to the top, and I uncovered a range of familiar situations. Male managers who could not accept a woman as a colleague without constantly reminding her that she was "different."

Women who could not make themselves heard in committee meetings and who felt left out. Bright women who hid their accomplishments. A female sales executive who felt that most women should not be hired for jobs like hers. A woman scientist who let another woman in her unit flounder without help. A woman faculty member who brought cookies to department meetings and mothered her colleagues.

All the characters were there, dressed in their sex roles. Yet I saw that even so the play was not about sex. It was about numbers. These women were all tokens, alone or nearly alone in a world of male peers and bosses. When people take on a token status—whether they are female scientists or male nurses or black executives in a white company—they share certain experiences that influence their behavior.

Tokens, by definition, stand out from the crowd. In one company I studied, the first 12 women to go to work among 400 men set the rumor mill in motion. They caused more talk and attracted more attention, usually for their physical attributes, than new male employees. The men tended to evaluate the women against their image of the ideal female rather than the ideal colleague, and the women, under relentless scrutiny, felt they could not afford to make mistakes.

When the token is a black man among whites, a similar reaction occurs. Shelly Taylor and Susan Fiske of Harvard set up an experiment in which they played a tape of group discussions to students. Then they showed pictures of the group and asked the students for their impressions of the discussants. Sometimes the photos showed a lone black in an all-white group and sometimes a mixed black-white group. Taylor and Fiske found that the students paid disproportionate attention to the token: they overemphasized his prominence in the group and exaggerated his personality traits. But when the students responded to integrated groups, they were no more likely to recall information about blacks than about whites, and they evaluated the attributes of the blacks as the same as those of the whites.

HOSTILE, RAUNCHY TALK

Tokens get attention, but they are isolated on the outskirts of the group. They are reminded constantly of how different they are, and what their proper place should be. Other employees sometimes respond to tokens by closing ranks and exaggerating the in-group culture. In several groups of sales trainees I observed, the men's talk got raunchier when token women were present, though they also added elaborate apologies and bows in the women's direction. Tokens have to listen to jokes about people like them, and they face subtle pressures to side with the majority against their kind. Male nurses report the same kind of disguised hostility from the women they work with, who constantly remind them that they do not belong and pose loyalty tests to see if they will side with women against other men. The token is never quite trusted by the rest of the group.

To win the group's trust, tokens often resort to acting out the stereotypical role that members of their sex or race are supposed to play. These roles require them to deny parts of themselves that don't fit the majority group's assumptions, and they make it difficult for the tokens to be ordinary workers doing their jobs. Token women, for instance, may wind up playing mother, sex object, pet, or iron maiden. Token men get caught, too. Lone blacks in groups of white workers, sociologist Everett Hughes found, may play the comedian. Taylor and Fiske's students saw the solo black as taking on special roles in the group, often highly stereotyped. And male nurses, according to Bernard Segal, get inveigled into doing the distasteful chores that the women didn't want to do, which were considered "men's work."

Tokens face additional pressures because they must work doubly hard to prove themselves. "Women must work twice as hard as men to be thought half as good," wrote suffragist Charlotte Whitton; "Luckily, this is not difficult." But it *is* difficult, and takes its psychological toll in emotional stress. Tokens have a shaky identity because of their precarious position; they can't behave in a totally natural way because they are on display all the time.

Many of the supposed personality traits of minority people in white male organizations, then, simply reflect their token status. To avoid the glare of visibility, some tokens try to hide themselves and their achievements. To escape the feeling of being outsiders, some tokens go overboard in adopting the attitudes of the insiders. To win trust and the comfort of being accepted, some play the stereotype that is expected of them.

Yet all these reactions—which are not necessarily conscious or intentional— are exactly those that prove to the majority that they were right all along. So tokens are kept to a numerical minimum, and another vicious spiral continues.

THE JOB MAKES THE WOMAN

What I am suggesting is that the job makes the man—and the woman. People bring much of themselves and their histories to their work, but I think we have overlooked the tremendous impact of an organization's structure on what happens to them once they are there.

If my approach is right, it suggests that change will not come from changing personalities or attitudes, and not from studying sex or race differences. Change will come only from interrupting the self-perpetuating cycles of blocked opportunity, powerlessness and tokenism.

Take the case of Linda S., a woman who had been a secretary in a large corporation for 16 years. Five years ago, she would have said that she never wanted to be anything but a secretary. She also would have told you that since she had recently had children she was thinking of quitting. She said secretarial work was not a good enough reason to leave the children.

Then came an affirmative-action program, and Linda was offered a promotion. She wavered. It would mean leaving her good female friends for a lonely life among male managers. Her friends thought she was abandoning them. She worried whether she could handle the job. But her boss talked her into it and promised to help, reassuring her that he would be her sponsor.

So Linda was promoted, and now she handles a challenging management job most successfully. Seeing friends is the least of her many reasons to come to work every day, and her ambitions have soared. She wants to go right to the top.

"I have 15 years left to work," she says. "And I want to move up six grades to corporate vice president—at least."

MOTIVATION, LEADERSHIP, AND ORGANIZATION: DO AMERICAN THEORIES APPLY ABROAD?

Geert Hofstede

A well-known experiment used in organizational behavior courses involves showing the class an ambiguous picture—one that can be interpreted in two different ways. One such picture represents either an attractive young girl or an ugly old woman, depending on the way you look at it. Some of my colleagues and I use the experiment, which demonstrates how different people in the same situaiton may perceive quite different things. We start by asking half of the class to close their eyes while we show the other half a slightly altered version of the picture— one in which only the young girl can be seen—for only five seconds. Then we ask those who just saw the young girl's picture to close their eyes while we give the other half of the class a five-second look at a version in which only the old woman can be seen. After this preparation we show the ambiguous picture to everyone at the same time.

The results are amazing—most of those "conditioned" by seeing the young girl first see only the young girl in the ambiguous picture, and those "conditioned" by seeing the old woman tend to see only the old woman. We then ask one of those who perceive the old woman to explain to one of those who perceive the young girl what he or she sees, and vice versa, until everyone finally sees both images in the picture. Each group usually finds it very difficult to get its views across to the other one and sometimes there's considerable irritation at how "stupid" the other group is.

CULTURAL CONDITIONING

I use this experiment to introduce a discussion on cultural conditioning. Basically, it shows that in five seconds I can condition half a class to see something different from what the other half sees. If this is so in the simple classroom situation, how much stronger should differences in perception of the same reality be between people who have been conditioned by different education and life experience—not for five seconds, but for twenty, thirty, or forty years?

I define culture as the collective mental programming of the people in an environment. Culture is not a characteristic of individuals; it encompasses a number of people who were conditioned by the same education and life experience. When we speak of the culture of a group, a tribe, a geographical region, a national minority, or a nation, culture refers to the collective mental programming that these people have in common; the programming that is different from that of other groups, tribes, regions, minorities or majorities, or nations.

Culture, in this sense of collective mental programming, is often difficult to change; if it changes at all, it does so slowly. This is so not only because it exists in the minds of the people but, if it is shared by a number of people, because it has become crystallized in the institutions these people have built together: their family structures, educational structures, religious organizations, associations, forms of government, work organizations, law, literature, settlement patterns, buildings and even, as I hope to show, scientific theories. All of these reflect common beliefs that derive from the common culture.

Although we are all conditioned by cultural influences at many different levels—family, social, group, geographical region, professional environment—this article deals specifically with the influence of our national environment: that is, our country. Most countries' inhabitants share a national character that's more clearly apparent to foreigners than to the nationals themselves; it represents the cultural mental programming that the nationals tend to have in common.

NATIONAL CULTURE IN FOUR DIMENSIONS

The concept of national culture or national character has suffered from vagueness. There has been little consensus on what represents the national culture of, for example, Americans, Mexicans, French, or Japanese. We seem to lack even the terminology to describe it. Over a period of six years, I have been involved in a large research project on national cultures. For a set of 40 independent nations, I have tried to determine empirically the main criteria by which their national cultures differed. I found four such criteria, which I label dimensions; these are Power Distance, Uncertainty Avoidance, Individualism-Collectivism, and Masculinity-Femininity. To understand the dimensions of national culture, we can compare it with the dimensions of personality we use when we describe individuals' behavior. In recruiting, an organization often tries to get an impression of a candidate's dimensions of personality, such as intelligence (high-low); energy level (active-passive); and emotional stability (stable-unstable). These distinctions can be refined through the use of certain tests, but it's essential to have a set of criteria whereby the characteristics of individuals can be meaningfully described. The dimensions of national culture I use represent a corresponding set of criteria for describing national cultures.

Characterizing a national culture does not, of course, mean that every person in the nation has all the characteristics assigned to that culture. Therefore, in describing national cultures we refer to the common elements within each nation—the national norm—but we are not describing the individuals. This should be kept in mind when interpreting the four dimensions explained in the following paragraphs.

348

The four dimensions of national culture were found through a combination of theoretical reasoning and massive statistical analysis, in what is most likely the largest survey material ever obtained with a single questionnaire. This survey material was collected between 1967 and 1973 among employees of subsidiaries of one large U.S.-based multinational corporation (MNC) in 40 countries around the globe. The total data bank contains more than 116,000 questionnaires collected from virtually everyone in the corporation, from unskilled workers to research Ph.D.s and top managers. Moreover, data were collected twice—first during a period from 1967 to 1969 and a repeat survey during 1971 to 1973. Out of a total of about 150 different survey questions (of the precoded answer type), about 60 deal with the respondents' beliefs and values; these were analyzed for the present study. The questionnaire was administered in the language of each country; a total of 20 language versions had to be made. On the basis of these data, each of the 40 countries could be given an index score for each of the four dimensions.

I was wondering at first whether differences found among employees of one single corporation could be used to detect truly national culture differences. I also wondered what effect the translation of the questionnaire could have had. With this in mind, I administered a number of the same questions from 1971 to 1973 to an international group of about 400 managers from different public and private organizations following management development courses in Lausanne, Switzerland. This time, all received the questionnaire in English. In spite of the different mix of respondents and the different language used, I found largely the same differences between countries in the manager group that I found among the multinational personnel. Then I started looking for other studies, comparing aspects of national character across a number of countries on the basis of surveys using other questions and other respondents (such as students) or on representative public opinion polls. I found 13 such studies; these compared between 5 and 19 countries at a time. The results of these studies showed a statistically significant similarity (correlation) with one or more of the four dimensions. Finally, I also looked for national indicators (such as per capital national income, inequality of income distribution, and government spending on development aid) that could logically be supposed to be related to one or more of the dimensions. I found 31 such indicators—of which the values were available for between 5 and 40 countries—that were correlated in a statistically significant way with at least one of the dimensions. All these additional studies (for which the data were collected by other people, not by me) helped make the picture of the four dimensions more complete. Interestingly, very few of these studies had even been related to each other before, but the four dimensions provide a framework that shows how they can be fit together like pieces of a huge puzzle. The fact that data obtained within a single MNC have the power to uncover the secrets of entire national cultures can be understood when it's known that the respondents form well-matched samples from their nations: They are employed by the same firm (or its subsidiary); their jobs are similar (I consistently compared the same occupations across the different countries); and their age categories and sex compositions were similar—only their nationalities differed. Therefore, it we look at differences in survey answers between multinational employees in countries A, B, C, and so on, the general factor that can account for the differences in the answers is national culture.

Power Distance

The first dimension of national culture is called *Power Distance.* It indicates the extent to which a society accepts the fact that power in institutions and organizations is distributed unequally. It's reflected in the values of the less powerful members of society as well as in those of the more powerful ones. A fuller picture

FIGURE 1 The Power Distance Dimension

Small Power Distance	Large Power Distance
Inequality in society should be minimized.	There should be an order of inequality in this world in which everybody has a rightful place: high and low are protected by this order.
All people should be interdependent.	A few people should be independent: most should be dependent.
Hierarchy means an inequality of roles, established for convenience.	Hierarchy means existential inequality.
Superiors consider subordinates to be "people like me."	Superiors consider subordinates to be a different kind of people.
Subordinates consider superiors to be "people like me."	Subordinates consider superiors to be a different kind of people.
Superiors are accessible.	Superiors are inaccessible.
The use of power should be legitimate and is subject to the judgment as to whether it is good or evil.	Power is a basic fact of society that antedates good or evil. Its legitimacy is irrelevant.
All should have equal rights.	Power-holders are entitled to privileges.
Those in power should try to look less powerful than they are.	Those in power should try to look as powerful as possible.
The system is to blame.	The underdog is to blame.
The way to change a social system is to redistribute power.	The way to change a social system is to dethrone those in power.
People at various power levels feel less threatened and more prepared to trust people.	Other people are a potential threat to one's power and can rarely be trusted.
Latent harmony exists between the powerful and the powerless.	Latent conflict exists between the powerful and the powerless.
Cooperation among the powerless can be based on solidarity.	Cooperation among the powerless is difficult to attain because of their low-faith-in-people norm.

of the difference between small Power Distance and large Power Distance societies is shown in Figure 1. Of course, this shows only the extremes; most countries fall somewhere in between.

Uncertainty Avoidance

The second dimension, *Uncertainty Avoidance,* indicates the extent to which a society feels threatened by uncertain and ambiguous situations and tries to avoid these situations by providing greater career stability, establishing more formal rules, not tolerating deviant ideas and behaviors, and believing in absolute truths and the attainment of expertise. Nevertheless, societies in which uncertainty avoidance is strong are also characterized by a higher level of anxiety and aggressiveness that creates, among other things, a strong inner urge in people to work hard. (See Figure 2.)

Individualism-Collectivism

The third dimension encompasses *Individualism* and its opposite, *Collectivism.* Individualism implies a loosely knit social framework in which people are

FIGURE 2 The Uncertainty Avoidance Dimension

Weak Uncertainty Avoidance	Strong Uncertainty Avoidance
The uncertainty inherent in life is more easily accepted and each day is taken as it comes.	The uncertainty inherent in life is felt as a continuous threat that must be fought.
Ease and lower stress are experienced.	Higher anxiety and stress are experienced.
Time is free.	Time is money.
Hard work, as such, is not a virtue.	There is an inner urge to work hard.
Aggressive behavior is frowned upon.	Aggressive behavior of self and others is accepted.
Less showing of emotions is preferred.	More showing of emotions is preferred.
Conflict and competition can be contained on the level of fair play and used constructively.	Conflict and competition can unleash aggression and should therefore be avoided.
More acceptance of dissent is entailed.	A strong need for consensus is involved.
Deviation is not considered threatening; greater tolerance is shown.	Deviant persons and ideas are dangerous; intolerance holds sway.
The ambiance is one of less nationalism.	Nationalism is pervasive.
More positive feelings toward younger people are seen.	Younger people are suspect.
There is more willingness to take risks in life.	There is great concern with security in life.
The accent is on relativism, empiricism.	The search is for ultimate, absolute truths and values.
There should be as few rules as possible.	There is a need for written rules and regulations.
If rules cannot be kept, we should change them.	If rules cannot be kept, we are sinners and should repent.
Belief is placed in generalists and common sense.	Belief is placed in experts and their knowledge.
The authorities are there to serve the citizens.	Ordinary citizens are incompetent compared with the authorities.

supposed to take care of themselves and of their immediate families only, while collectivism is characterized by a tight social framework in which people distinguish between in-groups and out-groups; they expect their ingroup (relatives, clan, organizations) to look after them, and in exchange for that they feel they owe absolute loyalty to it. A fuller picture of this dimension is presented in Figure 3.

Masculinity

The fourth dimension is called *Masculinity* even though, in concept, it encompasses its opposite pole, *Femininity*. Measurement in terms of this dimension express the extent to which the dominant values in society are "masculine"—that is, assertiveness, the acquisition of money and things, and *not* caring for others, the quality of life, or people. These values were labeled "masculine" because, *within* nearly all societies, men scored higher in terms of the values' positive sense than of their negative sense (in terms of assertiveness, for example, rather than its lack)—even though the society as a whole might veer toward the "feminine" pole. Interestingly, the more an entire society scores to the masculine side, the wider the gap between its "men's" and "women's" values (see Figure 4).

FIGURE 3 The Individualism Dimension

Collectivist	Individualist
In society, people are born into extended families or clans who protect them in exchange for loyalty.	In society, everybody is supposed to take care of himself/herself and his/her immediate family.
"We" consciousness holds sway.	"I" consciousness holds sway.
Identity is based in the social system.	Identity is based in the individual.
There is emotional dependence of individual on organizations and institutions.	There is emotional independence of individual from organizations or institutions.
The involvement with organizations is moral.	The involvement with organizations is calculative.
The emphasis is on belonging to organizations; membership is the ideal.	The emphasis is on individual initiative and achievement; leadership is the ideal.
Private life is invaded by organizations and clans to which one belongs; opinions are predetermined.	Everybody has a right to a private life and opinion.
Expertise, order, duty, and security are provided by organization or clan.	Autonomy, variety, pleasure, and individual financial security are sought in the system.
Friendships are predetermined by stable social relationships, but there is need for prestige within these relationships.	The need is for specific friendships.
Belief is placed in group decisions.	Belief is placed in individual decisions.
Value standards differ for in-groups and out-groups (particularism).	Value standards should apply to all universalism).

FIGURE 4 The Masculinity Dimension

Feminine	Masculine
Men needn't be assertive, but can also assume nurturing roles.	Men should be assertive. Women should be nurturing.
Sex roles in society are more fluid.	Sex roles in society are clearly differentiated.
There should be equality between the sexes.	Men should dominate in society.
Quality of life is important.	Performance is what counts.
You work in order to live.	You live in order to work.
People and environment are important.	Money and things are important.
Interdependence is the ideal.	Independence is the ideal.
Service provides the motivaiton.	Ambition provides the drive.
One sympathizes with the unfortunate.	One admires the successful achiever.
Small and slow are beautiful.	Big and fast are beautiful.
Unisex and androgyny are ideal.	Ostentatious manliness ("machismo") is appreciated.

A SET OF CULTURAL MAPS
OF THE WORLD

Research data were obtained by comparing the beliefs and values of employees within the subsidiaries of one large multinational corporation in 40 countries around the world. These countries represent the wealthy countries of the West and the larger, more prosperous of the Third World countries. The Socialist block countries are missing, but data are available for Yugoslavia (where the corporation is represented by a local, self-managed company under Yogoslavian law). It was possible, on the basis of mean answers of employees on a number of key questions, to assign an index value to each country on each dimension. As described in the box on page 349, these index values appear to be related in a statistically significant way to a vast amount of other data about these countries, including both research results from other samples and national indicator figures.

Because of the difficulty of representing four dimensions in a single diagram, the position of the countries on the dimensions is shown in Figures 5, 6, and 7 for two dimensions at a time. The vertical and horizontal axes and the circles around clusters of countries have been drawn subjectively, in order to show the degree of proximity of geographically or historically related countries. The three diagrams thus represent a composite set of cultural maps of the world.

Of the three "maps," those in Figure 5 (Power Distance × Uncertainty Avoidance) and Figure 7 (Masculinity × Uncertainty Avoidance) show a scattering of countries in all corners—that is, all combinations of index values occur. Figure 6 (Power Distance × Individualism), however, shows one empty corner: The combination of Small Power Distance and Collectivism does not occur. In fact, there is a tendency for Large Power Distance to be associated with Collectivism and for Small Power Distance with Individualism. However, there is a third factor that should be taken into account here: national wealth. Both Small Power Distance and Individualism go together with greater national weatlh (per capita gross national product). The relationship between Individualism and Wealth is quite strong, as Figure 6 shows. In the upper part (Collectivist) we find only the poorer countries, with Japan as a borderline exception. In the lower part (Individualism), we find only the wealthier countries. If we look at the poorer and wealthier countries separately, there is no longer any relationship between Power Distance and Individualism.

The 40 Countries: Abbreviations Used in Figures 5, 6, and 7

ARG	Argentina	FRA	France	JAP	Japan	SIN	Singapore
AUL	Australia	GBR	Great Britain	MEX	Mexico	SPA	Spain
AUT	Austria	GER	Germany (West)	NET	Netherlands	SWE	Sweden
BEL	Belgium	GRE	Greece	NOR	Norway	SWI	Switzerland
BRA	Brazil	HOK	Hong Kong	NZL	New Zealand	TAI	Taiwan
CAN	Canada	IND	India	PAK	Pakistan	THA	Thailand
CHL	Chile	IRA	Iran	PER	Peru	TUR	Turkey
COL	Colombia	IRE	Ireland	PHI	Philippines	USA	United States
DEN	Denmark	ISR	Israel	POR	Portugal	VEN	Venezuela
FIN	Finland	ITA	Italy	SAF	South Africa	YUG	Yugoslavia

FIGURE 5   The Position of the 40 Countries on the Power Distance and Uncertainty Avoidance Scales

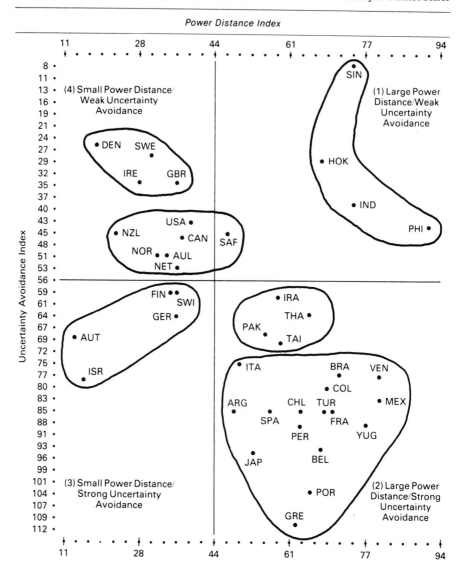

FIGURE 6 The Position of the 40 Countries on the Power Distance and Individualism Scales

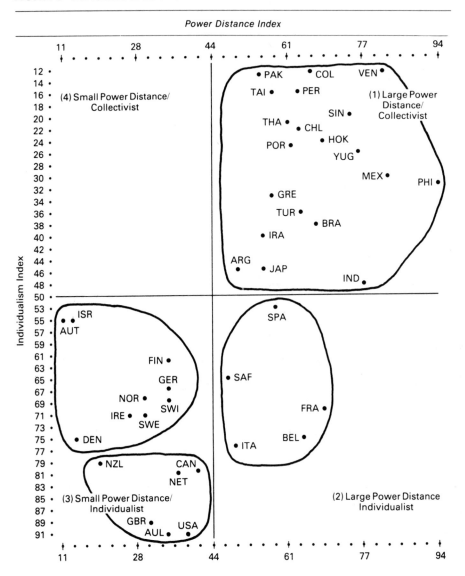

FIGURE 7 The Position of the 40 Countries on the Uncertainty Avoidance and Masculinity Scales

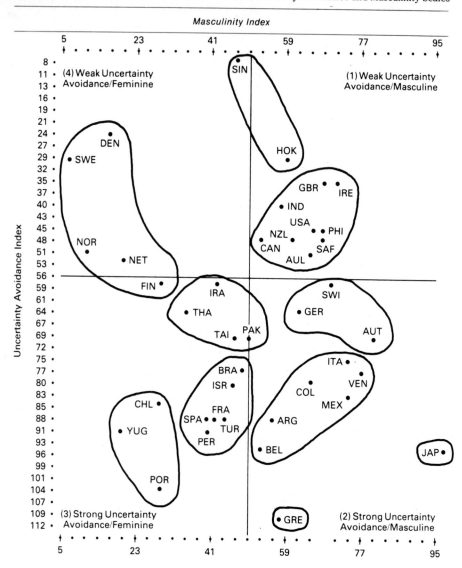

THE CULTURAL RELATIVITY
OF MANAGEMENT THEORIES

Of particular interest in the context of this discussion is the relative position of the United States on the four dimensions. Here is how the United States rates:

- On *Power Distance* at rank 15 out of the 40 countries (measured from below), it is below average but it is not as low as a number of other wealthy countries.
- On *Uncertainty Avoidance* at rank 9 out of 40, it is well below average.

- On *Individualism* at rank 40 out of 40, the United States is the single most individualist country of the entire set (followed closely by Australia and Great Britain).
- On *Masculinity* at rank 28 out of 40, it is well above average.

For about 60 years, the United States has been the world's largest producer and explorer of management theories covering such key areas as motivation, leadership, and organization. Before that, the centers of theorizing about what we now call "management" lay in the Old World. We can trace the history of management thought as far back as we want—at least to parts of the Old Testament of the Bible, and to ancient Greece (Plato's *The Laws* and *The Republic,* 350 B.C.). Sixteenth-century European "management" theorists include Niccolo Machiavelli (Italy) and Thomas More (Great Britain); early twentieth-century theorists include Max Weber (Germany) and Henri Fayol (France).

Today we are all culturally conditioned. We see the world in the way we have learned to see it. Only to a limited extent can we, in our thinking, step out of the boundaries imposed by our cultural conditioning. This applies to the author of a theory as much as it does to the ordinary citizen: Theories reflect the cultural environment in which they were written. If this is true, Italian, British, German, and French theories reflect the culture of Italy, Britain, Germany, and France of their day, and American theories reflect the culture of the United States of its day. Since most present-day theorists are middle-class intellectuals, their theories reflect a national intellectual middle-class culture background.

Now we ask the question: To what extent do theories developed in one country and reflecting the cultural boundaries of that country apply to other countries? Do American management theories apply in Japan? In India? No management theorist, to my knowledge, has ever explicitly addressed himself or herself to this issue. Most probably assume that their theories are universally valid. The availability of a conceptual framework built on four dimensions of national culture, in conjunction with the cultural maps of the world, makes it possible to see more clearly where and to what extent theories developed in one country are likely to apply elsewhere. In the remaining sections of this article I shall look from this viewpoint at most popular American theories of management in the areas of motivation, leadership, and organization.

MOTIVATION

Why do people behave as they do? There is a great variety of theories of human motivation. According to Sigmund Freud, we are impelled to act by unconscious forces within us, which he called our id. Our conscious conception of ourselves—our ego—tries to control these forces, and an equally unconscious internal pilot—our superego—criticizes the thoughts and acts of our ego and causes feelings of guilt and anxiety when the ego seems to be giving in to the id. The superego is the product of early socialization, mainly learned from our parents when we were young children.

Freud's work has been extremely influential in psychology, but he is rarely quoted in the context of management theories. The latter almost exclusively refer to motivation theories developed later in the United States, particularly those of David McClelland, Abraham Maslow, Frederick Herzberg, and Victor Vroom. According to McClelland, we perform because we have a need to achieve (the achievement motive). More recently, McClelland has also paid a lot of attention to the power motive. Maslow has postulated a hierarchy of human needs, from more "basic" to "higher": most basic are physiological needs, followed by security, social needs, esteem needs, and, finally, a need for "self-actualization." The latter incorporates McClelland's theory of achievement, but is defined in broader terms. Maslow's theory of the hierarchy of needs postulates that a higher need will become active only if the lower needs are sufficiently satisfied. Our acting is basically a rational activity by which we expect to fulfill successive levels of needs. Herzberg's two-factor theory of motivation distinguishes between hygienic factors (largely corresponding to Maslow's lower needs—physiological, security, social) and motivators (Maslow's higher needs—esteem, self-actualization); the hygienic factors have only the potential to motivate negatively (demotivate—they are necessary but not sufficient conditions), while only the motivators have the potential to motivate positively. Vroom has formalized the role of "expectancy" in motivation; he opposes "expectancy" theories and "drive" theories. The former see people as being *pulled* by the expectancy of some kind of result from their acts, mostly consciously. The latter (in accordance with Freud's theories) see people as *pushed* by inside forces—often unconscious ones.

Let us now look at these theories through culture-conscious glasses. Why has Freudian thinking never become popular in U.S. management theory, as has the thinking of McClelland, Maslow, Herzberg, and Vroom? To what extent do these theories reflect different cultural patterns? Freud was part of an Austrian middle-class culture at the turn of the century. If we compare present-day Austria and the United States on our cultural maps, we find the following:

- Austria scores considerably lower on Power Distance.
- Austria scores considerably higher on Uncertainty Avoidance.
- Austria scores considerably lower on Individualism.
- Austria scores considerably higher on Masculinity.

We do not know to what extent Austrian culture has changed since Freud's time, but evidence suggests that cultural patterns change very slowly. It is, therefore, not likely to have been much different from today's culture. The most striking thing about present-day Austrian culture is that it combines a fairly high Uncertainty Avoidance with a very low Power Distance (see Figure 5). Somehow the combination of high Uncertainty Avoidance with high Power Distance is more comfortable (we find this in Japan and in all Latin and Mediterranean countries— see Figure 5). Having a powerful superior whom we can both praise and blame is one way of satisfying a strong need for avoiding uncertainty. The Austrian culture, however (together with the German, Swiss, Israeli, and Finnish cultures), cannot rely on an external boss to absorb its uncertainty. Thus Freud's superego acts naturally as an inner uncertainty-absorbing device, an internalized boss. For strong

Uncertainty Avoidance countries like Austria, working hard is caused by an inner urge—it is a way of relieving stress. (See Figure 2.) The Austrian superego is reinforced by the country's relatively low level of Individualism (see Figure 6). The inner feeling of obligation to society plays a much stronger role in Austria than in the United States. The ultrahigh Individualism of the United States leads to a need to explain every act in terms of self-interest, and expectancy theories of motivation do provide this explanation—we always do something *because* we expect to obtain the satisfaction of some need.

The comparison between Austrian and U.S. culture has so far justified the popularity of expectancy theories of motivation in the United States. The combination in the United States of weak Uncertainty Avoidance and relatively high Masculinity can tell us more about why the achievement motive has become so popular in that country. David McClelland, in his book *The Achieving Society*, sets up scores reflecting how strong achievement need is in many countries by analyzing the content of children's stories used in those countries to teach the young to read. It now appears that there is a strong relationship between McClelland's need for achievement country scores and the combination of weak Uncertainty Avoidance and strong Masculinity charted in Figure 7. (McClelland's data were collected for two historic years—1925 and 1950—but only his 1925 data relate to the cultural map in Figure 7. It is likely that the 1925 stories were more traditional, reflecting deep underlying cultural currents; the choice of stories in 1950 in most countries may have been affected by modernization currents in education, often imported from abroad.)

Countries in the upper righthand corner of Figure 7 received mostly high scores on achievement need in McClelland's book; countries in the lower lefthand corner of Figure 7 received low scores. This leads us to the conclusion that the concept of the achievement motive presupposes two cultural choices—a willingness to accept risk (equivalent to weak Uncertainty Avoidance; see Figure 2) and a concern with performance (equivalent to strong Masculinity; see Figure 4). This combination is found exclusively in countries in the Anglo-American group and in some of their former colonies (Figure 7). One striking thing about the concept of achievement is that the word itself is hardly translatable into any language other than English; for this reason, the word could not be used in the questionnaire of the multinational corporation used in my research. The English-speaking countries all appear in the upper righthand corner of Figure 7.

If this is so, there is reason to reconsider Maslow's hierarchy of human needs in the light of the map shown in Figure 7. Quadrant 1 (upper righthand corner) in Figure 7 stands for *achievement motivation,* as we have seen (performance plus risk). Quadrant 2 distinguishes itself from quadrant 1 by strong Uncertainty Avoidance, which means *security motivation* (performance plus security). The countries on the feminine side of Figure 7 distinguish themselves by a focusing on quality of life rather than on performance and on relationships between people rather than on money and things (see Figure 4). This means *social motivation:* quality of life plus security in quadrant 3, and quality of life plus risk in quadrant 4. Now, Maslow's hierarchy puts self-actualization (achievement) plus esteem above social needs above security needs. This, however, is not the description of a universal human motivation process—it is the description of a value system, the value system of the U.S. middle class to which the author belonged. I suggest that if we want to continue thinking in terms of a hierarchy for countries in the lower righthand corner of Figure 7 (quadrant 2), security needs should rank at the top; for countries in the upper lefthand corner (quadrant 4), social needs should rank at the top, and for countries in the lower lefthand corner (quadrant 3) *both* security and social needs should rank at the top.

One practical outcome of presenting motivation theories is the movement toward humanization of work—an attempt to make work more intrinsically interesting to the workers. There are two main currents in humanization of work— one, developed in the United States and called *job enrichment,* aims at restructuring individual jobs. A chief proponent of job enrichment is Frederick Herzberg. The other current, developed in Europe and applied mainly in Sweden and Norway, aims at restructuring work into group work—forming, for example, such semi-autonomous teams as those seen in the experiments at Volvo. Why the difference in approaches? What is seen as a "human" job depends on a society's prevailing model of humankind. In a more masculine society like the United States, humanization takes the form of masculinization, allowing individual performance. In the more feminine societies of Sweden and Norway, humanization takes the form of feminization—it is a means toward more wholesome interpersonal relationships in its deemphasis of interindividual competition.

LEADERSHIP

One of the oldest theorists of leadership in world literature is Machiavelli (1468–1527). He described certain effective techniques for manipulation and remaining in power (including deceit, bribery, and murder) that gave him a bad reputation in later centuries. Machiavelli wrote in the context of the Italy of his day, and what he described is clearly a large Power Distance situation. We still find Italy on the larger Power Distance side of Figure 5 (with all other Latin and Mediterranean countries), and we can assume from historical evidence that Power Distances in Italy during the sixteenth century were considerably larger than they are now. When we compare Machiavelli's work with that of his contemporary, Sir Thomas More (1478–1535), we find cultural differences between ways of thinking in different countries even in the sixteenth century. The British More described in *Utopia* a state based on consensus as a "model" to criticize the political situation of his day. But practice did not always follow theory, of course: More, deemed too critical, was beheaded by order of King Henry VIII, while Machiavelli the realist managed to die peacefully in his bed. The difference in theories is nonetheless remarkable.

In the United States a current of leadership theories has developed. Some of the best known were put forth by the late Douglas McGregor (Theory X versus Theory Y), Rensis Likert (System 4 management), and Robert R. Blake with Jane S. Mouton (the Management Grid®). What these theories have in common is that they all advocate participation in the manager's decisions by his/her subordinates (participative management); however, the initiative toward participation is supposed to be taken by the manager. In a worldwide perspective (Figure 5), we can understand these theories from the middle position of the United States on the Power Distance side (rank 15 out of 40 countries). Had the culture been one of larger Power Distance, we could have expected more "Machiavellian" theories of leadership. In fact, in the management literature of another country with a larger Power Distance index score, France, there is little concern with participative management American style, but great concern with who has the power. However, in countries with smaller Power Distances than the United States (Sweden, Norway, Germany, Israel), there is considerable sympathy for models of management in which even the initiatives are taken by the subordinates (forms of industrial democracy) and with which there's little sympathy in the United States. In the approaches toward "industrial democracy" taken in these countries, we notice their differences on the second dimension, Uncertainty Avoidance. In weak Uncertainty Avoidance countries like Sweden, industrial democracy was started in the form of local experiments and only later was given a legislative framework. In strong Uncertainty Avoidance countries like Germany, industrial democracy was brought about by legislation first and then had to be brought alive in the organizations ("Mitbestimmung").

The crucial fact about leadership in any culture is that it is a complement to subordinateship. The Power Distance Index scores in Figure 5 are, in fact, based on the values of people as *subordinates,* not on the values of superiors. Whatever a naive literature on leadership may give us to understand, leaders cannot choose their styles at will; what is feasible depends to a large extent on the cultural conditioning of a leader's subordinates. Along these lines, Figure 8 describes the type of subordinateship that, other things being equal, a leader can expect to meet in societies at three different levels of Power Distance—subordinateship to which a leader must respond. The middle level represents what is most likely found in the United States.

Neither McGregor, nor Likert, nor Blake and Mouton allow for this type of cultural proviso—all three tend to be prescriptive with regard to a leadership style that, at best, will work with U.S. subordinates and with those in cultures—such as Canada or Australia—that have not too different Power Distance levels (Figure 5). In fact, my research shows that subordinates in larger Power Distance countries tend to agree more frequently with Theory Y.

A U.S. theory of leadership that allows for a certain amount of cultural relativity, although indirectly, is Fred Fiedler's contingency theory of leadership. Fiedler states that different leader personalities are needed for "difficult" and "easy" situations, and that a cultural gap between superior and subordinates is one of the factors that makes a situation "difficult." However, this theory does not address the kind of cultural gap in question.

In practice, the adaptation of managers to higher Power Distance environments does not seem to present too many problems. Although this is an unpopular message—one seldom professed in management development courses—managers moving to a larger Power Distance culture soon learn that they have to behave more autocratically in order to be effective, and tend to do so; this is borne out

FIGURE 8 Subordinateship for Three Levels of Power Distance

Small Power Distance	Medium Power Distance (United States)	Large Power Distance
Subordinates have weak dependence needs.	Subordinates have medium dependence needs.	Subordinates have strong dependence needs.
Superiors have weak dependence needs toward their superiors.	Superiors have medium dependence needs toward their superiors.	Superiors have strong dependence needs toward their superiors.
Subordinates expect superiors to consult them and may rebel or strike if superiors are not seen as staying within their legitimate role.	Subordinates expect superiors to consult them but will accept autocratic behavior as well.	Subordinates expect superiors to act autocratically.
Ideal superior to most is a loyal democrat.	Ideal superior to most is a resourceful democrat.	Ideal superior to most is a benevolent autocrat or paternalist.
Laws and rules apply to all and privileges for superiors are not considered acceptable.	Laws and rules apply to all, but a certain level of privileges for superiors is considered normal.	Everybody expects superiors to enjoy privileges; laws and rules differ for superiors and subordinates.
Status symbols are frowned upon and will easily come under attack from subordinates.	Status symbols for superiors contribute moderately to their authority and will be accepted by subordinates.	Status symbols are very important and contribute strongly to the superior's authority with the subordinates.

by the colonial history of most Western countries. But it is interesting that the Western ex-colonial power with the highest Power Distance norm—France—seems to be most appreciated by its former colonies and seems to maintain the best postcolonial relationships with most of them. This suggests that subordinates in a large Power Distance culture feel even more comfortable with superiors who are real autocrats than with those whose assumed autocratic stance is out of national character.

The operation of a manager in an environment with a Power Distance norm lower than his or her own is more problematic. U.S. managers tend to find it difficult to collaborate wholeheartedly in the "industrial democracy" processes of such countries as Sweden, Germany, and even the Netherlands. U.S. citizens tend to consider their country as the example of democracy, and find it difficult to accept that other countries might wish to develop forms of democracy for which they feel no need and that make major inroads upon managers' (or leaders') preogatives. However, the very idea of management preogatives is not accepted in very low Power Distance countries. This is, perhaps, best illustrated by a remark a Scandinavian social scientist is supposed to have made to Herzberg in a seminar: "You are against participation for the very reason we are in favor of it—one doesn't know where it will stop. We think that is good."

One way in which the U.S. approach to leadership has been packaged and formalized is management by objectives (MBO), first advocated by Peter Drucker in 1955 in *The Practice of Management.* In the United States, MBO has been used to spread a pragmatic results orientation throughout the organization. It has been considerably more successful where results are objectively measurable than where they can only be interpreted subjectively, and, even in the United States, it has been criticized heavily. Still, it has been perhaps the single most popular management technique "made in U.S.A." Therefore, it can be accepted as fitting U.S. culture. MBO presupposes:

- That subordinates are sufficiently independent to negotiate meaningfully with the boss (not-too-large Power Distance).
- That both are willing to take risks (weak Uncertainty Avoidance).
- That performance is seen as important by both (high Masculinity).

Let us now take the case of Germany, a below-average Power Distance country. Here, the dialogue element in MBO should present no problem. However, since Germany scores considerably higher on Uncertainty Avoidance, the tendency toward accepting risk and ambiguity will not exist to the same extent. The idea of replacing the arbitrary authority of the boss with the impersonal authority of mutually agreed upon objectives, however, fits the small Power Distance/strong Uncertainty Avoidance cultural cluster very well. The objectives become the subordinates' "superego." In a book of case studies about MBO in Germany, Ian R. G. Ferguson states that "MBO has acquired a different flavor in the German-speaking area, not least because in these countries the societal and political pressure toward increasing the value of man in the organization on the right to co-determination has become quite clear. Thence, MBO has been transliterated into Management by Joint Goal Setting (Führung durch Zielvereinbarung)." Ferguson's view of MBO fits the ideological needs of the German-speaking countries of the moment. The case studies in his book show elaborate formal systems with extensive ideological justification; the stress on *team* objectives is quite strong, which is in line with the lower individualism in these countries.

The other area in which specific information on MBO is available is France. MBO was first introduced in France in the early 1960s, but it became extremely popular for a time after the 1968 student revolt. People expected that this new technique would lead to the long-overdue democratization of organizations. Instead of DPO (Direction par Objectifs), the French name for MBO became DPPO (Direction *Participative* par Objectifs). So in France, too, societal developments affected the MBO system. However, DPPO remained, in general, as much a vain slogan as did Liberté, Egalité, Fraternité (Freedom, Equality, Brotherhood) after the 1789 revolt. G. Frank wrote in 1973, "I think that the career of DPPO is terminated, or rather that it has never started, and it won't ever start as long as we continue in France our tendency to confound ideology and reality. . . ." In a postcript to Frank's article, the editors of *Le Management* write: "French blue- and white-collar workers, lower-level and higher-level managers, and 'patrons' all belong to the same cultural system which maintain dependency relations from level to level. Only the deviants really dislike this system. The hierarchical structure protects against anxiety; DPO, however generates anxiety. . . ." The reason for the anxiety in the French cultural context is that MBO presupposes a depersonalized authority in the form of internalized objectives; but French people, from their early childhood onward, are accustomed to large Power Distances, to an authority that is highly personalized. And in spite of all attempts to introduce Anglo-Saxon management methods, French superiors do not easily decentralize and do not stop short-circuiting intermediate hierarchical levels, nor do French subordinates expect them to. The developments of the 1970s have severely discredited DPPO, which probably does injustice to the cases in which individual French organizations or units, starting from less exaggerated expectations, have benefited from it.

In the examples used thus far in this section, the cultural context of leadership may look rather obvious to the reader. But it also works in more subtle, less obvious ways. Here's an example from the area of management decision making: A prestigious U.S. consulting firm was asked to analyze the decision making process in a large Scandinavian "XYZ" corporation. Their report criticized the corporation's decision-making style, which they characterized as being, among other things, "intuitive" and "consensus based." They compared "observations of traditional XYZ practices" with "selected examples of practices in other companies." These "selected examples," offered as a model, were evidently taken from their U.S. clients and reflect the U.S. textbook norm—"fact based" rather than intuitive management, and "fast decisions based on clear responsibilities" rather than the use of informal, personal contacts, and the concern for consensus.

Is this consulting firm doing its Scandinavian clients a service? It follows from Figure 7 that where the United States and the Scandinavian culture are wide apart is on the Masculinity dimension. The use of intuition and the concern for consensus in Scandinavia are "feminine" characteristics of the culture, well embedded in the total texture of these societies. Stressing "facts" and "clear responsibilities" fits the "masculine" U.S. culture. From a neutral viewpoint, the reasons for criticizing the U.S. decision-making style are as good as those for criticizing the Scandinavian style. In complex decision-making situations, "facts" no longer exist independently from the people who define them, so "fact-based management" becomes a misleading slogan. Intuition may not be a bad method of deciding in such cases at all. And if the implementation of decisions requires the commitment of many people, even a consensus process that takes more time is an asset rather than a liability. But the essential element overlooked by the consultant is that decisions have to be made in a way that corresponds to the values of the environment in which they have to be effective. People in this consulting firm lacked insight into their own cultural biases. This does not mean that the Scandinavian corporation's management need not improve its decision making and could not learn from the consultant's experience. But this can be done only through a mutual recognition of cultural differences, not by ignoring them.

ORGANIZATION

The Power Distance × Uncertainty Avoidance map (Figure 5) is of vital importance for structuring organizations that will work best in different countries. For example, one U.S.-based multinational corporation has a worldwide policy that salary-increase proposals should be initiated by the employee's direct superior. However, the French management of its French subsidiary interpreted this policy in such a way that the superior's superior's superior—three levels above—was the one to initiate salary proposals. This way of working was regarded as quite natural by both superiors and subordinates in France. Other factors being equal, people in large Power Distance cultures prefer that decisions be centralized because even superiors have strong dependency needs in relation to their superiors; this tends to move decisions up as far as they can go (see Figure 8). People in small Power Distance cultures want decisions to be decentralized.

While Power Distance relates to centralization, Uncertainty Avoidance relates to formalization—the need for formal rules and specialization, the assignment of tasks to experts. My former colleague O. J. Stevens at INSEAD has done an interesting research project (as yet unpublished) with M.B.A. students from Germany, Great Britain, and France. He asked them to write their own diagnosis and solution for a small case study of an organizational problem—a conflict in one company between the sales and product development departments. The majority of the French referred the problem to the next higher authority (the president of the company); the Germans attributed it to the lack of a written policy, and proposed establishing one; the British attributed it to a lack of interpersonal communication, to be cured by some kind of group training.

Stevens concludes that the "implicit model" of the organization for most French was a pyramid (both centralized and formal); for most Germans, a well-oiled machine (formalized but not centralized); and for most British, a village market (neither formalized nor centralized). This covers three quadrants (2, 3, and 4) in Figure 5. What is missing is an "implicit model" for quadrant 1, which contains four Asian countries, including India. A discussion with an Indian colleague leads me to place the family (centralized, but not formalized) in this quadrant as the "implicit model" of the organization. In fact, Indian organizations tend to be formalized as far as relationships between people go (this is related to Power Distance), but not as far as workflow goes (this is Uncertainty Avoidance).

The "well-oiled machine" model for Germany reminds us of the fact that Max Weber, author of the first theory of bureaucracy, was a German. Weber pictures bureaucracy as a highly formalized system (strong Uncertainty Avoidance), in which, however, the rules protect the lower-ranking members against abuse of power by their superiors. The superiors have no power by themselves, only the power that their bureaucratic roles have given them as incumbents of the roles—the power is in the role, not in the person (small Power Distance).

The United States is found fairly close to the center of the map in Figure 5, taking an intermediate position between the "pyramid," "machine," and "market" implicit models—a position that may help explain the success of U.S. business operations in very different cultures. However, according to the common U.S. conception of organization, we might say that *hierarchy is not a goal by itself* (as it is in France) and that *rules are not a goal by themselves*. Both are means toward obtaining results, to be changed if needed. A breaking away from hierarchic and bureaucratic traditions is found in the development toward matrix organizations and similar temporary or flexible organization systems.

Another INSEAD colleague, André Laurent, has shown that French managers strongly disbelieve in the feasibility of matrix organizations, because they see them as violating the "holy" principle of unit of command. However, in the French subsidiary of a multinational corporation that has a long history of successful matrix management, the French managers were quite positive toward it; obviously, then, cultural barriers to organizational innovation can be overcome. German managers are not too favorably disposed toward matrix organizations either, feeling that they tend to frustrate their need for organizational clarity. This means that matrix organizations will be accepted *if* the roles of individuals within the organization can be defined without ambiguity.

The extreme position of the United States on the Individualism scale leads to other potential conflicts between the U.S. way of thinking about organizations and the values dominant in other parts of the world. In the U.S. Individualist conception, the relationship between the individual and the organization is essentially calculative, being based on enlightened self-interest. In fact, there is a strong historical and cultural link between Individualism and Capitalism. The capitalist system—based on self-interest and the market mechanism—was "invented" in Great Britain, which is still among the top three most Individualist countries in the world. In more Collectivist societies, however, the link between individuals and their traditional organizations is not calculative, but moral: It is based not on self-interest, but on the individual's loyalty toward the clan, organization, or society—which is supposedly the best guarantee of that individual's ultimate interest. "Collectivism" is a bad word in the United States, but "individualism" is as much a bad word in the writings of Mao Tse-tung, who writes from a strongly Collectivist cultural tradition (see Figure 6 for the Collectivist scores of the Chinese majority countries Taiwan, Hong Kong, and Singapore). This means that U.S. organizations may get themselves into considerable trouble in more Collectivist environments if they do not recognize their local employees' needs for ties of mutual loyalty between company and employee. "Hire and fire" is very ill perceived in these countries, if firing isn't prohibited by law altogether. Given the value position of people in more Collectivist cultures, it should not be seen as surprising if they prefer other types of economic order to capitalism—if capitalism cannot get rid of its Individualist image.

CONSEQUENCES FOR POLICY

So far we have seriously questioned the universal validity of management theories developed in one country—in most instances here, the United States.

On a practical level, this has the least consequence for organizations operating entirely within the country in which the theories were born. As long as the theories apply within the United States, U.S. organizations can base their policies for motivating employees, leadership, and organization development on these policies. Still, some caution is due. If differences in environmental culture can be shown to exist between countries, and if these constrain the validity of management theories, what about the subcultures within the country? To what extent do the familiar theories apply when the organization employs people for whom the theories were not, in the first instance, conceived—such as members of minority groups with a different educational level, or belonging to a different generation? If culture matters, an organization's policies can lose their effectiveness when its cultural environment changes.

No doubt, however, the consequences of the cultural relativity of management theories are more serious for the multinational organization. The cultural maps in Figures 5, 6, and 7 can help predict the kind of culture difference between subsidiaries and mother company that will need to be met. An important implication is that identical personnel policies may have very different effects in different countries—and within countries for different subgroups of employees. This is not only a matter of different employee values; there are also, of course, differences in government policies and legislation (which usually reflect quite clearly the country's different cultural position). And there are differences in labor market situations and labor union power positions. These differences—tangible as well as intangible—may have consequences for performance, attention to quality, cost, labor turnover, and absenteeism. Typical universal policies that may work out quite differently in different countries are those dealing with financial incentives, promotion paths, and grievance channels.

The dilemma for the organization operating abroad is whether to adapt to the local culture or try to change it. There are examples of companies that have successfully changed local habits, such as in the earlier mention of the introduction of matrix organization in France. Many Third World countries want to transfer new technologies from more economically advanced countries. If they are to work at all, these technologies must presuppose values that may run counter to local traditions, such as a certain discretion of subordinates toward superiors (lower Power Distance) or of individuals toward ingroups (more Individualism). In such a case, the local culture has to be changed; this is a difficult task that should not be taken lightly. Since it calls for a conscious strategy based on insight into the local culture, it's logical to involve acculturated locals in strategy formulations. Often, the original policy will have to be adapted to fit local culture and lead to the desired effect. We saw earlier how, in the case of MBO, this has succeeded in Germany, but generally failed in France.

A final area in which the cultural boundaries of home-country management theories are important is the training of managers for assignments abroad. For managers who have to operate in an unfamiliar culture, training based on home-country theories is of very limited use and may even do more harm than good. Of more importance is a thorough familiarization with the other culture, for which the organization can use the services of specialized crosscultural training institutes—or it can develop its own program by using host-country personnel as teachers.

ACKNOWLEDGMENTS

This article is based on research carried out in the period 1973–78 at the European Institute for Advanced Studies in Management, Brussels. The article itself was sponsored by executive search consultants Berndtson International S.A., Brussels. The author acknowledges the helpful comments of Mark Cantley, André Laurent, Ernest C. Miller, and Jennifer Robinson on an earlier version of it.

SELECTED BIBLIOGRAPHY

The first U.S. book about the cultural relativity of U.S. management theories is still to be written, I believe—which lack in itself indicates how difficult it is to recognize one's own cultural biases. One of the few U.S. books describing the process of cultural conditioning for a management readership is Edward T. Hall's *The Silent Language* (Fawcett, 1959, but reprinted since). Good reading also is Hall's article "The Silent Language in Overseas Business (*Harvard Business Review,* May–June 1960). Hall is an anthropologist and therefore a specialist in the study of culture. Very readable on the same subject are two books by the British anthropoligist Mary Douglas, *Natural Symbols: Exploration in Cosmology* (Vintage, 1973) and the reader *Rules and Meanings: The Anthropology of Everyday Knowledge* (Penguin, 1973). Another excellent reader is Theodore D. Weinshall's *Culture and Management* (Penguin, 1977).

On the concept of national character, some well-written professional literature is Margaret Mead's "National Character," in the reader by Sol Tax, *Anthropology Today* (University of Chicago Press, 1962), and Alex Inkeles and D. J. Levinson's, "National Character," in Lindzey and Aronson's *Handbook of Social Psychology,* second edition, volume 4 (Addison-Wesley, 1969). Critique on the implicit claims of universal validity of management theories comes from some foreign authors: An important article is Michel Brossard and Marc Maurice's "Is There a Universal Model of Organization Structure?" (*International Studies of Management and Organization,* Fall 1976). This journal is a journal of translations from non-American literature, based in New York, that often contains important articles on management issues by non-U.S. authors that take issue with the dominant theories. Another article is Gunnar Hjelholt's "Europe Is Different," in Geert Hofstede and M. Sami Kassem's reader, *European Contributions to Organization Theory* (Assen, Netherlands: Von Gorcum, 1976).

Some other references of interest: Ian R. G. Ferguson's *Management by Objectives in Deutschland* (Herder und Herder, 1973) (in German); G. Franck's "Epitaphe pour la DPO," in *Le Management,* November 1973 (in French); and D. Jenkin's *Blue- and White-Collar Democracy* (Doubleday, 1973).

Note: Details of Geert Hofstede's study of national cultures have been published in his book, *Culture's Consequences: International Differences in Work-Related Values* (Beverly Hills: Sage Publications, 1980).

12

Leadership and Organizational Culture

COMING TO A NEW AWARENESS OF ORGANIZATIONAL CULTURE
Edgar H. Schein

EVOLUTION AND REVOLUTION
Larry E. Greiner

THE 4 COMPETENCIES OF LEADERSHIP
Warren Bennis

COMING TO A NEW AWARENESS OF ORGANIZATIONAL CULTURE

Edgar H. Schein

PREVIEW

A. Organizational culture can be defined in terms of a dynamic model of how culture is learned, passed on, and changed.

1. Culture is the pattern of basic assumptions that a given group has invented, discovered, or developed in learning to cope with its problems of external adaptation and internal integration.
2. The pattern of basic assumptions is the cultural paradigm on which the perceptions, thoughts, and feelings of organizational members are based.
3. Culture exists in groups—sets of people who have shared significant problems, solved them, observed the effects of their solutions, and who have taken in new members.
4. Basic assumptions inherent in a culture serve to stabilize the group and are highly resistant to change.
5. Culture cannot serve its stabilizing function unless it is taught to new members.

Source: Reprinted from "Coming to a New Awareness of Organizational Culture" by E. H. Schein, *Sloan Management Review,* Winter 1981, pp. 3–16, by permission of the author and the publisher. Copyright © 1981 by the Sloan Management Review Association. All rights reserved.

B. Four approaches can be used in various combinations to decipher a culture's paradigm of assumptions.
   1. Interviews can analyze the process and content of socialization of new members.
   2. Interviewers can analyze responses to critical incidents in the organization's history.
   3. Beliefs, values, and assumptions of culture creators or carriers can be analyzed.
   4. Interviewers and organization members can jointly explore and analyze anomalies, or puzzling features, uncovered in interviews.
C. Cultures may serve different purposes at different stages in the development of an organization.
   1. Culture serves as a source of identity and strength for young and growing companies. Little chance exists for successfully changing culture at this stage.
   2. In organizational mid-life culture may be changed, but not without consideration of all sources of stability. Managers must decide whether to encourage diversity of subcultures to promote flexibility, or attempt to create a more homogeneous, stronger corporate culture.
   3. Maturity or decline resulting from excessive internal stability which prevents innovation may be combatted by changes in culture. This is a painful process, however, and one likely to elicit strong resistance.
   4. Attempts at culture management strategies must begin by considering the organizational life cycle.

The purpose of this article is to define the concept of organizational culture in terms of a dynamic model of how culture is learned, passed on, and changed. As many recent efforts argue that organizational culture is the key to organizational excellence, it is critical to define this complex concept in a manner that will provide a common frame of reference for practitioners and researchers. Many definitions simply settle for the notion that culture is a set of shared meanings that make it possible for members of a group to interpret and act upon their environment. I believe we must go beyond this definition: even if we knew an organization well enough to live in it, we would not necessarily know how its culture arose, how it came to be what it is, or how it could be changed if organizational survival were at stake.

The thrust of my argument is that we must understand the dynamic evolutionary forces that govern how culture evolves and changes. My approach to this task will be to lay out a formal definition of what I believe organizational culture is, and to elaborate each element of the definition to make it clear how it works.

ORGANIZATIONAL CULTURE: A FORMAL DEFINITION

Organizational culture is the *pattern of basic assumptions* that a *given group* has *invented, discovered, or developed in learning to cope* with its *problems of external adaptation and internal integration,* and that have *worked well enough to be considered valid,* and, therefore, to be *taught to new members* as the correct way to *perceive, think, and feel* in relation to those problems.

1. Pattern of Basic Assumptions

Organizational culture can be analyzed at several different levels, starting with the *visible artifacts*—the constructed environment of the organization, its architecture, technology, office layout, manner of dress, visible or audible behavior patterns, and public documents such as charters, employee orientation materials, stories (see Figure 1). This level of analysis is tricky because the data are easy to obtain but hard to interpret. We can describe "how" a group constructs its environment and "what" behavior patterns are discernible among the members, but we often cannot understand the underlying logic—"why" a group behaves the way it does.

To analyze *why* members behave the way they do, we often look for the *values* that govern behavior, which is the second level in Figure 1. But as values are hard to observe directly, it is often necessary to infer them by interviewing key members of the organization or to content analyze artifacts such as documents and charters.[1] However, in identifying such values, we usually note that they represent accurately only the manifest or *espoused* values of a culture. That is, they focus on what people *say* is the reason for their behavior, what they ideally would like those reasons to be, and what are often their rationalizations for their behavior. Yet, the underlying reasons for their behavior remain concealed or unconscious.[2]

To really *understand* a culture and to ascertain more completely the group's

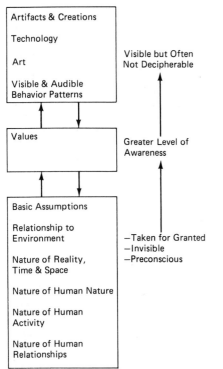

FIGURE 1 The Levels of Culture and Their Interaction

values and overt behavior, it is imperative to delve into the *underlying assumptions,* which are typically unconscious but which actually determine how group members perceive, think, and feel.[3] Such assumptions are themselves learned responses that originated as espoused values. But, as a value leads to a behavior, and as that behavior begins to solve the problem which prompted it in the first place, the value gradually is transformed into an underlying assumption about how things really are. As the assumption is increasingly taken for granted, it drops out of awareness.

Taken-for-granted assumptions are so powerful because they are less debatable and confrontable than espoused values. We know we are dealing with an assumption when we encounter in our informants a refusal to discuss something, or when they consider us "insane" or "ignorant" for bringing something up. For example, the notion that businesses should be profitable, that schools should educate, or that medicine should prolong life are assumptions, even though they are often considered "merely" values.

To put it another way, the domain of values can be divided into (1) ultimate, nondebatable, taken for granted values, for which the term "assumptions" is more appropriate; and (2) debatable, overt, espoused values, for which the term "values" is more applicable. In stating that basic assumptions are unconscious, I am not arguing that this is a result of repression. On the contrary, I am arguing that as certain motivational and cognitive processes are repeated and continue to work, they become unconscious. They can be brought back to awareness only through a kind of focused inquiry, similar to that used by anthropologists. What is needed are the efforts of both an insider who makes the unconscious assumptions and an outsider who helps to uncover the assumptions by asking the right kinds of questions.[4]

Cultural Paradigms: A Need for Order and Consistency. Because of the human need for order and consistency, assumptions become patterned into what may be termed cultural "paradigms," which tie together the basic assumptions about humankind, nature, and activities. A cultural paradigm is a set of inter-related assumptions that form a coherent pattern. Not all assumptions are mutually compatible or consistent, however. For example, if a group holds the assumption that all good ideas and products ultimately come from individual effort, it cannot easily assume simultaneously that groups can be held responsible for the results achieved, or that individuals will put a high priority on group loyalty. Or, if a group assumes that the way to survive is to conquer nature and to manipulate its environment aggressively, it cannot at the same time assume that the best kind of relationship among group members is one that emphasizes passivity and harmony. If human beings do indeed have a cognitive need for order and consistency, one can then assume that all groups will eventually evolve sets of assumptions that are compatible and consistent.

To analylze cultural paradigms, one needs a set of logical categories for studying assumptions. Table 1 shows such a set based on the original comparative study of Kluckhohn and Strodtbeck.[5] In applying these categories broadly to cultures, Kluckhohn and Strodtbeck note that Western culture tends to be oriented toward

TABLE 1 Basic Underlying Assumptions Around Which Cultural Paradigms Form

1. The Organization's Relationship to Its Environment. Reflecting even more basic assumptions about the relationship of humanity to nature, one can assess whether the key members of the organization view the relationship as one of dominance, submission, harmonizing, finding an appropriate niche, and so on.

2. The nature of Reality and Trust. Here are the linguistic and behavioral rules that define what is real and what is not, what is "fact," how truth is ultimately to be determined, and whether truth is "revealed" or "discovered"; basic concepts of time as linear or cyclical, monochronic or polychronic; basic concepts such as space as limited or infinite and property as communal or individual; and so forth.

3. The Nature of Human Nature. What does it mean to be "human" and what attributes are considered intrinsic or ultimate? Is human nature good, evil, or neutral? Are human beings perfectible or not? Which is better, Theory X or Theory Y?

4. The Nature of Human Activity. What is the "right" thing for human beings to do, on the basis of the above assumptions about reality, the environment, and human nature: to be active, passive, self-developmental, fatalistic, or what? What is work and what is play?

5. The nature of Human Relationshps. What is considered to be the "right" way for people to relate to each other, to distribute power and love? Is life cooperative or competitive; individualistic, group collaborative, or communal; based on traditional lineal authority, law, or chrisma; or what?

Source: Reprinted, by permission of the publisher, from "The Role of the Founder in Creating Organizational Culture," by Edgar H. Schein, *Organizational Dynamics.* Summer 1983 © 1983 Periodicals Division, American Management Association. All rights reserved.

an active mastery of nature, and is based on individualistic competitive relationships. It uses a future-oriented, linear, monochronic concept of time,[6] views space and resources as infinite, assumes that human nature is neutral and ultimately perfectible, and bases reality or ultimate truth on science and pragmatism.

In contrast, some Eastern cultures are passively oriented toward nature. They seek to harmonize with nature and with each other. They view the group as more important than the individual, are present or past oriented, see time as polychronic and cyclical, view space and resources as very limited, assume that human nature is bad but improvable, and see reality as based more on revealed truth than on empirical experimentation.

In this light, organizational culture paradigms are adapted versions of broader cultural paradigms. For example, Dyer notes that the GEM Corporation operates on the interlocking assumptions that: (1) ideas come ultimately from individuals; (2) people are responsible, motivated, and capable of governing themselves; however, truth can only be pragmatically determined by "fighting" things out and testing in groups; (3) such fighting is possible because the members of the organization view themselves as a family who will take care of each other. Ultimately, this makes it safe to fight and be competitive.[7]

I have observed another organization that operates on the paradigm that (1) truth comes ultimately from older, wiser, better educated, higher status members; (2) people are capable of loyalty and discipline in carrying out directives; (3) relationships are basically lineal and vertical; (4) each person has a niche that is his or her territory that cannot be invaded; and (5) the organization is a "solidary unit" that will take care of its members.

Needless to say, the manifest behaviors in these two organizations are totally different. In the first organization, one observes mostly open office landscapes, few offices with closed doors, a high rate of milling about, intense conversations and arguments, and a general air of informality. In the second organization, there is a hush in the air: everyone is in an office and with closed doors. Nothing is done except by appointment and with a prearranged agenda. When people of different ranks are present, one sees real deference rituals and obedience, and a general air of formality permeates everything.

Nonetheless, these behavioral differences make no sense until one has discovered and deciphered the underlying cultural paradigm. To stay at the level of artifacts or values is to deal with the *manifestations* of culture, but not with the cultural essence.

2. A Given Group

There cannot be a culture unless there is a group that "owns" it. Culture is embedded in groups, hence the creating group must always be clearly identified. If we want to define a cultural unit, therefore, we must be able to locate a group that is independently defined as the creator, host, or owner of that culture. We must be careful not to define the group in terms of the existence of a culture however tempting that may be, because we then would be creating a completely circular definition.

A given group is a set of people (1) who have been together long enough to have shared significant problems, (2) who have had opportunities to solve those problems and to observe the effects of their solutions, and (3) who have taken in new members. A group's culture cannot be determined unless there is such a definable set of people with a shared history.

The passing on of solutions to new members is required in the definition of culture because the decision to pass something on is itself a very important test of whether a given solution is shared and perceived as valid. If a group passes on with conviction elements of a way of perceiving, thinking, and feeling, we can assume that that group has had enough stability and has shared enough common experiences to have developed a culture. If, on the other hand, a group has not faced the issue of what to pass on in the process of socialization, it has not had a chance to test its own consensus and commitment to a given belief, value, or assumption.

The Strength of a Culture. The "strength" or "amount" of culture can be defined in terms of (1) the *homogeneity* and *stability* of group membership and (2) the *length* and *intensity* of shared experiences of the group. If a stable group has had a long, varied, intense history (i.e., if it has had to cope with many difficult survival problems and has succeeded), it will have a strong and highly differentiated culture. By the same token, if a group has had a constantly shifting membership or has been together only for a short time and has not faced any difficult issues, it will, by definition, have a weak culture. Although individuals within that group may have very strong individual assumptions, there will not be enough shared experiences for the group as a whole to have a defined culture.

By this definition, one would probably assess IBM and the Bell System as having strong cultures, whereas very young companies or ones which have had a high turnover of key executives would be judged as having weak ones. One should also note that once an organization has a strong culture, if the dominant coalition or leadership remains stable, the culture can survive high turnover at lower ranks because new members can be strongly socialized into the organization as, for example, in elite military units.

It is very important to recognize that cultural strength may or may not be correlated with effectiveness. Though some current writers have argued that strength is desirable,[8] it seems clear to me that the relationship is far more complex. The actual content of the culture and the degree to which its solutions fit the problems posed by the environment seem like the critical variables here, not strength. One can hypothesize that young groups strive for culture strength as a way of creating an identity for themselves, but older groups may be more effective with a weak total culture and diverse subcultures to enable them to be responsive to rapid environmental change.

This way of defining culture makes it specific to a given group. If a total corporation consists of stable, functional, divisional, geographic, or rank-based subgroups, then that corporation will have multiple cultures within it. It is perfectly possible for those multiple cultures to be in conflict with each other, such that one could not speak of a single corporate culture. On the other hand, if there has been common corporate experience as well, then one could have a strong corporate culture on top of various subcultures that are based in subunits. The deciphering of a given company's culture then becomes an empirical matter of locating where the stable social units are, what cultures each of those stable units have developed, and how those separate cultures blend into a single whole. The total culture could then be very homogeneous or heterogeneous, according to the degree to which subgroup cultures are similar or different.

It has also been pointed out that some of the cultural assumptions in an organization can come from the occupational background of the members of the organization. This makes it possible to have a managerial culture, an engineering culture, a science culture, a labor union culture, etc., all of which coexist in a given organization.[9]

3. Invented, Discovered, or Developed

Cultural elements are defined as learned solutions to problems. In this section, I will concentrate on the nature of the learning mechanisms that are involved.

Structurally, there are two types of learning situations: (1) positive problem-solving situations that produce positive or negative reinforcement in terms of whether the attempted solution works or not; and (2) anxiety-avoidance situations that produce positive or negative reinforcement in terms of whether the attempted solution does or does not avoid anxiety. In practice, these two types of situations are intertwined, but they are structurally different and, therefore, they must be distinguished.

In the positive problem-solving situation, the group tries out various responses until something works. The group will then continue to use this response until it ceases to work. The information that it no longer works is visible and clear. By contrast, in the anxiety-avoidance situation, once a response is learned because it successfully avoids anxiety, it is likely to be repeated indefinitely. The reason is that the learner will not willingly test the situation to determine whether the cause of the anxiety is still operating. Thus all rituals, patterns of thinking or feeling, and behaviors that may originally have been motivated by a need to avoid a painful, anxiety-provoking situation are going to be repeated, even if the causes of the original pain are no longer acting, because the avoidance of anxiety is, itself, positively reinforcing.[10]

To fully grasp the importance of anxiety reduction in culture formation, we have to consider, first of all, the human need for cognitive order and consistency, which serves as the ultimate motivator for a common language and shared categories of perception and thought.[11] In the absence of such shared "cognitive maps," the human organism experiences a basic existential anxiety that is intolerable—an anxiety observed only in extreme situations of isolation or captivity.[12]

Secondly, humans experience the anxiety associated with being exposed to hostile environmental conditions and to the dangers inherent in unstable social relationships, forcing groups to learn ways of coping with such external and internal problems.

A third source of anxiety is associated with occupational roles such as coal mining and nursing. For example, the Tavistock sociotechnical studies have shown clearly that the social structure and ways of operation of such groups can be conceptualized best as a "defense" against the anxiety that would be unleashed if work were done in another manner.[13]

If an organizational culture is composed of both types of elements—those designed to solve problems and those designed to avoid anxiety—it becomes necessary to analyze which is which if one is concerned about changing any of the elements. In the positive-learning situation, one needs innovative sources to find a better solution to the problem; in the anxiety-avoidance situation, one must first find the source of the anxiety and either show the learner that it no longer exists, or provide an alternative source of avoidance. Either of these is difficult to do.

In other words, cultural elements that are based on anxiety reduction will be more stable than those based on positive problem solving because of the nature of the anxiety reduction mechanism and the fact that human systems need a certain amount of stability to avoid cognitive and social anxiety.

Where do solutions initially come from? Most cultural solutions in new groups and organizations originate from the founders and early leaders of those organizations.[14] Typically, the solution process is an advocacy of certain ways of doing things that are then tried out and either adopted or rejected, depending on how well they work out. Initially, the founders have the most influence, but, as the group ages and acquires its own experiences, its members will find their own solutions. Ultimately, the process of discovering new solutions will be more a result of interactive, shared experiences. But leadership will always play a key role during these times when the group faces a new problem and must develop new responses to the situation. In fact, one of the crucial functions of leadership is to provide guidance at precisely those times when habitual ways of doing things no longer work, or when a dramatic change in the environment requires new responses.

At those times, leadership must not only insure the invention of new and better solutions, but must also provide some security to help the group tolerate the anxiety of giving up old, stable responses, while new ones are learned and tested. In the Lewinian change framework, this means that the "unfreezing stage" must involve both enough disconfirmation to motivate change and enough psychological safety to permit the individual or group to pay attention to the disconfirming data.[15]

4. Problems of External Adaptation and Internal Integration

If culture is a solution to the problems a group faces, what can we say about the nature of those problems? Most group theories agree it is useful to distinguish between two kinds of problems: (1) those that deal with the group's basic survival, which has been labeled the primary task, basic function, or ultimate mission of the group; and (2) those that deal with the group's ability to function as a group. These problems have been labeled socioemotional, group building and maintenance, or integration problems.[16]

Homans further distinguishes between the *external system* and the *internal system* and notes that the two are interdependent.[17] Even though one can distinguish between the external and internal problems, in practice both systems are highly interrelated.

External Adaptation Problems. Problems of external adaptation are those that ultimately determine the group's survival in the environment. While a part of the group's environment is "enacted," in the sense that prior cultural experience predisposes members to perceive the environment in a certain way and even to control that environment to a degree, these will always be elements of the environment (weather, natural circumstances, availability of economic and other resources, political upheavals) that are clearly beyond the control of the group and that will, to a degree, determine the fate of the group.[18] A useful way to categorize the problems of survival is to mirror the stages of the problem-solving cycle as shown in Table 2.[19]

TABLE 2   Problems of External Adaptation and Survival

Strategy:	Developing consensus on the *primary task, core mission, or manifest and latent functions of the group.*
Goals:	Developing consensus of *goals,* such goals being the concrete reflection of the core mission.
Means for Accomplishing Goals:	Developing consensus of the *means to be used* in accomplishing the goals—for example, division of labor, organization structure, reward system, and so forth.
Measuring Performance:	Developing consensus on the *criteria to be used in measuring how well the group is doing against its goals and targets*—for example, information and control systems.
Correction:	Developing consensus on *remedial or repair strategies* as needed when the group is not accomplishing its goals.

Source: Reprinted by permission of the publisher, from "The Role of the Founder in Creating Organizational Culture," by Edgar H. Schein, *Organizational Dynamics.* Summer 1983 © 1983 Periodicals Divisoin, American Management Association. All rights reserved.

The basic underlying assumptions of the culture from which the founders of the organization come will determine to a large extent the initial formulations of core mission, goals, means, criteria, and remedial strategies, in that those ways of doing things are the only ones with which the group members will be familiar. But as an organization develops its own life experience, it may begin to modify to some extent its original assumptions. For example, a young company may begin by defining its core mission to be to "win in the marketplace over all competition," but may at a later stage find that "owning its own niche in the marketplace," "coexisting with other companies," or even "being a silent partner in an oligopolistic industry" is a more workable solution to survival. Thus for each stage of the problem-solving cycle, there will emerge solutions characteristic of that group's own history, and those solutiuons or ways of doing things based on learned assumptions will make up a major portion of that group's culture.

Internal Integration Problems. A group or organization cannot survive if it cannot manage itself as a group. External survival and internal integration problems are, therefore, two sides of the same coin. Table 3 outlines the major issues of internal integration around which cultural solutions must be found.

While the nature of the solutions will vary from one organization to another,

TABLE 3 Problems of Internal Integration

Language:	*Common language and conceptual categories.* If members cannot communicate with and understand each other, a group is impossible by definition.
Boundaries:	Consensus on *group boundaries and criteria for inclusion and exclusion.* One of the most important areas of culture is the shared consensus of who is in, who is out, and by what criteria one determines membership.
Power & Status:	Consensus on *criteria for the allocation of power and status.* Each organization must work out its pecking order and its rules for how one gets, maintains, and loses power. This area of consensus is crucial in helping members manage their own feelings of aggression.
Intimacy:	Consensus on *criteria for intimacy, friendship, and love.* Every organization must work out its rules of the game for peer relationships, for relationships between the sexes, and for the manner in which openness and intimacy are to be handled in the context of managing the organization's tasks.
Rewards & Punishments:	Consensus on *criteria for allocation of rewards and punishments.* Every group must know what its heroic and sinful behaviors are; what gets rewarded with property, status, and power; and what gets punished through the withdrawal of rewards and, ultimately, excommunication.
Ideology:	Consensus of *ideology and "religion."* Every organization, like every society, faces unexplainable events that must be given meaning so that members can respond to them and avoid the anxiety of dealing with the unexplainable and uncontrollable.

by definition, every organization will have to face each of these issues and develop some kind of solution. However, because the nature of that solution will reflect the biases of the founders and current leaders, the prior experiences of group members, and the actual events experienced, it is likely that each organizational culture will be unique, even though the underlying issues around which the culture is formed will be common.[20]

An important issue to study across many organizations is whether an organization's growth and evaluation follows an inherent evolutionary *trend* (e.g., developing societies are seen as evolving from that of a community to more of a bureaucratic, impersonal type of system). One should also study whether organizational cultures reflect in a patterned way of the underlying technology, the age of the organization, the size of the organization, and the nature of the parent culture within which the organization evolves.

5. Assumptions That Work Well Enough To Be Considered Valid

Culture goes beyond the norms or values of a group in that it is more of an *ultimate* outcome, based on repeated success and a gradual process of taking things for granted. In other words, to me what makes something "cultural" is this "taken-for-granted" quality, which makes the underlying assumptions virtually undiscussable.

Culture is perpetually being formed in the sense that there is constantly some kind of learning going on about how to relate to the environment and to manage internal affairs. But this ongoing evolutionary process does not change those things that are so thoroughly learned that they come to be a stable element of the group's life. Since the basic assumptions that make up an organization's culture serve the secondary function of stabilizing much of the internal and external environment for the group, and since that stability is sought as a defense against the anxiety which comes with uncertainty and confusion, these deeper parts of the culture either do not change or change only very slowly.

6. Taught to New Members

Because culture serves the function of stabilizing the external and internal environment for an organization, it must be taught to new members. It would not serve its function if every generation of new members could introduce new perceptions, language, thinking patterns, and rules of interaction. For culture to serve its function, it must be perceived as correct and valid, and if it is perceived that way, it automatically follows that it must be taught to newcomers.

It cannot be overlooked that new members do bring new ideas and do produce culture change, especially if they are brought in at high levels of the organization. It remains to be settled empirically whether and how this happens. For example, does a new member have to be socialized first and accepted into a central and powerful position before he or she can begin to affect change? Or does a new member bring from the onset new ways of perceiving, thinking, feeling, and acting, which produce automatic changes through role innovation?[21] Is the manner in which new members are socialized influential in determining what kind of innovation they will produce?[22] Much of the work on innovation in organizations is confusing because often it is not clear whether the elements that are considered "new" are actually new assumptions, or simply new artifacts built on old cultural assumptions.

In sum, if culture provides the group members with a paradigm of how the world "is," it goes without saying that such a paradigm would be passed on without question to new members. It is also the case that the very process of passing on the culture provides an opportunity for testing, ratifying, and reaffirming it. For both of these reasons, the process of socialization (i.e., the passing on of the group's culture) is stratigically an important process to study if one wants to decipher what the culture is and how it might change.[23]

7. Perceive, Think, and Feel

The final element in the definition reminds us that culture is pervasive and ubiquitous. The basic assumptions about nature, humanity, relationships, truth, activity, time, and space cover virtually all human functions. This is not to say that a given organization's culture will develop to the point of totally "controlling" all of its members' perceptions, thoughts, and feelings. But the process of learning to manage the external and internal environment does involve all of one's cognitive and emotional elements. As cultural learning progresses, more and more of the person's responses will become involved. Therefore, the longer we live in a given culture, and the older the culture is, the more it will influence our perceptions, thoughts, and feelings.

By focusing on perceptions, thoughts, and feelings, I am also stating the importance of those categories relative to the category of *overt behavior*. Can one speak of a culture in terms of just the overt behavior patterns one observes? Culture is *manifested* in overt behavior, but the idea of culture goes deeper than behavior. Indeed, the very reason for elaborating an abstract notion like "culture" is that it is too difficult to explain what goes on in organizations if we stay at the descriptive behavioral level.

To put it another way, behavior is, to a large extent, a joint function of what the individual brings to the situation and the operating situational forces, which to some degree are unpredictable. To understand the cultural portion of what the individual brings to the situation (as opposed to the idiosyncratic or situational portions), we must examine the individual's pattern of perceptions, thoughts, and feelings. Only after we have reached a consensus at this inner level have we uncovered what is potentially *cultural*.

The Study of Organizational Culture and Its Implications. Organizational culture as defined here is difficult to study. However, it is not as difficult as studying a different society where language and customs are so different that one needs to live in the society to get any feel for it at all. Organizations exist in a parent culture, and much of what we find in them is derivative from the assumptions of the parent culture. But different organizations will sometimes emphasize or amplify different elements of a parent culture. For example, in the two companies previously mentioned, we find in the first an extreme version of the individual freedom ethic, and in the second one, an extreme version of the authority ethic, *both* of which can be derived from U.S. culture.

The problem of deciphering a particular organization's culture, then, is more a matter of surfacing assumptions, which will be recognizable once they have been uncovered. We will not find alien forms of perceiving, thinking, and feeling if the investigator is from the same parent culture as the organization that is being investigated. On the other hand, the particular pattern of assumptions, which we call an organization's cultural paradigm, will not reveal itself easily because it is taken for granted.

How then do we gather data and decipher the paradigm? Basically, there are four approaches that should be used in combination with one another:

1. Analyzing the Process and Content of Socialization of New Members. By interviewing "socialization agents," such as the supervisors and older peers of new members, one can identify some of the important areas of the culture. But some elements of the culture will not be discovered by this method because they are not revealed to newcomers or lower members.

2. Analyzing Responses to Critical Incidents in the Organization's History. By constructing a careful "organizational biography" from documents, interviews, and perhaps even surveys of present and past key members, it is possible to identify the major periods of culture formation. For each crisis or incident identified, it is then necessary to determine what was done, why it was done, and what the outcome was. To infer the underlying assumptions of the organization, one would then look for the major themes in the reasons given for the actions taken.

3. Analyzing Beliefs, Values, and Assumptions of "Culture Creators or Carriers." When interviewing founders, current leaders, or culture creators or carriers, one should initially make an open-ended chronology of each person's history in the organization—his or her goals, modes of action, and assessment of outcomes. The list of external and internal issues found in Tables 2 and 3 can be used as a checklist later in the interview to cover areas more systematically.

4. Jointly Exploring and Analyzing with Insiders the Anomalies or Puzzling Features Observed or Uncovered in Interviews. It is the *joint inquiry* that will help to disclose basic assumptions and help determine how they may interrelate to form the cultural paradigm.

The insider must be a representative of the culture and must be interested in disclosing his or her *own* basic assumptions to test whether they are in fact cultural prototypes. This process works best if one acts from observations that puzzle the outsider or that seem like anomalies because the insider's assumptions are most easily surfaced if they are contrasted to the assumptions that the outsider initially holds about what is observed.

While the first three methods mentioned above should enhance and complement one another, at least one of them should systematically cover all of the external adaptation and internal integration issues. In order to discover the underlying basic assumptions and eventually to decipher the paradigm, the fourth method is necessary to help the insider surface his or her own cultural assumptions. This is done through the outsider's probing and searching.[24]

If an organization's total culture is not well developed, or if the organization consists of important stable subgroups, which have developed subcultures, one must modify the above methods to study the various subcultures.[25] Furthermore, the organizational biography might reveal that the organization is at a certain point in its life cycle, and one would hypothesize that the functions that a given kind of culture plays vary with the life-cycle stage.[26]

Implications for Culture Management and Change. If we recognize organizational culture—whether at the level of the group or the total corporation—as a deep phenomenon, what does this tell us about when and how to change or manage culture? First of all, the evolutionary perspective draws our attention to the fact that the culture of a group may serve different functions at different times. When a group is forming and growing, the culture is a "glue"—a source of identity and strength. In other words, young founder-dominated companies need their cultures as a way of holding together their organizations. The culture changes that do occur in a young organization can best be described as clarification, articulation, and elaboration. If the young company's culture is genuinely maladaptive in relation to the external environment, the company will not survive anyway. But even if one identified needed changes, there is little chance at this stage that one could change the culture.

In organizational midlife, culture can be managed and changed, but not without considering all the sources of stability which have been identified above. The large diversified organization probably contains many functional, geographic, and other groups that have cultures of their own—some of which will confilct with each other. Whether the organization needs to enhance the diversity to remain flexible in the face of environmental turbulence, or to create a more homogeneous "strong" culture (as some advocate) becomes one of the toughest strategy decisions management confronts, especially if senior management is unaware of some of its own cultural assumptions. Some form of outside intervention and "culture consciousness raising" is probably essential at this stage to facilitate better strategic decisions.

Organizations that have reached a stage of maturity or decline resulting from mature markets and products or from excessive internal stability and comfort that prevents innovation[27] may need to change parts of their culture, provided they can obtain the necessary self-insight. Such managed change will always be a painful process and will elicit strong resistance. Moreover, change may not even be possible without replacing the large numbers of people who wish to hold on to all of the original culture.

No single model of such change exists: managers may successfully orchestrate change through the use of a wide variety of techniques, from outright coercion at one extreme to subtle seduction through the introduction of new technologies at the other extreme.[28]

SUMMARY AND CONCLUSIONS

I have attempted to construct a formal definition of organizational culture that derives from a dynamic model of learning and group dynamics. The definition highlights that culture: (1) is always in the process of formation and change;

(2) tends to cover all aspects of human functioning; (3) is learned around the major issues of external adaptation and internal integration; and (4) is ultimately embodied as an interrelated, patterned set of basic assumptions that deal with ultimate issues, such as the nature of humanity, human relationships, time, space, and the nature of reality and truth itself.

If we are to decipher a given organization's culture, we must use a complex interview, observation, and joint-inquiry approach in which selected members of the group work with the outsider to uncover the unconscious assumptions that are hypothesized to be the essence of the culture. I believe we need to study a large number of organizations using these methods to determine the utility of the concept or organizational culture and to relate cultural variables to other variables, such as strategy, organizational structure, and ultimately, organizational effectiveness.

If such studies show this model of culture to be useful, one of the major implications will be that our theories of organizational change will have to give much more attention to the opportunities and constraints that organizational culture provides. Clearly, if culture is as powerful as I argue in this article, it will be easy to make changes that are congruent with present assumptions, and very difficult to make changes that are not. In sum, the understanding of organizational culture would then become integral to the process of management itself.

FOOTNOTES*

1. J. Martin and C. Sield, "Organizational Culture and Counterculture: An Uneasy Symbiosis," *Organizational Dynamics,* Autumn 1983, pp. 52-64.
2. C. Argyris, "The Executive Mind and Double Loop Learning," *Organizational Dynamics,* Autumn 1982, pp. 5-22.
3. E. H. Schein, "Does Japanese Management Style Have a Message for American Managers?" *Sloan Management Review,* Fall 1981, pp. 55-68; E. H. Schein, "The Role of the Founder in Creating Organizational Culture," *Organizational Dynamics,* Summer 1983, pp. 13-28.
4. R. Evered and M. R. Louis, "Alternative Perspectives as the Organizational Sciences: 'Inquiry from the Inside' and 'Inquiry from the Outside,' " *Academy of Management Review* (1981):385, 395.
5. F. R. Kluckholm and F. L. Strodtbeck, *Variations in Value Orientations* (Evanston, Il.: Row Peterson, 1961). An application of these ideas to the study of organizations across cultures, as contrasted with the culture of organizations can be found in W. M. Evan, *Organization Theory* (New York: John Wiley & Sons, 1976). ch. 15. Other studies of cross-cultural comparisons are not reviewed in detail here. See for example: G. Hofstede, *Culture's Consequences* (Beverly Hills, CA: Sage Publications, 1980); G. W. England, *The Manager and His Values* (Cambridge, MA: Ballinger, 1975).
6. E. T. Hall, *The Silent Language* (New York: Doubleday, 1969).
7. W. G. Dyer, Jr., *Culture in Organizations: A Case Study and Analysis* (Cambridge, MA: Sloan School of Management, MIT, Working Paper #1279-82, 1982).

*The research on which this article is based was supported by the Chief of Naval Research, Psychology of Sciences Division (Code 452). Organizational Effectiveness Research Programs, Office of Naval Research, Arlington, VA 22217, under Contract Number N(XX)14 80-C-0905, NK 170-911.

Special thanks go to my colleagues Lotte Haydn, John Van Maanen, and Meryl Louis for helping me to think through this murky area; and to Gibb Dyer, Barbara Lawrence, Steve Barley, Jan Sanzchus, and Mary Nord whose research on organizational culture has begun to establish the utility of these ideas.

8. T. E. Deal and A. A. Kennedy, *Corporate Culture* (Reading, MA: Addison-Wesley, 1982); T. J. Peters and R. H. Waterman, Jr., *In Search of Excellence* (New York: Harper & Row, 1982).

9. J. Van Maanen and S. R. Barley, "Occupational Communities: Culture and Control in Organizations" (Cambridge, MA: Sloan School of Management, November 1982); L. Bailyn, "Resolving Contradictions in Technical Careers," *Technology Review,* November–December 1982, pp. 40–47.

10. R. L. Solomon and L. C. Wynne, "Traumatic Avoidance Learning: The Principles of Anxiety Conservation and Partial Irreversibility," *Psychological Review* 61, 1954, p. 353.

11. D. O. Hebb, "The Social Significance of Animal Studies," in *Handbook of Social Psychology,* G. Lindzey (Reading, MA: Addison-Wesley, 1954).

12. E. H. Schein, *Coercive Persuasion* (New York: Norton, 1961).

13. E. I. Trist and K. W. Bamforth, "Some Social and Psychological Consequences of the Long-Wall Method of Coal Getting," *Human Relations,* 1951, pp. 1–38; I. E. P. Menzies, "A Case Study in the Functioning of Social Systems as a Defense Against Anxiety," *Human Relations,* 1960, pp. 95–121.

14. A. M. Pettigrew, "On Studying Organizational Cultures," *Administrative Science Quarterly* (1979); 570 581; Schein (Summer 1983), pp. 13–28.

15. Schein (1961); E. H. Schein and W. G. Bennis, *Personal and Organizational Change through Group Methods* (New York: John Wiley & Sons, 1965).

16. A. K. Rice, *The Enterprise and Its Environment* (London: Tavistock, 1963); R. F. Babes, *Interaction Process Analysis* (Chicago, IL.: University of Chicago Press, 1950); T. Parsons, *The Social System* (Glencoe, IL.: The Free Press, 1951).

17. G. Homans, *The Human Group* (New York: Harcourt Brace, 1950).

18. K. E. Weick, "Cognitive Processes in Organizations," in *Research in Organizational Behavior,* ed. B. Staw (Greenwich, CT: JAI Press, 1979), pp. 41–74; J. Van Maanen, "The Self, the Situation, and the Rules of Interpersonal Relations," in *Essays in Interpersonal Dynamics,* W. G. Bennis, J. Van Maanen, E. H. Schein, and F. I. Steele (Homewood, IL: Dorsey Press, 1979).

19. E. H. Schein, *Process Consultation* (Reading, MA: Addison-Wesley, 1969).

20. When studying different organizations, it is important to determine whether the deeper paradigms that eventually arise in each organizational culture are also unique, or whether they will fit into certain categories such as those that the typological schemes suggest. For example, Handy describes a typology based on Harrison's work that suggests that organizational paradigms will revolve around one of four basic issues: (1) personal connections, power, and politics; (2) role structuring; (3) tasks and efficiency; or (4) existential here and now issues. See: C. Handy, *The Gods of Management* (London: Penguin, 1978); R. Harrison, "How to Describe Your Organization," *Harvard Business Review,* September–October 1972.

21. E. H. Schein, "The Role Innovator and His Education," *Technology Review,* October–November 1970, pp. 32–38.

22. J. Van Maanen and E. H. Schein, "Toward a Theory of Organizational Socialization," in *Research in Organizational Behavior,* Vol. 1, ed. B. Staw (Greenwich, CT: JAI Press, 1979).

23. Ibid.

24. Evered and Louis (1981).

25. M. R. Louis, "A Cultural Perspective on Organizations," *Human Systems Management* (1981): 246–258.

26. H. Schwartz and S. M. Davis, "Matching Corporate Culture and Business Strategy," *Organizational Dynamics,* Summer 1981, pp. 30–48; J. R. Kimberly and R. H. Miles, *The Organizational Life Cycle* San Francisco: Jossey Bass, 1981).

27. R. Katz, "The Effects of Group Longevity of Project Communication and Performance," *Administrative Science Quarterly* (1982): 27, 81–194.

28. A fuller explication of these dynamics can be found in my forthcoming book on organizational culture.

EVOLUTION AND REVOLUTION
AS ORGANIZATIONS GROW

Larry E. Greiner

A small research company chooses too complicated and formalized an organization structure for its young age and limited size. It flounders in rigidity and bureaucracy for several years and is finally acquired by a larger company.

Key executives of a retail store chain hold on to an organization structure long after it has served its purpose, because their power is derived from this structure. The company eventually goes into bankruptcy.

A large bank disciplines a "rebellious" manager who is blamed for current control problems, when the underlying cause is centralized procedures that are holding back expansion into new markets. Many younger managers subsequently leave the bank, competition moves in, and profits are still declining.

The problems of these companies, like those of many others, are rooted more in past decisions than in present events or outside market dynamics. Historical forces do indeed shape the future growth of organizations. Yet management, in its haste to grow, often overlooks such critical developmental questions as: Where has our organization been? Where is it now? And what do the answers to these questions mean for where we are going? Instead, its gaze is fixed outward toward the environment and the future—as if more precise market projections will provide a new organizational identity.

Companies fail to see that many clues to their future success lie within their own organizations and their evolving states of development. Moreover, the inability of management to understand its organization development problems can result in a company becoming "frozen" in its present stage of evolution, or, ultimately, in failure, regardless of market opportunities.

My position in this article is that the future of an organization may be less determined by outside forces than it is by the organization's history. In stressing the force of history on an organization, I have drawn from the legacies of European psychologists (their thesis being that individual behavior is determined primarily by previous events and experiences, not by what lies ahead). Extending this analogy of individual development to the problems of organization development, I shall discuss a series of developmental phases through which growing companies tend to pass. But, first let me provide two definitions.

1. The term *evolution* is used to describe prolonged periods of growth where no major upheaval occurs in organization practices.
2. The term *revolution* is used to describe those periods of substantial turmoil in organizational life.

As a company progresses through developmental phases, each evolutionary period creates its own revolution. For instance, centralized practices eventually lead to demands for decentralization. Moreover, the nature of management's solution to each revolutionary period determines whether a company will move forward into its next stage of evolutionary growth. As I shall show later, there are at least five phases of organization development, each characterized by both an evolution and a revolution.

KEY FORCES IN DEVELOPMENT

During the past few years a small amount of research knowledge about the phases of organization development has been building. Some of this research is very quantitative, such as time-series analyses that reveal patterns of economic performance over time.[1] The majority of studies, however, are case-oriented and use company records and interviews to reconstruct a rich picture of corporate development.[2] Yet both types of research tend to be heavily empirical without attempting more generalized statements about the overall process of development.

A notable exception is the historical work of Alfred D. Chandler, Jr., in his book *Strategy and Structure*.[3] This study depicts four very broad and general phases in the lives of four large U.S. companies. It proposes that outside market opportunities determine a company's strategy, which in turn, determines the company's organization structure. This thesis has a valid ring for the four companies examined by Chandler, largely because they developed in a time of explosive markets and technological advances. But more recent evidence suggests that organization structure may be less malleable than Chandler assumed; in fact, structure can play a critical role in influencing corporate strategy. It is this reverse emphasis on how organization structure affects future growth which is highlighted in the model presented in this article.

From an analysis of recent studies,[4] five key dimensions emerge as essential for building a model of organization development:

1. Age of the organization.
2. Size of the organization.
3. Stages of evolution.
4. Stages of revolution.
5. Growth rate of the industry.

I shall describe each of these elements separately, but first note their combined effect as illustrated in Exhibit 1. Note especially how each dimension influences the other over time; when all five elements begin to interact, a more complete and dynamic picture of organizational growth emerges.

After describing these dimensions and their interconnections, I shall discuss each evolutionary revolutionary phase of development and show (a) how each stage of evolution breeds its own revolution, and (b) how management solutions to each revolution determine the next stage of evolution.

EXHIBIT 1 Model of Organization Development

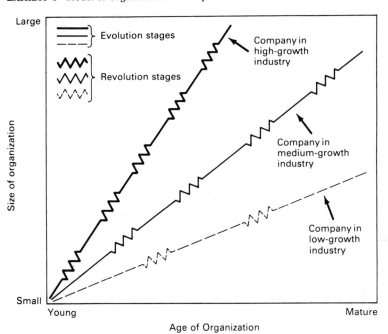

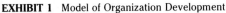

Age of the Organization

The most obvious and essential dimension for any model of development is the life span of an organization (represented as the horizontal axis in Exhibit 1). All historical studies gather data from various points in time and them make comparisons. From these observations, it is evident that the same organization practices are not maintained throughout a long time span. This makes a most basic point: management problems and principles are rooted in time. The concept of decentralization, for example, can have meaning for describing corporate practices at one time period but loses its descriptive power at another.

The passage of time also contributes to the institutionalization of managerial attitudes. As a result, employee behavior becomes not only more predictable but also more difficult to change when attitudes are outdated.

Size of the Organization

This dimension is depicted as the vertical axis in Exhibit 1. A company's problems and solutions tend to change markedly as the number of employees and sales volume increase. Thus, time is not the only determinant of structure; in fact, organizations that do not grow in size can retain many of the same management issues and practices over lengthy periods. In addition to increased size, however, problems of coordination and communication magnify, new functions emerge, levels in the management hierarchy multiply, and jobs become more interrelated.

Stages of Evolution

As both age and size increase, another phenomenon becomes evident: the prolonged growth that I have termed the evolutionary period. Most growing organizations do not expand for two years and then retreat for one year; rather, those that survive a crisis usually enjoy four to eight years of continuous growth without a major economic setback or severe internal disruption. The term evolution seems appropriate for describing these quieter periods because only modest adjustments appear necessary for maintaining growth under the same overall pattern of management.

Stages of Revolution

Smooth evolution is not inevitable; it cannot be assumed that organization growth is linear. *Fortune's* "500" list, for example, has had significant turnover during the last 50 years. Thus we find evidence from numerous case histories which reveals periods of substantial turbulence spaced between smoother periods of evolution.

I have termed these turbulent times the periods of revolution because they typically exhibit a serious upheaval of management practices. Traditional management practices, which were appropriate for a smaller size and earlier time, are brought under scrutiny by frustrated top managers and disillusioned lower-level managers. During such periods of crisis, a number of companies fail—those unable to abandon past practices and effect major organization changes are likely either to fold or to level off in their growth rates.

The critical task for management in each revolutionary period is to find a new set of organization practices that will become the basis for managing the next period of evolutionary growth. Interestingly enough, these new practices eventually sow their own seeds of decay and lead to another period of revolution. Companies therefore experience the irony of seeing a major solution in one time period become a major problem at a later date.

Growth Rate of the Industry

The speed at which an organization experiences phases of evolution and revolution is closely related to the market environment of its industry. For example, a company in a rapidly expanding market will have to add employees rapidly; hence, the need for new organization structures to accommodate large staff increases is accelerated. While evolutionary periods tend to be relatively short in fast-growing industries, much longer evolutionary periods occur in mature or slowly growing industries.

Evolution can also be prolonged, and revolutions delayed, when profits come easily. For instance, companies that make grievous errors in a rewarding industry can still look good on their profit and loss statements; thus they can avoid a change in management practices for a longer period. The aerospace industry in its infancy is an example. Yet revolutionary periods still occur, as one did in aerospace when profit opportunities began to dry up. Revolutions seem to be much more severe and difficult to resolve when the market environment is poor.

PHASES OF GROWTH

With the foregoing framework in mind, let us now examine in depth the five specific phases of evolution and revolution. As shown in Exhibit 2, each evolutionary period is characterized by the dominant *management style* used to achieve growth, while each revolutionary period is characterized by the dominant *management problem* that must be solved before growth can continue. The patterns presented in Exhibit 2 seem to be typical for companies in industries with moderate growth over a long time period; companies in faster growing industries tend to experience all five phases more rapidly, while those in slower growing industries encounter only two or three phases over many years.

It is important to note that *each phase is both an effect of the previous phase and a cause for the next phase.* For example, the evolutionary management style in Phase 3 of the exhibit is "delegation," which grows out of, and becomes the solution to, demands for greater "autonomy" in the preceding Phase 2 revolution. The style of delegation used in Phase 3, however, eventually provokes a major revolutionary crisis that is characterized by attempts to regain control over the diversity created through increased delegation.

The principal implication of each phase is that management actions are narrowly prescribed if growth is to occur. For example, a company experiencing

EXHIBIT 2 The Five Phases of Growth

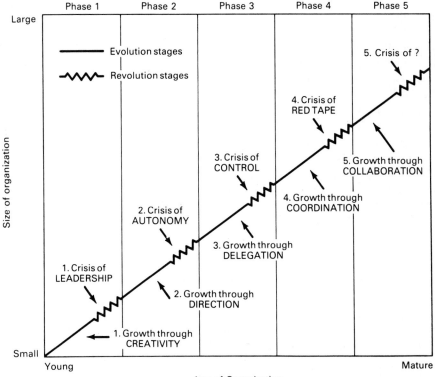

an autonomy crisis in Phase 2 cannot return to directive management for a solution—it must adopt a new style of delegation in order to move ahead.

Phase 1: Creativity...

In the birth stage of an organization, the emphasis is on creating both a product and a market. Here are the characteristics of the period of creative evolution:

- The company's founders are usually technically or entrepreneurially oriented, and they disdain management activities; their physical and mental energies are absorbed entirely in making and selling a new product.
- Communication among employees is frequent and informal.
- Long hours of work are rewarded by modest salaries and the promise of ownership benefits.
- Control of activities come from immediate marketplace feedback; the management acts as the customers react.

...& the leadership crisis: All of the foregoing individualistic and creative activities are essential for the company to get off the ground. But therein lies the problem. As the company grows, larger production runs require knowledge about the efficiencies of manufacturing. Increased numbers of employees cannot be managed exclusively through informal communication; new employees are not motivated by an intense dedication to the product or organization. Additional capital must be secured, and new accounting procedures are needed for financial control.

Thus the founders find themselves burdened with unwanted management responsibilities. So they long for the "good old days," still trying to act as they did in the past. And conficts between the harried leaders grow more intense.

At this point a crisis of leadership occurs, which is the onset of the first revolution. Who is to lead the company out of confusion and solve the managerial problems confronting it? Quite obviously, a strong manager is needed who has the necessary knowledge and skill to introduce new business techniques. But this is easier said than done. The founders often hate to step aside even though they are probably temperamentally unsuited to be managers. So here is the first critical developmental choice—to locate and install a strong business manager who is acceptable to the founders and who can pull the organization together.

Phase 2: Direction...

Those companies that survive the first phase by installing a capable business manager usually embark on a period of sustained growth under able and directive leadership. Here are the characteristics of this evolutionary period:

- A functional organization structure is introduced to separate manufacturing from marketing activities, and job assignments become more specialized.
- Accounting systems for inventory and purchasing are introduced.
- Incentives, budgets, and work standards are adopted.
- Communication becomes more formal and impersonal as a hierarchy of titles and positions builds.

- The new manager and his key supervisors take most of the responsibility for instituting direction, while lower-level supervisors are treated more as functional specialists than as autonomous decision-making managers.

  ...& the autonomy crisis: Although the new directive techniques channel employee energy more efficiently into growth, they eventually become inappropriate for controlling a larger, more diverse and complex organization. Lower-level employees find themselves restricted by a cumbersome and centralized hierarchy. They have come to possess more direct knowledge about markets and machinery than do the leaders at the top; consequently, they feel torn between following procedures and taking initiative on their own.

Thus the second revolution is imminent as a crisis develops from demands for greater autonomy on the part of lower-level managers. The solution adopted by most companies is to move toward greater delegation. Yet it is difficult for top managers who were previously successful at being directive to give up responsibility. Moreover, lower-level managers are not accustomed to making decisions for themselves. As a result, numerous companies flounder during this revolutionary period, adhering to centralized methods while lower-level employees grow more disenchanted and leave the organization.

Phase 3: Delegation...

The next era of growth evolves from the successful application of a decentralized organization structure. It exhibits these characteristics:

- Much greater responsibility is given to the managers of plants and market territories.
- Profit centers and bonuses are used to stimulate motivation.
- The top executives at headquarters restrain themselves to managing by exception, based on periodic reports from the field.
- Management often concentrates on making new acquisitions which can be lined up beside other decentralized units.
- Communication from the top is infrequent, usually by correspondence, telephone, or brief visits to field locations.

The delegation stage proves useful for gaining expansion through heightened motivation at lower levels. Decentralized managers with greater authority and incentive are able to penetrate larger markets, respond faster to customers, and develop new products.

  ...& the control crisis: A serious problem eventually evolves, however, as top executives sense that they are losing control over a highly diversified field operation. Autonomous field managers prefer to run their own shows without coordinating plans, money, technology, and manpower with the rest of the organization. Freedom breeds a parochial attitude.

Hence, the Phase 3 revolution is under way when top management seeks to regain control over the total company. Some top managements attempt a return to centralized management, which usually fails because of the vast scope of operations. Those companies that move ahead find a new solution in the use of special coordination techniques.

Phase 4: Coordination...

During this phase, the evolutionary period is characterized by the use of formal systems for achieving greater coordination and by top executives taking responsibility for the initiation and administration of these new systems. For example:

- Decentralized units are merged into product groups.
- Formal planning procedures are established and intensively reviewed.
- Numerous staff personnel are hired and located at headquarters to initiate company-wide programs of control and review for line managers.
- Capital expenditures are carefully weighed and parceled out across the organization.
- Each product group is treated as an investment center where return on invested capital is an important criterion used in allocating funds.
- Certain technical functions, such as data processing, are centralized at headquarters, while daily operating decisions remain decentralized.
- Stock options and companywide profit sharing are used to encourage identity with the firm as a whole.

All of these new coordination systems prove useful for achieving growth through more efficient allocation of a company's limited resources. They prompt field managers to look beyond the needs of their local units. While these managers still have much decision-making responsibility, they learn to justify their actions more carefully to a "watchdog" audience at headquarters.

...& the red-tape crisis: But a lack of confidence gradually builds between line and staff, and between headquarters and the field. The proliferation of systems and programs begins to exceed its utility; a red-tape crisis is created. Line managers, for example, increasingly resent heavy staff direction from those who are not familiar with local conditions. Staff people, on the other hand, complain about uncooperative and uninformed line managers. Together both groups criticize the bureaucratic paper system that has evolved. Procedures take precedence over problem solving, and innovation is dampened. In short, the organization has become too large and complex to be managed through formal programs and rigid systems. The Phase 4 revolution is under way.

Phase 5: Collaboration...

The last observable phase in previous studies emphasizes strong interpersonal collaboration in an attempt to overcome the red-tape crisis. Where Phase 4 was managed more through formal systems and procedures, Phase 5 emphasizes greater spontaneity in management action through teams and the skillful confrontation of interpersonal differences. Social control and self-discipline take over from formal control. This transition is especially difficult for those experts who created the old systems as well as for those line managers who relied on formal methods for answers.

The Phase 5 evolution, then, builds around a more flexible and behavioral approach to management. Here are its characteristics:

- The focus is on solving problems quickly through team action.
- Teams are combined across functions for task-group activity.
- Headquarters staff experts are reduced in number, reassigned, and combined in interdisplinary teams to consult with, not to direct, field units.
- A matrix-type structure is frequently used to assemble the right teams for the appropriate problems.
- Previous formal systems are simplified and combined into single multipurpose systems.
- Conferences of key managers are held frequently to focus on major problem issues.
- Educational programs are utilized to train managers in behavioral skills for achieving better teamwork and conflict resolution.
- Real-time information systems are integrated into daily decision making.
- Economic rewards are geared more to team performance than to individual achievement.
- Experiments in new practices are encouraged throughout the organization.

...& the ? crisis: What will be the revolution in response to this stage of evolution? Many large U.S. companies are now in the Phase 5 evolutionary stage, so the answers are critical. While there is little clear evidence, I imagine the revolution will center around the "psychological saturation" of employees who grow emotionally and physically exhausted by the intensity of teamwork and the heavy pressure for innovative solutions.

My hunch is that the Phase 5 revolution will be solved through new structures and programs that allow employees to periodically rest, reflect, and revitalize themselves. We may even see companies with dual organization structures: a "habit" structure for getting the daily work done, and a "reflective" structure for stimulating perspective and personal enrichment. Employees could then move back and forth between the two structures as their energies are dissipated and refueled.

One European organization has implemented just such a structure. Five reflective groups have been established outside the regular structure for the purpose of continuously evaluating five task activities basic to the organization. They report directly to the managing director, although their reports are made public throughout the organization. Membership in each group includes all levels and functions, and employees are rotated through these groups on a six-month basis.

Other concrete examples now in practice include providing sabbaticals for employees, moving managers in and out of "hot spot" jobs, establishing a four-day workweek, assuring job security, building physical facilities for relaxation *during* the working day, making jobs more interchangeable, creating an extra team on the assembly line so that one team is always off for reeducation, and switching to longer vacations and more flexible working hours.

The Chinese practice of requiring executives to spend time periodically on lower-level jobs may also be worth a nonideological evaluation. For too long U.S. management has assumed that career progress should be equated with an upward path toward title, salary, and power. Could it be that some vice presidents of marketing might just long for, and even benefit from, temporary duty in the field sales organization?

IMPLICATIONS OF HISTORY

Let me now summarize some important implications for practicing managers. First, the main features of this discussion are depicted in Exhibit 3, which shows the specific management actions that characterize each growth phase. These actions are also the solutions which ended each preceding revolutionary period.

EXHIBIT 3 Organization Practices during Evolution in the Five Phases of Growth

Category	PHASE 1	PHASE 2	PHASE 3	PHASE 4	PHASE 5
MANAGEMENT FOCUS	Make & sell	Efficiency of operations	Expansion of market	Consolidation of organization	Problem solving & innovation
ORGANIZATION STRUCTURE	Informal	Centralized & functional	Decentralized & geographical	Line-staff & product groups	Matrix of teams
TOP MANAGEMENT STYLE	Individualistic & entrepreneurial	Directive	Delegative	Watchdog	Participative
CONTROL SYSTEM	Market results	Standards & cost centers	Reports & profit centers	Plans & investment centers	Mutual goal setting
MANAGEMENT REWARD EMPHASIS	Ownership	Salary & merit increases	Individual bonus	Profit sharing & stock options	Team bonus

In one sense, I hope that many readers will react to my model by calling it obvious and natural for depicting the growth of an organization. To me this type of reaction is a useful test of the model's validity.

But at a more reflective level I imagine some of these reactions are more hindsight than foresight. Those experienced managers who have been through a developmental sequence can empathize with it now, but how did they react when in the middle of a stage of evolution or revolution? They can probably recall the limits of their own developmental understanding at that time. Perhaps they resisted desirable changes or were even swept emotionally into a revolution without being able to propose constructive solutions. So let me offer some explicit guidelines for managers of growing organizations to keep in mind.

Know Where You Are
in the Developmental Sequence

Every organization and its component parts are at different stages of development. The task of top management is to be aware of these stages; otherwise, it may not recognize when the time for change has come, or it may act to impose the wrong solution.

Top leaders should be ready to work with the flow of the tide rather than against it; yet they should be cautious, since it is tempting to skip phases out of impatience. Each phase results in certain strengths and learning experiences in the organization that will be essential for success in subsequent phases. A child prodigy, for example, may be able to read like a teenager, but he cannot behave like one until he ages through a sequence of experiences.

I also doubt that managers can or should act to avoid revolutions. Rather, these periods of tension provide the pressure, ideas, and awareness that afford a platform for change and the introdution of new practices.

Recognize the Limited Range of Solutions

In each revolutionary stage it becomes evident that this stage can be ended only by certain specific solutions; moreover, these solutions are different from those which were applied to the problems of the preceding revolution. Too often it is tempting to choose solutions that were tried before, which makes it impossible for a new phase of growth to evolve.

Management must be prepared to dismantle current structures before the revolutionary stage becomes too turbulent. Top managers, realizing that their own managerial styles are no longer appropriate, may even have to take themselves out of leadership positions. A good Phase 2 manager facing Phase 3 might be wise to find another Phase 2 organization that better fits his talents, either outside the company or with one of its newer subsidiaries.

Finally, evolution is not an automatic affair; it is a contest for survival. To move ahead, companies must consciously introduce planned structures that not only are solutions to a current crisis but also are fitted to the *next* phase of growth. This requires considerable self-awareness on the part of top management, as well as great interpersonal skill in persuading other managers that change is needed.

Realize That Solutions Breed New Problems

Managers often fail to realize that organizational solutions create problems for the future (i.e., a decision to delegate eventually causes a problem of control). Historical actions are very much determinants of what happens to the company at a much later date.

An awareness of this effect should help managers to evaluate company problems with greater historical understanding instead of "pinning the blame" on a current development. Better yet, managers should be in a position to *predict* future problems, and thereby to prepare solutions and coping strategies before a revolution gets out of hand.

A management that is aware of the problems ahead could well decide *not* to grow. Top managers may, for instance, prefer to retain the informal practices of a small company, knowing that this way of life is inherent in the organization's limited size, not in their congenial personalities. If they choose to grow, they may do themselves out of a job and a way of life they enjoy.

And what about the management of very large organizations? Can they find new solutions for continued phases of evolution? Or are they reaching a stage where the government will act to break them up because they are too large?

CONCLUDING NOTE

Clearly, there is still much to learn about processes of development in organizations. The phases outlined here are only five in number and are still only approximations. Researchers are just beginning to study the specific developmental problems of structure, control, rewards, and management style in different industries and in a variety of cultures.

One should not, however, wait for conclusive evidence before educating managers to think and act from a developmental perspective. The critical dimension of time has been missing for too long from our management theories and practices. The intriguing paradox is that by learning more about history we may do a better job in the future.

FOOTNOTES

1. See, for example, William H. Starbuck, "Organizational Metamorphosis," in *Promising Research Directions,* eds., R. W. Millman and M. P. Hottenstein (Tempe, Ariz., Academy of Management, 1968), p. 113.
2. See, for example, The *Grangesberg* case series, prepared by C. Roland Christensen and Bruce R. Scott, Case Clearing House, Harvard Business School.
3. *Strategy and Structure: Chapters in the History of the American Industrial Enterprise* (Cambridge, Mass., The M.I.T. Press, 1962).
4. I have drawn on many sources for evidence: (a) numerous cases collected at the Harvard Business School; (b) *Organization Growth and Development,* ed. William H. Starbuck (Middlesex, England, Penguin Books, Ltd., 1971), where several studies are cited: and (c) articles published in journals, such as Lawrence E. Fouraker and John M. Stopford, "Organization Structure and the Multinational Strategy," *Administrative Science Quarterly,* 1968, Vol. 13, No. 1, p. 47; and Malcolm S. Salter, "Management Appraisal and Reward Systems," *Journal of Business Policy,* 1971, Vol. 1, No. 4.

THE 4 COMPETENCIES OF LEADERSHIP

Warren Bennis

For nearly five years I have been researching a book on leadership. During this period, I have traveled around the country spending time with 90 of the most effective, successful leaders in the nation; 60 from corporations and 30 from the public sector.

My goal was to find these leaders' common traits, a task that has required

The material in this article is developed further in W. Bennis & B. Nanus. *Leaders,* NY: Harper & Row, 1985. Used with permission of the author.

much more probing than I expected. For a while I sensed much more diversity than commonality among them. The group comprises both left-brain and right-brain thinkers; some who dress for success and some who don't; well-spoken, articulate leaders and laconic, inarticulate ones; some John Wayne types and some who are definitely the opposite. Interestingly, the group includes only a few stereotypically charismatic leaders.

Despite the diversity, which is profound and must not be underestimated, I identified certain areas of competence shared by all 90. Before presenting those findings, though, it is important to place this study in context, to review the mood and events in the United States just before and during the research.

DECLINE AND MALAISE

When I left the University of Cincinnati late in 1977, our country was experiencing what President Carter called "despair" or "malaise." From 1960 to 1980, our institutions' credibility had eroded steadily. In an article about that period entitled, "Where Have All the Leaders Gone," I described how difficult the times were for leaders, including university presidents like myself.

I argued that, because of the complexity of the times, leaders felt impotent. The assassinations of several national leaders, the Vietnam war, the Watergate scandal, the Iranian hostage crisis and other events led to a loss of trust in our institutions and leaderships.

I came across a quotation in a letter Abigail Adams wrote to Thomas Jefferson in 1790: "These are the hard times in which a genius would wish to live." If, as she believed, great necessities summon great leaders, I wanted to get to know the leaders brought forth by the current malaise. In a time when bumper stickers appeared reading "Impeach Someone," I resolved to seek out leaders who were effective under these adverse conditions.

At the same time that America suffered from this leadership gap, it was suffering from a productivity gap. Consider these trends:

- In the 1960s, the average GNP growth was 4.1 percent; in the 1970s, it was 2.9 percent; in 1982, it was negative.
- The U.S. standard of living, the world's highest in 1972, now ranks fifth.
- In 1960, when the economies of Europe and Japan had been rebuilt, the U.S. accounted for 25 percent of the industrial nations' manufacturing exports and supplied 98 percent of its domestic markets. Now, the U.S. has less than a 20 percent share of the world market, and that share is declining.
- In 1960, U.S. automobiles had a 96 percent market share; today we have about 71 percent. The same holds true for consumer electronics; in 1960 it was 94.4 percent, in 1980 only 49 percent. And that was before Sony introduced the Walkman!

In addition to leadership and productivity gaps, a subtler "commitment gap" existed, that is, a reluctance to commit to one's work or employer.

The Public Agenda's recent survey of working Americans shows the following statistics. Less than one out of four jobholders (23 percent) says he or she currently works at full potential. Nearly half say they do not put much effort into their jobs above what is required. The overwhelming majority, 75 percent, say they could be significantly more effective on their job than they are now. And nearly 6 in 10 working Americans believe that "most people do not work as hard as they used to."

A number of observers have pointed out the considerable gap between the number of hours people are paid to work and the number of hours they spend on productive labor. Evidence developed recently by the University of Michigan indicates the gap may be widening. They found the difference between paid hours and actual working hours grew 10 percent between 1970 and 1980.

This increasing commitment gap leads to the central question: How can we empower the work force and reap the harvest of human effort?

If I have learned anything from my research, it is this: The factor that empowers the work force and ultimately determines which organizations succeed or fail is the leadership of those organizations. When strategies, processes or cultures change, the key to improvement remains leadership.

THE SAMPLE: 90 LEADERS

For my study, I wanted 90 effective leaders with proven track records. The final group contains 60 corporate executives, most, but not all, from Fortune 500 companies, and 30 from the public sector. My goal was to find people with leadership ability, in contrast to just "good managers"—true leaders who affect the culture, who are the social architects of their organiations and who create and maintain values.

Leaders are people who do the right thing; managers are people who do things right. Both roles are crucial, and they differ profoundly. I often observe people in top positions doing the wrong thing well.

Given my definition, one of the key problems facing American organizations and probably those in much of the industrialized world is that they are underled and overmanaged. They do not pay enough attention to doing the right thing, while they pay too much attention to doing things right. Part of the fault lies with our schools of management; we teach people how to be good technicians and good staff people, but we don't train people for leadership.

The group of 60 corporate leaders was not especially different from any profile of top leadership in America. The median age was 56. Most were white males, with six black men and six women in the group. The only surprising finding was that all the CEOs not only were married to their first spouse, but also seemed enthusiastic about the institution of marriage. Examples of the CEOS are Bill Weschnick, chairman and CEO of Arco, and the late Ray Kroc of McDonald's restaurants.

Public-sector leaders included Harold Armstrong, a genuine all-American hero who happened to be at the University of Cincinnati; three elected officials; two orchestra conductors; and two winning athletics coaches. I wanted conductors and coaches because I mistakenly believed they were the last leaders with complete control over their constituents.

After several years of observation and conversation, I have defined four competencies evident to some extent in every member of the group. They are:

- management of attention;
- management of meaning;
- management of trust;
- management of self.

MANAGEMENT OF ATTENTION

One of the traits most apparent in these leaders is their ability to draw others to them, because they have a vision, a dream, a set of intentions, an agenda, a time of reference. They communicate an extraordinary focus of commitment, which attracts people to them. One of these leaders was described as making people want to join in with him; he enrolls them in his vision.

Leaders, then, manage attention through a compelling vision that brings others to a place they have not been before. I came to this understanding in a roundabout way, as this anecdote illustrates.

One of the people I most wanted to interview was one of the few I couldn't seem to reach. He refused to answer my letters or phone calls. I even tried getting in touch with the members of the board. He is Leon Fleischer, a well-known child prodigy who grew up to become a prominent pianist, conductor and musicologist. What I did not know about him was that he had lost the use of his right hand and no longer performed.

When I called him originally to recruit him for the University of Cincinnati faculty, he declined and told me he was working with orthopedic specialists to regain the use of his hand. He did visit the campus, and I was impressed with his commitment to staying in Baltimore, near the medical institution where he received therapy.

Fleischer was the only person who kept turning me down for an interview, and finally I gave up. A couple of summers later I was in Aspen, Colorado while Fleischer was conducting the Aspen Music Festival. I tried to reach him again, even leaving a note on his dressing room door, but I got no answer.

One day in downtown Aspen, I saw two perspiring young cellists carrying their instruments and offered them a ride to the music tent. They hopped in the back of my jeep, and, as we rode, I questioned them about Fleischer.

"I'll tell you why he is so great," said one. "He doesn't waste our time."

Fleischer finally agreed not only to be interviewed but to let me watch him rehearse and conduct music classes. I linked the way I saw him work with that simple sentence, "He doesn't waste our time." Every moment Fleischer was before the orchestra, he knew exactly what sound he wanted. He didn't waste time because his intentions were always evident. What united him with the other musicians was their concern with intention and outcome.

When I reflected on my own experience, it struck me that when I was most effective, it was because I knew what I wanted. When I was ineffective, it was because I was unclear about it.

So, the first leadership competency is the management of attention through a set of intentions or a vision, not in a mystical or religious sense, but in the sense of outcome, goal or direction.

MANAGEMENT OF MEANING

To make dreams apparent to others, and to align people with them, leaders must communicate their vision. Communication and alignment work together.

Consider, for example, the contrasting styles of Presidents Reagan and Carter. Ronald Reagan is called "the great communicator"; one of his speech writers said Reagan can read the phone book and make it interesting. The reason is that Reagan uses metaphors with which people can identify.

In his first budget message, for example, Reagan described a trillion dollars by comparing it to piling up dollar bills beside the Empire State Building. Reagan, to use one of Alexander Haig's coinages, "tangibilitated" the idea. Leaders make ideas tangible and real to others, so they can support them. For no matter how marvelous the vision, the effective leader must use a metaphor, a word or a model to make that vision clear to others.

In contrast, President Carter was boring. Carter was one of our best informed presidents; he had more facts at his finger tips than almost any other president. But he never made the meaning come through the facts.

I interviewed an assistant secretary of commerce appointed by Carter, who told me that after four years in his administration, she still did not know what Jimmy Carter stood for. She said that working for him was like looking through the wrong side of a tapestry; the scene was blurry and indistinct.

The leader's goal is not mere explanation or clarification but the creation of meaning. My favorite baseball joke is exemplary: In the ninth inning of a key playoff game, with a 3 and 2 count on the batter, the umpire hesitates a split second in calling the pitch. The batter whirls around angrily and says, "Well, what was it?" The umpire barks back, "It ain't *nothing* until *I* call it!"

The more far-flung and complex the organization, the more critical is the ability. Effective leaders can communicate ideas through several organizational layers, across great distances, even through the jamming signals of special interest groups and opponents.

When I was a university president, a group of administrators and I would hatch what we knew was a great idea. Then we would do the right thing: delegate, delegate, delegate. But when the product or policy finally appeared, it scarcely resembled our original idea.

This process occurred so often that I gave it a name: The Pinocchio Effect. (I am sure Geppetto had no idea how Pinocchio would look when he finished carving him.) The Pinocchio Effect leaves us surprised. Because of inadequate communication, results rarely resemble our expectations.

We read and hear so much about information that we tend to overlook the importance of meaning. Actually, the more bombarded a society or organization, the more deluged with facts and images, the greater its thirst for meaning. Leaders integrate facts, concepts and anecdotes into meaning for the public.

Not all the leaders in my group are word masters. They get people to understand and support their goals in a variety of ways.

The ability to manage attention and meaning comes from the whole person. It is not enough to use the right buzz word or a cute technique, or to hire a public relations person to write speeches.

Consider, instead, Frank Dale, publisher of the Los Angeles afternoon newspaper, *The Herald Examiner*. Dale's charge was to cut into the market share of his morning competitor, *The L.A. Times*. When he first joined the newspaper a few years ago, he created a campaign with posters picturing the *Herald Examiner* behind and slightly above the *Times*. The whole campaign was based on this potent message of how the *Herald Examiner* would overtake the *Times*.

I interviewed Dale at his office, and when he sat down at his desk and fastened around him a safety belt like those on airplanes, I couldn't supress a smile. He did this to remind me and everybody else of the risks the newspaper entailed. His whole person contributed to the message.

No one is more cynical than a newspaper reporter. You can imagine the reactions that traveled the halls of the *Herald Examiner* building. At the same time, nobody forgot what Frank Dale was trying to communicate. And that is the management of meaning.

MANAGEMENT OF TRUST

Trust is essential to all organizations. The main determinant of trust is reliability, what I call constancy. When I talked to the board members or staffs of these leaders, I heard certain phrases again and again: "She is all of a piece." "Whether you like it or not, you always know where he is coming from, what he stands for."

When John Paul II visited this country, he gave a press conference. One reporter asked how the Pope could account for allocating funds to build a swimming pool at the papal summer palace. He responded quickly: "I like to swim. Next question." He did not rationalize about medical reasons or claim he got the money from a special source.

A recent study showed people would much rather follow individuals they can count on, even when they disagree with their viewpoint, than people they agree with but who shift positions frequently. I cannot emphasize enough the significance of constancy and focus.

Margaret Thatcher's reelection in Great Britain is another excellent example. When she won office in 1979, observers predicted she quickly would revert to defunct Labor Party policies. She did not. In fact, not long ago a *London Times* article appeared headlined (parodying Christopher Fry's play) "The Lady's Not for Returning." She has not turned; she has been constant, focused and all of the piece.

MANAGEMENT OF SELF

The fourth leadership competency is management of self, knowing one's skills and deploying them effectively. Management of self is critical; without it, leaders and managers can do more harm than good. Like incompetent doctors, incompetent managers can make life worse, make people sicker and less vital. (The term *iatrogenic,* by the way, refers to illness *caused* by doctors and hospitals.) Some managers give themselves heart attacks and nervous breakdowns; still worse, many are "carriers," causing their employees to be ill.

Leaders know themselves; they know their strengths and nurture them. They also have a faculty I think of as the Wallenda Factor.

The Flying Wallendas are perhaps the world's greatest family of aerialists and tightrope walkers. I was fascinated when, in the early 1970s, 71-year old Karl Wallenda said that for him living is walking a tightrope, and everything else is waiting. I was struck with his capacity for concentration on the intention, the task, the decision.

I was even more intrigued when, several months later, Wallenda fell to his death while walking a tightrope between two high-rise buildings in San Jaun. With a safety net, Wallenda fell, still clutching the balancing pole he warned his family never to drop lest it hurt somebody below.

Later, Wallenda's wife said that before her husband fell, for the first time since she had known him he was concentrating on falling, instead of on walking the tightrope. He personally supervised the attachment of the guide wires, which he never had done before.

Like Wallenda before his fall, the leaders in my group seemed unacquainted with the concept of failure. What you or I might call a failure, they referred to as a mistake. I began collecting synonyms for the word failure mentioned in the interviews, and I found more than 20: mistake, error, false start, bloop, flop, loss, miss, foul-up, stumble, botch, bungle. . .but not failure.

One CEO told me that if she had a knack for leadership, it was the capacity to make as many mistakes as she could as soon as possible, and thus get them out of the way. Another said that a mistake is simply "another way of doing things." These leaders learn from and use something that doesn't go well: it is not a failure but simply the next step.

When I asked Harold Williams, president of the Getty Foundation, to name the experience that most shaped him as a leader, he said it was being passed over for the presidency of Norton Simon. When it happened, he was furious and demanded reasons, most of which he considered idiotic. Finally, a friend told him that some of the reasons were valid and he should change. He did, and about a year and a half later became president.

Or consider coach Ray Meyer of DePaul University, whose team finally lost at home after winning 29 straight home games. I called him to ask how he felt. He said, "Great. Now we can start to concentrate on winning, not on *not* losing."

Consider Broadway producer Harold Prince, who calls a press conference the morning after his show opens, before reading the reviews, to announce his next play. Or Susan B. Anthony, who said, "Failure is impossible." Or Fletcher

Byrum, who, after 22 years as president of Coopers, was asked about his hardest decision. He replied that he did not know what a hard decision was; that he never worried, that he accepted the possibility of being wrong. Byrum said that worry was an obstacle to clear thinking.

The Wallenda Factor is an approach to life; it goes beyond leadership and power in organizations. These leaders all have it.

EMPOWERMENT: THE EFFECTS
OF LEADERSHIP

Leadership can be felt throughout an organization. It gives pace and energy to the work and empowers the work force. Empowerment is the collective effect of leadership. In organizations with effective leaders, empowerment is most evident in four themes:

- *People feel significant.* Everyone feels that he or she makes a difference to the success of the organization. The difference may be small—prompt delivery of potato chips to a mom-and-pop grocery store or developing a tiny but essential part for an airplane. But where they are empowered, people feel that what they do has meaning and significance.
- *Learning and competence matter.* Leaders value learning and mastery, and so do people who work for leaders. Leaders make it clear that there is no failure, only mistakes that give us feedback and tell us what to do next.
- *People are part of a community.* Where there is leadership, there is a team, a family, a unity. Even people who do not especially like each other feel the sense of community. When Neil Armstrong talks about the Apollo explorations, he describes how a team carried out an almost unimaginably complex set of interdependent tasks. Until there were women astronauts, the men referred to this feeling as "brotherhood." I suggest they rename it "family."
- *Work is exciting.* Where there are leaders, work is stimulating, challenging, fascinating and fun. An essential ingredient in organizational leadership is pulling rather than pushing people toward a goal. A "pull" style of influence attracts and energizes people to enroll in an exciting vision of the future. It motivates through identification, rather than through rewards and punishments. Leaders articulate and embody the ideals toward which the organization strives.

People cannot be expected to enroll in just any exciting vision. Some visions and concepts have more staying power and are rooted more deeply in our human needs than others. I believe the lack of two such concepts in modern organizational life is largely responsible for the alienation and lack of meaning so many experience in their work.

One of these is the concept of quality. Modern industrial society has been oriented to quantity, providing more goods and services for everyone. Quantity is measured in money; we are a money-oriented society. Quality often is not measured at all, but is appreciated intuitively. Our response to quality is a feeling. Feelings of quality are connected intimately with our experience of meaning, beauty and value in our lives.

Closely linked to the concept of quality is that of dedication, even love, of our work. This dedication is evoked by quality and is the force that energizes high-performing systems. When we love our work, we need not be managed by hopes of reward or fears of punishment. We can create systems that facilitate our work, rather than being preoccupied with checks and controls of people who want to beat or exploit the system.

And that is what the human resources profession should care most about.

13
Leadership and Decision Making

LEADERSHIP REVISITED
Victor H. Vroom

THE SCIENCE OF MUDDLING THROUGH
C. E. Lindblom

LEADERSHIP REVISITED

Victor H. Vroom

RESEARCH ON LEADERSHIP TRAITS

Early research on the question of leadership had roots in the psychology of individual differences and in the personality theory of that time. The prevailing theory held that differences among people could be understood in terms of their traits—consistencies in behavior exhibited over situations. Each person could be usefully described on such dimensions as honesty-dishonesty, introversion-extroversion or masculine-feminine. In extrapolating this kind of theory to the study of leadership, it seemed natural to assume that there was such a thing as a trait of leadership, i.e., it was something that people possessed in different amounts. If such differences existed, they must be measurable in some way. As a consequence, psychologists set out, armed with a wide variety of psychological tests, to measure differences between leaders and followers. A large number of studies were conducted including comparisons of bishops with clergymen, sales

Source: E. L. Case and F. G. Zimmer (eds.) *Man and Work in Society.* New York: Van Nostrand Reinhold Company, 1975, pps. 221–233. Reprinted by permission.

managers with salesmen and railway presidents with station agents. Since occupancy of a leadership position may not be a valid reflection of the degree of leadership, other investigators pursued a different tack by looking at the relationship between personal traits of leaders and criteria for their effectiveness in carrying out their positions.

If this search for the measurable components of this universal trait of leadership had been effective, the implications for society would have been considerable. The resulting technology would have been of countless value in selecting leaders in all of our social institutions and would have eliminated errors inevitably found on the subjective assessments which typically guide this process. But the search was largely unsuccessful and the dream of its byproduct—a general technology of broader selection—was unrealized. The results, which have been summarized elsewhere (Bass, 1960; Gibb, 1969; Stogdill, 1948), cast considerable doubt on the usefulness of the concept of leadership as a personality trait. They do not imply that individual differences have nothing to do with leadership, but rather that their significance must be evaluated in relation to the situation.

Written more than 25 years ago, Stogdill's conclusions seem equally applicable today.

> The pattern of personal characteristics of the leader must bear some relevant relationship to the characteristics, activities and goals of the followers...It becomes clear that an adequate analysis of leadership involves not only a study of leaders, but also of situations. (1948, pp. 64–65)

The study of leadership based on personality traits had been launched on an oversimplified premise. But as Stogdill's conclusions were being written, social scientists at Ohio State University and at the University of Michigan were preparing to launch another and quite different attack on the problem of leadership. In these ventures, the focus was not on personal traits but on leader behavior and leadership style. Effective and ineffective leaders may not be distinguishable by a battery of psychological tests but may be distinguished by their characteristic behavior patterns in their work roles.

RESEARCH ON EFFECTIVE
LEADERSHIP METHODS

The focus on behavior of the leader rather than his personal traits was consistent with Lewin's classic dictum that behavior is a function of both person and environment (Lewin, 1951) and of growing recognition that the concept of trait provided little room for environmental or situational influences on behavior. Such a focus also envisioned a greater degree of consistency in behavior across situations than has been empirically demonstrated (Hartshorne and May, 1928; Mischel, 1968; Vroom and Yetton, 1973).

If particular patterns of behavior or leadership styles were found which consistently distinguished leaders of effective and ineffective work groups, the payoff to organizations and to society would have been considerable, but of a different nature than work based on the trait approach. Such results would have less obvious implications for leader selection but would have significant import for leader development and training. Knowledge of the behavior patterns which characterize effective leaders would provide a rational basis for the design of educational programs in an attempt to instill these patterns in actual or potential leaders.

Space does not permit a detailed account of the Ohio State and Michigan research or of its offshoots in other institutions. It is fair to say, however, that the success of this line of inquiry in developing empirically based generalization about effective leadership styles is a matter of some controversy. There are some who see in the results a consistent pattern sufficient to constitute the basis of technologies or organization design or leader development. Likert (1967), reviewing the program of research at Michigan, finds support for what he calls System 4, a participative group-based conception of management. Similarly, Blake and Mouton (1964), with their conceptual roots in the Ohio State research program, argue that the effective leader exhibits concern for both production and employees (their 9–9 style) and have constructed a viable technology of management and organization development based on that premise.

On the other hand, other social scientists including the present writer (Korman, 1966; Sales, 1966; Vroom, 1964) have reviewed the evidence resulting from these studies and commented lamentably on the variability in results and the difficulty in making from them any definitive statements about effective leadership behavior without knowledge of the situation in which the behavior has been exhibited.

At first glance, these would appear to be two directly opposing interpretations of the same results, but that would probably be too strong a conclusion. The advocates of general leadership principles have stated these principles in such a way that they are difficult to refute by empirical evidence and at the same time provide considerable latitude for individual interpretation. To say that a leader should manage in such a way that personnel at all levels feel real responsibility for the attainment of the organization's goal (Likert, 1967) or alternatively that he should exhibit concern for both production and his employees (Blake and Mouton, 1964) are at best general blueprints for action rather than specific blueprints indicating how these objectives should be achieved. The need for adapting these principles to the demands of the situation is recognized by most social scientists. For example, Likert writes:

> Supervision is. . . always a relative process. To be effective and to communicate as intended, a leader must always adapt his behavior to take into account the expectations, values, and interpersonal skills of those with whom he is interacting. . . . There can be no specific rules of supervision which will work well in all situations. Broad principles can be applied in the process of supervision and furnish valuable guides to behavior. These principles, however, must be applied always in a manner that takes fully into account the characteristics of the specific situation and of the people involved. (1961, p. 95)

To this writer, the search for effective methods of supervision management and leadership has come close to foundering on the same rocks as the trait approach.

It too has failed to deal explicitly with differences in situational requirements for leadership. If the behavioral sciences are to make a truly viable contribution to the management of the contemporary organization, they must progress beyond an advocacy of power equalization with appropriate caveats about the need for consideration of situational differences and attempt to come to grips with the complexities of the leadership process.

INVESTIGATION ON LEADERSHIP STYLES

These convictions, whether right or wrong, provided the basis for a new approach to the investigation of leadership style—its determinants and consequences— launched about six years ago by the author and Phillip Yetton, then a graduate student at Carnegie Mellon University. We set ourselves two goals: (1) to formulate a normative or prescriptive model of leader behavior which incorporated situational characteristics in an explicit manner and which was consistent with existing empirical evidence concerning the consequences of alternative approaches; and (2) to launch an empirical attack on the determinants of leader behavior which would reveal the factors both within the person and in the situation which influence leaders to behave in various ways.

In retrospect, these goals were ambitious ones and the reader will have to judge for himself the extent to which either has been achieved. We attempted to make the task more manageable by focusing on one dimension of leader behavior— the degree to which the leader encourages the participation of his subordinates in decision-making. This dimension was chosen both because it was at the core of most prescriptive approaches to leadership and because a substantial amount of research had been conducted on it.

The first step was to review that evidence in detail. No attempt will be made here to repeat that review. (The reader interested in this question may consult Lowin, 1968; Vroom, 1964; or Wood, 1974.) Instead, we will restrict our attention to a summary of the major conclusions which appeared justifiable by the evidence.

1. Involvement of subordinates in "group decision-making" is costly in terms of time. Autocratic decision-making processes are typically faster (and thus of potential value in emergency or crisis situations) and invariabley require less investment in man-hours of the group in the process of decision-making than methods which provide greater opportunities for participation by subordinates, particularly those decision processes which require consensus by the group.

2. Participation by subordinates in decision-making creates greater acceptance of decisions which in turn is reflected in better implementation. There is a wide range of circumstances under which "people support what they helped to build." Increasing the opportunity for subordinates to have a significant voice in decisions which affect them results in greater acceptance and commitment to the decisions, which will in turn be reflected in more effective and reliable implementation of the decision.

3. The effects of increased participation by subordinates in decision making on the quality or rationality of decisions tend to be positive, although the effects

408

are likely to depend on several identifiable factors. Extensive research has been conducted on group and individual problem solving. Group decisions tend to be higher in quality when the relevant information is widely distributed among group members, when the problem is unstructured, and when there exists a mutual interest or common goal among group members.

4. Involvement of subordinates in decision making leads to growth and development of subordinates. This consequence of participation has been least researched and its assertion here is based primarily on theoretical rather than empirical grounds. It is different from the three previous factors (time, acceptance, and quality of decision) in its long-term nature.

From this general research foundation a normative model was constructed. The model utilized five decision processes which vary in the amount of opportunity afforded subordinates to participate in decision making. These processes are shown in Table 1.

TABLE 1 Types of Management Decision Styles

AI	You solve the problem or make the decision yourself using information available to you at that time.
AII	You obtain necessary information from subordinate(s) and then decide on a solution to the problem yourself. You may or may not tell subordinates what the problem is in getting the information from them. The role played by your subordinates in making the decision is clearly one of providing the necessary information to you, rather than generating or evaluating alternative solutions.
CI	You share the problem with relevant subordinates individually, getting their ideas and suggestions without bringing them together as a group. Then you make the decision which may or may not reflect your subordinates' influence.
CII	You share the problem with your subordinates as a group, collectively obtaining their ideas and suggestions. Then, *you* make the decision which may or may not reflect your subordinates' influence.
GII	You share the problems with your subordinates as a group. Together you generate and evaluate alternatives and attempt to reach agreement (consensuss) on a solution. Your role is much like that of chairman. You do not try to influence the group to adopt "your" solution and are willing to accept and implement any solution which has the support of the entire group.

The model to be described is a contingency model. It rests on the assumption that no one decision-making process is best under all circumstances, and that its effectiveness is dependent upon identifiable properties of the situation. However, it is different from other contingency models in the fact that the situational characteristics are attributes of the particular problem or decision rather than more general role characteristics. To distinguish this type of situational variable from others we have designated them as problem attributes. These attributers are the building blocks of the model and represent the means of diagnosing the nature of the problem or decision at hand so as to determine the optimal decision process.

The most recent form of the model is shown in Figure 1. It is expressed here in the form of a decision tree. The problem attributes are arranged along the top and are shown here in the form of yes-no questions. To use the model to deter-

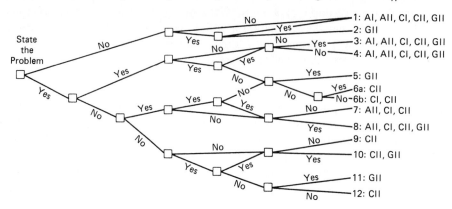

A B C D E F G H

State the Problem

1: AI, AII, CI, CII, GII
2: GII
3: AI, AII, CI, CII, GII
4: AI, AII, CI, CII, GII
5: GII
6a: CII
6b: CI, CII
7: AII, CI, CII
8: AII, CI, CII, GII
9: CII
10: CII, GII
11: GII
12: CII

A. Is there a quality requirement such that one solution is likely to be more rational than another?
B. Do I have sufficient info to make a high quality decision?
C. Is the problem structured?
D. Is acceptance of decision by subordinates critical to effective implementation?
E. If I were to make the decision by myself, is it reasonably certain that it would be accepted by my subordinates?
F. Do subordinates share the organizational goals to be attained in solving this problem?
G. Is conflict among subordinates likely in preferred solutions? (This question is irrelevant to individual problems.)
H. Do subordinates have sufficient info to make a high quality decision?

FIGURE 1 Decision-Process Flow Chart for Group Problems

mine the decision process, one starts at the left-hand side of the diagram and asks the question pertaining to attribute *A*. The answer (yes or no) will determine the path taken. When a second box is encountered, the question pertaining to that attribute is asked and the process continued until a terminal node is reached. At that node one will find a number (indicating problem type) and a feasible set of decision processes.

For some problem types only one decision process is shown; for others there are two, three, four or even all five processes. The particular decision processes shown are those that remain after a set of seven rules has been applied. The roles function to protect both the quality and the acceptance by eliminating methods that have a substantial likelihood of jeopardizing either of these two components of an effective decision. The interested reader should consult Vroom and Yetton (1973) for a detailed statement in both verbal and mathematical form, of these rules.

If more than one alternative remains in the feasible set, there are a number of bases for choosing among them. One of them is time, the methods are arranged in ascending order of the time in man-hours which they require. Accordingly, a time minimizing model (which we have termed Model A) would select that alternative that is farthest to the left within the feasible set. An alternative to minimizing time is maximizing development of subordinates. This model (which we have termed Model B) would select that decision process which is farthest to the right within the feasible set.

While we have attempted to phrase the questions pertaining to the problem attributes in as meaningful a fashion as possible, the reader should keep in mind that they are really surrogates for more detailed specifications of the underlying variables. The reader interested in more information on the meaning of the attributes, the threshold for yes-no judgments or their rationale for inclusion in the model should consult Vroom and Yetton (1973). Illustrations of the models' application to concrete cases can be found in Vroom (1973); Vroom and Yetton (1973); and Vroom and Jago (1974).

The model shown in Figure 1 is intended to apply to a domain of managerial decision-making which Maier, Solem, and Maier (1957) refer to as group problems, i.e., problems which have potential effects on all or a substantial subset of the manager's subordinates. Recently, we have become interested in extending the model to "individual problems," i.e., those affecting only one subordinate. For these decisions, the first three decision processes shown in Table 1 represent potentially reasonable alternatives, but there are at least two other variable alternatives not yet represented. One of these we have called GI, which is a form of group decision involving only a single subordinate. (A GI manager shares the problem with the subordinate and together they analyze the problem and arrive at a mutually satisfactory solution.) The other, which we have designated as DI, consists of delegating the problem or decision to the subordinate.

Many of the considerations used in building the model for group problems—such as problem attributes and rules—could easily be adapted to the domain of individual problems. There remained, however, one major structural difference. For group problems, there was a tradeoff between the short-run consideration of time efficiency (which favored autocratic methods) and longer-range considerations involving subordinate development (which favored participative methods). The reader will recall that Model A and Model B represented two extreme modes of resolution of that tradeoff. For individual problems, the differences in time requirements of the five processes (AI, AII, CI, GI, DI) are not nearly as large and the alternative which provides the greatest amount of subordinate influence or participation, DI, can hardly be argued to be least time efficient. This difference in the correlation between time efficiency and participation for individual and group problems required an adjustment in the location of DI in the ordering of alternatives in terms of time. Model A and Model B retain their original meaning from the earlier model, but they are no longer polar opposites.

Figure 2 contains a model also expressed as a decision tree which purports to guide choices among decision processes for both individual and group problems. The only difference lies in the specifications of two feasible sets (one for group and one for individual problems) for each problem type.

Is the model in its present form an adequate guide to practice? Would managers make fewer errors in their choices of decision processes if they were to base them on the model? We would be less than honest if we said we knew the answers to such questions. Most managers who have had sufficient training in the use of the model to be able to use it reliably report that it is a highly useful guide, although there are occasionally considerations not presently contained in the model—such as geographical dispersion of subordinates—which prevent implementation of its recommendations. Some research has been conducted in an attempt

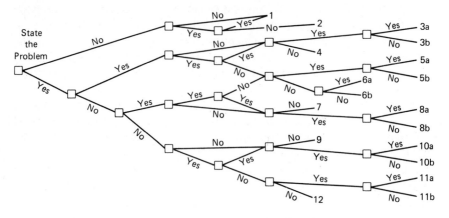

The feasible set is shown for each problem type for Group (G) and Individual (I) problems.

$1\begin{vmatrix}\text{G: AI, AII, CI, CII, GII}\\ \text{I: AI, DI, AII, CI, GI}\end{vmatrix}$ $5a\begin{vmatrix}\text{G: GII}\\ \text{I: DI, GI}\end{vmatrix}$ $8a\begin{vmatrix}\text{G: AII, CI, CII, GII}\\ \text{I: DI, AII, CI, GI}\end{vmatrix}$ $11a\begin{vmatrix}\text{G: GII}\\ \text{I: DI, GI}\end{vmatrix}$

$2\begin{vmatrix}\text{G: GII}\\ \text{I: DI, GI}\end{vmatrix}$ $5b\begin{vmatrix}\text{G: GII}\\ \text{I: DI, GI}\end{vmatrix}$ $8b\begin{vmatrix}\text{G: AII, CI, CII, GII}\\ \text{I: AII, CI, GI}\end{vmatrix}$ $11b\begin{vmatrix}\text{G: GII}\\ \text{I: GI}\end{vmatrix}$

$3a\begin{vmatrix}\text{G: AI, AII, CI, CII, GII}\\ \text{I: AI, DI, AII, CI, GI}\end{vmatrix}$ $6a\begin{vmatrix}\text{G: CII}\\ \text{I: CI, GI}\end{vmatrix}$ $9\begin{vmatrix}\text{G: CII}\\ \text{I: CI}\end{vmatrix}$ $12\begin{vmatrix}\text{G: CII}\\ \text{I: CI, GI}\end{vmatrix}$

$3b\begin{vmatrix}\text{G: AI, AII, CI, CII, GII}\\ \text{I: AI, AII, CI, GI}\end{vmatrix}$ $6b\begin{vmatrix}\text{G: CI, CII}\\ \text{I: CI, GI}\end{vmatrix}$ $10a\begin{vmatrix}\text{G: CII, GII}\\ \text{I: DI, CI, GI}\end{vmatrix}$

$4\begin{vmatrix}\text{G: AI, AII, CI, CII}\\ \text{I: AI, AII, CI}\end{vmatrix}$ $7\begin{vmatrix}\text{G: AII, CI, CII}\\ \text{I: CI, GI}\end{vmatrix}$ $10b\begin{vmatrix}\text{G: CII, GII}\\ \text{I: CI, GI}\end{vmatrix}$

A. Is there a quality requirement such that one solution is likely to be more rational than another?
B. Do I have sufficient info to make a high quality decision?
C. Is the problem structured?
D. Is acceptance of decision by subordinates critical to effective implementation?
E. If I were to make the decision by myself, is it reasonably certain that it would be accepted by my subordinates?
F. Do subordinates share the organizational goals to be attained in solving this problem?
G. Is conflict among subordinates likely in preferred solutions? (This question is irrelevant to individual problems.)
H. Do subordinates have sufficient info to make a high quality decision?

FIGURE 2   Decision-Process Flow Chart for Both Individual and Group Problems

to establish the validity of the model (see Vroom and Yetton, 1973: 182–84), but the results, while promising, are not conclusive. Perhaps the most convincing argument for the development of models of this kind is that they can serve as a guide for research that can identify their weaknesses and that superior models can later be developed.

The reader will note that flexibility in leader behavior is one of the requirements of use of the model. To use it effectively, the leader must adapt his approach to the situation. But how flexible are leaders in the approaches they use? Do they naturally try and vary their approach with the situation? Is it possible to develop such flexibility through training? These questions were but a few of those which guided the next phase of our inquiry into how leaders do in fact behave and into the factors both within the leader himself and in the situations with which he deals which cause him to share decision-making power with his subordinates.

Two different research methods have been used in an attempt to answer questions such as these. The first investigation utilized a method that can be referred to as "recalled problems." Over 500 managers from 11 different countries representing a variety of firms were asked to provide a written description of a problem that they had recently had to solve. These varied in length from one paragraph to several pages and covered virtually every facet of managerial decision making. For each case, the manager was asked to indicate which of the decision processes shown in Table 1 he used to solve the problem. Finally, each manager was asked to answer the questions corresponding to the problem attributes used in the normative model with his own case in mind.

These data made it possible to determine the frequency with which the managers' decision process was similar to that of the normative model and the factors in their description of the situation which were associated with the use of each decision process. This investigation provided results which were interesting but also led to the development of a second more powerful method for investigating the same questions. This method, which will be termed "standardized problems," used some of the actual cases, each of which depicts a manager faced with a problem to solve or decision to make. In each case, a leader would be asked to assume the role of the manager faced with the situation described and to indicate which decision process he would use if faced with that situation.

Several such sets of cases have been developed. In early research, each set consisted of thirty cases, but more recently longer sets of forty-eight and fifty-four cases have been used. Composition of each set of standardized cases was in accordance with multifactorial experimental design. Cases varied in terms of each of the eight problem attributes used in the normative model, and variation in each attribute was independent of each other attribute. This feature permits the assessment of the effects of each of the problem attributes on the decision processes used by a given manager.

The cases themselves spanned a wide range of managerial problems including production scheduling, quality control, portfolio management, personnel allocation, and research and development project selection. To date, several thousand managers in the United States and abroad have been studied using this approach.

RESULTS AND CONCLUSIONS

To summarize everything learned in the course of this research is well beyond the scope of this reading, but it is possible to discuss some of the highlights. Since the results obtained from the two research methods—recalled and standardized problems—are consistent, the major results can be presented independent of the method used.

Perhaps the most striking finding is the weakening of the widespread view that participativeness is a general trait that individual managers exhibit in different amounts. To be sure, there were differences among managers in their general tendencies to utilize participative methods as opposed to autocratic ones. On the standardized problems, these differences accounted for about 10 percent of the total variance in the decision processes observed. Furthermore, those managers who tended to use more participative methods such as CII and GII with group problems also tended to use more participative methods like delegation for dealing with individual problems.

However, these differences in behavior between managers were small in comparison with differences within managers. On the standardized problems, no manager has indicated that he would use the same decision process on all problems or decisions, and most use all methods under some circumstances. Taking managers' reports of their behavior in concrete situations, it is clear that they are striving to be flexible in their approaches to different situations.

Some of this variance in behavior within managers can be attributed to widely shared tendencies to respond to some situations by sharing power and others by retaining it. It makes more sense to talk about participative and autocratic situations than it does to talk about participative and autocratic managers. In fact, on the standardized problems, the variance in behavior across problems or cases is from three to five times as large as the variance across managers.

What are the characteristics of an autocratic as opposed to a participative situation? An answer to this question would constitute a partial descriptive model of this aspect of the decision-making process and has been the goal of much of the research conducted. From observations of behavior on both recalled problems and on standardized problems, it is clear that the decision-making process employed by a typical manager is influenced by a large number of factors, many of which also show up in the normative model. Following are several conclusions substantiated by the results on both recalled and standardized problems.

Managers use decision processes providing less opportunity for participation (1) when they possess all the necessary information rather when they lack some of the needed information; (2) when the problem they face is well-structured rather than unstructured; (3) when their subordinates' acceptance of the decision is not critical for the effective implementation of the decision or when the prior probability of acceptance of an autocratic decision is high; and (4) when the personal goals of their subordinates are not congruent with the goals of the organization as manifested in the problem.

These findings concern relatively common or widely shared ways of dealing with organizational problems. The results also strongly suggest that managers have ways of "tailoring" their decision process to the situation that distinguish one manager from another. Theoretically, these can be thought of as differences among managers in decision rules that they employ about when to encourage participation.

Consider, for example, two managers who have identical distributions of the use of the five decision processes shown in Table 1 on a set of thirty cases. In a sense, they are equally participative (or autocratic). However, the situation in which they permit or encourage participation in decision making on the part of their subordinates may be very different. One may restrict the participation of his subordinates to decisions without a quality requirement, whereas the other may restrict their participation to problems with a quality requirement. The former would be more inclined to use participative decision processes (like GI) on such decisions as what color the walls should be painted or when the company picnic should be held. The latter would be more likely to encourage participation in decision making on decisions that have a clear and demonstrable impact on the organization's success in achieving its external goals.

Use of the standardized problem set permits the assessment of such differences in decision rules that govern choices among decision-making processes. Since the cases are selected in accordance with an experimental design, they can indicate differences in the behavior of managers attributable not only to the existence of a quality requirement in the problem but also in the effects of acceptance requirements, conflict, information requirements, and the like.

The research using both recalled and standardized problems has also permitted the examination of similarities and differences between the behavior of the normative model and the behavior of a typical manager. Such an analysis reveals, at the very least, what behavioral changes could be expected if managers began using the normative model as the basis for choosing their decision-making processes.

A typical manager says he would (or did) use exactly the same decision process as that shown in Figure 1 in about 40 percent of the group problems. In two-thirds of the situations, his behavior is consistent with the feasible set of methods proposed in the model. However, in the remaining one-third of the situations, his behavior violates at least one of the seven rules underlying the model. Results show significantly higher agreement with the normative model for individual problems than for group problems.

The rules designed to protect the acceptance or commitment of the decision have substantially higher probabilities of being violated than do the rules designed to protect the quality or rationality of the decision. Assuming for the moment that these two sets of rules have equal validity, these findings strongly suggest that the decisions made by typical managers are more likely to prove ineffective due to deficiencies of acceptance by subordinates than due to deficiencies in decision quality.

Another striking difference between the behavior of the model and of the typical manager lies in the fact that the former shows far greater variance with the situation. If a typical manager voluntarily used the model as the basis for choosing his methods of making decisions, he would become both more autocratic and more participative. He would employ autocratic methods more frequently in situations in which his subordinates were unaffected by the decision and participative methods more frequently when his subordinates' cooperation and support were critical and/or their information and expertise were required.

It should be noted that the typical manager to whom we have been referring is merely a statistical average of the several thousand who have been studied over the last three or four years. There is a great deal of variation around that average. As evidenced by their behavior on standardized problems, some managers are already behaving in a manner that is highly consistent with the model, while others behavior is clearly at variance with it.

The research program that has been summarized was conducted in order to shed new light on the causes and consequences of decision-making processes used by leaders in formal organizations. In the course of research, it was realized that the data collection procedures, with appropriate additions and modifications, might also serve a useful function in leadership development. From this realization evolved an important byproduct of the research activities—a new approach to leadership training based on the concepts in the normative model and the empirical methods of the descriptive research.

A detailed description of this training program and of initial attempts to evaluate its effectiveness may be found in Vroom and Yetton (1973, chap. 8). It is based on the premise that one of the critical skills required of all leaders is the ability to adapt their behavior to the demands of the situation and that a component of this skill involves selecting the appropriate decision-making process for each problem or decision they confront. The purpose of the program is not to "train" managers to use the model in their everyday decision-making activities. Instead the model serves as a device for encouraging managers to examine their leadership styles and for coming to a conscious realization of their own, often implicit, choices among decision processes, including their similarity and dissimilarity with the model. By helping managers to become aware of their present behavior and of alternatives to it, the training provides a basis for rethinking their leadership style to be more consistent with goals and objectives. Succinctly, the training is intended to transform habits into choices rather than to program a leader with a particular method of making choices.

A fundamental part of the program in its present form is the use of a set of standardized cases previously described in connection with the descriptive phase of the research. Each participant specifies the decision process he would employ if he were the leader described in the case. His responses to the entire set of cases are processed by computer, which generates a highly detailed analysis of his leadership style. The responses for all participants in a single course are typically processed simultaneously, permitting the calculation of differences between the person and others in the same program.

In its latest form, a single computer printout for a person consists of seven 15″ by 11″ pages, each filled with graphs and tables highlighting different features of his behavior. Understanding the results requires a detailed knowledge of the concepts underlying the model, something already developed in one of the previous phases of the training program. The printout is accompanied by a manual that aids in explaining the results and provides suggested steps to be followed in extracting the full meaning from the printout.

Following are a few of the questions that the printout answers:

1. How autocratic or participative am I in my dealings with subordinates in the program?
2. What decision processes do I use more or less frequently than the average?
3. How close does my behavior come to that of the model? How frequently does my behavior agree with the feasible set? What evidence is there that my leadership style reflects the pressure of time as opposed to a concern with the development of my subordinates? How do I compare in these respects with other participants in the program?
4. What rules do I violate most frequently and least frequently? On what cases did I violate these rules? Does my leadership style reflect more concern with getting decisions that are high in quality or with getting decisions that are accepted?

When a typical manager receives his printout, he immediately goes to work trying to understand what it tells him about himself. After most of the major results have been understood, he goes back to the set of cases to reread those on which he has violated rules. Typically, managers show an interest in discussing and comparing their results with others in the program. Gatherings of four to six people comparing their results and their interpretations of them, often for several hours at a stretch, were such a common feature that they have recently been institutionalized as part of the procedure.

It should be emphasized that this method of providing feedback on their leadership style is just one part of the total training experience which encompasses over thirty hours over a period of three successive days. To date, no long-term evaluations of its effectiveness has been undertaken, but initial results appear quite promising.

SUMMARY

How far has the understanding of leadership progressed in the 50 years since the Hawthorne Studies? The picture that has been painted in this reading is one of false starts stemming from oversimplified conceptions of the process. An encouraging sign, however, is the increased interest in contingency theories or models incorporating both leader and situational variables. In this reading I have spent much time describing one kind of contingency model; Professor Fiedler, who accompanies me on this panel, has developed another form of contingency model.

These two models share a number of qualities, but are different in several important aspects. I believe that Professor Fiedler sees much greater consistency and less flexibility in leader behavior than is required by the normative model or exhibited in managers' statements of how they would behave on the problem set. I suspect that we also have substantially different views on the potential for modification of leadership style through training and development.

Both of these are fascinating and important questions, and I for one would enjoy exploring them during our later discussion. But there is one prediction about which I feel quite confident. Fifty years from now, both contingency models will be found wanting in detail if not in substance. If either Professor Fiedler or I am remembered at that time, it will be for the same reason that we meet to commemorate the Hawthorne Studies this week—the kinds of questions we posed rather than the specific answers we provided.

REFERENCES

Bass, B. M. *Leadership, Psychology and Organizational Behavior.* New York: Harper, 1960.

Blake, R., and Mouton, J. *The Managerial Grid,* Houston: Gulf, 1964.

Gibb, C. A. "Leadership," in *Handbook of Social Psychology,* edited by G. Lindzey and E. Aronson, vol. 4. Reading, Mass.: Addison-Wesley, 1969.

Hartshone, H., and May, M. A. *Studies in Deceit.* New York: Macmillan, 1928.

Korman, A. K. " 'Consideration,' 'Initiating Structure,' and Organizational Criteria— A Review," *Personnel Psychology* 19 (1966).

Lewin, K. *Field Theory in Social Science,* edited by D. Cartwright. New York: Harper, 1941.

Likert, R. *New Patterns of Management.* New York: McGraw-Hill, 1961.

Likert, R. *The Human Organization.* New York: McGraw-Hill, 1967.

Lowin, A. "Participative Decision-Making: A Model, Literature Critique, and Prescriptions for Research." *Organizational Behavior and Human Performance* 3 (1968).

Mischel, W. *Personality and Assessment.* New York: Wiley, 1968.

Maier, N. R. F.; Solem, A. R.; and Maier, A. A. *Supervisory and Executive Development: A Manual for Role Playing.* New York: Wiley, 1954.

Sales, S. M. "Supervisory Style and Productivity: Review and Theory." *Personnel Psychology* 19 (1966).

Stogdill, R. M. "Personal Factors Associated with Leadership: A Survey of the Literature. *Journal of Psychology* 25 (1948).

Vroom, V. H. *Work and Motivation.* New York: Wiley, 1964.

Vroom, V. H. "A New Look at Management Decision-Making." *Organizational Dynamics* 1 (1973).

Vroom, V. H. , and Jago, A. G. "Decision-Making as a Social Process: Normative and Descriptive Models of Leader Behavior." *Decision Science,* 1974.

Vroom, V. H. , and Yetton, P. W. "A Normative Model of Leadership Style. In *Readings in Managerial Psychology,* edited by H. J. Leavitt and L. Pondy, 2d ed. Chicago: University of Chicago Press, 1973.

Wood, M. J. "Power Relationships and Group Decision Making in Organizations." *Psychological Bulletin,* 1974.

THE SCIENCE OF 'MUDDLING THROUGH'

C. E. Lindblom

Suppose an administrator is given responsibility for formulating policy with respect to inflation. He might start by trying to list all related values in order of importance, e.g., full employment, reasonable business profit, protection of small savings, prevention of a stock-market crash. Then all possible policy outcomes could be rated as more or less efficient in attaining a maximum of these values. This would of course require a prodigious inquiry into values held by members of society and an equally prodigious set of calculations on how much of each value is equal to how much of each other value. He could then proceed to outline all possible policy alternatives. In a third step, he would undertake systematic comparison of his multitude of alternatives to determine which attains the greatest amount of values.

In comparing policies, he would take advantage of any theory available that generalized about classes of policies. In considering inflation, for example, he would compare all policies in the light of the theory of prices. Since no alternatives are beyond his investigation, he would consider strict central control and the abolition of all prices and markets on the one hand and elimination of all public con-

Source: Reprinted with permission from *Public Administration Review,* ©1959 by the American Society for Public Administration (ASPA), 1120 G Street NW, Suite 500, Washington, DC 20005. All rights reserved.

trols with reliance completely on the free market on the other, both in the light of whatever theoretical generalizations he could find on such hypothetical economies. Finally, he would try to make the choice that would in fact maximize his values.

An alternative line of attack would be to set as his principal objective, either explicitly or without conscious thought, the relatively simple goal of keeping prices level. This objective might be compromised or complicated by only a few other goals, such as full employment. He would in fact disregard most other social values as beyond his present interest, and he would for the moment not even attempt to rank the few values that he regarded as immediately relevant. Were he pressed, he would quickly admit that he was ignoring many related values and many possible important consequences of his policies.

As a second step, he would outline those relatively few policy alternatives that occurred to him. He would then compare them. In comparing his limited number of alternatives, most of them familiar from past controversies, he would not ordinarily find a body of theory precise enough to carry him through a comparison of their respective consequences. Instead he would rely heavily on the record of past experience with small policy steps to predict the consequences of similar steps extended into the future.

Moreover, he would find that the policy alternatives combined objectives or values in different ways. For example, one policy might offer price-level stability at the cost of some risk of unemployment; another might offer less price stability but also less risk of unemployment. Hence, the next step in his approach—the final selection—would combine into one the choice among values and the choice among instruments for teaching values. It would not, as in the first method of policy making, approximate a more mechanical process of choosing the means that best satisfied goals that were previously clarified and ranked. Because practitioners of the second approach expect to achieve their goals only partially, they would expect to repeat endlessly the sequence just described, as conditions and aspirations changed and as accuracy of prediction improved.

BY ROOT OR BY BRANCH

For complex problems, the first of these two approaches is of course impossible. Although such an approach can be described, it cannot be practiced except for relatively simple problems, and even then only in a somewhat modified form. It assumes intellectual capacities and sources of information that men simply do not possess, and it is even more absurd as an approach to policy when the time and money that can be allocated to a policy problem is limited, as is always the case. Of particular importance to public administrators is the fact that public agencies are in effect usually instructed not to practice the first method. That is to say, their prescribed functions and constraints—the politically or legally possible—restrict their attention to relatively few values and relatively few alternative policies among the countless alternatives that might be imagined. It is the second method that is practiced.

Curiously, however, the literatures of decision making, policy formulation, planning, and public administration formalize the first approach rather than the second, leaving public administrators who handle complex decisions in the position of practicing what few preach. For emphasis I run some risk of overstatement. True enough, the literature is well aware of limits on man's capacities and of the inevitability that policies will be approached in some such style as the second. But attempts to formalize rational policy formulation—to lay out explicitly the necessary steps in the process—usually describe the first approach and not the second.[1]

The common tendency to describe policy formulation even for complex problems as though it followed the first approach has been strengthened by the attention given to, and successes enjoyed by, operations research, statistical decision theory, and systems analysis. The hallmarks of these procedures, typical of the first approach, are clarity of objective, explicitness of evaluation, a high degree of comprehensiveness of overview, and, wherever possible, quantification of values for mathematical analysis. But these advanced procedures remain largely the appropriate technqiues of relatively small-scale problem solving where the total number of variables to be considered is small and value problems restricted. Charles Hitch, head of the Economic Division of RAND Corporation, one of the leading centers for application of these techniques, has written:

> I would make the empirical generalization from my experience at RAND and elsewhere that operations research is the art of sub-optimizing, i.e., of solving some lower-level problems, and that difficulties increase and our special competence diminishes by an order of magnitude with every level of decision making we attempt to ascend. The sort of simple explicit model which operations researchers are so proficient in using can certainly reflect most of the significant factors influencing traffic control on the George Washington Bridge, but the proportion of the relevant reality which we can represent by any such model or models in studying, say, a major foreign-policy decision, appears to be almost trivial.[2]

Accordingly, I propose in this paper to clarify and formalize the second method, much neglected in the literature. This might be described as the method of *successful limited comparisons*. I will contrast it with the first approach, which might be called the rational-comprehensive method.[3] More impressionistically and briefly—and therefore generally used in this article—they could be characterized as the 'branch method' and 'root method', the former continually building out from the current situation, step by step and by small degrees; the latter starting from fundamentals anew each time, building on the past only as experience is embodied in a theory, and always prepared to start completely from the ground up.

---

[1] James G. March and Herbert A. Simon similarly characterize the literature. They also take some important steps, as have Simon's other recent articles, to describe a less heroic model of policy making. See March and Simon (1958), p. 137.

[2] Hitch (1957), p. 718. Hitch's dissent is from particular points made in the article to which his paper is a reply, his claim that operations research is for low-level problems is widely accepted. For examples of the kind of problems to which operations research is applied, see C. W. Churchman, R. L. Ackoff, and E. L. Arnoff (1957), and J. F. McCloskey and J. M. Coppinger (1956).

[3] I am assuming that administrators often make policy and advise in the making of policy and am treating decision making and policy making as synonymous for purposes of this paper.

Let us put the characteristics of the two methods side by side in simplest terms.

Rational-comprehensive (Root)	Successive limited comparisons (Branch)
1(a) Clarification of values or objectives distinct from and usually prerequisite to empirical analysis or alternative policies.	1(b) Selection of value goals and empirical analysis of the needed action are not distinct from one another but are closely intertwined.
2(a) Policy formulation is therefore approached through means-end analysis: first the ends are isolated, then the means to achieve them are sought.	2(b) Since means and ends are not distinct, means-end analysis is often inappropriate or limited.
3(a) The test of a 'good' policy is that it can be shown to be the most appropriate means to desired ends.	3(b) The test of a 'good' policy is typically that various analysis find themselves directly agreeing on a policy (without their agreeing that it is the most appropriate means to an agreed objective).
4(a) Analysis is comprehensive: every important relevant factor is taken into account.	4(b) Analysis is drastically limited: (i) Important possible outcomes are neglected. (ii) Important alternative potential policies are neglected. (iii) Important affected values are neglected.
5(a) Theory is often heavily relied upon.	5(b) A succession of comparisons greatly reduces or eliminates reliance on theory.

Assuming that the root method is familiar and understandable, we proceed directly to clarification of its alternative by contrast. In explaining the second, we shall be describing how most administrators do in fact approach complex questions, for the root method, the 'best' way as a blueprint or model, is in fact not workable for complex policy questions, and administrators are forced to use the method of successive limited comparisons.

INTERTWINING EVALUATION AND EMPIRICAL ANALYSIS: 1(b)

The quickest way to understand how values are handled in the method of successive limited comparisons is to see how the root method often breaks down in *its* handling of values or objectives. The idea that values should be clarified, and in advance of the examination of alternative policies, is appealing. But what happens when we attempt it for complex social problems? The first difficulty is that on many critical values or objectives, citizens disagree, congressmen disagree, and public administrators disagree. Even where a fairly specific objective is prescribed for the administrator, there remains considerable room for disagreement on subobjectives. Consider, for example, the conflict with respect to locating public housing, described in Meyerson and Banfield's study of the Chicago Housing Authority

(1955)—disagreement which occurred despite the clear objective of providing a certain number of public housing units in the city. Similarly conflicting are objectives in highway location, traffic control, minimum wage administration, development of tourist facilities in national parks, or insect control.

Administrators cannot escape these conflicts by ascertaining the majority's preference, for preferences have not been registered on most issues; indeed, there often *are* no preferences in the absence of public discussion sufficient to bring an issue to the attention of the electorate. Furthermore, there is a question of whether intensity of feeling should be considered as well as the number of persons preferring each alternative. By the impossibility of doing otherwise, administrators often are reduced to deciding policy without clarifying objectives first.

Even when an administrator resolves to follow his own values as a criterion for decisions, he often will not know how to rank them when they conflict with one another, as they usually do. Suppose, for example, that an administrator must relocate tenants living in tenements scheduled for destruction. One objective is to empty the buildings fairly promptly, another is to find suitable accommodation for persons displaced, another is to avoid friction with residents in other areas in which a large influx would be unwelcome, another is to deal with all concerned through persuasion if possible, and so on.

How does one state even to oneself the relative importance of these partially conflicting values? A simple ranking of them is not enough; one needs ideally to know how much of one value is worth sacrificing for some of another value. The answer is that typically the administrator chooses—and must choose—directly among policies in which these values are combined in different ways. He cannot first clarify his values and then choose among policies.

A more subtle third point underlies both the first two. Social objectives do not always have the same relative values. One objective may be highly prized in one circumstance, another in another circumstance. If, for example, an administrator values highly both the dispatch with which his agency can carry through its projects *and* good public relations, it matters little which of the two possibly conflicting values he favors in some abstract or general sense. Policy questions arise in forms which put to administrators such a question as: given the degree to which we are or are not already achieving the values of dispatch and the values of good public relations, is it worth sacrificing a little speed for a happier clientele, or is it better to risk offending the clientele so that we can get on with our work? The answer to such a question varies with circumstances.

The value problem is, as the example shows, always a problem of adjustments at a margin. But there is no practicable way to state marginal objectives or values except in terms of particular policies. That one value is preferred to another in one decision situation does not mean that it will be preferred in another decision situation in which it can be had only at great sacrifice of another value. Attempts to rank or order values in general and abstract terms so that they do not shift from decision to decision end up by ignoring the relevant marginal preferences. The significance of this third point thus goes very far. Even if all administrators had at hand an agreed set of values, objectives, and constraints, and an agreed ranking of these values, objectives, and constraints, their marginal values in actual choice situations would be impossible to formulate.

Unable consequently to formulate the relevant values first and then choose among policies to achieve them, administrators must choose directly among alternative policies that offer different marginal combinations of values. Somewhat paradoxically, the only practicable way to disclose one's relevant marginal values even to oneself is to describe the policy one chooses to achieve them. Except roughly and vaguely, I know of no way to describe—or even to understand—what my relative evaluations are for, say, freedom and security, speed and accuracy in governmental decisions, or low taxes and better schools than to describe my preferences among specific policy choices that might be made between the alternatives in each of the pairs.

In summary, two aspects of the process by which values are actually handled can be distinguished. The first is clear: evaluation and empirical analysis are intertwined; that is, one chooses among values and among policies at one and the same time. Put a little more elaborately, one simultaneously chooses a policy to attain certain objectives and chooses the objectives themselves. The second aspect is related but distant: the administrator focuses his attention on marginal or incremental values. Whether he is aware of it or not, he does not find general formulations of objectives very helpful and in fact makes specific marginal or incremental comparisons. Two policies, X and Y, confront him. Both promise the same degree of attainment of objectives $a, b, c, d,$ and e. But X promises him somewhat more of f than does Y, while Y promises him somewhat more of g than does X. In choosing between them, he is in fact offered the alternative of a marginal or incremental amount of f at the expense of a marginal or incremental amount of g. The only values that are relevant to his choice are these increments by which the two policies differ; and, when he finally chooses between the two marginal values, he does so by making a choice between policies.[4]

As to whether the attempt to clarify objectives in advance of policy selection is more or less rational than the close intertwining of marginal evaluation and empirical analysis, the principal difference established is that for complex problems the first is impossible and irrelevant, and the second is both possible and relevant. The second is possible because the administrator need not try to analyze any values except the values by which alternative policies differ and need not be concerned with them except as they differ marginally. His need for information on values or objectives is drastically reduced as compared with the root method; and his capacity for grasping, comprehending, and relating values to one another is not strained beyond the breaking point.

RELATIONS BETWEEN MEANS AND ENDS: 2(*b*)

Decision making is ordinarily formalized as a means-ends relationship: means are conceived to be evaluated and chosen in the light of ends finally selected independently of and prior to the choice of means. This is the means-ends relation-

---

[4]The line of argument is, of course, an extension of the theory of market choice, especially the theory of consumer choice, to public policy choices.

ship of the root method. But it follows from all that has just been said that such a means-ends relationship is possible only to the extent that values are agreed upon, are reconcilable, and are stable at the margin. Typically, therefore, such a means-ends relationship is absent from the branch method, where means and ends are simultaneously chosen.

Yet any departure from the means-ends relationships of the root method will strike some readers as inconceivable. For it will appear to them that only in such a relationship is it possible to determine whether one policy choice is better or worse than another. How can an administrator know whether he has made a wise or foolish decision if he is without prior values or objectives by which to judge his decision? The answer to this question calls up the third distinctive difference between root and branch methods: how to decide the best policy.

THE TEST OF 'GOOD' POLICY: 3(*b*)

In the root method, a decision is 'correct,' 'good,' or 'rational' if it can be shown to attain some specified objective, where the objective can be specified without simply describing the decision itself. Where objectives are defined only through the marginal or incremental approach to values described above, it is still sometimes possible to test whether a policy does in fact attain the desired objectives; but a precise statement of the objectives takes the form of a description of the policy chosen or some alternative to it. To show that a policy is mistaken one cannot offer an abstract argument that important objectives are not achieved; one must instead argue that another policy is more to be preferred.

So far, the departure from customary ways of looking at problem solving is not troublesome, for many administrators will be quick to agree that the most effective discussion of the correctness of policy does take the form of comparison with other policies that might have been chosen. But what of the situation in which administrators cannot agree on values or objectives, either abstractly or in marginal terms? What then is the rest of 'good' policy? For the root method, there is no test. Agreement on objectives failing, there is no standard of 'correctiveness.' For the method of successive limited comparisons, the test is agreement on policy itself, which remains possible even when agreement on values is not.

It has been suggested that continuing agreement in Congress on the desirability of extending old-age insurance stems from liberal desires to strengthen the welfare programs of the federal government and from conservative desires to reduce union demands for private pension plans. If so, this is an excellent demonstration of the case with which individuals of different ideologies often can agree on concrete policy. Labor mediators report a similar phenomenon: the contestants cannot agree on criteria for settling their disputes but can agree on specific proposals. Similarly, when one administrator's objective turns out to be another's means, they often can agree on policy. Agreement on policy thus becomes the only practicable test of the policy's correctness. And for one administrator to seek to win the other over to agreement on ends as well would accomplish nothing and create quite unnecessary controversy.

If agreement directly on policy as a test for 'best' policy seems a poor substitute for testing the policy against its objectives, it ought to be remembered that objectives themselves have no ultimate validity other than they are agreed upon. Hence agreement is the test of 'best' policy in both methods. But where the root method requires agreement on what elements in the decision constitute objectives and on which of these objectives should be sought, the branch method falls back on agreement wherever it can be found. In an important sense, therefore, it is not irrational for an administrator to defend a policy as good without being able to specify what it is good for.

NON-COMPREHENSIVE ANALYSIS: 4(*b*)

Ideally, rational-comprehensive analysis leaves out nothing important. But it is impossible to take everything important into consideration unless 'important' is so narrowly defined that analysis is in fact quite limited. Limits on human intellectual capacities and on available information set definite limits to man's capacity to be comprehensive. In actual fact, therefore, no one can practice the rational-comprehensive method for really complex problems, and every administrator faced with a sufficiently complex problem must find ways drastically to simplify.

An administrator assisting in the formulation of agricultural economic policy cannot in the first place be competent on all possible policies. He cannot even comprehend one policy entirely. In planning a soil-bank program, he cannot successfully anticipate the impact of higher or lower farm income on, say, urbanization—the possible consequent loosening of family ties, the possible consequent need for revisions in social security and further implications for tax problems arising out of new federal responsibilities for social security and municipal responsibilities for urban services. Nor, to follow another line of repercussions, can he work through the soil-bank program's effects on prices for agricultural products in foreign markets and consequent implications for foreign relations, including those arising out of economic rivalry between the United States and the U.S.S.R.

In the method of successive limited comparisons, simplification is systematically achieved in two principal ways. First, it is achieved through limitation of policy comparisons to those policies that differ in relatively small degree from policies presently in effect. Such a limitation immediately reduces the number of alternatives to be investigated and also drastically simplifies the character of the investigation of each. For it is not necessary to undertake fundamental inquiry into an alternative and its consequences; it is necessary only to study those respects in which the proposed alternative and its consequences differ from the status quo. The empirical comparison of marginal differences among alternative policies that differ only marginally is, of course, a counterpart to the incremental or marginal comparison of values discussed above.[5]

[5]A more precise definition of incremental policies and a discussion of whether a change that appears 'small' to one observer might be seen differently by another is to be found in C. E. Lindblom (1958), p. 298.

Relevance As Well As Realism

It is a matter of common observation that in western democracies public administrators and policy analysts in general do largely limit their analyses to incremental or marginal differences in policies that are chosen to differ only incrementally. They do not do so, however, solely because they desperately need some way to simplify their problems; they also do so in order to be relevant. Democracies change their policies almost entirely through incremental adjustments. Policy does not move in leaps and bounds.

The incremental character of political change in the United States has often been remarked. The two major political parties agree on fundamentals; they offer alternative policies to the voters only on relatively small points of difference. Both parties favor full employment, but they define it somewhat differently; both favor the development of waterpower resources, but in slightly different ways; and both favor unemployment compensation, but not the same level of benefits. Similarly, shifts of policy within a party take place largely through a series of relatively small changes, as can be seen in their only gradual acceptance of the idea of governmental responsibility for support of the unemployed, a change in party positions beginning in the early thirties and culminating in a sense in the Employment Act of 1946.

Party behavior is in turn rooted in public attitudes, and political theorists cannot conceive of democracy's surviving in the United States in the absence of fundamental agreement on potentially disruptive issues, with consequent limitation of policy debates to relatively small differences in policy.

Since the policies ignored by the administrator are politically impossible and so irrelevant, the simplification of analysis achieved by concentrating on policies that differ only incrementally is not a capricious kind of simplification. In addition, it can be argued that, given the limits on knowledge within which policy makers are confined, simplifying by limiting the focus to small variations from present policy makes the most of available knowledge. Because policies being considered are like present and past policies, the administrator can obtain information and claim some insight. Non-incremental policy proposals are therefore typically not only politically irrelevant but also unpredictable in their consequences.

The second method of simplification of analysis is the practice of ignoring important possible consequences of possible policies, as well as the values attached to the neglected consequences. If this appears to disclose a shocking shortcoming of successive limited comparisons, it can be replied that, even if the exclusions are random, policies may nevertheless be more intelligently formulated than through futile attempts to achieve a comprehensiveness beyond human capacity. Actually, however, the exclusions, seeming arbitrary or random from one point of view, need be neither.

Achieving a Degree of Comprehensiveness

Suppose that each value neglected by one policy-making agency were a major concern of at least one other agency. In that case, a helpful division of labor would be achieved, and no agency need find its task beyond its capacities. The shortcomings of such a system would be that one agency might destroy a value either before another agency could be activated to safeguard it or in spite of another agency's efforts. But the possibility that important values may be lost is present in any form of organization, even where agencies attempt to comprehend in planning more than is humanly possible. The virtue of such a hypothetical division of labor is that every important interest or value has its watchdog. And these watchdogs can protect the interests in their jurisdiction in two quite different ways: first, by redressing damages done by other agencies; and second, by anticipating and heading off injury before it occurs.

In a society like that of the United States in which individuals are free to combine to pursue almost any possible common interest they might have and in which government agencies are sensitive to the pressures of these groups, the system described in approximated. Almost every interest has its watchdog. Without claiming that every interest has a sufficiently powerful watchdog, it can be argued that our system often can assure a more comprehensive regard for the values of the whole society than any attempt at intellectual comprehensiveness.

In the United States, for example, no part of government attempts a comprehensive overview of policy on income distribution. A policy nevertheless evolves, and one responding to a wide variety of interests. A process of mutual adjustment among farm groups, labor unions, municipalities and school boards, tax authorities, and government agencies with responsibilities in the fields of housing, health, highways, national parks, fire, and policy accomplishes a distribution of income in which particular income problems neglected at one point in the decision processes become central at another point.

Mutual adjustment is more pervasive than the explicit forms it takes in negotiation between groups; it persists through the mutual impacts of groups upon one another even where they are not in communication. For all the imperfections and latent dangers in this ubiquitous process of mutual adjustment, it will often accomplish an adaptation of policies to a wider range of interests than could be done by one group centrally. Note, too, how the incremental pattern of policy making fits with the multiple pressure pattern. For when decisions are only incremental—closely related to known policies—it is easier for one group to anticipate the kind of moves another might make and easier too for it to make correction for injury already accomplished.[6]

Even partisanship and narrowness, to use pejorative terms, will sometimes be assets to rational decision making, for they can doubly ensure what one agency neglects, another will not; they specialize personnel to distinct points of view. The claim is valid that effective rational coordination of the federal administration, if possible to achieve at all, would require an agreed set of values[7]—if 'rational' is defined as the practice of the root method of decision making. But a high degree of administrative coordination occurs as each agency adjusts its policies to the

[6]The link between the practice of the method of successive limited comparisons and mutual adjustment of interests in a highly fragmented decision-making process adds a new facet to pluralist theories of government and administration.

[7]See Herbert Simon, Donald W. Smithburg, and Victor A. Thompson (1950), p. 434.

concerns of the other agencies in the process of fragmented decision making I have just described.

For all the apparent shortcomings of the incremental approach to policy alternatives with its arbitrary exclusion coupled with fragmentation, when compared to the root method, the branch method often looks far superior. In the root method, the inevitable exclusion of factors is accidental, unsystematic, and not defensible by any argument so far developed, while in the branch method the exclusions are deliberate, systematic, and defensible. Ideally, of course, the root method does not exclude; in practice it must. Nor does the branch method necessarily neglect long-run considerations and objectives. It is clear that important values must be omitted in considering policy, and sometimes the only way long-run objectives can be given adequate attention is through the neglect of short-run considerations. But the values omitted can be either long-run or short-run.

SUCCESSION OF COMPARISONS: 5(*b*)

The final distinctive element in the branch method is that the comparisons, together with the policy choice, proceed in a chronological series. Policy is not made once and for all; it is made and remade endlessly. Policy making is a process of successive approximation to some desired objectives in which what is desired itself continues to change under reconsideration. It is at best a very rough process. Neither social scientists nor politicians nor public administrators yet know enough about the social world to avoid repeated error in predicting the consequences of policy moves. A wise policy maker consequently expects that his policies will achieve only part of what he hopes and at the same time will produce unanticipated consequences he would have preferred to avoid. If he proceeds through a *succession* of incremental changes, he avoids serious lasting mistakes in several ways.

In the first place, past sequences of policy steps have given him knowledge about the probable consequences of further similar steps. Second, he need not attempt big jumps toward his goals that would require predictions beyond his or anyone else's knowledge, because he never expects his policy to be a final resolution of a problem. His decision is only one step, one that if successful can quickly be followed by another. Third, he is in effect able to test his previous predictions as he moves on to each further step. Lastly, he often can remedy a past error fairly quickly—more quickly than if policy proceeded through more distinct steps widely spaced in time.

Compare this comparative analysis of incremental changes with the aspiration to employ theory in the root method. Man cannot think without classifying, without subsuming one experience under a more general category of experiences. The attempt to push categorization as far as possible and to find general propositions which can be applied to specific situations is what I refer to with the word 'theory.' Where root analysis often leans heavily on theory in this sense, the branch method does not.

The assumption of root analysis is that theory is the most systematic and economical way to bring relevant knowledge to bear on a specific problem. Granting the assumption, an unhappy fact is that we do not have adequate theory to apply to problems in any policy area, although theory is more adequate in some areas—monetary policy, for example—than in others. Comparative analysis, as in the branch method, is sometimes a systematic alternative to theory.

Suppose an administrator must choose among a small group of policies that differ only incrementally from each other and from present policy. He might aspire to 'understand' each of the alternatives—for example, to know all the consequences of each aspect of each policy. If so, he would indeed require theory. In fact, however, he would usually decide that, *for policy-making purposes,* he need know, as explained above, only the consequences of each of those aspects of the policies in which they differed from one another. For this much more modest aspiration, he requires no theory (although it might be helpful, if available), for he can proceed to isolate probable differences by examining the differences in consequences associated with past differences in policies, a feasible program because he can take his observations from a long sequence of incremental changes.

For example, without a more comprehensive social theory about juvenile delinquency than scholars have yet produced, one cannot possible understand the ways in which a variety of public policies—say on education, housing, recreation, employment, race relations, and policing—might encourage or discourage delinquency. And one needs such an understnading if one undertakes the comprehensive overview of the problem prescribed in the models of the root method. If, however, one merely wants to mobilize knowledge sufficient to assist in a choice among a small group of similar policies—alternative policies on juvenile court procedures, for example—one can do so by comparative analysis of the results of similar past policy moves.

THEORISTS AND PRACTITIONERS

This difference explains—in some cases at least—why the administrator often feels that the outside expert or academic problem solver is sometimes not helpful and why they in turn often urge more theory on him. And it explains why an administrator often feels more confident when 'flying by the seat of his pants' than when following the advice of theorists. Theorists often ask the administrator to go the long way round to the solution of his problems, in effect ask him to follow the best canons of the scientific method, when the administrator knows that the best available theory will work less well than more modest incremental comparisons. Theorists do not realize that the administrator is often in fact practicing a systematic method. It would be foolish to push this explanation too far, for sometimes practical decision makers are pursuing neither a theoretical approach nor successive comparisons, or any other systematic method.

It may be worth emphasizing that theory is sometimes of extremely limited helpfulness in policy making for at least two rather different reasons. It is greedy for facts; it can be constructed only through a great collection of observations. And it is typically insufficiently precise for application to a policy process that moves through small changes. In contrast the comparative method both economizes on the need for facts and directs the analyst's attention to just those facts that are relevant to the fine choices faced by the decision maker.

With respect to precision of theory, economic theory serves as an example. It predicts that an economy without money or prices would in certain specified ways misallocate resources, but this finding pertains to an alternative far removed from the kind of policies on which administrators need help. Yet it is not precise enough to predict the consequences of policies restricting business mergers, and this is the kind of issue on which the administrators need help. Only in relatively restricted areas does economic theory achieve sufficient precision to go far in resolving policy questions; its helpfulness in policy making is always so limited that it requires supplementation through comparative analysis.

SUCCESSIVE COMPARISON AS A SYSTEM

Successive limited comparisons is, then, indeed a method or system; it is not a failure of method for which administrators ought to apologize. Nonetheless, its imperfections, which have not been explored in this paper, are many. For example, the method is without a built-in safeguard for all relevant values, and it also may lead the decision maker to overlook excellent policies for no other reason than that they are not suggested by the chain of successive policy steps leading up to the present. Hence, it ought to be said that under this method, as well as under some of the most sophisticated variants of the root method—operations research, for example—policies will continue to be as foolish as they are wise.

Why then bother to describe the method in all the above detail? Because it is in fact a common method of policy formulation, and is, for complex problems, the principal reliance of administrators as well as of other policy analysts.[8] And because it will be superior to any other decision-making method available for complex problems in many circumstances, certainly superior to a futile attempt at superhuman comprehensiveness. The reaction of the public administrator to the exposition of method doubtless will be less a discovery of a new method than a better acquaintance with an old. But by becoming more conscious of their practice of this method, administrators might practice it with more skill and know when to extend or constrict its use. (That they sometimes practice it effectively and sometimes may not explain the extremes of opinion on 'muddling through,' which is both praised as a highly sophisticated form of problem solving and denounced

---

[8]Elsewhere I have explored this same method of policy formation as practiced by academic analysts of policy (C. E. Lindblom, 1958). Although it has been here presented as a method for public administrators, it is no less necessary to analysts more removed from immediate policy questions, despite their tendencies to describe their own analytical efforts as though they were in the rational-comprehensive method with an especially heavy use of theory. Similarly, this same method is inevitably resorted to in personal problem solving, where means and ends are sometimes impossible to separate, where aspirations or objectives undergo constant development, and where drastic simplification of the complexity of the real world is urgent if problems are to be solved in the time that can be given to them. To an economist accustomed to dealing with the marginal or incremental concept in market processes, the central idea in the method is that both evaluation and empirical analysis are incremental. Accordingly I have referred to the method elsewhere as 'the incremental method.'

as no method at all. For I suspect that in so far as there is a system in what is known as 'muddling through,' this method is it.)

One of the noteworthy incidental consequences of clarification of the method is the light it throws on the suspicion an administrator sometimes entertains that a consultant or adviser is not speaking relevantly and responsibly when in fact by all ordinary objective evidence he is. The trouble lies in the fact that most of us approach policy problems within a framework given by our view of a chain of successive policy choices made up to the present. One's thinking about appropriate policies with respect, say, to urban traffic control is greatly influenced by one's knowledge of the incremental steps taken up to the present. An administrator enjoys an intimate knowledge of his past sequences that 'outsiders' do not share, and his thinking and that of the 'outsider' will consequently be different in ways that may puzzle both. Both may appear to be talking intelligently, yet each may find the other unsatisfactory. The relevance of the policy chain of succession is even more clear when an American tries to discuss, say, antitrust policy with a Swiss, for the chains of policy in the two countries are strikingly different and the two individuals consequently have organized their knowledge in quite different ways.

If this phenomenon is a barrier to communication, an understanding of it promises an enrichment of intellectual interaction in policy formulation. Once the source of difference is understood, it will sometimes be stimulating for an administrator to seek out a policy analyst whose recent experience is with a policy chain different from his own.

This raises again a question only briefly discussed above on the merits of like-mindedness among government administrators. While much of organization theory argues the virtues of common values and agreed organizational objectives, for complex problems in which the root method is inapplicable, agencies will want among their own personnel two types of diversification: administrators whose thinking is organized by reference to policy chains other than those familiar to most members of the organization and, even more commonly, administrators whose professional or personal values or interests create diversity of view (perhaps coming from different specialties, social classes, geographical areas) so that, even within a single agency, decision making can be fragmented and parts of the agency can serve as watchdogs for other parts.

REFERENCES

Churchman, C. W., Ackoff, R. L., and Arnoff, E. L. (1957), *Introduction to Operations Research,* Wiley.

Hitch, C. (1957), 'Operations Research and National Planning: a Dissent,' *Operations Research,* 5, October.

Lindblom, C. E. (1958), 'Policy Analysis,' *American Economic Review,* 48, June.

March, J. G., and Simon, H. A. (1958), *Organizations,* Wiley.

McCloskey, J. F., and Coppinger, J. M. (eds.) (1956). *Operations Research for Management,* Johns Hopkins Press, vol. 2.

Meyerson, M., and Banfield, E. C. (1955), *Politics, Planning, and the Public Interest,* Free Press.

Simon, H. A., Smithburg, D. W., and Thompson, V. A. (1950), *Public Administration,* Knopf.

14
Leadership, Power and Influence

THE LEADERSHIP CHALLENGE—
A CALL FOR THE TRANSFORMATIONAL LEADER
Noel M. Tichy
David O. Ulrich

WHO GETS POWER—AND HOW THEY HOLD ONTO IT:
A STRATEGIC CONTINGENCY MODEL OF POWER
Gerald R. Salancik
Jeffrey Pfeffer

LEADERSHIP: THE MANAGEMENT OF MEANING
Linda Smircich
Gareth Morgan

THE LEADERSHIP CHALLENGE—A CALL FOR THE TRANSFORMATIONAL LEADER

Noel M. Tichy
David O. Ulrich

Some optimists are heralding in the age of higher productivity, a transition to a service economy, and a brighter competitive picture for U.S. corporations in world markets. We certainly would like to believe that the future will be brighter, but our temperament is more cautious. We feel that the years it took for most U.S. companies to get "fat and flabby" are not going to be reversed by a crash diet for one or two years. Whether we continue to gradually decline as a world competitive economy will largely be determined by the quality of leadership in the top echelons of our business and government organizations. Thus, it is our belief that now is the time for organizations to change their corporate lifestyles.

To revitalize organizations such as General Motors, American Telephone and Telegraph, General Electric, Honeywell, Ford, Burroughs, Chase Manhattan Bank, Citibank, U.S. Steel, Union Carbide, Texas Instruments, and Control Data—just to mention a few companies currently undergoing major transformations—a new brand of leadership is necessary. Instead of managers who continue to move organizations along historical tracks, the new leaders must *transform* the organizations and head them down new tracks. What is required of this kind of leader is an ability to help the organization develop a vision of what it can be, to mobilize the organization to accept and work toward achieving the new vision, and to institutionalize the changes that must last over time. Unless the creation of this breed of leaders becomes a national agenda, we are not very optimistic about the revitalization of the U.S. economy.

We call these new leaders transformational leaders, for they must create something new out of something old: out of an old vision, they must develop and communicate a new vision and get others not only to see the vision but also to commit themselves to it. Where transactional managers make only minor adjustments in the organization's mission, structure, and human resource management, transformational leaders not only make major changes in these areas but they also evoke fundamental changes in the basic political and cultural systems of the organization. The revamping of the political and cultural systems is what most distinguishes the transformational leader from the transactional one.

Lee Iacocca: A Transformational Leader

One of the most dramatic examples of transformational leadership and organizational revitalization in the early 1980s has been the leadership of Lee Iacocca, the chairman of Chrysler Corporation. He provided the leadership to transform a company from the brink of bankruptcy to profitability. He created a vision of success and mobilized large factions of key employees toward enacting that vision while simultaneously downsizing the workforce by 60,000 employees. As a result of Iacocca's leadership, by 1984 Chrysler had earned record profits, had attained high levels of employee morale, and had helped employees generate a sense of meaning in their work.

Until Lee Iacocca took over at Chrysler, the basic internal political structure had been unchanged for decades. It was clear who reaped what benefits from the organization, how the pie was to be divided, and who could exercise what power. Nonetheless, Mr. Iacocca knew that he needed to alter these political traditions, starting with a new definition of Chrysler's link to external stakeholders. Therefore, the government was given a great deal of control over Chrysler in return for the guaranteed loan that staved off bankruptcy. Modification of the political system required other adjustments, including the "trimming of fat" in the management ranks, limiting financial rewards for all employees, and receiving major concessions for the UAW. An indicator of a significant political shift was the inclusion of Douglas Frazer on the Chrysler Board of Directors as part of UAW concessions.

Equally dramatic was the change in the organization's cultural system. First, the company had to recognize its unique status as a recipient of a federal bailout. This bailout came with a stigma, thus Mr. Iacocca's job was to change the company's cultural values from a loser's to a winner's feeling. Still, he realized that employees were not going to be winners unless they could, in cultural norms, be more efficient and innovative than their competitors. The molding and shaping of the new culture was clearly and visibly led by Mr. Iacocca, who not only used internal communication as a vehicle to signal change but also used his own personal appearance in Chrysler ads to reinforce these changes. Quickly, the internal culture was transformed to that of a lean and hungry team looking for victory. Whether Chrysler will be able to sustain this organizational phenomenon over time remains to be seen. If it does, it will provide a solid corporate example of what Burns referred to as a transforming leader.[1]

Lee Iacocca's high visibility and notoriety may be the *important* missing elements in management today: there seems to be a paucity of transformational leader role models at all levels of the organization.

ORGANIZATIONAL DYNAMICS OF CHANGE

Assumption One: Trigger Events Indicate Change Is Needed

Organizations do not change unless there is a trigger which indicates change is needed. This trigger can be as extreme as the Chrysler impending bankruptcy or as moderate as an abstract future-oriented fear that an organization may lose its competitiveness. For example, General Electric's trigger for change is a view that by 1990 the company will not be world competitive unless major changes occur in productivity, innovation, and marketing. Thus, Chairman Jack Welch sees his role as that of transforming GE even though it does not face imminent doom. Nonetheless, the trick for him is to *activate* the trigger; otherwise, complacency may prevail. Similarly, for AT&T, technological, competitive, and political forces have led it to undertake its massive transformation. For General Motors, economic factors of world competition, shifting consumer preferences, and technological change have driven it to change.

In a decade of increased information, international competition, and technological advances, triggers for change have become commonplace and very pressing. However, not all potential trigger events lead to organizational responses, and not all triggers lead to change. Nonetheless, the trigger must create a *felt* need in organizational leaders. Without this felt need, the "boiled frog phenomenon" is likely to occur.

The Boiled Frog. This phenomenon is based on a classic experiment in biology. A frog which is placed in a pan of cold water but which still has the freedom to jump out can be boiled if the temperature change is gradual, for it is not aware of the barely detectable changing heat threshold. In contrast, a frog dropped in a pot of boiling water will immediately jump out: it has a felt need to survive. In a similar vein, many organizations that are insensitive to gradually changing organizational thresholds are likely to become "boiled frogs"; they act in ignorant bliss of environmental triggers and eventually are doomed to failure. This failure, in part, is a result of the organization having no felt need to change.

Assumption Two: A Change Unleashes Mixed Feelings

A felt need for change unleashes a mix of forces, both a positive impetus for change as well as a strong negative individual and organizational resistance.

432

These forces of resistance are generated in each of three interrelated systems—technical, political, cultural—which must be managed in the process of organizational transitions (see Table 1).[2] Individual and organizational resistance to change in these three systems must be overcome if an organization is to be revitalized.[3]

Managing technical systems refers to managing the coordination of technol-

TABLE 1 A List of Technical, Political, and Cultural System Resistances

---

Technical System Resistances include:

Habit and inertia. Habit and inertia cause task-related resistance to change. Individuals who have always done things one way may not be politically or culturally resistant to change, but may have trouble, for technical reasons, changing behavior patterns. Example: some office workers may have difficulty shifting from electric typewriters to word processors.

Fear of the unknown or loss of organizational predictability. Not knowing or having difficulty predicting the future creates anxiety and hence resistance in many individuals. Example: the introduction of automated office equipment has often been accompanied by such resistances.

Sunk costs. Organizations, even when realizing that there are potential payoffs from a change, are often unable to enact a change because of the sunk costs of the organization's resources in the old way of doing things.

Political System Resistances include:

Powerful coalitions. A common threat is found in the conflict between the old guard and the new guard. One interpretation of the exit of Archie McGill, former president of the newly formed AT&T American Bell, is that the backlash of the old-guard coalition exacted its price on the leader of the new-guard coalition.

Resource limitations. In the days when the economic pie was steadily expanding and resources were much less limited, change was easier to enact as every part could gain—such was the nature of labor management agreements in the auto industry for decades. Now that the pie is shrinking decisions need to be made as to who shares a smaller set of resources. These zero-sum decisions are much more politically difficult. As more and more U.S. companies deal with productivity, downsizing, and divesture, political resistance will be triggered.

Indictment quality of change. Perhaps the most significant resistance to change comes from leaders having to indict their own past decisions and behaviors to bring out a change. Example: Roger Smith, chairman and CEO of GM, must implicitly indict his own past behavior as a member of senior management when he suggests changes in GM's operations. Psychologically, it is very difficult for people to change when they were party to creating the problems they are trying to change. It is much easier for a leader from the outside, such as Lee Iacocca, who does not have to indict himself every time he says something is wrong with the organization.

Cultural System Resistances include:

Selective perception (cultural filters). An organization's culture may highlight certain elements of the organization, making it difficult for members to conceive of other ways of doing things. An organization's culture channels that which people perceive as possible; thus, innovation may come from outsiders or deviants who are not as channeled in their perceptions.

Security based on the past. Transition requires people to give up the old ways of doing things. There is security in the past, and one of the problems is getting people to overcome the tendency to want to return to the "good old days." Example: today, there are still significant members of the white-collar workforce at GM who are waiting for the "good old days" to return.

Lack of climate for change. Organizations often vary in their conduciveness to change. Cultures that require a great deal of conformity often lack much receptivity to change. Example: GM with its years of internally developed managers must overcome a limited climate for change.

---

ogy, capital, information, and people in order to produce products or services desired and used in the external marketplace. Managing political systems refers to managing the allocation of organizational rewards such as money, status, power, and career opportunities and to exercise power so employees and departments perceive equity and justice. Managing cultural systems refers to managing the set of shared values and norms which guides the behavior of members of the organization.

When a needed change is perceived by the organizational leaders, the dominant group in the organization must experience a dissatisfaction with the status quo. For example, in the late 1970s John DeButts, chairman and chief executive officer of AT&T, was not satisfied with the long-term viability of AT&T as a regulated telephone monopoly in the age of computers and satellite communication systems. Likewise, when Roger Smith became CEO at General Motors in the early 1980s, he could hardly be satisfied with presiding over GM's first financial loss since the depression. In these two cases, the felt need provided the impetus for transition; yet, such impetus is not uniformly positive.

The technical, political, and cultural resistances are most evident during early stages of an organizational transformation. At GM the early 1980s were marked by tremendous uncertainty concerning many technical issues such as marketing strategy, production strategy, organization design, factory automation, and development of international management. Politically, many powerful coalitions were threatened. The UAW was forced to make wage concessions and accept staffing reductions. The white-collar workers saw their benefits being cut and witnessed major layoffs within the managerial ranks. Culturally, the once dominant managerial style no longer fit the environmental pressures for change: the "GM way" was no longer the right way.

One must be wary of these resistances to change as they can lead to organizational stagnation rather than revitalization. In fact, some managers at GM in late 1983 were waiting for "the good old days" to return. Such resistance exemplifies a dysfunctional reaction to the felt need. As indicated in Figure 1, a key to whether resistant forces will lead to little or inadequate change and hence organizational decline or revitalization lies in an organization's leadership. Defensive, transactional leadership will not rechannel the resistant forces. A case in point is International Harvester which appears to have had a defensive transactional leadership. Thus, in the early 1980s, International Harvester lacked a new vision which would inspire employees to engage in new behaviors. In contrast, Lee Iacocca has been a transformational leader at Chrysler by creating a vision, mobilizing employees, and working toward the institutionalization of Chrysler's transition.

Assumption Three: Quick-Fix Leadership Leads to Decline

Overcomiing resistance to change requires transformational leadership, not defensive, transactional managers who are in search of the one minute quick fix. The transformational leader needs to avoid the trap of simple, quick-fix solutions to major organizational problems. Today, many versions of this quick-fix mentality abound: the book, *One Minute Manager,* has become a best seller in companies

434

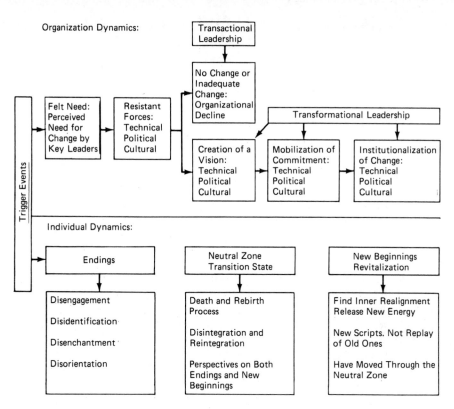

Organization Dynamics:

| Transactional Leadership |

| No Change or Inadequate Change: Organizational Decline |

| Felt Need: Perceived Need for Change by Key Leaders | Resistant Forces: Technical Political Cultural |

Transformational Leadership

| Creation of a Vision: Technical Political Cultural | Mobilization of Commitment: Technical Political Cultural | Institutionalization of Change: Technical Political Cultural |

Trigger Events

Individual Dynamics:

| Endings | Neutral Zone Transition State | New Beginnings Revitalization |

| Disengagement

Disidentification

Disenchantment

Disorientation | Death and Rebirth Process

Disintegration and Reintegration

Perspectives on Both Endings and New Beginnings | Find Inner Realignment Release New Energy

New Scripts. Not Replay of Old Ones

Have Moved Through the Neutral Zone |

FIGURE 1 Transformational Leadership

in need of basic transformation.[4] Likewise, *In Search of Excellence* has become a cookbook for change.[5] In fact, a number of CEOs have taken the eight characteristics of the "excellent" companies and are trying to blindly impose them on their organizations without first examining their appropriateness. For example, many faltering organizations try to copy such company practices at Hewlett-Packard's (HP) statement of company values. Because they read that HP has a clearly articulated statement of company values—the HP equivalent of the ten commandments—they want to create their list of ten commandments. The scenario which has been carried out in many major U.S. firms in the past year goes something like this: the CEO wants to develop the company value statement, so he organizes an off-site meeting in order to spend a couple of days developing the company XYZ corporate value statement. The session is usually quite enlightening—managers become quite thoughtful, and soul-searching takes place. At the end of the session, the group is able to list the XYZ company's "ten commandments." The CEO is delighted that they are now well on the way to a major cultural change. He brings the ten commandments back to the corporation and calls in the staff to begin the communication program so that all company employees can learn the new cultural values. This about ends the transformational process.

The problem with the ten-commandments quick fix is that the CEOs tend to overlook the lesson Moses learned several thousand years ago—namely, getting the ten commandments written down and communicated is the easy part; getting them implemented is the challenge. How many thousands of years has it been since Moses received the ten commandments, and yet today there still seems to be an implementation challenge. Transformational leadership is different from defensive, transactional leadership. Lee Iacocca did not have to read about what others did to find a recipe for his company's success.

Assumption Four: Revitalization Requires Transformational Leadership

There are three identifiable programs of activity associated with transformational leadership.

1. Creation of a Vision.   The transformational leader must provide the organization with a vision of a desired future state. While this task may be shared with other key members of the organization, the vision remains the core responsibility of the transformational leader. The leader needs to integrate analytic, creative, intuitive, and deductive thinking. Each leader must create a vision which gives direction to the organization while being congruent with the leader's and the organization's philosophy and style.

For example, in the early 1980s at GM, after several years of committee work and staff analysis, a vision of the future was drafted which included a mision statement and eight objectives for the company. This statement was the first articulation of a strategic vision for General Motors since Alfred Sloan's leadership. This new vision was developed consistently with the leadership philosophy and style of Roger Smith. Many people were involved in carefully assessing opportunities and constraints for General Motors. Meticulous staff work culminated in committee discussions to evoke agreement and commitment to the mission statement. Through this process a vision was created which paved the way for the next phases of the transformation at GM.

At Chrysler, Lee Iacocca developed a vision without committee work or heavy staff involvement. Instead, he relied more on his intuitive and directive leadership, philosophy, and style. Both GM and Chrysler ended up with a new vision because of transformational leaders proactively shaping a new organization mission and vision. The long-term challenge to organizational revitalization is not "how" the visions are created but the extent to which the visions correctly respond to environmental pressures and transitions within the organization.

2. Mobilization of Commitment.   Here, the organization, or at least a critical mass of it, accepts the new mission and vision and makes it happen. At General Motors, Roger Smith took his top 900 executives on a five-day retreat to share and discuss the vision. The event lasted five days not because it takes that long to share a one-paragraph mission statement and eight objectives, but because the process of evolving commitment and mobilizing support requires a great deal of dialogue and exchange. It should be noted that mobilization of commitment must go well beyond five-day retreats; nevertheless, it is in this phase that transformational leaders get deeper understanding of their *followers*. Maccoby acknowledges that leaders who guide organizations through revitalization are distinct from previous leaders and gamesmen who spearheaded managers to be winners in the growth days of the 1960s and early 1970s. Today, Maccoby argues:

> The positive traits of the gamesman, enthusiasm, risk taking, meritocratic fairness, fit America in a period of unlimited economic growth, hunger for novelty, and an unquestioned career ethic. The negative traits for manipulation, seduction, and the perpetual adolescent need for adventure were always problems, causing distrust and unnecessary crises. The gamesman's daring, the willingness to innovate and take risks are still needed. Companies that rely on conservative company men in finance to run technically based organizations (for example, auto and steel) lose the competitive edge. But unless their negative traits are transformed or controlled, even gifted gamesmen become liabilities as leaders in a new economic reality. A period of limited resources and cutbacks, when the team can no longer be controlled by the promise of more, and one person's gains may be another's loss, leadership with values of caring and integrity and a vision of self-development must create the trust that no one will be penalized for cooperation and that sacrifice as well as rewards are equitable.[6]

After transformational leaders create a vision and mobilize commitment, they must determine how to institutionalize the new mission and vision.

3. Institutionalization of Change. Organizations will not be revitalized unless new patterns of behavior within the organization are adopted. Transformational leaders need to transmit their vision into reality, their mission into action, their philosophy into practice. New realities, action, and practices must be shared throughout the organization. Alterations in communication, decision making, and problem-solving systems are tools through which transitions are shared so that visions become a reality. At a deeper level, institutionalization of change requires shaping and reinforcement of a new culture that fits with the revitalized organization. The human resource systems of selection, development, appraisal, and reward are major levers for institutionalizing change.

INDIVIDUAL DYNAMICS OF CHANGE

The previous section outlined requisite processes for organizational revitalization. Although organizational steps are necessary, they are not sufficient in creating an implementing change. In managing transitions, a more problematic set of forces which focuses on individual psychodynamics of change must be understood and managed. Major transitions unleash powerful conflicting forces in people. The change invokes simultaneous positive and negative personal feelings of fear and hope, anxiety and relief, pressure and stimulation, leaving the old and accepting a new direction, loss of meaning and new meaning, threat to self-esteem and new sense of value. The challenge for transformational leaders is to recognize these mixed emotions, act to help people move from negative to positive emotions, and mobilize and focus energy that is necessary for individual renewal and organizational revitalization.

Figure 1 provides a set of concepts for understanding the individual dynamics of transitions. The concepts, drawn from the work by Bridges, propose a three-phase process of individual change: first come endings, followed by neutral zones, and then new beginnings.[7] During each of these phases, an identifiable set of psychological tasks can be identified which individuals need to successfully complete in order to accept change.

THE THREE-PHASE PROCESS

Endings.   All individual transitions start with endings. Endings must be accepted and understood before transitions can begin. Employees who refuse to accept the fact that traditional behaviors have ended will be unable to adopt new behaviors. The first task is to disengage, which often accompanies a physical transaction. For example, when transferring from one job to another, individuals must learn to accept the new physical setting and disengage from the old position: when transferred employees continually return to visit former colleagues, this is a sign that they have inadequately disengaged. The second task is to disidentify. Individual self-identity is often tied to a job position in such a way that when a plant manager is transferred to corporate staff to work in the marketing department, he or she must disidentify with the plant and its people and with the self-esteem felt as a plant manager. At a deeper personal level, individual transactions require disenchantment. Disenchantment entails recognizing that the enchantment or positive feelings associated with past situations will not be possible to replicate in the future. Chrysler, GM, AT&T, or U.S. Steel employees who remember the "good old days" need to become disenchanted with those feelings: the present reality is different and self-worth cannot be recaptured by longing for or thinking about the past. A new enchantment centered on new circumstances needs to be built. Finally, individuals need to experience and work through disorientation which reflects the loss of familiar trappings. As mature organizations become revitalized, individuals must disengage, disidentify, disenchant, and disorient with past practices and discover in new organizations a new sense of worth or value.

To help individuals cope with endings, transformational leaders need to replace past glories with future opportunities. However, leaders must also acknowledge individual resistances and senses of loss in a transitional period while encouraging employees to face and accept failures as learning opportunities. Holding on to past accomplishments and memories without coming to grips with failure and the need to change may be why companies such as W. T. Grant, International Harvester, and Braniff were unsuccessful at revitalization. There is a sense of dying in all endings, and it does not help to treat transactions as if the past can be buried without effort. Yet, one should see the past as providing new directions.

Neutral Zone.   The key to individuals being able to fully change may be in the second phase which Bridges terms the neutral zone.[8] This phase can be interpreted as a seemingly unproductive "time out" when individuals feel disconnected from people and things of the past and emotionally unconnected with the present. In reality, this phase is a time of reorientation where individuals complete endings and begin new patterns of behavior. Often Western culture, especially in the U.S., avoids this experience and treats the neutral zone like a busy street, to be crossed as fast as possible and certainly not a place to contemplate and experience. However, running across the neutral zone too hurriedly does not allow the ending to occur nor the new beginning to properly start. A death and rebirth process is necessary so that organizational members can work through the disintegration and reintegration. To pass through the neutral zone requires taking the time and thought to gain perspective on both the ending—what went wrong, why it needs to be changed, and what must be overcome in both attitude and behavioral change—and the new beginning—what the new priorities are, why they are needed, and what new attitudes and behaviors will be required. It is in this phase that the most skillful transformational leadership is called upon.

A timid, bureaucratic leader who often reels in the good old days will not provide the needed support to help individuals cross through the neutral zone. On the other hand, the militaristic dictatorial leader who tries to force a "new beginning" and does not allow people to work through their own feelings and emotions may also fail to bring about change. The purported backlash toward the "brash" Archie McGill at American Bell in June 1983 may have been an example of trying to force people through the neutral zone in order to get to a new beginning. Archie McGill was known to rant and rave about the stodgy, old fashioned, and noninnovative "bell-shaped men" at AT&T. While he was trying to help and lead individuals to become innovative and marketing orientated, he may not have allowed them to accept the endings inherent in the transition. Although his enthusiasm may have been well placed, he may have lacked the sensitivity to individual endings and neutral phases of transactions.

Failure to lead individuals through the neutral zone may result in aborted new beginnings. In 1983, International Harvester appeared to be stuck in the neutral zone. In order for International Harvester to make a new beginning, it must enable people to find a new identification with the future organization while accepting the end of the old organization. Such a transformation has successfully occurred at Chrylsler Corporation where morale and esprit de corps grew with the new vision implanted by Lee Iacocca. In the end, organizational revitalization can only occur if individuals accept past failures and engage in new behaviors and attitudes.

New Beginnings. After individuals accept endings by working through neutral zones, they are able to work with new enthusiasm and commitment. New beginnings are characterized by employees learning from the past rather than reveling in it, looking for new scripts rather than acting out old ones, and being positive and excited about current and future work opportunities rather than dwelling on past successes or failures. When Mr. Iacocca implemented his vision at Chrysler, many long-term employees discovered new beginnings. They saw the new Chrysler as an opportunity to succeed, and they worked with a renewed vigor.

WHAT QUALITIES DO TRANSFORMATIONAL
LEADERS POSSESS?

So what does it take to transform an organization's technical, political, and cultural systems? The transformational leader must possess a deep understanding, whether it be intuitive or learned, of organizations and their place both in society at large and in the lives of individuals. The ability to build a new institution requires the kind of political dialogue our founding fathers had when Jefferson, Hamilton, Adams, and others debated issues of justice, equity, separation of powers, checks and balances, and freedom. This language may sound foreign to corporate settings but when major organization revitalization is being undertaken, all of these concepts merit some level of examination. At Chrysler, issues of equity, justice, power, and freedom underlay many of Mr. Iacocca's decisions. Thus, as a start, transformational leaders need to understand concepts of equity, power, freedom, and the dynamics of decision making. In addition to modifying systems, transformational leaders must understand and realign cultural systems.

In addition to managing political and cultural systems, transformational leaders must make difficult decisions quickly. Leaders need to know when to push and when to back off. Finally, transformational leaders are often seen as creators of their own luck. These leaders seize opportunities and know when to act so that casual observers may perceive luck as a plausible explanation for their success; whereas, in reality it is a transformational leader who knows when to jump and when not to jump. Again, Mr. Iacocca can be viewed either as a very lucky person or as the possessor of a great ability to judge when to act and when not to act.

THE SIGNIFICANCE
OF CORPORATE CULTURES

Much has been written about organizational cultures in recent years.[9] We suggest that every organization has a culture, or a patterned set of activities that reflects the organization's underlying values. Cultures don't occur randomly. They occur because leaders spend time on and reward some behaviors and practices more than others. These practices become the foundation of the organization's culture. At HP, for example, Bill Hewlett and Dave Packard spent time wandering around, informally meeting with and talking to employees. Such leadership behavior set the HP cultural tone of caring about and listening to people. Similarly, Tom Watson, Sr., at IBM spent a great deal of time with customers. His pratice led to a company culture of commitment to customers. Indeed, corporate cultures exist. Leaders can shape cultures by carefully monitoring where and how they spend their time and by encouraging and rewarding employees to behave in certain ways.

Culture plays two central roles in organizations. First, it provides organizational members with a way of understanding and making sense of events and symbols. Thus, when employees are confronted with certain complex problems, they "know" how to approach them the "right" way. Like the Eskimos who have a vocabulary that differentiates the five types of snow, organizations create vocabularies to describe how things are done in the organization. At IBM, it is very clear to all insiders how to form a task force and to solve problems since task forces and problem solving are a way of life in IBM's culture.

Second, culture provides meaning. It embodies a set of values which helps justify why certain behaviors are encouraged at the exclusion of other behaviors. Companies with strong cultures have been able to commit people to the organization and have them identify very personally and closely with the organization's success. Superficially, this is seen in the "hoopla" activities associated with an IBM sales meeting, a Tupperware party, or an Amway distributor meeting. Outsiders often ridicule such activities, yet they are part of the process by which some successful companies manage cultural meaning. On one level, corporate culture is analogous to rituals carried out in religious groups. The key point in assessing culture is to realize that in order to transform an organization the culture that provides meaning must be assessed and revamped. The transformational leader needs to articulate new values and norms and then to use multiple change levers ranging from role modeling, symbolic acts, creation of rituals, and revamping of human resource systems and management processes to support new cultural messages.

CONCLUSION

Based on the premise that the pressures for basic organizational change will intensify and not diminish, we strongly believe that transformational leadership, not transactional management, is required for revitalizing our organizations. Ultimately, it is up to our leaders to choose the right kind of leadership and corporate lifestyle.

REFERENCES

1. See J. M. Burns, *Leadership* (New York: Harper & Row, 1978).
2. See N. M. Tichy, *Managing Strategic Change: Technical, Political and Cultural Dynamics* (New York: John Wiley & Sons, 1983).
3. Ibid.
4. See K. H. Blanchard and S. Johnson, *The One Minute Manager* (New York: Berkeley Books, 1982).
5. See T. J. Peters and R. J. Waterman, Jr., *In Search of Excellence* (New York: Harper & Row, 1982).
6. See M. Maccoby, *The Leader* (New York: Ballentine Books, 1981).
7. See W. Bridges, *Making Sense of Life's Transitions* (New York: Addison-Wesley, 1980).
8. Ibid.
9. See: T. E. Deal and A. A. Kennedy, *Corporate Cultures* (Reading, MA: Addison-Wesley, 1982); "Corporate Culture: The Hard-to-Change Values That Spell Success or Failure," *Business Week,* 27 October 1980, pp. 148–160; W. Ulrich, "HRM and Culture: History, Rituals, and Myths," *Human Resource Management* (23/2) Summer 1984.

WHO GETS POWER—AND HOW THEY HOLD ON TO IT: A STRATEGIC CONTINGENCY MODEL OF POWER

Gerald R. Salancik
Jeffrey Pfeffer

Power is held by many people to be a dirty word or, as Warren Bennis has said, "It is the organization's last dirty secret."

This article will argue that traditional "political" power, far from being a dirty business, is, in its most naked form, one of the few mechanisms available for aligning an organization with its own reality. However, institutionalized forms of power—what we prefer to call the cleaner forms of power: authority, legitimization, centralized control, regulations, and the more modern "mangement information systems"—tend to buffer the organization from reality and obscure the demands of its environment. Most great states and institutions declined, not because they played politics, but because they failed to accommodate to the political realities they faced. Political processes, rather than being mechanisms for unfair and unjust allocations and appointments, tend toward the realistic resolution of conflicts among interests. And power, while it eludes definition, is easy enough to recognize by its consequences—the ability of those who possess power to bring about the outcomes they desire.

The model of power we advance is an elaboration of what has been called strategic-contingency theory, a view that sees power as something that accrues to organizational subunits (individuals, departments) that cope with critical organizational problems. Power is used by subunits, indeed, used by all who have it, to enhance their own survival through control of scarce critical resources, through the placement of allies in key positions, and through the definition of organizational problems and policies. Because of the processes by which power develops and is used, organizations become both more aligned and more misaligned with their environments. This contradiction is the most interesting aspect of organizational power, and one that makes administration one of the most precarious of occupations.

WHAT IS ORGANIZATIONAL POWER?

You can walk into most organizations and ask without fear of being misunderstood, "Which are the powerful groups or people in this organization?" Although many organizational informants may be *unwilling* to tell you, it is unlikely they will be *unable* to tell you. Most people do not require explicit definitions to know what power is.

Power is simply the ability to get things done the way one wants them to be done. For a manager who wants an increased budget to launch a project that he thinks is important, his power is measured by his ability to get that budget. For an executive vice-president who wants to be chairman, his power is evidenced by his advancement toward his goal.

People in organizations not only know what you are talking about when you ask who is influential but they are likely to agree with one another to an amazing extent. Recently, we had a chance to observe this in a regional office of an insurance company. The office had 21 department managers; we asked ten of these managers to rank all 21 according to the influence each one had in the organization. Despite the fact that ranking 21 things is a difficult task, the managers sat down and began arranging the names of their colleagues and themselves in a column. Only one person bothered to ask, "What do you mean by influence?" When told "power," he responded, "Oh," and went on. We compared the rankings of all ten managers and found virtually no disagreement among them in the managers ranked among the top five or the bottom five. Differences in the rankings came from department heads claiming more influence for themselves than their colleagues attributed to them.

Such agreement on those who have influence, and those who do not, was not unique to this insurance company. So far we have studied over 20 very different organizations—universities, research firms, factories, banks, retailers, to name a few. In each one we found individuals able to rate themselves and their peers on a scale of influence or power. We have done this both for specific decisions and for general impact on organizational policies. Their agreement was unusually high, which suggests that distributions of influence exist well enough in everyone's mind to be referred to with ease—and we assume with accuracy.

WHERE DOES ORGANIZATIONAL POWER COME FROM?

Earlier we stated that power helps organizations become aligned with their realities. This hopeful prospect follows from what we have dubbed the strategic-contingencies theory of organizational power. Briefly, those subunits most able to cope with the organization's critical problems and uncertainties acquire power. In its simplest form, the strategic-contingencies theory implies that when an organization faces a number of lawsuits that threaten its existence, the legal department will gain power and influence over organizational decisions. Somehow other organizational interest groups will recognize its critical importance and confer upon it a status and power never before enjoyed. This influence may extend beyond handling legal matters and into decisions about product design, advertising production, and so on. Such extensions undoubtedly would be accompanied by appropriate, or acceptable, verbal justifications. In time, the head of the legal department may become the head of the corporation, just as in times past the vice-president for marketing had become the president when market shares were a worrisome problem and, before him, the chief engineer, who had made the production line run as smooth as silk.

Stated in this way, the strategic-contingencies theory of power paints an appealing picture of power. To the extent that power is determined by the critical uncertainties and problems facing the organization and, in turn, influences decisions in the organization, the organization is aligned with the realities it faces. In short, power facilitates the organization's adaptation to its environment—or its problems.

We can cite many illustrations of how influence derives from a subunit's ability to deal with critical contingencies. Michel Crozier described a French cigarette factory in which the maintenance engineers had a considerable say in the plant-wide operation. After some probing he discovered that the group possessed the solution to one of the major problems faced by the company, that of trouble-shooting the elaborate, expensive, and irrascible automated machines that kept breaking down and dumbfounding everyone else. It was the one problem that the plant manager could in no way control.

The production workers, while troublesome from time to time, created no insurmountable problems; the manager could reasonably predict their absenteeism or replace them when necessary. Production scheduling was something he could deal with since, by watching inventories and sales, the demand for cigarettes was known long in advance. Changes in demand could be accommodated by slowing down or speeding up the line. Supplies of tobacco and paper were also easily dealt with through stockpiles and advance orders.

The one thing that management could neither control nor accommodate to, however, was the seemingly happenstance breakdowns. And the foremen couldn't instruct the workers what to do when emergencies developed since the maintenance department kept its records of problems and solutions locked up in a cabinet or in its members' heads. The breakdowns were, in truth, a critical source of uncertainty for the organization, and the maintenance engineers were the only ones who could cope with the problem.

The engineers' strategic role in coping with breakdowns afforded them a considerable say on plant decisions. Schedules and production quotas were set in consultation with them. And the plant manager, while formally their boss, accepted their decisions about personnel in their operation. His submission was to his credit, for without their cooperation he would have had an even more difficult time in running the plant.

Ignoring Critical Consequences

In this cigarette factory, sharing influence with the maintenance workers reflected the plant manager's awareness of the critical contingencies. However, when organizational members are not aware of the critical contingencies they face, and do not share influence accordingly, the failure to do so can create havoc. In one case, an insurance company's regional office was having problems with the performance of one of its departments, the coding department. From the outside, the department looked like a disaster area. The clerks who worked in it were somewhat dissatisfied; their supervisor paid little attention to them, and they resented the hard work. Several other departments were critical of this manager, claiming that she was inconsistent in meeting deadlines. The person most critical was the claims manager. He resented having to wait for work that was handled by her department, claiming that it held up his claims adjusters. Having heard the rumors about dissatisfaction among her subordinates, he attributed the situation to poor supervision. He was second in command in the office and therefore took up the issue with her immediate boss, the head of administrative services. They consulted with the personnel manager and the three of them concluded that the manager needed leadership training to improve her relations with her subordinates. The coding manager objected, saying it was a waste of time, but agreed to give more priority to the claims department's work. Within a week after the training, the results showed that her workers were happier but that the performance of her department had decreased, save for the people serving the claims department.

About this time, we began, quite independently, a study of influence in this organization. We asked the administrative services director to draw up flow charts of how the work of one department moved on to the next department. In the course of the interview, we noticed that the coding department began or interceded in the work flow of most of the other departments and casually mentionned to him. "The coding manager must be very influential." He said "No, not really. Why would you think so?" Before we could reply he recounted the story of her leadership training and the fact that things were worse. We then told him that it seemed obvious that the coding department would be influential from the fact that all the other departments depended on it. It was also clear why productivity had fallen. The coding manager took the training seriously and began spending more time raising her workers' spirits than she did worrying about the problems of all the departments that depended on her. Giving priority to the claims area only exaggerated the problem, for their work was getting done at the expense of the work of the other departments. Eventually the company hired a few more clerks to relieve the pressure in the coding department and performance returned to a more satisfactory level.

Originally we got involved with this insurance company to examine how the influence of each manager evolved from his or her department's handling of critical organizational contingencies. We reasoned that one of the most important contingencies faced by all profit-making organizations was that of generating income. Thus we expected managers would be influential to the extent to which they contributed to this function. Such was the case. The underwriting managers, who wrote the policies that committed the premiums, were the most influential; the claims managers who kept a lid on the funds flowing out, were a close second. Least influential were the managers of functions unrelated to revenue, such as mailroom and payroll managers. And contrary to what the administrative services manager believed, the third most powerful department head (out of 21) was the woman in charge of the coding function, which consisted of rating, recording, and keeping track of the codes of all policy applications and contracts. Her peers attributed more influence to her than could have been inferred from her place on the organization chart. And it was not surprising, since they all depended on her department. The coding department's records, their accuracy and the speed with which they could be retrieved, affected virtually every other operating department in the insurance office. The underwriters depended on them in getting the contracts straight; the typing department depended on them in preparing the formal contract document; the claims department depended on them in adjusting claims; and accounting depended on them for billing. Unfortunately, the "bosses" were not aware of these dependencies, for unlike the cigarette factory, there were no massive breakdowns that made them obvious, while the coding manager, who was a hard-working but quiet person, did little to announce her importance.

The cases of this plant and office illustrate nicely a basic point about the source of power in organizations. The basis for power in an organization derives from the ability of a person or subunit to take or not take actions that are desired by others. The coding manager was seen as influential by those who depended on her department, but not by the people at the top. The engineers were influential because of their role in keeping the plant operating. The two cases differ in these respects: The coding supervisor's source of power was not as widely recognized as that of the maintenance engineers, and she did not use her source of power to influence decisions; the maintenance engineers did. Whether power is used to influence anything is a separate issue. We should not confuse this issue with the fact that power derives from a social situation in which one person has a capacity to do something and another person does not, but wants it done.

POWER SHARING IN ORGANIZATIONS

Power is shared in organizations; and it is shared out of necessity more than out of concern for principles of organizational development or participatory democracy. Power is shared because no one person controls all the desired activities in the organization. While the factory owner may hire people to operate his noisy machines, once hired they have some control over the use of the machinery. And thus they have power over him in the same way he has power over them. Who has more power over whom is a mooter point than that of recognizing the inherent nature of organizing as a sharing of power.

Let's expand on the concept that power derives from the activities desired in an organization. A major way of managing influence in organizations is through the designation of activities. In a bank we studied, we saw this principle in action. This bank was planning to install a computer system for routine credit evaluation. The bank, rather progressive-minded, was concerned that the change would have adverse effects on employees and therefore surveyed their attitudes.

The principal opposition to the new system came, interestingly, not from the employees who performed the routine credit checks, some of whom would be relocated because of the change, but from the manager of the credit department. His reason was quite simple. The manager's primary function was to give official approval to the applications, catch any employee mistakes before giving approval, and arbitrate any difficulties the clerks had in deciding what to do. As a consequence of his role, others in the organization, including his superiors, subordinates, and colleagues, attributed considerable importance to him. He, in turn, for example, could point to the low proportion of credit approvals, compared with other financial institutions, that resulted in bad debts. Now, to his mind, a wretched machine threatened to transfer his role to a computer programmer, a man who knew nothing of finance and who, in addition, had ten years less seniority. The credit manager eventually quit for a position at a smaller firm with lower pay, but one in which he would have more influence than his redefined job would have left him with.

Because power derives from activities rather than individuals, an individual's or subgroup's power is never absolute and derives ultimately from the context of the situation. The amount of power an individual has at any one time depends, not only on the activities he or she controls, but also on the existence of other persons or means by which the activities can be achieved and on those who determine what ends are desired and, hence, on what activities are desired and critical for the organization. One's own power always depends on other people for these two reasons. Other people, or groups or organizations, can determine the definition of what is a critical contingency for the organization and can also undercut the uniqueness of the individual's personal contribution to the critical contingencies of the organization.

Perhaps one can best appreciate how situationally dependent power is by examining how it is distributed. In most societies, power organizes around scarce and critical resources. Rarely does power organize around abundant resources. In the United States, a person doesn't become powerful because he or she can drive a car. There are simply too many others who can drive with equal facility. In certain villages in Mexico, on the other hand, a person with a car is accredited with enormous social status and plays a key role in the community. In addition to scarcity, power is also limited by the need for one's capacities in a social system. While a racer's ability to drive a car around a 90° turn at 80 mph may be sparsely distributed in a society, it is not likely to lend the driver much power in the society. The ability simply does not play a central role in the activities of the society.

The fact that power revolves around scarce and critical activities, of course, makes the control and organization of those activities a major battleground in struggles for power. Even relatively abundant or trivial resources can become the bases for power if one can organize and control their allocation and the definition of what is critical. Many occupational and professional groups attempt to do just this in modern economies. Lawyers organize themselves into associations, regulate the entrance requirements for novitiates, and then get laws passed specifying situations that require the services of an attorney. Workers had little power in the conduct of industrial affairs until they organized themselves into closed and controlled systems. In recent years, women and blacks have tried to define themselves as important and critical to the social system, using law to reify their status.

In organizations there are obviously opportunities for defining certain activities as more critical than others. Indeed, the growth of managerial thinking to include defining organizational objectives and goals has done much to foster these opportunities. One sure way to liquidate the power of groups in the organization is to define the need for their services out of existence. David Halberstam presents a description of how just such a thing happened to the group of correspondents that evolved around Edward R. Murrow, the brilliant journalist, interviewer, and war correspondent of CBS News. A close friend of CBS chairman and controlling stockholder William S. Paley, Murrow, and the news department he directed, were endowed with freedom to do what they felt was right. He used it to create some of the best documentaries and commentaries ever seen on television. Unfortunately, television became too large, too powerful, and too suspect in the eyes of the federal government that licensed it. It thus became, or at least the top executives believed it had become, too dangerous to have in-depth, probing commentary on the news. Crisp, dry, uneditorializing headliners were considered safer. Murrow was out and Walter Cronkite was in.

The power to define what is critical in an organization is no small power. Moreover, it is the key to understanding why organizations are either aligned with their environments or misaligned. If an organization defines certain activities as critical when in fact they are not critical, given the flow of resources coming into the organization, it is not likely to survive, at least in its present form.

Most organization managers evolve a distribution of power and influence that is aligned with the critical realities they face in the environment. The environment, in turn, includes both the internal environment, the shifting situational contexts in which particular decisions get made, and the external environment that it can hope to influence but is unlikely to control.

THE CRITICAL CONTINGENCIES

The critical contingencies facing most organizations derive from the environmental context within which they operate. This determines the available needed resources and thus determines the problems to be dealt with. That power organizes around handling these problems suggests an important mechanism by which organizations keep in tune with their external environments. The strategic contingencies model implies that subunits that contribute to the critical resources of the organization will gain influence in the organization. Their influence presumably is then used to bend the organization's activities to the contingencies that determine its resources. This idea may strike one as obvious. But its obviousness in no way diminishes its importance. Indeed, despite its obviousness, it escapes the notice of many organizational analysts and managers, who all too frequently think of the organization in terms of a descending pyramid, in which all the departments in one tier hold equal power and status. This presumption denies the reality that departments differ in the contributions they are believed to make to the overall organization's resources, as well as to the fact that some are more equal than others.

Because of the importance of this idea to organizational effectiveness, we decided to examine it carefully in a large midwestern university. A university offers an excellent site for studying power. It is composed of departments with nominally equal power and is administered by a central executive structure much like other bureaucracies. However, at the same time it is a situation in which the departments have clearly defined identities and face diverse external environments. Each department has its own bodies of knowledge, its own institutions, its own sources of prestige and resources. Because the departments operate in different external environments, they are likely to contribute differentially to the resources of the overall organization. Thus a physics department with close ties to NASA may contribute substantially to the funds of the university; and a history department with a renowned historian in residence may contribute to the intellectual credibility or prestige of the whole university. Such variations permit one to examine how these various contributions lead to obtaining power within the university.

We analyzed the influence of 29 university departments throughout an 18-month period in their history. Our chief interest was to determine whether departments that brought more critical resources to the university would be more powerful than departments that contributed fewer or less critical resources.

To identify the critical resources each department contributed, the heads of all departments were interviewed about the importance of seven different resources to the university's success. The seven included undergraduate students (the factor determining size of the state allocations by the university), national prestige, administrative expertise, and so on. The most critical resource was found to be contract and grant monies received by a department's faculty for research or consulting services. At this university, contract and grants contributed somewhat less than 50 percent of the overall budget, with the remainder primarily coming from state appropriations. The importance attributed to contract and grant monies, and the rather minor importance of undergraduate students, was not surprising for this particular university. The university was a major center for graduate education; many of its departments ranked in the top ten of their respective fields. Grant and contract monies were the primary source of discretionary funding available for maintaining these programs of graduate education, and hence for maintaining the university's prestige. The prestige of the university itself was critical both in recruiting able students and attracting top-notch faculty.

From university records it was determined what relative contributions each of the 29 departments made to the various needs of the university (national prestige, outside grants, teaching). Thus, for instance, one department may have contributed to the university by teaching 7 percent of the instructional units, bringing in 2 percent of the outside contracts and grants, and having a national ranking of 20. Another department, on the other hand, may have taught one percent of the instructional units, contributed 12 percent to the grants, and be ranked the third best department in its field within the country.

The question was: Do these different contributions determine the relative power of the departments within the university? Power was measured in several ways; but regardless of how measured, the answer was "Yes." Those three resources together accounted for about 70 percent of the variance in subunit power in the university.

But the most important predictor of departmental power was the department's contribution to the contracts and grants of the university. Sixty percent of the variance in power was due to this one factor, suggesting that the power of departments derived primarily from the dollars they provided for graduate education, the activity believed to be the most important for the organization.

THE IMPACT OF ORGANIZATIONAL POWER ON DECISION MAKING

The measure of power we used in studying this university was an analysis of the responses of the department heads we interviewed. While such perceptions of power might be of interest in their own right, they contribute little to our understanding of how the distribution of power might serve to align an organization with its critical realities. For this we must look to how power actually influences the decisions and policies of organizations.

While it is perhaps not absolutely valid, we can generally gauge the relative importance of a department of an organization by the size of the budget allocated to it relative to other departments. Clearly it is of importance to the administrators of those departments whether they get squeezed in a budget crunch or are given more funds to strike out after new opportunities. And it should also be clear that when those decisions are made and one department can go ahead and try new approaches while another must cut back on the old, then the deployment of the resources of the organization in meeting its problems is most directly affected.

Thus our study of the university led us to ask the following questions. Does power lead to influence in the organization? To answer this question, we found it useful first to ask another one, namely: Why should department heads try to influence organizational decisions to favor their own departments to the exclusion of other departments? While this second question may seem a bit naive to anyone who has witnessed the political realities of organizations, we posed it in a context of research on organizations that sees power as an illegitimate threat to the neater rational authority of modern bureaucracies. In this context, decisions are not believed to be made because of the dirty business of politics but because of the overall goals and purposes of the organization. In a university, one reasonable basis for decision making is the teaching workload of departments and the demands that follow from that workload. We would expect, therefore, that departments with heavy student demands for courses would be able to obtain funds for teaching. Another reasonable basis for decision making is quality. We would expect, for that reason, that departments with esteemed reputations would be able to obtain funds both because their quality suggests they might use such funds effectively and because such funds would allow them to maintain their quality. A rational model of bureaucracy intimates, then, that the organizational decisions taken would favor those who perform the stated purposes of the organization—teaching undergraduates and training professional and scientific talent—well.

The problem with rational models of decision making, however, is that what is rational to one person may strike another as irrational. For most departments, resources are a question of survival. While teaching undergraduates may seem to be a major goal for some members of the university, developing knowledge may seem so to others; and to still others, advising governments and other institutions about policies may seem to be the crucial business. Everyone has his own idea of the proper priorities in a just world. Thus goals rather than being clearly defined and universally agreed upon are blurred and contested throughout the organization. If such is the case, then the decisions taken on behalf of the organization as a whole are likely to reflect the goals of those who prevail in political contests, namely, those with power in the organization.

Will organizational decisions always reflect the distribution of power in the organization? Probably not. Using power for influence requires a certain expenditure of effort, time, and resources. Prudent and judicious persons are not likely to use their power needlessly or wastefully. And it is likely that power will be used to influence organizational decisions primarily under circumstances that both require and favor its use. We have examined three conditions that are likely to affect the use of power in organizations: scarcity, criticality, and uncertainty. The first suggests that subunits will try to exert influence when the resources of the organization are scarce. If there is an abundance of resources, then a particular department or a particular individual has little need to attempt influence. With little effort, he can get all he wants anyway.

The second condition, criticality, suggests that a subunit will attempt to influence decisions to obtain resources that are critical to its own survival and activities. Criticality implies that one would not waste effort, or risk being labeled obstinate, by fighting over trivial decisions affecting one's operations.

An office manager would probably balk less about a threatened cutback in copying machine usage than about a reduction in typing staff. An advertising department head would probably worry less about losing his lettering artist than his illustrator. Criticality is difficult to define because what is critical depends on people's beliefs about what is critical. Such beliefs may or may not be based on experience and knowledge and may or may not be agreed upon by all. Scarcity, for instance, may itself affect conceptions of criticality. When slack resources drop off, cutbacks have to be made—those "hard decisions," as congressmen and resplendent administrators like to call them. Managers then find themselves scrapping projects they once held dear.

The third condition that we believe affects the use of power is uncertainty: When individuals do not agree about what the organization should do or how to do it, power and other social processes will affect decisions. The reason for this is simply that, if there are no clear-cut criteria available for resolving conflicts of interest, then the only means for resolution is some form of social process, including power, status, social ties, or some arbitrary process like flipping a coin or drawing straws. Under conditions of uncertainty, the powerful manager can argue his case on any grounds and usually win it. Since there is no real consensus, other contestants are not likely to develop counter arguments or amass sufficient opposition. Moreover, because of his power and their need for access to the resources he controls, they are more likely to defer to his arguments.

Although the evidence is slight, we have found that power will influence the allocations of scarce and critical resources. In the analysis of power in the university, for instance, one of the most critical resources needed by departments is the general budget. First granted by the state legislature, the general budget is later allocated to individual departments by the university administration in response to requests from the department heads. Our analysis of the factors that contribute to a department getting more or less of this budget indicated that subunit power was the major predictor, overriding such factors as student demand for courses, national reputations of departments, or even the size of a department's faculty. Moreover, other research has shown that when the general budget has been cut back or held below previous uninflated levels, leading to monies becoming more scarce, budget allocations mirror departmental powers even more closely.

Student enrollment and faculty size, of course, do themselves relate to budget allocations, as we would expect since they determine a department's need for resources, or at least offer visible testimony of needs. But departments are not always able to get what they need by the mere fact of needing them. In one analysis it was found that high-power departments were able to obtain budget without regard to their teaching loads and, in some cases, actually in inverse relation to their teaching load. In contrast, low-power departments could get increases in budget only when they could justify the increases by a recent growth in teaching load, and then only when it was far in excess of norms for other departments.

General budget is only one form of resources that is allocated to departments. There are others such as special grants for student fellowships or faculty research. These are critical to departments because they affect the ability to attract other resources, such as outstanding faculty or students. We examined how power influenced the allocations of four resources department heads had described as critical and scarce.

When the four resources were arrayed from the most to the least critical and scarce, we found that departmental power best predicted the allocations of the most critical and scarce resources. In other words, the analysis of how power influences organizational allocations leads to this conclusion. Those subunits most likely to survive in times of strife are those that are more critical to the organization. Their importance to the organization gives them power to influence resource allocations that enhance their own survival.

HOW EXTERNAL ENVIRONMENT IMPACTS EXECUTIVE SELECTION

Power not only influences the survival of key groups in an organization, it also influences the selection of individuals to key leadership positions, and by such a process further aligns the organization with its environmental context.

We can illustrate this with a recent study of the selection and tenure of chief administrators in 57 hospitals in Illinois. We assumed that since the critical problems facing the organization would enhance the power of certain groups at the expense of others, then the leaders to emerge should be those most relevant to the context of the hospitals. To assess this we asked each chief administrator about his professional background and how long he had been in office. The replies were then related to the hospitals' funding, ownership, and competitive conditions for patients and staff.

One aspect of a hospital's context is the source of its budget. Some hospitals, for instance, are run much like other businesses. They sell bed space, patient care, and treatment services. They charge fees sufficient both to cover their costs and to provide capital for expansion. The main source of both their operating and capital funds is patient billings. Increasingly, patient billings are paid for, not by patients, but by private insurance companies. Insurers like Blue Cross dominate and represent a potent interest group outside a hospital's control but critical to its income. The insurance companies, in order to limit their own costs, attempt to hold down the fees allowable to hospitals, which they do effectively from their positions on state rate boards. The squeeze on hospitals that results from fees increasing slowly while costs climb rapidly more and more demands the talents of cost accountants or people trained in the technical expertise of hospital administration.

By contrast, other hospitals operate more like social service institutions, either as government healthcare units (Bellevue Hospital in New York City and Cook County Hospital in Chicago, for example) or as charitable institutions. These hospitals obtain a large proportion of their operating and capital funds, not from privately insured patients, but from government subsidies or private donations. Such institutions rather than requiring the talents of a technically efficient administrator are likely to require the savvy of someone who is well integrated into the social and political power structure of the community.

Not surprisingly, the characteristics of administrators predictably reflect the funding context of the hospitals with which they are associated. Those hospitals with larger proportions of their budget obtained from private insurance companies were most likely to have administrators with backgrounds in accounting and least likely to have administrators whose professions were business or medicine. In contrast, those hospitals with larger proportions of their budget derived from private donations and local governments were most likely to have administrators with business or professional backgrounds and least likely to have accountants. The same held for formal training in hospital management. Professional hospital administrators could easily be found in hospitals drawing their incomes from private insurance and rarely in hospitals dependent on donations or legislative appropriations.

As with the selection of administrators, the context of organizations has also been found to affect the removal of executives. The environment, as a source of organizational problems, can make it more or less difficult for executives to demonstrate their values to the organization. In the hospitals we studied, long-term administrators came from hospitals with few problems. They enjoyed amicable and stable relations with their local business and social communities and suffered little competition for funding and staff. The small city hospital director who attended civic and Elks meetings while running the only hospital within a 100-mile radius, for example, had little difficulty holding on to his job. Turnover was highest in hospitals with the most problems, a phenomenon similar to that observed in a study of industrial organizations in which turnover was highest among executives in industries with competitive environments and unstable market conditions. The interesting thing is that instability characterized the industries rather than the individual firms in them. The troublesome conditions in the individual firms were attributed, or rather misattributed, to the executives themselves.

It takes more than problems, however, to terminate a manager's leadership. The problems themselves must be relevant and critical. This is clear from the way in which an administrator's tenure is affeccted by the status of the hospital's operating budget. Naively we might assume that all administrators would need to show a surplus. Not necessarily so. Again, we must distinguish between those hospitals that depend on private donations for funds and those that do not. Whether an endowed budget shows a surplus or deficit is less important than the hospital's relations with benefactors. On the other hand, with a budget dependent on patient billing, a surplus is almost essential; monies for new equipment or expansion must be drawn from it, and without them quality care becomes more difficult and patients scarcer. An administrator's tenure reflected just these considerations. For those hospitals dependent upon private donations, the length of an administrator's term depended not at all on the status of the operating budget but was fairly predictable from the hospital's relations with the business community. On the other hand, in hospitals dependent on the operating budget for capital financing, the greater the deficit the shorter was the tenure of the hospital's principal administrators.

CHANGING CONTINGENCIES
AND ERODING POWER BASES

The critical contingencies facing the organization may change. When they do, it is reasonable to expect that the power of individuals and subgroups will change in turn. At times the shift can be swift and shattering, as it was recently for powerholders in New York City. A few years ago it was believed that David Rockefeller was one of the ten most powerful people in the city, as tallied by *New York* magazine, which annually sniffs out power for the delectation of its readers. But that was before it was revealed that the city was in financial trouble, before Rockefeller's Chase Manhattan Bank lost some of its own financial luster, and before brother Nelson lost some of his political influence in Washington. Obviously David Rockefeller was no longer as well positioned to help bail the city out. Another loser was an attorney with considerable personal connections to the political and religious leaders of the city. His talents were no longer in much demand. The persons with more influence were the bankers and union pension fund executors who fed money to the city; community leaders who represent blacks and Spanish-Americans, in contrast, witnessed the erosion of their power bases.

One implication of the idea that power shifts with changes in organizational environments is that the dominant coalition will tend to be that group that is most appropriate for the organization's environment, as also will the leaders of an organization. One can observe this historically in the top executives of industrial firms in the United States. Up until the early 1950s, many top corporations were headed by former production line managers or engineers who gained prominence because of their abilities to cope with the problems of production. Their success, however, only spelled their demise. As production became routinized and mechanized, the problem of most firms became one of selling all those goods they so efficiently produced. Marketing executives were more frequently found in corporate boardrooms. Success outdid itself again, for keeping markets and production steady and stable requires the kind of control that can only come from acquiring competitors and suppliers or the invention of more and more appealing products—ventures that typically require enormous amounts of capital. During the 1960s, financial executives assumed the seats of power. And they, too, will give way to others. Edging over the horizon are legal experts, as regulation and antitrust suits are becoming more and more frequent in the 1970s, suits that had their beginnings in the success of the expansion generated by prior executives. The more distant future, which is likely to be dominated by multinational corporations, may see former secretaries of state and their minions increasingly serving as corporate figureheads.

THE NONADAPTIVE CONSEQUENCES OF ADAPTATION

From what we have said thus far about power aligning the organization with its own realities, an intelligent person might react with a resounding ho-hum, for it all seems too obvious. Those with the ability to get the job done are given the job to do.

However, there are two aspects of power that make it more useful for understanding organizations and their effectiveness. First, the "job" to be done has a way of expanding itself until it becomes less and less clear what the job is. Napoleon began by doing a job for France in the war with Austria and ended up Emperor, convincing many that only he could keep the peace. Hitler began by promising an end to Germany's troubling postwar depression and ended up convincing more people than is comfortable to remember that he was destined to be the savior of the world. In short, power is a capacity for influence that extends far beyond the original bases that created it. Second, power tends to take on institutionalized forms that enable it to endure well beyond its usefulness to an organization.

There is an important contradiction in what we have observed about organizational power. On the one hand we have said that power derives from the contingencies facing an organization and that when those contingencies change so do the bases for power. On the other hand we have asserted that subunits will tend to use their power to influence organizational decisions in their own favor, particularly when their own survival is threatened by the scarcity of critical resources. The first statement implies that an organization will tend to be aligned with its environment since power will tend to bring to key positions those with capabilities relevant to the context. The second implies that those in power will not give up their positions so easily; they will pursue policies that guarantee their continued domination. In short, change and stability operate through the same mechanism, and, as a result, the organization will never be completely in phase with its environment or its needs.

The study of hospital administrators illustrates how leadership can be out of phase with reality. We argued that privately funded hospitals needed trained technical administrators more so than did hospitals funded by donations. The need as we perceived it was matched in most hospitals, but by no means in all. Some organizations did not conform with our predictions. These deviations imply that some administrators were able to maintain their positions independent of their suitability for those positions. By dividing administrators into those with long and short terms of office, one finds that the characteristics of longer-termed administrators were virtually unrelated to the hospital's context. The shorter-termed chiefs on the other hand had characteristics more appropriate for the hospital's problems. For a hospital to have a recently appointed head implies that the previous administrator had been unable to endure by institutionalizing himself.

One obvious feature of hospitals that allowed some administrators to enjoy a long tenure was a hospital's ownership. Administrators were less entrenched when their hospitals were affiliated with and dependent upon larger organizations, such as governments or churches. Private hospitals offered more secure positions for administrators. Like private corporations, they tend to have more diffused ownership, leaving the administrator unopposed as he institutionalizes his reign. Thus he endures, sometimes at the expense of the performance of the organization. Other research has demonstrated that corporations with diffuse ownership have poorer earnings than those in which the control of the manager is checked by a dominant shareholder. Firms that overload their boardrooms with more insiders than are appropriate for their context have also been found to be less profitable.

A word of caution is required about our judgment of "appropriateness." When we argue some capabilities are more appropriate for one context than another, we do so from the perspective of an outsider and on the basis of reasonable assumptions as to the problems the organization will face and the capabilities they will need. The fact that we have been able to predict the distributon of influence and the characteristics of leaders suggests that our reasoning is not incorrect. However, we do not think that all organizations follow the same pattern. The fact that we have not been able to predict outcomes with 100 percent accuracy indicates they do not.

MISTAKING CRITICAL CONTINGENCIES

One thing that allows subunits to retain their power is their ability to name their functions as critical to the organization when they may not be. Consider again our discussion of power in the university. One might wonder why the most critical tasks were defined as graduate education and scholarly research, the effect of which was to lend power to those who brought in grants and contracts. Why not something else? The reason is that the more powerful departments argued for those criteria and won their case, partly because they were more powerful.

In another analysis of this university, we found that all departments advocate self-serving criteria for budget allocation. Thus a department with large undergraduate enrollments argued that enrollments should determine budget allocations, a department with a strong national reputation saw prestige as the most reasonable basis for disturbing funds, and so on. We further found that advocating such self-serving criteria actually benefited a department's budget allotments but, also, it paid off more for departments that were already powerful.

Organizational needs are consistent with a current distribution of power also because of a human tendency to categorize problems in familiar ways. An accountant sees problems with organizational performance as cost accountancy problems or inventory flow problems. A sales manager sees them as problems with markets, promotional strategies, or just unaggressive sales people. But what is the truth?

Since it does not automatically announce itself, it is likely that those with prior credibility, or those with power, will be favored as the enlightened. This bias, while not intentionally self-serving, further concentrates power among those who already possess it, independent of changes in the organization's context.

INSTITUTIONALIZING POWER

A third reason for expecting organizational contingencies to be defined in familiar ways is that the current holders of power can structure the organization in ways that institutionalize themselves. By institutionalization we mean the establishment of relatively permanent structures and policies that favor the influence of a particular subunit. While in power, a dominant coalition has the ability to institute constitutions, rules, procedures, and information systems that limit the potential power of others while continuing their own.

The key to institutionalizing power always is to create a device that legitimates one's own authority and diminishes the legitimacy of others. When the "Divine Right of Kings" was envisioned centuries ago it was to provide an unquestionable foundation for the supremacy of royal authority. There is generally a need to root the exercise of authority in some higher power. Modern leaders are no less affected by this need. Richard Nixon, with the aid of John Dean, reified the concept of executive privilege, which meant in effect that what the President wished not to be discussed need not be discussed.

In its simpler form, institutionalization is achieved by designating positions or roles for organizational activities. The creation of a new post legitimizes a function and forces organization members to orient to it. By designating how this new post relates to older, more established posts, moreover, one can structure an organization to enhance the importance of the function in the organization. Equally, one can diminish the importance of traditional functions. This is what happened in the end with the insurance company we mentioned that was having trouble with its coding department. As the situation unfolded, the claims director continued to feel dissatisfied about the dependency of his functions on the coding manager. Thus he instituted a reorganization that resulted in two coding departments. In so doing, of course, he placed activities that affected his department under his direct control, presumably to make the operation more effective. Similarly, consumer-product firms enhance the power of marketing by setting up a coordinating role to interface production and marketing functions and then appoint a marketing manager to fill the role.

The structures created by dominant powers sooner or later become fixed and unquestioned features of the organization. Eventually, this can be devastating. It is said that the battle of Jena in 1806 was lost by Frederick the Great, who died in 1786. Though the great Prussion leader had not direct hand in the disaster, his imprint on the army was so thorough, so embedded in its skeletal underpinnings, that the organization was inappropriate for others to lead in different times.

Another important source of institutionalized power lies in the ability to structure information systems. Setting up committees to investigate particular organizational issues and having them report only to particular individuals or groups, facilitates their awareness of problems by members of those groups while limiting the awareness of problems by the members of other groups. Obviously, those who have information are in a better position to interpret the problems of an organization, regardless of how realistically they may, in fact, do so.

Still another way to institutionalize power is to distribute rewards and resources. The dominant group may quiet competing interest groups with small favors and rewards. The credit for this artful form of cooptation belongs to Louis XIV. To avoid usurpation of his power by the nobles of France and the Fronde that had so troubled his father's reign, he built the palace at Versailles to occupy them with hunting and gossip. Awed, the courtiers basked in the reflected glories of the "Sun King" and the overwhelming setting he had created for his court.

At this point, we have not systematically studied the institutionalization of power. But we suspect it is an important condition that mediates between the environment of the organization and the capabilities of the organization for dealing with that environment. The more institutionalized power is within an organization, the more likely an organization will be out of phase with the realities it faces. President Richard Nixon's structuring of his White House is one of the better documented illustrations. If we go back to newspaper and magazine descriptions of how he organized his office from the beginning in 1968, most of what occurred subsequently follows almost as an afterthought. Decisions flowed through virtually only the small White House staff; rewards, small presidential favors of recognition, and perquisites were distributed by this staff to the loyal; and information from the outside world—the press, Congress, the people on the streets—was filtered by the staff and passed along only if initialed "bh." Thus it was not surprising that when Nixon met war protestors in the early dawn, the only thing he could think to talk about was the latest football game, so insulated had he become from their grief and anger.

One of the more interesting implications of institutionalized power is that executive turnover among the executives who have structured the organization is likely to be a rare event that occurs only under the most pressing crisis. If a dominant coalition is able to structure the organization and interpret the meaning of ambiguous events like declining sales and profits or lawsuits, then the "real" problems to emerge will easily be incorporated into traditional molds of thinking and acting. If opposition is designed out of the organization, the interpretations will go unquestioned. Conditions will remain stable until a crisis develops, so overwhelming and visible that even the most adroit rhetorician would be silenced.

IMPLICATIONS FOR THE MANAGEMENT OF POWER IN ORGANIZATIONS

While we could derive numerous implications from this discussion of power, our selection would have to depend largely on whether one wanted to increase one's power, decrease the power of others, or merely maintain one's position. More important, the real implications depend on the particulars of an organizational situation. To understand power in an organization one must begin by looking out-side it—into the environment—for those groups that mediate the organization's outcomes but are not themselves within its control.

Instead of ending with homilies, we will end with a reversal of where we began. Power, rather than being the dirty business it is often made out to be, is probably one of the few mechanisms for reality testing in organizations. And the cleaner forms of power, the institutional forms, rather than having the virtues they are often credited with, can lead the organization to become out of touch. The real trick to managing power in organizations is to ensure somehow that leaders can-not be unaware of the realities of their environments and cannot avoid changing to deal with those realities. That, however, would be like designing the "self-liquidating organization," an unlikely event since anyone capable of designing such an instrument would be obviously in control of the liquidation.

Management would do well to devote more attention to determining the critical contingencies of their environments. For if you conclude, as we do, that the environment sets most of the structure influencing organizational outcomes and problems, and that power derives from the organization's activities that deal with those contingencies, then it is the environment that needs managing, not power. The first step is to construct an accurate model of the environment, a process that is quite difficult for most organizations. We have recently started a project to aid administration in systematically understanding their environments. From this experience, we have learned that the most critical blockage to perceiving an organization's reality accurately is a failure to incorporate those with the relevant expertise into the process. Most organizations have the requisite experts on hand but they are positioned so that they can be comfortably ignored.

One conclusion you can, and probably should, derive from our discussion is that power—because of the way it develops and the way it is used—will always result in the organization suboptimizing its performance. However, to this grim absolute, we add a comforting caveat: If any criteria other than power were the basis for determining an organization's decisions, the results would be even worse.

SELECTED BIBLIOGRAPHY

The literature on power is at once both voluminous and frequently empty of con-tent. Some is philosophical musing about the concept of power, while other writing contains popularized palliatives for acquiring and exercising influence. Machiavelli's The Prince, if read carefully, remains the single best prescriptive treatment of power and its use. Most social scientists have approached power descriptively, attempt-ing to understand how it is acquired, how it is used, and what its effects are. Meyer Zald's edited collection Power in Organizations (Vanderbilt University Press, 1970) is one of the more useful sets of thoughts about power from a sociological perspec-tive, while James Tedeschi's edited book, The Social Influences Processes (Aldine-Atherton, 1972) represents the social psychological approach to understanding power and influence. The strategic contingencies' approach with its emphasis on the importance of uncertainty for understanding power in organizations, is described by David Hickson and his colleagues in "A Strategic Contingencies Theory of Intraorganizational Power" (*Administrative Science Quarterly,* December 1971, pp. 216–229).

Unfortunately, while many have written about power theoretically, there have been few empirical examinations of power and its use. Most of the work has taken the form of case studies. Michel Crozier's *The Bureaucratic Phenomenon* (University of Chicago Press, 1964) is important because it describes a group's source of power as control over critical activities and illustrates how power is not strictly derived from hierarchical position. J. Victor Baldridge's *Power and Conflict in the University* (John Wiley & Sons, 1971) and Andrew Pettigrew's study of computer purchase decisions in one English firm (*Politics of Organizational Decision-Making,* Tavistock, 1973) both present insights into the acquisition and use of power in specific instances. Our work has been more empirical and comparative, testing more explicitly the ideas presented in this article. The study of university decision making is reported in articles in the June 1974, pp. 135–151, and December 1974, pp. 453–473, issues of the *Administrative Science Quarterly,* the insurance firm study in J. G. Hunt and L. L. Larson's collection, *Leadership Frontiers* (Kent State University Press, 1975), and the study of hospital administrator succession will appear in 1977 in the *Academy of Management Journal.*

LEADERSHIP:
THE MANAGEMENT OF MEANING

Linda Smircich
Gareth Morgan

The concept of leadership permeates and structures the theory and practice of organizations and hence the way we shape and understand the nature of organized action, and its possibilities. In fact, the concept and practice of leadership, and variant forms of direction and control, are so powerfully ingrained into popular thought that the absence of leadership is often seen as an absence of organization. Many organizations are paralyzed by situations in which people appear for direction, feeling immobilized and disorganized by the sense that they are not being led. Yet other organizations are plagued by the opposite situation characterized in organizational vernacular as one of "all chiefs, no Indians"—the situation where the majority aspire to lead and few to follow. Thus, successful acts of organization are often seen to rest in the synchrony between the initiation of action and the appeal for direction; between the actions of leaders and the receptivity and responsiveness of followers.

In this paper we focus on understanding the phenomenon of leadership, not merely to improve the practice of leadership, but as a means for understanding the phenomenon of organization. For, in leading, managers enact a particular form of social reality with far-reaching, but often poorly understood and appreciated, consequences. We engage in our analysis to reveal how concepts and ideas that dominate management theory and ideology shape managerial practice and the reality of organization. Our appraoch is to analyze leadership as a distinctive kind of social practice, present a case study of leadership in an organizational context, and analyze its consequences for understanding the basic nature of modern corporate life.

THE PHENOMENON OF LEADERSHIP

Leadership is realized in the process whereby one or more individuals succeeds in attempting to frame and define the reality of others. Indeed, leadership situations may be conceived as those in which there exists an *obligation* or a perceived *right* on the part of certain individuals to define the reality of others.

This process is most evident in unstructured group situations where leadership emerges in a natural and spontaneous manner. After periods of interaction, unstructured leaderless groups typically evolve common modes of interpretation and shared understandings of experience that allow them to develop into a social organization (Bennis & Shepard, 1965). Individuals in groups that evolve this way attribute leadership to those members who structure experience in meaningful ways. Certain individuals, as a result of personal inclination or the emergent expectations of others, find themselves adopting or being obliged to take a leadership role by virtue of the part they play in the definition of the situation. They emerge as leaders because of their role in framing experience in a way that provides a viable basis for action, e.g., by mobilizing meaning, articulating and defining what has previously remained implicit or unsaid, by inventing images and meanings that provide a focus for new attention, and by consolidating, confronting, or changing prevailing wisdom (Peters, 1978; Pondy, 1976). Through these diverse means, individual actions can frame and change situations, and in so doing enact a system of shared meaning that provides a basis for organized action. The leader exists as a formal leader only when he or she achieves a situation in which an obligation, expectation, or right to frame experience is presumed, or offered and accepted by others.

Leadership, like other social phenomena, is socially constructed through interaction (Berger & Luckmann, 1966), emerging as a result of the constructions and actions of both leaders and led. It involves a complicity or process of negotiation through which certain individuals, implicity or explicitly, surrender their power to define the nature of their experience to others. Indeed, leadership depends on the existence of individuals willing, as a result of inclination or pressure, to surrender, at least in part, the powers to shape and define their own reality. If a group situation embodies competing definitions of reality, strongly held, no clear pattern of leadership evolves. Often, such situations are characterized by struggles among those who aspire to define the situation. Such groups remain loosely coupled networks of interaction, with members often feeling that they are "disorganized" because they do not share a common way of making sense of their experience.

Leadership lies in large part in generating a point of reference, against which a feeling of organization and direction can emerge. While in certain circumstances the leader's image of reality may be hegemonic, as in the case of charismatic or totalitarian leaders who mesmerize their followers, this is by no means always the case. For the phenomenon of leadership in being interactive is by nature dialectical. It is shaped through the interaction of at least two points of reference, i.e., of leaders and of led.

This dialectic is often the source of powerful internal tensions within leadership situations. These manifest themselves in the conflicting definitions of those who aspire to define reality and in the fact that while the leader of a group may forge a unified pattern of meaning, that every same pattern often provides a point of reference for the negation of leadership (Sennet, 1980). While individuals may look to a leader to frame and concretize their reality, they may also react against, reject, or change the reality thus defined. While leadership often emerges as a result of expectations projected on the emergent leader by the led, the surrender of power involved provides the basis for negation of the situation thus created. Much of the tension in leadership situations stems from this source. Although leaders draw their power from their ability to define the reality of others, their inability to control completely provides seeds of disorganization in the organization of meaning they provide.

The emergence of leadership in unstructured situations thus points toward at least four important aspects of leadership as a phenomenon. First, leadership is essentially a social process defined through interaction. Second, leadership involves a process of defining reality in ways that are sensible to the led. Third, leadership involves a dependency relationship in which individuals surrender their powers to interpret and define reality to others! Fourth, the emergence of formal leadership roles represents an additional stage of institutionalization, in which rights and obligations to define the nature of experience and activity are recognized and formalized.

LEADERSHIP IN FORMALIZED SETTINGS

The main distinguishing feature of formal organization is that the way in which experience is to be structured and defined is built into a stock of taken for granted meanings, or "typifications" in use (Schutz, 1967) that underlie the everyday definition and reality of the organization. In particular, a formal organization is premised upon shared meanings that define roles and authority relationships that institutionalize a pattern of leadership. In essence, formal organization truncates the leadership process observed in natural settings, concretizing its characteristics as a mode of social organization into sets of predetermined roles, relationships, and practices, providing a blueprint of how the experience of organizational members is to be structured.

Roles, for example, institutionalize the interactions and definitions that shape the reality of organization life. Rules, conventions, and work practices present ready-made typifications through which experience is to be made sensible. Authority relationships legitimize the pattern of dependency relations that characterize the process of leadership, specifying who is to define organizational reality, and in what circumstances. Authority relationships institutionalize a hierarchical pattern of interaction in which certain individuals are expected to define the experience of others—to lead, and others to have their experience defined—to follow. So powerful is this process of institutionalized leadership and the expectation that someone has the right and obligation to define reality, that leaders are held to account if they do not lead "effectively." Those expecting to be led, for example, often rationalize their own inaction or ineffectivenes by scapegoating through statements such as "she is a poor manager" or "he is messing things up." On the other hand, occupancy of an authority role presents the leader in every situation with an existential dilemma—how to define and strucutre the element of organizational reality encountered at a given time. Formal organizations are often heavily populated by those who feel obliged to define the reality and experience of others in a way that is consistent with their idea of "being a good leader." To fail in this obligation is to fail in one's organizational role.

In these ways, patterns of formal organization institutionalize aspects of the leadership process within the context of a unified structure that specifies patterns of desired interaction, sense making, and dependency. As in the case of leadership as an emergent process, formal structures of organized action also contain a dialectical tension between the pattern of action and meaning that the structure seeks to establish, and the tendency of individuals to reinterpret, or even react against, the structure thus defined. While submitting to the dominant pattern of meaning, individuals frequently strive to develop patterns of their own, a phenomenon well documented in studies of the so-called "informal organization" (Roethlisberger & Dickson, 1939).

It is this inherent tension that calls for the development of a mediating form of leadership, bridging the gulf between the requirements of institutionalized structure and the natural inclinations of its human agents. It is this form of leadership that we most often recognize as leadership in informal organizations—the interpersonal process linking structure and the human beings who inhabit this structure. The person that is most easily recognized as an organizational leader is one who rises above and beyond the specification of formal structure to provide members of the organization with a sense that they are organized, even amidst an everyday feeling that at a detailed level everything runs the danger of falling apart.

Similarly, successful corporate leaders who give direction to the organization in a strategic sense frequently do so by providing an image or pattern of thinking in a way that has meaning for those directly involved (Quinn, 1980). This is reflected in part in Selznick's (1957) conception of leadership as involving the embodiment of organizational values and purpose. Strategic leadership, in effect, involves providing a conception and direction for organizational process that goes above and beyond what is embedded in the fabric of organization as a structure, i.e., a reified and somewhat static pattern of meaning.

Formal organization thus embodies at least two distinctive, yet complementary aspects of the phenomon of leadership: (1) the structure of organization institutionalizes the leadership process into a network of roles, often in an overconcretized and dehumanizing form; (2) mediating or interpersonal leadership—what is most evident as leadership in action, operationalizes the principles of leadership as an emergent process within the context of the former. This is usually as a means of transcending the limitations of the former for containing the dialectical tension that it embodies, and as a means of giving the whole coherence and direction over time. These two aspects of leadership have been well recognized in leadership research (Katz & Kahn, 1966) and are frequently interpreted and studied in terms of a relationship between "initiating structure" and "consideration" (e.g., Stogdill, 1974).

The phenomenon of leadership in formal organizations has been conceptualized and studied in many ways. Leadership research has sought for an understanding of leadership in terms of the personal traits of leaders (Mann, 1959), in terms of situations in which they lead (Fiedler, 1967), in terms of what they do (Mintzberg, 1973) or some combination thereof. Such approaches to the study of leadership tap into important attributes of what leadership may involve in a day to day practice, particularly in terms of action requirements, and identify those practices most likely to work in different situations. Other approaches have viewed leadership as a process of exchange and influence (Barnard, 1938; Jacobs, 1971), and attempts have been made to understand the nature of the interactions and transactions necessary for effective leadership to occur (Bougon, Note 1). In the remainder of this paper, we wish to supplement these views with an approach to studying leadership that focuses on the way detailed interactive situations acquire meaningful form.

LEADERSHIP AS THE MANAGEMENT OF MEANING

A focus on the way meaning in organized settings is created, sustained, and changed provides a powerful means of understanding the fundamental nature of leadership as a social process. In understanding the way leadership actions attempt to shape and interpret situations to guide organizational members into a common interpretation of reality, we are able to understand how leadership works to create an important foundation for organized activity. This process can be most easily conceptualized in terms of a relationship between figure and ground. Leadership action involves a moving figure—a flow of actions and utterances (i.e., what leaders do) within the context of a moving ground—the actions, utterances, and general flow of experience that constitute the situation being managed. Leadership as a phenomenon is identifiable within its wider context as a form of action that seeks to shape its context.

Leadership works by influencing the relationship between figure and ground, and hence the meaning and definition of the context as a whole. The actions and utterances of leaders guide the attention of those involved in a situation in ways that are consciously or unconsciously designed to shape the meaning of the situation. The actions and utterances draw attention to particular aspects of the overall flow of experience, transforming what may be complex and ambiguous into something more discrete and vested with a specific pattern of meaning. This is what Schutz (1967) has referred to as a "bracketing" of experience, and Goffman

(1974) as a "framing" of experience, and Bateson (1972) and Weick (1979) as the "punctuation of contexts." The actions and utterances of leaders frame and shape the context of action in such a way that the members of that context are able to use the meaning thus created as a point of reference for their own action and understanding of the situation.

This process can be represented schematically in terms of the model presented in Figure 1. When leaders act they punctuate contexts in ways that provide a focus for the creation of meaning. Their action isolates an element of experience, which can be interpreted in terms of the context in which it is set. Indeed, its meaning is embedded in its relationship with its context. Consider, for example, the simple situation in which someone in a leadership role loses his or her temper over the failure of an employee to complete a job on time. For the leader this action embodies a meaning that links the event to context in a significant way, e.g., "This employee has been asking for a reprimand for a long time"; "This was an important job"; "This office is falling apart." For the employees in the office, the event may be interpreted in similar terms, or a range of different constructions placed upon the situation, e.g., "Don't worry about it, he always loses his temper from time to time"; "She's been under pressure lately because of problems at home."

The leader's action may generate a variety of interpretations that set the basis for meaningful action. It may serve to redefine the context into a situation where the meeting of deadlines assumes greater significance, or merely serves as a brief interruption in daily routine, soon forgotten. As discussed earlier, organized situations are often characterized by complex patterns of meaning, based on rival interpretations of the situation. Different members may make sense of situations with the aid of different interpretive schemes, establishing "counter-realities," a source of tension in the group situation that may set the basis for change of an innovative or disintegrative kind. These counterrealities underwrite much of the political activities within organizations, typified by the leader's loyal lieutenants—the "yes men" accepting and reinforcing the leader's definition of the situation and the "rebels" or "out" groups forging and sustaining alternative views.

Effective leadership depends upon the extent to which the leader's defini-

FIGURE 1 Leadership: A Figure-Ground Relationship Which Creates Figure-Ground Relationships

Framing Experience ⟶	*Interpretation* ⟶	*Meaning and Action*
Leadership action creates a focus of attention within the ongoing stream of experience which characterizes the total situation.	The action assumes significance, i.e., is interpreted within its wider context. The leader has a specific figure-ground relation in mind in engaging in action; other members of the situation construct their own interpretation of this action.	Action is grounded in the interpretive process which links figure and ground.
Such action "brackets" and "frames" an element of experience for interpretation and meaningful action.		

tion of the situation, e.g., "People in this office are not working hard enough," serves as a basis for action by others. It is in this sense that effective leadership rests heavily on the framing of the experience of others, so that action can be guided by common conceptions as to what should occur. The key challenge for a leader is to manage meaning in such a way that individuals orient themselves to the achievement of desirable ends. In this endeavor the use of language, ritual, drama, stories, myths, and symbolic construction of all kinds may play an important role (Pfeffer, 1981; Pondy, Frost, Morgan & Dandridge, 1982; Smircich, 1982). They constitute important tools in the management of meaning. Through words and images, symbolic actions and gestures, leaders can structure attention and evoke patterns of meaning that give them considerable control over the situation being managed. These tools can be used to forge particular kinds of figure-ground relations that serve to create appropriate modes of organized action. Leadership rests as much in these symbolic modes of action as in those instrumental modes of management, direction, and control that define the substance of the leader's formal organizational role.

A CASE STUDY IN THE MANAGEMENT OF MEANING

In order to illustrate the way leadership involves the management of meaning, we present here a case study drawn from an ethnographic study of the executive staff of an insurance company. The company was a division of a larger corporation (10,000 employees), was 11 years old, and employed 200 people. The case focuses on the way the president of the insurance company, Mr. Hall, sought to structure the experience of staff members by creating a particular figure-ground relationship—"Operation June 30th" (OJ30). OJ30 emerged as a prominent organizational event during the fieldwork and provided a focus for studying the process of leadership in action, in this instance, one of limited success.

Methodology

The research was conducted by one of the authors during the summer of 1979. An agreement was reached whereby the researcher was invited to spend six weeks in the insurance company as an observer of the executive staff. The purpose of the research was to learn about the ways of life within the 10-member top management group, to uncover the structures of meaning in use in the setting, and to synthesize an image of the group's reality.

The specific techniques used to gather data in the setting, consistent with the ethnographic tradition (Bogdan & Taylor, 1975; Schatzman & Strauss, 1973; Smircich, Note 2), were oriented toward understanding the realms of intersubjective meaning which gave that organization a semblance of unity and character to its membership.

In this study the researcher maintained the work hours of the organization. Early on she met individually with each of the staff members and explained the project as an attempt to learn about their organization. Each day's activity consisted of observing the management staff in a variety of situations: staff meetings, planning sessions, interactions with their subordinates, on coffee breaks, and in casual conversation. The guiding principle in this endeavor was to obtain a multi-sided view of the situation in order to build a holistic image of the group's understanding of itself. Toward the end of the stay in the company, tape recorded conversations/interviews were held with all staff members, including the president. The raw data from this study consist of daily field notes, documents, tapes of conversations, and the researcher's experience of the situation.

During the field work, the organization was in the midst of OJ30, and it was a prominent topic of discussion by the staff and in the researcher's conversations with the staff. For the purposes of this paper, the data were culled for all references to the OJ30 program so that an account of the situation from multiple viewpoints could be presented.

Ideally, the research would have proceeded in a way that allowed the researcher to reflect back to the group the many-sided image of the meaning system in use that had emerged. As the case study shows, the president's unwillingness to proceed with this aspect of the research was representative of the way of life he strived to maintain in the organization and in that sense provides a form of validation for some of the data presented here.

The Background to Operation June 30th

"Operation June 30th" was integrated by Mr. Hall, the president, in direct response to complaints by the district sales managers that the agents in the field were not getting adequate service from the home office. Insurance claims, applications, endorsements, and renewals were not being handled promptly. The agents were getting complaints from their customers about long delays; consequently, they submitted second and third work requests that only served to make the volume of paperwork greater. The slowdown in processing of paperwork also meant that the agents' commission checks were slow in going out so that they did not receive their commission in the month of sale.

After hearing the frustration of the Sales Department, Hall considered what might be done.[2] He conferred with the vice-president of administrative operations and the vice-president of claims and asked them if they thought it would be possible to have processing operations current by June 30th, the end of the fiscal year. President Hall then wrote an announcement (Figure 2), showed it to the vice-presidents for their comments and approval, and released it to the district sales managers.

With the initiation of OJ30, makeshift posters proclaiming "Operation June 30th Goals Week of June ____" were attached to file cabinets in the operations area. To bring the workflow up to date, overtime work (evenings and Saturdays) was expected, and other departments were encouraged to help out wherever possible by loaning people during the week or by urging their people to come in on the weekends. Each week at the staff meeting a status report was made by the vice-president of operations on the number of files that had been processed through each of the operating units.

At Hall's staff meeting of July 2nd, the vice-president of operations declared OJ30 a "success." During that meeting an energetic discussion about how to express

WHAT:	A special program designed to bring all insurance processing activities up to date by June 30, 1979.
WHY:	The present work backlog is having an adverse impact on total insurance operations.
HOW:	1. All departments will make a concerted effort to eliminate all backlogs. The goal is to have work conditions current in all departments by June 30. 2. All insurance home office employees who have the time will be expected to "volunteer" to assist other departments by performing certain assigned processing tasks until June 30. Procedures relative to this will be developed.
TIMING:	Operation June 30 will commence on Monday, May 14 and will terminate on Saturday, June 30.
PRIORITY:	This program has the highest priority. Nothing else in insurance is of more importance.
REPORTS:	Each staff member will report in writing weekly to Mr. Hall on the status of work conditions in his or her department.

FIGURE 2 Operation June 30

gratitude to the employees took place. The company ultimately provided a free lunch for the employees to thank them for their efforts, and a written statement of progress was prepared for the district sales managers. But privately some staff members expressed quite differing views about what had occurred. In fact some held the opinion that the whole affair was a failure because it did not address the real problems in the company.

OJ30 was a focus for the construction of different interpretations of reality. While the president and some of his staff constructed the situation in one way, other members forged their own view of the situation through the interplay of quite a different figure-ground relationship. It is instructive to examine the way the dynamics of the leadership process in this situation are reflected in the constructions of those involved.

Operation June 30:
An Attempt to Manage Meaning

How OJ30 structured meaning is reflected in the way it was created, named, and managed as a significant event within day to day work life. OJ30 was presented to staff members in a way that attempted to orient attention away from the current situation to a desired future state. No attempt was made to analyze or interpret the significance of the backlog of work; the intent was just to eliminate it. This is reflected in the president's choice of language in the creation and naming of Operation June 30th. In the announcement the backlog was labelled "adverse," but not otherwise interpreted. The backlog is defined as the problem, and OJ30 was conceived as a military style operation to overcome it, implying a gathering of troops for an all-out assault. The name chosen by the president was not oriented to an explanation of the present conditions (e.g., "Operation Backlog" or "Operation Clean Sweep") but instead served to focus attention on a desired future state.

Moreover, the inclusion of a date gave the program the status of a concrete event with an end point.

In this effort the president chose to emphasize certain temporal, perceptual ("special program," "highest priority") and interpersonal horizons ("concerted effort," "volunteer") to serve as context. By choosing a future time horizon, a perceptual space of tightness/closeness to respond to urgency, and an interpersonal horizon of smoothness and nonconflict, the president implied that the message of Operation June 30th was one of a forward focus. He placed no blame for current conditions and viewed the organization as a team, each member having an important role. When the vice-president of operations declared Operation June 30th a success, Hall saw the free lunch as an appropriate way to draw the event to a close.

This same pattern of emphasis was reflected in other examples of the president's talk, as in this instance of elaborating his management philosophy:

> We all need each other. You really don't go very far unless everybody's got their shoulder to the wheel. . . . You can't overdo this (teamwork) to the point where you threaten to suppress some spirited debate in an organization. . . . You could have people not speaking their minds just because they feel they might undermine the teamwork philosophy, or the image you're trying to build. That would be wrong, because you've got to have some confrontation between people as you go along, as long as it doesn't get personal. This is what I keep saying to the staff. You can't get personal about these things, because once you get personal and take on a person individually and affect your relationship, then you've injected a little poison into the outfit. But at long as you're sincere and you're talking about the issues instead of personalities, then debate should be encouraged if you're going to make the best decisions. . . and the main thing is just to keep the personalities out of it.

The president does not speak of his role in terms of charting the direction of the organization but instead focuses his efforts at establishing and maintaining internal harmony. His approach toward OJ30 was quite consistent with his focus.

The Staff Members' Reactions.   Although the president sought to shape a reality of cooperation and urgency in the face of adverse conditions, it is apparent from the talk of executive staff that he did not succeed in generating these feelings among these staff members. Indeed, the reality for them was basically one of disharmony, disaffection, and noninvolvement. This is evidenced by remarks of the vice-president of operations, whose department was the main focus of Operation June 30th.

> Tom (the president) talks about "sprinting to the finish," "we all have to put our shoulder to the wheel," but you know that nobody responds. . . . To tell you the truth, I'm pretty fed up, I'm agitated by working every Saturday that I've been working, and to see very few other people who are helping or anything. . . . "

The vice-president of operations maintained a chart to keep track of who had been helping during Operation June 30th and expressed dissatisfaction with what it showed. "See, Director of Personnel, all dashes by his name, he hasn't helped out. . . . We have no team around here."

The president's use of military imagery was noted by the director of personnel but not seen as effective.

> It's (OJ30) probably a good thing in a lot of ways because say somebody attacked our country, we got called into a world war. . . . I kind of thought that when this initially came out it would serve as a common cause, a unification of the different forces we have in the company. It started off in that direction, but it's eased up quite a bit.

There was no urgency about OJ30 for the staff members. "We'll be in the same boat on July 30th," said one executive and he explained why.

> As long as. . . the president or someone else that has some involvement with that department doesn't challenge them, everyone's going to think everything is fine. And it will be, until some agents or some insured. . . begin to ask more questions as to why this isn't being done. I know for a fact that they aren't up-to-date. I could go over there and find errors.

But at the July 2nd staff meeting this same executive did not question the vice-president of operations' description of OJ30 as a success, justifying his own behavior by saying his department was not directly involved and that it was the president's responsibility to check and ask questions. But he believed the president incapable of doing so because he didn't know what to look for. In his own way, this executive also participated in burying the problems, but he saw that as the only option available to him.

The Staff Members' Interpretations.   The executive staff members rejected the meaning that the president sought to attach to the OJ30 program. They made sense of the project not in terms of some desired future state of task performance, but against the background of what they knew and felt about their organization.[3]

They were not a team, but instead a group in which conflict was represented but close to the surface. Their group enacted a continued pattern of not dealing with problems effectively. The executive staff attributed this pattern to the preferences and style of the president. They considered him "too trusting" and "not wanting to hear if things are bad." Although he espoused that "you have to have some confrontation between people," he and the staff participated in avoiding confrontation.

To the executive staff, OJ30 was symbolic of the way of life in their organization. It represented one more instance of the president's continued reluctance to deal fully and directly with problems. He may have labelled OJ30 "highest priority" and attempted to mobilize their energies, but he got little more than business as usual. For the staff did not interpret it as an occasion in which to behave in tight and helpful coordination. They made sense of OJ30, not as an organization imperative emphasizing interdependence, but as an organizational malaise encouraging an isolationist response.

The executive staff expressed feelings of powerlessness; they saw no way to do things differently. For them it was a choice of resigning or going along with the way it is. Neither alternative seemed attractive. They shared a common understanding of the expected mode of behavior, basically a passive posture and a shared perception of the president's preferences. Paradoxically, the president's attempt to manage the meaning of OJ30 ("everybody get their shoulder to the wheel") was actually sabotaged by his staff's adherence to what they saw as the "real" organizational value—the value which Hall, to them, embodied: If you do nothing, no harm will come to you.

The Competing Interpretations of Reality. Figure 3 presents a summary of the competing interpretive schemes through which the president and his executive staff made sense of the OJ30 project. For the president, OJ30 sought to define the situation in a way that created a high priority, future-oriented program addressed to the question, "What do we do now?" His interpretation of the final "success" of the program was framed against the relative success of OJ30 in getting rid of the backlog of work. For the staff, OJ30 was framed against an understanding of why they were "in a mess" and had a very different significance. It was just another sign of the inadequate way the fragmented organization was being run. They saw it as the act of a manager who was afraid to confront the real issues, who insisted on seeing the organization as a team, whereas the reality was that of a poorly managed group characterized by narrow self-interest, and noncooperation at anything but a surface level. OJ30 for them was symbolic of the status quo, and hence they were not effectively mobilized into action.

FIGURE 3 Competing Interpretation of OJ30

Framing Experience	Interpretation	Meaning and Action
	The President's Interpretation	*For the President*
OJ30 frames significant elements of work experience (work backlog, customer and staff complaints) in a form that makes them amenable to action.	OJ30 provides an opportunity for the company to work together in the resolution of a problem. It will solve the problem and help develop a cooperative spirit.	OJ30 does much to clear the backlog of work and can be judged a success. Meaning framed against an *idealized image*
	The Staff Member's Interpretation	*For Staff Members*
	OJ30 represents another futile act which will do nothing to solve the organization's basic problems. It symbolizes the way we do things here.	Will call for no more than minimal action; do not take too seriously for it can't do much to remedy the basic problem. Meaning framed against *past history*

IMPLICATIONS FOR THE THEORY AND PRACTICE OF CONTEMPORARY ORGANIZATION

The OJ30 case illustrates a leadership action concerned with managing the meaning of a particular situation. As an action designed to catch up on a work-flow problem, OJ30 was partially successful, for it did generate extra work from many staff who felt obliged to do something in conformity with the president's wishes. As an action designed to define the meaning of a situation, it was for the most part a failure, for it was interpreted by the executive staff in a manner that ran counter to what the president desired. Indeed the president's most powerful impact on the pattern of meaning within the organization was of a negative kind—his inaction and avoidance of problems creating an atmosphere of drifting and inaction.

At the surface our analysis may lead to the conclusion that Hall was a weak and ineffective leader. But to quickly judge him so is to risk losing sight of the larger dynamics that are at work in this leadership situation. Although Hall's view of organizational reality is not shared by the executive staff, he exerted a major impact on the broader definition of the situation. His style and presence provided the most powerful point of reference for action. The executive staff in this case adopts a passive nonconfronting posture, living a somewhat uncomfortable organizational reality defined and symbolized by the president. Hall provides evidence of how even weak leadership, by its fundamental nature, involves the definitions of situations.

Leaders symbolize the organized situation in which they lead. Their actions and utterances project and shape imagery in the minds of the led, which is influential one way or another in shaping actions within the setting as a whole. This is not to deny the importance of the voluntary nature of the enactments and sense-making activities initiated by members of the situation being managed. Rather, it is to recognize and emphasize the special and important position accorded to the leader's view of the situation in the frame of reference of others. Leaders, by nature of their leadership role, are provided with a distinctive opportunity to influence the sense making of others. Our case study illustrates the importance of the leader recognizing the nature of his or her influence and managing the meaning of situations in a constructive way. At a minimum this involves that he or she (a) attempt to deal with the equivocality that permeates many interactive situations; (b) attend to the interpretive schemes of those involved, and (c) embody through use of appropriate language, rituals, and other forms of symbolic discourse, the meanings and values conducive to desired modes of organized action. A focus on leadership as the management of meaning encourages us to develop a theory for the practice of leadership in which these three generalizations are accorded a central role.

Our analysis also draws attention to the role of power as a defining feature of the leadership process. With the OJ30 case we see the way power relations embedded in a leadership role oblige others to take particular note of the sense-making activities emanating from that role. We have characterized this in terms of a dependency relation between leaders and led, in which the leader's sense-making activities assume priority over the sense-making activities of others.

The existence of leadership depends on and fosters this dependency, for insofar as the leader is expected to define the situation, others are expected to surrender that right. As we have noted, leadership as a phenomenon depends upon the existence of people who are prepared to surrender their ability to define their reality to others. Situations of formal leadership institutionalize this pattern into a system of rights and obligations whereby the leader has the prerogative to define reality, and the led to accept that definition as a frame of reference for orienting their own activity.

Organized action in formal settings constitutes a process of enactment and sense making on the part of those involved, but one shaped in important ways by the power relations embedded in the situation as a whole. Leadership and the organizational forms to which it gives rise enact a reality that expresses a power relationship. An understanding of the power relationship embedded in all enactment processes is thus fundamental for understanding the nature of organization as an enacted social form, for enactments express power relationships.

Thus our analysis of the leadership process tells us much about the nature of organization as a hierarchical phenomenon. Most patterns of formal organization institutionalize the emergent characteristics of leadership into roles, rules, and relations that give tangible and enduring form to relationships between leaders and led. Our analysis of leadership as a social phenomenon based on interaction, sense making, and dependency implies a view of much modern organization in which these factors are seen as defining features. To see leadership as the management of meaning is to see organizations as networks of managed meanings, resulting from those interactive processes through which people have sought to make sense of situations.

The view of leadership and organization provides a framework for reconsidering the way leadership has been treated in organizational research. By viewing leadership as a relationship between traits, roles, and behaviors and the situations in which they are found, or as a transactional process involving the exchange of rewards and influence, most leadership research has focused upon the dynamics and surface features of leadership as a tangible social process. The way leadership as a phenomenon involves the structuring and transformation of reality has with notable exceptions (e.g., Burns, 1978), been ignored, or at best approached tangentially. The focus on the exchange of influence and rewards has rarely penetrated to reveal the way these processes are embedded in, and reflect a deeper structure of power-based meaning and action. Leadership is not simply a process of acting or behaving, or a process of manipulating rewards. It is a process of power-based reality construction and needs to be understood in these terms.

The concept of leadership is a central building block of the conventional wisdom of organization and management. For the most part the idea that good organization embodies effective leadership practice passes unquestioned. Our analysis here leads us to question this wisdom and points toward the unintended consequences that leadership situations often generate.

The most important of these stem from the dependency relations that arise when individuals surrender their power and control over the definition of reality to others. Leaders may create situations in which individuals are crippled by purposelessness and inaction when left to guide efforts on their own account. Leadership may actually work against the development of self-responsibility, self-initiative, and self-control, in a manner that parallels Argyris's (1957) analysis of the way the characteristics of bureaucratic organization block potentialities for full human development. These blocks arise whenever leadership actions divert individuals from the process of defining and taking responsibility for their own action and experience.

Leadership situations may generate a condition of "trained inaction" in the led, a variant form of Veblen's (1904) "trained incapacity," observed by Merton (1968) as a dominant characteristic of the bureaucratic personality. This trained inaction is clearly illustrated in the OJ30 study where the executive staff experienced problems in their work situation as something beyond their control. The situation here emanates from the way a relatively weak leader defines the situation; but it is equally evident in situations of strong, dominating leadership illustrated in a graphic but extreme way in situations such as the tragedy in Jonestown, Guyana.

An awareness of the dependency relationships that characterize leadership situations sensitizes us to potentially undesirable consequences and also points toward ways in which leadership action can be directed for the avoidance of such states through the creation of patterns of meaning construction that facilitate constructive tension and innovation rather than passivity. In this regard our analysis points toward an important focus for both the practice of contemporary organization and for future research—on the processes through which the management of meaning in organized situations can develop in ways that enhance, rather than deny, the ability of individuals to take responsibility for the definition and control of their world.

It is important to investigate forms of organized action that depart from the traditional leadership model. We are persuaded to suggest that the study of non-leadership situations would focus attention on a phenomenon of some importance.

Patterns of organization that replace hierarchical leadership with patterns of more equalized interaction in which each has an obligation to define what is happening, and respond accordingly, changes the very basis of organization. Such arrangements increase the adaptive capacity of organization through what Emery and Trist (1972) have described as a redundancy of functions. These embody a model of human development in line with the ability of human beings to take responsibility for their actions. In situations characterized by hierarchical dependency, those in leadership roles are obliged to interpret and assimilate all that there is to observe and understand about a situation before initiating the action of others. In situations of more equalized power, this obligation and ability is more widely spread. Members of a situation are unable to look to authority relations to solve problems; adaptive capacities have to be developed at the level at which they are needed, increasing the learning and adaptive ability of the whole. Autonomous work groups and leaderless situations of all kinds present concrete opportunities for the study of emergent principles of organization that offer alternatives to the dependency relations that have permeated Western culture as an organizational norm.

The conventional wisdom that organization and leadership are by definition intertwined has structured the way we see and judge alternative modes of organized action. Approaching this subject from a perspective that treats organization as a phenomenon based on the management of meaning, we can begin to see

474

and understand the importance of developing and encouraging alternative means through which organized action can be generated and sustained.

NOTES

1. A minor qualification is appropriate here in that certain charismatic leaders may inspire others to restructure their reality in creative ways. The dependency relation is evident, however, in that the individual takes the charismatic leader as a point of reference in this process.

2. The president of the insurance company had been involved in the day to day management of the company for 18 months. Previously, all nine executive staff members had reported to an executive vice-president so that the president could devote his attention to external relationships. When the executive vice-president died in January 1978, a decision was made not to replace him. Instead, all executive staff members reported directly to the president. The executive staff was a stable group; all had been employed in the company for no less than seven years.

3. The staff members were concerned about the equivocality surrounding the cause of the backlog. In a conversation with the researcher, the director of sales asked himself, "How did the company get into this position?" And replied, "It started two years ago with the decision to microfilm. It ate us up. I could have my head handed to me for this, the president backed it." The sales director expressed the view that the past decision to install microfilming equipment and to microfilm all stored records as well as microfilm all incoming work had been the major factor in the operating departments falling so far behind in the processing of work. The other executives agreed with this interpretation.

REFERENCE NOTES

1. Bougon, M. *Schemata, leadership, and organizational behavior.* Doctoral dissertation. Cornell University, 1980.
2. Smircich, L. Studying organizations as cultures. In G. Morgan (Ed.), *Organizational research strategies: Links between theory and method.* Unpublished manuscript.

REFERENCES

Argyris, C. *Personality and organization.* New York: Harper, 1957.
Barnard, C. *The functions of the executive.* Cambridge, Mass.: Harvard University Press, 1938.
Bateson, G. *Steps to an ecology of mind.* New York: Ballantine Books, 1972.
Bennis, W. G., & Shepherd, H. A. A theory of group development. *Human Relations,* 1965, 9, 415–457.
Berger, P., & Luckmann, T. *The social construction of reality.* New York: Anchor Books, 1966.
Bogdan. R., & Taylor, S. J. *Introduction to qualitative methods.* New York: Wiley, 1975.
Burns, J. M. *Leadership.* New York: Harper & Row, 1978.
Emery, F. E., & Trist, E. L. *Towards a social ecology.* Harmondsworth: Penguin, 1973.
Fiedler, F. E. *A theory of leadership effectiveness.* New York: McGraw-Hill, 1967.
Goffman, E. *Frame analysis.* New York: Harper Colophon Books, 1974.
Jacobs, T. O. *Leadership and exchange in formal organizations.* Alexandria, Va.: Human Resources Organization, 1971.
Katz, D., & Kahn, R. L. *The social psychology of organizations.* New York: Wiley, 1966.

Mann, R. D. A review of the relationships between personality and performance in small groups. *Psychological Bulletin,* 1959, *56,* 241–270.

Merton, R. K. *Social theory and social structure.* (enlarged ed.). New York: Free Press, 1968.

Mintzberg, H. *The nature of managerial work.* Englewood Cliffs, N.J.: Prentice-Hall, 1973.

Peters. T. J. Symbols, patterns and settings: An optimistic case for getting things done. *Organizational Dynamics,* 1978, 3–22.

Pfeffer, J. Management as symbolic action: The creation and maintenance of organizational paradigms. *Research in Organizational Behavior,* 1981, *3,* 1–52.

Pondy, L. R. Leadership is a language game. In M. McCall & M. Lombardo (Eds.), *Leadership: Where else can we go?* Durham, N.C.: Duke University Press, 1976.

Pondy, L. R., Frost, P., Morgan, G., & Dandridge, T. (Eds.). *Organizational symbolism.* Greenwich, Conn.: JAI Press, 1982.

Quinn, J. B. *Strategies for change.* New York: Irwin, 1980.

Roethlisberger, F. J., & Dickson, W. J. *Management and the worker.* Cambridge, Mass.: Harvard Unviersity Press, 1939.

Schatzman, L., & Strauss, A. *Fieldwork.* Englewood Cliffs, N.J.: Prentice-Hall, 1973.

Schutz, A. *Collected papers I: The problem of social reality.* (2nd ed.). The Hague: Martinus Nijhoff, 1967.

Selznick, P. *Leadership in administration.* New York: Harper & Row, 1957.

Sennett, R. *Authority.* New York: Knopf, 1980.

Smircich, L. Organizations as shared meanings. In Pondy, L. R., Frost, P., Morgan, G. & Dandridge, T. (Eds.). *Organizational symbolism.* Greenwich, Conn.: JAI Press, 1982.

Stogdill, R. M. *Handbook of leadership: A survey of theory and research.* New York: The Free Press, 1974.

Veblen, T. *The theory of business enterprise.* Clifton, N.J.: Augustus M. Kelly, 1975 (originally published 1904).

Weick, K., *The social psychology of organizing.* Reading, Mass.: Addison-Wesley, 1979.

15

Supervision and Employee Development

JAPANESE MANAGEMENT:
PRACTICES AND PRODUCTIVITY
Nina Hatvany
Vladimir Pucik

FIRMS WITH A SUPERIOR LEADERSHIP CAPACITY:
PRACTICES THAT CREATE BETTER THAN AVERAGE MANAGEMENT TEAMS
John P. Kotter

OVERCOMING THE DYSFUNCTION OF MbO
Steven Kerr

JAPANESE MANAGEMENT: PRACTICES AND PRODUCTIVITY

Nina Hatvany
Vladimir Pucik

The [United States] is the most technically advanced country and the most affluent one. But capital investment alone will not make the difference. In any country the quality of products and the productivity of workers depend on management. When Detroit changes its management system we'll see more powerful American competitors.

—Hideo Sugiura, Executive Vice President
Honda Motor Co.

Productivity—or output per worker—is a key measure of economic health. When it increases, the economy grows in real terms and so do standards of living. When it declines, real economic growth slows or stagnates. Productivity is the result of many factors, including investment in capital goods, technological innovation, and workers' motivation.*

Source: Reprinted with permission from *Organizational Dynamics,* Spring 1981, © 1981 by AMACOM, A division of American Management Associations. All rights reserved.

*The authors would like to thank Mitsuyo Hanada, Blair McDonald, William Newman, William Ouchi, Thomas Rochl, Michael Tushman, and others for their helpful comments on earlier drafts of this paper. We are grateful to Citibank, New York, and the Japan Foundation, Tokyo, for their financial support of the work in the preparation of this paper.

After a number of years of sluggish productivity growth, the United States now trails most other major industrial nations in the rise in output per worker, although it still enjoys the best overall rate. This state of affairs is increasingly bemoaned by many critics in both academic and business circles. Some reasons suggested to "explain" the U.S. decline in productivity rankings include excessive government regulation, tax policies discouraging investment, increases in energy costs, uncooperative unions, and various other factors in the business environment.

Some observers, however—among them Harvard professors Robert Hayes and William J. Abernathy—put the blame squarely on American managers. They argue that U.S. firms prefer to service existing markets rather than develop a superior product or process technology, and, perhaps most important, focus on short-run returns on investment rather than long-term growth and research and development strategy. Too many managers are setting and meeting short-term, market-driven objectives instead of adopting the appropriate time-horizon needed to plan and execute the successful product innovations needed to sustain worldwide competitiveness.

The performance of the American manufacturing sector is often contrasted with progress achieved by other industrialized countries—particularly Japan. Japan's productivity growth in manufacturing has been nearly three times the U.S. rate over the past two decades—the average annual growth rate between 1960 and 1978 was 7.8 percent. In the last five years alone, the productivity index has increased by more than 40 percent and most economists forecast similar rates for the 1980s. Such impressive results deserve careful examination.

Students of the Japanese economy generally point out that Japanese investment outlays as a proportion of gross national product are nearly twice as large as those in the United States, and this factor is backed by a high personal savings ratio and the availability of relatively cheap investment funds. Also, a massive infusion of imported technology contributed significantly to the growth of productivity in Japan. Among noneconomic factors, the Japanese political environment seems to support business needs, especially those of advanced industries. In addition, the "unique" psychological and cultural characteristics of the Japanese people are frequently cited as the key reason for Japan's success.

It is indeed a well-known fact that absenteeism in most Japanese companies is low, turnover rates are about half the U.S. figures, and employee commitment to the company is generally high. But although cultural factors are important in any context, we doubt that any peculiarities of Japanese people (if they exist) have much impact on their commitment or productivity. In fact, several recent research studies indicate that Japanese and American workers show little or no difference in the personality attributes related to performance. Rather, we join Robert Hayes and William Abernathy in believing that, in this context, productivity stems from the superior management systems of many Japanese firms. But the focus of our analysis is not on such areas as corporate marketing and production strategies. Instead, we will examine management practices in Japan as they affect one key company asset: human resources.

Our analysis is guided by our experience with subsidiaries of Japanese firms in the United States. Typically, these companies are staffed by a small group of

Japanese managers with varying levels of autonomy relative to the company's parent. The rest of the employees are American. Although they operate in an alien culture, many of these subsidiaries are surprisingly successful. While it is often very difficult to measure the performance of newly established operations, it is no secret that production lines in several Japanese subsidiaries operate at the same productivity rate as those in Japan (for example, the Sony plant in San Diego).

This example—as well as others—serves to demonstrate that what works in Japan can often work in the United States. The techniques used by the management of Japanese subsidiaries to motivate their American workers seem to play an important part in the effort to increase productivity. Therefore, a careful examination of management practices in Japan is useful not only for a specialist interested in cross-cultural organization development, but also for the management practitioner who is losing to foreign competition even on his or her homeground. What is it that the Japanese do better?

Our discussion attempts to answer this question by presenting a model of the Japanese management system that rests on a few elements that can be examined in different cultural settings. The model will be used to highlight the relationship between the management strategies and techniques observed in Japan and positive work outcomes, such as commitment and productivity. Our review is not intended to be exhaustive, but rather to suggest the feasibility of integrating findings from Japan with more general concepts and theories. We will therefore focus on relationships that may be verified by observations of behavior in non-Japanese, especially U.S., settings.

We propose that positive work outcomes emanate from a complex set of behavioral patterns that are not limited to any specific culture. The emphasis is on management practices as a system and on the integration of various strategies and techniques to achieve desired results. We hope thus to provide an alternative to statements—often cited but never empirically supported—that the high commitment and productivity of Japanese employees is primarily traceable to their cultural characteristics.

A MANAGEMENT SYSTEM FOCUSED ON HUMAN RESOURCES

Most managers will probably agree that management's key concern is the optimal utilization of a firm's various assets. These assets may vary—financial, technological, human, and so on. Tradeoffs are necessary because utilization of any one asset may result in underutilization of another. We propose that in most Japanese companies, *human assets are considered to be the firm's most important and profitable assets in the long run.* Although the phrase itself sounds familiar, even hollow, to many American managers and OD consultants, it is important to recognize that this management orientation is backed up by a well-integrated system of strategies and techniques that translate this abstract concept into reality.

First, long-term and secure employment is provided, which attracts employees of the desired quality and induces them to remain with the firm. Second, a company philosophy is articulated that shows concern for employee needs and stresses cooperation and teamwork in a unique environment. Third, close attention is given both to hiring people who will fit well with the particular company's values and to integrating employees into the company at all stages of their working life. These general strategies are expressed in specific management techniques. Emphasis is placed on continuous development of employee skills; formal promotion is of secondary importance, at least during the early career stages. Employees are evaluated on a multitude of criteria—often including group performance results—rather than on individual bottomline contribution. The work is structured in such a way that it may be carried out by groups operating with a great deal of autonomy. Open communication is encouraged, supported, and rewarded. Information about pending decisions is circulated to all concerned before the decisions are actually made. Active observable concern for each and every employee is expressed by supervisory personnel (Figure 1). Each of these management practices, either alone or in combination with the others, is known to have a positive influence on commitment to the organization and its effectiveness.

We will discuss these practices as we have observed them in large and medium-size firms in Japan and in several of their subsidiaries in the United States. Although similar practices are often also in evidence in small Japanese companies, the long-term employment policies in these firms are more vulnerable to drops in economic activity and the system's impact is necessarily limited.

FIGURE 1   Japanese Management Paradigm

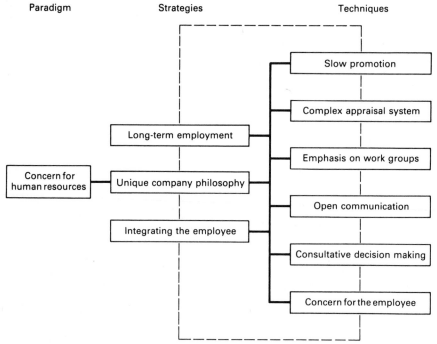

Strategies

Once management adopts the view that utilizing human assets is what matters most in the organization's success, several strategies have to be pursued to secure these assets in the desired quality and quantity. These strategies involve the following:

Provide Secure Employment.   Although Japanese companies typically provide stable and long-term employment, many smaller firms find it difficult to do so in times of recession. The policy calls for hiring relatively unskilled employees (often directly from high schools or universities), training them on the job, promoting from within, and recognizing seniority.

The implicit guarantee of the employee's job, under all but the most severe economic circumstances, is a marked departure from conventional managerial thinking about the need to retain flexibility in work force size in order to respond efficiently to cyclical variations in demand. However, this employment system, at least as practiced in large corporations in Japan, is far from being inflexible. Several techniques can be applied to ride out recession with a minimum burden of labor cost while keeping a maximum number of regular workers on their jobs—a freeze on new hiring, solicitation of voluntary retirement sweetened by extra benefits, use of core employees to replace temporaries and subcontractors doing nonessential work, and so forth. Thus a labor force cut of approximately 10 to 15 percent in a short time period is not an unusual phenomenon. In addition, across-the-board salary and bonus cuts for all employees, including the management, would follow if necessary.

Japanese managers believe that job security has a positive impact on morale and productivity, limits turnover and training costs, and increases the organization's cohesiveness. For that reason, they are willing to accept its temporary negative effect in a period of reduced demand. Long-term employment security is also characteristic of all the U.S. subsidiaries that we have visited. Layoffs and terminations occur extremely rarely. For example, the Kikkoman Company instituted across-the-board wage cuts in an attempt to preserve employment during the last recession. Murata instituted a four-day workweek, and at Matsushita's Quasar plant, a number of employees were shifted from their regular work to functions such as repairs, maintenance, and service. It should be noted that there are several well-known U.S. corporations—for example, IBM and Hewlett-Packard—that follow similar practices when the alternative would be layoff.

In Japanese companies, even poor performers are either retrained or transferred, instead of simply being dismissed. The plant manager in an electronics component factory explained how the company copes with personal failures: "We give a chance to improve even if there has been a big mistake. For example, the quality control manager didn't fit, so we transferred him to sales engineering and now he is doing fine."

Research on behavior in organizations suggest that the assumptions of Japanese managers and some of their U.S. colleagues about the positive impact of job security are, at least to some degree, justified. It has been shown that long tenure is positively associated with commitment to the organization, which in turn reduces turnover. High commitment in conjunction with a binding choice (employees of large firms in Japan have difficulty finding jobs of the same quality elsewhere, given the relatively stable labor market) also leads to high satisfaction, but whether this contributes to high productivity still remains to be proved. It is, however, necessary to view the policy of secure employment as a key condition for the implementation of other management strategies and techniques that have a more immediate impact on the organization's effectiveness.

Articulate a Unique Company Philosophy. A philosophy that is both articulated and carried through presents a clear picture of the organization's objectives, norms, and values—and thus helps transform commitment into productive effort. Familiarity with organizational goals gives direction to employees' actions, sets constraints on their behavior, and enhances their motivation. The understanding of shared meanings and beliefs expressed in the company philosophy binds the individual to the organization and, at the same time, stimulates the emergence of goals shared with others, as well as the stories, myths, and symbols that form the fabric of a company philosophy. William Ouchi and Raymond Price suggest that an organizational philosophy is an elegant informational device that provides a form of control at once pervasive and effective; at the same time it provides guidance for managers by presenting a basic theory of how the firm should be managed.

An explicit management philosophy of how work should be done can be found in many successful corporations in both Japan and the United States; examples in the United States include IBM, Texas Instruments, and U.S. Homes. Nevertheless, it is fair to say that the typical Japanese firm's management philosophy has a distinct flavor. It usually puts a heavy emphasis on cooperation and teamwork within a corporate "family" that is unique and distinct from that of any other firm. In return for an employee's effort, the family's commitment to the employee is translated into company determination to avoid layoffs and to provide a whole range of supplementary welfare benefits for the employee and his or her family. Naturally, without reasonable employment security, the fostering of team spirit and cooperation would be impossible. The ideal is thus to reconcile two objectives: pursuit of profits and perpetuation of the company as a group.

In a number of cases, a particular management philosophy that originated with the parent company in Japan is also being actively disseminated in its U.S. subsidiaries. Typically, claims of uniqueness range from the extent of the company's concern for employees' work lives to the quality of service to the customer. We quote from the in-house literature issued by one of the fastest growing Japanese-owned electronics component makers in California:

> *Management Philosophy:* Our goal is to strive toward both the material and the spiritual fulfillment of all employees in the Company, and through this successful fulfillment, serve mankind in its progress and prosperity.
>
> *Management Policy:* Our purpose is to fully satisfy the needs of our customers and in return gain a just profit for ourselves. We are a family united in common bonds and singular goals. One of these bonds is the respect and support we feel for our fellow family co-workers.

Integrate Employees Into the Company.   The benefits of an articulated company philsophy are lost, however, if it's not properly communicated to employees or if it's not visibly supported by management's behavior. A primary function of the company's socialization effort, therefore, is to ensure that employees have understood the philsophy and seen it in action. Close attention is given to hiring people who are willing to endorse the values of the particular company and to the employees' integration into the organization at all stages of their working life. The development of cohesiveness within the firm, based on the acceptance of goals and values, is a major focus of personnel policies in many Japanese firms.

Because employees are expected to remain in the company for a major part of their careers, careful selection is necessary to ensure that they fit well into the company climate. In many U.S.-based Japanese firms also, new hires at all levels are carefully screened with this aspect in mind. As in Japan, basic criteria for hiring are moderate views and a harmonious personality, and for that reason a large proportion of new hires comes from employee referrals. In general, "virgin" workforces are preferred, since they can readily be assimilated into each company's unique environment as a community.

The intensive socialization process starts with the hiring decision and the initial training program and continues in various forms thereafter. Over time, the employee internalizes the various values and objectives of the firm, becomes increasingly committed to them, and learns the formal and informal rules and procedures, particularly through job rotation. That process usually includes two related types of job transfers. First, employees are transferred to new positions to learn additional skills in on-the-job training programs. These job changes are planned well in advance for all regular employees, including blue-collar workers. Second, transfers are part of a long-range, experience-building program through which the organization develops its future managers; such programs involve movement across departmental boundaries at any stage of an employee's career.

While employees rotate semilaterally from job to job, they become increasingly socialized into the organization, immersed in the company philosophy and culture, and bound to a set of shared goals. Even in the absence of specific internal regulations that might be too constraining in a rapidly changing environment, a well-socialized manager who has held positions in various functions and locations within the firm has a feel for the organization's needs.

Techniques

The basic management orientation and strategies that we have just discussed are closely interrelated with specific management techniques used in Japanese firms and in their subsidiaries in the United States. The whole system is composed of a set of interdependent employment practices in which the presence of one technique complements as well as influences the effectiveness of others. This interdependence, rather than a simple cause-effect relationship, is the key factor that helps maintain the organization's stability and effectiveness. Additional environmental variables may determine which of the strategies or techniques will require most attention from top management, but in their impact on the organization no single technique listed below is of prime importance.

Slow Promotion, Job Rotation, and Internal Training. All Japanese subsidiaries that we have visited have seniority-based promotion systems. At one of them, a medium-sized motorcycle plant, a seniority-based promotion system has been reinstituted after an experiment with a merit-based system proved highly unpopular with employees. Training is conducted, as expected, mostly on the job, and as one textile company executive noted, career paths are flexible: "You can get involved in what you want to do." Hiring from outside into upper-level positions is rare. According to another Japanese plant manager: "We want someone who understands the management system of the company. We want to keep the employees with us; we want to keep them happy."

Although promotion is slow, early informal identification of the elite is not unusual and carefully planned lateral job transfers add substantial flexibility to job assignments. Not all jobs are equally central to the workflow in an organization, so employees—even those with the same status and salary—can be rewarded or punished by providing or withholding positions in which they could acquire the skills needed for future formal promotions.

Job rotation in U.S.-based Japanese firms seems less planned or structured than in Japan and more an ad hoc reaction to organizational needs—but in general, the emphasis on slow promotion and job rotation creates an environment in which an employee becomes a generalist rather than a specialist in a particular functional area. For the most part, however, these general skills are unique to the organization. Several of the Japanese manufacturers that invested in the United States were forced to simplify their product technology because they were not able to recruit qualified operators versatile enough to meet their needs, and there was not enough time to train them internally.

In Japan, well-planned job rotation is the key to the success of an in-company training program that generally encompasses all the firm's employees. For some categories of highly skilled blue-collar workers training plans for a period of up to ten years are not unusual. Off-the-job training is often included, again for managers and nonmanagers alike. However, whether such an extensive training system will be transferred to U.S. subsidiaries remains to be seen.

In addition to its impact on promotion and training, job rotation also promotes the development of informal communication networks that help in coordinating work activities across functional areas and in resolving problems speedily. This aspect of job rotation is especially important for managerial personnel. Finally, timely job rotation relieves an employee who has become unresponsive to, or bored with, the demands of his or her job.

Some observers argue that deferred promotion may frustrate highly promising, ambitious employees. However, the personnel director of a major trading company has commented: "The secret of Japanese management, if there is any, is to make everybody feel as long as possible that he is slated for the top position in the firm—thereby increasing his motivation during the most productive period of his employment." The public identification of "losers," who of course far outnumber "winners" in any hierarchical organization, is postponed in the belief that the increased output of the losers, who are striving hard to do well and still hoping to beat the odds, more than compensates for any lags in the motivation of the impatient winners. By contrast, top management in many American organizations is preoccupied with identifying rising stars as soon as possible and is less concerned about the impact on the losers' morale.

Complex Appraisal System. In addition to emphasizing the long-term perspective, Japanese companies often establish a complex appraisal system that includes not only individual performance measures tied to the bottom line, but also measures of various desirable personality traits and behaviors—such as creativity, emotional maturity, and cooperation with others as well as team performance results. In most such companies, potential, personality, and behavior, rather than current output, are the key criteria, yet the difference is often merely symbolic. Output measures may easily be "translated" into such attributes as leadership skills, technical competence, relations with others, and judgment. This approach avoids making the employee feel that the bottom line, which may be beyond his or her control, in part or in whole, is the key dimension of evaluation. Occasional mistakes, particularly those made by lower-level employees, are considered part of the learning process.

At the same time, evaluations do clearly discriminate among employees because each employee is compared with other members of an appropriate group (in age and status) and ranked accordingly. The ranking within the cohort is generally not disclosed to the employees, but of course it can be partially inferred from small salary differentials and a comparison of job assignments. At least in theory, the slow promotion system should allow for careful judgments to be made even on such subjective criteria as the personality traits of honesty and seriousness. However, the authors' observations suggest that ranking within the cohort is usually established rather early in one's career and is generally not very flexible thereafter.

Employees are not formally separated according to their ability until later in their tenure; ambitious workers who seek immediate recognition must engage in activities that will get them noticed. Bottom-line performance is not an adequate criterion because, as noted, it is not the only focus of managerial evaluation. This situation encourages easily observable behavior, such as voluntary overtime, that appears to demonstrate willingness to exert substantial effort on the organization's behalf. The evaluation process becomes to a large degree self-selective.

Several other facets of this kind of appraisal system deserve our attention. Because evaluations are based on managerial observations during frequent, regular interactions with subordinates, the cost of such an evaluation system is relatively low. When behavior rather than bottom-line performance is the focus of evaluation, means as well as ends may be assessed. This very likely leads to a better match between the direction of employee efforts and company objectives, and it encourages a long-term perspective. Finally, since group performance is also a focus of evaluation, peer pressure on an employee to contribute his or her share to the group's performance becomes an important mechanism of performance control. Long tenure, friendship ties, and informal communication networks enable both superiors and peers to get a very clear sense of the employee's performance and potential relative to others.

Among the management techniques characteristic of large Japanese enterprises, the introduction of a complex appraisal system is probably the least visible in their U.S. subsidiaries. Most of their U.S.-based affiliates are relatively young; thus long-term evaluation of employees, the key point in personnel appraisal as practiced in Japan, is not yet practicable. Furthermore, the different expectations of American workers and managers about what constitutes a fair and equitable appraisal system might hinder acceptance of the parent company's system.

Emphasis on Work Groups. Acknowledging the enormous impact of groups on their members—both directly, through the enforcement of norms, and indirectly, by affecting the beliefs and values of members—Japanese organizations devote far greater attention to structural factors that enhance group motivation and cooperation than to the motivation of individual employees. Tasks are assigned to groups, not to individual employees, and group cohesion is stimulated by delegating responsibility to the group not only for getting the tasks performed, but also for designing the way in which they get performed. The group-based performance evaluation has already been discussed.

Similarly, in the U.S.-based Japanese firms that we have visited, the group rather than an individual forms the basic work unit for all practical purposes. Quality of work and speed of job execution are key concerns in group production meetings that are held at least monthly, and even daily in some companies. The design function, however, is not yet very well developed; many workers are still relative newcomers unfamiliar with all aspects of the advanced technology. Intergroup rivalry is also encouraged. In one capacitor company, a group on a shift that performs well consistently is rewarded regularly. Sometimes news of a highly productive group from another shift or even from the Japanese parent is passed around that shop floor to stimulate the competition.

In Japan, group autonomy is encouraged by avoiding any reliance on experts to solve operational problems. One widely used group-based technique for dealing with such problems is quality control (QC) circles. A QC circle's major task is to pinpoint and solve a particular workshop's problem. Outside experts are called in only to educate group members in the analytical tools for problem solving or to provide a specialized technical service. Otherwise, the team working on the problem operates autonomously, with additional emphasis on self-improvement activities that will help achieve group goals. Fostering motivation through direct employee participation in the work process design is a major consideration in the introduction of QC circles and similar activities to the factory floor.

Nevertheless, work-group autonomy in most work settings is bound by clearly defined limits, with the company carefully coordinating team activities by controlling the training and evaluation of members, the size of the team, and the scope and amount of production. Yet within these limits, teamwork is not only part of a company's articulated philosophy, it actually forms the basic fabric of the work process. Job rotation is encouraged both to develop each employee's skills and to fit the work group's needs.

From another perspective, the group can also assist in developing job-relevant knowledge by direct instruction and by serving as a model of appropriate behavior. The results of empirical studies suggest that structuring tasks around work groups not only may improve performance, but also may contribute to increased esteem and a sense of identity among group members. Furthermore, this process of translating organizational membership into membership in a small group seems, in general, to result in higher job satisfaction, lower absenteeism, lower turnover rates, and fewer labor disputes.

Open and Extensive Communication. Even in the Japanese-owned U.S. companies, plant managers typically spend at least two hours a day on the shop floor and are readily available for the rest of the day. Often, foremen are deliberately deprived of offices so they can be with their subordinates on the floor throughout the whole day, instructing and helping whenever necessary. The same policy applies to personnel specialists. The American personnel manager of a Japanese motorcycle plant, for example, spends between two and four hours a day on the shop floor discussing issues that concern employees. The large number of employees he is able to greet by their first name testifies to the amount of time he spends on the floor. "We have an open-door policy—but it's their door, not management's" was his explanation of the company's emphasis on the quality of face-to-face vertical communication.

Open communication is also inherent in the Japanese work setting. Open work spaces are crowded with individuals at different hierarchical levels. Even high-ranking office managers seldom have separate private offices. Partitions, cubicles, and small side rooms are used to set off special areas for conferences with visitors or small discussions among the staff. In one Japanese-owned TV plant on the West Coast, the top manager's office is next to the receptionist—open and visible to everybody who walks into the building, whether employee, supplier, or customer.

Open communication is not limited to vertical exchanges. Both the emphasis on team spirit in work groups and the network of friendships that employees develop during their long tenure in the organization encourage the extensive face-to-face communication so often reported in studies involving Japanese companies. Moreover, job rotation is instrumental in building informal lateral networks across departmental boundaries. Without these networks, the transfer of much job-related information would be impossible. These informal networks are not included in written work manuals; thus they are invisible to a newcomer; but their use as a legitimate tool to get things done is implicitly authorized by the formal contact system. Communication skills and related factors are often the focus of yearly evaluations. Frequently, foreign observers put too much emphasis on vertical ties and other hierarchical aspects of Japanese organizations. In fact, the ability to manage lateral communication is perhaps even more important to effective performance, particularly at the middle-management level.

Consultative Decision Making. Few Japanese management practices are so misunderstood by outsiders as is the decision-making process. The image is quite entrenched in Western literature on Japanese organizations: Scores of managers huddle together in endless discussion until consensus on every detail is reached, after which a symbolic document, "ringi," is passed around so they can affix their seals of approval on it. This image negates the considerable degree of decentralization for most types of decisions that is characteristic in most subsidiaries we have visited. In fact, when time is short, decisions are routinely made by the manager in charge.

Under the usual procedure for top-management decision making, a proposal is initiated by a middle manager (but often under the directive of top management). This middle manager engages in informal discussion and consultation with peers and supervisors. When all are familiar with the proposal, a formal request for a decision is made and, because of earlier discussions, is almost inevitably ratified—often in a ceremonial group meeting or through the "ringi" procedure. This implies not unanimous approval, but unanimous consent to its implementation.

This kind of decision making is not participative in the Western sense of the word, which encompasses negotiation and bargaining between a manager and subordinates. In the Japanese context, negotiations are primarily lateral between the departments concerned with the decision. Within the work group, the emphasis is on including all group members in the process of decision making, not on achieving consensus on the alternatives. Opposing parties are willing to go along, with the consolation that their viewpoint may carry the day the next time around.

However, the manager will usually not implement his or her decision "until others who will be affected have had sufficient time to offer their views, feel that they have been fairly heard, and are willing to support the decision even though they may not feel that it is the best one," according to Thomas P. Rohlen. Those outside the core of the decision-making group merely express their acknowledgment of the proposed course of action. They do not participate; they do not feel ownership of the decision. On the other hand, the early communication of the proposed changes helps reduce uncertainty in the organization. In addition, prior information on upcoming decisions gives employees an opportunity to rationalize and accept the outcomes.

Japanese managers we have interviewed often expressed the opinion that it is their American partners who insist on examining every aspect and contingency of proposed alternatives, while they themselves prefer a relatively general agreement on the direction to follow, leaving the deatils to be solved on the run. Accordingly, the refinement of a proposal occurs during its early implementation stage.

Although the level of face-to-face communication in Japanese organizations is relatively high, it should not be confused with participation in decision making. Most communication concerns routine tasks; thus it is not surprising that research on Japanese companies indicates no relationship between the extent of face-to-face communication and employees' perceptions of how much they participate in decision making.

Moreover, consultation with lower-ranking employees does not automatically imply that the decision process is "bottom up," as suggested by Peter Drucker and others. Especially in the case of long-term planning and strategy, the initiative comes mostly from the top. Furthermore, consultative decision making does not diminish top management's responsibility for a decision's consequences. Although the ambiguities of status and centrality may make it difficult for outsiders to pin-point responsibility, it is actually quite clear within the organization. Heads still roll to pay for mistakes, albeit in a somewhat more subtle manner than is customary in Western organizations: Departure to the second- or third-ranking subsidiary is the most common punishment.

Concern for the Employee. It is established practice for managers to spend a lot of time talking to employees about everyday matters. Thus they develop a feeling for employees' personal needs and problems, as well as for their perform-ance. Obviously, gaining this intimate knowledge of each employee is easier when an employee has long tenure, but managers do consciously attempt to get to know their employees, and they place a premium on providing time to talk. The quality of relationships developed with subordinates is also an important factor on which a manager is evaluated.

Various company-sponsored cultural, athletic, and other recreational acti-vities further deepen involvement in employees' lives. The heavy schedule of com-pany social affairs is ostensibly voluntary, but virtually all employees participate. Typically, an annual calendar of office events might include two overnight trips, monthly Saturday afternoon recreation, and an average of six office parties—all at company expense. A great deal of drinking goes on at these events and much good fellowship is expressed among the employees.

Finally, in Japan the company allocates substantial financial resources to pay for benefits for all employees, such as a family allowance and various com-muting and housing allowances. In addition, many firms provide a whole range of welfare services ranging from subsidized company housing for families and dormitories for unmarried employees, through company nurseries and company scholarships for employees' children, to mortgage loans, credit facilities, savings plans, and insurance. Thus employees often perceive a close relationship between their own welfare and the company's financial welfare. Accordingly, behavior for the company's benefit that may appear self-sacrificing is not at all so; rather, it is in the employee's own interest.

Managers in U.S.-based companies generally also voiced a desire to make life in the company a pleasant experience for their subordinates. As in Japan, managers at all levels show concern for employees by sponsoring various recrea-tional activities or even taking them out to dinner to talk problems over. Again, continuous open communication gets special emphasis. However, company benefits are not as extensive as in Japan because of a feeling that American employees prefer rewards in the form of salary rather than the "golden handcuff" of benefits. Furthermore, the comprehensive government welfare system in the United States apparently renders such extensive benefits superfluous.

In summary, what we observed in many Japanese companies is an integrated system of management strategies and techniques that reinforce one another because of the systemic management orientation to the quality of human resources. In addi-tion to this system's behavioral consequences, which we have already discussed, a number of other positive outcomes have also been reported in research studies on Japanese organizations.

For example, when the company offers desirable employment conditions designed to provide job security and reduce voluntary turnover, the company benefits not only from the increased loyalty of the workforce, but also from a reduction in hiring, training, and other costs associated with turnover and replacement. Because employees enjoy job security, they do not fear technical innovation and may, in fact, welcome it—especially if it relieves them of tedious or exhausting manual tasks. In such an atmosphere, concern for long-term growth, rather than a focus on immediate profits, is also expected to flourish.

An articulated philosophy that expresses the company's family atmosphere as well as its uniqueness enables the employee to justify loyalty to the company and stimulates healthy competition with other companies. The management goals symbolized in company philosophy can give clear guidance to the employee who's trying to make the best decision in a situation that is uncertain.

Careful attention to selection and the employee's fit into the company results in a homogeneous workforce, easily able to develop the friendship ties that form the basis of information networks. The lack of conflict among functional divisions and the ability to communicate informally across divisions allow for rapid interdivisional coordination and the rapid implementation of various company goals and policies.

The other techniques we've outlined reinforce these poitive outcomes. Slow promotion reinforces a long-range perspective. High earnings in this quarter need not earn an employee an immediate promotion. Less reliance on the bottom line means that an employee's capabilities and behaviors over the long term become more important in their evaluation. Groups are another vehicle by which the company's goals, norms, and values are communicated to each employee. Open communication is the most visible vehicle for demonstrating concern for employees and willingness to benefit from their experience, regardless of rank. Open communication is thus a key technique that supports consultative decision making and affects the quality of any implementation process. Finally, caring about employees' social needs encourages identification with the firm and limits the impact of personal troubles on performance.

What we have described is a system based on the understanding that in return for the employee's contribution to company growth and well-being, the profitable firm will provide a stable and secure work environment and protect the individual employee's welfare even during a period of economic slowdown.

The Transferability of Japanese Management Practices

As in Japan, a key managerial concern in all U.S.-based Japanese companies we have investigated was the quality of human resources. As one executive put it, "We adapt the organization to the people because you can't adapt people to the organization." A number of specific instances of how Japanese management techniques are being applied in the United States were previously cited. Most personnel policies we've observed were similar to those in Japan, although evaluation systems and job-rotation planning are still somewhat different, probably because of the youth of the subsidiary companies. Less institutionalized concern for employee welfare was also pointed out.

The experience of many Japanese firms that have established U.S. subsidiaries suggests that the U.S. workers are receptive to many management practices introduced by Japanese managers. During our interviews, many Japanese executives pointed out that the productivity level in their U.S. plants is on a level similar to that in Japan—and occasionally even higher. Other research data indicate that American workers in Japanese-owned plants are even more satisfied with their work conditions than are their Japanese or Japanese-American colleagues.

The relative success of U.S.-based Japanese companies in transferring their employment and management practices to cover the great majority of their U.S. workers is not surprising when we consider that a number of large U.S. corporations have created management systems that use some typical Japanese techniques. Several of these firms have an outstanding record of innovation and rapid growth. A few examples are Procter & Gamble, Hewlett-Packard, and Cummins Engine.

William Ouchi and his colleagues call these firms Theory Z organizations. Seven key characteristics of Theory Z organizations are the following:

1. Long-term employment.
2. Slow evaluation and promotion.
3. Moderately specialized careers.
4. Consensual decision making.
5. Individual responsibility.
6. Implicit, informal control (but with explicit measures).
7. Holistic concern for the employee.

The Theory Z organization shares several features with the Japanese organization, but there are differences: In the former, responsibility is definitely individual, measures of performance are explicit, and careers are actually moderately specialized. However, Ouchi tells us little about communication patterns in these organizations, the role of the work group, and some other features important in Japanese settings.

Here's an example of a standard practice in the Theory Z organization that Ouchi studied in depth:

> [The Theory Z organization] calculated the profitability of each of its divisions, but it did not operate a strict profit center or other marketlike mechanism. Rather, decisions were frequently made by division managers who were guided by broader corporate concerns, even though their own divisional earnings may have suffered as a result.

A survey by Ouchi and Jerry Johnson showed that within the electronics industry perceived corporate prestige, managerial ability, and reported corporate earnings were all strongly positively correlated with the "Z-ness" of the organization.

It is also significant that examples of successful implementation of the Japanese system can be found even in Britain, a country notorious for labor-management conflict. In our interpretation, good labor-management relations—even the emergence of a so-called company union—is an effect, rather than a cause, of the mutually beneficial, reciprocal relationship enjoyed by the employees of the firm. Thus we see the co-existence of our management paradigm with productivity in companies in Japan, in Japanese companies in the United States and Europe, and in a number of indigenous U.S. companies. Although correlation does not imply cause, such a causal connection would be well supported by psychological theories. Douglas McGregor summarizes a great deal of research in saying: "Effective performance results when conditions are created such that the members of the organization can achieve their own goals best by directing their efforts toward the success of the enterprise."

CONCLUSION

Many cultural differences exist, of course, between people in Japan and those in Western countries. However, this should not distract our attention from the fact that human beings in all countries also have a great deal in common. In the workplace, all people value decent treatment, security, and an opportunity for emotional fulfillment. It is to the credit of Japanese managers that they have developed organizational systems that, even though far from perfect, do respond to these needs to a great extent. Also to their credit is the fact that high motivation and productivity result at the same time.

The strategies and techniques we have reviewed constitute a remarkably well-integrated system. The management practices are highly congruent with the way in which tasks are structured, with individual members' goals, and with the organization's climate. Such a fit is expected to result in a high degree of organizational effectiveness or productivity. We believe that the management paradigm of concern for human resources blends the hopes of humanistic thinkers with the pragmatism of those who need to show a return on investment. The evidence strongly suggests that this paradigm is both desirable and feasible in Western countries and that the key elements of Japanese management practices are not unique to Japan and can be successfully transplanted to other cultures. The linkage between human needs and productivity is nothing new in Western management theory. It required the Japanese, however, to translate the idea into a successful reality.

SELECTED BIBLIOGRAPHY

Robert Hayes and William Abernathy brought the lack of U.S. innovation to public attention in their article, "Managing Our Way to Economic Decline" (*Harvard Business Review,* July–August 1980).

Thomas P. Rohlen's book, *For Harmony and Strength: Japanese White-Collar Organization in Anthropological Perspective* (Berkeley: University of California Press, 1974), is a captivating description of the Japanese management system as seen in a regional bank. Peter Drucker has written several articles on the system, including

"What We Can Learn from Japanese Management" (*Harvard Business Review,* March–April 1971). His thoughts are extended to the United States by the empirical work of Richard Pascale, "Employment Practices and Employee Attitudes: A Study of Japanese and American Managed Firms in the U.S." (*Human Relations,* July 1978).

For further information on the Theory Z organization see "Type Z Organization: Stability in the Midst of Mobility" by William Ouchi and Alfred Jaeger (*Academy of Management Review,* April 1978), "Types of Organizational Control and Their Relationship to Emotional Well-Being" by William Ouchi and Jerry Johnson (*Administrative Science Quarterly,* Spring 1978), and "Hierarchies, Clans, and Theory Z: A New Perspective on Organization Development" by William Ouchi and Raymond Price (*Organizational Dynamics,* Autumn 1978).

Douglas McGregor explains the importance of a fit between employee and organizational goals in *The Human Side of Enterprise* (New York: McGraw-Hill, 1960).

FIRMS WITH A SUPERIOR LEADERSHIP CAPACITY: PRACTICES THAT CREATE BETTER-THAN-AVERAGE MANAGEMENT TEAMS

John P. Kotter

It is not entirely clear whether there are any firms today that do a truly exceptional job of attracting, developing, retaining, and motivating leadership talent. Nevertheless, some corporations clearly do achieve a level of success that is much superior (relatively) to others. Considerable evidence supports that conclusion—from the Executive Resources Questionnaire, the interviews done for this book, the *Fortune* Reputation Study, and elsewhere.

If we are to improve current practice related to creating a leadership capacity within management groups and help firms break out of the syndrome seen in the West Products case, it would be useful to know what some corporations actually do to create those better-than-average management teams.

WHAT THE MANAGERIALLY STRONGER FIRMS DO DIFFERENTLY: EVIDENCE FROM THE QUESTIONNAIRE

A casual reading of management, leadership, and human resources literature can generate dozens of hypotheses regarding what is most important to creating a superior leadership capacity within management. Some writers imply that hiring standards are the key; bring in the right people, and everything else takes care of itself. Others focus on development; provide challenging job assignments to people early in their careers, and the leaders will emerge and grow. Some point to formal

Source: Reprinted with permission of The Free Press, a Division of Macmillan, Inc. from *The Leadership Factor* by John P. Kotter. Copyright (c) 1988 by John P. Kotter, Inc.

systems—succession planning, high potential identification, or compensation reviews. Others suggest that more informal practices, such as the amount of mentoring and coaching provided, are key.

The Executive Resources Questionnaire provides one basis for testing those hypotheses. The survey asks an overall question about the quality of a firm's management, as well as more specific questions about practices that affect the quality. Because there is a relatively broad range of responses to that first question (quality of management), we can see which (if any) of the more specific programs and practices seem to be associated with differences in that quality.

Tables 1 and 2 summarize the results of a vary basic analysis of this sort. An examination of the first table shows that firms with superior managements are said to do a better job, on average, of attracting, developing, retaining, and motivating leadership talent (that is, *all four* aspects of the process). They achieve those results, the second table further suggests, by employing nothing less than dozens of more adequate practices.

More specifically, the detailed data (upon which Table 2 is based) say that those firms attract the people they need by having more adequate college recruiting efforts, programs for high potentials, training/educational opportunities, promotional opportunities, compensation, work environments, and reputations. They then hire the right people by having a more adequate sense of what they need to support business objectives, by keeping hiring standards high, and by having more hiring-level managers who can spot potential.

According to questionnaire data, those firms develop that talent by focusing scarce development resources on those who have the most potential. They spot that potential with more adequate performance appraisal processes, succession planning processes, and programs designed specifically to identify potential. They also tend to offer more opportunities to young people to get exposure to higher levels of management and have more executives at higher levels who can adequately spot young people with potential. They target development resources by more adequately identifying exactly what the development needs of those employees are.

TABLE 1 A Comparison of the "Stronger" Management Firms with All Others*

	Stronger Management Firms	All Other Firms
1. How good a job is the company doing with respect to recruiting and hiring a sufficient number of people into the firm who have the potential of someday providing effective leadership in important management positions?	2.8 (1 = excellent, 5 = poor)	3.4
2. How good a job is the company doing with respect to developing employees with potential?	3.0	3.3
3. How good a job is the company doing with respect to retaining and motivating those employees?	2.8	3.4

*Only firms in which twenty or more executives completed the questionnaire are included in this analysis. Firm scores are the simple mean of all the executives' responses. This and the next table compare the four firms scoring highest on item 57 (the "Stronger Management Firms") with fourteen lower-scoring firms.

494

TABLE 2 A Comparison of Programs and Practices: From the Executive Resources Questionnaire

	Number of Areas in Which Stronger Firms Have:		
	More Adequate Practices	Equally Adequate Practices	Less Adequate Practices
1. Regarding fifteen programs and practices that affect the recruitment and hiring of people with leadership potential	14	1	0
2. Regarding nineteen programs and practices that affect the training and development of those people	15	4	0
3. Regarding twelve programs and practices that affect the retention and motivation of such people	12	0	0

They then meet those needs in many ways, including adding responsibilities to jobs, creating special jobs, using inside and outside training, transferring people between functions and divisions, mentoring and coaching employees, giving those people feedback on development progress, and giving them instruction in how to manage their own development.

Firms with better-than-average management retain and motivate the people they develop, according to questionnaire data, by having more adequate practices for them in the areas of compensation, promotion opportunities, development opportunities, and training opportunities. They also provide them with more adequate information on job openings in the firm and have higher-quality career planning discussions with them. And they offer those people a considerably better work environment.

In other words, the questionnaire data suggest that no single program or small set of practices is key to creating a stronger-than-average leadership capacity within management. Good succession planning, excellent college recruiting, or superior economic incentives, by themselves, appear not to be sufficient. The firms with better-than-average management seem to do a more adequate job in dozens of areas that affect the hiring, development, and retention of talent.

WHAT FIFTEEN FIRMS DO DIFFERENTLY: EVIDENCE FROM THE "BEST PRACTICES STUDY"

That questionnaire-based conclusion receives further support with information from a second source: a more in-depth study of fifteen firms.

Those firms were chosen using data from *Fortune's* Reputation Study. The 1985 version of that survey asked hundreds of "experts" to rate 250 corporations on a number of dimensions, two of which were (1) the quality of the firms' management and (2) the firms' success of attracting, developing, and retaining talented employees. The twenty firms that were ranked the highest on those two dimensions are shown in Table 3. Fifteen of those firms were included in a "Best Practices" study as background for this book (the table identifies which fifteen). In

TABLE 3 Firms Rated Highest on Two Dimensions[a] in the 1985 Fortune Reputation Study

Firm	Rating (1–10 Scale)[b]	Included in This Study
1. IBM	8.75	Yes
2. Dow Jones	8.4	Yes
3. Hewlett-Packard	8.4	Yes
4. Coca Cola	8.35	Yes
5. Morgan Guaranty	8.3	Yes
6. Anheuser-Busch	8.3	Yes
7. 3M	8.2	Yes
8. General Electric	8.15	Yes
9. Boeing	8.0	No
10. Citicorp	7.9	Yes
11. Standard Oil of Indiana	7.9	No
12. General Motors	7.8	Yes
13. Du Pont	7.75	Yes
14. Merck	7.7	Yes
15. General Mills	7.65	Yes
16. Johnnson & Johnson	7.6	Yes
17. Kodak	7.55	No
18. Abbott	7.55	No
19. Delta	7.55	No
20. First Boston	7.5	Yes

[a]"Quality of Management" and "Ability to Attract, Develop, and Keep Talented People."
[b]10 = excellent. Mean score on the two dimensions combined.

using that procedure, it was not assumed that the fifteen firms had managements that were excellent in any absolute sense, nor that they had the best leadership capacity within their managements in a relative sense (relative to all other firms). It was assumed *only* that the fifteen represented a good sample of corporations with better-than-average managements.

Eight or more top executives were interviewed in each of the fifteen firms, typically for an hour each. The two core questions that structured the discussions were: (1) What do you do to attract and retain people with some leadership potential? (2) What do you do to develop and broaden those people?

The responses from the 150 interviews are entirely consistent with the questionnaire data. There are no big "secrets to success." These firms just do a lot of little things differently from the norm in business today. For our purposes here, a discussion of all the practices will be grouped into five sessions relating to: a sophisticated recruiting effort, an attractive work environment, challenging opportunities, early identification, and planned development.

A SOPHISTICATED RECRUITING EFFORT

Interviews from the "Best Practices" study suggest, first of all, that the fifteen firms do a superior job of recruiting sufficient people who have the potential of providing them with leadership at some time in the future. They do so by using a half-dozen practices that are slightly different from the norm today in business.

The first practice is to let line management drive the recruiting effort. At these firms, human resource professionals aid in the process, providing coordination and administrative support, but they do not seem to run the process. Line management does, including some fairly senior people. At General Mills, for example, even the chairman sometimes visits key colleges. At First Boston, the managing director who heads the recruiting effort literally spends half his time on recruiting. At Mercke, the CEO himself devotes considerable time and effort to recruiting people who can help provide technical leadership in the firm. Although obviously expensive in terms of senior management time, most executives in these firms seem convinced it is necessary. A typical comment from one of those businessmen:

> Our current senior management is in the best position to know how many and what kind of people will be needed to run the business in the future; they understand where our business strategy is taking us better than anyone. They also are better able to spot the kind of quality minds and interpersonal abilities we want in young people; in a sense, it takes one to know one. And they are in a much better position to sell the company than are lower-level managers or personnel staff.

Second, many of these corporations target a limited number of colleges and universities that they feel are a good source of future leadership, and then they treat those schools much as they would major customers. Hewlett-Packard, for example, focuses on thirty schools for its corporate recruiting effort and works hard to develop good relationships with those schools by (among other things) networking with their faculties and donating computer equipment. When managed well, those efforts appear to pay off handsomely.

Third, most of these firms seem to work especially hard to keep hiring standards high across the entire company. IBM, for example, quantifies certain measures of the quality of incoming hires, sets targets on those measures, and then "inspects" on a regular basis how well each hiring department is doing. Merck brings all high-potential recruiting candidates to corporate headquarters to meet some senior managers who are thought to have a good sense of the firm's hiring standards. General Mills does that too, and if any of those senior executives vote no on a candidate, they seriously consider not making an offer despite plenty of "yes" votes. Morgan Guaranty brings all new recruits to a lengthy training program in New York; if any of its offices are diluting hiring standards, it becomes rather obvious by the end of the program. The exact practices vary from firm to firm, but the main objective seems to remain the same: Keep standards from slipping because of short-term economic pressures.

A fourth practice that appears to distinguish most of these firms is that they actually pay some attention to leadership potential when recruiting. Morgan Guaranty, for example, asks everyone who interviews candidates to fill out a one-page "Prospective Employee—Interview Evaluation." The form gently reminds people to "keep in mind" four factors that have little to do with the technical components of banking; one of those factors is "leadership potential." "With all the well-educated and talented people we hire," an investment banker recently reported, "you'd think we would be guaranteed plenty of leadership and management potential. But it's not true. Unless we focus on that explicitly, we end up with a lot of smart technicians who often lack common sense and basic interpersonal skills."

A fifth practice commonly found at these firms might be called the well-managed "close." As one General Mills executive reported:

> When we find someone we really want, we work hard to close the sale. For example, if we meet such people at one of our informal wine and cheese gatherings, we'll immediately send a follow-up letter and invite them to Minneapolis. When they are here, we'll make sure they have lunch with a recent graduate of their school or someone from their home town. We will then make them an offer at the end of the day—no, "We'll get back to you in a few weeks" stuff. Then, if they don't accept immediately, we might fly them and their spouses back to corporate to see the community and meet the chairman. In between, there will be all the appropriate follow-up letters and calls.

Finally, these firms usually evaluate their overall recruiting at least once a year. Many generate statistics on offers made to offers accepted, or offers lost to key competitors, and then compare those statistics to historical averages. Some, like Du Pont, look at more indirect indices, such as how many relatively new hires are rated on the yearly performance appraisal as having high potential.

ATTRACTIVE WORK ENVIRONMENT

A few years ago I visited a former student who works for Hewlett-Packard. By job standards, he was doing very well at the time. At age thirty-four, he was in charge of hundreds of people and a sizable budget. But by salary standards, he was making 25 percent less than the average person who graduated in his MBA class. When I questioned him about this, he admitted that he wished he made more money. He also volunteered that he had considered on several occasions leaving HP for startup ventures. But he hadn't. I asked why.

The long answer the young man provided basically boiled down to this: Hewlett-Packard has been a good place for a talented person to work. People are treated well. Competence is respected. Bureaucracy and political games are minimized. Individual initiative is recognized and rewarded. It is technically a very exciting place for people with engineering backgrounds. etc. etc.

What is so interesting about that response is that it is not at all unusual at the fifteen "Best Practice" firms. When one asks executives at those firms how they attract and retain good people, almost always they say "because it's a great place to work." Why they think it's a great place to work seems to vary somewhat from firm to firm and from individual to individual. What remains constant is their belief that it's "fun" for someone with leadership potential to work there.

Perhaps the most common answer regarding what makes a work environment fun is "lack of politics." By that, people typically mean the environment is friendly. ("When someone gets the knife out around here it is made of rubber.") They also mean that results are what count, not covert alliances or form. And they mean that people actually try to help each other. "I could get a job at (another prestigious newspaper)," a Dow Jones manager says, "but I'm not interested. Politics here are 10 percent of what they are over there. We don't have their warring factions. I mean, who wants to have to put up with that? It's not worth it."

Executives also often mention honesty or integrity as an important feature of a good work environment. Johnson & Johnson people, for example, often refer to the fact that they usually live up to the high ethical standards outlined in their "credo," and that makes J&J's environment very attractive. Executives at other firms sometimes talk about other corporate values, such as a dedication to quality (one hears that often at Dow Jones and Anheuser-Busch). They talk about the lack of bureaucracy or the informality. They talk about the quality of their fellow workers. They sometimes refer to the nice location of the workplace (e.g., 3M in Minneapolis, Coke in Atlanta) or the aesthetics of the work environment (Morgan Guaranty). And they often point out that "people are treated well around here."

For example, one of the frequent complaints one hears from lower-level managers in many firms is that they feel "trapped." Here is a very typical comment:

> I have almost no idea what job openings exist or will exist outside my department. That kind of information just doesn't circulate at my level. So my capacity to get a good opportunity in some other part of the company is almost completely under the control of my bosses. Unfortunately, they don't have much incentive to want to find those opportunities for me. So I'm trapped in a narrow and vertical career path, which in the long run won't be good for me. And the speed of my movement on this path is a function of strong forces I don't control. It's not a good situation. It's driving me to look for opportunities outside the company.

The fifteen firms studied here seem to do a much better job than average of minimizing that problem by providing high potentials (and often others too) with information on job openings throughout the company. Hewlett-Packard, for example, has worked to maintain a labor market inside the company that is at least as open and accessible as external markets. Most people really appreciate those efforts, and such practices facilitate lateral movement for development purposes (more on that later).

CHALLENGING OPPORTUNITIES

Interviews at the fifteen "Best Practice" firms are replete with references to the importance of "challenging opportunities." One gets the sense that challenging entry-level jobs help attract good people in the first place, and challenging promotion opportunities help firms hold onto those people, because people with leadership potential love new challenges and hate old routines. The challenges, in turn, both stretch people and allow them, often early in their careers, to exercise some leadership. And that, of course, is at the heart of development.

Those interviewed say that challenging opportunities are created in a number of ways. In many firms, decentralization is the key. By definition, decentralization pushes responsibility lower in an organization and in the process creates more challenging jobs at lower levels. Johnson & Johnson, 3M, HP, General Electric, and a number of other well-known firms have used that approach quite successfully in the past.

Some of those same firms also have created as many small units as possible so there are lots of challenging little general management jobs available. Hewlett-Packard, GE, and J&J are said to have benefited greatly over the years from that approach.

In a similar vein, many of the firms seem to develop additional challenging opportunities by stressing growth through new products: 3M has even had a policy over the years that at least 25 percent of its revenue should come from products introduced within the last five years. That encourages small new ventures, which in turn offer hundreds of opportunities to test and stretch young people with leadership potential.

Some of those same firms have also worked hard to minimize bureaucracy and rigid structures so that it's easier to enhance jobs with additional challenges. As an executive at Coca Cola recently put it:

> If I hire an MBA as a brand manager, because we are not highly compartmentalized and structured, he or she can make that job into almost anything. The person is not in a box. We can make the job as big and challenging as is necessary to really turn that person on.

In a similar way, more and more companies, like Du Pont, seem to be using task force assignments to generate additional challenge in jobs.

Other firms, including some that face limits to how much they can decentralize responsibility into small units, have created specific jobs to challenge people with leadership potential. Perhaps the most obvious example is administrative assistant (or executive assistant) jobs. Anheuser-Busch has created about thirty such jobs. IBM has even more, and has obviously benefited from the practice. The last few presidents and many of the current executive staff at IBM had AA jobs early in their careers.

When all of those techniques still do not produce enough opportunities, perhaps because the business (or part of the business) is not growing, these firms then (more often than the norm in business today) take the painful actions needed to free up promotion possibilities. That sometimes means making early retirement attractive to certain people. And it always means coming to grips with "blockers"—people who have no chance of further promotion, are a long way from retirement, and are not performing well in their current assignments.

EARLY IDENTIFICATION

Equipping people with what they will need to provide effective leadership takes time, often lots of time. As such, it is not entirely surprising to find that the fifteen firms seem to do a far better job than average of identifying people with some leadership potential early in their careers and identifying just what will be needed to stretch and develop that potential.

The methods most of those firms use are surprisingly straightforward. They go out of their way to make young employees and people at lower levels in their organizations visible to senior management. Senior managers then judge for themselves who has potential and what the development needs of those people are. Executives then discuss their tentative conclusions openly and candidly, among themselves, in an effort to draw more and more accurate judgments. "Scientific" techniques seem to be rarely employed. The key is: look, talk, and think.

To make younger employees visible to senior management, a variety of techniques are said to be utilized. Here are the most common, each described by an executive whose firm uses that approach:

> We regularly take young people who someone thinks has potential and put them on special projects that conclude with presentations to senior management. I can still remember making a presentation when I was thirty years old to a group that included the chairman of the company.
>
> *An executive at Johnson & Johnson*

> Once a month, I have a luncheon with one of my key functional managers, and I always ask that he or she bring some high-potential employees along. At certain staff meetings, I do the same thing. This allows me to get to know a lot of young people and to draw my own conclusions about potential, strengths, and weaknesses.
>
> *An executive at Coca Cola*

> We don't let the organizational structure constrain us. We always go right to the individual who has information we need. This puts us in contact with a lot of lower-level and more junior employees, and gives us a firsthand feeling for who they are and what they are good at.
>
> *An executive at Dow Jones*

> We have many recognition programs in this company. These programs often bring good people to the attention of senior management. They make good people more visible, which is very helpful.
>
> *An executive at General Mills*

> One of the things we do is to set up situations which allow our divisions to put their best people "on stage." And then we take a hard look. In this way, you can spot promising young people, and once you know their names, you can go out of your way to get to know them better.
>
> *An executive at Hewlett-Packard*

> Our top people make it a habit to get out to our plants on a regular basis. This gives them a chance to meet and to talk to younger employees. It makes folks visible to senior executives who would never meet them otherwise.
>
> *An executive at Anheuser-Busch*

Those kinds of practices provide senior managers with information on people who might have leadership potential. Those executives then usually share and discuss that information among themselves, either informally or formally, on a regular basis.

The Management Council at Hewlett-Packard (the top twenty-eight people), for example, has had regular discussions about the middle management at the company, and the discussions are reported to be "very open." Large firms tend to try to do that sort of thing in a very systematic way. At Du Pont, for example, the sixteen senior department heads meet once a month for two hours. At a typical meeting, the agenda will include a discussion of the half-dozen people one of those executives thinks are "highly promotable." Before every meeting, a picture and biography for those six people are sent to all sixteen department heads. At the meeting, everyone who knows those people is expected to speak up, especially those who have concerns or questions about a person's potential (e.g., "When Harry worked for us five years ago, he only performed at an average level. What has happened to him recently that led you to think so highly of him?''). People who don't know the candidate being discussed are also expected to be aggressive in their questioning (e.g., "How does she compare to George Smith?" "How well did he do in his one staff assignment?'').

PLANNED DEVELOPMENT

Armed with a better-than-average sense of who has some leadership potential and what needs to be developed in those people, executives in the "Best Practices" firms then spend much more time than firms like West Products planning for that development. Sometimes that is done as a part of a formal succession planning or high-potential development process. Often it is done more informally. In either case, the key ingredient appears to be an intelligent assessment of what feasible development opportunities fit each candidate's needs.

"Developmental opportunities," in the sense that the term is being used here, include:

- New job assignments (promotions and lateral moves)
- Formal training (inside the firm, at a public seminar, or at a university)
- Task force or committee assignments
- Mentoring or coaching from a senior executive
- Attendance at meetings outside one's core responsibility
- Special projects
- Special developmental jobs (e.g., executive assistant jobs)

With the fifteen firms studied here, one finds those opportunities used more systematically than is the norm in business today. One finds (as this writer did) a Ph.D. organic chemist (at Coke) working as an executive's administrative assistant as part of a conscious strategy to broaden that person. One finds bankers (in Morgan and Citicorp) or functional heads (at J&J) systematically shipped off to foreign offices to give them international experience and a chance to run a small operation by themselves. One finds technically trained people (at Du Pont) moved from research to manufacturing to marketing to general management to corporate staff, and then into executive line jobs. One finds people (at IBM) regularly attending some type of educational experience. One finds, again and again, what appears to be considerable intelligent effort being expended to develop and broaden people so that they will someday have what it takes to provide leadership in complex executive jobs.

One also finds some effort in these firms not just to plan for development in a generic sense, but to plan for the kind of development that will support future business strategies. Sometimes that is done very formally (e.g., strategic business planning is somehow tied to succession planning). Often it is more informal. It is not clear how effective those efforts are, but some executives clearly think they are important.

And when formal training is used—and it seems to be used a great deal in these firms—it is never employed as a substitute for experience. Unlike in firms like West Products, where training is often used as a "quick fix," in these firms training both leverages past experiences (that is, it helps people to learn more from them) and prepares people to learn more from future assignments (in making them more aware of certain things).

THE FINDINGS IN PERSPECTIVE

The findings in this chapter are consistent with Peters and Waterman's notion that successful firms do a lot of little things a little better, as well as the Center for Creative Leadership work on how effective executives are developed. Even more fundamentally. . .these findings have a certain logic to them. The business environment today is asking many people to help provide leadership. Doing that effectively is often extremely difficult. Indeed, the assets one needs to provide effective leadership in big jobs form a long list. . .Trying to find and equip many people with the tools they will need to provide that leadership might therefore logically be a large and very complicated task, one that should require a great effort in a lot of different areas. And that is essentially what the evidence in this chapter says. . .(as summarized in Exhibit 1).

To put the magnitude of the task in perspective, let us remember that it seems to take all of this effort to produce what we have been calling "better-than-average" managements. That is, we have no evidence to suggest that any of the firms in the "Best Practices" study have managements that are, at least on the leadership dimension, excellent in any absolute sense. These firms simply have managements

EXHIBIT 1 How Practices Create a Leadership Capacity in Management

that are better able to supply leadership in competitively intense industries than in the norm today in business. Just imagine what might be required to produce truly excellent managements.

OVERCOMING THE DYSFUNCTIONS OF MbO

Steven Kerr

Despite tremendous interest in Management by Objectives (MbO) and its extensive use in industry as a developmental tool, "research examining the planning, implementation and evaluation of MbO systems has been surprisingly scarce."[1] When the very natural tendency for change agents to write about and for journals to publish successes rather than failures is taken into account, it is even more clear that little is really known about the dysfunctions which often plague MbO introductions and implementations.

There are two major problems with trying to evaluate MbO. One is that "Management by Objectives" is really a catch-all title for several different, if related, approaches.[2] The other is that, when introduced as a total system of management, MbO constitutes a simultaneous assault upon the organization's authority, reward communications and control systems, changing so many variables at once that careful study is all but impossible.

I am not prepared to claim without definitive data that Management by Objectives is or is not working in organizations today. Based on a review of the MbO literature and on related research, however, and aided by personal contact with MbO in four organizations (twice as an employee, twice as a consultant), I am prepared to suggest that most MbO efforts are accompanied by a number of dysfunctions, dysfunctions serious enough in many cases to keep the system from performing efficiently.

MbO is often sold as a total managerial system. I hope to show that MbO is *not* likely to be effective when employed as a total system. I hope to show also that the typical MbO process contains logical inconsistencies and makes implicit assumptions which are contrary to things we know about organizations and about people.

The purposes of this article are (1) to discuss the weaknesses underlying the MbO process, and (2) to suggest how MbO can be modified so as to permit its successful use in organizations.

Source: Reprinted with permission of the author and publisher from *Management by Objectives,* Vol. 5, No. 1, 1976.

[1] Henry L. Tosi and William J. Bigoness, "MbO and Personality: A Search for Comparability," *Management by Objectives,* 3, Number 4, 1974, p. 44.

[2] Harry Levinson, "Management by Whose Objectives?" *Harvard Business Review,* July-August 1970, p. 125.

Although there are several varieties of "Management by Objectives," in general MbO features "joint goal-setting between those at each level of management and those at the next higher level, the expression of objectives whenever possible in quantifiable terms such as dollars, units, and percentages, and the subsequent measurement and comparison of actual performance with the agreed-upon objectives."[3]

MbO is certainly intuitively appealing; why else would so many firms incur the heavy costs of its adoption in the absence of conclusive evidence of its worth? However, its intuitive appeal masks several important shortcomings and deficiencies. Some of the explicit claims and implicit assumptions that have been made on behalf of MbO are presented below.

Assumption 1: "Joint" Goal-Setting
Among Hierarchical Unequals Is Possible

This premise lies at the heart of the MbO philosophy, and presumes that the superior can comfortably go from his "boss-judge" role to one of "friend-helper" (and, presumably, back again). It is claimed of one participative system, for example, that evaluation meetings between the boss and his subordinates can be "strictly man-to-man in character... In listening to the subordinate's review of performance, problems, and failings, the manager is automatically cast in the role of *counselor*. This role for the manager, in turn, results naturally in a problem-solving discussion."[4]

The assumption that such schizoid behavior can be induced on any kind of regular basis is naive. The research literature[5] provides abundant evidence that hierarchical status differences produce some very predictable effects upon interaction patterns, subordinate defensiveness, and quantity and quality of communications, and these effects "stack the deck" against joint goal-setting by unequals. Bennis has summarized some of the difficulties involved:

> Two factors seem to be involved... The superior as a helper, trainer, consultant, and co-ordinator; and the superior as an instrument and arm of reality, a man with power over the subordinate... For each actor in the relationship, a *double reference* is needed... The double reference approach requires a degree of maturity, more precisely a commitment to maturity, on the part of both the superior and subordinate that exceeds that of any other organizational approach... It is suggestive that psychiatric patients find it most difficult to see the psychiatrist both as a human being and helper and an individual with certain perceived powers. The same difficulty exists in the superior-subordinate relationship.[6]

[3]Alan C. Filley, Robert J. House and Steven Kerr, *Managerial Process and Organizational Behavior* (Glenview, Ill., Scott, Foresman, 1976) (2nd edition, in press).

[4]Herbert H. Meyer, Emanuel Kay, and John R. P. French, Jr., "Split Roles in Performance Appraisal," *Harvard Business Review,* Janaury–February 1965, p. 129.

[5]See for example Peter M. Blau and W. Richard Scott, *Formal Organizations* (San Francisco, Chandler, 1962), pp. 121-124 and 242-244.

[6]Warren G. Bennis, "Leadership Theory and Administrative Behavior: The Problem of Authority," *Administrative Science Quarterly,* 1960, pp. 285-287.

Assumption 2: MbO Can Be Effective
at the Lowest Managerial Levels

Proponents have contended that successful implementation will enable MbO to permeate the entire organization, and be effective even at the lowest level of management. However, several studies have concluded that this filtering-down process very often fails to occur, and that the lower the hierarchical status of the manager the less influence he can exert, and the less he is likely to be a genuine participant in the goal-setting process.[7] In part this reflects the inherent problems of attempting joint goal-setting among hierarchical unequals.

Another reason for the failure of MbO to be effective at the lower managerial levels is an illogicality in the process itself. It is that even if we assume truly democratic, participative goal-setting at the very top of the firm (say, between the president and his divisional vice-presidents), their meetings must still ultimately produce firm, hard goals for the months ahead. The most collegial atmosphere in the world cannot keep these goals, once agreed upon, from being perceived as commitments by the parties concerned. These commitments must then serve as lower limits, as monkeys on the back of any vice-president who then seeks to establish democratic, participative goal-setting with his own subordinates. Having agreed with the president that 12 percent growth in sales is a fair goal for the coming year, the marketing vice-president is unlikely to accept his sales manager's carefully-worded argument that 9 percent is better. While lower-level managers may enjoy the fiction of participation, they will probably soon realize that most of their objectives have already been "locked in" by meetings held at higher levels. They of course retain the freedom to set objectives even more challenging than those agreed upon higher up; they will seldom be able to set objectives less challenging.

Varying the goal-setting sequence can serve to alter this chain of events, but will seldom improve upon it. For example, some MbO proponents claim that "simultaneous goal-setting" at all managerial levels produces genuine participation. However, the ensuing problems of coordination and communications border on the unreal. The marketing vice-president might under these conditions meet with the president, and agree "tentatively" that 12 percent sales growth sounded pretty good for the next year. After meeting with his sales manager, who preferred 9 percent, he would again meet with the president to renegotiate. If 10 percent were now agreed on he would once more meet with the sales manager, to democratically explain why 9 percent was too low. Meanwhile, however, the sales manager would have held meetings with his district managers, and perhaps become convinced that 9 percent was too high. At this point the marketing vice-president would presumably return to his "friend-helper" the president for another round of "joint" goal-setting.

The only way to insure that low-level managers have influence is for them to initiate the process, by communicating to their superior the goals they wish to

[7]See for example John M. Ivancevich, "A Longitudinal Assessment of Management by Objectives," *Administrative Science Quarterly,* 1972, pp. 126–138. More recently, Raia, and Tosi and Carroll have published results which agree.

pursue during the coming period. Their superior would then set his objectives based upon their objectives, and so on up the line. This gain in low-level influence may be costly, however, since the firm's goals are essentially being set by those at the bottom of the hierarchy, who (usually) are less educated, trained, and experienced, and who may possess inadequate information. Technical drawbacks aside, this alternative is likely to be politically unacceptable to managers at the top. It is therefore no surprise that many studies have shown MbO to be increasingly ineffective at successively lower levels.

Assumption 3: MbO Is An Aid in
Evaluating and Rewarding Performance

Management by Objectives is often used in conjunction with management appraisal programs. Some writers recommend linking it directly to the compensation program, under the assumption that MbO provides "a means of measuring the true contribution of managerial and professional personnel."[8] However, this assumption calls to mind some impossible-to-answer questions, and very often leads to information suppression and risk-avoidance behavior, particularly in highly uncertain and rapidly changing organizational units.

The impossible-to-answer questions include:

1. How do you tell whether the goals whose accomplishment you are rewarding are challenging?

Padding by subordinates of time it will take or money it will cost may be detectable when the superior has technical expertise in the area for which the objective is being set, and when the task depends on technology which is stable and predictable. There are numerous instances, however, in engineering, marketing, product development and other areas, when even the most astute superior will be unable to determine whether target dates have a built-in safety factor.

2. How do you insure that all your subordinates have goals which are of equal difficulty?

If MbO is to be useful as an evaluation-compensation tool, subordinates must perceive that they have a fair chance to obtain organizational rewards. Yet it is virtually impossible to devise any system which will provide for goals which are equally challenging.

3. What do you do when conditions change?

Suppose that a new competitor or a new credit rating comes along, and what formerly were challenging goals suddenly become easy goals, or impossible goals. In a truly stable environment this may not be a daily concern, but in our age of continuous "future shock" stable environments are becoming unusual. Even a modest technological development or a small change in company policy can eliminate the challenge from objectives previously set. Do we now reward for goal-attainment when a ten-year-old could also have been successful? Do we punish non-attainment of objectives which have become herculean in difficulty? Or do we spend the better part of every afternoon negotiating?

[8]George S. Odiorne, *Management by Objectives—A System of Managerial Leadership* (New York, Pitman, 1965), p. 55.

4. Is exceeding the objective good?

Even aside from the fact that conditions continually change, this question is more difficult than it may seem. In one firm I am familiar with, the completion of a task in seven weeks when it was forecasted to take ten weeks brings mild *disapproval* rather than praise. The rationale is credible enough; it is that others with whom the goal-setter interacts are not expecting the guidebook, product, software package or whatever to be ready, and so cannot take advantage of the fact that it is ready. This organization takes a position that deviations from standard *in either direction* are usually undesirable. While this may or may not be the best approach, the point is that it is seldom possible to determine whether early completion of a task is an indication of good performance or of bad planning. That the individual worked like the dickens is seldom sufficient to resolve this dilemma.

5. How do you "objectively" reward performance under MbO?

Proponents of Management by Objectives take special pains to avoid this question, since it is obviously one for which there is no answer. Odiorne, for example, asserts that MbO "determines who should get the *pay* increases. . . The increases are allocated on the basis of the results achieved against agreed-upon goals at the beginning of the period."[9] The problem with this, however, is that no formula for comparing "results achieved against agreed-upon goals" exists. Researchers have correctly cautioned that "evaluations should rarely be based on whether or not the objective is accomplished or on the sheer number accomplished. . .," and have listed other factors that must be taken into accounting, including:

- proper allocation of time to given objectives
- type and difficulty of objectives
- creativity in overcoming obstacles
- efficient use of resources
- use of good management practices in accomplishing objectives (cost reduction, delegation, good planning, etc.)
- avoidance of conflict-inducing or unethical practices[10]

Certainly it is necessary to consider these and other factors; otherwise subordinates could better themselves by taking shortcuts which negatively affect total organizational effectiveness. But take another look at the above list of "other factors" to be considered. Have you seen a list which calls for greater *subjectivity?* Could you possibly establish *objective* measures of whether "proper" time was allocated to given objectives, whether "creativity" was used to overcome obstacles, or whether "good" management practices were used? In short, MbO leaves you as dependent on subjectivity as you were before, only with the additional problem that expectations of "fair" and "objective" evaluation and reward systems have been created, making employee dissatisfaction more likely.

If the added objectivity promised by Management by Objectives typically

[9]Ibid., p. 66.

[10]Stephen J. Carroll and Henry L. Tosi, Jr., *Management by Objectives: Applications and Research,* (New York: Macmillan, 1973), p. 83.

turns out to be illusory, the information suppression and risk-avoidance behavior often brought on by linking MbO to rewards is certainly no illusion. Common sense suggests that many employees will build margins for error into their cost estimates and target dates, and in this case common sense is supported by research.[11] Even workers high in need for Achievement will often create safety cushions, while privately setting moderate-risk objectives against which they can compete. I have seen or heard of many cases where employees set objectives on projects which were virtually or actually completed. You may be quick to brand such actions unethical; can you as quickly deny that they are rational responses to a system which requests of employees that they voluntarily set challenging, risky goals, only to face smaller paychecks and possibly damaged careers if these goals are not accomplished?

Assumption 4: Objectives Should Be as Specific as Possible

MbO encourages goal-setting in extremely quantitative fashion, with intermediate and final results all expressed in dollars, dates, or percentages. While such quantification is often possible and desirable, MbO encourages it to the extent that goal displacement and inefficiency sometimes result. Studies indicate that the MbO process can cause employees to over-concentrate their efforts in areas for which objectives have been written, to the virtual exclusion of other activities.[12] Since it is seldom possible to write quantifiable objectives about innovation, creativity, and interpersonal-relations, employees under MbO are seldom evaluated in these areas, and may consequently worry little about coming up with new ideas or improving relations with other organizational units.

Even in areas for which objectives do exist, excessive emphasis on quantifiable objectives encourages (and, when linked to compensation, rewards) performance in accordance with the *letter,* not the *spirit,* of the objective. Attempting to measure and reward accuracy in paying surgical claims, for example, one insurance firm requires that managers set objectives about the number of returned checks and letters of complaint received from policyholders. However, underpayments are likely to provoke cries of outrage from the insured, while overpayments are often accepted in courteous silence. Since it is often impossible to tell from the physician's statement which of two surgical procedures, with different allowable benefits, was performed, and since writing for clarification will interfere with other objectives concerning "percentage of claims paid within two days of receipt," the new hire in more than one claims section is soon acquainted with the informal norm: "When in doubt, pay it out!"[13] The managers of these sections regularly meet or exceed their objectives in the areas of both quality (accuracy) and quantity. But at what cost to the organization?

[11]See for example Stephen J. Carroll and Henry L. Tosi, "Goal Characteristics and Personality Factors in a Management-by-Objectives Program," *Administrative Science Quarterly,* 1970, pp. 295–305.

[12]See for example Anthony P. Raia, "A Second Look at Management Goals and Controls," *California Management Review,* 1966, pp. 49–58.

[13]Steven Kerr, "On the Folly of Rewarding A, While Hoping for B," *Academy of Management of Journal,* 1975.

Assumption 5: MbO Is Useful
in a Dynamic, Changing Environment

Certainly, the dynamic environment is where new systems of planning, evaluation and communications are most needed. We already know quite a bit about managing the stable, highly-certain segments of business, and a variety of techniques such as PERT are available to us and work particularly well when parameters are known. MbO, however, is less useful when conditions are changing and the future is uncertain. We have already suggested that risk-avoidance by subordinates will most often occur under conditions of uncertainty, and we have also pointed out that under such circumstances goal difficulty is so likely to change that systematic reward and punishment under MbO is impossible.

One reviewer of the MbO literature found that "the most striking result is the emphasis on the need for goal clarity (low role conflict and ambiguity) if Management by Objectives is to be an effective planning procedure."[14] Low role conflict and ambiguity can be fairly well established by SOPs and job descriptions in the stable, highly-certain parts of most firms; they are nearly impossible to come by in uncertain areas. MbO, after all, attempts to produce a mutually-acceptable job description, and "no matter how detailed the job description, it is essentially static, that is, a series of statements. . .The more complex the task and the more flexible a man must be in it, the less any fixed statement of job elements will fit what he does. . ."[15]

I have to this point tried to demonstrate that Management by Objectives is a sometimes overrated, flawed system which may introduce more problems than it solves. Rather than join those who attribute its failures to "errors in implementation," "not enough time," or "lack of top management support," I believe its difficulties stem from the fact that it depends upon assumptions which are contrary to what we think we know about organizations and about people.

Of course, if you are *not* knee-deep in pseudoparticipation, caution-crazy subordinates and make-believe objectivity, don't let me convince you you're sick when you're not. In this age of situational theories it is no more possible to state that something will not work than to claim it always will. However, if you *are* having problems of the kind I have described, and if you buy my argument that MbO is at least partially responsible, you may still feel that sunk cost and political realities argue against trying to quit cold turkey. The remainder of this article is therefore aimed at separating those parts of MbO worth keeping from those which ought to be discarded.

FEATURES WORTH KEEPING

1. Conscious emphasis on goal-setting. Considerable research suggests that systematic, periodic goal-setting positively affects performance, and can alter an organization's activities-oriented approach in favor of one that is more results-oriented.

[14]John B. Miner, *The Management Process: Theory, Research and Practice,* (New York, Macmillan, 1973).
[15]Levinson, *op cit.* p. 126.

2. Frequent interaction and feedback between superior and subordinates. These have been found to be related to "higher goal success, improvement in relationships with the boss, goal clarity, a feeling of supportiveness and interest from one's superior, a feeling that one can participate in matters affecting him, and satisfaction with the superior."[16] Feedback frequency is particularly important "to managers low in self-assurance, cautious in decision making, and with jobs involving frequent change."[17]

3. Opportunities for participation. Although it is erroneous to assume that hierarchically-unequal individuals can comfortably engage in joint goal-setting, this does not mean that all forms of participation are impossible. Even chances to give advice about matters which will ultimately be decided higher up often have favorable effects upon subordinate attitudes. While not all workers respond positively to participation, studies indicate that performance will seldom suffer merely because of such opportunities.

One way to improve participation under MbO might be for the peer group to develop their objectives as a group. Status differentials are likely to be less important, freeing individuals of the need to be cautious and deferential.[18] Peer-group goal-setting should serve to minimize duplication of objectives and reduce paperwork. Successful negotiation with the boss should be easiser, since group support would tend to offset the boss's higher rank. Communications would be facilitated and the present weakness of MbO to reward for *individual* goals accomplished, even at the expense of overall harmony or efficiency, would be resolved.

Another way to improve participation under MbO is for the organization to provide training to all subordinates and, especially, to all managers who will be required to operate under the system. The skills and attitudes necessary for MbO to be effective are neither intuitive nor "natural" to individuals brought up in traditionally bureaucratic organizations. Both book learning and simulated experiences will probably be necessary before those who will be living with the system become competent even to try it. This point should be obvious as to be unworthy of mention; yet comparatively few MbO change agents include systematic skills and attitude training as part of their programs.

FEATURES TO DISCARD

1. Linking MbO to the compensation system. The only areas where tying MbO to rewards will not tend to induce risk-avoidance and goal displacement are those where conditions are so predictable that no deceit is possible. In these areas, however, incentive plans and piecework, commission, and bonus systems are already available.

2. Using MbO as an "objective" way to measure performance. While re-

[16]Stephen J. Carroll, Jr. and Henry L. Tosi, "The Relation of Characteristics of the Review Process as Moderated by Personality and Situational Factors to the Success of the 'Management by Objectives' Approach," *Academy of Management Proceedings,* 1969, p. 141.

[17]Tosi and Bigoness, *op cit.,* p. 46.

[18]Levinson, *op cit.,* makes this point, as does Robert A. Howell, "A Fresh Look at Management by Objectives," *Business Horizons,* 1967, p. 55.

questing that managers in their feedback sessions with subordinates totally suppress consideration of whether agreed-upon objectives have been met is probably futile, formal comparison of goals accomplished against goals set should definitely be avoided. Such comparisons *will not* enable performance reviews to be carried out on a more objective basis, but *will* cause the risk-avoidance and goal-displacement behavior described above.

3. Focusing attention upon only those objectives which can easily be quantitifed. Objectives should be written "in every area where performance and results directly and vitally affect the survival and prosperity of the business."[19] This is true *whether or not* quantification is possible! Numerous instances could be cited where performance suffered either because non-quantifiable objectives were ignored altogether or because some simple-minded number (e.g., patents as *the* measure of creativity) was substituted for them.[20] Conversely, performance may be improved by keeping in mind that "although in many areas the qualitative aspects of output may have to be assessed largely in terms of value judgments, the discipline of prescribing standards of performance and of testing results against them can improve the control process."[21]

4. Making Personnel Division responsible for maintenance. Once it is decided that MbO will not be used as an instrument of evaluation and reward, the rationale for active involvement by Personnel largely vanishes. Such involvement will serve mainly to increase both the volume of required paperwork and the level of threat perceived by lower-level participants.

5. Forms, forms, and more forms. The problem of excessive paperwork has been found to be a major impediment to the effective use of MbO.[22] Once the notion of utilizing MbO for evaluation and control is abandoned, surprisingly few forms are really necessary.

6. Pre-packaged programs and costly consultants. Although these may (or may not) be necessary for successful introduction and maintenance of the change-everything-at-once-and-see-what-happens king-sized version of MbO, they are probably unnecessary for the "mini-MbO" that will remain once "features to discard" one to four are followed.

CONCLUSIONS

In sum:

1. Management by Objectives is at present a high-cost long-run package whose success is by no means guaranteed, which generates many side effects impossible to predict or control. Two competent researchers speak of MbO as a "complex organizational change process which may be painful and time-consuming,"[23]

[19]Peter F. Drucker, *The Practice of Management,* (New York: Harper & Row, 1954).

[20]For examples see Kerr, *op cit.*

[21]C. J. Hancock, "MbO Raises Management Effectiveness in Government Service," *Management by Objectives,* 3, Number 4, 1974, p. 12.

[22]See for example Anthony P. Raia, *Managing by Objectives* (Glenview, Ill.: Scott, Foresman, 1974.)

[23]Henry L. Tosi and Stephen J. Carroll, "Some Structural Factors Related to Goal Influence in the Management by Objectives Process," *Business Topics,* Spring, 1969, p. 50.

and another points out that "it will take four to five years to achieve a fully effective Management by Objectives system."[24]

2. Management by Objectives is yet another technique that requires friendly, helpful superiors, honest and mature subordinates, and a climate of mutual trust. Carvalho has cautioned that "successful implementation of MbO requires, even demands, that all managers have a fundamental results-oriented attitude," as well as "an attitude which accepts collaboration, co-operation, and joint sharing of responsibilities as the norm rather than the exception." He goes on to state that such attitudes are hardly commonplace in most organizations today, and that to develop them, a "mini-cultural revolution" will probably be needed.[25] And we have already taken note of Bennis' opinion that the double reference approach necessary for MbO to work "requires a degree of maturity, more precisely a commitment to maturity, on the part of both the superior and subordinate that exceeds that of any other organizational approach."[26] In short, *MbO often works best for those individuals who need it least.*

3. Management by Objectives is best suited to those static environments in which we already have sufficient technology to manage competently. Rapidly changing conditions and high role conflict and ambiguity seriously impair its usefulness. *MbO often works best in those situations where we need it least.*

4. We must stop pretending that MbO adds much to our ability to reward and evaluate. It is unlikely to be effective when employed as a "total" management system. Its strength lies in its emphasis on goal-setting, its provision for feedback and interaction, and its opportunities for participation. These features can and should be maintained, but not at a cost of jolting the organization with massive and simultaneous changes. A good illustration of the point is given by Lasagna, who described the problems which afflicted his organization as a result of attempting to use MbO for too many purposes. He reports that they had much better success when they substituted a mini-MbO which was not tied to evaluation and compensation.[27]

The advantages that would accrue to users of a "mini-system" of MbO are due to the fact that such an approach would introduce fewer new variables, require less time to take effect, cost far less and minimize unpredictable side effects. It would be particularly effective in combating the increase in employee anxiety and defensiveness which so often accompanies MbO introduction. Furthermore, a mini-MbO would be less likely to cause management to forget that the system is in no sense a cure-all, but is rather just another tool in the managerial kit. Finally, a "mini-system" of MbO would for the first time enable scientific study of costs and benefits to be conducted, so that we may at last discover whether or not Management by Objectives is worth its cost.

[24]Robert A. Howell, "Managing by Objectives—A Three Stage System," *Business Horizons,* February 1970, p. 45. See also F. D. Barrett, "The MbO Time Trip," *Business Quarterly,* Autumn 1972.

[25]G. F. Carvalho, "Installing MbO: A New Perspective on Organizational Change," *Human Resources Management,* Spring, 1972, pp. 23–30.

[26]Bennis, *op cit.,* p. 286.

[27]John B. Lasagna, "Make Your MbO Pragmatic," *Harvard Business Review,* November–December 1971, pp. 64–69.

16

Performance Appraisal

PERFORMANCE APPRAISAL REVISITED
Edward E. Lawler III
Allan M. Mohrman, Jr.
Susan M. Resnick

ON THE FOLLY OF REWARDING A WHILE HOPING FOR B
Steven Kerr

PERFORMANCE APPRAISAL REVISITED

Edward E. Lawler III
Allan M. Mohrman, Jr.
Susan M. Resnick

For decades performance appraisal has been a much discussed and studied practice. It is also one that has produced a great deal of frustration and a never-ending search for the "right" system. As part of this search, organizations seem to be regularly changing their systems in the hope that they will find the answer. Our study reports on the results of one company's search and suggests that the system may not be the solution.

One of the most influential series of studies was done by the General Electric (GE) Company during the early 1960s. Publication of these results in a *Harvard Business Review* article in 1965 led a number of corporations to revise their performance appraisal practices, and in important respects changed the way appraisal is conceptualized by researchers and managers (Meyer, Kay and French, 1965). Among the key recommendations in this article were to separate pay discussions from performance appraisal and to use a process called *work planning and review*. In this process, specific objectives are identified in advance of a performance period; then, at the end of the period, results are reviewed against these objectives.

Source: Reprinted by permission of the publisher, from *Organizational Dynamics,* Summer 1984, © 1984. American Management Association, New York. All rights reserved.

The years since the publication of the seminal GE study have seen performance appraisal emerge as an increasingly important issue in organizations. Growing concern about productivity and legal issues surrounding age, sex, and race discrimination have brought the performance appraisal practices of organizations into even sharper focus. In addition, current thinking about effective human resources management more and more places performance appraisal at the center of integrated human resources management systems. For example, it is often noted that performance appraisal needs to be very clearly related to the pay system, the career-development system, and the selection system and, in turn, needs to flow from the way job design is approached in the organization.

Finally, it is important that the appraisal system measure and reward behaviors that support the organization's strategic objectives. Thus, if an organization wishes to have an integrated human resources management system that supports its business plan, performance appraisal of some form or another is a necessity, not an option. Further, it is something that should not be done poorly. Its inputs are so vital to the successful operation of other human resources management systems that, if it is done poorly, the overall human resources management system is destined to be ineffective.

At least two perspectives must be accounted for in assessing any performance appraisal system. There is (1) the effectiveness of the system as judged by the management or the appraisers and there is (2) the effectiveness of the system as judged by the subordinate employees or the appraisers. Ideally, performance appraisal should meet the needs of both. If it is to meet the needs of employees, it must help them know the organization's official view of their work, their chances for advancement and salary increases within the organization, and ways they can improve their performance to better meet their own and the organization's goals. If it is to meet the typical goals of the organization, performance appraisal must help the organization utilize the skills of its employees, and motivate and develop them to perform effectively.

Although increased interests in performance appraisals has led to a great deal of research, much of it has focused only on the mechanics of measurement and the appraisal forms. Research, for example, has compared the advantages of five-point versus seven-point scales versus management by objectives system, and so on. For years we have suspected that research focusing on the form itself and on the mechanics of appraisal is missing many important issues involved in designing and managing performance appraisal systems.

Thus, when the General Electric Company asked us if we would be interested in doing a study on the impact and the organizational role of their performance appraisal practices, we were delighted. It promised the opportunity to look at a corporation that for several decades has seriously studied and worked on performance appraisal, and a chance to go beyond focusing only on the nuts and bolts of the performance appraisal system in the context of an organization and its jobs and to test emerging notions of the multiple functions of performance appraisal.

After briefly describing the study, we will discuss what managers and employees believed the performance appraisal system should be like and should accomplish; then we will discuss actual performance appraisal practices and some determinants of appraisal effectiveness. Finally, we make recommendations for organizations that are considering changing their performance appraisal systems. Our recommendations are not based solely on our GE experience, however. We have since done similar research in a number of other organizational settings. Our findings continue to confirm the patterns first noted at GE.

STUDY DESCRIPTION

Interviews, questionnaires, and personnel records served as the major data sources for the study. We interviewed personnel executives and other top level executives, with numerous manager-subordinate pairs among them. In addition, we collected questionnaire data from 700 manager-subordinate pairs from all levels of management and all functional areas in the "exempt" population. In half the cases, the person being appraised was also responsible for appraising the performance of others. Half of the pairs we studied completed questionnaires both before and after a performance appraisal while other pairs completed questionnaires only after the event. This was done in order to eliminate from our results any effects of filling out a questionnaire before the appraisal. Interestingly, this proved unnecessary as the results were the same for both groups. Therefore, the results reported in Exhibits 1-5, while based on a sample size of 320 manager-subordinate pairs who filled out the "before" and "after" questionnaires, also reflect the responses of the 400 pairs who filled out an "after only" version of the questionnaire.

Often, researchers question whether research findings from a single organization can be generalized. This study minimized such concerns by including many different types of organizations within the General Electric Corporation. We intentionally picked nine very different businesses in the company. This is exemplified by the fact that performance appraisal was done in widely varying ways in these sites. For example, performance appraisal was conducted at regular intervals at eight sites, but only sometimes at one site. We found more than 50 different performance appraisal forms in use across the nine sites, along with variations in such features as how often and when the performance appraisal was done. (One organization even gave its appraisers a booklet containing ten different forms and told them to pick the one they preferred.) Additional variations involved whether and how appraisal was linked with pay, manpower planning, promotion, and the job itself.

When studied 20 years ago, few GE employees could cite any examples of constructive action—or even significant improvement—that stemmed from suggestions received in a performance appraisal interview with their boss. Today, as Exhibit 1 shows, managers and subordinates believe that appraisal practices do indeed make a difference to the organization as a whole by fostering motivation, productive changes in behavior, and increased understanding. Both groups believe that their appraisals provide accurate feedback and are based on general agreement about performance criteria (although subordinates were considerably less sanguine than the managers). But, like their colleagues 20 years ago, only a minority in each group thought these practices would occur if they were not organizational requirements.

EXHIBIT 1 General Beliefs About Performance Appraisal[1]

		Disagree	Neutral	Agree
1. PA *should* be done *only* for the subordinate's personal development.	appraisers	78	7	15
	subordinates	71	9	20
2. Salary and promotion decisions *should* be based on PA results.	appraisers	5	3	92
	subordinates	12	3	85
3. Salary and promotion decisions *are* based on PA results.	appraisers	24	8	68
	subordinates	41	10	49
4. PA practices provide accurate feedback to the subordinate and superiors and subordinates agree on what constitutes good or poor performance.	appraisers	22	6	72
	subordinates	36	8	55
5. PA makes a difference. It motivates employees, leads to more productive behavior, and increases understanding about the subordinate's role.	appraisers	17	9	74
	subordinates	25	13	62
6. Superiors and subbordinates carry out PA activities only because the organization requires it.	appraisers	35	8	57
	subordinates	28	9	63
7. Subordinates' PA *should* be based on goals previously agreed to by the superior and subordinate.	appraisers	4	3	93
	subordinates	8	5	87
8. A subordinate's self-appraisal *should* be an important part of PA.	appraisers	6	4	90
	subordinates	8	6	86

[1]Percents of those answering the questions are reported.

In addition to documenting attitudes, the earlier General Electric study made recommendations about the appropriate practice of performance appraisal. One recommendation was that appraisal should be based on mutually agreed-upon goals. Interestingly, when asked about specific practices that should be part of the appraisal process, the GE employees now mention that performance appraisal should be based on goals previously agreed to by the appraiser and the subordinate. And, in the spirit of the earlier recommendations, today's appraisers and subordinates believe that an employee's self-appraisal should be an important part of performance appraisal. In contrast to the recommendations of the earlier study, there is strong support for the proposition that performance evaluation should be integrated with other human resources systems. The GE respondents believed evaluations should be done for more than developmental purposes and should be an important determinant of salary and promotions.

Appraisers and subordinates had differing beliefs in three areas concerning the purposes of performance appraisal (see Exhibit 2). Appraisers, more than subordinates, believed that one purpose of performance appraisal should be to allow subordinates to have input on the definition of work; subordinates, more than appraisers, believed that a purpose was to explain and communicate pay decisions and to mutually plan future work goals. These discrepancies in beliefs suggest the differing needs appraisers and subordinates bring to performance appraisal. For example, because employees look to the performance appraisal session to let them know how they stand vis-à-vis the other human resources systems,

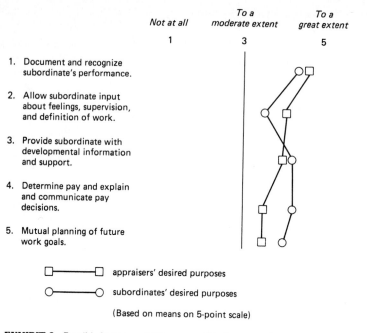

	Not at all	To a moderate extent	To a great extent
	1	3	5

1. Document and recognize subordinate's performance.

2. Allow subordinate input about feelings, supervision, and definition of work.

3. Provide subordinate with developmental information and support.

4. Determine pay and explain and communicate pay decisions.

5. Mutual planning of future work goals.

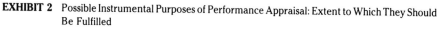

□——————□ appraisers' desired purposes

○——————○ subordinates' desired purposes

(Based on means on 5-point scale)

EXHIBIT 2 Possible Instrumental Purposes of Performance Appraisal: Extent to Which They Should Be Fulfilled

and what the future holds for them, the discussion of pay is more salient to them than to management.

Overall, the data from General Electric show a fairly consistent and well-developed set of beliefs about performance appraisal. Despite the fact that a variety of practices and procedures are used within the company, the overall view is clear that performance appraisal should be done, that it has an organizational impact, that it needs to be organizationally required, that it should be based on goals, and that it should determine such things as pay and promotion. The data also highlight the fact that appraisers and subordinates bring different needs and hopes to the appraisal event.

THE PRACTICE OF PERFORMANCE APPRAISAL

Having looked at what appraisers and subordinates believe should happen in performance appraisal, we now turn to a discussion of what they actually experience.

In general, performance appraisal interviews were called on short notice and took less than a hour. These results seem to indicate a rather casual approach to performance appraisal and thus are of some significance in and of themselves. They become more interesting, however, when we compare the participants' views about what occurred in the appraisal and their reactions to the event.

Overall, the subordinates' attitude toward the appraisal event was much more negative than that of the appraisers. Although appraisers tended to know about the appraisal in advance, subordinates were more often surprised. Appraisers also tended to see the appraisal meeting as lasting much longer than did the subordinates. In general appraisers were satisfied with the duration of time while subordinates would have liked more. Subordinates also saw more distractions and interruptions and generally felt the appraisal did not get the time that it warranted.

On the positive side, both parties at least agreed that the appraisal took place. In other companies we have studied, there is sometimes no agreement on whether the appraisal has taken place! The superior typically reports that it has, while the subordinate says it hasn't. One director of human resources, frustrated by employees' complaints that they hadn't received performance appraisals and by their managers' insistence on having given the appraisals, suggested that managers keep a banner in their upper left-hand drawer—a banner that reads, "This is your performance appraisal." The banner can be unfurled and placed over their desk at the appropriate time. In addition to this solution, there are other, less theatrical and more effective ones for improving the practice of performance appraisal in the eyes of the subordinate.

Appraisers were quite clear that things really important to them were discussed in the appraisal event. For example, 82 percent said that such matters were discussed to a great extent. The situation was quite different with respect to subordinates: Only 46 percent of them felt that things important to them were discussed to a great extent.

With respect to decision making, subordinates (much more than appraisers) saw the most important decisions as being made primarily by the appraisers. Similarly, with respect to communication, the subordinates saw communication as coming mostly from their appraiser; appraisers saw the communication patterns as more balanced.

As mentioned earlier, both appraisers and their subordinates were in agreement that performance appraisals should be based on previously agreed-to goals and subordinates' self-appraisals. In practice, however, these expectations were not always fulfilled. Self-appraisals, for example, were used to only a moderate extent or less in about half the appraisals. While slightly over half the appraisers believed that the appraisal was based on predetermined goals to more than a moderate extent, only one-third of the subordinates corroborated these observations.

Earlier we noted that, in order to meet the needs of the subordinate *and* the organization, the appraisal had to deal with a number of issues. Exhibit 3 shows the reported content of the discussion during the performance appraisal session. In general, appraisers report giving more attention to each topic than do subordinates. Nevertheless, they do tend to agree on which areas get the most attention and which get the least. Both agree that strengths in past performance got the most attention while salary received the least.

This is quite consistent with respondents' beliefs that the primary purpose of performance appraisal is to document a subordinate's performance. It is also consistent with the recommendations of the earlier GE study to separate discussion of salary from the performance appraisal session. However, it is in conflict with what needs to happen if the appraisal is to meet the needs of the sub-

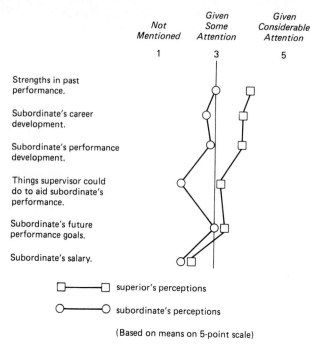

	Not Mentioned	Given Some Attention	Given Considerable Attention
	1	3	5

Strengths in past performance.

Subordinate's career development.

Subordinate's performance development.

Things supervisor could do to aid subordinate's performance.

Subordinate's future performance goals.

Subordinate's salary.

☐——☐ superior's perceptions

○——○ subordinate's perceptions

(Based on means on 5-point scale)

EXHIBIT 3 Discussion During Appraisal: How Much Was Each of These Areas Discussed?

ordinate and to provide the kind of data that link it to other human resources management systems.

In summary, although there are significant disagreements between managers and employees about what goes on during performance appraisal, some general conclusions can be reached. Performance appraisals seem to be events that focus on performance and content important to appraisers, take place in a relatively short period of time, and are not, according to subordinates, necessarily scheduled in advance. In addition, they usually do not include an employee's self-appraisal or a discussion of salary—and, depending on whom you ask, they may or may not be based on mutually agreed-to goals.

EFFECTIVENESS OF THE APPRAISAL PROCESS

Both appraisers and subordinates were asked to judge the extent to which the five possible purposes shown in Exhibit 2 were accomplished by their appraisal. Exhibit 4 shows the responses for appraisers and Exhibit 5 shows them for the appraisers' subordinates. As can be seen, appraisers were generally more satisfied that the appraisal met their purposes than the subordinates were that it met theirs. The overall pattern suggests that existing performance appraisal practices were most effective in documenting performance and recognizing it. But the appraisal

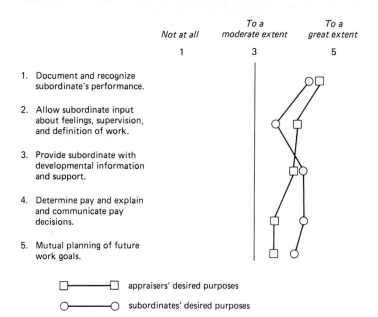

	To a	To a
	moderate extent	great extent
Not at all		

1. Document and recognize
   subordinate's performance.

2. Allow subordinate input
   about feelings, supervision,
   and definition of work.

3. Provide subordinate with
   developmental information
   and support.

4. Determine pay and explain
   and communicate pay
   decisions.

5. Mutual planning of future
   work goals.

□————□ appraisers' desired purposes

○————○ subordinates' desired purposes

(Based on means on 5-point scale)

EXHIBIT 4 Appraisers' Desired Instrumental Purposes Vs. Perceived Occurrences

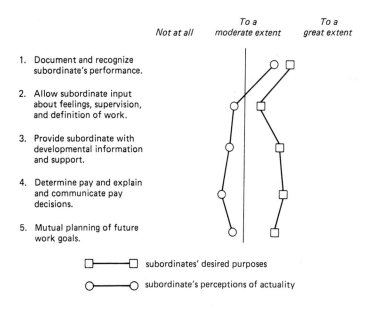

1. Document and recognize
   subordinate's performance.

2. Allow subordinate input
   about feelings, supervision,
   and definition of work.

3. Provide subordinate with
   developmental information
   and support.

4. Determine pay and explain
   and communicate pay
   decisions.

5. Mutual planning of future
   work goals.

□————□ subordinates' desired purposes

○————○ subordinate's perceptions of actuality

EXHIBIT 5 Subordinates' Desired Instrumental Purposes Vs. Perceived Occurrences

clearly failed to deal with pay, planning, and developmental issues as fully as the subordinates would have liked. In other words, the performance appraisal system is falling short in meeting the employees' needs.

In interviews with manager-subordinate pairs, a discrepancy commonly arises. Managers feel that they have spent time discussing the larger picture of the subordinate's career and life within the organization. Yet when subordinates are asked about the amount of time spent discussing their development and career, they frequently say they would have liked more, or that it was not discussed at all, or that it was discussed only in passing.

At first, these opposite reactions surprised us. In fact, there was an initial question on whether the interview schedule was correct—whether the two people involved really were an appraiser-subordinate pair. Then we considered the amount of time spent on the subordinate's development at work in general. In the hustle-bustle of the work day, a subordinate's development is often forgotten. So subordinates often look forward to the performance appraisal session as a time to focus on *their* work and *their* development. Their managers, however, have a different perspective: one of managing a unit, having their own performance judged (one H.R. director commented, "After all, we are all subordinates, aren't we?"), and being unsure of what their own career path or future in the organization looks like; thus they have generally offered all that they know (which may not be much) or that they are comfortable sharing. It is not surprising, then, that we interviewed subordinates who hungered for information about their career development in the organization, or out of the organization, and felt shortchanged by their appraisal in this regard. Nor is it surprising that this hunger tends to come particularly from younger employees, generally in their twenties; from women returning to work; or from employees of all ages in companies undergoing reorganization.

These unmet needs are reflected in the subordinates' satisfaction—or dissatisfaction—with the appraisal system. Only about half of them report being satisfied with the appraisal or feeling good about the way it was conducted. In comparison, over 80 percent of the appraisers report being satisfied or feeling good about the event.

Other data collected to test the effectiveness of the appraisal process also showed great differences between appraisers and subordinates. Not only do a substantial majority of appraisers report learning from the event themselves, they also feel that the appraisal gave subordinates a clearer understanding of their duties and responsibilities, a clearer idea of what is expected of them, and other useful information.

The subordinates were much less likely to see these positive results from the appraisal event. For example: Although 53 percent of the managers reported that the employees' behavior improved after the appraisal, only 41 percent of the employees felt that this was the case.

With respect to the subordinate's overall performance rating, a familiar pattern appeared. That is, subordinates tended to rate their own performance much higher than did the appraisers. Our study of this issue, however, did not stop with simply asking appraisers and subordinates to rate the subordinates' performance. We also asked them both before and after the appraisal to estimate what they thought each other's appraisal of the subordinate's performance was. Interestingly, we found that both before and after the appraisal the subordinate had a clear, generally accurate perception of the appraiser's point of view. The superior was not as accurate about the subordinate's view, but was aware that an important discrepancy existed. Thus, although they disagreed on the absolute level of the subordinate's performance, they were both aware that some disagreement existed, and the subordinates knew rather accurately the nature and extent of the disagreement. This is a particularly important point because it suggests that although appraisers are frequently going to be in the position of delivering a negative message, the message typically does not come as a surprise to the subordinate.

In summary, the appraisal process gets very different marks depending on whether the perspective is that of appraisers or that of subordinates. Appraisers, who of course are largely in control of the event, feel that it generally meets their needs. On the other hand, subordinates recognize the importance of the process, but feel that it falls short of meeting their needs.

DETERMINANTS OF PERFORMANCE APPRAISAL EFFECTIVENESS

Given these differing views of performance appraisal and the need for it to serve the purposes of both parties, we decided to determine both (1) the characteristics that leave both appraisers and subordinates with a perception of positive outcomes form the appraisal process and (2) those that merely lead subordinates to feel their needs are met (since our research suggests that if either party's needs are likely to go unmet it is the subordinates'). In looking for these characteristics we focused on the organizational context and the processes and procedures of the performance appraisal system.

Climate

The general climate of the organization seemed to have a significant impact on how well the performance appraisal process went. When the climate was one of high trust, support, and openness, appraisers and subordinates alike saw performance appraisal as going better. In these instances both reported greater emphasis on the subordinate's development, greater participation and contribution by the subordinate, and a higher degree of trust, openness, and constructiveness during the appraisal interview. In other words, in an environment of high trust the performance appraisal system is more likely to meet the individual subordinate's developmental needs.

Another organization studied illustrates how the climate or culture of the organization created its own definition for mutual goal setting. The organization was highly autocratic and hierarchical; subordinates had rarely been asked their opinion about anything, particularly their own performance. (In fact, these subordinates were so unused to stating their opinions that when an attitude survey was administered which asked what they thought should be accomplished by performance appraisal systems, there was an inordinate amount of missing data.) In interviews of several manager-and-subordinate pairs about a new appraisal system based on mutual goal setting, the managers typically reported that mutual goal setting took place, while the subordinates typically reported being "goaled." This organization's culture leads its people to conclude that mutual goal setting occurs when the subordinate is present while the manager presents the goals.

Job Content

The content of the subordinate's job was another important factor in determining how the appraisal went. In general, jobs that met the characteristics of being enriched tended to have better performance appraisals. Enriched tasks exhibit these characteristics: people performing them have a whole piece of work to do and are responsible for the methods and procedures used in carrying out this whole piece of work and (2) the jobs themselves allow feedback—that is, subordinates know from the work itself whether or not they accomplished their tasks and the precise results of their labors. Specifically, subordinates who thought of their jobs as being enriched were more satisfied and enthusiastic about the appraisal; felt they had participated and contributed; and felt the atmosphere to have been trusting, friendly, and open. On the other hand, there was no evidence that appraisers saw the outcome of the appraisal process more favorably when the content of the subordinate's job was enriched.

Subordinates also rated the degree to which their jobs were clear, well specified, and well defined. When subordinates saw well-defined job procedures, goals, priorities, and responsibilities, they felt not only that the appraisal achieved the same qualities perceived by those with enriched jobs, but also that it led to a higher degree of learning, more focus on development, more discussion of ways to improve weaknesses, more discussion of future goals, and more discussion of how managers could aid employees. In short, well-specified jobs led to constructive appraisal events. As was the case with enriched jobs, appraisers did not tend to report more favorable outcomes when jobs were well specified.

In sum, subordinates who view their jobs as enriched or well-specified are more likely to perceive the performance appraisal as meeting their needs. Job content, however, seemed to have little impact on the appraiser's reaction.

Pay Discussion

Having discussed contextual issues and their relationship to performance appraisal, we now turn our attention to a discussion of procedural issues and their impact. As mentioned, an important recommendation of the initial General Electric study was the separation of pay and performance appraisal discussions. Earlier we mentioned the employees' desire for pay discussions and the fact that salary was infrequently discussed during the appraisal session. A natural question then becomes, "Does the discussion of pay during the performance appraisal make a difference to the effectiveness of the appraisal?"

As the earlier General Electric study suggested, we found that the discussion of pay does make a difference. However, implications of the data are different from what the earlier study suggested. Discussion of salary change seemed to make the event go slightly but significantly better for both parties, particularly in the employee's eyes. A number of reasons for this suggest themselves—including the fact that discussing pay makes the event a more serious one and thus causes better preparation. In addition, the information content needed to justify a salary action gives the employee something to which he or she can respond. Finally, as already stressed, subordinates feel that a pay discussion *should* be part of the appraisal event. Therefore, the discussion of pay helps subordinates fulfill their needs.

Appraisal Forms

The design of appraisal systems almost always begins (and often ends) with the design of the appraisal form to be used. As indicated, we found more than 50 different forms being used in the nine GE organizations. We even found managers who secretly used forms they had developed or brought with them from other companies. Many forms were hybrids, combinations, and recombinations of one another and of almost all prominent approaches to appraisal forms in general use. Overall, we found that form content had little if any effect on the actual appraisal event.

Work Planning

Another major recommendation of the initial General Electric study was the use of a work planning and review process. Performance appraisal research has long held that the use of such a *process* will lead to performance improvement. Nevertheless, many system administrators have painstakingly designed a form and assumed a process would ensue. Fortunately, this study gave us the opportunity to investigate not only the impact of work planning, but also the impact a form can have on the way the appraisal is done.

When we compared appraisals using forms with work-planning components and those not mentioning work planning, we found no difference in the extent to which work planning and associated practices such as goal setting took place. Form content had no effect on perceptions of whether work planning actually took place. We have found many superiors in GE and elsewhere who are expert at getting the form filled out and signed without having *the process* take place. Nevertheless, when the process of work planning was done it did lead to performance improvement and to a generally more successful appraisal in the eyes of both the parties.

Subordinate Input

Although the form had no effect, two procedures did affect perceptions of work planning. If the subordinate compiled information before the review, or if the appraisal form was completed during or after the appraisal session, both manager and employee perceived that work planning took place. In addition to affecting perceptions of work planning, these procedures led to a greater feeling of ownership by subordinates for the performance appraisal event. These findings, combined with several others, tend to confirm the validity of the point made in numerous articles on performance appraisals—namely, that the more active the subordinate is and the more influence the subordinate has on the appraisal process, the more likely it is that the appraisal process will meet all its objectives.

RECOMMENDATIONS

Our results suggest some general advice that can be given to any organization. First, they suggest that performance appraisal should be a key link in the overall human resources management strategy. Both managers and subordinates think that it should have an important overall role and that it should accomplish a number of objectives vital to organizational effectiveness. These include defining work roles, motivating performance, and aiding the subordinate's development. In order to accomplish all these, a performance appraisal cannot be a casual activity. It must be an important part of the culture and activities in the organization. The tone set by appraisal has important ramifications throughout all other processes of human resource management. General Electric, as a result of the research, decided to continue to put a strong emphasis on performance appraisal as a management tool rather than to diminish their focus on it.

Our data strongly suggest that the answer to doing a performance appraisal well lies in focusing on the process of the appraisal and on the organizational context in which the event takes place, not on the form or system. This recommendation is in direct contrast to the emphasis usually placed on the form.

Issues like culture, job design, the relationship between pay and performance, the timing of career-development discussions, and the degree to which the process encourages subordinates to become equal partners all seem to be more important than the form used. Let us briefly comment on what may need to be done in each of these areas.

1. In the area of culture, appraisal seems to be influenced by a number of larger trends and factors that cannot be treated here, but some specifics are worth mentioning. At the very least, top management needs to take performance appraisal seriously, to explicitly fit it to the prevailing culture and human resource strategy, to evaluate how well it does fit, to encourage practices that do fit, and to reward superiors and subordinates who do it well. All this has a decided impact on whether supervisors take it seriously and spend the time and effort needed to do it well. It is also important that superiors at higher managerial levels model the type of appraisal behavior they wish superiors lower down in the organization to demonstrate. In short, appraisal needs to be real and effective at higher organizational levels.

2. It seems clear that poor job designs can make performance appraisals ineffective. This suggests that a strong emphasis be placed on early definition of the nature of the job for which a subordinate is to be held accountable and on how performance on that job is going to be measured. Here, work on job enrichment seems appropriate and, as such, should be an integral part of the job definition process. In the absence of well-defined and well-designed jobs, the appraisal process is doomed from the beginning. To the extent that jobs cannot be predefined—and there are good reasons to legitimately expect this in some

settings—the appraisal system needs to recognize that the appraisal itself will in part need to function as a process of job definition. If both parties are to agree on the definition and design of the job, then the appraisal processs will benefit from mutual participation.

3. Our data suggest that pay actions and consequences should be a natural part of the appraisal discusison. Efforts to separate them seem to be more counter-productive than productive, no matter how well intentioned—especially in organizational contexts that stress pay for performance. Thus our recommendation is that they be made an important part of the appraisal process.

4. Our data suggst that the area that gets the least attention—yet is very important to subordinates—is career development. Some parts of General Electric successfully handled this as a different process. Our suggestion is that other organizations should do this as well. That is, at a different time and as part of a different system, organizations should put into place a joint process in which superiors and subordinates work through the kind of career opportunities that exist, the kind of developmental needs the subordinates have, and the kind of career track that a subordinate can reasonably aspire to. This is, appropriately, part of another future-oriented system that is integrated into the overall human resources management system. Nevertheless, as in the case of pay, past performance is an important element in career discussions and vice versa. Superiors should therefore talk about such connections during the appraisal event. This should be particularly emphasized when a merit promotion policy is in effect.

5. Specific steps should be built into the procedure to assure that the subordinate is an active partner in defining the performance appraisal process. We found appraisals more effective, for example, when the subordinate shared a self-appraisal of his or her performance with the supervisor before a final appraisal judgment was reached. For this to happen, it is important that the subordinate participate in defining the job and pinpointing the measures that will be used in the performance appraisal. In short, if the appraisal process is to be of mutual benefit, it must be a mutual process; therefore, anything that encourages this two-way exchange of information is desirable. This is, of course, one way to get the manager out of the role of judge so that he or she can help the subordinate take responsibility for the outcome of the overall process. If subordinates are to become an active part of the appraisal process, *they* (and not just the appraisers) need training and orientation for this role.

CONCLUSIONS

Overall, the study results point out just how complex the performance appraisal process is and emphasize the importance of doing it well. It is not an optional activity for organizations that want to have an effective human resources management system. It is significant that a corporation like General Electric, which has spent decades improving its performance appraisal process, is still questioning how well it is doing performance appraisals. Somewhat discouragingly, the data show a considerable gap between what their system might accomplish and what it actually accomplishes. GE's willingness to take an objective look at such an important part of their human resources management system is greatly to GE's credit. It is also to their credit that they acted upon the study results and made important changes in their corporate policy. In many respects, General Electric can serve as a model for other corporations.

Finally, with respect to the specifics of performance appraisal, several important messages emerge. Quick fixes that make alterations in forms are no more likely to be successful here than are quick fixes in other areas. Performance appraisal in an organization is only as good as its overall human resources climate, strategy, and policies, and especially its processes of fitting it to these. It is unrealistic to expect to have an effective performance appraisal system where jobs are poorly designed, the culture is negative, and subordinates are asked to be passive and do what they are told.

Performance appraisal is both a personal event between two people who have an ongoing relationship and a bureaucratic event that is needed to maintain an organization's human resource management system. Therefore, it is a major mechanism for integrating the individual and the organization. As such, it will always be subject to contradictory purposes, misperceptions, miscommunications, and some ineffectiveness. On the other hand, our data suggest that there are some ways to make it go better and that it is worth investing time and effort to do it well. At best, it's two people sharing their perceptions of each other, their relationships, their work, and their organization—sharing that results in better performance, better feelings, and a more effective organization. At its worst, it is one person in the name of the organization trying to force his or her will on another with the result of miscommunication, misperception, disappointment, and alienation. The best is achievable, but only with considerable effort, careful design, constant attention to process, and support by top management.

SELECTED BIBLIOGRAPHY

The following is offered as suggested reading for those interested in pursuing the topic of performance appraisal:

D. L. DeVries, A. M. Morrison, S. L. Shullman, and M. L. Gerlach's *Performance Appraisal on the Line* (Wiley-Interscience, 1981).

G. P. Latham and K. N. Wexley's *Increasing Productivity Through Performance Appraisal* (Addison-Wesley, 1981).

E. E. Lawler's *Pay and Organization Development* (Addison-Wesley, 1981).

H. H. Meyer, E. Kay, and J. R. P. French's "Split Roles in Performance Appraisal" (*Harvard Business Review,* January–February 1965).

A. M. Mohrman and E. E. Lawler's "Motivation and Performance Appraisal Behavior," a chapter in *Performance Measurement and Theory,* F. Landy and S. Zedeck (eds.) (Erlbaum, 1983).

ON THE FOLLY OF REWARDING A, WHILE HOPING FOR B

Steven Kerr

Whether dealing with monkeys, rats, or human beings, it is hardly controversial to state that most organisms seek information concerning what activities are rewarded, and then seek to do (or at least pretend to do) those things, often to the virtual exclusion of activities not rewarded. The extent to which this occurs of course will depend on the perceived attractiveness of the rewards offered, but neither operant nor expectancy theorists would quarrel with the essence of this notion.

Nevertheless, numerous examples exist of reward systems that are fouled up in that behaviors which are rewarded are those which the rewarder is trying to *discourage,* while the behavior he desires is not being rewarded at all.

In an effort to understand and explain this phenomenon, this paper presents examples from society, from organizations in general, and from profit-making firms in particular. Data from a manufacturing company and information from an insurance firm are examined to demonstrate the consequences of such reward systems for the organizations involved, and possible reasons why such reward systems continue to exist are considered.

SOCIETAL EXAMPLES

Politics

Official goals are "purposely vague and general and do not indicate...the host of decisions that must be made among alternative ways of achieving official goals and the priority of multiple goals..." (8, p. 66). They usually may be relied on to offend absolutely no one, and in this sense can be considered high-acceptance, low-quality goals. An example might be "build better schools." Operative goals are higher in quality but lower in acceptance, since they specify where the money will come from, what alternative goals will be ignored, etc.

The American citizenry supposedly wants its candidates for public office to set forth operative goals, making their proposed programs "perfectly clear," specifying sources and uses of funds, etc. However, since operative goals are lower in acceptance, and since aspirants to public office need acceptance (from at least 50.1 percent of the people), most politicians prefer to speak only of officials goals, at least until after the election. They of course would agree to speak at the operative level if "punished" for not doing so. The electorate could do this by refusing to support candidates who do not speak at the operative level.

Instead, however, the American voter typically punishes (withholds support from) candidates who frankly discuss where the money will come from, rewards politicians who speaks only of official goals, but hopes that candidates (despite

Source: Reprinted from *Academy of Management Journal,* 1975, vol. 18, pp. 769–83.

the reward system) will discuss the issues operatively. It is academic whether it was moral for Nixon, for example, to refuse to discuss his 1968 "secret plan" to end the Vietnam war, his 1972 operative goals concerning the lifting of price controls, the reshuffling of his cabinet, etc. The point is that the reward system made such refusal rational.

It seems worth mentioning that no manuscript can adequately define what is "moral" and what is not. However, examination of costs and benefits, combined with knowledge of what motivates a particular individual, often will suffice to determine what for him is "rational."[1] If the reward system is so designed that it is irrational to be moral, this does not necessarily mean that immorality will result. But is this not asking for trouble?

War

If some oversimplification may be permitted, let it be assumed that the primary goal of the organization (Pentagon, Luftwaffe, or whatever) is to win. Let it be assumed further that the primary goal of most individuals on the front lines is to get home alive. Then there appears to be an important conflict in goals—personally rational behavior by those at the bottom will endanger goal attainment by those at the top.

But not necessarily! It depends on how the reward system is set up. The Vietnam war was indeed a study of disobedience and rebellion, with terms such as "fragging" (killing one's own commanding officer) and "search and evade" becoming part of the military vocabulary. The difference in subordinates' acceptance of authority between World War II and Vietnam is reported to be considerable, and veterans of the Second World War often have been quoted as being outraged at the mutinous actions of many American soldiers in Vietnam.

Consider, however, some critical differences in the reward system in use during the two conflicts. What did the GI in World War II want? To go home. And when did he get to go home? When the war was won! If he disobeyed the orders to clean out the trenches and take the hills, the war would not be won and he would not go home. Furthermore, what were his chances of attaining his goal (getting home alive) if he obeyed the orders compared to his chances if he did not? What is being suggested is that the rational soldier in World War II, *whether patriotic or not,* probably found it expedient to obey.

Consider the reward system in use in Vietnam. What did the man at the bottom want? To go home. And when did he get to go home? When his tour of duty was over! This was the case *whether or not* the war was won. Furthermore, concerning the relative chance of getting home alive by obeying orders compared to the chance if they were disobeyed, it is worth noting that a mutineer in Vietnam was far more likely to be assigned rest and rehabilitation (on the assumption that fatigue was the cause) than he was to suffer any negative consequence.

In his description of the "zone of indifference," Barnard stated that "a person

---

[1] In Simon's (10, pp. 76–77) terms, a decision is "subjectively rational" if it maximizes an individual's valued outcomes so far as his knowledge permits. A decision is "personally rational" if it is oriented toward the individual's goals.

can and will accept a communication as authoritative only when...at the time of his decision, he believes it to be compatible with his personal interests as a whole" (1, p. 165). In light of the reward system used in Vietnam, would it not have been personally irrational for some orders to have been obeyed? Was not the military implementing a system which *rewarded* disobedience, while *hoping* that soldiers (despite the reward system) would obey orders?

Medicine

Theoretically, a physician can make either of two types of error, and intuitively one seems as bad as the other. A doctor can pronounce a patient sick when he is actually well, thus causing him needless anxiety and expense, curtailment of enjoyable foods and activities, and even physical danger by subjecting him to needless medication and surgery. Alternately, a doctor can label a sick person well, and thus avoid treating what may be a serious, even fatal ailment. It might be natural to conclude that physicians seek to minimize both types of error.

Such a conclusion would be wrong.[2] It is estimated that numerous Americans are presently afflicted with iatrogenic (physician *caused*) illnesses (9). This occurs when the doctor is approached by someone complaining of a few stray symptoms. The doctor classifies and organizes these symptoms, gives then a name, and obligingly tells the patient what further symptoms may be expected. This information often acts as a self-fulfilling prophecy, with the result that from that day on the patient for all practical purposes is sick.

Why does this happen? Why are physicians so reluctant to sustain a type 2 error (pronouncing a sick person well) that they will tolerate many type 1 errors? Again, a look at the reward system is needed. The punishments for a type 2 error are real: guilt, embarrassment, and the threat of lawsuit and scandal. On the other hand, a type 1 error (labeling a well person sick) "is sometimes seen as sound clinical practice, indicating a healthy conservative approach to medicine" (9, p. 69). Type 1 errors also are likely to generate increased income and a stream of steady customers who, being well in a limited physiological sense, will not embarrass the doctor by dying abruptly.

Fellow physicians and the general public therefore are really *rewarding* type 1 errors and at the same time *hoping* fervently that doctors will try not to make them.

GENERAL ORGANIZATIONAL EXAMPLES

Rehabilitation Centers and Orphanages

In terms of the prime beneficiary classification (2, p. 42) organizations such as these are supposed to exist for the "public-in-contact," that is, clients. The orphanage therefore theoretically is interested in placing as many children as possible in good homes. However, often orphanages surround themselves with so many rules concerning the adoption that it is nearly impossible to pry a child out of the

[2]In one study (4) of 14,867 films for signs of tuberculosis, 1,216 positive readings turned out to be clinically negative; only 24 negative readings proved clinically active, a ratio of 50 to 1.

place. Orphanages may deny adoption unless the applicants are a married couple, both of the same religion as the child, without history of emotional or vocational instability, with a specified minimum income and a private room for the child, etc.

If the primary goal is to place children in good homes, then the rules ought to constitute means toward that goal. Goal displacement results when these "means become ends-in-themselves that displaces the original goals" (2, p. 229).

To some extent these rules are required by law. But the influence of the reward system on the orphanage's management should not be ignored. Consider, for example, that the:

1. Number of children enrolled often is the most important determinant of the size of the allocated budget.
2. Number of children under the director's care also will affect the size of his staff.
3. Total organizational size will determine largely the director's prestige at the annual conventions, in the community, etc.

Therefore, to the extent that staff size, total budget, and personal prestige are valued by the orphanage's executive personnel, it becomes rational for them to make it difficult for children to be adopted. After all, who wants to be the director of the smallest orphanage in the state?

If the reward system errs in the opposite direction, paying off only for placements, extensive goal displacement again is likely to result. A common example of vocational rehabilitation in many states, for example, consists of placing someone in a job for which he has little interest and few qualifications, for two months or so, and then "rehabilitating" him again in another position. Such behavior is quite consistent with the prevailing reward system, which pays off for the number of individuals placed in any position for 60 days or more. Rehabilitation counselors also confess to competing with one another to place relatively skilled clients, sometimes ignoring persons with few skills who would be harder to place. Extensively disabled clients find that counselors often prefer to work with those whose disabilities are less severe.[3]

Universities

Society *hopes* that teachers will not neglect their teaching responsibilities but *rewards* them almost entirely for research and publications. This is most true at the large and prestigious universities. Clichés such as "good research and good teaching go together" notwithstanding, professors often find that they must choose between teaching and research-oriented activities when allocating their time. Rewards for good teaching usually are limited to outstanding teacher awards, which are given to only a small percentage of good teachers and which usually bestow little money and fleeting prestige. Punishments for poor teaching also are rare.

Rewards for research and publications, on the other hand, and punishments for failure to accomplish these, are commonly administered by universities at which teachers are employed. Furthermore, publication-oriented resumés usually will be

[3]Personal interviews conducted during 1972–73.

well received at other universities, whereas teaching credentials, harder to document and quantify, are much less transferable. Consequently it is rational for university teachers to concentrate on research, even if to the detriment of teaching and at the expense of their students.

By the same token, it is rational for students to act based upon the goal displacement which has occurred within universities concerning what they are rewarded for. If it is assumed that a primary goal of a university is to transfer knowledge from teacher to student, then grades become identifiable as a means toward that goal, serving as motivational, control, and feedback devices to expedite the knowledge transfer. Instead, however, the grades themselves have become much more important for entrance to graduate school, successful employment, tuition refunds, parental respect, etc., than the knowledge or lack of knowledge they are supposed to signify.

It therefore should come as no surprise that information has surfaced in recent years concerning fraternity files for examinations, term-paper writing services, organized cheating at the service academics, and the like. Such activities constitute a personally rational response to a reward system which pays off for grades rather than knowledge.

BUSINESS-RELATED EXAMPLES

Ecology

Assume that the president of XYZ Corporation is confronted with the following alternatives:

1. Spend $11 million for antipollution equipment to keep from poisoning fish in the river adjacent to the plant; or
2. Do nothing, in violation of the law, and assume a one in ten chance of being caught, with a resultant $1 million fine plus the necessity of buying the equipment.

Under this not unrealistic set of choices it requires no linear program to determine that XYZ Corporation can maximize its probabilities by flouting the law. Add the fact that XYZ's president is probably being rewarded (by creditors, stockholders, and other salient parts of his task environment) according to criteria totally unrelated to the number of fish poisoned, and his probable course of action becomes clear.

Evaluation of Training

It is axiomatic that those who care about a firm's well-being should insist that the organization get fair value for its expenditures. Yet it is commonly known that firms seldom bother to evaluate a new GRID, MBO, job enrichment program, or whatever, to see if the company is getting its money's worth. Why? Certainly it is not because people have not pointed out that this situation exists; numerous practitioner-oriented articles are written each year to just this point.

The individuals (whether in personnel, manpower planning, or wherever) who normally would be responsible for conducting such evaluations are the same ones often charged with introducing the change effort in the first place. Having convinced top management to spend the money, they usually are quite animated afterwards in collecting arigorous vignettes and anecdotes about how successful the program was. The last thing many desire is a formal systematic and revealing evaluation. Although members of top management may actually *hope* for such systematic evaluation, their reward systems continue to *reward* ignorance in this area. And if the personnel department abdicates its responsibility, who is to step into the breach? The change agent himself? Hardly! He is likely to be too busy collecting anecdotal "evidence" of his own, for use with his next client.

Miscellaneous

Many additional examples could be cited of systems which in fact are rewarding behaviors other than those supposedly desired by the rewarder. A few of these are described briefly below.

Most coaches disdain to discuss individual accomplishments, preferring to speak of teamwork, proper attitude, and a one-for-all spirit. Usually, however, rewards are distributed according to individual performance. The college basketball player who feeds his teammates instead of shooting will not compile impressive scoring statistics and is less likely to be drafted by the pros. The ballplayer who hits to right field to advance the runners will win neither the batting nor home run titles, and will be offered smaller raises. It therefore is rational for players to think of themselves first, and the team second.

In business organizations where rewards are dispensed for unit performance or for individual goals achieved, without regard for overall effectiveness, similar attitudes often are observed. Under most Management by Objectives (MBO) systems, goals in areas where quantification is difficult often go unspecified. The organization therefore often is in a position where it *hopes* for employee effort in the areas of team building, interpersonal relations, creativity, etc., but it formally *rewards* none of these. In cases where promotions and raises are formally tied to MBO, the system itself contains a paradox in that it "asks employees to set challenging, risky goals, only to face smaller paychecks and possibly damaged careers if these goals are not accomplished" (5, p. 40).

It is *hoped* that administrators will pay attention to long-run costs and opportunities and will institute programs which will bear fruit later on. However, many organizational reward systems pay off for short-run sales and earnings only. Under such circumstances it is personally rational for officials to sacrifice long-term growth and profit (by selling off equipment and property, or by stifling research and development) for short-term advantages. This probably is most pertinent in the public sector, with the result that many public officials are unwilling to implement programs which will not show benefits by election time.

As a final, clear-cut example of a fouled-up reward system, consider the cost-plus contract or its next of kin, the allocation of next year's budget as a direct function of this year's expenditures. It probably is conceivable that those who award such budgets and contracts really hope for economy and prudence in spending.

It is obvious, however, that adopting the proverb "to him who spends shall more be given," rewards not economy, but spending itself.

TWO COMPANIES' EXPERIENCES

A Manufacturing Organization

A midwest manufacturer of industrial goods had been troubled for some time by aspects of its organizational climate it believed dysfunctional. For research purposes, interviews were conducted with many employees and a questionnaire was administered on a company-wide basis, including plants and offices in several American and Canadian locations. The company strongly encouraged employee participation in the survey, and made available time and space during the work-day for completion of the instrument. All employees in attendance during the day of the survey completed the questionnaire. All instruments were collected directly by the researcher, who personally administered each session. Since no one employed by the firm handled the questionnaires, and since respondent names were not asked for, it seems likely that the pledge of anonymity given was believed.

A modified version of the Expect Approval scale (7) was included as part of the questionnaire. The instrument asked respondents to indicate the degree of approval or disapproval they could expect if they performed each of the described actions. A seven-point Likert scale was used, with 1 indicating that the action would probably bring strong disapproval and 7 signifying likely strong approval.

Although normative data for this scale from studies of other organizations are unavailable, it is possible to examine fruitfully the data obtained from this survey in several ways. First, it may be worth noting that the questionnaire data corresponded closely to information gathered through interviews. Furthermore, as can be seen from the results summarized in Table 1, sizable differences between various work units, and between employees at different job levels within the same work unit, were obtained. This suggests that response bias effects (social desirability in particular loomed as a potential concern) are not likely to be severe.

Most importantly, comparisons between scores obtained on the Expect Approval scale and a statement of problems which were the reason for the survey revealed that the same behaviors which managers in each division thought dysfunctional were those which lower level employees claimed were rewarded. As compared to job levels 1 to 8 in Division B (see Table 1), those in Division A claimed a much higher acceptance by management of "conforming" activities. Between 31 and 37 percent of Division A employees at levels 1-8 stated that going along with the majority, agreeing with the boss, and staying on everyone's good side brought approval; only once (level 5-8 responses to one of the three items) did a majority suggest that such actions would generate disapproval.

Furthermore, responses from Division A workers at levels 1-4 indicate that behaviors geared toward risk avoidance were as likely to be rewarded as to be punished. Only at job levels 9 and above was it apparent that the reward system was positively reinforcing behaviors desired by top management. Overall, the same "tendencies toward conservatism and apple-polishing at the lower levels" which

TABLE 1 Summary of Two Divisions' Data Relevant to Conforming and Risk-Avoidance Behaviors (extent to which subjects expect approval)

Dimension	Item	Division and Sample	Total Responses	Percentage of Workers Responding		
				1, 2, or 3 (Disapproval)	4	5, 6, or 7 (Approval)
Risk avoidance	Making a risky decision based on the best information at the time, but which turns out wrong.	A, levels 1–4 (lowest)	127	61	25	14
		A, levels 5–B	172	46	31	23
		A, levels 9 and above	17	41	30	30
		B, levels 1–4 (lowest)	31	56$	26	16
		B, levels 5–B	19	42	41	16
		B, levels 9 and above	10	50	20	30
Risk	Setting extremely high and challenging standards and goals, and then narrowly failing to make them.	A, levels 1–4	122	47	28	25
		A, levels 5–B	168	33	26	41
		A, levels 9+	17	24	6	70
		B, levels 1–4	31	48	23	29
		B, levels 5–8	18	17	33	50
		B, levels 9+	10	30	0	70

Statement	Category				
Setting goals which are extremely easy to make and then making them.	A, levels 1–4	124	35	30	35
	A, levels 5–8	171	47	27	26
	A, levels 9+	17	70	24	6
	B, levels 1–4	31	58	26	16
	B, levels 5–8	19	63	16	21
	B, levels 9+	10	80	09	20
Being a "yes man" and always agreeing with the boss.	A, levels 1–4	126	46	17	37
	A, levels 5–8	180	54	14	31
	A, levels 9+	17	88	12	0
	B, levels 1–4	32	53	28	19
	B, levels 5–8	19	68	21	11
	B, levels 9+	10	80	10	10
Always going along with the majority.	A, levels 1–4	125	40	29	35
	A, levels 5–8	170	47	31	32
	A, levels 9+	17	70	12	18
	B, levels 1–4	31	61	23	16
	B, levels 5–8	19	68	11	21
	B, levels 9+	10	80	10	10

TABLE 1 *(continued)*

Dimension	Item	Division and Sample	Total Responses	Percentage of Workers Responding		
				1, 2, or 3 (Disapproval)	4	5, 6, or 7 (Approval)
	Being careful to stay on the good side of everyone, so that everyone agrees that you are a great guy.	A, levels 1–4	124	45	18	37
		A, levels 5–8	173	45	22	33
		A, levels 9+	17	64	6	30
		B, levels 1–4	31	54	23	23
		B, levels 5–8	19	73	11	16
		B, levels 9+	10	80	10	10

divisional management had complained about during the interviews were those claimed by subordinates to be the most rational course of action in light of the existing reward system. Management apparently was not getting the behaviors it was *hoping* for, but it certainly was getting the behaviors it was perceived by subordinates to be *rewarding*.

An Insurance Firm

The Group Health Claims Division of a large eastern insurance company provides another rich illustration of a reward system which reinforces behaviors not desired by top management.

Attempting to measure and reward accuracy in paying surgical claims, the firm systematically keeps track of the number of returned checks and letters of complaint received from policyholders. However, underpayments are likely to provoke cries of outrage from the insured, while overpayments often are accepted in courteous silence. Since it often is impossible to tell from the physician's statement which of two surgical procedures, with different allowable benefits, was performed, and since writing for clarifications will interfere with other standards used by firm concerning "percentage of claims paid within two days of receipt," the new hire in more than one claims section is soon acquainted with the informal norm: "When in doubt, pay it out!"

The situation would be even worse were it not for the fact that other features of the firm's reward system tend to neutralize those described. For example, annual "merit" increases are given to all employees, in one of the following three amounts:

1. If the worker is "outstanding" (a select category, into which no more than two employees per section may be placed): 5 percent
2. If the worker is "above average" (normally all workers not "outstanding" are so rated): 4 percent
3. If the worker commits gross acts of negligence and irresponsibility for which he might be discharged in many other companies: 3 percent.

Now, since (a) the difference between the 5 percent theoretically attainable through hard work and the 4 percent attainable merely by living until the review data is small and (b) since insurance firms seldom dispense much of a salary increase in cash (rather, the worker's insurance benefits increase, causing him to be further overinsured), many employees are rather indifferent to the possibility of obtaining the extra one percent reward and therefore tend to ignore the norm concerning indiscriminant payments.

However, most employees are not indifferent to the rule which states that, should absences or latenesses total three or more in any six-month period, the entire 4 or 5 percent due at the next "merit" review must be forfeited. In this sense the firm may be described as *hoping* for performance, while *rewarding* attendance. What it gets, of course, is attendance. (If the absence-lateness rule appears to the reader to be stringent, it really is not. The company counts "times" rather than "days" absent, and a ten-day absence therefore counts the same as one lasting two days. A worker in danger of accumulating a third absence within six months merely has to remain ill (away from work) during his second absence until his first absence is more than six months old. The limiting factor is that at some point his salary ceases, and his sickness benefits take over. This usually is sufficient to get the younger workers to return, but for those with 20 or more years' service, the company provides sickness benefits of 90 percent of normal salary, tax-free! Therefore. . . .)

CAUSES

Extremely diverse instances of systems which reward behavior A although the rewarder apparently hopes for behavior B have been given. These are useful to illustrate the breadth and magnitude of the phenomenon, but the diversity increases the difficulty of determining commonalities and establishing causes. However, four general factors may be pertinent to an explanation of why fouled-up reward systems seem to be so prevalent.

Fascination with an "Objective" Criterion

It has been mentioned elsewhere that:

> Most "objective" measures of productivity are objective only in that their subjec- tive elements are (a) determined in advance, rather than coming into play at the time of the formal evaluation, and (b) well concealed on the rating instrument itself. Thus industrial firms seeking to devise objective rating systems first decide, in an arbitrary manner, what dimensions are to be rated, . . . usually including some items having little to do with organizational effectiveness while excluding others that do. Only then does Personnel Division churn out official-looking documents on which all dimensions chosen to be rated are assigned point values, categories, or whatever (6, p. 92).

Nonetheless, many individuals seek to establish simple, quantifiable standards against which to measure and reward performance. Such efforts may be successful in highly predictable areas within an organization, but are likely to cause goal displacement when applied anywhere else. Overconcern with attendance and lateness in the insurance firm and with number of people placed in the vocational rehabilitation division may have been largely responsible for the problems described in those organizations.

Overemphasis on Highly Visible Behaviors

Difficulties often stem from the fact that some parts of the task are highly visible while other parts are not. For example, publications are easier to demonstrate than teaching, and scoring baskets and hitting home runs are more readily observ- able than feeding teammates and advancing base runners. Similarly, the adverse consequences of pronouncing a sick person well are more visible than those sustained by labeling a well person sick. Team-building and creativity are other examples of behaviors which may not be rewarded simply because they are hard to observe.

Hypocrisy

In some of the instances described the rewarder may have been getting the desired behavior, notwithstanding claims that the behavior was not desired. This may be true, for example, of management's attitude toward apple polishing in the manufacturing firm (a behavior which subordinates felt was rewarded, despite management's avowed dislike of the practice). This also may explain politicians' unwillingness to revise the penalties for disobedience of ecology laws, and the failure of top management to devise reward systems which would cause systematic evaluation of training and developing programs.

Emphasis on Morality or Equity
Rather than Efficiency

Some consideration of other factors prevents the establishment of a system which rewards behaviors desired by the rewarder. The felt obligation of many Americans to vote for one candidate or another, for example, may impair their ability to withhold support from politicians who refuse to discuss the issues. Simlarly, the concern for spreading the risks and costs of wartime military service may outweigh the advantage to be obtained by commiting personnel to combat until the war is over.

It should be noted that only with respect to the first two causes are reward systems really paying off for other than desired behaviors. In the case of the third and fourth causes the system *is* rewarding behaviors desired by the rewarder, and the systems are fouled up only from the standpoints of those who believe the rewarder's public statements (cause 3), or those who seek to maximize efficiency rather than other outcomes (cause 4).

CONCLUSIONS

Modern organization theory requires a recognition that the members of organizations and society possess divergent goals and motives. It therefore is unlikely that managers and their subordinates will seek the same outcomes. Three possible remedies for this potential probelm are suggested.

Selection

It is theoretically possible for organizations to employ only those individuals whose goals and motives are wholly consonant with those of management. In such cases the same behaviors judged by subordinates to be rational would be perceived by management as desirable. State-of-the-art reviews of selection techniques, however, provide scant grounds for hope that such an approach would be successful (for example, see 12).

Training

Another theoretical alternative is for the organization to admit those employees whose goals are not consonant with those of management and then, through training, socialization, or whatever, alter employee goals to make them consonant. However, research on the effectiveness of such training programs, though limited, provides further grounds for pessimism (for example, see 3).

Altering the Reward System

What would have been the result if:

1. Nixon had been assured by his advisors that he could not win reelection except by discussing the issues in detail?
2. Physicians' conduct was subjected to regular examination by review boards for type 1 errors (calling healthy people ill) and to penalties (fines, censure, etc.) for errors of either type?
3. The President of XYZ Corporation had to choose between (a) spending $11 million for antipollution equipment, and (b) incurring a 50-50 chance of going to jail for five years?

Managers who complain that their workers are not motivated might do well to consider the possibility that they have installed reward systems which are paying off for behaviors other than those they are seeking. This, in part, is what happened in Vietnam, and this is what regularly frustrates societal efforts to bring about honest politicians, civic-minded managers, etc. This certainly is what happened in both the manufacturing and the insurance companies.

A first step for such managers might be to find out what behaviors currently are being rewarded. Perhaps an instrument similar to that used in the manufacturing firm could be useful for this purpose. Chances are excellent that these managers will be surprised by what they find—that their firms are not rewarding what they assume they are. In fact, such undesirable behavior by organizational members as they have observed may be explained largely by the reward systems in use.

This is not to say that all organizational behavior is determined by formal rewards and punishments. Certainly it is true that in the absence of formal reinforcement some soldiers will be patriotic, some presidents will be ecology minded, and some orphanage directors will care about children. The point, however, is that in such cases the rewarder is not *causing* the behaviors desired but is only a fortunate bystander. For an organization to *act* upon its members, the formal reward system should positively reinforce desired behaviors, not consititute an obstacle to be overcome.

It might be wise to underscore the obvious fact that there is nothing really new in what has been said. In both theory and practice these matters have been mentioned before. Thus in many states Good Samaritan laws have been installed to protect doctors who stop to assist a stricken motorist. In states without such laws it is commonplace for doctors to refuse to stop, for fear of involvement in a subseuqent lawsuit. In college basketball additional penalties have been instituted against players who foul their opponents deliberately. It has long been argued by Milton Friedman and others that penalties should be altered so as to make it irrational to disobey the ecology laws, and so on.

By altering the reward system the organization escapes the necessity of selecting only desirable people or of trying to alter undersirable ones. In Skinnerian terms (as described in 11, p. 704), "As for responsibility and goodness—as commonly defined—no one. . .would want or need them. They refer to a man's behaving well despite the absence of positive reinforcement that is obviously sufficient to explain it. Where such reinforcement exists, 'no one needs goodness.' "

REFERENCES

1. Barnard, Chester I. *The Functions of the Executive.* Cambridge, Mass.: Harvard University Press, 1964.
2. Blau, Peter M., and W. Richard Scott. *Formal Organizations.* San Francisco: Chandler, 1962.
3. Fiedler, Fred E. "Predicting the Effects of Leadership Training and Experience from the Contingency Model," *Journal of Applied Psychology,* vol. 56 (1972), pp. 114–19.
4. Garland, L. H. "Studies of the Accuracy of Diagnostic Procedures," *American Journal Roentgenological Radium Therapy Nuclear Medicine,* vol. 82 (1959), pp. 25–38.
5. Kerr, Steven. "Some Modifications in MBO as an OD Strategy," *Academy of Management Proceedings,* 1973, pp. 39–42.
6. Kerr, Steven. "What Price Objectivity?" *American Sociologist,* vol. 8 (1973), pp. 92–93.
7. Litwin, G. H., and R. A. Stringer, Jr. *Motivation and Organizational Climate.* Boston: Harvard University Press, 1968.
8. Perrow, Charles. "The Analysis of Goals in Complex Organizations," in A. Etzioni, ed., *Readings on Modern Organizations.* Englewood Cliffs, N.J.: Prentice-Hall, 1969.
9. Scheff, Thomas J. "Decision Rules, Types of Error, and Their Consequences in Medical Diagnosis," in F. Massarik and P. Ratoosh, eds., *Mathematical Explorations in Behavioral Science.* Homewood, Ill.: Irwin, 1965.
10. Simon, Herbert A. *Administrative Behavior.* New York: Free Press, 1957.
11. Swanson, G. E. "Review Symposium: Beyond Freedom and Dignity," *American Journal of Sociology,* vol. 78 (1972), pp. 702–05.
12. Webster, E. *Decision Making in the Employment Interview.* Montreal: Industrial Relations Center, McGill University, 1964.

17

Organizational Analysis

A CONGRUENCE MODEL FOR DIAGNOSING ORGANIZATIONAL BEHAVIOR
David A. Nadler
Michael Tushman

STRUCTURE IS NOT ORGANIZATION
Robert H. Waterman, Jr.
Thomas J. Peters
Julien R. Phillips

A CONGRUENCE MODEL FOR DIAGNOSING ORGANIZATIONAL BEHAVIOR

David A. Nadler
Michael Tushman

Managers perform their jobs within complex social systems called organizations. In many senses, the task of the manager is to influence behavior in a desired direction, usually toward the accomplishment of a specific task or performance goal. Given this definition of the managerial role, skills in the diagnosis of patterns of organizational behavior become vital. Specifically, the manager needs to be able to *understand* the patterns of behavior that are observed, to *predict* in what direction behavior will move (particularly in the light of managerial action), and to use this knowledge to *control* behavior over the course of time.

The understanding, prediction, and control of behavior by managers occurs, of course, in organizations every day. The problem with managerial control of behavior as frequently practiced is that the understanding-prediction-control sequence is based on the intuition of the individual manager. This intuitive approach is usually based on models of behavior or organization which the manager carries

Source: Reprinted by permission of the authors.

around in his/her head—models that are often naive and simplistic. One of the aims of this paper will be to develop a model of organizations, based on behavioral science research, that is both systematic and useful.

The model to be discussed in this paper will serve two ends. It will provide a way of systematically thinking about behavior in organizations as well as provide a framework within which the results of research on organizational behavior can be expressed.

Effective managerial action requires that the manager be able to diagnose the system s/he is working in. Since all elements of social behavior cannot be dealt with at once, the manager facing this "blooming-buzzing" confusion must simplify reality—that is, develop a model of organizational functioning. The diagnostic model will present one way of simplifying social reality that still retains the dynamic nature of organizations. The model will focus on a set of key organizational components (or variables) and their relationships as the primary determinants of behavior. The diagnosis of these key components will provide a concise snapshot of the organization. However, organizations do not stand still. The diagnostic model will preserve the changing nature of organizations by evaluating the effects of feedback on the nature of the key components and their relationships. In all, the diagnostic model will provide a way of thinking about organizations by focusing on a set of key variables and their relationships over time. The model will therefore not consider all the complexity of organizational behavior. To be useful in real settings, insight from the model must be supplemented with clinical data and managerial insight.

Besides as a way of thinking about organizational behavior, the diagnostic model can also serve as a vehicle to organize a substantial portion of research on organizational behavior. An increased awareness of the research results concerning the relationships between the key components should help the manager make the link between diagnosing the situation and making decisions for future action. The model, then, cannot only help the manager to diagnose and describe organizational behavior, but it can provide an effective way to organize and discuss behavioral science research results that may be of use to managers.

While the diagnostic model is a potentially powerful managerial tool, it must be seen as a developing tool. Parts of the model are less well developed than others (e.g., the informal organization). As research in organizational behavior advances, so, too, should the development of this diagnostic model. Finally, no claim is made that this model is the most effective way of organizing reality. It is suggested, however, that models of organizational behavior are important and that they ought to (1) deal with several variables and their relationships, and (2) take into account the dynamic nature of organizations.

In conclusion, the premise of this article is that effective management requires that the manager be able to systematically diagnose, predict, and control behavior. The purpose of this paper is to present a research-based (as opposed to intuitive) model of organizational behavior that can be used to diagnose organizations as well as to integrate behavioral science research results. The model should therefore be of use to practitioners in organizations as well as to students in the classroom.

BASIC ASSUMPTIONS OF THE MODEL

The diagnostic model that will be discussed here is based on a number of assumptions about organizational life. These assumptions are as follows:

1. *Organizations are dynamic entities.* Organizations exist over time and space, and the activities that make up organizations are dynamic. There are many definitions of organizations, such as Schein's (1970) statement that

> an organization is the rational coordination of the activities of a number of people for the achievement of some common explicit purpose or goal, through division of labor and function, and through a hierarchy of authority and responsibility.

While definitions like this are adequate to define what an organization is, they are static in nature and do not enable one to grasp how the different components of organization interact with each other over time. An adequate model of organizations must reflect the dynamic nature of organizational behavior.

2. *Organizational behavior exists at multiple levels.* There are different levels of abstraction at which organizational behavior can be examined. Specifically, behavior occurs at the *individual,* the *group,* and the *organizational systems* levels. Behavior that is attributable to each of these levels can be identified and isolated (that is, one can see the behavior of individuals as different from the behavior of groups or of organizations themselves). At the same time, these three levels interact with each other, organizational-level behavior being affected by the behavior of individuals, group-level behavior being affected by the organizational-level phenomena, and so on.

3. *Organizational behavior does not occur in a vacuum.* Organizations are made up of both social and technical components and thus have been characterized as sociotechnical systems (Emery and Trist, 1960). The implication of this is that any approach to looking at behavior must also take into account the technical components of the organization—such issues as the nature of the task and the technology. Since the organization is dependent on inputs, knowledge, and feedback from the environment, our model must also take into account the constraints of the organization's task environment (e.g., to what extent the market is changing).

4. *Organizations have the characteristics of open social systems.* Organizations have the characteristics of systems that are composed of interrelated components and conduct transactions with a larger environment. Systems have a number of unique behavioral characteristics, and thus a model of organizational behavior must take into account the systemic nature of organizations.

OPEN-SYSTEMS THEORY

The point made above about open-systems theory is a crucial one which needs to be explored in more depth. The basic premise is the characteristics of systems that are seen in both the physical and social sciences (Von Bertalanffy, 1962; Buckley, 1967) are particularly valuable when looking at organizations. Social organizations, it is claimed, can be viewed as systems (Katz and Kahn, 1966) with a number of key systems characteristics.

What is a system and what are systems characteristics? In the simplest of terms, a system is a "set of interrelated elements." These elements are interdependent such that changes in the nature of one component may lead to changes in the nature of the other components. Further, because the system is embedded wih larger systems, it is dependent on the larger environment for resources, information, and feedback. Another way of looking at a system is to define it as a mechanism that imports some form of energy input from the environment, which submits that input to some kind of transformation process, and which produces some kind of energy output back to the environment (Katz and Kahn, 1966). The notion of open systems also implies the existence of some boundary differentiating the system from the larger environment in which it is embedded. These system boundaries are usually not rigid. This familiar view of a system can be seen in Figure 1. Closed systems, on the other hand, are not dependent on the environment and are more deterministic in nature. Closed systems tend to have more rigid boundaries and all transactions take place within the system, guided by unitary goals and rationality. (An example approaching a closed system would be a terrarium, completely self-contained and insulated from the larger enviroinment.)

A more extensive definition of open systems has been presented by Katz and Kahn (1966) in the form of a listing of characteristics of open social systems. An adapted list of these characteristics is as follows:

1. *Importation of energy.* A system functions by importing energy (information, products, materials, etc.) from the larger environment.

2. *Throughput.* Systems move energy through them, largely in the form of transformation processes. These are often multiple processes (i.e., decisions, material manipulation, etc.)

3. *Output.* Systems send energy back to the larger environment in the form of products, services, and other kinds of outcomes which may or may not be intended.

4. *Cycles of events over time.* Systems function over time and thus are dynamic in nature. Events tend to occur in natural repetitive cycles of input, throughput, and output, with events in sequence occurring over and over again.

5. *Equilibrium seeking.* Systems tend to move toward the state where all components are in equilibrium—where a steady state exists. When changes are made that result in an imbalance, different components of the system move to restore the balance.

6. *Feedback.* Systems use information about their output to regulate their input and transformation processes. These informational connections also exist between system components, and thus changes in the functioning of one component will lead to changes in other system components (second-order effects).

7. *Increasing differentiation.* As systems grow, they also tend to increase their dif-

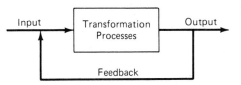

FIGURE 1 The Elementary Systems Model

ferentiation; more components are added, more feedback loops, more transformation processes. Thus, as systems get larger, they also get more complex.

8. *Equifinality*. Different system configurations may lead to the same end point, or conversely, the same end state may be reached by a variety of different processes.

9. *System survival requirements*. Because of the inherent tendency of systems to "run down" or dissipate their energy, certain functions must be performed (at least at minimal levels) over time. These requirements include (a) goal achievement, and (b) adaptation (the ability to maintain balanced successful transactions with the environment).

A SPECIFIC SYSTEMS MODEL

Open-systems theory is a general framework for conceptualizing organizational behavior over time. It sensitizes the manager to a basic model of organizations (i.e., input-throughput-output-feedback) as well as to a set of basic organizational processes (e.g., equilibrium, differentiation, equifinality). While systems concepts are useful as an overall perspective, they do not help the manager systematically diagnose specific situations or help him/her apply research results to specific problems. A more concrete model must be developed that takes into account system-theory concepts and processes and helps the manager deal with organizational reality.

According to Figure 1, organizations (or some other unit of interest, e.g., a department or factory) take some set of inputs, work on these inputs through some sort of transformation process, and produce output that is evaluated and responded to the environment. While managers must attend to the environment and input considerations, they must specifically focus on what the organization does to produce output. That is, managers are intimately involved in what systems theory terms the *transformation processes*. It is the transformation processes, then, that the model will specifically focus on. Given the cycle of processes from input to feedback, the model will focus on the more specific variables and processes that affect how the organization takes a given set of inputs and produces a set of organizational outputs (e.g., productivity, innovation, satisfaction). While the diagnostic model will specifically focus on the determinants of the transformation processes and their relationships to outputs, it must be remembered that these processes are part of a more general model of organizational behavior that takes inputs, outputs, and the environment into account (see Figure 1).

The model focuses on the critical system characteristic of dependence. Organizations are made up of components or parts that interact with each other. These components exist in states of relative balance, consistency, or "fit" with each other. The different parts of the organization can fit well together and thus function effectively; or fit poorly, leading to problems. Given the central nature of fit in the model, we shall talk about it as a *congruence model* of organizational behavior, since effectiveness is a function of the congruence of the various components.

This concept of congruence between organizational components is not a new one. Leavitt (1965), for example, identifies four major components of organization as being people, tasks, technology, and structure. The model presented here builds on this view and also draws from models developed and used by Seiler (1967), Lawrence and Lorsch (1969), and Lorsch and Sheldon (1972).

What we are concerned about is modeling the *behavioral* system of the organization—the system of elements that ultimately produce patterns of behavior. In its simplest form, what inputs does the system have to work with, what are the major components of the system and the nature of their interactions, and what is the nature of the system output?

The congruence model is based on the system's assumptions outlined above. The inputs to the system (see Figure 2) are those factors that at any one point in time are relatively fixed or given. Three major classes of inputs can be identified: (1) the environment of the system, (2) the resources available to the system, and (3) the organizational strategies that are developed over time.

The transformation process of the system is seen as the interaction between four major components of the organizational system. These components are (1) the tasks of the organization, (2) the individuals in the organizational system, (3) the organizational arrangements, and (4) the informal organization.

The outputs are the results of the interactions among the components, given the inputs. Several major outputs can be identified, including individual affect and behavior, group behavior, and the effectiveness of total system functioning. Looking at the total system, particular attention is paid to the system's ability to attain its goals, to utilize available resources, and to successfully adapt over time. Explicit in the model are feedback loops running from the outputs and the transformation process. The loops represent information flow about the nature of the system output and the interaction of system components. The information is available for use to make modifications in the nature of systems inputs or components.

FIGURE 2 The Systems Model as Applied to Organizational Behavior

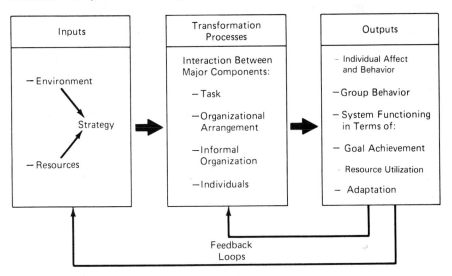

In understanding the model, it is therefore important to understand what makes up the system inputs, components, and outputs and how they relate to each other. In particular, it is important for the manager to understand how system components relate to each other since these relationships are particularly critical for influencing behavior.

The Nature of Inputs

Inputs are important since at any point in time they are the fixed or given factors that influence organizational behavior. The inputs provide both constraints and opportunities for managerial action. While the diagnosis of organizational behavior is focused primarily on the understanding of the interactions among system components, an understanding of the nature of the inputs is still important. The major classes of inputs that constrain organizational behavior are listed in Table 1. A brief description of these inputs is as follows:

1. *Environmental inputs.* Organizations as open systems carry on constant transactions with the environment. Specifically, three factors in the environment of the specific organization are important. First, there are the various groups, organizations, and events that make up the external environment. This includes the functioning of product, service, and capital markets; the behavior of competitors and suppliers; governmental regulation; and the effect of the larger culture. Second, the organization may be embedded within another larger formal system. For example, a factory that is being considered may be part of a larger multinational corporation or of a larger corporate division. These larger "supra-systems" form an important part of the environment of the organization. Third, both the internal and external environment can be described according to a number of dimensions that appear to impact the functioning of organizations (Emery and Trist, 1965). Specifically, the issues of stability and homogeneity of the environment are important.

2. *Resources.* Another important input is composed of the resources that are available to the organization. Any organization has a range of resources

TABLE 1 Dimension of System Inputs

Environment	Resources	Strategy

External environment
  Markets
  Government
  Financial institutions
  Competitors
  Suppliers
  Labor unions
  The larger culture, etc.
Internal environment
  Immediate supra-systems
Environmental characteristics
  Stability
  Homogeneity
	Capital
	Raw materials
	Technologies
	People
	Intangibles
		Critical decisions in the past
		  Identification of environmental
		    opportunities and distinctive
		    competences
		  Organizational mission
		  Long-range and short-range goals
		  Plans

available as inputs. Major categories for classifying resources would include capital resources (including liquid capital, physical plant, property, etc.), raw materials (the material on which the organization will perform the transformation process), technologies (approaches or procedures for performing the transformation), people, and various intangible resources.

3. *Strategy*. Over time, organizations develop ways of utilizing their resources that deal effectively with the constraints, demands, and opportunities of the environment. They develop plans of action that centrally define what the organization will attempt to do in relation to the larger systems in which it is embedded. These plans of action are called strategies and are another major input.

While all three inputs are important, one, however, has a very critical primary effect upon the nature of one of the components, and therefore it ultimately affects all the components and their interactions. This input is strategy.

As has been said, an organization as an open system functions within a larger environment. That environment provides opportunities for action, it provides constraints on activities, and it makes demands upon the organization's capacities. The organization faces the environment with a given set of resources of various kinds: human, technological, managerial, and so on. The process of determining how those resources can best be used to function within the environment is generally called strategy determination (see Newman and Logan, 1976, or Andrews, 1971). The organization identifies opportunities in the environment where its distinctive competence or unique set of resources will provide it with a competitive advantage.

Some organizations develop strategies through formalized and complex processes of long-range strategic planning, while other organizations may give no or little conscious attention to strategy at all. Further, the process of strategy formulation can itself be seen as the output of intraorganizational processes (e.g., Bower, 1970; Mintzberg, 1973). The point is, however, that organizations have strategies, whether they be implicit or explicit, formal or informal. The point for organizational behavior is that the strategy of an organization is probably the single most important input (or constraint set) to the behavioral system. The strategy and the elements of that strategy (goals or plans) essentially define the *task* of the organization, one of the major components of the behavioral system (see Figure 3). From one perspective, all organizational behavior is concerned with implementation of strategies through the performance of tasks. Individuals, formal organizational arrangements, and informal organizational arrangements are all important because of their relationship to the tasks that need to be performed.

FIGURE 3 The Role of Strategy as the Primary Input to the Model

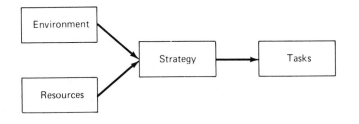

The inputs listed above therefore provide opportunities, provide constraints, and may even make demands upon the organization. Given these inputs, the issue of how the organization functions to make use of the opportunities and constraints provided by the inputs is perhaps the most central issue of managerial and organizational behavior.

The Nature of Organizational Components

Assuming a set of inputs, the transformation process occurs through the interaction of a number of basic components of organization. The major components (listed with their subdimensions in Table 2) are as follows:

1. *Task component.* This component concerns the nature of the tasks or jobs that must be performed by the organization, by groups, and by individuals. Major dimensions of tasks include the extent and nature of interdependence between task performers, the level of required skills, the degree of autonomy, the extent of feedback, the variability of the task, the potential meaningfulness of the task, and the types of information needed to adequately perform the task.

2. *Individuals component.* This component obviously refers to the individuals who are members of the organization. The major dimensions of this component relate to the systematic differences in individuals which have relevance for organizational behavior. Such dimensions include background or demographic variables such as skill levels, levels of education, and so on, and individual differences in need strength, personality, or perceptual biases.

3. *Organizational arrangements.* This includes all the formal mechanisms used by the organization to direct structure or control behavior. Major dimensions include leadership practices, microstructure (how specific jobs, systems, or subcomponents are structured), and macrostructure (how whole units, departments, and organizations are structured).

4. *Informal organization.* In addition to the formal prescribed structure that exists in the system, there is an informal social structure that tends to emerge over time. Relevant dimensions of the informal organization include the functioning of informal group structures, the quality of intergroup relations, and the operation of various political processes throughout the organization.

Organizations can therefore be looked at as a set of components, including the task, the individuals, the organizational arrangements, and the informal organization. (For the complete model, see Figure 4.) To be useful, however, the model must go beyond the simple listing and description of these components and describe the dynamic relationship that exists among the various components.

The Concept of Fit. Between each pair of inputs there exists a degree of congruence, or "fit." Specifically, the congruence between two components is defined as follows:

> The degree to which the needs, demands, goals, objectives and/or structures of one component are consistent with the needs, demands, goals, objectives and/or structures of another component.

TABLE 2 Basic Characteristics of Behavioral System Components

Task	Individuals	Organizational Arrangements	Informal Organization
Organizational tasks	Response capabilities	Subunits	Small-group functioning
Complexity	Intelligence	Grouping of tasks and roles	Norms
Predictability	Skills and abilities	Unit composition	Informal goals
Required interdependence	Experience	Unit design	Communication patterns
	Training	Formal leadership in the unit	Cohesiveness
		Physical arrangements, etc.	Informal group structures
Subunit and individual tasks	Psychological differences	Coordination and control	Intergroup relations
Complexity	Need strength	Goals	Conflict/cooperation
Predictability	Attitudes	Plans	Information flows
Required interdependence	Perceptual biases	Hierarchy	Perceptions
Autonomy	Expectations	Reward systems	Orgnaizational level
Feedback	Background differences	Personnel systems	Networks, cliques, and
Task variety		Control systems	coalitions
Task identity		Integrator roles and groups	Conflicting interest groups
Task meaningfulness			Power distribution
Task skill demands			Ideology and values

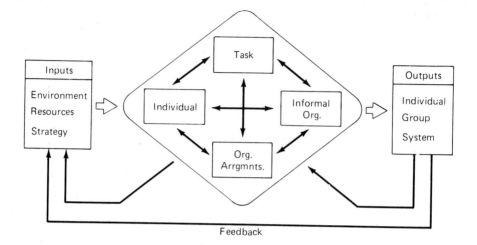

FIGURE 4 A Congruence Model for Diagnosing Organizational Behavior

Thus fit (indicated by the double-headed arrows in Figure 4) is a measure of the congruence between pairs of components. Because components cover a range of different types of phenomena, however, fit can be more clearly defined only by referring to specific fits between specific pairs of components. In each case research results can be used as a guide to evaluate whether the components are in a state of high consistency or high inconsistency. An awareness of these fits is critical since inconsistent fits will be related to dysfunctional behavior.

Specific definitions of congruence and examples of research on the nature of these fits is presented in Table 3. For each of the six fits among the components, more information is provided about the specific issues that need to be examined to determine the level of consistency between the components. Citations are given for examples of the research relevant to each of these relationships.

The Congruence Hypothesis. Just as each pair of components has a degree of high or low congruence, so does the aggregate model display a relatively high or low total system congruence. Underlying the model is a basic hypothesis about the nature of its and their relationship to behavior. This hypothesis is as follows:

> Other things being equal, the greater the total degree of congruence of fit between the various components, the more effective will be organizational behavior at multiple levels. Effective organizational behavior is defined as behavior which leads to higher levels of goal attainment, utilization of resources, and adaptation.

The implications of the congruence hypothesis in this model is that the manager needs to adequately diagnose the system, determine the location and nature of inconsistent fits, and plan courses of action to change the nature of those fits without bringing about dysfunctional second-order effects. The model also implies that different configurations of the key components can lead to effective behavior (consistent with the system characteristics of equifinality). Therefore, the ques-

TABLE 3 Definitions of Fits and Examples of Research

Fit	The Issues	Examples of Research on the Fits
Individual-organization	To what extent individual needs are met by the organizational arrangements; to what extent individuals hold clear or distorted perceptions of organizational structures; the convergence of individual and organizational goals.	Argyris (1957), Vroom (1959), Tannenbaum and Allport (1956), Schein (1970)
Individual-task	To what extent the needs of individuals are met by the tasks; to what extent individuals have skills and abilities to meet task demands.	Turner and Lawrence (1965), Hackman and Lawler (1971), Hackman and Oldham (1975)
Individual-informal organization	To what extent individual needs are met by the informal organization; to what extent the informal organization makes use of individual resources, consistent with informal goals.	Whyte (1955), Hackman and Morris (1976), Gouldner (1954), Crozier (1964), Trist and Bamforth (1951)
Task-organization	Whether the organizational arrangements are adequate to meet the demands of the task; whether organizational arrangements tend to motivate behavior consistent with task demands.	Burns and Stalker (1961), Woodward (1965), Lawrence and Lorsch (1969), Vroom and Yetton (1973)
Task-informal organization	Whether the informal organization structure facilitates task performance or not; whether it hinders or promotes meeting the demands of the task.	Blake, Shepard and Mouton, (1964), Blau (1956), Trist and Bamforth (1951), Burns and Stalker (1961), Gouldner, 1954
Organization-informal organization	Whether the goals, rewards, and structures of the informal organization are consistent with those of the formal organization.	Roethlisberger and Dickson (1939), Dalton (1959), Likert (1967), Crozier (1964), Strauss (1962)

tion is not finding the "one best way" of managing, but of determining effective combinations of inputs that will lead to congruent fits.

This process of diagnosing fit and identifying combinations of inputs to produce congruence is not necessarily an intuitive process. A number of situations that lead to consistent fits have been defined in the research literature (for example, see some of the research cited in Table 3). Thus, in many cases fit is something that can be defined, measured, and quantified in many organizational systems. The basic point is that goodness of fit is based upon theory and research rather than intuition. In most cases, the theory provides considerable guidance about what leads to congruence relationships (although in some areas the research is more abundant than others; the research on informal organization, for example, has been sparse in recent years). The implication is that the manager who is attempting to diagnose behavior needs to become familiar with critical findings of the relevant research so that s/he can evaluate the nature of fits in a particular system.

The Nature of Outputs

The model indicates that the outputs flow out of the interaction of the various components. Any organizational system produces a number of different outputs.

For general diagnostic purposes, however, four major classes of outputs are particularly important:

1. *Individual behavior and effect.* A crucial issue is how individuals behave, specifically with regard to their organizational membership behavior (for example, absenteeism, lateness, turnover) and with regard to performance of designated tasks. Individuals also have effective responses to the work environment (levels of satisfaction, for example) which also are of consequence. Other individual behavior such as nonproductive behavior, drug usage, off-the-job activities, and so on, are also outputs of the organization in many cases.

2. *Group and intergroup behavior.* Beyond the behavior of individuals, the organization is also concerned with the performance of groups or departments. Important considerations would include intergroup conflict or collaboration and the quality of intergroup communication.

3. *System-functioning.* At the highest level of abstraction is the question of how well the system as a whole is functioning. The key issues here include (1) how well is the system attaining its desired goals of production, output, return on investment, etc.; (2) how well the organization is utilizing available resources; and (3) how well is the organization adapting (i.e., maintaining favorable transactions with the environment over time).

USING THE DIAGNOSTIC MODEL

Given the diagnostic model, the final question to be addressed here is how the model can be put to use. A number of authors have observed that the conditions facing organizations are always changing and that managers must therefore continually engage in problem identification and problem-solving activities (e.g., Schein, 1970)). These authors suggest that managers must gather data on the performance of their organization, compare the ideal to the actual performance levels, develop and choose action plans, and then implement and evaluate these action plans. These problem-solving phases link together to form a *problem-solving process* if the evaluation phase is seen as the beginning of the next diagnostic phase. For long-term organizational viability, this problem-solving process must be continually reaccomplished (Schein, 1970; Weick, 1969). The basic phases of this problem-solving process are outlined in Figure 5.

How does the diagnostic model relate to this problem-solving process? The problem-solving process requires diagnosis, the generation of action plans, and the evaluation of the action plans. *Each of these steps requires a way of looking at organizations to guide the analysis.* To the extent that the diagnostic model integrates system-theory concepts and presents a specific model of organizations, the model can be used as the core of the problem-solving process. The model can therefore be used as a framework to guide the diagnosis, the evaluation of alternative actions, and the evaluation and feedback of the results of a managerial action. Further, to the extent that the manager is familiar with the research results bearing on the different fits in the model, s/he will be better able to both diagnose the situation and evaluate alternative action plans. In short, the problem-solving

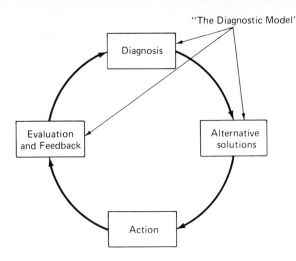

FIGURE 5 Basic Phases of Using the Diagnostic Model

process, along with the research-based use of the diagnostic model, can be used as an effective managerial tool.

Given the problem-solving process and the diagnostic model, it is possible to identify and describe a number of discrete steps in the problem-solving cycle. These steps can be organized into three phases: (1) diagnosis, (2) alternative solutions-action, and (3) evaluation-feedback. The basis phases and their component steps will be outlined here.

The Diagnostic Phase

This phase is premised on the idea that any managerial action must be preceded by a systematic diagnosis of the system under investigation. This phase can be broken into four distinct, but related, steps.

1. *Identify the system.* Before any detailed analysis can begin it is important to identify the system being considered. The unit of analysis must be clearly specified (i.e., project, division, organization). The boundaries of the focal unit, its membership, and what other units constitute the layer system should be considered.

2. *Determine the nature of the key variables.* Having defined the system, the next step is to use the data in the situation (or case) to determine the nature of the inputs and the four key components. The analyst should focus on the underlying dimensions of each variable. The diagnosis should focus not on an exhaustive description of each component but on the dimensions the analyst considers most important in the particular situation. The question could be phrased: In this situation, what are the most salient characteristics of the key components that are affecting the observed behavior?

3. *Diagnose the state of fits and their relationship to behaviors (i.e., outputs).* This step is the most critical in the diagnosis phase. It really involves two related stages: (a) diagnosing fits between the components, and (b) considering the link between the fits and system output.

a. Using experience, observations, and relevant research knowledge, the manager must evaluate each of the fit lines in the model. The analyst must focus on the extent to which the key components are consistent (or fit) with each other. For instance, to what extent are the organizational arrangements consistent with the demands of the task?

b. Fits (or lack of fits) between the key components have consequences in terms of system behavior. This step makes the fit-to-behavior link explicit. That is, given the diagnoses of the various fits, the analyst must then relate the fits to behaviors observed in the system (e.g., conflict, performance, stress, satisfaction). This is a particular key step since managerial action will be directed at the inconsistent fits to improve some aspect of the organization's behavior.

4. *Identifying critical system problems.* Based on the diagnosis of fits and their behavioral consequences, the final diagnostic step is to relate the set of behaviors to system outputs (goal achievement, resource utilization, and adaptation). Given these outputs, the manager must then evaluate which system behaviors require managerial attention and action.

The diagnostic phase forces the analyst to make a set of decisions. The analyst must decide the unit of analysis, make decisions as to the most salient characteristics of each of the key variables, make decisions as to the relationships between the key components and their effects on behavior, and relate the observed behaviors to system outputs and decide on the system's most pressing problems. None of these decisions are clear cut—each involves managerial discretion. It follows that there is no one best diagnosis of any set of organizational conditions. The final point to be made in the diagnosis phase is that diagnosis makes a difference. The manager's diagnosis must lead to a set of actions. Different diagnoses will therefore usually lead to different actions.

Alternative Solutions—Action Plan Phase

Diagnosis leads to a consideration of potential managerial actions. This alternative action phase can be separated into three stages.

5. *Generate alternative solutions.* Having identified critical problems and the relationship between fits and behavior, the next step is to generate a range of possible managerial actions. These actions or interventions will be directed at the inconsistent fits, which will in turn affect the behaviors under consideration.

Action plans for a particular situation may differ. There may be different diagnoses or there may be a number of interventions or organizational arrangements leading to the same end point (following from the system characteristic of equifinality). In short, there is not likely to be one most appropriate set of managerial actions to deal with a particular set of conditions.

6. *Evaluating alternative strategies.* While there usually is not one single most appropriate managerial action to deal with a particular situation, the various alternatives can be evaluated for their relative merits. To what extent do the solutions deal with the inconsistent fits? Does one solution deal with the inconsistent fits more comprehensively? Are there dysfunctional second-order (i.e., latent) consequences of the action—for instance, will changing the task dimensions deal with

an inconsistent task-informal organization fit but adversely affect the task-individual fit? In short, given the highly interdependent nature of open systems, the manager must systematically evaluate the alternative actions. Based on theory, research, and experience, the manager must make predictions about the possible effects of different strategies. The manager should therefore focus on the extent to which the intervention deals with the critical system problem *as well as* with the possibilities of latent consequences of the intervention. This exercise of prediction should provide a way of evaluating the relative strengths and weaknesses of the alternative actions.

7. *Choice of strategies to be implemented.* Given the explicit evaluation of the different approaches, the final step in this phase is to weigh the various advantages and disadvantages of the alternative actions and choose an action plan to be implemented.

Evaluation and Feedback Phase

The diagnosis and alternative solution-action phases leave the manager with an action plan to deal with the critical system problem(s). The final phase in using the diagnostic model deals with the implementation of the action plan and with the importance of evaluation, feedback, and adjustment of strategy to meet emergent system requirements.

8. *Implementation of strategies.* This step deals explicitly with issues that arise in introducing change into an ongoing system. This step recognizes the need to deal with the response of organizations to change. To what extent will the intervention be accepted and worked on as opposed to resisted and sabotaged? There is an extensive literature dealing with the implementation of change programs (e.g., Walton, 1975; Rogers and Shoemaker, 1971; French and Bell, 1973). While these considerations cannot be dealt with here, it is important to highlight the potential problems of translating plans and strategies into effective action.

9. *Evaluation and feedback.* After implementing a strategy, it is important to continue the diagnostic activity and to explicitly evaluate the actual vs. the ideal (or predicted) impact of the intervention on the system. Feedback concerning the organization's or the environment's response to the action can then be used to adjust the intervention to better fit the system's requirements and/or deal with any unanticipated consequences of the change. In a sense, then, step 9 closes the loop and starts the diagnosis-alternatives-action-evaluation cycle again (see Figure 5).

In conclusion, we have discussed a number of discrete, though related, steps for using the diagnostic model. The model provides a way of systematically diagnosing organizations. This diagnosis can then be used as an integral part of a problem-solving strategy for the organization. Further, the model can assist the manager in evaluating alternative solutions (i.e., what fits are dealt with) as well as evaluating the effects of the managerial actions (i.e., what fits were affected). Since organizations are made up of processes that must recur over time, the manager must continually go through the kind of problem-solving strategy indicated in Figure 5. If this adaptive-coping kind of scheme is critical for organizational viability over time (see Schein, 1970), the diagnostic model can be seen as a concrete research-based tool to facilitate the diagnosis of the system *and* to provide a base for evaluating alternative actions and the consequences of those actions.

The diagnostic model and the problem-solving cycle are ways of structuring and dealing with the complex reality of organizations. Given the indeterminate nature of social systems, there is no one best way of handling a particular situation. The model and problem-solving cycle do, however, force the manager to make a number of decisions and to think about the consequences of those decisions. If the diagnostic model and problem-solving process have merit, it is up to the manager to use these tools along with his/her experiences to make the appropriate set of diagnostic, evaluative, and action decisions over time.

SUMMARY

This article has attempted to briefly outline a model for diagnosing organizational behavior. The model is based on the assumption that organizations are open social systems and that an interaction of inputs leads to behavior and various outputs. The model presented is one based on the theory and research literature in organizational behavior and thus assumes that the manager using the model has some familiarity with the concepts coming out of this literature. Together with a process for its use, the model provides managers with a potentially valuable tool in the creation of more effective organizations.

REFERENCES

Andrews, K. R. *The concept of corporate strategy.* Homewood, Ill.: Dow Jones-Irwin, 1971.

Argyris. C. *Personality and organization: The conflict between system and the individual.* New York: Harper & Row, 1957.

Blake, R. R., Shephard, H. A., and Mouton, J. S. *Managing intergroup conflict in industry.* Houston, Tex.: Gulf, 1964.

Blau, P. M. *The dynamics of bureaucracy.* Chicago: University of Chicago Press, 1955.

Bower, J. L. *Managing the resource allocation process.* Cambridge, Mass.: Harvard University Graduate School of Business Administration, Division of Research, 1970).

Buckley, W. *Sociology and modern systems theory.* Englewood Cliffs, N.J.: Prentice-Hall, 1967.

Burns, T., and Stalker, G. M. *The management of innovation.* London: Tavistock Publications, 1961.

Crozier, R. *The bureaucratic phenomenon.* Chicago: University of Chicago Press, 1964.

Dalton, M. *Men who manage,* New York: Wiley, 1959.

Duncan, R. Characteristics of organizational environments. *Administrative Science Quarterly,* 1972, *17,* 313–327.

Emery. F. E., and Trist, E. L. Socio-technical systems. In *Management sciences models and techniques,* Vol. II. London: Pergamon Press, 1960.

Emery, F. E., and Trist, E. L. The causal texture of organizational environments, *Human Relations,* 1965, *18,* 21–32.

French, W. L., and Bell, C. H. *Organization development.* Englewood Cliffs, N.J.: Prentice-Hall, 1973.

Gouldner, A. *Patterns of industrial bureaucracy.* New York: Free Press, 1954.

Katz, D., and Kahn, R. L. *The social psychology of organizations.* New York: John Wiley & Sons, 1966.

Hackman, J. R., and Lawler, E. E. Employee reactions to job characteristics, *Journal of Applied Psychology,* 1971, *55,* 259–286.

Hackman, J. R., and Morris, C. G. Group tasks, group interaction process and group performance effectiveness: A review and proposed integration. In L. Berkowitz (ed.), *Advances in experimental social psychology.* New York: Academic Press, 1976.

Hackman, J. R., and Oldham, G. R. Development of the job diagnostic survey. *Journal of Applied Psychology,* 1975, *60,* 159–170.

Lawrence, P. R., and Lorsch, J. W. *Organization and environment: Managing differentiation and integration.* Homewood, Ill.: Richard D. Irwin, 1969.

Leavitt, H. J. Applied organizational change in industry. In J. G. March (ed.), *Handbook of organizations.* Chicago: Rand McNally, 1965, 1144–1170.

Likert, R. *The human organization: Its management and value.* New York: McGraw-Hill, 1967.

Lorsch, J. W., and Sheldon, A. The individual in the organization: A systems view. In J. W. Lorsch and P. R. Lawrence (eds.), *Managing group and intergroup relations.* Homewood, Ill.: Irwin-Dorsey, 1972.

Mintzberg, H. *The nature of managerial work.* New York: Harper & Row, 1973.

Newman, W. H., and Logan, J. P. *Strategy, policy, and central management,* 7th ed. Cincinnati, Ohio: South-Western Publishing Co., 1976.

Roethlisberger, F. J., and Dickson, W. J. *Management and the worker.* Cambridge, Mass.: Harvard University Press, 1939 (also New York: Wiley, 1964).

Rogers, E. M., and Shoemaker, F. F. *Communciation of innovations: A cross-cultural approach.* New York: Free Press, 1971.

Schein, E. H. *Organizational psychology.* Englewood Cliffs, N.J.: Prentice-Hall, 1970.

Seiler, J. A. *Systems analysis in organizational behavior.* Homewood, Ill.: Irwin-Dorsey, 1967.

Strauss, G. Tactics of lateral relationships. *Administrative Science Quarterly,* 1962, *7,* 161–186.

Tannenbaum, A. S., and Allport, F. H. Personality structure, and group structure: An interpretative study of their relationship through an event structure hypothesis, *Journal of Abnormal and Social Psychology,* 1956, *53,* 272–280.

Trist, E. L., and Bamforth, R. Some social and psychological consequences of the long wall method of coal-getting. *Human Relations,* 1951, *4,* 3–38.

Turner, A. N., and Lawrence, P. R. *Industrial jobs and the worker.* Boston: Harvard University School of Business Administration, 1965.

Von Bertalanffy, L. *General systems theory: Foundations, development, applications,* rev. ed. New York: Braziller, 1968.

Vroom, V. H. Some personality determinants of the effects of participation. *Journal of Abnormal and Social Psychology,* 1959, *59,* 322–327.

Vroom, V. H., and Yetton, P. W. *Leadership and decision making.* Pittsburgh, Pa.: University of Pittsburg Press, 1973.

Walton, R. E. The diffusion of new work structures: Explaining why success didn't take. *Organizational Dynamics,* 1975 (Winter), 3–22.

Weick, K. E. *The social psychology of organizing.* Reading, Mass.: Addison-Wesley, 1969.

Whyte, W. F. (ed.) *Money and motivation. An analysis of incentives in industry.* New York: Harper & Row, 1955.

Woodward, J. *Industrial organization: Theory and practice.* New York: Oxford University Press, 1965.

STRUCTURE IS NOT ORGANIZATION

Robert H. Waterman, Jr.
Thomas J. Peters
Julien R. Phillips

The Belgian surrealist René Magritte painted a series of pipes and titled the series *Ceci n'est pas une pipe:* this is not a pipe. The picture of the thing is not the thing. In the same way, a structure is not an organization. We all know that, but like as not, when we reorganize what we do is to restructure. Intellectually all managers and consultants know that much more goes on in the process of organizing than the charts, boxes, dotted lines, position descriptions, and matrices can possibly depict. But all too often we behave as though we didn't know it; if we want change we change the structure.

Early in 1977, a general concern with the problems of organization effectiveness, and a particular concern about the nature of the relationship between structure and organization, led us to assemble an internal task force to review our client work. The natural first step was to talk extensively to consultants and client executives around the world who were known for their skill and experience in organization design. We found that they too were dissatisfied with conventional approaches. All were disillusioned about the usual structural solutions, but they were also skeptical about anyone's ability to do better. In their experience, the techniques of the behavioral sciences were not providing useful alternatives to structural design. True, the notion that structure follows strategy (get the strategy right and the structure follows) looked like an important addition to the organizational tool kit; yet strategy rarely seemed to dictate unique structural solutions. Moreover, the main problem in strategy had turned out to be execution: getting it done. And that, to a very large extent, meant *organization*. So the problem of organization effectiveness threatened to prove circular. The dearth of practical additions to old ways of thought was painfully apparent.

OUTSIDE EXPLORATIONS

Our next step was to look outside for help. We visited a dozen business schools in the United States and Europe and about as many superbly performing companies. Both academic theorists and business leaders, we found, were wrestling with the same concerns.

Our timing in looking at the academic environment was good. The state of theory is in great turmoil but moving toward a new consensus. Some researchers

Source: Reprinted from *Business Horizons,* June 1980. Copyright 1980 by the Foundation for the School of Business at Indiana University. Used with permission.

The authors want to offer special acknowledgement and thanks to Anthony G. Athos of Harvard University, who was instrumental in the development of the 7-S framework and who, in his capacity as our consultant, helped generally to advance our thinking on organization effectiveness.

continue to write about structure, particularly its latest and most modish variant, the matrix organization. But primarily the ferment is around another stream of ideas that follow from some startling premises about the limited capacity of decision makers to process information and reach what we usually think of as "rational" decisions.

The stream that today's researchers are tapping is an old one, started in the late 1930s by Fritz Roethlisberger and Chester Barnard, then both at Harvard (Barnard had been president of New Jersey Bell). They challenged rationalist theory, first—in Roethlisberger's case—on the shop floors of Western Electric's Hawthorne plant. Roethlisberger found that simply *paying attention* provided a stimulus to productivity that far exceeded that induced by formal rewards. In a study of workplace hygiene, they turned the lights up and got an expected productivity increase. Then to validate their results they turned the lights down. But something surprising was wrong: productivity went up again. Attention, they concluded, not working conditions per se, made the difference.

Barnard, speaking from the chief executive's perspective, asserted that the CEO's role is to harness the social forces in the organization, to shape and guide values. He described good value-shapers as *effective* managers, contrasting them with the mere manipulators of formal rewards who dealt only with the narrower concept of *efficiency*.

Barnard's words, though quickly picked up by Herbert Simon (whom we'll come back to later), lay dormant for thirty years while the primary management issues focused on decentralization and structure—the appropriate and burning issue of the time.

But then, as the decentralized structure proved to be less than a panacea for all time, and its substitute, the matrix, ran into worse trouble, Barnard's and Simon's ideas triggered a new wave of thinking. On the theory side, it is exemplified by the work of James March and Karl Weick, who attacked the rational model with a vengeance. Weick suggests that organizations learn—and adapt—very slowly. They pay obsessive attention to internal cues long after their practical value has ceased. Important business assumptions are buried deep in the minutiae of organizational systems and other habitual routines whose origins have been long obscured by time. March goes further. He introduced, only slightly facetiously, the garbage can as an organizational metaphor. March pictures organizational learning and decision making as a stream of choices, solutions, decision makers, and opportunities interacting almost randomly to make decisions that carry the organization toward the future. His observations about large organizations parallel Truman's about the presidency: "You issue orders from this office and if you can find out what happens to them after that, you're a better man that I am."

Other researchers have accumulated data which support this unconventional view. Henry Mintzberg made one of the few rigorous studies of how senior managers actually use time. They don't block out large chunks of time for planning, organizing, motivating, and controlling as some suggest they should. Their time, in fact, is appallingly but perhaps necessarily fragmented. Andrew Pettigrew studied the politics of strategic decision and was fascinated by the inertial properties of organizations. He showed that organizations frequently hold onto faulty assumptions about their world for as long as a decade, despite overwhelming evidence that it has changed and they probably should too.

In sum, what the researchers tell us is: "We can explain why you have problems." In the face of complexity and multiple competing demands, organizations simply can't handle decision making in a totally rational way. Not surprisingly, then, a single blunt instrument-like structure—is unlikely to prove the master tool that can change organizations with best effect.

Somewhat to our surprise, senior executives in the top-performing companies that we interviewed proved to be speaking very much the same language. They were concerned that the inherent limitations of structural approaches could render their companies insensitive to an unstable business environment marked by rapidly changing threats and opportunities from every quarter—competitors, governments, and unions at home and overseas. Their organizations, they said, had to learn how to build capabilities for rapid and flexible response. Their favored tactic was to choose a temporary focus, facing perhaps one major issue this year and another next year or the year after. Yet at the same time, they were acutely aware of their peoples' needs for a stable, unifying value system—a foundation for long-term continuity. Their task, as they saw it, was largely one of preserving internal stability while adroitly guiding the organization's responses to fast-paced external change.

Companies such as IBM, Kodak, Hewlett-Packard, GM, Du Pont, and P&G, then, seem obsessive in their attention to maintaining a stable culture. At the same time, these giants are more responsive than their competitors. Typically, they do not seek responsiveness through major structural shifts. Instead, they seem to rely on a series of temporary devices to focus the attention of the entire organization for a limited time on a single priority goal or environmental threat.

SIMON AS EXEMPLAR

Thirty years ago, in *Administrative Behavior,* Herbert Simon (a 1977 Nobel laureate) anticipated several themes that dominate much of today's thinking about organization. Simon's concepts of "satisficing" (settling for adequate instead of optimal solutions) and "the limits of rationality" were, in effect, nails in the coffin of economic man. His ideas, if correct, are crucial. The economic man paradigm has not only influenced the economists but has also influenced thought about the proper organization and administration of most business enterprises—and, by extension, public administration. Traditional thought has it that economic man is basically seeking to maximize against a set of fairly clear objectives. For organization planners the implications of this are that one can specify objectives, determine their appropriate hierarchy, and then logically determine the "best" organization.

Simon labeled this the "rational" view of the administrative world and said, in effect, that it was all right as far as it went but that it had decided limits. For one, most organizations cannot maximize—the goals are really not that clear. Even if they were, most business managers do not have access to complete information, as the economic model requires, but in reality operate with a set of relatively simple decision rules in order to *limit* the information they really need to process to make most decisions. In other words, the rules we use in order to get on with it in big organizations limit our ability to optimize anything.

Suppose the goal is profit maximization. The definition of profit and its maximization varies widely even within a single organization. Is it earnings growth, quality of earnings, maximum return on equity, or the discounted value of the future earnings stream—and if so, at what discount rate? Moreover, business organizations are basically large social structures with diffuse power. Most of the individuals who make them up have different ideas of what the business ought to be. The few at the top seldom agree entirely on the goals of their enterprise, let alone on maximization against one goal. Typically they will not push their views so hard as to destroy the social structure of their enterprise and, in turn, their own power base.

All this leaves the manager in great difficulty. While the research seems valid and the message of complexity rings true, the most innovative work in the field is descriptive. The challenge to the manager is how to organize better. His goal is organization effectiveness. What the researchers are saying is that the subject is much more complex than any of our past prescriptive models have allowed for. What none has been able to usefully say is, "OK, here's what to do about it."

THE 7-S FRAMEWORK

After a little over a year and a half of pondering this dilemma, we began to formulate a new framework for organizational thought. As we and others have developed it and tested it in teaching, in workshops, and in direct problem solving over the past year, we have found it enormously helpful. It has repeatedly demonstrated its usefulness both in diagnosing the causes of organizational malaise and in formulating programs for improvement. In brief, it seems to work.

Our assertion is that productive organization change is not simply a matter of structure, although structure is important. It is not so simple as the interaction between strategy and structure, although strategy is critical too. Our claim is that effective organizational change is really the relationship between structure, strategy, systems, style, skills, staff, and something we call superordinate goals. (The alliteration is intentional: it serves as an aid to memory.)

Our central idea is that organization effectiveness stems from the interaction of several factors—some not especially obvious and some underanalyzed. Our framework for organization change, graphically depicted in the following exhibit, suggests several important ideas:

- First is the idea of a multiplicity of factors that influence an organization's ability to change and its proper mode of change. Why pay attention to only one or two, ignoring the others? Beyond structure and strategy, there are at least five other identifiable elements. The division is to some extent arbitrary, but it has the merit of acknowledging the complexity identified in the research and segmenting it into manageable parts.
- Second, the diagram is intended to convey the notion of the interconnectedness of the variables—the idea is that it's difficult, perhaps impossible, to make significant

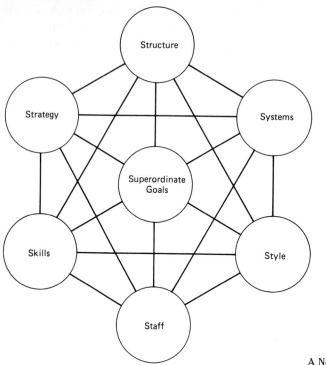

A New View of Organization

progress in one area without making progress in the others as well. Notions of organization change that ignore its many aspects or their interconnectedness are dangerous.

- In a recent article on strategy, *Fortune* commented that perhaps as many as 90 percent of carefully planned strategies don't work. If that is so, our guess would be that the failure is a failure in execution, resulting from inattention to the other S's. Just as a logistics bottleneck can cripple a military strategy, inadequate systems or staff can make paper tigers of the best-laid plans for clobbering competitors.

- Finally, the shape of the diagram is significant. It has no starting point or implied hierarchy. A priori, it isn't obvious which of the seven factors will be the driving force in changing a particular organization at a particular point in time. In some cases, the critical variable might be strategy. In others, it could be systems or structure.

Structure

To understand this model of organization change better, let us look at each of its elements, beginning—as most organization discussions do—with structure. What will the new organization of the 1980s be like? If decentralization was the trend of the past, what is next? Is it matrix organization? What will "Son of Matrix" look like? Our answer is that those questions miss the point.

To see why, let's take a quick look at the history of structural thought and development. The basic theory underlying structure is simple. Structure divides tasks and then provides coordination. It trades off specialization and integration. It decentralizes and then recentralizes.

The old structural division was between production and sales. The chart showing this was called a functional organization. Certain principles of organization, such as one-man/one-boss, limited span of control, grouping of like activities, and commensurate authority and responsibility, seemed universal truths.

What happened to this simple idea? Size and complexity. A company like General Electric has grown over a thousandfold in both sales and earnings in the past eighty years. Much of its growth has come through entry into new and diverse businesses. At a certain level of size and complexity, a functional organization, which is dependent on frequent interaction among all activities, breaks down. As the number of people or businesses increases arithmetically, the number of interactions required to make things work increases geometrically. A company passing a certain size and complexity threshold must decentralize to cope.

Among the first to recognize the problem and explicitly act on it was Du Pont in 1921. The increasing administrative burden brought about by its diversification into several new product lines ultimately led the company to transform its highly centralized, functionally departmental structure into a decentralized, multidivisional one. Meanwhile, General Motors, which has been decentralized from the outset, was learning how to make a decentralized structure work as more than just a holding company.

However, real decentralization in world industry did not take place until much later. In 1950, for example, only about 20 percent of the *Fortune 500* companies were decentralized. By 1970, 80 percent were decentralized. A similar shift was taking place throughout the industrialized world.

Today three things are happening. First, because of the portfolio concept of managing a business, spun off from General Electric research (which has now become PIMS), companies are saying, "We can do more with our decentralized structure than control complexity. We can shift resources, act flexibly—that is, manage strategically."

Second, the dimensions along which companies want to divide tasks have multiplied. Early on, there were functional divisions. Then came product divisions. Now we have possibilities for division by function, product, market, geography, nation, strategic business unit, and probably more. The rub is that as the new dimensions are added, the old ones don't go away. An insurance company, for example, can organize around market segments, but it still needs functional control over underwriting decisions. The trade-offs are staggering if we try to juggle them all at once.

Third, new centralist forces have eclipsed clean, decentralized divisions of responsibility. In Europe, for example, a company needs a coherent union strategy. In Japan, especially, companies need a centralized approach to the government interface. In the United States, regulation and technology force centralization in the interest of uniformity.

This mess has produced a new organization form: the matrix, which purports, at least in concept, to reconcile the realities of organizational complexity with the imperatives of managerial control. Unfortunately, the two-dimensional matrix model is intrinsically too simple to capture the real situation. Any spatial model that really did capture it would be incomprehensible.

Matrix does, however, have one well-disguised virtue: it calls attention to the central problem in structuring today. That problem is not the one on which most organization designers spend their time—that is, how to divide up tasks. It is one of emphasis and coordination—how to make the whole thing work. The challenge lies not so much in trying to comprehend all the possible dimensions of organization structure as in developing the ability to focus on those dimensions which are currently important to the organization's evolution—and to be ready to refocus as the crucial dimensions shift. General Motors' restless use of structural change—most recently the project center, which led to their effective downsizing effort—is a case in point.

The General Motors solution has a critical attribute—the use of a temporary overlay to accomplish a strategic task. IBM, Texas Instruments, and others have used similar temporary structural weapons. In the process, they have meticulously preserved the shape and spirit of the underlying structure (e.g., the GM division or the TI Product Customer Center). We regularly observe those two attributes among our sample of top performers: the use of the temporary and the maintenance of the simple underlying form.

We speculate that the effective "structure of the eighties" will more likely be described as "flexible" or "temporary"; this matrix-like property will be preserved even as the current affair with the formal matrix structure cools.

Strategy

If structure is not enough, what is? Obviously, there is strategy. It was Alfred Chandler who first pointed out that structure follows strategy, or more precisely, that a strategy of diversity forces a decentralized structure.[1] Throughout the past decade, the corporate world has given close attention to the interplay between strategy and structure. Certainly, clear ideas about strategy make the job of structural design more rational.

By "strategy" we mean those actions that a company plans in response to or anticipation of changes in its external environment—its customers, its competitors. Strategy is the way a company aims to improve its position vis-à-vis competition—perhaps through low-cost production or delivery, perhaps by providing better value to the customer, perhaps by achieving sales and service dominance. It is, or ought to be, an organization's way of saying: "Here is how we will create unique value."

As the company's chosen route to competitive success, strategy is obviously a central concern in many business situations—especially in highly competitive industries where the game is won or lost on share points. But "structure follows strategy" is by no means the be-all and end-all of organization wisdom. We find too many examples of large, prestigious companies around the world that are replete with strategy and cannot execute any of it. There is little if anything wrong with their structures; the causes of their inability to execute like in other dimensions of our framework. When we turn to nonprofit and public-sector organizations,

---

[1] Alfred D. Chandler, Jr., *Strategy and Structure: Chapters in the History of the American Industrial Enterprise* (Cambridge, Mass.: MIT Press, 1962).

moreover, we find that the whole meaning of "strategy" is tenuous—but the problem of organizational effectiveness looms as large as ever.

Strategy, then, is clearly a critical variable in organization design—but much more is at work.

Systems

By systems we mean all the procedures, formal and informal, that make the organization go, day by day and year by year: capital budgeting systems, training systems, cost accounting procedures, budgeting systems. If there is a variable in our model that threatens to dominate the others, it could well be systems. Do you want to understand how an organization really does (or doesn't) get things done? Look at the systems. Do you want to change an organization without disruptive restructuring? Try changing the systems.

A large consumer goods manufacturer was recently trying to come up with an overall corporate strategy. Textbook portfolio theory seemed to apply: Find a good way to segment the business, decide which segments in the total business portfolio are most attractive, invest most heavily in those. The only catch: Reliable cost data by segment were not to be had. The company's management information system was not adequate to support the segmentation.

Again, consider how a bank might go about developing a strategy. A natural first step, it would seem, would be to segment the business by customer and product to discover where the money is made and lost and why. But in trying to do this, most banks almost immediately come up against an intractable costing problem. Because borrowers are also depositors, because transaction volumes vary, because the balance sheet turns fast, and because interest costs are half or more of total costs and unpredictable over the long term, costs for various market segments won't stay put. A strategy based on today's costs could be obsolete tomorrow.

One bank we know has rather successfully sidestepped the problem. Its key to future improvement is not strategy but the systems infrastructure that will allow account officers to negotiate deals favorable to the bank. For them the system *is* the strategy. Development and implementation of a superior account profitability system, based on a return-on-equity tree, has improved their results dramatically. "Catch a fish for a man and he is fed for a day; teach him to fish and he is fed for life": The proverb applies to organizations in general and to systems in particular.

Another intriguing aspect of systems is the way they mirror the state of an organization. Consider a certain company we'll call International Wickets. For years management has talked about the need to become more market oriented. Yet astonishingly little time is spent in their planning meetings on customers, marketing, market share, or other issues having to do with market orientation. One of their key systems, in other words, remains *very* internally oriented. Without a change in this key system, the market orientation goal will remain unattainable no matter how much change takes place in structure and strategy.

To many business managers the word "systems" has a dull, plodding, middle-management sound. Yet it is astonishing how powerfully systems changes can enhance organizational effectiveness—without the disruptive side effects that so often ensue from tinkering with structure.

Style

It is remarkable how often writers, in characterizing a corporate management for the business press, fall back on the word "style." Tony O'Reilly's style at Heinz is certainly not AT&T's, yet both are successful. The trouble we have with style is not in recognizing its importance, but in doing much about it. Personalities don't change, or so the conventional wisdom goes.

We think it important to distinguish between the basic personality of a top-management team and the way that team comes across to the organization. Organizations may listen to what managers say, but they believe what managers do. Not words, but patterns of actions are decisive. The power of style, then, is essentially manageable.

One element of a manager's style is how he or she chooses to spend time. As Henry Mintzberg has pointed out, managers don't spend their time in the neatly compartmentalized planning, organizing, motivating, and controlling modes of classical management theory.[2] Their days are a mess—or so it seems. There's a seeming infinity of things they might devote attention to. No top executive attends to all of the demands on his time; the median time spent on any one issue is nine minutes.

What can a top manager do in nine minutes? Actually, a good deal. He can signal what's on his mind; he can reinforce a message; he can nudge people's thinking in a desired direction. Skillful management of his inevitably fragmented time is, in fact, an immensely powerful change lever.

By way of example, we have found differences beyond anything attributable to luck among different companies' success rations in finding oil or mineral deposits. A few years ago, we surveyed a fairly large group of the finders and nonfinders in mineral exploration to discover what they were doing differently. The finders almost always said their secret was "top-management attention." Our reaction was skeptical: "Sure, that's the solution to most problems." But subsequent hard analysis showed that their executives *were* spending more time in the field, *were* blocking out more time for exploration discussions at board meetings, and *were* making more room on their own calendars for exploration-related activities.

Another aspect of style is symbolic behavior. Taking the same example, the successful finders typically have more people on the board who understand exploration or have headed exploration departments. Typically they fund exploration more consistently (that is, their year-to-year spending patterns are less volatile). They define fewer and more consistent exploration targets. Their exploration activities typically report at a higher organizational level. And they typically articulate better reasons for exploring in the first place.

A chief executive of our acquaintance is fond of saying that the way you recognize a marketing-oriented company is that "everyone talks marketing." He doesn't mean simply that an observable preoccupation with marketing is the end result, the final indication of the company's evaluation toward the marketplace. He means that it can be the lead. Change in orientation often starts when enough

[2]Henry Mintzberg, "The Manager's Job: Folklore and Fact," *Harvard Business Review,* July/August 1975: 49-61.

people talk about it before they really know what "it" is. Strategic management is not yet a crisply defined concept, but many companies are taking it seriously. If they talk about it enough, it will begin to take on specific meaning for their organizations—and those organizations will change as a result.

This suggests a second attribute of style that is by no means confined to those at the top. Our proposition is that a corporation's style, as a reflection of its culture, has more to do with its ability to change organization or performance than is generally recognized. One company, for example, was considering a certain business opportunity. From a strategic standpoint, analysis showed it to be a winner. The experience of others in the field confirmed that. Management went ahead with the acquisition. Two years later it backed out of the business, at a loss. The acquisition had failed because it simply want's consistent with the established corporate culture of the parent organization. It didn't fit their view of themselves. The will to make it work was absent.

Time and again strategic possibilities are blocked—or slowed down—by cultural constraints. One of today's more dramatic examples is the Bell System, where management has undertaken to move a service-oriented culture toward a new and different kind of marketing. The service idea, and its meaning to AT&T, is so deeply embedded in the Bell System's culture that the shift to a new kind of marketing will take years.

The phenomenon at its most dramatic comes to the fore in mergers. In almost every merger, no matter how closely related the businesses, the task of integrating and achieving eventual synergy is a problem no less difficult than combining two cultures. At some level of detail, almost everything done by two parties to a merger will be done differently. This helps explain why the management of acquisitions is so hard. If the two cultures are not integrated, the planned synergies will not accrue. On the other hand, to change too much too soon is to risk uprooting more tradition than can be replanted before the vital skills of the acquiree wither and die.

Staff

Staff (in the sense of people, not line/staff) is often treated in one of two ways. At the hard end of the spectrum, we talk of appraisal systems, pay scales, formal training programs, and the like. At the soft end, we talk about morale, attitude, motivation, and behavior.

Top management is often, and justifiably, turned off by both these approaches. The first seems too trivial for their immediate concern ("Leave it to the personnel department"), the second too intractable ("We don't want a bunch of shrinks running around, stirring up the place with more attitude surveys").

Our predilection is to broaden and redefine the nature of the people issue. What do the top-performing companies do to foster the process of developing managers? How, for example, do they shape the basic values of their management cadre? Our reason for asking the question at all is simply that no serious discussion of organization can afford to ignore it (although many do). Our reason for framing the question around the development of managers is our observation that the superbly performing companies pay extraordinary attention to managing what might be called the socialization process in their companies. This applies especially to the way they introduce young recruits into the mainstream of their organizations and to the way they manage their careers as the recruits develop into tomorrow's managers.

The process for orchestrating the early careers of incoming managers, for instance, at IBM, Texas Instruments, P&G, Hewlett-Packard, or Citibank is quite different from its counterpart in many other companies we know around the world. Unlike other companies, which often seem prone to sidetrack young but expensive talent into staff positions or other jobs out of the mainstream of the company's business, these leaders take extraordinary care to turn young managers' first jobs into first opportunities for contributing in practical ways to the nuts-and-bolts of what the business is all about. If the mainstream of the business is innovation, for example, the first job might be in new-products introduction. If the mainstream of the business is marketing, the MBA's first job could be sales or product management.

The companies who use people best rapidly move their managers into positions of real responsibility, often by the early- to mid-thirties. Various active support devices like assigned mentors, fast-track programs, and carefully orchestrated opportunities for exposure to top management are hallmarks of their management of people.

In addition, these companies are all particularly adept at managing, in a special and focused way, their central cadre of key managers. At Texas Instruments, Exxon, GM, and GE, for instance, a number of the very most senior executives are said to devote several weeks of each year to planning the progress of the top few hundred.

These, then, are a few examples of practical programs through which the superior companies manage people as aggressively and concretely as others manage organization structure. Considering people as a pool of resources to be nurtured, developed, guarded, and allocated is one of the many ways to turn the "staff" dimension of our 7-S framework into something not only amenable to, but worthy of practical control by senior management.

We are often told, "Get the structure 'right' and the people will fit" or "Don't compromise the 'optimum' organization for people considerations." At the other end of the spectrum we are earnestly advised, "The right people can make any organization work." Neither view is correct. People do count, but staff is only one of our seven variables.

Skills

We added the notion of skills for a highly practical reason: It enables us to capture a company's crucial attributes as no other concept can do. A strategic description of a company, for example, might typically cover markets to be penetrated or types of products to be sold. But how do most of us characterize companies? Not by their strategies or their structures. We tend to characterize them by what they do best. We talk of IBM's orientation to the marketplace, its prodigious customer service capabilities, or its sheer market power. We talk of Du Pont's research prowess, Procter & Gamble's product management capability,

ITT's financial controls, Hewlett-Packard's innovation and quality, and Texas Instruments' project management. These dominating attributes, or capabilities, are what we mean by skills.

Now why is this distinction important? Because we regularly observe that organizations facing big discontinuities in business conditions must do more than shift strategic focus. Frequently they need to add a new capability, that is to say, a new skill. The Bell System, for example, is currently striving to add a formidable new array of marketing skills. Small copier companies, upon growing larger, find that they must radically enhance their service capabilities to compete with Xerox. Meanwhile Xerox needs to enhance its response capability in order to fend off a host of new competition. These dominating capability needs, unless explicitly labeled as such, often get lost as the company "attacks a new market" (strategy shift) or "decentralizes to give managers autonomy" (structure shift).

Additionally, we frequently find it helpful to *label* current skills, for the addition of a new skill may come only when the old one is dismantled. Adopting a newly "flexible and adaptive marketing thrust," for example, may be possible only if increases are accepted in certain marketing or distribution costs. Dismantling some of the distracting attributes of an old "manufacturing mentality" (that is, a skill that was perhaps crucial in the past) may be the only way to insure the success of an important change program. Possibly the most difficult problem in trying to organize effectively is that of weeding out old skills—and their supporting systems, structures, etc.—to ensure that important new skills can take root and grow.

Superordinate Goals

The word "superordinate" literally means "of higher order." By superordinate goals, we mean guiding concepts—a set of values and aspirations, often unwritten, that goes beyond the conventional formal statement of corporate objectives.

Superordinate goals are the fundamental ideas around which a business is built. They are its main values. But they are more as well. They are the broad notions of future direction that the top management team wants to infuse throughout the organization. They are the way in which the team wants to express itself, to leave its own mark. Examples would include Theodore Vail's "universal service" objective, which has so dominated AT&T; the strong drive to "customer service" which guides IBM's marketing; GE's slogan, "Progress is our most important product," which encourages engineers to tinker and innovate throughout the organization; Hewlett-Packard's "innovative people at all levels in the organization"; Dana's obsession with productivity, as a total organization, not just a few at the top; and 3M's dominating culture of "new products."

In a sense, superordinate goals are like the basic postulates in a mathematical system. They are the starting points on which the system is logically built, but in themselves are not logically derived. The ultimate test of their value is not their logic but the usefulness of the system that ensues. Everyone seems to know the importance of compelling superordinate goals. The drive for their accomplishment pulls an organization together. They provide stability in what would otherwise be a shifting set of organization dynamics.

Unlike the other six S's, superordinate goals don't seem to be present in all, or even most, organizations. They are, however, evident in most of the superior performers.

To be readily communicated, superordiante goals need to be succinct. Typically, therefore, they are expressed at high levels of abstraction and may mean very little to outsiders who don't know the organization well. But for those inside, they are rich with significance. Within an organization, superordinate goals, if well articulated, make meanings for people. And making meanings is one of the main functions of leadership.

CONCLUSION

We have passed rapidly through the variables in our framework. What should the reader have gained from the exercise?

We started with the premise that solutions to today's thorny organizing problems that invoke only structure—or even strategy and structure—are seldom adequate. The inadequacy stems in part from the inability of the two-variable model to explain why organizations are so slow to adapt to change. The reasons often lie among our other variables: systems that embody outdated assumptions, a management style that is at odds with the stated strategy, the absence of a superordinate goal that binds the organization together in pursuit of a common purpose, the refusal to deal concretely with "people problems" and opportunities.

At its most trivial, when we merly use the framework as a checklist, we find that it leads into new terrain in our efforts to understand how organizations really operate or to design a truly comprehensive change program. At a minimum, it gives us a deeper bag in which to collect our experiences.

More importantly, it suggests the wisdom of taking seriously the variables in organizing that have been considered soft, informal, or beneath the purview of top management interest. We believe that style, systems, skills, superordinate goals can be observed directly, even measured—if only they are taken seriously. We think that these variables can be at least as important as strategy and structure in orchestrating major change; indeed, that they are almost critical for achieving necessary, or desirable, change. A shift in systems, a major retraining program for staff, or the generation of top-to-bottom enthusiasm around a new superordinate goal could take years. Changes in strategy and structure, on the surface, may happen more quickly. But the pace of real change is geared to all seven S's.

At its most powerful and complex, the framework forces us to concentrate on interactions and fit. The real energy required to redirect an institution comes when all the variables in the model are aligned. One of our associates looks at our diagram as a set of compasses. "When all seven needles are all pointed the same way," he comments, "you're looking at an *organized* company."

18
Organization Design

MANAGING INNOVATION: CONTROLLED CHAOS
James Brian Quinn

SOCIOTECHNICAL CONSIDERATIONS FOR THE DEVELOPMENT
OF THE SPACE STATION: AUTONOMY AND THE HUMAN ELEMENT IN SPACE
Claudia Bird Schoonhoven

RESTORING AMERICAN COMPETITIVENESS:
LOOKING FOR NEW MODELS OF ORGANIZATIONS
Tom Peters

MANAGING INNOVATION: CONTROLLED CHAOS

James Brian Quinn

Management observers frequently claim that small organizations are more innovative than large ones. But is this commonplace necessarily true? Some large enterprises are highly innovative. How do they do it? Can lessons from these companies and their smaller counterparts help other companies become more innovative?

This article proposes some answers to these questions based on the initial results of an ongoing 2½ year worldwide study. The research sample includes both well-documented small ventures and large U.S., Japanese, and European companies and programs selected for their innovation records. More striking than the cultural differences among these companies are the similarities between innovative small and large organizations and among innovative organizations in different countries. Effective management of innovation seems much the same, regardless of national boundaries or scale of operations.

There are, of course, many reasons why small companies appear to produce a disproportionate number of innovations. First, innovation occurs in a probabilistic setting. A company never knows whether a particular technical result can be achieved and whether it will succeed in the marketplace. For every new solution that succeeds, tens to hundreds fail. The sheer number of attempts—most by small-scale entrepreneurs—means that some ventures will survive. The 90% to 99% that fail are distributed widely throughout society and receive little notice.

On the other hand, a big company that wishes to move a concept from invention to the marketplace must absorb all potential failure costs itself. This risk may be socially or managerially intolerable, jeopardizing the many other products, projects, jobs, and communities the company supports. Even if its innovation is successful, a big company may face costs that newcomers do not bear, like converting existing operations and customer bases to the new solution.

By contrast, a new enterprise does not risk losing an existing investment base or cannibalizing customer franchises built at great expense. It does not have to change an internal culture that has successfully supported doing things another way or that has developed intellectual depth and belief in the technologies that led to past successes. Organized groups like labor unions, consumer advocates, and government bureaucracies rarely monitor and resist a small company's moves as they might a big company's. Finally, new companies do not face the psychological pain and the economic costs of laying off employees, shutting down plants and even communities, and displacing supplier relationships built with years of mutual commitment and effort. Such barriers to change in large organizations are real, important, and legitimate.

The complex products and systems that society expects large companies to undertake further compound the risks. Only big companies can develop new ships or locomotives; telecommunication networks; or systems for space, defense, air traffic control, hospital care, mass foods delivery, or nationwide computer interactions. These large-scale projects always carry more risk than single-product introductions. A billion-dollar development aircraft, for example, can fail if one inexpensive part in its 100,000 components fails.

Clearly, a single enterprise cannot by itself develop or produce all the parts needed by such large new systems. And communications among the various groups making design and production decisions on components are always incomplete. The probability of error increases exponentially with complexity, while the system innovator's control over decisions decreases significantly—further escalating potential error costs and risks. Such forces inhibit innovation in large organizations. But proper management can lessen these effects.

OF INVENTORS & ENTREPRENEURS

A close look at innovative small enterprises reveals much about the successful management of innovation. Of course, not all innovations follow a single pattern. But my research—and other studies in combination—suggest that the following factors are crucial to the success of innovative small companies.

Need Orientation

Inventor-entrepreneuers tend to be "need or achievement oriented."[1] They

[1] David McClelland, *The Achieving Society* (New York: Halsted Press, 1976); Gene Bvlinksy, *The Innovation Millionaires* (New York: Scribner's, 1976).

576

believe that if they "do the job better," rewards will follow. They may at first focus on their own view of market needs. But lacking resources, successful small entrepreneurs soon find that it pays to approach potential customers early, test their solutions in users' hands, learn from these interactions, and adapt designs rapidly. Many studies suggest that effective technological innovation develops hand-in-hand with customer demand.[2]

Experts and Fanatics

Company founders tend to be pioneers in their technologies and fanatic when it comes to solving problems. They are often described as "possessed" or "obsessed," working toward their objectives to the exclusion even of family or personal relationships. As both experts and fanatics, they perceive probabilities of success as higher than others do. And their commitment allows them to persevere despite the frustrations, ambiguities, and setbacks that always accompany major innovations.

Long Time Horizons

Their fanaticism may cause inventor-entrepreneurs to underestimate the obstacles and length of time to success. Time horizons for radical innovations make them essentially "irrational" from a present value viewpoint. In my sample, delays between intervention and commercial production ranged from 3 to 25 years.[3] In the late 1930s, for example, industrial chemist Russell Marker was working on steroids called sapogenins when he discovered a technique that would degrade one of these, diosgenin, into the female sex hormone progesterone. By processing some ten tons of Mexican yams in rented and borrowed lab space, Marker finally extracted about four pounds of diosgenin and started a tiny business to produce steroids for the laboratory market. But it was not until 1962, over 23 years later, that Syntex, the company Marker founded, obtained FDA approval for its oral contraceptive.

For both psychological and practical reasons, inventor-entrepreneuers generally avoid early formal plans, proceed step-by-step, and sustain themselves by other income and the momentum of the small advances they achieve as they go along.

Low Early Costs

Innovators tend to work in homes, basements, warehouses, or low-rent facilities whenever possible. They incur few overhead costs; their limited resources go directly into their projects. They pour nights, weekends, and "sweat capital" into their endeavors. They borrow whatever they can. They invent cheap equipment and prototype processes, often improving on what is available in the marketplace. If one approach fails, few people know; little time or money is lost.

[2]Eric von Hippel, "Get New Products From Customers," HBR March–April 1982, p. 117.

[3]A study at Battelle found an average of 19.2 years between invention and commercial production. Battelle Memorial Laboratories, "Science, Technology, and Innovation" Report to the National Science Foundation 1973; R. C. Dean, "The Temporal Mismatch Innovation's Pace vs. Management's Time Horizon," *Research Management,* May 1974, p. 13.

All this decreases the costs and risks facing a small operation and improves the present value of its potential success.

Multiple Approaches

Technology tends to advance through a series of random—often highly intuitive—insights frequently triggered by gratuitous interactions between the discoverer and the outside world. Only highly committed entrepreneurs can tolerate (and even enjoy) this chaos. They adopt solutions wherever they can be found, unencumbered by formal plans or PERT charts that would limit the range of their imaginations. When the odds of success are low, the participation and interaction of many motivated players increase the chance that one will succeed.

A recent study of initial public offerings made in 1962 shows that only 2% survived and still looked like worthwhile investments 20 years later.[4] Small-scale entrepreneurship looks efficient in part because history only records the survivors.

Flexibility and Quickness

Undeterred by committees, broad approvals, and other bureaucratic delays, the inventor-entrepreneur can experiment, test, recycle, and try again with little time lost. Because technological progress depends largely on the number of successful experiments accomplished per unit of time, fast-moving small entrepreneurs can gain both timing and performance advantages over clumsier competitors. This responsiveness is often crucial in finding early markets for radical innovations where neither innovators, market researchers, nor users can quite visualize a product's real potential. For example, Edison's lights first appeared on ships and in baseball parks; Astroturf was intended to convert the flat roofs and asphalt of playgrounds of city schools into more humane environments; and graphite and boron composites designed for aerospace unexpectedly found their largest markets in sporting goods. Entrepreneurs quickly adjusted their entry strategies to market feedback.

Incentives

Inventor-entrepreneurs can foresee tangible personal rewards if they are successful. Individuals often want to achieve a technical contribution, recognition, power, or sheer independence, as much as money. For the original, driven personalities who create significant innovations, few other paths offer such clear opportunities to fulfill all their economic, psychological, and career goals at once. Consequently, they do not panic or quit when others with solely monetary goals might.

Availability of Capital

One of America's great competitive advantages is its rich variety of sources to finance small, low-probability ventures. If entrepreneurs are turned down by one source, other sources can be sought in myriads of creative combinations.

[4]Business Economics Group, W. R. Grace & Co., 1983.

Professionals involved in such financings have developed a characteristic approach to deal with the chaos and uncertainty of innovation. First, they evaluate a proposal's conceptual validity: If the technical problems can be solved, is there a real business there for someone and does it have a large upside potential? Next, they concentrate on people: Is the team thoroughly committed and expert? Is it the best available? Only then do these financiers analyze specific financial estimates in depth. Even then, they recognize that actual outcomes generally depend on subjective factors, not numbers.[5]

Timeliness, aggressiveness, commitment, quality of people, and the flexibility to attack opportunities not at first perceived are crucial. Downside risks are minimized, not by detailed controls, but by spreading risks among multiple projects, keeping early costs low, and gauging the tenacity, flexibility, and capability of the founders.

BUREAUCRATIC BARRIERS TO INNOVATION

Less innovative companies and, unfortunately, most large corporations operate in a very different fashion. The most notable and common constraints on innovation in larger companies include:

Top Management Isolation

Many senior executives in big companies have little contact with conditions on the factory floor or with customers who might influence their thinking about technological innovation. Since risk perception is inversely related to familiarity and experience, financially oriented top managers are likely to perceive technological innovations as more problematic than acquisitions that may be just as risky but that will appear more familiar.[6]

Intolerance of Fanatics

Big companies often view entrepreneurial fanatics as embarrassments or troublemakers. Many major cities are now ringed by companies founded by these "nonteam" players—often to the regret of their former employers.

Short Time Horizons

The perceived corporate need to report a continuous stream of quarterly profits conflicts with the long time spans that major innovations normally require. Such pressures often make publicly owned companies favor quick marketing fixes,

---

[5]Christina C. Pence, *How Venture Capitalists Make Venture Decisions* (Ann Arbor, Mich.: UMI Research Press, 1982).

[6]Robert H. Hayes and David A. Garvin, "Managing as if Tomorrow Mattered," HBR May-June 1982, p. 70; Robert H. Hayes and William J. Abernathy, "Managing Our Way to Economic Decline," HBR July-August 1980, p. 67.

cost cutting, and acquisition strategies over process, product, or quality innovations that would yield much more in the long run.

Accounting Practices

By assessing all its direct, indirect, overtime, and service costs against a project, large corporations have much higher development expenses compared with entrepreneurs working in garages. A project in a big company can quickly become an exposed political target, its potential net present value may sink unacceptably, and an entry into small markets may not justify its sunk costs. An otherwise viable project may soon founder and disappear.

Excessive Rationalism

Managers in big companies often seek orderly advance through early market research studies or PERT planning. Rather than managing the inevitable chaos of innovation productively, these managers soon drive out the very things that lead to innovation in order to prove their announced plans.

Excessive Bureaucracy

In the name of efficiency, bureaucratic structures require many approvals and cause delays at every turn. Experiments that a small company can perform in hours may take days or weeks in large organizations. The interactive feedback that fosters innovation is lost, important time windows can be missed, and real costs and risks rise for the corporation.

Inappropriate Incentives

Reward and control systems in most big companies are designed to minimize surprises. Yet innovation, by definition, is full of surprises. It often disrupts well-laid plans, accepted power patterns, and entrenched organizational behavior at high costs to many. Few large companies make millionaires of those who create such disruptions, however profitable the innovations may turn out to be. When control systems neither penalize opportunities missed nor reward risks taken, the results are predictable.

HOW LARGE INNOVATIVE COMPANIES DO IT

Yet some big companies are continuously innovative. Although each such enterprise is distinctive, the successful big innovators I studied have developed techniques that emulate or improve on their smaller counterparts' practices. What are the most important patterns?

Atmosphere and Vision

Continuous innovation occurs largely because top executives appreciate innovation and manage their company's value system and atmosphere to support it.

For example, Sony's founder, Masaru Ibuka, stated in the company's "Purposes of Incorporation" the goal of a "free, dynamic, and pleasant factory...where sincerely motivated personnel can exercise their technological skills to the highest level." Ibuka and Sony's chairman, Akio Morita, inculcated the "Sony spirit" through a series of unusual policies: hiring brilliant people with nontraditional skills (like an opera singer) for high management positions, promoting young people over their elders, designing a new type of living accommodation for workers, and providing visible awards for outstanding technical achievements.

Because familiarity can foster understanding and psychological comfort, engineering and scientific leaders are often those who create atmospheres supportive of innovation, especially in a company's early life. Executive vision is more important than a particular management background—as IBM, Genentech, AT&T, Merck, Elf Aquitaine, Pilkington, and others in my sample illustrate. CEOs of these companies value technology and include technical experts in their highest decision circles.

Innovative managements—whether technical or not—project clear long-term visions for their organizations that go beyond simple economic measures. As Intel's chairman, Gordon Moore, says: "We intend to be the outstandingly successful innovative company in this industry: We intend to continue to be a leader in this revolutionary (semiconductor) technology that is changing the way this world is run." Genentech's original plan expresses a similar vision: We expect to be the first company to commercialize the [rDNA] technology, and we plan to build a major profitable corporation by manufacturing and marketing needed products that benefit mankind. The future uses of genetic engineering are far reaching and many. Any product produced by a living organism is eventually within the company's reach."

Such visions, vigorously supported, are not "management fluff," but have many practical implications. They attract quality people to the company and give focus to their creative and entrepreneurial drives. When combined with sound internal operations, they help channel growth by concentrating attention on the actions that lead to profitability, rather than on profitability itself. Finally, these visions recognize a realistic time frame for innovation and attract the kind of investors who will support it.

Orientation to the Market

Innovative companies tie their visions to the practical realities of the marketplace. Although each company uses techniques adapted to its own style and strategy; two elements are always present: a strong market orientation at the very top of the company and mechanisms to ensure interactions between technical and marketing people at lower levels. At Sony, for example, soon after technical people are hired, the company runs them through weeks of retail selling. Sony engineers become sensitive to the ways retail sales practices, product displays, and nonquantifiable customer preferences affect success. Similarly, before AT&T's recent divestiture, Bell Laboratories had an Operating Company Assignment Program to rotate its researchers through AT&T and Western Electric development and production facilities. And it had a rigorous Engineering Complaint System that collected technical problems from operating companies and required Bell Labs to specify within a few weeks how it would resolve or attack each problem.

From top to bench levels in my sample's most innovative companies, managers focus primarily on seeking to anticipate and solve customers' emerging problems.

Small, Flat Organizations

The most innovative large companies in my sample try to keep the total organization flat and project teams small. Development teams normally include only six or seven key people. This number seems to constitute a critical mass of skills while fostering maximum communication and commitment among members. According to research done by my colleague, Victor McGee, the number of channels of communication increases as $n[2(n-1)-1]$. Therefore:

For team size	=	1	2	3	4	5	6	7	8	9	10	11
Channels	=	1	2	9	28	75	186	441	1016	2295	5110	11253

Innovative companies also try to keep their operating divisions and total technical units small—below 400 people. Up to this number, only two layers of management are required to maintain a span of control over 7 people. In units much larger than 400, people quickly lose touch with the concept of their product or process, staffs and bureaucracies tend to grow, and projects may go through too many formal screens to survive. Since it takes a chain of yesses and only one no to kill a project, jeopardy multiplies as management layers increase.

Multiple Approaches

At first one cannot be sure which of several technical approaches will dominate a field. The history of technology is replete with accidents, mishaps, and chance meetings that allowed one approach or group to emerge rapidly over others. Leo Baekelund was looking for a synthetic shellac when he found Bakelite and started the modem plastics industry. At Syntex, researchers were not looking for an oral contraceptive when they created 19-norprogesterone, the precursor to the active ingredient in half of all contraceptive pills. And the microcomputer was born because Intel's Ted Hoff "happened" to work on a complex calculator just when Digital Equipment Corporation's PDP8 architecture was fresh in his mind.

Such "accidents" are involved in almost all major technological advances. When theory can predict everything, a company has moved to a new stage, from development to production. Murphy's law works because engineers design for what they can foresee; hence what fails is what theory could not predict. And it is rare that the interactions of components and subsystems can be predicted over the lifetime of operations. For example, despite careful theoretical design work, the first high performance jet engine literally tore itself to pieces on its test stand, while others failed in unanticipated operating conditions (like an Iranian sandstorm).

Recognizing the inadequacies of theory, innovative enterprises seem to move faster from paper studies to physical testing than to noninnovative enterprises. When possible, they encourage several prototype programs to proceed in parallel.

Sony pursued 10 major options in developing its videotape recorder technology. Each option had two to three subsystem alternatives. Such redundancy helps the company cope with uncertainties in development, motivates people through competition, and improves the amount and quality of information available for making final choices on scale-ups or introductions.

Developmental Shoot-Outs

Many companies structure shoot-outs among competing approaches only after they reach the prototype stages. They find this practice provides more objective information for making decisions, decreases risk by making choices that best reflect marketplace needs, and helps ensure that the winning option will move ahead with a committed team behind it. Although many managers worry that competing approaches may be inefficient, greater effectiveness in choosing the right solution easily outweighs duplication costs when the market rewards higher performance or when large volumes justify increased sophistication. Under these conditions, parallel development may prove less costly because it both improves the probability of success and reduces development time.

Perhaps the most difficult problem in managing competing projects lies in reintegrating the members of the losing team. If the company is expanding rapidly or if the successful project creates a growth opportunity, losing team members can work on another interesting program or sign on with the winning team as the project moves toward the marketplace. For the shoot-out system to work continuously, however, executives must create a climate that honors high-quality performance whether a project wins or loses, reinvolves people quickly in their technical specialties or in other projects, and accepts and expects rotation among tasks and groups.

At Sony, according to its top R&D manager, the research climate does not penalize the losing team: "We constantly have several alternative projects going. Before the competition is over, before there is a complete loss, we try to smell the potential outcome and begin to prepare for that result as early as possible. Even after we have consensus, we may wait for several months to give the others a chance. Then we begin to give important jobs (on the other programs) to members of the losing groups. If your team doesn't win, you may still be evaluated as performing well. Such people have often received my 'crystal award' for outstanding work. We never talk badly about these people. Ibuka's principle is that doing something, even if it fails, is better than doing nothing. A strike-out at Sony is OK, but you must not just stand there. You must swing at the ball as best you can."

Skunkworks

Every highly innovative enterprise in my research sample emulated small company practices by using groups that functioned in a skunkworks style. Small teams of engineers, technicians, designers, and model makers were placed together with no intervening organizational or physical barriers to developing a new product from idea to commercial prototype stages. In innovative Japanese companies, top managers often worked hand-in-hand on projects with young engineers. Surprisingly, *ringi* decision making was not evident in these situations. Soichiro Honda was known for working directly on technical problems and emphasizing his technical points by shouting at his engineers or occasionally even hitting them with wrenches!

The skunkworks approach eliminates bureaucracies, allows fast, unfettered communications, permits rapid turnaround times for experiments, and instills a high level of group identity and loyalty. Interestingly, few successful groups in my research were structured in the classic "venture group" form, with a careful balancing of engineering, production, and marketing talents. Instead they acted on an old truism: introducing a new product or process to the world is like raising a healthy child—it needs a mother (champion) who loves it, a father (authority figure with resources) to support it, and pediatricians (specialists) to get it through difficult times. It may survive solely in the hands of specialists, but its chances of success are remote.

Interactive Learning

Skunkworks are as close as most big companies can come to emulating the highly interactive and motivating learning environment that characterizes successful small ventures. But the best big innovators have gone even farther. Recognizing that the random, chaotic nature of technological change cuts across organizational and even institutional lines, these companies tap into multiple outside sources of technology as well as their customers' capabilities. Enormous external leverages are possible. No company can spend more than a small share of the world's $200 billion devoted to R&D. But like small entrepreneurs, big companies can have much of that total effort cheaply if they try.

In industries such as electronics, customers provide much of the innovation on new products. In other industries, such as textiles, materials or equipment suppliers provide the innovation. In still others, such as biotechnology, universities are dominant, while foreign sources strongly supplement industries such as controlled fusion. Many R&D units have strategies to develop information for trading with outside groups and have teams to cultivate these sources.[7] Large Japanese companies have been notably effective at this. So have U.S. companies as diverse as Du Pont, AT&T, Apple Computer, and Genentech.

An increasing variety of creative relationships exist in which big companies participate—as joint ventures, consortium members, limited partners, guarantors of first markets, major academic funding sources, venture capitalists, spin-off equity holders, and so on. These rival the variety of inventive financing and networking structures that individual entrepreneurs have created.

Indeed, the innovative practices of small and large companies look even more alike. This resemblance is especially striking in the interactions between companies and customers during development. Many experienced big companies are relying less on early market research and more on interactive development with lead customers. Hewlett-Packard, 3M, Sony, and Raychem frequently introduce radic-

---

[7]In *Managing the Flow of Technology* (Cambridge: MIT Press, 1977), Thomas J. Allen illustrates the enormous leverage provided such technology accessors (called "gatekeepers") in R&D organizations.

ally new products through small teams that work closely with lead customers. These teams learn from their customers' needs and innovations, and rapidly modify designs and entry strategies on this information.

Formal market analyses continue to be useful for extending product lines, but they are often misleading when applied to radical innovations. Market studies predicted that Haloid would never sell more than 5,000 xerographic machines, that Intel's microprocessor would never sell more than 10% as many units as there were minicomputers, and that Sony's transistor radios and miniature television sets would fail in the marketplace. At the same time, many eventual failures such as Ford's Edsel, IBM's FS system, and the supersonic transport were studied and planned exhaustively on paper, but lost contact with customers' real needs.

A STRATEGY FOR INNOVATION

The flexible management practices needed for major innovations often pose problems for established cultures in big companies. Yet there are reasonable steps managers in these companies can take. Innovation can be bred in a surprising variety of organizations, as many examples show. What are its key elements?

An Opportunity Orientation

In the 1981–1983 recession, many large companies cut back or closed plants as their "only available solution." Yet I repeatedly found that top managers in these companies took these actions without determining firsthand why their customers were buying from competitors, discerning what niches in their markets were growing, or tapping the innovations their own people had to solve problems. These managers foreclosed innumerable options by defining the issue as cost cutting rather than opportunity seeking. As one frustrated division manager in a manufacturing conglomerate put it: "If management doesn't actively seek or welcome technical opportunities, it sure won't hear about them."

By contrast, Intel met the challenge of the last recession with its "20% solution." The professional staff agreed to work one extra day a week to bring innovations to the marketplace earlier than planned. Despite the difficult times, Intel came out of the recession with several important new products ready to go—and it avoided layoffs.

Entrepreneurial companies recognize that they have almost unlimited access to capital and they structure their practices accordingly. They let it be known that if their people come up with good ideas, they can find the necessary capital—just as private venture capitalists or investment bankers find resources for small entrepreneurs.

Structuring for Innovation

Managers need to think carefully about how innovation fits into their strategy and structure their technology, skills, resources, and organizational commitments accordingly. A few examples suggest the variety of strategies and alignments possible:

- Hewlett-Packard and 3M develop product lines around a series of small, discrete, freestanding products. These companies form units that look like entrepreneurial start-ups. Each has a small team, led by a champion, in low-cost facilities. These companies allow many different proposals to come forward and test them as early as possible in the marketplace. They design control systems to spot significant losses on any single entry quickly. They look for high gains on a few winners and blend less successful, smaller entries into prosperous product lines.

- Other companies (like AT&T or the oil majors) have had to make large system investments to last for decades. These companies tend to make long-term needs forecasts. They often start several programs in parallel to be sure of selecting the right technologies. They then extensively test new technologies in use before making systemwide commitments. Often they sacrifice speed of entry for long-term low cost and reliability.

- Intel and Dewey & Almy, suppliers of highly technical specialties to OEM, develop strong technical sales networks to discover and understand customer needs in depth. These companies try to have technical solutions designed into customers' products. Such companies have flexible applied technology groups working close to the marketplace. They also have quickly expandable plant facilities and a cutting-edge technology (not necessarily basic research) group that allows rapid selection of currently available technologies.

- Dominant producers like IBM or Matsushita are often not the first to introduce new technologies. They do not want to disturb their successful product lines any sooner than necessary. As market demands become clear, these companies establish precise price-performance windows and form overlapping project teams to come up with the best answer for the marketplace. To decrease market risks, they use product shoot-outs as close to the market as possible. They develop extreme depth in production technologies to keep unit costs low from the outset. Finally, depending on the scale of the market entry, they have project teams report as close to the top as necessary to secure needed management attention and resources.

- Merck and Hoffman-LaRoche, basic research companies, maintain laboratories with better facilities, higher pay, and more freedom than most universities can afford. These companies leverage their internal spending through research grants, clinical grants, and research relationships with universities throughout the world. Before they invest $20 million to $50 million to clear a new drug, they must have reasonable assurance that they will be first in the marketplace. They take elaborate precautions to ensure that the new entry is safe and effective, and that it cannot be easily duplicated by others. Their structures are designed to be on the cutting edge of science, but conservative in animal testing, clinical evaluation, and production control.

These examples suggest some ways of linking innovation to strategy. Many other examples, of course, exist. Within a single company, individual divisions may have different strategic needs and hence different structures and practices. No single approach works well for all situations.

Complex Portfolio Planning

Perhaps the most difficult task for top managers is to balance the needs of existing lines against the needs of potential lines. This problem requires a portfolio strategy much more complex than the popular four-box Boston Consulting

Group matrix found in most strategy texts. To allocate resources for innovation strategically, managers need to define the broad, long-term actions within and across divisions necessary to achieve their visions. They should determine which positions to hold at all costs, where to fall back, and where to expand initially and in the more distant future.

A company's strategy may often require investing most resources in current lines. But sufficient resources should also be invested in patterns that ensure intermediate and long-term growth; provide defenses against possible government, labor, competitive, or activist challenges; and generate needed organizational technical, and external relations flexibilities to handle unforeseen opportunities or threats. Sophisticated portfolio planning within and among divisions can protect both current returns and future prospects—the two critical bases for that most cherished goal, high price-earnings ratios.

AN INCREMENTALIST APPROACH

Such managerial techniques can provide a strategic focus for innovation and help solve many of the timing, coordination, and motivation problems that plague large, bureaucratic organizations. Even more detailed planning techniques may help in guiding the development of the many small innovations that characterize any successful business. My research reveals, however, that few, if any, major innovations result from highly structured planning systems. Within the broad framework I have described, major innovations are best managed as incremental, goal-oriented, interactive learning processes.[8]

Several sophisticated companies have labeled this approach "phased program planning." When they see an important opportunity in the marketplace (or when a laboratory champion presses them), top managers outline some broad, challenging goals for the new programs: "to be the first to prove whether rDNA is commercially feasible for this process," or "to create an economic digital switching system for small country telephone systems." These goals have few key timing, cost, or performance numbers attached. As scientists and engineers (usually from different areas) begin to define technical options, the programs' goals become more specific—though managers still allow much latitude in technical approaches.

As options crystallize, managers try to define the most important technical sequences and critical decision points. They may develop "go, no go" performance criteria for major program phases and communicate these as targets for project teams. In systems innovations, for example, performance specifications must be set to coordinate the interactions of subsystems. Successful companies leave open for as long as possible exactly how these targets can be achieved.

While feeding resources to the most promising options, managers frequently keep other paths open. Many of the best concepts and solutions come from projects

[8]For a further discussion of incrementalism, see James Brian Quinn, "Managing Strategies Incrementally," *Omega* 10, no. 6, (1982), p. 613; and *Strategies for Change: Logical Incrementalism* (Homewood, Ill.: Dow Jones-Irwin, 1980).

partly hidden or "bootlegged" by the organization. Most successful managers try to build some slacks or buffers into their plans to hedge their bets, although they hesitate to announce these actions widely. They permit chaos and replication in early investigations, but insist on much more formal planning and controls as expensive development and scale-up proceed. But even at these later stages, these managers have learned to maintain flexibility and to avoid the tyranny of paper plans. They seek inputs from manufacturing, marketing, and customer groups early. Armed with this information, they are prepared to modify their plans even as they enter the marketplace. A European executive describes this process of directing innovation as "a somewhat orderly tumult that can be managed only in an incremental fashion."

Why Incrementalism?

The innovative process is inherently incremental. As Thomas Hughes says, "Technological systems evolve through relatively small steps marked by an occasional stubborn obstacle and by constant random breakthroughs interacting across laboratories and borders."[9] A forgotten hypothesis of Einstein's became the laser in Charles Townes's mind as he contemplated azaleas in Franklin Square. The structure of DNA followed a circuitous route through research in biology, organic chemistry, X-ray crystallography, and mathematics toward its Nobel Prize-winning conception as a spiral staircase of amino acids and bases. Such rambling trails are characteristic of virtually all major technological advances.

At the outset of the attack on a technical problem, an innovator often does not know whether his problem is tractable, what approach will prove best, and what concrete characteristics the solution will have if achieved. The logical route, therefore, is to follow several paths—though perhaps with varying degrees of intensity—until more information becomes available. Not knowing precisely where the solution will occur, wise managers establish the widest feasible network for finding and assessing alternative solutions. They keep many options open until one of them seems sure to win. Then they back it heavily.

Managing innovation is like a stud poker game, where one can play several hands. A player has some idea of the likely size of the pot at the beginning, knows the general but not the sure route to winning, buys one card (a project) at a time to gain information about probabilities and the size of the pot, closes hands as they become discouraging, and risks more only late in the hand as knowledge increases.

Political & Psychological Support

Incrementalism helps deal with the psychological, political, and motivational factors that are crucial to protect success. By keeping goals broad at first, a manager avoids creating undue opposition to a new idea. A few concrete goals may be projected as a challenge. To maintain flexibility, intermediate steps are not developed in detail. Alternate routes can be tried and failures hidden. As early

---

[9]Thomas Hughes, "The Inventive Continuum," *Science 84.* November 1984, p. 83.

problems are solved, momentum, confidence, and identity build around the new approach. Soon a project develops enough adherents and objective data to withstand its critics' opposition.

As it comes more clearly into competition for resources, its advocates strive to solve problems and maintain its viability. Finally, enough concrete information exists for nontechnical managers to compare the programs fairly with more familiar options. The project now has the legitimacy and political clout to survive—which might never have happened if its totality has been disclosed or planned in detail at the beginning. Many sound technical projects have died because their managers did not deal with the politics of survival.

Chaos Within Guidelines

Effective managers of innovation channel and control its main directions. Like venture capitalists, they administer primarily by setting goals, selecting key people, and establishing a few critical limits and decision points for intervention rather than by implementing elaborate planning or control systems. As technology leads or market needs emerge, these managers set a few—most critical—performance targets and limits. They allow their technical units to decide how to achieve these, subject to defined constraints and reviews at critical junctures.

Early bench-scale project managers may pursue various options, making little attempt at first to integrate each into a total program. Only after key variables are understood—and perhaps measured and demonstrated in lab models—can more precise planning be meaningful. Even then, many factors may remain unknown; chaos and competition can continue to thrive in the pursuit of the solution. At defined review points, however, only those options that can clear performance milestones may continue.

Choosing which projects to kill is perhaps the hardest decision in the management of innovation. In the end, the decision is often intuitive, resting primarily on a manager's technical knowledge and familiarity with innovation processes. Repeatedly, successful managers told me, "Anyone who thinks he can quantify this decision is either a liar or a fool...There are too many unknowables, variables...Ultimately, one must use intuition, a complex feeling, calibrated by experience...We'd be foolish not to check everything, touch all the bases. That's what the models are for. But ultimately it's a judgment about people, commitment, and probabilities...You don't dare use milestones too rigidly."

Even after selecting the approaches to emphasize, innovative managers tend to continue a few others as smaller scale "side bets" or options. In a surprising number of cases, these alternatives prove winners when the planned option fails.

Recognizing the many demands entailed by successful programs, innovative companies find special ways to reward innovators. Sony gives "a small but significant" percentage of a new product's sales to its innovating teams. Pilkington, IBM, and 3M's top executives are often chosen from those who have headed successful new product entries. Intel lets its Magnetic Memory Group operate like a small company, with special performance rewards and simulated stock options, GE, Syntex, and United Technologies help internal innovators establish new companies and take equity positions in "nonrelated" product innovations.

Large companies do not have to make their innovators millionaires, but rewards should be visible and significant. Fortunately, most engineers are happy with the incentives that Tracy Kidder calls "playing pinball"—giving widespread recognition to a job well done and the right to play in the next exciting game.[10] Most innovative companies provide both, but increasingly they are supplementing these with financial rewards to keep their most productive innovators from jumping outside.

MATCH MANAGEMENT TO THE PROCESS

Management practices in innovative companies reflect the realities of the innovation process itself. Innovation tends to be individually motivated, opportunistic, customer responsive, tumultuous, nonlinear, and interactive in its development. Managers can plan overall directions and goals, but surprises are likely to abound. Consequently, innovative companies keep their programs flexible for as long as possible and freeze plans only when necessary for strategic purposes such as timing. Even then they keep options open by specifying broad performance goals and allowing different technical approaches to compete for as long as possible.

Executives need to understand and accept the tumultuous realities of innovation, learn from the experiences of other companies, and adapt the most relevant features of these others to their own management practices and cultures. Many features of small company innovators are also applicable in big companies. With top-level understanding, vision, a commitment to customers and solutions, a genuine portfolio strategy, a flexible entrepreneurial atmosphere, and proper incentives for innovative champions, many more large companies can innovate to meet the severe demands of global competition.

[10]Tracy Kidder, *The Soul of a New Machine* (Boston: Little, Brown, 1981).

SOCIOTECHNICAL CONSIDERATIONS FOR THE DEVELOPMENT OF THE SPACE STATION: AUTONOMY AND THE HUMAN ELEMENT IN SPACE*

Claudia Bird Schoonhoven

INTRODUCTION

A permanent space station is now being designed for astronauts to assemble in space. Planned for operation in about 1995, this important achievement is the beginning of humans working and living in space for long periods of time. To prepare for long-term habitation in outer space, one must ask: How does one organize a space station? More specifically, two questions have been raised about autonomy and the human element in space. In order to maximize individual and mission performance, (1) to what extent should the space station operate independently from "ground control" and (2) to what extent should machines operate independently from direct, "real-time" control by humans? When considering these issues, one is actually asking how best to design organizations for high levels of performance (effectiveness) for the least cost (efficiency). To address these questions, this article will consider the organization and management of the space station, including the station's relations with ground operations.

The concern for the space station is with organizational design—that is, with ensuring that the right people are focusing on the right tasks, that they have the proper information, technology, incentives, and controls to perform these tasks effectively and efficiently, and that their efforts are coordinated so that the organization's overall objectives are accomplished. This is called designing for organizational performance and effectiveness. A variable of special concern is technology—in particular information technology in the form of computers, expert systems, and robotic tools for performing tasks with the assistance of computer-programmed machines. This makes the design of an effective space organization a sociotechnical systems (STS) issue.

This article will move beyond an exclusive focus on the "man-machine interface," a common end point in space systems design. Organizations are systems of complex, interrelated variables. Organization research, theory, and practice indicates that negative consequences result when a single-minded focus is placed on only "man-machine" relations. To ignore the systemic properties of organizations when designing a part of the organization is to invite unintended, negative conse-

Source: Reprinted from the *Journal of Applied Behavioral Sciences,* 1986, with permission of the author and publisher.

*The research reported in this article was supported by the National Aeronautics and Space Administration (NASA) and the American Society for Engineering Education (ASEE). Codirected by the Stanford University department of aeronautics and astronautics and by the NASA Ames Research Center, the research project focused on autonomy and the human element in space. The support of NASA and ASEE is gratefully acknowledged. The writing of this article was facilitated by a sabbatical award from San Jose State University and the Stanford Graduate School of Business's sponsorship of visiting scholars. I especially wish to thank Dean Marshall Burak, James G. March, Eugene J. Webb, and Dean Robert K. Jaedicke.

quences. One treats the human-machine interface in isolation only at one's peril.

Although much about social organization remains to be discovered, we do know a fair amount about the behavior of people in formal, complex organizational settings and about how organizations tend to operate under various conditions. A major point to be emphasized is that both social and organizational systems are subject to design choices in much the same way that physical and technological factors are subject to design choices (Kotter, Schlesinger, & Sathe, 1979). This article addresses the organizational context of the human-machine "interface" and its influence on human performance. By providing some insights from the field of organizational theory and STS analysis, I hope to inform NASA's decision-making process regarding autonomy and the human element in space.

The following sections will describe alternate approaches to organizational design and management, along with some consequences of these approaches.

APPROACHES TO ORGANIZATIONAL DESIGN AND EFFECTIVENESS

Scientific Management and the "Strike in Space"

Scientific management developed as an early approach to organizational design (Taylor, 1911), yet it nonetheless flourishes today in modern organizations. Emphasizing the optimum use of the technical subsystem, the man-machine interface is a central contemporary focus of this approach. Recall that scientific management rationalizes the technical system of the organization by splitting traditional worker responsibility for work planning and design into planning, which is retained as a management responsibility, and work execution consistent with the plan, which remains the workers' responsibility. Managers plan and workers work, a distinction rigidly maintained because functional specialization combined with superior aptitude for each function are thought to produce optimum output. This view has led to autocratic decision and authority structures, because workers are viewed as incapable of the intellectual tasks of planning and decision making.

Focusing exclusively on the technical subsystem as a means for ensuring optimum production prohibits the manager or organizational designer from anticipating certain interdependencies between the technical subsystem and the social structure of the organization. The consequence of work plans and work organization focused tightly on the man-machine interaction alone does not simply produce unimplemented plans, but rather considerable unanticipated strife, inefficiency, and substantially increased costs of producing the desired product or service.

For example, scientific management principles apparently were involved in what has become known as the "strike in space," which occurred during NASA's 1973 Skylab activities (Balbaky, 1980). On Friday, December 27, 1973, the Apollo 3 astronauts conducted the first day-long, sit-down strike in space, closing down communication with mission control for 24 hours and refusing to work until management in mission control had set priorities for its work demands. To maximize mission objectives in this final leg of the program, ground control had removed virtually all slack from the astronauts' schedule of activities and treated the men as if they were robots. To accomplish all planned activities, ground control shortened the times allowed for meals and setting up experiments and made no allowance for unsystematically stowed equipment. Favorite leisure activities—watching the sun and earth—were forbidden (Cooper, 1976; Weick, 1976). Neil Hutchinson, flight director of the mission, reported, "We lay out the whole day for them, and the astronauts normally follow it to a 'T.' What we've done is we've learned how to maximize what you can get out of a man in one day" (Cooper, 1976, p. 61).

Mission control saw further that it was necessary for the ground to control work schedules. "So many jobs interfere with one another!" Hutchinson said, after the third crew had returned to earth. "With so many constraints, I'd say they're bound to screw something up!' " (Cooper, 1976, p. 122). This is not simply a matter of determining who makes up the work schedule and who has superior knowledge about interrelated elements in the system. This is a fundamental organizational problem of determining how to distribute authority for the Skylab activities between the ground and space. As designed, the Skylab crew members had no autonomy and discretion in determining the pace and sequence of their work, no local control over the conditions of work. This derives from a conception of the worker held either explicitly or implicitly by managers within NASA at the time of Skylab which has far-reaching implications for the management of the forthcoming space station. The cost to NASA for the short-lived 24-hour strike in space was $2,520,000 calculated at $35,000 per "astronaut-hour" in space. Work productivity fell to zero during that period and worker morale was damaged, as were relations with mission control. By any standards, the organizational subunit suffered a severe drop in effectiveness and efficiency during that period.

A centralized, bureaucratic structure such as that governing the Skylab's operations is not inappropriate for an organization as long as its tasks are routine and the technology well understood. In such cases, workers can still be treated well and the leadership can be participative. As tasks or environments change, however, the rules and procedures must be appropriate for the changed circumstances, and this is perhaps the biggest failing of bureaucratic, centralized structures. Therefore, a centralized, bureaucratic structure is not the organization design of choice for near-term space station efforts.

When tasks are nonroutine, however—as they generally are in space missions—centralized, rule-based structures are inefficient and often ineffective, as fixed rules are applied inappropriately to changed circumstances. Instead, discretion must be high at the level at which the unprogrammed decisions are required. A correspondingly high cognitive load will fall on the work force, and the knowledge required will be extensive. In organizations faced with nonroutine tasks, be they because of environmental or technological uncertainty, being "efficient" is not the relevant criteria. The efficiency of problem solving and the discovery of novel solutions under changing circumstances is what is relevant for these organizations. Notice, too, that a new concept has been introduced: that of the organization's environment The environment presents problems and opportunities for the organization and is a major stimulator of change in organization structures. This suggests that past organizational arrangements may not be entirely appropriate for the environment of space, about which much is still unknown, for such an environment does not easily forgive errors.

Two conclusions can be drawn from this organizational experience. First, a more balanced view, often referred to as the sociotechnical systems approach to organizational design and change, ought to be taken (Miller & Rice, 1967; Trist, 1960; Trist & Bamforth, 1951). Rather than thinking of technical and social systems separately, attention should be given to both when designing organizations because of their mutual interdependence in organizations. Second, there is no one best way to design an organization. The appropriate design depends upon a complex set of interrelations between an organization's designated technologies, tasks, goals, work force characteristics, and environment. This approach is known as a "contingency" approach to organizational design, after the work of Thompson (1967) and Lawrence and Lorsch (1967).

APPLYING SOCIOTECHNICAL SYSTEMS AND ORGANIZATIONAL THEORY TO SPACE STATION DESIGN

Equifinality

Several issues are important in deciding the appropriate level of autonomy for the space station. The first design recommendation is to not make prematurely fixed decisions regarding the proper structure for the space station, which will then be relied upon in an unexamined, unquestioned way as "the one best way" to structure and manage a space station. Twenty years of organizational research has demonstrated that no single way of structuring successful organizations exists. The idea of "equifinality," which is a systems concept, emphasizes that often more than one single path to the same outcome exists. There are several satisfactory ways to structure the situation initially, with different strengths and weaknesses, which will be explored below. Similarly, there are several ways of structuring a situation that are unlikely to be successful.

Thus far, I have referred to "the" space station as if there will be only one. Several varieties of space stations are likely to be developed in the near future, and they may be specialized according to mission. The commercialization of space has become newsworthy. There undoubtedly will be purely commercial ventures in space as the high costs of space missions are increasingly shifted to the private sector. For example, the commercialization of space has become so newsworthy that a publication dedicated to the subject has been launched (*Commercial Space*, 1985). Since there have been purely military shuttle missions, a high probability exists that some space stations will have predominantly military missions. This simply extends my original recommendation that different ways of organizing will be appropriate for space stations as a generic set, depending upon which goals and missions are pursued, the degree of task specialization, the technology in place, and so forth.

Morphogenesis

Another design consideration is to regard the organization structure of the space station as adaptive and changing rather than as fixed. The systems concept "morphogenesis" refers to those processes that elaborate or change the system, such as growth, learning, and structural differentiation (Scott, 1981). Morphogenesis reminds us that organizational form is capable of adaptation over time. The structure of the space station will need to accommodate changing levels of technology, modification in the number and mix of space station missions, associated shifts in the number and characteristics of the astronauts and other crew members, and increasing knowledge of space. The apparently hostile and unforgiving characteristics of the space environment are likely to become less problematic as more routine technologies are developed to solve the problems of surviving in space. This is likely to make the environment less hostile, eventually. This recommendation is particularly applicable to the groundstation division of labor. With sufficient funding, technical knowledge is likely to advance rapidly, which in turn will make it possible to shift more and more functions to the station itself. Weick (1979) reminds us that organizations continue to exist only if they maintain a balance between flexibility and stability.

Computer Technology
and Organization Structure

Decisions regarding the level of computer power to locate on the space station, and which data banks will be accessible on a discretionary basis either on board or on ground, will strongly influence the extent to which those on the station will be capable of autonomous decision making. Research in organizations has shown that power derives from control over physical access to computer hardware and to the computers' computational and data storage capabilities (Whisler, 1967). Early studies of the impact of computer technology on organizations focused on the shift and scramble of the organizations' power structure. When computer installation was dominated by large system, mainframe computers, usually only "one" computer was available, and it was a valued resource. As a consequence, the decision as to where to physically locate the computer and who had administrative control over its access and use had strong implications for the relative authority and control that organizational segment would subsequently achieve (Whisler, 1970). Power within the organization thus derived from control over the computer. A sour ᵥ of political power in an organization is simply control over essential information in the system (Hickson, Hinings, Lee, Scheck, & Pennings, 1971; Pfeffer, 1978, 1982)

Similar to these research findings has been the manner in which NASA has elected to implement computer capabilities in spacecraft. For the most part, the most powerful and extensive computer facilities have remained on the ground, in mission control and in related ground-based space operating centers. Computer monitoring and control of space craft functions and operations have been ground based for many reasons, including weight limitations. If full decision-making autonomy of the space station and its work force were to become a goal of NASA's, this goal could not be achieved unless most essential data processing capabilities resided on board the space station itself. Without unrestricted access to the requisite data, the space station is unlikely to achieve its potential for autonomy. Therefore, if NASA chooses to locate substantial computerized data banks on the ground, for example, the structures possible in the space station will be constrained. That microelectronics technology makes possible extensive redundant, distributed systems on board the station does not change the fact that control over the accessibility of data will be a source of organizational power.

Professional Workers, Technology and Organization Structure

Research on the relationship between technology and organizational structure has found that greater technical complexity is associated with greater structural complexity, except when professionals constitute a significant part of the work force (Bell, 1967; Blau, Heydebrand, & Stauffer, 1966; Pugh, 1969). For example, research "think tanks," law firms, and medical clinics have comparatively "flat," undifferentiated authority structures. This alternative structures complexity into the individuals' job responsibilities by introducing greater complexity into the repertoire of the worker. As a consequence, task complexity is confronted with more highly qualified and flexible performers: professionals. This response is particularly effective when the work is also uncertain, a condition making preplanning and subdivision of the work risky at best under the changing circumstances (Scott, 1981).

As technical and mission complexity have increased, NASA has begun to recruit increasingly larger numbers of scientifically trained workers with Ph.D. degrees, medical degrees, degrees in engineering, and specialized training in space research applications. Because of the complexity of future missions and the high level of problem-solving ability that will be required, this trend is likely to continue. Astronauts recruited from among the scientifically trained have a high educational attainment, a high intelligence quotient, and work attitudes strongly influenced by an achievement orientation. Astronauts in this latter category come from occupations categorized as "professional." When task complexity is dealt with by the decision to hire professionally trained workers, what are the appropriate organizational structures within which professionals work most effectively?

Professionals work in formal organizations under two general types of structures: autonomous and heteronomous authority structures. In autonomous professional organizations such as general hospitals, universities, and "think tanks," administrators delegate to the professionals responsibility for defining and implementing goals and for setting and maintaining performance standards, and the professionals organize themselves to assume these responsibilities (Scott, 1965). A clear division of labor exists between tasks for which the professionals and the administrators assume responsibility. Administrators keep the organization functioning, but they do not control professional tasks (Goss, 1961). Substantial discretion and autonomy are granted to the professionals, who are subject only to collegial review and control review and control systems (Clark, 1963; Freidson, 1975; Scott, 1981; Smigel, 1964).

In heteronomous structures of mixed authority, professional employees are subordinated to the administrative structure (Scott, 1965). Professional autonomy is substantially greater than that usually allocated to nonprofessionals, but substantially less than that which professionals enjoy in autonomous professional organizations. Discretion is more circumscribed, and professionals are subject to administrative supervision and evaluation. For example, consider professionals within libraries, secondary schools, social welfare agencies, or engineering firms. For these professionals, the reduced level of professional autonomy is strongly related to the external political and social power of their occupations (Etzioni, 1969; Kornhauser, 1962; Miller, 1967; Montagna, 1968). Autonomous and heteronomous structures can be found within organizational subunits and between entire organizations. Thus scientists and engineers in the research and development section of a manufacturing organization are likely to be organized heteronomously. A structure of general rules and hierarchical supervision surrounds their work, however, and managers who are members of their professions provide the administration.

What does all this suggest for the organization of the space station and its relations with the ground? Because the on-board tasks will be complex, both conceptually and technologically, with a substantial amount of real-time problem solving indicative of substantial information processing and task uncertainty, the space station crew will actually consist of professionally trained workers. The literature indicates that professionals work most effectively in either autonomous or heteronomous authority structures (Farris, 1973; Friedson, 1975; Hall, 1975; Scott, 1965, 1981). In both cases, substantial decision-making authority is allocated to the workers, as are high discretion regarding the time and pacing of their work and levels of technical decisions, and decision making is decentralized to the subunit where the work is performed. The decision process is likely to be advisory, collaborative, and collegial, with influence based upon holding relevant knowledge rather than superior organizational position. This suggests that a space station administrator or commander may be responsible for the physical facilities and integrity of the work setting, much as hospital administrators must govern the physical plant and hotel facilities but do not direct the technical work. This also suggests that the relationship between the ground and the space station should be a supportive one, much in the way in which corporations provide the resources (i.e., equipment, technology, and facilities) for carrying out research and development work.

Structures not supported by the research on professionals and contingent organizing are highly bureaucratic organizations characterized by centralized decision making, careful and close supervision of the workers, worker behavior governed by standardized rules or "by the book," and low levels of discretion and decision autonomy for the workers. This strongly suggests that the military command model is inappropriate, unless the space station crew conducts a specialized military mission without performing scientific research or applications.

Simultaneous Loose and Tight Coupling:
The Problem of System Survival

At least one important issue not covered in the research noted above has consequences for the organization of the space station. To what extent will the external environment of space, currently considered hostile and unforgiving of errors, introduce unanticipated novelties into the work setting? When the timing and sequence of events cannot be predicted and/or when uncertainties occur requiring quick decision making, these circumstances are thought to preclude the use of collaborative or participative decision making because of pressures for a rapid response. In situations such as this, the issue is neither effectiveness nor efficiency, but the survival of the system. In such circumstances, the military command model of tightly controlled behavior is often suggested. Because the external environment of space is so important to the organization of the station, what can be referred to as simultaneous loose and tight coupling may be a useful set of concepts to invoke in this situation.

Loose coupling of organizational elements refers to the absence of tight and rigid connections among the several components of organizations and assumes that many of these elements are capable of autonomous action (Weick, 1976). Loose coupling is a variable; hence, we speak of the degree of loose coupling in organizations. Weick suggests ways in which the loose coupling of an organization's structure may be highly adaptive and thus promote survival of the system. When the structures of a system's subunits are allowed to vary independently—and thus human behavior within the subunits also varies—this may provide more sensitive mechanisms for detecting variations in the environment. Should problems develop with one subelement of the system, it can be more easily sealed off or severed from the rest of the system. Moreover, adjustment by individuals or separate departments to environmental disturbances allows the rest of the system to function with greater stability. This indicates, contrary to the military command model, that highly discretionary and autonomous behavior may be appropriate structural elements for the space station, even under conditions of external threat.

Self-Designing Systems

One alternative to the dilemma of tight versus loose coupling is to allow the astronauts to "self-design" their own organizations. Weick (1977) argues that features of the Skylab "strike in space" go beyond conventional organizational concepts. Although advance planning for the Skylab had dealt with what to do in space, less attention had been paid to "planning how to plan what to do." The astronauts did not seem to have any solution-generating process on board, except that of trial and error and working to the limits of human energy. The one-day strike got results of "the most unimaginative sort." It did not result in a discrediting of the previous organizational design in which the ground control planned and directed activities and Skylab astronauts executed them, nor did rearrangement of activities and responsibilities occur as a result of the strike.

Weick explains that with organizational "self-design" the designers integrate themselves into the design: "The likelihood is that sensitive self-design would have taken astronaut needs into account more consistently over a much greater portion of the mission." Although designing the organization (planning) and implementing plans seem to be separate activities, the processes of designing and implementing feed back to one another: Implementation clarifies design and design clarifies implementation (1977). Weick's ideas are ones NASA might want to consider in designing the space station's organizational arrangements. At the least, they suggest that research that solicits the ideas of past and future space travelers is necessary for organizational design of future space stations. This must include the ideas of those who managed and were closely associated with mission control on earth. Their joint perceptions of the ground control-space station relationship should be probed.

Crew Selection:
Skewed Sex Ratios and Responses
to Tokens in Work Settings

Until recently, all astronauts in the U.S. space program were white men. NASA has recently added women and members of ethnic and racial minority groups to the corps for the first time. In 1983, Sally Ride became the first U.S. woman in space, the only woman among a crew of white men, and this constitutes a structural condition of tokenism. The choice to send crews into space with what are called "tokens" has consequences for the interaction dynamics, the mental health, the level of aggression, and the actual performance of the mission. Since the space station will present conditions of long-term isolation and confinement, a socially structured condition of tokenism could have serious negative consequences for future space missions. Research on this matter will be summarized briefly below.

Research has shown that the relative numbers of socially and culturally different people in a group are critical in shaping the social interaction. This research should not be confused with that evaluating the effects of gender on sexual or intimate behavior. I refer instead to research on the proportions of relative numbers of different types of persons in a group. "Skewed" groups contain a preponderance of one type—the numerical dominants—over another: the relative tokens (Kanter, 1977).

Kanter investigated female tokens in a male-dominated sales force of a large industrial corporation. The women in the sales force were under strong performance pressures, and they operated under a number of handicaps in the work setting. They were socially isolated, which resulted in their exclusion from important task-learning opportunites. This exclusion in turn inhibited their opportunities for strong task performance in interaction with their more experienced male peers. Performance pressure on the tokens gave them less room for error. In response to tokenism, underachievement or overachievement was common among the tokens.

When informal interaction is crucial to success, be it in industrial sales or close living and working on a space station, the performance of tokens is likely to be variable compared to that of members of the majority group, at least while the tokens are in the structured situation of being a numerical minority. Tokens undergo substantial personal stress, and they need to expend extra energy to maintain satisfactory relationships in work situations such as these. Among the causes of this stress are unsatisfactory social relationships, unstable self-images, frustration over rewards, and social ambiguity. They find it difficult to self-disclose information of a personal nature, which is considered a requisite for psychological well-being. The dynamics of tokenism help to perpetuate the system that keeps members of the token's category in short supply. The presence of a few does not necessarily pave the way for others; indeed, this often has the opposite effect.

As a design consideration, token members of a minority social category should not be isolated in space station missions. In the case of gender, including numbers of types of persons closer to the natural occurrence of these categories on earth will promote more balanced behavior by both men and women. Then the social isolation and psychological stress felt by tokens will likely be reduced. There should be no substantial differences in performance, for pressures to overachieve or to shirk from view will be removed for the tokens. Social relationships between the two proportions should be facilitated for both the dominant class and the members of minority groups. Overachievers from the token groups should no longer fear retaliation for outperforming those from the dominant group, and those in the dominant group would no longer suffer public humiliation for being outperformed by the high-achieving tokens. More natural displays of excellence would occur, with appropriate acceptance and encouragement of excellent performance among the crew members.

Human Factors Engineering and the Organization of NASA

Charles Perrow (1983, 1985) has analyzed failures of equipment and systems in which human factors appear to have been neglected. He rejects the notion that designers of such equipment are unaware of human factors or are contemptuous of them. Rather, he argues that the nature of the organization has an impact on the attention given to human factors. He suggests that design engineers, as well as other organizational members, respond to the rewards, sanctions, and prevailing belief systems of top management. Top managers have the option of requiring that designers use the principles of human factors in their designs by structuring the reward system so that it is in the designers' interests to take these principles into account.

I suggest that the work of human factors engineers and design engineers be tightly integrated organizationally within NASA to facilitate the requisite flow of information between the two functions. It has been recognized by others and implied during my own research that human factors engineers are viewed as "qualitative and soft," in contrast to the "quantitative and hard" design engineers (Meister & Farr, 1967; Perrow, 1983). In high-technology organizations, "soft" translates into lower status. A lower social value is placed on "soft" disciplines, and thus lower, often nominal influence on decision making results as a consequence. The social valuation process characteristic of organizations helps guarantee that most engineering design decisions will be informed by scientific management principles rather than by "softer" human factors, will be tightly focused on the man-machine interaction, and will likely discount social and organizational variables. I do not recommend that human factors engineering emphasize ever-more quantitative ergonomic factors, but instead recommend that top managers give explicit support to necessarily qualitative, human, socially oriented factors through the multiple signalling devices available to high-level executives and administrators, such as being certain that key human factors people attend and occasionally chair meetings concerned with design specifications.

It is generally good policy to have the users and maintainers of equipment involved in the early decision and subsequent design stages of automated equipment. NASA has been commended by behavioral scientists in the past for the extent to which "the users"—that is, the astronauts—have been consulted in design decisions. To ensure that this process continues and is an extensively relied-upon policy, top managers of NASA might consider clearly stating their expectations and facilitating organizational arrangements that allow close collaboration between users, design engineers, and human factors engineers. This might include modifying the existing organizational structure and granting rewards for the desired behavior. In other systems, many "high-technology" equipment decisions and designs have not been well informed by user input (Perrow, 1985). Indeed, the attribution of "operator error" in the face of system failures is widespread in most systems, especially in high-technology systems. This is an easy view to take, and one that should be resisted. In many high-technology organizations, design engineers work separately, insulated from the external costs and consequences of their designs. Costs to the user include excessive fatigue, boredom, excessive work load, isolation, frustration, and, above all, accidents for the operators. Were operators to participate in design reviews, were designers brought into contact with experienced operators, were designers required to operate their equipment somewhat or see it in operation, the externalization would be reduced.

As an alternative to the traditional division of labor in which managers plan and workers execute, responsibility for planning work might be shifted to the status of a joint responsibility of both management and the workers (astronauts) or delegated as much as possible to the workers themselves. Focusing on the technical subsystem alone—the technology and the operators—as a means for creating optimum production is a trap easily fallen into. Work plans made exclusively by management and its scheduling engineers typically produce unimplemented plans, considerable unanticipated strife, inefficiency, and substantially increased costs, as was shown in the Skylab experience. Conversely, allocating responsibility for work planning to the workers—especially workers of the intellectual, educational, and motivational caliber of the NASA astronauts—more easily integrates two interrelated subsystems of the organization; the technical subsystem and the social subsystem.

Many organizations neglect, if not deliberately defeat, the extremely flexible and creative capabilities of the human component of the system. "For want of a robot, stands an operator" (Perrow, 1983). As a design alternative, NASA might take greater advantage of the flexible and creative qualitites of its astronauts as decisions are made regarding divisions of labor between humans and machines and regarding the ability of the space station personnel to self-manage their operations independently of ground control. One finds too little evidence that Swain's list (Swain & Guttman, no date) of "man (sic) and machine advantages" has been relied upon seriously in the design of equipment and in the degree to which astronauts have been allowed to self-image their work in space.

Human-Machine Interface Within
the Space Station Context

With microprocessors readily available, the opportunity to distribute computer processing throughout the space station and its environs is a reality. When decisions are made to locate terminals, microcomputers, and the like, consideration should be given to the extent to which computer location contributes to the isolation of the workers. Some isolation may be necessary because of the environmental requirements of various tasks, such as biological experimentation, and some intermittent isolation may be desired because of needs for privacy related to working in a relatively cramped environment. Beyond these isolation requirements, I recommend that astronauts not be inadvertently isolated from their peers by an arbitrary placement of equipment. The isolation of workers and work groups promotes tunnel vision and stereotypes and undermines the ability of the organization as a whole to produce integrated work focused on the organization's goals.

Having people monitor machines is an increasing outcome of the machine automation process. Such monitoring can result in the degradation of skills necessary for intervention in the system during failures and particularly during crises (Perrow, 1985). It is also alleged to promote inattention. NASA might consider designs that require the coordination of activity by two or more operators, thereby promoting higher levels of required attendance. More extensive information inquiry capability could also be designed into automatic systems. For example, expert systems currently being developed provide more information to the operation and thereby increase the responsible decision capacity of the operator. This could slow the skills atrophy process. Finely tuned decision making is needed during periods of high work load or crises.

Lessons from Skylab

What general principles can be drawn from applying STS theory and organizational analysis to the design of space stations with respect to questions of machine automation and human autonomy? Machine automation should be used, whenever technologically feasible, to relieve humans of routine tasks that are dull, monotonous, and dangerous. Some work, however, will remain after the engineering of a system that will be residual, and this is typically assigned to a human operator. When a task or set of tasks is being engineered for machine automation on the space station, it is important that as much of the monotony of the task be absorbed by the machine as possible. This is a design rule that is cost effective, since it capitalizes on the strengths of human beings—strengths which are costly to recreate in robots, given current and projected levels of machine technology. "The strong points of the human element are its large memory capacity, its large repertory of responses, its flexibility in relating these responses to information inputs, and its ability to react creatively when the unexpected is encountered" (Haberstroh, 1965, p. 1176).

602

Second, it is important that the "residual" work remaining after automation for humans be interesting and challenging. When a division of labor is being allocated between humans and machines, it is important that all the "interesting, challenging stuff" not be allocated to the machine. When work is divided, it is broken down into simpler, specialized tasks. Narrowly defined, noncomplex, specialized tasks are boring tasks for humans. Instead of being relieved of routine, monotonous tasks, the workers will have been forced, through engineering decisions, to handle even duller, more narrowly defined jobs after automation. This is a frequent problem with decisions dividing labor between humans and robots.

Third, if it is technologically feasible to automate only part of a routine job, it may be preferable to decide not to automate that task on the space station at all. Many tasks involve complex interrelationships, even though they are frequently executed operations regarded as routine. Complexity is derived from two sources: the number of elements that must be taken into account and the degree of interrelatedness and interdependence between the elements. It is better to leave the complexity and interest in the work to the human by not dividing the labor between humans and machines, if one is forced by the existing technology to give the most interesting part of the work to the machine. Thus, when an automation decision is being made, if the manager making the decision and the engineer providing the technological design would not be willing to do the tasks remaining after automation themselves, they should not automate and divide the labor in the proposed manner.

After automation or partial automation of a set of tasks, it is common to treat the human operators as extensions of the machines. In true scientific management fashion, managers and engineers often attempt to program the humans using the machines as tools to gain increased speed and efficiency from the human workers. The goal is to maximize the output of the human as a system component. The operation of computer-controlled assembly lines in which production control, management, or industrial engineers set the pace of the line is a case in point, as is the programmed scheduling of astronauts' time and attention on the Skylab (Cooper, 1976).

NEEDED AREAS OF STUDY

Many have remarked on the extent to which the Soviets have undertaken social and behavioral research and have used its findings in the Russian space program to a far greater extent than we have in the United States (Bluth, 1981; Connor, Harrison, & Atkins, 1983). NASA's administrators have already begun to reflect on these issues. For example, Stan Sadin has remarked that concerns about behavioral matters may be more central in the USSR than in the U.S. space programs: "...it now seems clear that the stage is set for extending a research analysis of interrelated selection, training, and organizational problems..." (1982, p. V137). The main point is that there exists far too little reliable information on the social and organizational problems related to the space station as a technological context for work. In brief, I recommend that research be undertaken on the following issues.

External Environment

The external environment of space is currently conceptualized as hostile and unforgiving of errors. The issue is to determine the extents to which the space environment is likely to introduce uncertainties into the work setting requiring quick decision making on which system survival depends. When the issue is survival of the system rather than mission effectiveness of efficiency, what is the appropriate organizing mode? Under "normal" working conditions in the space station, there is substantial research to guide recommendations for structure and organization. Under "abnormal," unpredictable environmental circumstances, the appropriate organizing mode is less clear and needs to be researched. Much could be learned from intensive case analyses to discover how past space travelers conceptualize these issues.

Second, the relationship between structure under normal work circumstances and that invoked during a period of system survival must be considered. There are sufficient examples of earth-based societies in which martial law was invoked during periods of crisis only to become institutionalized over time as the "normal" structure. Crises provide opportunities for substantial power shifts. These issues should be analyzed prior to space station habitation rather than discovered when the need occurs during an actual crisis in space.

Organizational Design

Research that solicits the ideas of past and future space travelers and the earth-based managers of space missions regarding the organizational design of future space stations is imperative. The extent to which "self-design" is feasible should be pursued, in addition to a focus on structures that have already been implemented and experienced.

Social Relationships

Research is needed on the interactions between the formal (work) organization's structure and the social living structure under conditions of isolation, confinement, and a hostile external environment. Our concern is with the social relationships among people who also live where they work, because the space station may be the ultimate company town. What are the likely interactions between the off-duty social structure and the formal organization of the work? How does the interacting set of variables influence (a) mission performance and (b) the mental and emotional health of the space workers? A recent court case reversing the U.S. Coast Guard's disciplinary handling of two ship-based officers' professional and personal, off-duty relationships suggests the need for research on such issues. Since the Coast Guard officers involved were a man and a woman and the woman was a structural token, sex-skewed ratio dynamics may be relevant here.

Tokens and Balanced Ratios

Based on Kanter's work (1977a, b), research should investigate when a work group moves from a numerically skewed, rare token-dominant majority structure to a balanced position. This is necessary to inform managerial decisions regarding the desirable gender and racial balance among astronauts necessary for making up crews for space station missions. This will facilitate recruiting, selection, and development decisions for the astronaut corps, and the knowledge will help NASA missions avoid the negative consequences of the dynamics of tokenism reviewed above. Research should also investigate whether team development and individual training of astronauts prior to a crew's departure for space can ameliorate the effects of tokenism. Organizations do not always have available the appropriate mix of requisite skills, balanced by a "non-token" distribution of gender and ethnicity, among their crew members. Thus it is likely that sex-skewed crews will be embarking on missions at least for the near future. For this reason, training interventions ought to be researched as a potentially intervening set of variables affecting the dynamics of tokenism.

Robotics

The past ten years of microelectronic progress has made possible the development of electromechanical productivity-enhancing units called robots and robotic systems. Since preliminary robotic devices have been developed for work in the space station context and more are likely to be, the conditions under which humans and intelligent machines interact productively ought to be investigated. The most common application of robotic knowledge has been in industry, especially in manufacturing settings. Since the installed base of robotic flexible manufacturing systems (FMS) has grown substantially in recent years, these organizational settings offer researchers the opportunity to study the interactions between humans and intelligent machines within a complex technological system.

Minimally, data are needed on conditions promoting the safety of the human participants in the system, taking into account the degree of control the workers exercise over the machines in the robotic system. Another set of issues concerns the ways worker characteristics, including skills, educational attainment, and knowledge, have shifted with the introduction of robots. How has the manager-knowledge worker relationship—or relations among the workers themselves—been modified with the introduction of intelligent machines? What are managerial and worker attitudes toward the intelligent machines, particularly in high-performing organizational settings? These questions suggest a multivariate approach for examining the conditions under which strong performance is facilitated when intelligent machines become a significant element in the organizational system.

REFERENCES

Balbaky, E.M.L. (1980). *Strike in space* (Case No. 1–431–008). Unpublished report, Harvard Business School, Boston.

Bell, G. D. (1967). Determining the span of control. *American Journal of Sociology, 73,* 100–109.

Blau, P. M., Heyderbrand, W. V., & Stauffer, R. E. (1966). The structure of small bureaucracies. *American Sociological Review, 31,* 179–191.

Bluth, B. J. (1981, Fall). Sociological aspects of permanent manned occupancy in space. *AIAA Student Journal.*

Clark, B. R. (1963). Faculty organization and authority. In T. F. Lunsford (Ed.), *The study of academic administration* (pp. 37-51). Boulder, CO: Western Interstate Commission for Higher Education.

Commercial Space. (1985, January). New York: McGraw-Hill.

Connor, M. M., Harrison, A. A., & Atkins, F. R. (1983). *Living aloft: Human requirements for extended space flight.* National Aeronautics and Space Administration R. P.

Cooper, H. (1976). *A house in space.* New York: Holt, Rinehart, and Winston.

Etzioni, A. (1969). *The semi-professions and their organization.* New York: Free Press.

Farris, G. (1973). The technical supervisor. *Technology Review, 75*(5).

Freidson, E. (1975). *Doctoring together? A study of professional social control.* New York: Elsevier.

Goss, M.E.W. (1961, February). Influence and authority among physicians in an out-patient clinic. *American Sociological Review, 26,* 39-50.

Haberstroh, C. J. (1965). Organization design and systems analysis. In J. G. March (Ed.), *Handbook of organizations* (pp. 1171-1121j). Chicago: Rand McNally.

Hall, R. H. (1975). *Occupations and the social structure* (2nd ed.). Englewood Cliffs, NJ: Prentice-Hall.

Hickson D. J., Hinings, C. R., Lee, C. A., Schenck, R. E., & Pennings, J. M. (1971). A strategic contingencies' theory of intraorganizational power. *Administrative Science Quarterly, 16,* 216-229.

Kanter, R. M. (1977a). *Men and women of the corporation.* New York: Basic Books.

Kanter, R. M. (1977b, March). Skewed sex ratios and responses to token women. *American Journal of Sociology, 82*(5), 965-990.

Kornhauser, W. (1962). *Scientists in industry: Conflict and accommodation.* Berkeley, CA: University of California Press.

Kotter, J. P., Schlesinger, L., & Sathe, V. (1979). *Organization text, cases, and readings in the management of organizational design and change.* Homewood, IL: Richard D. Irwin.

Lawrence, P., & Lorsch, J. (1967). Differentiation and integration in complex organizations. *Administrative Science Quarterly, 12,* 1-47.

Meister, D., & Farr, D. E. (1967). The utilization of human factors information by designers. *Human Factors,* 71-87.

Miller, E. J., & Rice, A. K. (1967). *Systems of organization: The control of task and sentient boundaries.* London: Tavistock.

Montagna, P. D. (1968). Professionalism and bureaucratization in large profitable organizations. *American Journal of Sociology, 72,* 138-145.

Perrow, C. (1983). The organizational context of human factors. *Administrative Science Quarterly, 28,* 521-524.

Perrow, C. (1985). *Normal accidents: Living with high risk technologies.* New York: Basic Books.

Pfeffer, J. (1978). The micropolitics of organizations. In M. Meyer & Associates (Eds.). *Environments and organizations* (pp. 29-50). San Franscisco: Jossey-Bass.

Pfeffer, J. (1983). *Power.* Mansfield, MA: Pitman.

Pfeffer, J., & Liebiebici, H. (1973). The effect of competition on some dimensions of organizational structure. *Social Forces, 52,* 268-279.

Pugh, D. S., Hickson, D. J., & Hinings, C. R. (1969). An empirical taxonomy of structures of work organizations. *Administrative Science Quarterly, 14,* 115-126.

Sadin, S. (1982, August). Previous NASA workshop recommendations on the roles of automation and man in space. In M. Montemerlo & A. Cron (Eds.). *Space human factors.* NASA Office of Aeronautics and Space Technology.

Scott, W. R. (1965). Reactions to supervision in heteronomous professional organizations. *Administrative Science Quarterly, 14,* 115-126.

Scott, W. R. (1981). *Organizations: Rational, natural, and open systems.* Englewood Cliffs, NJ: Prentice-Hall.

Smigel, E. O. (1964). *The Wall Street lawyer: Professional organization man?* New York: Free Press.

Swain, A. D., & Guttman, H. E. (No date). *Handbook of human reliability analysis with nuclear power plant applications.* Albuquerque, NM: Sandia Laboratories.

Taylor, F. W. (1911). *The principles of scientific management.* New York: Harper.

Thompson, J. D. (1967). *Organizations in action.* New York: McGraw-Hill.

Trist, E. (1960). *Sociotechnical systems.* London: Tavistock.

Trist, E., & Bamforth, K. W. (1951). Some social and psychological consequences of the longwall method of coal-getting. *Human Relations, 4,* 3–38.

Weick, K. (1976, March). Educational organizations as loosely coupled systems. *Administrative Science Quarterly, 21,* 1–19.

Weick, K. (1977). Organizational design: Organizations as self-designing systems. *Organizational Dynamics,* 31–46.

Weick, K. (1979). *The social psychology of organizing* (2nd ed.). Reading, MA: Addison-Wesley.

Whisler, T. (1967). The impact of information technology on organizational control. In C. A. Meyers (Ed.), *The impact of computers on management* (pp. 16–49). Cambridge, MA: The MIT Press.

Whisler, T. (1970). *The impact of computers on organizations.* New York: Praeger.

RESTORING AMERICAN COMPETITIVENESS: LOOKING FOR NEW MODELS OF ORGANIZATIONS

Tom Peters

Every day brings new reports of lousy American product or service quality, vis-à-vis our foremost overseas competitors. The news of buyers rejecting our products pours in from Des Moines; Miami; Santa Clara County, California; Budapest; Zurich; and even Beijing. Industry after industry is under attack—old manufacturers and new, as well as the great hope of the future, the service industry. Change on an unimagined scale is a must, and islands of good news—those responding with alacrity—are available for our inspection. But it is becoming increasingly clear that the response is not coming fast enough. For instance, even the near-freefall of the dollar does not seem to be enough to make our exports attractive or reduce our passion for others' imports.

"Competitiveness is a microeconomic issue," the chairman of Toyota Motors stated recently. By and large, I agree. There are things that Washington, Bonn, Tokyo, Sacramento, Harrisburg, and Albany can do to help. But most of the answers lie within—that is, within the heads and hearts of our own managers.

Source: Reprinted from *The Academy of Management Executive,* 1988, with the permission of the author and publisher.

NEEDED: NEW MODELS

If we are to respond to wildly altered business and economic circumstances, we need entirely new ways of thinking about organizations. The familiar "military model"—the hierarchical, or "charts and boxes" structure—is not bearing up. It is a structure designed for more placid settings, and derived in times when you knew who the enemy was (not today's nameless or faceless Libyan terrorists or religious fanatics led by an old man in Teheran), and had time to prepare a response to your problems. (It took us Americans several years to gear up to win World War II—a luxury we can no longer afford in this era of nuclear capability.)

Likewise, peacetime economic wars of yore were marked by near certainty. Americans brought cheap energy to the fray, and were blessed by a vast "free trade" market at home. And for the first six decades of this century, we knew who our competitors were—a few big, domestic concerns. We knew where their leaders went to school, what cereals they ate for breakfast. Today, almost every U.S. industry has its competitors, from low-cost Malaysia to high-cost Switzerland, topped off by scores of tiny domestic competitors. Every industry now has—and keeps getting—new, unknown competitors. Moreover, the reality of exchange rates, interest rates, rates of inflation, prices of energy, and the ever-reconfigured microprocessor means that all of everything is up for grabs, unknown, constantly gyrating.

But remember that the American colonists broke away from their British masters in a war that featured the use of guerilla tactics. Popular mythology has it that the British insisted on lining up in rigid, straight-line formations to do battle, sorting bright red coats. By contrast, Ethan Allen and his fabled Green Mountain Boys eschewed formations, hid behind trees, and used their skill as crack shots while victoriously scampering through icy woods of the Hampshire Grants (now Vermont). Perhaps we again need organizations that evince the spunk and agility of the Green Mountain Boys rather than the formality of the British—a formality that was out of touch, with the new competitive reality in 18th century colonial wars and is out of touch, now, with the reality of the new economic wars.

Pictures, so it is said, are worth a thousand words. I believe that, and this article is devoted to describing two pictures, or "organizational maps." Neither looks much like a traditional organization chart: there is no square box at the top labeled "Chairman" (or "Vice-Chairman," or "Chief Executive Officer," or "President," and so on). Both charts break tradition in that they include customers, suppliers, distributors, and franchisees. The layouts are circular, moving from customers in toward the corporate chieftains at the circle's center. But beyond the circular scheme, the two bear little resemblance to one another.

EXHIBIT 1: THE INFLEXIBLE, RULE-DETERMINED, MASS PRODUCER OF THE PAST

Let's begin with an assessment of Exhibit 1. Start with *a*, the corporate center policy. This is the traditional, invisible, impersonal, generally out-of-touch corporate hub. The tininess of the circle representing the corporate center suggests both tightness

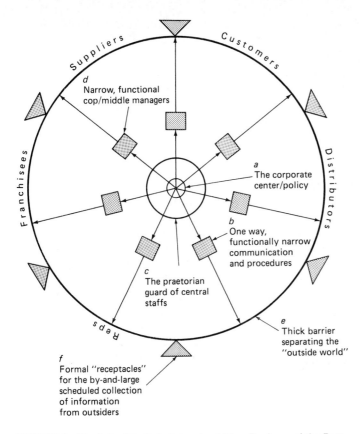

Suppliers

Customers

d
Narrow, functional
cop/middle managers

a
The corporate
center/policy

Distributors

b
One way,
functionally narrow
communication
and procedures

Franchisees

c
The praetorian
guard of central
staffs

Reps

e
Thick barrier
separating the
"outside world"

f
Formal "receptacles"
for the by-and-large
scheduled collection
of information
from outsiders

EXHIBIT 1 The Inflexible, Rule-determined, Mass Producer of the Past:
All Persons Know Their Place

and narrowness of scope; communication to the outside world (in or beyond the firm's official boundary) is usually via formal declaration—the policy manual or the multivolume plan, by and large determined on high—and communicated via the chain of command (i.e., downward). Within this tiny circle lie the "brains of the organization." It is here, almost exclusively, that the long term thinking, planning, and peering into the future takes place.

Move on to *b*—one-way, functionally narrow communciation via rules and procedures. Most communication in this generic organization type is highly channeled (hence the straight line) and top-down (note the direction of the arrow-heads). So communication and "control" are principally via rulebook, procedure manual, union contract, or the endless flow of memos providing guidance and demanding an endless stream of microinformation from the line. Moreover, the communication rarely "wobbles" around the circle (look ahead to Exhibit 2 for a dramatic contrast); that is, the lion's share of the communicating is restricted to the narrow functional specialty (operations, engineering, marketing, etc.), more or less represented by the individual arrows.

Then comes c, the praetorian guard of central corporate staffs. The corporate center is tightly protected (note the thick line) by a phalanx of brilliant, MBA-trained, virgin (no line-operating experience), analysis-driven staffs. If the isolation of the corporate chieftains in their plush-carpeted executive suites were not enough, this group seals them off once and for all. It masticates any input from below (i.e., the field) into 14-color desktop-published graphics, with all the blood, sweat, tears, and frustrated customer feedback drained therefrom. On those occasions when the senior team attempts to reach out directly, the staff is as good at cutting its superiors off ("Don't bother, we'll do a study of that marketplace—no need to visit") as it is at cutting off unexpurgated flow from below to the chief and his or her most senior cohorts.

Next, per d, are the functionally narrow cop/middle managers. My graphic description is a lumpy (substantial) square, located in the midst of the linear communication flow between the top and the bottom (the bottom, as in last and least— the first line of supervision and the front line). The middle manager, as his or her role is traditionally conceived, sits directly athwart the virtually sole communication channel between the top and the bottom. He or she is, first and foremost, the guardian of functional turf and prerogatives and the *next* block in the communication channel—remember that the praetorian guard was substantial block #1. The "cop" notion is meant to be represented by both the solidity of the block and its direct positioning in the downward communication flow. The middle manager is a filter of data, coming both from the bottom (infrequently) and from the top (much more frequently). The middle manager's job, as depicted here, is seen as vertically oriented (largely confined to the function in question and to passing things up and down) rather than horizontally oriented.

A thick, opaque barrier—e—marks the transition from the firm to the outside world of suppliers, customers, distributors, franchisees, reps, and so on. The barrier is very impermeable. Communication, especially informal communication does not flow readily across it, either from the customer "in" or from the front line of the organization "out."

Which leads directly to the idea of f—formal "receptacles" from the scheduled collection of information from outsiders. Of course the old, inflexible organization does communicate with the outside world. But the communication tends to be formal, coming mainly from market research or from orderly interaction via salespeople. Both the timing and the format of the communication is predetermined. Even competitive analysis is rigid, hierarchical, and focused—a formal competitive analysis unit that audits known competitors, mainly on a scheduled basis.

These six attributes are hardly an exhaustive examination of the old-style organization, but they do capture many of its outstanding attributes and orientation—static, formal, top-down oriented, and rule-and-policy determined. It is orderly to a fault (a dandy trait in a different world). To be sure, this depiction is stylized and therefore somewhat unfair, but my observations argue that it captures a frightening amount of the truth in today's larger organizations.

EXHIBIT 2: THE FLEXIBLE, POROUS, ADAPTIVE, FLEET-OF-FOOT ORGANIZATION OF THE FUTURE

It takes but a glance to appreciate the radically different nature of Exhibit 2—it's a mess! So, welcome to the real world in today's more innovative businesses: start-ups, mid-size firms, and the slimmed-down business units of bigger firms. To the world of The Limited, Benetton, or the Gap in retailing. To the world of Compaq, Sun Microsystems, or the ASIC divisions of Intel or Motorola in computer systems. To the world of steelmakers Worthington Industries, Chaparral, and Nucor. To the world of Weaver Popcorn, Johnsonville Sausage, Neutrogena, ServiceMaster, and University National Bank & Trust of Palo Alto, California. To the world of somewhat ordered chaos, somewhat purposeful confusion; the world, above all, of flexibility, adaptiveness, and action. Or to a new world violently turned upside down.

Begin with *a*—the new-look corporate guidance system, a vital vision, philosophy, set of core values, and an out-and-about senior management team (see *b* and *c* on page 612). First, the innermost circle depicting the corporate center in Exhibit 2 is obviously bigger than its computer in Exhibit 1. My point is frightfully difficult to describe. I pictured the traditional corporate center in Exhibit 1 as out of touch, shrivelled, formalistic, and ruled by very tight policy and a constraining rather than opportunistic plan, with contacts inside and outside the enterprise conveyed in written format, usually via brisk, impatient, and bloodless staffers (the praetorian guard). But the visual image that comes to mind for the center of Exhibit 2 is of a glowing, healthy, breathing corporate center. People from below regularly wander in without muss or fuss, and those at the top are more often than not out wandering. Customers and suppliers are as likely to be members of the executive floor (which, happily, doesn't really exist as a physical entity) as are the members of the senior team. But above all, the glow comes from management's availability, informality, energy, hustle, and the clarity of (and excitement associated with) the competitive vision, philosophy, or core values. Rule here is not written, but by example, by role model, by spirited behavior, and by fun—the vigorous pursuit of a worthwhile competitive idea, whether the firm is a bank, local insurance agency, or superconductor outfit.

Next, as previously anticipated, comes *b*—top management "wandering" across functional barriers and out to the front line in the firm. First, all the communication lines in Exhibit 2 are portrayed as zigzagging and wavy, with reason: To be as flexible and adaptive as required by tomorrow's competitive situation demands the wholesale smashing of traditional barriers and functional walls, both up and down and from side to side. So, this particular wavy line not only depicts the chief and his or her senior cohorts wandering about, but it shows them purposefully disrespecting those functional spokes (in fact, there are no formal functional spokes in this organization chart). And, of course, the even more significant point is that the chiefs' (and their lieutenants') wandering regularly takes them to where

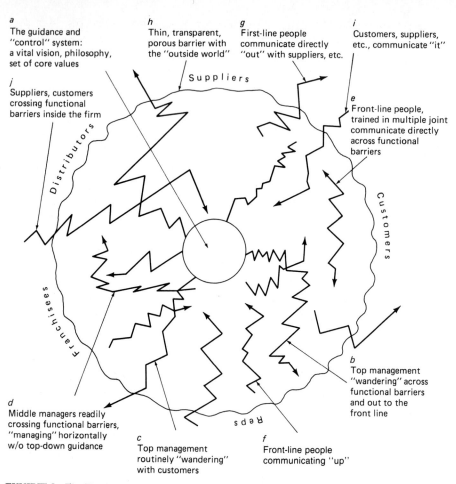

a
The guidance and "control" system: a vital vision, philosophy, set of core values

h
Thin, transparent, porous barrier with the "outside world"

g
First-line people communicate directly "out" with suppliers, etc.

i
Customers, suppliers, etc., communicate "it"

j
Suppliers, customers crossing functional barriers inside the firm

Suppliers

Distributors

e
Front-line people, trained in multiple joint communicate directly across functional barriers

Customers

Franchisees

b
Top management "wandering" across functional barriers and out to the front line

d
Middle managers readily crossing functional barriers, "managing" horizontally w/o top-down guidance

Reps

c
Top management routinely "wandering" with customers

f
Front-line people communicating "up"

EXHIBIT 2 The Flexible, Porous, Adaptive, Fleet-of-Foot Organization of the Future: Every Person is "Paid" to be Obstreperous, a Disrespecter of Formal Boundaries, to Hustle and to Be Engaged Fully with Engendering Swift Action, Constantly Improving Everything

the action is—at the front line, in the distribution center at 2 a.m., at the reservation center, at the night clerk's desk, in the factory, in the lab, or on the operations center floor.

Top management's "somewhat aimless ambling," as I like to call it, is not just restricted to the inside portion of the chart. Therefore, *c* depicts top management "wandering" with customers. Of course, the primary point is that top management is out and about—hanging out in the dealerships, with suppliers, and in general with customers, both big and small. But, again, the waviness of the line suggests a clarification; that is, the senior management visit here is not restricted to the stilted, formal "visit a customer a day" sort of affairs that mark all too many traditional top-management teams. Instead, it is the semi-unplanned visit; the drop-in to the dealer, supplier, or customer; or the largely unscheduled "ride around" with a salesperson on his or her normal, daily route.

As important as any of the contrasts between Exhibits 1 and 2 is *d*—middle managers routinely crossing functional barriers and managing horizontally without specific top-down guidance. Moving fast to implement anything, particularly engaging in fast-paced new product and service development, demands much faster, much less formal, and much less defensive communcation across traditional organization boundaries. Thus, the chief role for the middle manager of the future (albeit much fewer in number than in today's characteristically bloated middle-management ranks) is horizontal management rather than vertical management. The latter, as suggested in Exhibit 1, principally involves guarding the sanctity of the functional turf, providing any number of written reasons why function *x* is already overburdened and can't help function *y* at this particular juncture. In the new arrangement, the middle manager is paid proactively to grease skids between functions; that is, to be out of the office working with other functions to accomplish, not block, swift action taking. Once more, the zigzag nature of the line is meant to illustrate an essential point: Communication across functional barriers should be natural, informal, proactive, and helpful, not defensive and not preceded by infinite checking with the next layer(s) of management.

Perhaps the biggest difference involves *e*—frontline people, trained in multiple jobs, also routinely communicating across previously impenetrable functional barriers. The frontline person in Exhibit 1 has not only been cut off from the rest of the world by the button-down chieftains, praetorian guards, and turf-guarding middle managers, but also by a lack of training and cross-training, a history of not being listened to, and a last layer of cop—an old-school, Simon Legree, first-line supervisor. The role of the new-look frontline person sets all this on its ear. First, he or she is "controlled" not by a supervisor, middle management, or procedure book, but rather by the clarity and excitement of the vision, its daily embodiment by wandering senior managers, an extraordinary level of training, the obvious respect she or he is given, and the self-discipline that almost automatically accompanies exceptional grants of autonomy.

Not only is the frontline person encouraged to learn numerous jobs within the context of the work team, but she or he is also encouraged, at the frontline, to cross functional boundaries. Only regular frontline boundary crossing, in a virtually inhibited fashion, will bring forth the pace of action necessary for survival today. More formally, in the new regime you would expect to see frontline people as members of quality or productivity improvement teams that involve four or five functions. Informally, you would routinely observe the frontline person talking with the purchasing officer, a quality expert, or an industrial engineer (who she or he called in for advice, not vice versa) or simply chatting with members of the team 75 feet down the line—always at work on improvement projects that disdain old divisions of labor/task.

Move on to *f* and *g*, which take this frontline person two nontraditional steps further. First, *f*—frontline people communicating "up." The key to unlocking extraordinary productivity and quality improvements lies within the heads of the persons who live with the task, the persons on the firing line. Thus, in the new-look organization it becomes more commonplace for the frontline person to be communicating up, perhaps even two or three levels of management up (and one prays that there are no more than that in total) or all the way to the top on occasion.

And then—virtually unheard of outside sales and service departments today—the "average" person, per g, will routinely be out and about; that is, frontline people communicating directly with suppliers, customers, etc. Who is the person who best knows the problem with defective supplier material? Obviously, it's the frontline person who lives with it eight hours a day. With a little bit of advice and counsel from team members, and perhaps some occasional help from a middle manager (and following a bunch of perpetual training), who is the best person to visit the supplier—yes, take on a multiday visit that includes discussions with senior supplier management? Answer: It's again obvious—the first-line person or persons who suffer daily at the scene of the supplier's crime.

Now let's turn to the boundary, h—a thin, transparent permeable barrier to the outside world. This is yet another extraordinary distinction between the old-look and the new-look outfit. Recall Exhibit 1: The external barrier was thick, impermeable, and penetrated only at formal "receptacles." The new barrier is thin and wavy. Both the thinness and the imprecision are meant to suggest that there will be regular movement across it, in both directions. Frontline people, and senior people without prior notification, will be heading out with only semiplanned routines. Likewise, "external" colleagues will be regularly hanging out inside the firm (see i and j below). To be sure, the firm does exist as a legal entity: it is incorporated, and people are on its payroll. But more than any other factor, the idea of the firm turned inside out—the tough, recalcitrant hide that separates from "them" (customers, suppliers, etc.) ripped off—is the image I'm trying to convey. NIH (not invented here) in no longer tolerable. The firm must be permeable to (that it listen to with ease and respect and act upon) ideas from competitors, both small and large, foreign and domestic from interesting noncompetitors; from suppliers, customers, franchisees, reps, dealers, frontline people, and suppliers' frontline persons; and from joint venture partners. It must become virtually impossible to put one's finger on the outside organization boundary. Flow to and fro, by virtually everyone, all the time, and largely informally (i.e., leading to fast improvement without muss, fuss, and memos) must become the norm.

Next we move to i—customers, suppliers, etc. communicating (talking, hanging out, and participating "in"). The movement from adversarial to new nonadversarial/partnership relations with outsiders of all stripes is one of the biggest shifts required of American firms. Right now, the big (or small) business organization is typically the site of unabated warfare: top management versus lower management, management versus franchisees, company versus dealers and, above all, company versus suppliers. This must stop—period. Cleaning out the bulk of the distracting praetorian guard and middle management will obviously help, but achieving an attitude of partnership is at the top of the list of requirements, truly "living" a permeable organizational barrier. Customers and suppliers (and their people at all levels) must be part of any new product or service design teams. Even more routinely, customers, suppliers, franchisees, and reps ought to be part of day-to-day productivity and quality improvement teams. Once again, to compete today means to improve constantly, to invest fast; stripping away the impermeable barriers is the sine qua non of speedy implementation.

Which leads directly to *i*—suppliers, customers, etc., crossing functional barriers to work, and help, inside the firm. The idea of *i* was fine and dandy, but not enough. Customers shouldn't just be in the firm; they must be part of its most strategic internal dealings. The supplier shouldn't be shunted off to the purchasing person. Rather, he should be working with cost accountants, factory or operations center people, marketing teams, and new product and service design teams. Moreover, the wavy line suggests that the communication will be informal, not stilted.

There is no doubt that Exhibit 2, taken as a whole, appears anarchic. To a large extent, this must be so. To move faster in the face of radical uncertainty (competitors; energy, money, and currency costs; revolutionary technologies; and world instability) means that more chaos, more anarchy is required.[1] But that is only half the story. Return to Exhibit 2, idea *a*—the corporate guidance system in the new-look firm. Recall my halting effort to describe it as a glowing sun, an energy center. In fact, the control in Exhibit 2 may be much tighter than in the traditional Exhibit 1 organization. Instead of a bunch of stilted, formalistic baloney and out-of-touch leaders, the new control as noted is the energy, excitement, spirit, hustle, and clarity of the competitive vision that emanates from the corporate center. So when the newly empowered frontline person goes out to experiment—for example, to work with a supplier or with a multifunction team on quality or productivity improvement—she or he is, in fact, tightly controlled or guided by the attitudes, beliefs, energy, spirit, and so on, of the vital competitive vision. Moreover, that frontline person is extraordinarily well trained, unlike in the past, and remarkably well informed (for example, almost no performance information is kept secret from him or her). So, it's not at all a matter of tossing people out into a supplier's operation and saying, "We gotta be partners, now." The frontline person "out there" is someone who has seen senior management face to face (and smelled their enthusiasm); a person who has served on numerous multifunction teams; a person whose learning and training is continuous; a person who has just seen last month's divisional P&L in all its gory (or glorious) detail, following a year-long accounting course for all frontline "hands." Thus, there can be an astonishing high degree of controlled flexibility and informality, starting with the frontline and outsiders, in our new-look (Exhibit 2) organization. But there is also an astonishing amount of hard work required—perpetually clarifying the vision, living the vision, wandering, chatting, listening, *and* providing extraordinary and continuous training, for example—that must precede and/or accompany all this. So, perhaps "purposeful chaos," or something closely akin, is the best description of the Exhibit 2 new-look firm.

---

[1]See R. C. Conant and R. W. Ashby, "Every Good Regulator of a System Must be a Model of that System." *International Journal of Systems Science,* 1970, 1(2), 89–97. There is a compelling theoretical as well as pragmatic basis for the idea. In 1970. Conant and Ashby posited the Law of Requisite Variety, which has become the cornerstone of information theory. In layman's terms, it means that you have to be as messy as the surrounding situation. In a volatile world, we must have more sensors, processing information faster and leading to faster (and by definition more informal) action taking.

The ultimate point that underlies this brief contrast between and description of the two models is the nonoptional nature of the Exhibit 2 approach. Americans are getting kicked, battered, and whacked about in industry after industry. We must change, and change fast. The two charts discussed here are radically different, and although I'm not sure that Exhibit 2 is entirely "correct," I am sure that the radical difference between the two is spot on.

19
Job Design and Job Involvement

FROM CONTROL TO COMMITMENT IN THE WORKPLACE
Richard E. Walton

A NEW STRATEGY FOR JOB ENRICHMENT
J. Richard Hackman
Greg Oldham
Robert Janson
Kenneth Purdy

DEMING'S REDEFINITION OF MANAGEMENT
Myron Tribus

FROM CONTROL TO COMMITMENT IN THE WORKPLACE

Richard E. Walton

The larger shape of institutional change is always difficult to recognize when one stands right in the middle of it. Today, throughout American industry, a significant change is underway in long-established approaches to the organization and management of work. Although this shift in attitude and practice takes a wide variety of company-specific forms, its larger shape—its overall pattern—is already visible if one knows where and how to look.

Consider, for example, the marked differences between two plants in the chemical products division of a major U.S. corporation. Both make similar products and employ similar technologies, but that is virtually all they have in common.

The first, organized by businesses with an identifiable product or product line, divides its employees into self-supervising 10- to 15-person work teams that are collectively responsible for a set of related tasks. Each team member has the training to perform many or all of the tasks for which the team is accountable, and pay reflects the level of mastery of required skills. These teams have received assurances that management will go to extra lengths to provide continued employment in any economic downturn. The teams have also been thoroughly briefed on such issues as market share, product costs, and their implications for the business.

Not surprisingly, this plant is a top performer economically and rates well on all measures of employee satisfaction, absenteeism, turnover, and safety. With its employees actively engaged in identifying and solving problems, it operates with fewer levels of management and fewer specialized departments than do its sister plants. It is also one of the principal suppliers of management talent for these other plants and for the division manufacturing staff.

In the second plant, each employee is responsible for a fixed job and is required to perform up to the minimum standard defined for that job. Peer pressure keeps new employees from exceeding the minimum standards and from taking other initiatives that go beyond basic job requirements. Supervisors, who manage daily assignments and monitor performance, have long since given up hope for anything more than compliance with standards, finding sufficient difficulty in getting their people to perform adequately most of the time. In fact, they and their workers try to prevent the industrial engineering department, which is under pressure from top plant management to improve operations, from using changes in methods to "jack up" standards.

A recent management campaign to document an "airtight case" against employees who have excessive absenteeism or sub-par performance mirrors employees' low morale and high distrust of management. A constant stream of formal grievances, violations of plant rules, harassment of supervisors, wildcat walkouts, and even sabotage has prevented the plant from reaching its productivity and quality goals and has absorbed a disproportionate amount of division staff time. Dealings with the union are characterized by contract negotiations on economic matters and skirmishes over issues of management control.

No responsible manager, of course, would ever wish to encourage the kind of situation at this second plant, yet the determination to understand its deeper causes and to attack them at their root does not come easily. Established modes of doing things have an inertia all their own. Such an effort is, however, in process all across the industrial landscape. And with that effort comes the possibility of a revolution in industrial relations every bit as great as that occasioned by the rise of mass production the better part of a century ago. The challenge is clear to those managers willing to see it—and the potential benefits, enormous.

APPROACHES TO WORK-FORCE MANAGEMENT

What explains the extraordinary differences between the plants just described? Is it that the first is new (built in 1976) and the other old? Yes and no. Not all new plants enjoy so fruitful an approach to work organization; not all older plants have such intractable problems. Is it that one plant is unionized and the other not? Again, yes and no. The presence of a union may institutionalize conflict and lackluster performance, but it seldom causes them.

At issue here is not so much age or unionization but two radically different strategies for managing a company's or a factory's work force, two incompatible views of what managers can reasonably expect of workers and of the kind of partnership they can share with them. For simplicity, I will speak of these profound differences as reflecting the choice between a strategy based on imposing *control* and a strategy based on eliciting *commitment*.

The 'Control' Strategy

The traditional—or control-oriented—approach to work-force management took shape during the early part of this century in response to the division of work into small, fixed jobs for which individuals could be held accountable. The actual definition of jobs, as of acceptable standards of performance, rested on "lowest common denominator" assumptions about workers' skill and motivation. To monitor and control effort of this assumed caliber, management organized its own responsibilities into a hierarchy of specialized roles buttressed by a top-down allocation of authority and by status symbols attached to positions in the hierarchy.

For workers, compensation followed the rubric of "a fair day's pay for a fair day's work" because precise evaluations were possible when individual job requirements were so carefully prescribed. Most managers had little doubt that labor was best thought of as a variable cost, although some exceptional companies guaranteed job security to head off unionization attempts.

In the traditional approach, there was generally little policy definition with regard to employee voice unless the work force was unionized, in which case damage control strategies predominated. With no union, management relied on an open-door policy, attitude surveys, and similar devices to learn about employees' concerns. If the work force was unionized, then management bargained terms of employment and established an appeal mechanism. These activities fell to labor relations specialists, who operated independently from line management and whose very existence assumed the inevitability and even the appropriateness of an adversarial relationship between workers and managers. Indeed, to those who saw management's exclusive obligation to be to a company's shareowners and the ownership of property to be the ultimate source of both obligation and prerogative, the claims of employees were constraints, nothing more.

At the heart of this traditional model is the wish to establish order, exercise control, and achieve efficiency in the application of the work force. Although it has distant antecedents in the bureaucracies of both church and military, the model's real father is Frederick W. Taylor, the turn-of-the-century "father of scientific management," whose views about the proper organization of work have long influenced management practice as well as the reactive policies of the U.S. labor movement.

Recently, however, changing expectations among workers have prompted a growing disillusionment with the apparatus of control. At the same time, of course, an intensified challenge from abroad has made the competitive obsolescence of this strategy clear. A model that assumes low employee commitment and that is designed to produce reliable if not outstanding performance simply cannot match the standards of excellence set by world-class competitors. Especially in a high-wage country like the United States, market success depends on a superior level of performance, a level that, in turn, requires a deep commitment, not merely the obedience—if you could obtain it—of workers. And as painful experience shows, this commitment cannot flourish in a work-place dominated by the familiar model of control.

The 'Commitment' Strategy

Since the early 1970s, companies have experimented at the plant level with a radically different work-force strategy. The more visible pioneers—among them, General Foods at Topeka, Kansas; General Motors at Brookhaven, Mississippi; Cummins Engine at Jamestown, New York; and Procter & Gamble at Lima, Ohio—have begun to show how great and productive the contribution of a truly committed work force can be. For a time, all new plants of this sort were nonunion, but by 1980 the success of efforts undertaken jointly with unions—GM's cooperation with the UAW at the Cadillac plant in Livonia, Michigan, for example—was impressive enough to encourage managers of both new and existing facilities to rethink their approach to the work force.

Stimulated in part by the dramatic turnaround at GM's Tarrytown assembly plant in the mid-1970s, local managers and union officials are increasingly talking about common interests, working to develop mutual trust, and agreeing to sponsor quality-of-work-life (QWL) or employee involvement (EI) activities. Although most of these ventures have been initiated at the local level, major exceptions include the joint effort between the Communication Workers of America and AT&T to promote QWL throughout the Bell System and the UAW-Ford EI program centrally directed by Donald Ephlin of the UAW and Peter Pestillo of Ford. In the nonunion sphere, the spirit of these new initiatives is evident in the decision by workers of Delta Airlines to show their commitment to the company by collecting money to buy a new plane.

More recently, a growing number of manufacturing companies has begun to remove levels of plant hierarchy, increase managers' spans of control, integrate quality and production activities at lower organizational levels, combine production and maintenance operations, and open up new career possibilities for workers. Some corporations have even begun to chart organizational renewal for the entire company. Cummins Engine, for example, has ambitiously committed itself to inform employees about the business, to encourage participation by everyone, and to create jobs that involve greater responsibility and more flexibility.

In this new commitment-based approach to the work force, jobs are designed to be broader than before, to combine planning and implementation, and to include efforts to upgrade operations, not just maintain them. Individual responsibilities are expected to change as conditions change, and teams, not individuals, often are the organizational units accountable for performance. With management hierarchies relatively flat and differences in status minimized, control and lateral coordination depend on shared goals, and expertise rather than formal position determines influence.

People Express, to cite one example, started up with its management hierarchy limited to three levels, organized its work force into three- or four-person groups, and created positions with exceptionally broad scope. Every full-time employee is a "manager": flight managers are pilots who also perform dispatching and safety checks; maintenance managers are technicians with other staff responsibilities; customer service managers take care of ticketing, security clearance, passenger boarding, and in-flight service. Everyone, including the officers, is expected to rotate among functions to boost all workers' understanding of the business and to promote personal development.

Under the commitment strategy, performance expectations are high and serve not to define minimum standards but to provide "stretch objectives," emphasize continuous improvement, and reflect the requirements of the marketplace. Accordingly, compensation policies reflect less the old formulas of job evaluation than the heightened importance of group achievement, the expanded scope of individual contribution, and the growing concern for such questions of "equity" as gain sharing, stock ownership, and profit sharing. This principle of economic sharing is not new. It has long played a role in Dana corporation, which has many unionized plants, and is a fundamental part of the strategy of People Express, which has no union. Today, Ford sees it as an important part of the company's transition to a commitment strategy.

Equally important to the commitment strategy is the challenge of giving employees some assurance of security, perhaps by offering them priority in training and retraining as old jobs are eliminated and new ones created. Guaranteeing employees access to due process and providing them the means to be heard on such issues as production methods, problem solving, and human resource policies and practices is also a challenge. In unionized settings, the additional tasks include making relations less adversarial, broadening the agenda for joint problem solving and planning, and facilitating employee consultation.

Underlying all these policies is a management philosophy, often embodied in a published statement, that acknowledges the legitimate claims of a company's multiple stakeholders—owners, employees, customers, and the public. At the center of this philosophy is a belief that eliciting employee commitment will lead to enhanced performance. The evidence shows this belief to be well-grounded. In the absence of genuine commitment, however, new management policies designed for a committed work force may well leave a company distinctly more vulnerable than would older policies based on the control approach. The advantages—and risks—are considerable.

THE COSTS OF COMMITMENT

Because the potential leverage of a commitment-oriented strategy on performance is so great, the natural temptation is to assume the universal applicability of that strategy. Some environments, however, especially those requiring intricate teamwork, problem solving, organizational learning, and self-monitoring, are better suited than others to the commitment model. Indeed, the pioneers of the deep commitment strategy—a fertilizer plant in Norway, a refinery in the United Kingdom, a paper mill in Pennsylvania, a pet-food processing plant in Kansas—were all based on continuous process technologies and were all capital and raw material intensive. All provided high economic leverage to improvements in workers' skills and attitudes, and all could offer considerable job challenge.

Is the converse true? Is the control strategy appropriate whenever—as with convicts breaking rocks with sledgehammers in a prison yard—work can be completely prescribed, remains static, and calls for individual, not group, effort? In practice, managers have long answered yes. Mass production, epitomized by the assembly line, has for years been thought suitable for old-fashioned control.

But not any longer. Many mass producers, not least the automakers, have recently been trying to reconceive the structure of work and to give employees a significant role in solving problems and improving methods. Why? For many reasons, including to boost in-plant quality, lower warranty costs, cut waste, raise machine utilization and total capacity with the same plant and equipment, reduce operating and support personnel, reduce turnover and absenteeism, and speed up implementation of change. In addition, some managers place direct value on the fact that the commitment policies promote the development of human skills and individual self-esteem.

The benefits, economic and human, of worker commitment extend not only to continuous-process industries but to traditional manufacturing industries as well. What, though, are the costs? To achieve these gains, managers have had to invest extra effort, develop new skills and relationships, cope with higher levels of ambiguity and uncertainty, and experience the pain and discomfort associated with changing habits and attitudes. Some of their skills have become obsolete, and some of their careers have been casualties of change. Union officials, too, have had to face the dislocation and discomfort that inevitably follow any upheaval in attitudes and skills. For their part, workers have inherited more responsibility and, along with it, greater uncertainty and a more open-ended possibility of failure.

Part of the difficulty in assessing these costs is the fact that so many of the following problems inherent to the commitment strategy remain to be solved.

Employment Assurances

As managers in heavy industry confront economic realities that make such assurances less feasible and as their counterparts in fiercely competitive high-technology areas are forced to rethink early guarantees of employment security, pointed questions await.

Will managers give lifetime assurances to the few, those who reach, say, 15 years' seniority, or will they adopt a general no-layoff policy? Will they demonstrate by policies and practices that employment security, though by no means absolute, is a higher priority item than it was under the control approach? Will they accept greater responsibility for outplacement?

Compensation

In one sense, the more productive employees under the commitment approach deserve to receive better pay for their better efforts, but how can managers balance this claim on resources with the harsh reality that domestic pay rates have risen to levels that render many of our industries uncompetitive internationally? Already, in such industries as trucking and airlines, new domestic competitors have placed companies that maintain prevailing wage rates at a significant disadvantage. Experience shows, however, that wage freezes and concession bargaining create obstacles to commitment, and new approaches to compensation are difficult to develop at a time when management cannot raise the overall level of play.

Which approach is really suitable to the commitment model is unclear. Traditional job classifications place limits on the discretion of supervisors and encourage workers' sense of job ownership. Can pay systems based on employees' skill levels, which have long been used in engineering and skilled crafts, prove widely effective? Can these systems make up in greater mastery, positive motivation, and work-force flexibility what they give away in higher average wages?

In capital-intensive businesses, where total payroll accounts for a small percentage of costs, economics favor the move toward pay progression based on deeper and broader mastery. Still, conceptual problems remain with measuring skills, achieving consistency in pay decisions, allocating opportunities for learning new skills, trading off breadth and flexibility against depth, and handling the effects of "topping out" in a system that rewards and encourages personal growth.

There are also practical difficulties. Existing plants cannot, for example, convert to a skill-based structure overnight because of the vested interests of employees in the higher classifications. Similarly, formal profit- or gain-sharing plans like the Scanlon Plan (which shares gains in productivity as measured by improvements in the ratio of payroll to the sales value of production) cannot always operate. At the plant level, formulas that are responsive to what employees can influence, that are not unduly influenced by factors beyond their control, and that are readily understood, are not easy to devise. Small stand-alone businesses with a mature technology and stable markets tend to find the task least troublesome, but they are not the only ones trying to implement the commitment approach.

Yet another problem, very much at issue in the Hyatt-Clark bearing plant, which employees purchased from General Motors in 1981, is the relationship between compensation decisions affecting salaried managers and professionals, on the one hand, and hourly workers, on the other. When they formed the company, workers took a 25% pay cut to make their bearings competitive but the managers maintained and, in certain instances increased, their own salaries in order to help the company attract and retain critical talent. A manager's ability to elicit and preserve commitment, however, is sensitive to issues of equity, as became evident once again when GM and Ford announced huge executive bonuses in the spring of 1984 while keeping hourly wages capped.

Technology

Computer-based technology can reinforce the control model or facilitate movement to the commitment model. Applications can narrow the scope of jobs or broaden them, emphasize the individual nature of tasks or promote the work of groups, centralize or decentralize the making of decisions, and create performance measures that emphasize learning or hierarchical control.

To date, the effects of this technology on control and commitment have been

EXHIBIT Work-force strategies

	Control	Transitional	Commitment
Job design principles	Individual attention limited to performing individual job.	Scope of individual responsibility extended to upgrading system performance, via participative problem-solving groups in QWL, EI, and quality circle programs.	Individual responsibility extended to upgrading system performance.
	Job design deskills and fragments work and separates doing and thinking.	No change in traditional job design or accountability.	Job design enhances content of work, emphasizes whole task, and combined doing and thinking.
	Accountability focused on individual.		Frequent use of teams as basic accountable unit.
	Fixed job definition.		Flexible definition of duties. contingent on changing conditions.
Performance expectations	Measured standards define minimum performance. Stability seen as desirable.		Emphasis placed on higher, "stretch objectives," which tend to be dynamic and oriented to the marketplace.
Management organization: structure, systems, and style	Structure tends to be layered, with top-down controls.	No basic changes in approaches to structure, control, or authority.	Flat organization structure with mutual influence systems.
	Coordination and control rely on rules and procedures.		Coordination and control based more on shared goals, values, and traditions.
	More emphasis on prerogatives and positional authority.		Management emphasis on problem solving and relevant information and expertise.
	Status symbols distributed to reinforce hierarchy.	A few visible symbols change.	Minimum status differentials to de-emphasize inherent hierarchy.

EXHIBIT Work-force strategies (continued)

	Control	Transitional	Commitment
Compensation policies	Variable pay where feasible to provide individual incentive.	Typically no basic changes in compensation concepts.	Variable rewards to create equity and to reinforce group achievements: gain sharing, profit sharing.
	Individual pay geared to job evaluation.		Individual pay linked to skills and mastery.
	In downturn, cuts concentrated on hourly payroll.	Equality of sacrifice among employee groups.	Equality of sacrifice.
Employment assurances	Employees regarded as variable costs.	Assurances that participation will not result in loss of job.	Assurances that participation will not result in loss of job.
		Extra effort to avoid layoffs.	High commitment to avoid or assist in reemployment.
			Priority for training and retaining existing work force.
Employee voice policies	Employee input allowed on relatively narrow agenda. Attendant risks emphasized. Methods include open-door policy, attitude surveys, grievance procedures, and collective bargaining in some organizations.	Addition of limited, ad hoc consultation mechanisms. No change in corporate governance.	Employee participation encouraged on wide range of issues. Attendant benefits emphasized. New concepts of corporate governance.
	Business information distributed on strictly defined "need to know" basis.	Additional sharing of information.	Business data shared widely.
Labor-management relations	Adversarial labor relations; emphasis on interest conflict.	Thawing of adversarial attitudes; joint sponsorship of QWL or EI; emphasis on common fate.	Mutuality in labor relations; joint planning and problem solving on expanded agenda.
			Unions, management, and workers redefine their respective roles.

largely unintentional and unexpected. Even in organizations otherwise pursuing a commitment strategy, managers have rarely appreciated that the side effects of technology are not somehow "given" in the nature of things or that they can be actively managed. In fact, computer-based technology may be the least deterministic, most flexible technology to enter the workplace since the industrial revolution. As it becomes less hardware-dependent and more software-intensive and as the cost of computer power declines, the variety of ways to meet business requirements expands, each with a different set of human implications. Management has yet to identify the potential role of technology policy in the commitment strategy, and it has yet to invent concepts and methods to realize that potential.

Supervisors

The commitment model requires first-line supervisors to facilitate rather than direct the work force, to impart rather than merely practice their technical and administrative expertise, and to help workers develop the ability to manage themselves. In practice, supervisors are to delegate away most of their traditional functions—often without having received adequate training and support for their new team-building tasks or having their own needs for voice, dignity, and fulfillment recognized.

These dilemmas are even visible in the new titles many supervisors carry— "team advisers" or "team consultants," for example—most of which imply that supervisors are not in the chain of command, although they are expected to be directive if necessary and assume functions delegated to the work force if they are not being performed. Part of the confusion here is the failure to distinguish the behavioral style required of supervisors from the basic responsibilities assigned them. Their ideal style may be advisory, but their responsibilities are to achieve certain human and economic outcomes. With experience, however, as first-line managers become more comfortable with the notion of delegating what subordinates are ready and able to perform, the problem will diminish.

Other difficulties are less tractable. The new breed of supervisors must have a level of interpersonal skill and conceptual ability often lacking in the present supervisory work force. Some companies have tried to address this lack by using the position as an entry point to management for college graduates. This approach may succeed where the work force has already acquired the necessary technical expertise, but it blocks a route of advancement for workers and sharpens the dividing line between management and other employees. Moreover, unless the company intends to open up higher level positions for these college-educated supervisors, they may well grow impatient with the shift work of first-line supervision.

Even when new supervisory roles are filled—and filled successfully—from the ranks, dilemmas remain. With teams developed and functions delegated, to what new challenges do they turn to utilize fully their own capabilities? Do those capabilities match the demands of the other managerial work they might take on? If fewer and fewer supervisors are required as their individual span of control extends to a second and a third work team, what promotional opportunities exist for the rest? Where do they go?

Union-Management Relations

Some companies, as they move from control to commitment, seek to decertify their unions and, at the same time, strengthen their employees' bond to the company. Others—like GM, Ford, Jones & Laughlin, and AT&T—pursue cooperation intensified in the late 1970s, as improved work-force effectiveness could not by itself close the competitive gap in many industries and wage concessions became necessary. Based on their own analysis of competitive conditions, unions sometimes agreed to these concessions but expanded their influence over matters previously subject to management control.

These developments open up new questions. Where companies are trying to preserve the nonunion status of some plants and yet promote collaborative union relations in others, will unions increasingly force the company to choose? After General Motors saw the potential of its joint QWL program with the UAW, it signed a neutrality clause (in 1976) and then an understanding about automatic recognition in new plants (in 1979). If forced to choose, what will other managements do? Further, where union and management have collaborated in promoting QWL, how can the union prevent management from using the program to appeal directly to the workers about issues, such as wage concessions, that are subject to collective bargaining?

And if, in the spirit of mutuality, both sides agree to expand their joint agenda, what new risks will they face? Do union officials have the expertise to deal effectively with new agenda items like investment, pricing, and technology? To support QWL activities, they already have had to expand their skills and commit substantial resources at a time when shrinking employment has reduced their membership and thus their finances.

THE TRANSITIONAL STAGE

Although some organizations have adopted a comprehensive version of the commitment approach, most initially take on a more limited set of changes, which I refer to as a "transitional" stage or approach. The challenge here is to modify expectations, to make credible the leaders' stated intentions for further movement, and to support the initial changes in behavior. These transitional efforts can achieve a temporary equilibrium, provided they are viewed as part of a movement toward a comprehensive commitment strategy.

The cornerstone of the transitional stage is the voluntary participation of employees in problem-solving groups like quality circles. In unionized organizations, union-management dialogue leading to a jointly sponsored program is a condition for this type of employee involvement, which must then be supported by additional training and communication and by a shift in management style. Managers must also seek ways to consult employees about changes that affect them and to assure them that management will make every effort to avoid, defer, or minimize layoffs from higher productivity. When volume-related layoffs or concessions on pay are unavoidable, the principle of "equality of sacrifice" must apply to all employee groups, not just the hourly work force.

As a rule, during the early stages of transformation, few immediate changes can occur in the basic design of jobs, the compensation system, or the management system itself. It is easy, of course, to attempt to change too much too soon. A more common error, especially in established organizations, is to make only "token" changes that never reach a critical mass. All too often managers try a succession of technique-oriented changes one by one: job enrichment, sensitivity training, management by objectives, group brainstorming, quality circles, and so on. Whatever the benefits of these techniques, their value to the organization will rapidly decay if the management philosophy—and practice—does not shift accordingly.

A different type of error—"overreaching"—may occur in newly established organizations based on commitment principles. In one new plant, managers allowed too much peer influence in pay decisions; in another, they underplayed the role of first-line supervisors as a link in the chain of command; in a third, they over-emphasized learning of new skills and flexibility at the expense of mastery in critical operations. These design errors by themselves are not fatal, but the organization must be able to make mid-course corrections.

RATE OF TRANSFORMATION

How rapidly is the transformation in work-force strategy, summarized in the *Exhibit,* occurring? Hard data are difficult to come by, but certain trends are clear. In 1970, only a few plants in the United States were systematically revising their approach to the work force. By 1975, hundreds of plants were involved. Today, I estimate that at least a thousand plants are in the process of making a comprehensive change and that many times that number are somewhere in the transitional stage.

In the early 1970s, plant managers tended to sponsor what efforts there were. Today, company presidents are formulating the plans. Not long ago, the initiatives were experimental; now they are policy. Early change focused on the blue-collar work force and on those clerical operations that most closely resemble the factory. Although clerical change has lagged somewhat—because the control model has not produced such overt employee disaffection, and because management has been slow to recognize the importance of quality and productivity improvement—there are signs of a quickened pace of change in clerical operations.

Only a small fraction of U.S. workplaces today can boast of a comprehensive commitment strategy, but the rate of transformation continues to accelerate, and the move toward commitment via some explicit transitional stage extends to a still larger number of plants and offices. This transformation may be fueled by economic necessity, but other factors are shaping and pacing it—individual leadership in management and labor, philosophical choices, organizational competence in managing change, and cumulative learning from change itself.

SUGGESTED READINGS

Irving Bluestone, "Labor's Stake in Improving the Quality of Working Life," *The Quality of Working Life and the 1980s,* ed. Harvey Kolodny and Hans van Beinum (New York: Praeger, 1983).

Robert H. Guest, "Quality of Work Life—Learning from Tarrytown," HBR July–August 1979, p. 76.

Janice A. Klein, "Why Supervisors Resist Employee Involvement," HBR September–October 1984, p. 87.

John F. Runcie, " 'By Days I Make the Cars'," HBR May–June 1980, p. 106.

W. Earl Sasser and Frank S. Leonard, "Let First-Level Supervisors Do Their Job," HBR March–April 1980, p. 113.

Leonard A. Schlesinger and Janice A. Klein, "The First-Line Supervisor: Past, Present and Future," *Handbook of Organizational Behavior,* ed. Jay W. Lorsch (Englewood Cliffs, N.J.: Prentice-Hall, 1983).

Richard E. Walton, "Work Innovations in the United States," HBR July–August 1979, p. 88; "Improving the Quality of Work Life," HBR May–June 1974, p. 12; "How to Counter Alienation in the Plant," HBR November–December 1972, p. 70.

Richard E. Walton and Wendy Vittori, "New Information Technology: Organizational Problem or Opportunity?" *Office: Technology and People,* No. 1, 1983, p. 249.

Richard E. Walton and Leonard A. Schlesinger, "Do Supervisors Thrive in Participative Work Systems?" *Organizational Dynamics,* Winter 1979, p. 25.

A NEW STRATEGY FOR JOB ENRICHMENT

J. Richard Hackman
Greg Oldham
Robert Janson
Kenneth Purdy

...We present here a new strategy for going about the redesign of work. The strategy is based on three years of collaborative work and cross-fertilization among the authors—two of whom are academic researchers and two of whom are active practitioners in job enrichment. Our approach is new, but it has been tested in many organizations. It draws on the contributions of both management practice and psychological theory, but it is firmly in the middle ground between them. It builds on and complements previous work by Herzberg and others, but provides for the first time a set of tools for *diagnosing* existing jobs—and a map for translating the diagnostic results into specific action steps for change.

What we have, then, is the following:

1. A theory that specifies when people will get personally "turned on" to their work. The theory shows what kinds of jobs are most likely to generate excitement and commitment about work, and what kinds of employees it works best for.

Source: California Management Review, Summer 1975, pp. 57–71.

2. A set of action steps for job enrichment based on the theory, which prescribe in concrete terms what to do to make jobs more motivating for the people who do them.

3. Evidence that the theory holds water and that it can be used to bring about measurable—and sometimes dramatic—improvements in employee work behavior, in job satisfaction, and in the financial performance of the organizational unit involved.

THE THEORY BEHIND THE STRATEGY

What Makes People Get Turned On To Their Work?

For workers who are really prospering in their jobs, work is likely to be a lot like play. Consider, for example, a golfer at a driving range, practicing to get rid of a hook. His activity is *meaningful* to him; he has chosen to do it because he gets a "kick" from testing his skills by playing the game. He knows that he alone is *responsible* for what happens when he hits the ball. And he has *knowledge of the results* within a few seconds.

Behavioral scientists have found that the three "psychological states" experienced by the golfer in the above example also are critical in determining a person's motivation and satisfaction on the job.

Experienced Meaningfulness. The individual must perceive his work as worthwhile or important by some system of values he accepts.

Experienced Responsibility. He must believe that he personally is accountable for the outcomes of his efforts.

Knowledge of Results. He must be able to determine, on some fairly regular basis, whether or not the outcomes of his work are satisfactory.

When these three conditions are present, a person tends to feel very good about himself when he performs well. And those good feelings will prompt him to try to continue to do well—so he can continue to earn the positive feelings in the future. That is what is meant by "internal motivation"—being turned on to one's work because of the positive internal feelings that are generated by doing well, rather than being dependent on external factors (such as incentive pay or compliments from the boss) for the motivation to work effectively.

What if one of the three psychological states is missing? Motivation drops markedly. Suppose, for example, that our golfer has settled in at the driving range to practice for a couple of hours. Suddenly a fog drifts in over the range. He can no longer see if the ball starts to tail off to the left a hundred yards out. The satisfaction he got from hitting straight down the middle—and the motivation to try to correct something whenever he didn't—are both gone. If the fog stays, it's likely that he soon will be packing up his clubs.

The relationship between the three psychological states and on-the-job outcomes is illustrated in Figure 1. When all three are high, then internal work motiva-

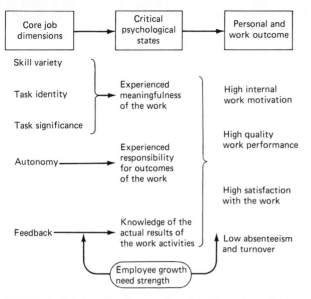

FIGURE 1 Relationships Among Core Job Dimensions, Critical Psychological States, and On-The-Job Outcomes

tion, job satisfaction, and work quality are high, and absenteeism and turnover are low.

What Job Characteristics Make It Happen?

Recent research has identified live "core" characteristics of jobs that elicit the psychological states described above.[1-3] These five core job dimensions provide the key to objectively measuring jobs and to changing them so that they have high potential for motivating people who do them.

Toward Meaningful Work. Three of the five core dimensions contribute to a job's meaningfulness for the worker:

1. Skill variety. The degree to which a job requires the worker to perform activities that challenge his skills and abilities. When even a single skill is involved, there is at least a seed of potential meaningfulness. When several are involved, the job has the potential of appealing to more of the whole person, and also of avoiding the

[1] A. N. Turner and P. R. Lawrence. *Industrial Jobs and the Worker* (Cambridge, Mass.: Harvard Graduate School of Business Administration, 1965).

[2] J. R. Hackman and E. E. Lawler, "Employee Reactions to Job Characteristics," *Journal of Applied Psychology Monograph,* 1971, pp. 259–286.

[3] J. R. Hackman and G. R. Oldham. *Motivation Through the Design of Work: Test of a Theory,* Technical Report No. 6 (New Haven, Conn.: Department of Administrative Sciences, Yale University, 1974).

monotony of performing the same task repeatedly, no matter how much skill it may require.

2. Task identity. The degree to which the job requires completion of a "whole" and identifiable piece of work—doing a job from beginning to end with a visible outcome. For example, it is clearly more meaningful to an employee to build complete toasters than to attach electrical cord after electrical cord, especially if he never sees a completed toaster. (Note that the whole job, in this example, probably would involve greater skill variety as well as task identity.)

3. Task significance. The degree to which the job has a substantial and perceivable impact on the lives of other people, whether in the immediate organization or the world at large. The worker who tightens nuts on aircraft brake assemblies is more likely to perceive his work as significant than the worker who fills small boxes with paper clips—even though the skill levels involved may be comparable.

Each of these three jobs dimensions represents an important route to experienced meaningfulness. If the job is high in all three, the worker is quite likely to experience his job as very meaningful. It is not necessary, however, for a job to be very high in all three dimensions. If the job is low in any one of them, there will be a drop in overall experienced meaningfulness. But even when two dimensions are low the worker may find the job meaningful if the third is high enough.

Toward Personal Responsibility. A fourth core dimension leads a worker to experience increased responsibility in his job. This is *autonomy,* the degree to which the job gives the worker freedom, independence, and discretion in scheduling work and determining how he will carry it out. People in highly autonomous jobs know that they are personally responsible for successes and failures. To the extent that their autonomy is high, then, how the work goes will be felt to depend more on the individual's own efforts and initiatives—rather than on detailed instructions from the boss or from a manual of job procedures.

Toward Knowledge of Results. The fifth and last core dimension is *feedback.* This is the degree to which a worker, in carrying out the work activities required by the job, gets information about the effectiveness of his efforts. Feedback is most powerful when it comes directly from the work itself—for example, when a worker has the responsibility for gauging and otherwise checking a component he has just finished, and learns in the process that he has lowered his reject rate by meeting specifications more consistently.

The Overall "Motivating Potential" of a Job. Figure 1 shows how the five core dimensions combine to affect the psychological states that are critical in determining whether or not an employee will be internally motivated to work effectively. Indeed, when using an instrument to be described later, it is possible to compute a "motivating potential score" (MPS) for any job. The MPS provides a single summary index of the degree to which the objective characteristics of the job will prompt high internal work motivation. Following the theory outlined above, a job high in motivating potential must be high in at least one (and hopefully more) of the three dimensions that lead to experienced meaningfulness and high in both autonomy and feedback as well. The MPS provides a quantitative index of the degree to which this is in fact the case (see Appendix for detailed formula). As will be seen later, the MPS can be very useful in diagnosing jobs and in assessing the effectiveness of job-enrichment activities.

Does the Theory Work for Everybody?

Unfortunately not. Not everyone is able to become internally motivated in his work, even when the motivating potential of a job is very high indeed.

Research has shown that the *psychological needs* of people are very important in determining who can (and who cannot) become internally motivated at work. Some people have strong needs for personal accomplishment, for learning and developing themselves beyond where they are now, for being stimulated and challenged, and so on. These people are high in "growth-need strength."

Figure 2 shows diagrammatically the proposition that individual growth needs have the power to moderate the relationship between the characteristics of jobs and work outcomes. Many workers with high growth needs will turn on eagerly when they have jobs that are high in the core dimensions. Workers whose growth needs are not so strong may respond less eagerly—or, at first, even balk at being "pushed" or "stretched" too far.

Psychologists who emphasize human potential argue that everyone has within him at least a spark of the need to grow and develop personally. Steadily accumulating evidence shows, however, that unless that spark is pretty strong, chances are it will get snuffed out by one's experiences in typical organizations. So, a person who has worked for 20 years in stulifying jobs may find it difficult or impossible to become internally motivated overnight when given the opportunity.

We should be cautious, however, about creating rigid categories of people based on their measured growth-need strength at any particular time. It is true that we can predict from these measures who is likely to become internally motivated on a job and who will be less willing or able to do so. But what we do not know yet is whether or not the growth-need "spark" can be rekindled for those individuals who have had their growth needs dampened, by years of growth-depressing experience in their organizations.

Since it is often the organization that is responsible for currently low levels of growth desires, we believe that the organization also should provide the individual with the chance to reverse that trend whenever possible, even if that means putting a person in a job where he may be "stretched" more than he wants to be. He can

FIGURE 2 The Moderating Effect of Employee Growth-Need Strength

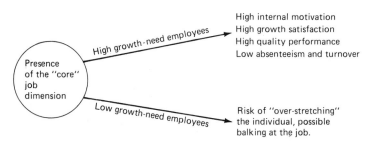

633

always move back later to the old job—and in the meantime the embers of his growth needs just might burst back into flame, to his surprise and pleasure, and for the good of the organization.

FROM THEORY TO PRACTICE: A TECHNOLOGY FOR JOB ENRICHMENT

When job enrichment fails, it often fails because of inadequate *diagnosis* of the target job and employees' reactions to it. Often, for example, job enrichment is assumed by management to be a solution to "people problems" on the job and is implemented even though there has been no diagnostic activity to indicate that the root of the problem is in fact how the work is designed. At other times, some diagnosis is made—but it provides no concrete guidance about what specific aspects of the job require change. In either case, the success of job enrichment may wind up depending more on the quality of the intuition of the change agent—or his luck—than on a solid base of data about the people and the work.

In the paragraphs to follow, we outline a new technology for use in job enrichment which explicitly addresses the diagnostic as well as the action components of the change process. The technology has two parts: (1) a set of diagnostic tools that are useful in evaluating jobs and people's reactions to them prior to change—and in pinpointing exactly what aspects of specific jobs are most critical to a successful change attempt; and (2) a set of "implementing concepts" that provide concrete guidance for action steps in job enrichment. The implementing concepts are tied directly to the diagnostic tools; the output of the diagnostic activity specifies which action steps are likely to have the most impact in a particular situation.

The Diagnostic Tools

Central to the diagnostic procedure we propose is a package of instruments to be used by employees, supervisors, and outside observers in assessing the target job and employees' reactions to it.[4] These instruments gauge the following:

1. The objective characteristics of the jobs themselves, including both an overall indication of the "motivating potential" of the job as it exists (that is, the MPS score) and the score of the job on each of the five core dimensions described previously. Because knowing the strengths and weaknesses of the job is critical to any work-redesign effort, assessments of the job are made by supervisors and outside observers as well as the employees themselves—and the final assessment of a job uses data from all three sources.
2. The current levels of motivation, satisfaction, and work performance of employees on the job. In addition to satisfaction with the work itself, measures are taken of how people feel about other aspects of the work setting, such as pay, supervision, and relationships with co-workers.
3. The level of growth-need strength of the employees. As indicated earlier, employees who have strong growth needs are more likely to be more responsive to job enrich-

[4]J. R. Hackman and G. R. Oldham, "Development of the Job Diagnostic Survey," *Journal of Applied Psychology*, 1975, pp. 159–70.

ment than employees with weak growth needs. Therefore, it is important to know at the outset just what kinds of satisfactions the people who do the job are (and are not) motivated to obtain from their work. This will make it possible to identify which persons are best to start changes with, and which may need help in adapting to the newly enriched job.

What, then, might be the actual steps one would take in carrying out a job diagnosis using these tools? Although the approach to any particular diagnosis depends upon the specifics of the particular work situation involved, the sequence of questions listed below is fairly typical.

Step 1. Are Motivation and Satisfaction Central to the Problem?

Sometimes organizations undertake job enrichment to improve the work motivation and satisfaction of employees when in fact the real problem with work performance lies elsewhere—for example, in a poorly designed production system, in an error-prone computer, and so on. The first step is to examine the scores of employees on the motivation and satisfaction portions of the diagnostic instrument. (The questionnaire taken by employees is called the Job Diagnostic Survey and will be referred to hereafter as the JDS.) If motivation and satisfaction are problematic, the change agent would continue to Step 2; if not, he would look to other aspects of the work situation to identify the real problem.

Step 2. Is the Job Low in Motivating Potential?

To answer this question, one would examine the motivating potential score of the target job and compare it to the MPS's of other jobs to determine whether or not *the job itself* is a probable cause of the motivational problems documented in Step 1. If the job turns out to be low on the MPS, one would continue to Step 3; if it scores high, attention should be given to other possible reasons for the motivational difficulties (such as the pay system, the nature of supervision, and so on).

Step 3. What Specific Aspects of the Job Are Causing the Difficulty?

This step involves examining the job on each of the five core dimensions to pinpoint the specific strengths and weaknesses of the job as it is currently structured. It is useful at this stage to construct a "profile" of the target job, to make visually apparent where improvements need to be made. An illustrative profile for two jobs (one "good" job and one job needing improvement) is shown in Figure 3.

Job A is an engineering maintenance job and is high on all of the core dimensions; the MPS of this job is a very high 260. (MPS scores can range from 1 to about 350; an "average" score would be about 125.) Job enrichment would not be recommended for this job; if employees working on the job were unproductive and unhappy, the reasons are likely to have little to do with the nature or design of the work itself.

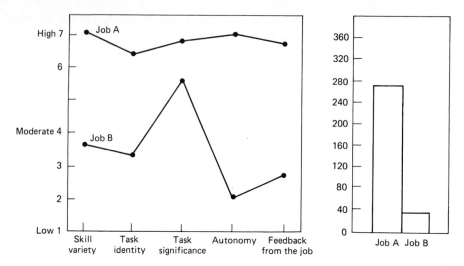

FIGURE 3 The JDS Diagnostic Profile for a "Good" and a "Bad" Job

Job B, on the other hand, has many problems. This job involves the routine and repetitive processing of checks in the "back room" of a bank. The MPS is 30, which is quite low—and indeed, would be even lower if it were not for the moderately high task significance of the job. (Task significance is moderately high because the people are handling large amounts of other people's money, and therefore the quality of their efforts potentially has important consequences for their unseen clients.) The job provides the individuals with very little direct feedback about how effectively they are doing it; the employees have little autonomy in how they go about doing the job; and the job is moderately low in both skill variety and task identity.

For Job B, then, there is plenty of room for improvement—and many avenues to examine in planning job changes. For still other jobs, the avenues for change often turn out to be considerably more specific: for example, feedback and autonomy may be reasonably high, but one or more of the core dimensions that contribute to the experienced meaningfulness of the job (skill variety, task identity, and task significance) may be low. In such a case, attention would turn to ways to increase the standing of the job on these latter three dimensions.

Step 4. How "Ready" Are the Employees for Change?

Once it has been documented that there is need for improvement in the job—and the particularly troublesome aspects of the job have been identified then it is time to begin to think about the specific action steps which will be taken to enrich the job. An important factor in such planning is the level of growth needs of the employees, since employees high on growth needs usually respond more readily to job enrichment than do employees with little need for growth. The JDS provides a direct measure of the growth-need strength of the employees. This measure can be very helpful in planning how to introduce the changes to the people (for instance, cautiously versus dramatically), and in deciding who should be among the first group of employees to have their jobs changed.

In actual use of the diagnostic package, additional information is generated which supplements and expands the basic diagnostic questions outlined above. The point of the above discussion is merely to indicate the kinds of questions which we believe to be most important in diagnosing a job prior to changing it. We now turn to how the diagnostic conclusions are translated into specific job changes.

The Implementing Concepts

Five "implementing concepts" for job enrichment are identified and discussed below.[5] Each one is a specific action step aimed at improving both the quality of the working experience for the individual and his work productivity. They are: (1) forming natural work units; (2) combining tasks; (3) establishing client relationships; (4) vertical loading; (5) opening feedback channels.

The links between the implementing concepts and the core dimensions are shown in Figure 4—which illustrates our theory of job enrichment, ranging from the concrete action steps through the core dimensions and the psychological states to the actual personal and work outcomes.

After completing the diagnosis of a job, a change agent would know which of the core dimensions were most in need of remedial attention. He could then turn to Figure 4 and select those implementing concepts that specifically deal with the most troublesome parts of the existing job. How this would take place in practice will be seen below.

FIGURE 4   The Full Model: How Use of the Implementing Concepts Can Lead to Positive Outcomes

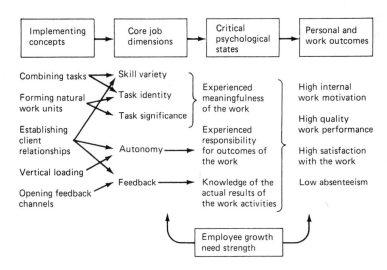

[5]R. W. Walters and Associates. *Job Enrichment for Results* (Cambridge, Mass.: Addison-Wesley Publishing Co. Inc., 1975).

Forming Natural Work Units. The notion of distributing work in some logical way may seem to be an obvious part of the design of any job. In many cases, however, the logic is one imposed by just about any consideration except jobholder satisfaction and motivation. Such considerations include technological dictates, level of worker training or experience, "efficiency" as defined by industrial engineering, and current workload. In many cases the cluster of tasks a worker faces during a typical day or week is natural to anyone *but* the worker.

For example, suppose that a typing pool (consisting of one supervisor and ten typists) handles all work for one division of a company. Jobs are delivered in rough draft or dictated form to the supervisor, who distributes them as evenly as possible among the typists. In such circumstances the individual letters, reports, and other tasks performed by a given typist in one day or week are randomly assigned. There is no basis for identifying with the work or the person or department for whom it is performed, or for placing any personal value upon it.

The principle underlying natural units of work, by contrast, is "ownership"—a worker's sense of continuing responsibility for an identifiable body of work. Two steps are involved in creating natural work units. The first is to identify the basic work items. In the typing pool, for example, the items might be "pages to be typed." The second step is to group the items in natural categories. For example, each typist might be assigned continuing responsibility for all jobs requested by one or several specific departments. The assignments should be made, of course, in such a way that workloads are about equal in the long run. (For example, one typist might end up with all the work from one busy department, while another handles jobs from several smaller units.)

At this point we can begin to see specifically how the job-design principles relate to the core dimensions (cf., Figure 4). The ownership fostered by natural units of work can make the difference between a feeling that work is meaningful and rewarding and the feeling that it is irrelevant and boring. As the diagram shows, natural units of work are directly related to two of the core dimensions: task identity and task signficance.

A typist whose work is assigned naturally rather than randomly—say, by departments—has a much greater chance of performing a whole job to completion. Instead of typing one section of a large report, the individual is likely to type the whole thing, with knowledge of exactly what the product of the work is (task identity). Furthermore, over time the typist will develop a growing sense of how the work affects co-workers in the department serviced (task significance).

Combining Tasks. The very existence of a pool made up entirely of persons whose sole function is typing reflects a fractionalization of jobs that has been a basic precept of "scientific management." Most obvious in assemblyline work, fractionalization has béen applied to nonmanufacturing jobs as well. It is typically justified by efficiency, which is usually defined in terms of either low costs or some time-and-motion type of criteria.

It is hard to find fault with measuring efficiency ultimately in terms of cost-effectiveness. In doing so, however, a manager should be sure to consider *all* the costs involved. It is possible, for example, for highly fractionalized jobs to meet all the time-and-motion criteria of efficiency, but if the resulitng job is so unrewarding that performing it day after day leads to high turnover, absenteeism, drugs and alcohol, and strikes, then productivity is really lower (and costs higher) than data on efficiency might indicate.

The principle of combining tasks, then, suggests that whenever possible existing and fractionalized tasks should be put together to form new and larger modules of work. At the Medfield, Massachusetts plant of Corning Glass Works the assembly of a laboratory hot plate has been redesigned along the lines suggested here. Each hot plate now is assembled from start to finish by one operator, instead of going through several separate operations that are performed by different people.

Some tasks, if combined into a meaningfully large module of work, would be more than an individual could do by himself. In such cases, it is often useful to consider assigning the new larger task to a small *team* of workers—who are given great autonomy for its completion. At the Racine, Wisconsin plant of Emerson Electric, the assembly process for trash disposal appliances was restructured this way. Instead of a sequence of moving the appliance from station to station, the assembly now is done from start to finish by one team. Such teams include both men and women to permit switching off the heavier and more delicate aspects of the work. The team responsible is identified on the appliance. In case of customer complaints, the team often drafts the reply.

As a job-design principle, task combination, like natural units of work, expands the task identity of the job. For example, the hot-plate assembler can see and identify with a finished product ready for shipment, rather than a nearly invisible junction of solder. Moreover, the more tasks that are combined into a single worker's job, the greater the variety of skills he must call on in performing the job. So task combination also leads directly to greater skill variety—the third core dimension that contributes to the overall experienced meaningfulness of the work.

Establishing Client Relationships. One consequence of fractionalization is that the typical worker has little or no contact with (or even awareness of) the ultimate user of his product or service. By encouraging and enabling employees to establish direct relationships with the clients of their work, improvements often can be realized simultaneously on three of the case dimensions. Feedback increases because of additional opportunities for the individual to receive praise or criticism of his work outputs directly. Skill variety often increases because of the necessity to develop and exercise one's interpersonal skills in maintaining the client relationship. And autonomy can increase because the individual often is given personal responsibility for deciding how to manage his relationships with the clients of his work.

Creating client relationships is a three-step process. First, the client must be identified. Second, the most direct contact possible between the worker and the client must be established. Third, criteria must be set up by which the client can judge the quality of the product or service he receives. And whenever possible, the client should have a means of relaying his judgments directly back to the worker.

The contact between worker and client should be as great as possible and as frequent as necessary. Face-to-face contact is highly desirable, at least occasionally. Where that is impossible or impractical, telephone and mail can suffice. In any case, it is important that the performance criteria by which the worker will be rated by the client must be mutually understood and agreed upon.

Vertical Loading. Typically the split between the "doing" of a job and the "planning" and "controlling" of the work has evolved along with horizontal fractionalization. Its rationale, once again, has been "efficiency through specialization." And once again, the excess of specialization that has emerged has resulted in unexpected but significant costs in motivation, morale, and work quality. In vertical loading, the intent is to partially close the gap between the doing and the controlling parts of the job—and thereby reap some important motivational advantages.

Of all the job-design principles, vertical loading may be the single most crucial one. In some cases, where it has been impossible to implement any other changes, vertical loading alone has had significant motivational effects.

When a job is vertically loaded, responsibilities and controls that formerly were reserved for high levels of management are added to the job. There are many ways to accomplish this:

- Return to the job holder greater discretion in settling schedules, deciding on work methods, checking on quality, and advising or helping to train less experienced workers.
- Grant additional authority. The objective should be to advance workers from a position of no authority or highly restricted authority to positions of reviewed, and eventually, near-total authority for his own work.
- Time management. The job holder should have the greatest possible freedom to decide when to start and stop work, when to break, and how to assign priorities.
- Troubleshooting and crisis decisions. Workers should be encouraged to seek problem solutions on their own, rather than calling immediately for the supervisor.
- Financial controls. Some degree of knowledge and control over budgets and other financial aspects of a job can often be highly motivating. However, access to this information frequently tends to be restricted. Workers can benefit from knowing something about the costs of their jobs, the potential effect upon profit, and various financial and budgetary alternatives.

When a job is vertically loaded it will inevitably increase in *autonomy*. And as shown in Figure 4, this increase in objective personal control over the work will also lead to an increased feeling of personal responsibility for the work, and ultimately to higher internal work motivation.

- Opening feedback channels. In virtually all jobs there are ways to open channels of feedback to individuals or teams to help them learn whether their performance is improving, deteriorating, or remaining at a constant level. While there are numerous channels through which information about performance can be provided, it generally is better for a worker to learn about his performance *directly as he does his job*—rather than from management on an occasional basis.

Job-provided feedback usually is more immediate and private than supervisor-supplied feedback, and it increases the worker's feelings of personal control over his work in the bargain. Moreover, it avoids many of the potentially disruptive interpersonal problems that can develop when the only way a worker has to find out how he is doing is through direct messages or subtle cues from the boss.

Exactly what should be done to open channels for job-provided feedback will vary from job to job and organization to organization. Yet in many cases the changes involve simply removing existing blocks that isolate the worker from naturally occurring data about performance—rather than generating entirely new feedback mechanisms. For example:

- Establishing direct client relationships often removes blocks between the worker and natural external sources of data about his work.
- Quality-control efforts in many organizations often eliminate a natural source of feedback. The quality check on a product or service is done by persons other than those responsible for the work. Feedback to the workers—if there is any—is belated and diluted. It often fosters a tendency to think of quality as "someone else's concern." By placing quality control close to the worker (perhaps even in his own hands), the quantity and quality of data about performance available to him can dramatically increase.
- Tradition and established procedure in many organizations dictate that records about performance be kept by a supervisor and transmitted up (not down) in the organizational hierarchy. Sometimes supervisors even check the work and correct any errors themselves. The worker who made the error never knows it occurred—and is denied the very information that could enhance both his internal work motivation and the technical adequacy of his performance. In many cases it is possible to provide standard summaries of performance records directly to the worker (as well as to his superior), thereby giving him personally and regularly the data he needs to improve his performance.
- Computers and other automated operations sometimes can be used to provide the individual with data now blocked from him. Many clerical operations, for example, are now performed on computer consoles. These consoles often can be programmed to provide the clerk with immediate feedback in the form of a CRT display or a printout indicating that an error has been made. Some systems even have been programmed to provide the operator with a positive feedback message when a period of error-free performance has been sustained.

Many organizations simply have not recognized the importance of feedback as a motivator. Data on quality and other aspects of performance are viewed as being of interest only to management. Worse still, the *standards* for acceptable performance often are kept from workers as well. As a result, workers who would be interested in following the daily or weekly ups and downs of their performance, and in trying accordingly to improve, are deprived of the very guidelines they need to do so. They are like the golfer we mentioned earlier, whose efforts to correct his hook are stopped dead by fog over the driving range.

THE STRATEGY IN ACTION: HOW WELL DOES IT WORK?

So far we have examined a basic theory of how people get turned on to their work; a set of core dimensions of jobs that create the conditions for such internal work motivation to develop on the job; and a set of five implementing concepts that are the action steps recommended to boost a job on the core dimensions and thereby increase employee motivation, satisfaction, and productivity.

The remaining question is straightforward and important: *Does it work?* In reality, that question is twofold. First, does the theory itself hold water, or are we barking up the wrong conceptual tree? And second, does the change strategy really lead to measurable differences when it is applied in an actual organizational setting?

This section summarizes the findings we have generated to date on these questions.

Is the Job-Enrichment Theory Correct?

In general, the answer seems to be yes. The JDS instrument has been taken by more than 1,000 employees working on about 100 diverse jobs in more than a dozen organizations over the last two years. These data have been analyzed to test the basic motivational theory—and especially the impact of the core job dimensions on worker motivation, satisfaction, and behavior on the job. An illustrative overview of some of the findings is given below.[6]

1. People who work on jobs high on the core dimensions are more motivated and satisfied than are people who work on jobs that score low on the dimensions. Employees with jobs high on the core dimensions (MPS scores greater than 240) were compared to those who held unmotivating jobs (MPS scores less than 40). As shown in Figure 5, employees with high MPS jobs were higher on (a) the three psychological states, (b) internal work motivation, (c) general satisfaction, and (d) "growth" satisfaction.

FIGURE 5 Employee Reactions to Jobs High and Low in Motivating Potential for Two Banks and a Steel Firm

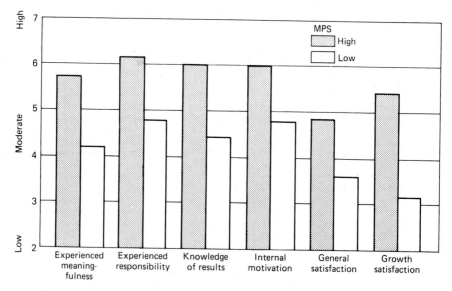

[6]Hackman and Oldham, *Motivation.*

2. Figure 6 shows that the same is true for measures of actual behavior at work—absenteeism and performance effectiveness—although less strongly so for the performance measure.

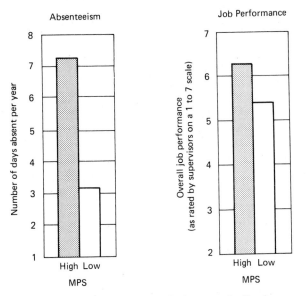

FIGURE 6 Absenteeism and Job Performance for Employees with Jobs High and Low in Motivating Potential

3. Responses to jobs high in motivating potential are more positive for people who have strong growth needs than for people with weak needs for growth. In Figure 7 the linear relationship between the motivating potential of a job and employees' level of internal work motivation is shown, separately for people with high versus low growth needs as measured by the JDS. While both groups of employees show increases in internal motivation as MPS increases, the rate of increase is significantly greater for the group of employees who have strong needs for growth.

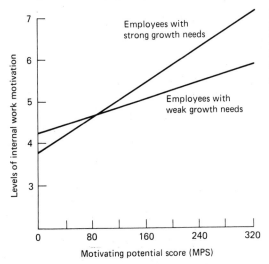

FIGURE 7 Relationship Between the Motivating Potential of a Job and the Internal Work Motivation of Employees (shown separately for employees with strong versus weak growth-need strength.)

How Does the Change Strategy Work in Practice?

The results summarized above suggest that both the theory and the diagnostic instrument work when used with real people in real organizations. In this section, we summarize a job-enrichment project conducted at The Travelers Insurance Companies, which illustrates how the change procedures themselves work in practice.

The Travelers project was designed with two purposes in mind. One was to achieve improvements in morale, productivity, and other indicators of employee well-being. The other was to test the general effectiveness of the strategy for job enrichment we have summarized in this article.

The work group chosen was a keypunching operation. The group's function was to transfer information from printed or written documents onto punched cards for computer input. The work group consisted of 98 keypunch operators and verifiers (both in the same job classification), plus seven assignment clerks. All reported to a supervisor who, in turn, reported to the assistant manager and manager of the data-input division.

The size of individual punching orders varied considerably, from a few cards to as many as 2,500. Some work came to the work group with a specified delivery date, while other orders were to be given routine service on a predetermined schedule.

Assignment clerks received the jobs from the user departments. After reviewing the work for obvious errors, omissions, and legibility problems, the assignment clerk parceled out the work in batches expected to take about one hour. If the clerk found the work not suitable for punching it went to the supervisor, who either returned the work to the user department or cleared up problems by phone. When work went to operators for punching, it was with the instruction, "Punch only what you see. Don't correct errors, no matter how obvious they look."

Because of the high cost of computer time, keypunched work was 100 percent verified—a task that consumed nearly as many manhours as the punching itself. Then the cards went to the supervisor, who screened the jobs for due dates before sending them to the computer. Errors detected in verificaiton were assigned to various operators at random to be corrected.

The computer output from the cards was sent to the originating department, accompanied by a printout of errors. Eventually the printout went back to the supervisor for final correction.

A great many phenomena indicated that the problems being experienced in the work group might be the result of poor motivation. As the only person performing supervisory functions of any kind, the supervisor spent most of his time responding to crisis situations, which recurred continually. He also had to deal almost daily with employees' salary grievances or other complaints. Employees frequently showed apathy or outright hostility toward their jobs.

Rates of work output, by accepted work-measurement standards, were inadequate. Error rates were high. Due dates and schedules frequently were missed. Absenteeism was higher than average, especially before and after weekends and holidays.

The single, rather unusual exception was turnover. It was lower than the company-wide average for similar jobs. The company has attributed this fact to a poor job market in the base period just before the project began, and to an older, relatively more settled work force—made up, incidentally, entirely of women.

The Diagnosis

Using some of the tools and techniques we have outlined, a consulting team from the Management Services Department and from Roy W. Walters & Associates concluded that the keypunch-operator's job exhibited the following serious weaknesses in terms of the core dimensions.

Skill Variety. There was none. Only a single skill was involved—the ability to punch adequately the data on the batch of documents.

Task Identity. Virtually nonexistent. Batches were assembled to provide an even workload, but not whole identifiable jobs.

Task Significance. Not apparent. The keypunching operation was a necessary step in providing service to the company's customers. The individual operator was isolated by an assignment clerk and a supervisor from any knowledge of what the operation meant to the using department, let alone its meaning to the ultimate customer.

Autonomy. None. The operators had no freedom to arrange their daily tasks to meet schedules, to resolve problems with the using department, or even to correct, in punching, information that was obviously wrong.

Feedback. None. Once a batch was out of the operator's hands, she had no assured chance of seeing evidence of its quality or inadequacy.

Design of the Experimental Trial

Since the diagnosis indicated that the motivating potential of the job was extremely low, it was decided to attempt to improve the motivation and productivity of the work group through job enrichment. Moreover, it was possible to design an experimental test of the effects of the changes to be introduced: the results of changes made in the target work group were to be compared with trends in a control work group of similar size and demographic make-up. Since the control group was located more than a mile away, there appeared to be little risk of communication between members of the two groups.

A base period was defined before the start of the experimental trial period, and appropriate data were gathered on the productivity, absenteeism, and work attitudes of members of both groups. Data also were available on turnover, but since turnover was already below average in the target group, prospective changes in this measure were deemed insignificant.

An educational session was conducted with supervisors, at which they were given the theory and implementing concepts and actually helped to design the job changes themselves. Out of this session came an active plan consisting of about 25 change items that would significantly affect the design of the target jobs.

The Implementing Concepts and the Changes

Because the job as it existed was rather uniformly low on the core job dimensions, all five of the implementing concepts were used in enriching it.

Natural Units of Work. The random batch assignment of work was replaced by assigning to each operator continuing responsibility for certain accounts—either particular departments or particular recurring jobs. Any work for those accounts now always goes to the same operator.

Task Combination. Some planning and controlling functions were combined with the central task of keypunching. In this case, however, these additions can be more suitably discussed under the remaining three implementing concepts.

Client Relationships. Each operator was given several channels of direct contact with clients. The operators, not their assignment clerks, now inspect their documents for correctness and legibility. When problems arise, the operator, not the supervisor, takes them up with the client.

Feedback. In addition to feedback from client contact, the operators were provided with a number of additional sources of data about their performance. The computer department now returns incorrect cards to the operators who punched them, and operators correct their own errors. Each operator also keeps her own file of copies of her errors. These can be reviewed to determine trends in error frequency and types of errors. Each operator receives weekly a computer printout of her errors and productivity, which is sent to her directly, rather than given to her by the supervisor.

Vertical Loading. Besides consulting directly with clients about work questions, operators now have the authority to correct obvious coding errors on their own. Operators may set their own schedules and plan their daily work, as long as they meet schedules. Some competent operators have been given the option of not verifying their work and making their own program changes.

Results of the Trial

The results were dramatic. The number of operators declined from 90 to 60. This occurred partly through attrition and partly through transfer to other departments. Some of the operators were promoted to higher-paying jobs in departments whose cards they had been handling—something that had never occurred before. Some details of the results are given below.

Quantity of Work. The control group, with no job changes made, showed an increase in productivity of 8.1 percent during the trial period. The experimental group showed an increase of 39.6 percent.

Error rates.   To assess work quality, error rates were recorded for about 40 operators in the experimental group. All were experienced, and all had been in their jobs before the job-enrichment program began. For two months before the study, these operators had a collective error rate of 1.53 percent. For two months toward the end of the study, the collective error rate was 0.99 percent. By the end of the study the number of operators with poor performance had dropped from 11.1 percent to 5.5 percent.

Absenteeism.   The experimental group registered a 24.1 percent decline in absences. The control group, by contrast, showed a 29 percent *increase.*

Attitudes Toward the Job.   An attitude survey given at the start of the project showed that the two groups scored about average, and nearly identically, in nine different areas of work satisfaction. At the end of the project the survey was repeated. The control group showed an insignificant 0.5 percent improvement, while the experimental group's overall satisfaction score rose 16.5 percent.

Selective Elimination of Controls.   Demonstrated improvements in operator proficiency permitted them to work with fewer controls. Travelers estimates that the reduction of controls had the same effect as adding seven operators—a saving even beyond the effects of improved productivity and lowered absenteeism.

Role of the Supervisor.   One of the most significant findings in the Travelers experiment was the effect of the changes on the supervisor's job, and thus on the rest of the organization. The operators took on many responsibilities that had been reserved at least to the unit leaders and sometimes to the supervisor. The unit leaders, in turn, assumed some of the day-to-day supervisory functions that had plagued the supervisor. Instead of spending his days supervising the behavior of subordinates and dealing with crises, he was able to devote time to developing feedback systems, setting up work modules and spearheading the enrichment effort—in other words, managing. It should be noted, however, that helping supervisors change their own work activities when their subordinates' jobs have been enriched is itself a challenging task. And if appropriate attention and help are not given to supervisors in such cases, they rapidly can become disaffected—and a job-enrichment "backlash" can result.[7]

SUMMARY

By applying work-measurement standards to the changes wrought by job enrichment—attitude and quality, absenteeism, and selective administration of controls—Travelers was able to estimate the total dollar impact of the project.

[7]E. E. Lawler III, J. R. Hackman, and S. Kaufman, "Effects of Job Redesign: A Field Experiment." *Journal of Applied Social Psychology,* (1973), pp. 49–62.

Actual savings in salaries and machine rental charges during the first year totaled $64,305. Potential savings by further application of the changes were put at $91,937 annually. Thus, by almost any measure used—from the work attitudes of individual employees to dollar savings for the company as a whole—The Travelers test of the job-enrichment strategy proved a success.

CONCLUSIONS

In this article we have presented a new strategy for the redesign of work in general and for job enrichment in particular. The approach has four main characteristics:

1. It is grounded in a basic psychological theory of what motivates people in their work.
2. It emphasizes that planning for job changes should be done on the basis of *data* about the jobs and the people who do them—and a set of diagnostic instruments is provided to collect such data.
3. It provides a set of specific implementing concepts to guide actual job changes, as well as a set of theory-based rules for selecting *which* action steps are likely to be most beneficial in a given situation.
4. The strategy is buttressed by a set of findings showing that the theory holds water, that the diagnostic procedures are practical and informative, and that the implementing concepts can lead to changes that are beneficial both to organizations and to the people who work in them.

We believe that job enrichment is moving beyond the stage where it can be considered "yet another management fad." Instead, it represents a potentially powerful strategy for change that can help organizations achieve their goals for higher quality work—and at the same time further the equally legitimate needs of contemporary employees for a more meaningful work experience. Yet there are pressing questions about job enrichment and its use that remain to be answered.

Prominent among these is the question of employee participation in planning and implementing work redesign. The diagnostic tools and implementing concepts we have presented are neither designed nor intended for use only by management. Rather, our belief is that the effectiveness of job enrichment is likely to be enhanced when the tasks of diagnosing and changing jobs are undertaken *collaboratively* by managing and by the employees whose work will be affected.

Moreover the effects of work redesign on the broader organization remain generally unchartered. Evidence now is accumulating that when jobs are changed, turbulence can appear in the surrounding organization—for example, in supervisory-subordinate relationships, in pay and benefit plans, and so on. Such turbulence can be viewed by management either as a problem with job enrichment, or as an opportunity for further and broader organizational development by teams of managers and employees. To the degree that management takes the latter view, we believe, the oft-espoused goal of achieving basic organizational change through the redesign of work may come increasingly within reach.

The diagnostic tools and implementing concepts we have presented are useful in deciding on and designing basic changes in the jobs themselves. They do not address the broader issues of who plans the changes, how they are carried out, and how they are followed up. The way these broader questions are dealt with, we believe, may determine whether job enrichment will grow up—or whether it will die an early and unfortunate death, like so many other fledgling behavioral-science approaches to organizational change.

APPENDIX

For the algebraically inclined, the Motivating Potential Score is computed as follows:

$$MPS = \left[\frac{\text{Skill variety} + \text{Task identity} + \text{Task significance}}{3} \times \text{Autonomy} + \text{Feedback} \right]$$

It should be noted that in some cases the MPS score can be *too* high for positive job satisfaction and effective performance—in effect overstimulating the person who holds the job. This paper focuses on jobs which are toward the low end of the scale—and which potentially can be improved through job enrichment.

Acknowledgements. The authors acknowledge with great appreciation the editorial assistance of John Hickey in the preparation of this paper, and the help of Kenneth Brousseau, Daniel Feldman, and Linda Frank in collecting the data that are summarized here. The research activities reported were supported in part by the Organizational Effectiveness Research Program of the Office of Naval Research, and the Manpower Administration of the U.S. Department of Labor, both through contracts to Yale University.

DEMING'S REDEFINITION OF MANAGEMENT

Myron Tribus

Recent publications in the *Harvard Business Review* and the popular press have indicated American management practices as the principal reason behind America's decline in international competitiveness. The problem seems to lie in the self-image of managers. Everyone, of course, has an image of what his or her job requires. People need self-images; they help them decide how to behave in different cir-

Source: Reprinted from Massachusetts Institute of Technology Center for Advanced Engineering Study.

cumstances. It seems that many managers do not have images that correspond to their true responsibilities.

I was inspired to this line of inquiry by a conversation with Dr. W. Edwards Deming, well known for his contributions to Japanese productivity and quality of manufacture. I asked him, "Suppose I were the president of a major corporation and I became convinced of the superiority of your methods. What would you advise me to do, if I warranted to take advantage of them, starting tomorrow?"

Dr. Deming leaned forward, looked me straight in the eye in his unique way, and said: "Oh! You want someone to explain your job to you, is that it?"

Subsequently, I went to the library to look for definitions of the manager's job. A great deal has been written about management, but very few authors have defined the job operationally.

Many people define the manager's job something like this: The manager has to see that everything gets done that should be done and prevent things that shouldn't happen from happening. More succinctly, Harry Truman had a small sign on his desk that said, "The Buck Stops Here." That description is accurate, for in the end the manager is responsible for everything that goes on in his or her domain. Such broad definitions are not useful.

A more useful approach is to ask: "What are the essential responsibilities that a manager may not delegate?" These responsibilities define the core of the manager's job.

Dr. Deming has prepared a list containing fourteen points, which, in his experience, are essential to quality and productivity and cannot be delegated by a manager. This paper starts from Dr. Deming's fourteen points (although not in the order he gives). It is only a beginning on the task of defining the job of a manager. At the end I shall return to the question of what needs to be done to complete the definition. Deming's points are discussed extensively in his new book, *Quality, Productivity, and Competitive Position,* and several of his publications.

PROVIDE CONTINUITY
AND CONSISTENCY OF PURPOSE

No one but the manager can set the goals and aspirations of the organization. Sometimes it is said, "We have to decide what business we are in." This is not enough. The manager must decide what kind of organization the company is to become. The manager must articulate the goals and strategies of the company in such a way that the public, the employees, the vendors, and the customers understand what to expect from the company.

At the entrance to the Newport News Shipyards there stood a sign:

"We shall build great ships.
At a profit if we can
At a loss if we must
but we shall build great ships."

When the shipyard was purchased by a conglomerate, the sign was removed with the statement: "We do not intend to build at a loss." Later the sign was restored.

The manager who removed the sign articulated the goals of the company. But managers should realize that the goals will be interpreted by the workers at all levels and will determine how they behave. Goals that invite the workers to cut corners will not lead to high-quality, competitive products.

The manager's behavior sets the style for others to follow. Only the manager can decide if the performance of the organization is satisfactory. Only the manager can make the decision to improve it.

The manager must not only articulate a purpose for the organization. The manager must also do whatever is required to ensure that the purpose is followed with integrity, altering it as circumstances dictate.

The statement of purpose must be credible, operational, and inspirational. It should provide a basis for everyone in the organization to want to work for a common purpose.

Two executives stand out in my mind as examples of the two extremes. The late Joe Wilson, founder of the Xerox Corporation, was extraordinarily able in setting forth what he wanted the company to be. His death led to a discontinuity in this ability, which, in my opinion, has led to some of the difficulties experienced by that organization today.

At the other extreme, I recall a CEO who made the following statement to an assembly of his managers:

"Never forget, gentlemen: The purpose of this company is to make money."

Not only is such a statement inadequate as a guide to decision making, it is an invitation to everyone to put his or her own career aspirations first, to jump ship at the earliest good opportunity, and to look outside the company for life's nonmonetary rewards. It is inadequate because it does not address the question, Are profits today more important than in the future? How are the employees to regard the company's future competitive position?

This way of providing guidance to a company can have unfortunate consequences, some of which have been discussed elsewhere.

DETERMINE THAT EVERYONE IN THE ORGANIZATION UNDERSTANDS WHAT THE CUSTOMERS WANT

The manager may delegate to someone in the organization the marketing function and the task of gathering information about customer preferences, marketability, and so forth. But no one else can see that the results of such studies are diffused throughout the organization and actually put to use. Only the manager can judge if the information provided is appropriate and appropriately used.

Too many managers think of the system for which they are responsible as operation in a *linear fashion*:

DESIGN IT   MAKE IT   TRY TO SELL IT

A more accurate image of how the system should work is taken from computer programming. The manager should think of the system as being in an endless *DO LOOP*:

START: DESIGN IT
          MAKE IT
          TEST IT
          SELL IT
          TEST IT IN THE MARKETPLACE
          FIND OUT WHAT THE CUSTOMERS WANT
          GO TO START

The manager must be *involved in these judgments.* They cannot be delegated.

IMPROVE THE QUALITY OF THE OUTPUT OF THE SYSTEM

This is probably the most misunderstood aspect of the manager's job in America today.

The workers work *in* a system. The job of the manager is to work *on* the system, to improve it and thereby to improve the quality of the output and decrease its cost. The quality of the output is determined by:

The quality of the inputs
    The information
    The materials
    The supplies
    The delivery
    The storage
    The handling

The design and operation of the system
    The relation between engineering and manufacturing
    The relation between sales and manufacturing
    The relation between purchasing and manufacturing
    The relation between marketing and engineering
    In short:
    The relations among all parts of the system

The training and education of all employees
    On-the-job training
    Supervisory training
    Professional training

Statistical control of quality
    Inspection methods
    Feedback and control for quality
    Materials acceptability

Many of these aspects may be delegated, of course, but only the manager can take the responsibility to *harmonize* the activities of the different parts of the system. Only the manager can judge the adequacy of the answers to such questions as these:

Are the specifications to the purchasing department adequate? Is the reward system for purchasing agents driving them to the lowest bidder regardless of quality? Are the purchased materials, instruments, supplies always the best for the job? Why not?

Is the information on which product specifications are based adequate? If the information is inadequate, who should take action? If the information is inadequate, who knows and acts?

One of the more common errors is to confuse quality of product with quality of process. It is often possible to obtain a high-quality product from a low-quality process, just by inspecting thoroughly enough and rejecting enough of the output. Of course, costs will rise under such a system. On the other hand, a high-quality *process* will produce high-quality output at a lower cost simply because there will be fewer delays, less rework, less wasted human effort, less wasted space, and less wasted material. In a high-quality *process* everything works right the first time. The work goes smoothly and productivity rises; not just the productivity of labor but also of capital and of management.

Another error is to fail to distinguish between high technology products and high technology production processes. In the manufacture of tissue paper, to cite an obviously low technology *product,* the manufacturing equipment of successfully competing companies will be of very high quality and technology. To compete in a market in which the cost of the raw material is a substantial fraction of the cost of the finished product, it is essential to run it efficiently, with statistical quality control. Otherwise the productivity of the capital investment will be too low to compete.

Unfortunately, this confusion between quality of product and quality of process causes many managers to believe that higher quality means higher cost. In their search for cost savings, they often indulge in false economies. It is especially unfortunate when the manager can say, truthfully, "We have no complaints on the quality of our product." The issue is quality of *process,* not quality of *product.*

The worst case of all is when it is said, "People have always complained about that."

ENSURE THAT EVERYONE IN THE COMPANY, FROM THE CHAIRMAN OF THE BOARD TO THE LOWEST LEVEL EMPLOYEE, UNDERSTANDS STATISTICAL REASONING AND CAN USE ELEMENTARY STATISTICS

Of all Dr. Deming's points, this one is the most resisted at first and endorsed most solidly in the end.

"Those who fear sin the most,
are those who have the least acquaintance with it."
                                   Anon.

Modern systems of people and machines used for production, sales, distribution, and managing are subject to many disturbances. Any quantity that can be measured in connection with these processes will be found to vary. These variations combine in ways that can only be described and understood through the use of statistics.

It should go without saying that managerial decisions should be based on valid, relevant *data*. Managers, and all who are involved with gathering, discussing, and deciding on data, should be able to reason statistically. Is the drop in sales this month meaningful? With what is it to be correlated? Is the sudden increase in orders attributable to the new advertising or the weather? Is the increase in orders sufficient basis for working an extra shift? What faith shall we put into a proposed correlation between defects and material purchased from a vendor who swears he is not at fault? People who do not understand even how to *discuss* such issues are a menace in these systems. Understanding variation is at the very heart of understanding the application of statistics to business.

Consider, for example, the related problems of inventory control, number of employees, and getting orders out on time. When an order is filled, each part of the organization will estimate the time required. This time estimate will be set at a level that gives a reasonable probability for meeting it. Just how much cushion is included will depend very much on the penalties for failure and the rewards for success.

For a delivery to occur "on time," the following events must each occur "on time":

The order must be written up—on time.
The items to be made must be described—on time.
Materials must be ordered—on time.
Materials must be delivered—on time.
Instructions to the workers must be given—on time.
Machines must be ready—on time.
Workers must be ready—on time.
Parts must be inspected—on time.
The completed system must be inspected—on time.
The system must be packaged for shipment—on time.
The product must be delivered—on time.

If the product is to be produced on time, each step should be done on time. Unless each job is watched over very carefully and priorities in each department changed on a daily basis, if the probability of achieving the schedule at each stage is 0.95, for the eleven steps taken together the probability that the schedule will be met is:

$$(0.95)^{11} = 0.57$$

If each organization sets its own schedule at a more comfortable level, one in which 99 percent of the tasks are done on time, the probability of completing the entire task on time still only rises to 0.89.

If the quality of the process is defined to include the ability to meet schedules, it is clear why increasing the quality of the process reduces cost. The gains from getting control over the time of the process are much greater than indicated by just the throughput.

Inventory, floor space, record keeping, conferences of people spending time to fix things up are all reduced.

The essence of gaining such control is understanding the *statistics of variation*. No company could afford the army of statisticians it would take to study, in fine detail, all of the industrial processes of a company. Even if such an army were available, it could not possibly persuade the workers to adopt the changes that would be suggested from an analysis done by "outsiders." On the other hand, if the workers are themselves part of the observing team and participants in the analysis of the data, both the cost of observation and of implementation will be reduced. Managers must first be instilled with the belief that current levels of variation are unacceptable, and they can and must be substantially improved.

Too many people believe that these ideas apply only to the factory floor. But, as Lester Thurow keeps pointing out, the factory floor employs fewer and fewer workers and their productivity is a constant source of inquiry. On average the productivity of American factory workers is higher than the workers in Japan, though the Japanese are said to be gaining. Where we have a disadvantage is in the size of the office staff used to support the factory. Unless the productivity of these workers is addressed, the overall productivity of the organization will not increase. The concepts of statistical quality control used to increase productivity have been applied to banks, for example. They may be used in the service industries as well as factories. As economists, such as Lester Thurow, keep pointing out, the work force is now more engaged in the production of services than of goods. Since it is goods we export, the inefficiencies in the service sector are added to the cost of what we sell. Therefore, the most rewarding applications of these ideas are likely to be in administrative areas.

The level of statistics that needs to be taught to the workers is not high. Based on Japanese and American experience, it probably will suffice if *everyone* understands the following statistical techniques:

1. How to read and construct a histogram.
2. How to read a process flow chart.
3. How to construct an Ishekawa ("fishbone") chart.
4. How to understand a Pareto chart.
5. How to read x-bar and R-bar charts.
6. Scatter plots (correlating x and y).

Each of these techniques may be taught in a short time, as part of on-the-job problem solving. Of course, these elementary tools are not enough. They should be supported by higher level abilities from consulting statisticians, either in-house or from outside.

INVITE EMPLOYEES TO BE PARTNERS
IN SYSTEM IMPROVEMENT

Although the manager is responsible for the improvement of the *system*, the job cannot be done by the manager alone. To the extent that everyone in the organization understands statistical reasoning, the manager can make everyone else in the system a partner in the improvement process. The responsibility to observe and gather data can be delegated to the lowest possible levels. Suggestions for improvements will result, and where they can be adopted at the lower levels, the manager should install procedures to allow people at these levels to implement them. But the manager must remain involved in the process because proposed changes will often involve procedures that cut across departmental lines. If the tools for the job are inadequate or the materials are inappropriate, purchasing may need to change its policies or practices.

The workers are *in* the system. They can observe it and propose changes. Only the manager works *on* the system and can judge and implement the changes.

Improvements will not come without management involvement. They will be made on a project-by-project basis. Management must provide leadership or the workers will not be able to participate. When the workers discover "common causes" (as Dr. Deming calls those causes of defects that are in the system itself), they will need the help of management to remove them. And only the managers can initiate those actions that reveal the special causes, in which workers may need more training or better supervision.

There are many benefits that flow from this responsibility. The modern movement toward "quality of work life" improvements fall naturally into place. But most of all, it will be possible to reach the record-breaking productivities that have been achieved only if the manager involves the employees as partners in improving the system, and not just the work.

REPLACE MASS INSPECTION
WITH QUALITY CONTROL

Only the manager can make the policy decision to place responsibility for quality on the workers and not on an army of inspectors. Sometimes, of course, there are legal requirements for inspection, as in some aspects of federal procurement. Wherever it is possible to do so, the inspection procedure should be delegated to the workers involved with the product, and they should be trained to carry out this function.

This philosophy should extend from purchasing through manufacturing, sales, delivery, and maintenance. It should be applied in the office as well. The office is already a complex system of people and machines. It, too, can be improved by this approach.

If everyone waits until something has gone wrong, the time to figure out what went wrong and how to fix it will be excessive and expensive. If time is spent seeing that things do not go wrong, time will not have to be spent fixing things. It is that simple.

Quality control procedures require a deeper understanding of each and every step of an industrial process. To commit to statistical quality control in place of mass inspection is to begin a never-ending search for improvement. Ultimately it will involve everyone in the observation and measurement of the statistical variations of the work under their control.

The first benefits will be the transfer of inspectors to the work force, the reduction of wasted effort, improved quality, and greater productivity.

MAKE CONTINUOUS IMPROVEMENTS A GOAL OF THE COMPANY STOP USING NUMERICAL TARGETS AND SLOGANS TO "MOTIVATE" THE WORKERS

This is probably the hardest practice for American managers to give up. American managers are habituated to using slogans ("Zero Defects") and to "negotiating" performance improvements ("Managing by Objectives"). It appears heretical to suggest that the practice is itself counterproductive.

The technique does not bear up under scrutiny, however. As every soldier knows, the only target to which one should make a commitment is one that is clearly attainable. And once attained, it will be foolish to exceed it. Next time demands will be raised.

The reason most managers seem to like these methods is that they have an air of crispness and authority about them that sets the boss apart from the worker. "I gave my people tough targets, and by God, they met them. Shows what they can do when you put the pressure on."

"I did my part. I set a goal. Now you do your part and meet it."

The output of a system is just that, the output of a system. Very few activities are entirely under the control of the workers in the system. The manager is (or should be) part of the system, not apart from it.

The slogan "Zero Defects" has no meaning for people searching out and correcting causes of defects. In general the people do not cause defects. The system causes them. Management can remove them; sloganeering cannot.

TEACH THE EMPLOYEES TO BE PROBLEM SOLVERS: SET AN EXAMPLE

The manager should be able to identify the barriers to quality improvement (and cost reduction—they amount to the same thing). The manager cannot do this alone and should teach subordinates to help with this process. This means the manager must be capable of being a "problem finder" and "problem solver" and teaching others how to define and solve problems. A good manager knows how to interpret statistical information to determine when the solution is to be sought in design of the product, maintenance, machines for production, training for workers, testing, materials handling, shipping, records keeping, marketing, sales, order handling, inventory control, or information systems. Possibilities for improvement exist in all of these activities (and more) and in the interfaces between them.

One of the important side benefits from teaching everyone to be a "problem finder and solver" (at their level) is that the organization becomes ready for innovation. As Utterback has shown, as an industry matures, its production processes tend to become fixed. There is greater and greater commitment to fixed hardware, fixed choices of materials, fixed procedures, fixed organizations, fixed processes, practices, and protocols. Everyone settles into a routine, bureaucracies are formed. When circumstances force a change, everyone resists.

On the other hand, if the organization is *habituated* to the constant search for improvement, for better ways, it will be much less resistant to the introduction of new ideas. Such a major cultural change in an organization takes years. Do not expect results overnight. It took the Japanese twenty to thirty years.

INSTITUTE TRAINING: EVALUATE THE ADEQUACY OF TRAINING

All too often workers are presumed adequately trained if no one complains. On the other hand, it may also be mistakenly assumed that more training is needed when in fact the process is not in control. In such cases the added training may not accomplish anything worthwhile.

Modern methods of training involve evaluation as well as instruction. This means determining:

> If the workers understand how the characteristics of their output affect customer satisfaction and company cost.
> If the workers can use statistical methods at the appropriate level.
> If the workers understand the technology they are using (welding, glueing, machining, measuring, word processing, and so on)
> If the workers are able to work together in groups.
> If the workers are capable problem solvers.

Modern methods are aimed not at sorting out the "good" from the "bad" and setting pay rates but rather at finding out whether additional training would be beneficial, and if so, of what kind.

ESTABLISH A "QUALITY PHILOSOPHY"

Only the manager can decide what level of quality is adequate.

In the emerging era of international competition, the levels of performance of products will be continually raised. Consumers will not accept defective workmanship, unsuited materials, poor maintenance, unreliability, delays, mistakes in handling and order filling, and unresponsiveness. Organizations that do not meet this challenge will simply disappear.

Everyone in the organization must believe that the management is devoted to quality, or the organization will not produce quality output. Cost cutting in maintenance as a way to bolster a quarterly dividend will send an unmistakable message throughout the organization.

It takes time to build quality habits into an organization. It takes education and training. It takes managerial example. The concept must be translated into action at every level of the organization. The example must flow through the various levels of management. Therefore the top management must be involved in training the intermediate and lower levels of management and in seeing the reward mechanisms (promotions and salary) are consistent with this objective.

Because so many American managers neglect this responsibility in favor of the quarterly dividend, it will be an especially difficult challenge to change their habits. In my judgment we should learn to recognize their approach to management for what it is: *bad management.*

Why some boards of directors pay such huge salaries to executives who obviously, by their words and actions, have no interest in this part of their responsibilities is, for me, one of the great dilemmas of our time.

The workers must feel that they are in a genuine partnership with the management in the quest of high quality.

STOP THE PRACTICE OF BUYING FROM THE LOWEST BIDDER

The practice of purchasing from the lowest bidder as a means to stimulate competition among vendors is destructive to the quest for high quality. Only the manager can investigate and change these practices, for the behavior of the purchasing agents is determined by the reward system within which they work.

Purchasing agents should purchase on quality as well as price. Quality can be judged by examining the statistical quality control charts that should accompany every purchase. Such charts show the variability in the manufacturing process and therefore give an indication of how suited the purchased goods will be to the production process into which they go. This information should be the basis for joint discussions involving the vendor, manufacturing, engineering, and, on some occasions, the research staff (and often the company statistician) seeking opportunities for improvement. A smaller number of vendors involved in a cooperative effort to reduce costs and improve quality is much better than a swarm of vendors intent only on reducing costs and with no long-term interest in the success of the purchaser.

DRIVE OUT FEAR

If the workers believe that increased productivity means they will be fired, they will certainly resist productivity increases. Not until the company is demonstrably on the verge of bankruptcy will they accept changes. The only way for the management to enlist the workers' help will be to form a genuine partnership in which everyone—workers, supervisors, managers—everyone has the same job security. Only the management can determine the priority it attaches to responsibilities to its four constituencies:

The stockholders
The customers
The public
The workers

In my opinion, the responsibilities should be in this order:

The public
The workers
The customers
The stockholders

The order in which these are regulated will be understood from the actions of management, and the workers will react accordingly.

The manager should strive toward a method of pay and rewards that helps the workers identify with the prosperity of the company. They should not only be unafraid of improving productivity, they should see, in a tangible way, how it benefits them.

CONCLUSION

In my opinion it is time to define anew what we mean by "good management." The idea that management is to be judged from the quarterly or even the annual bottom line is too simplistic. It represents an abdication of responsibility. Chrysler's problems this year were laid down a decade ago, when the bottom line looked quite favorable. The whole system of rewards for executives needs to be reconsidered. Ideas like Thurow's who suggests that retirement benefits for executives should be keyed to profits *after* retirement deserves careful consideration. The rewards will reflect how well we think they are doing their jobs, and this calls for better definitions than we now have. I believe that most executives would welcome a change in the system, which rewards them for building something that has a good chance of outlasting them, and to their credit.

Today, under the pressure of Japanese competition, we can sense in American managers a renewed interest in productivity and quality. It is said in many quarters that not only must American managers change their ways, they must also change their attitudes, especially toward labor. Today's managers come mostly from colleges and universities and do not have experience on the factory floor. Nor do they often have experience at the lowest levels of the firm and the people who work there. The ultimate levels of quality and productivity will be achieved only by people who know how to work as a team, and that means having respect for one another. Years of adversarial relations must now be overcome, and this will require new initiatives on the part of leaders of both management and labor. It begins with a new respect for one another. But in the end, respect will not be enough.

The degree of trust and confidence required for people to participate in productivity and quality improvements requires more than mere trust. It requires caring and genuine affection. This may be the hardest change in self-image required. America may have to wait for a new generation of managers, for those who grew up and became successful under the old rules may not be able to change. Time is precious. Those who can make the transition should be helped to do so, now.

20
Managing Change

STRATEGIES FOR LARGE SYSTEM CHANGE
Richard Beckhard

MANAGING THE HUMAN SIDE OF CHANGE
Rosabeth Moss Kanter

RULES OF THUMB FOR CHANGE AGENTS
Herbert A. Shepard

STRATEGIES FOR LARGE SYSTEM CHANGE

Richard Beckhard

INTRODUCTION

The focus of this article is on assisting large organization change through consultative or training interventions. As used below, "client" refers to an organization's leader(s) and "consultant" refers to the intervenor or change facilitator. Note that the consultant can come from within or from outside the organization.

Intervention is defined here as behavior which affects the *ongoing social processes* of a system. These processes include:

1. Interaction between individuals.
2. Interaction between groups.

Source: Reprinted by permission of the author and publisher from *Sloan Management Review,* Winter 1975.

This article is adapted from a chapter by the author in *Laboratory Method of Changing and Learning,* Benne, Bradford, Gibb, and Lippitt, editors, Spring 1975 from Science and Behavior Books, Palo Alto, California.

3. The procedures used for transmitting information, making decisions, planning actions, and setting goals.
4. The strategies and policies guiding the system, the norms, or the unwritten ground rules or values of the system.
5. The attitudes of people toward work, the organization, authority, and social values.
6. The distribution of effort within the system. Interventions can affect any one or several of these processes.

The first part of this article describes a model of diagnosis and strategy planning which has had high utility for the author during the past several years. The second part examines a number of actual strategies in organization and large system change and the issues of where to begin change and how to maintain change.[1]

A MODEL FOR CHANGE PLANNING

The following model is far from perfect. However, its use seems to enable one to ask the "right" questions and to obtain answers that yield a basis for relatively trustworthy judgment on early interventions into the large system. For convenience the model will be discussed under four headings.

Defining the Change Problem

When a change effort is initiated, either the client and/or the consultant, or some other part of the system has determined that there is some need for change. An initial diagnostic step concerns analyzing what these needs are and whether they are shared in different parts of the system. For example, let us suppose top management in an organization sees as a major need the improvement of the supervisory behavior of middle management and, simultaneously, the personnel staff in the organization sees as a *prior* need a change in the behavior of the top management and a change in the reward system. These are two very different perceptions of the priority of need for initial change, but a common perception that there is a need for change in the organization does exist. As a part of determining the need for change, it is also useful to collect some information from various parts of the system in order to determine the strength of the need.

There are two distinct ways of defining the change problem. The first considers the *organization* change needed or desired. For example, does the need concern changing the state of morale, the way work is done, the communication system, the reporting system, the structure or location of the decision making, the effectiveness of the top team, the relationships between levels, the way goals are set, or something else? The second considers what *type* of change is desired and what the hierarchy or rank-ordering of these types is. One should ask whether the primary initial change requires a change:

---

[1]For a more detailed explanation of the author's views concerning organization development and intervention, see Beckhard [1].

663

1. Of attitudes? Whose?
2. Of behavior? By whom and to what?
3. Of knowledge and understanding? Where?
4. Of organization procedures? Where?
5. Of practices and ways of work?

Rank-ordering the various types of change helps to determine which early interventions are most appropriate.

Having defined the change problem or problems from the viewpoint of both organizational change and change process, one can look at the organization system and subsystems to determine which are primarily related to the particular problem. The appropriate systems may be the organizational hierarchy, may be pieces of it, may be systems both inside and outside of the formal structure, or may be some parts of the formal structure and not other parts. A conscious identification of those parts of the total system which primarily affect or are affected by the particular change helps to reduce the number of subsystems to be considered and also helps to clarify directions for early intervention.

Determining Readiness and Capability for Change

Readiness as stated here means either attitudinal or motivational energy concerning the change. Capability means the physical, financial, or organizational capacity to make the change. These are separate but interdependent variables.

In determining readiness for change, there is a formula developed by David Gleicher of Arthur D. Little that is particularly helpful. The formula can be described mathematically as $C = (abd) > x$, where C = change, a = level of dissatisfaction with the status quo, b = clear or understood desired state, d = practical first steps toward a desired state, and x = "cost" of changing. In other words, for change to be possible and for commitment to occur there has to be enough dissatisfaction with the current state of affairs to mobilize energy toward change. There also has to be some fairly clear conception of what the state of affairs would be if and when the change were successful. Of course, a desired state needs to be consistent with the values and priorities of the client system. There also needs to be some client awareness of practical first steps, or starting points, toward the desired state.

An early diagnosis by the consultant of which of these conditions does not exist, or does not exist in high strength, may provide direct clues concerning where to put early intervention energy. For example, if most of the system is not really dissatisfied with the present state of things, then early interventions may well need to aim toward increasing the level of dissatisfaction. On the other hand, there may be plenty of dissatisfaction with the present state, but no clear picture of what a desired state might be. In this case, early interventions might be aimed at getting strategic parts of the organization to define the ideal or desired state. If both of these conditions exist but practical first steps are missing, then early intervention strategy may well be to pick some subsystem, e.g., the top unit or a couple of experimental groups, and to begin improvement activities.

The following case illustrates these ideas. A general manager was concerned that the line managers were not making good use of the resources of the staff specialists. He felt that the specialists were not aggressive enough in offering their help. He had a practical first step in mind: send the staff out to visit the units on a systematic basis and have them report to him after their visits. The manager sent a memo to all staff and line heads announcing the plan. Staff went to the field and had a variety of experiences, mostly frustrating. The general manager got very busy on other priorities and did not hold his planned follow-up meetings. After one round of visits, the staff stopped its visits except in rare cases. Things returned to normal. An analysis showed that the general manager's real level of dissatisfaction with the previous state of affairs was not high enough to cause him to invest personal energy in follow-up reporting, so the change did not last.

Capability as defined here is frequently but not always outside of personal control. For example, a personnel or training manager may be ready to initiate a management development program but have low capability for doing it because he has no funds or support. The president of an organization may have only moderate or low readiness to start a management development program but may have very high capability because he can allocate the necessary resources. Two subordinates in an organization may be equally ready and motivated towards some change in their own functioning or leadership skills. One may have reached the ceiling of his capabilities and the other may not. Looking at this variable is an important guideline in determining interventions.

Identifying the Consultant's Own
Resources and Motivation for the Change

In addition to defining the client and system status, and determining with the client the rank-ordering of change priorities, it is necessary for the consultant to be clear with himself and with the client about what knowledge and skills he brings to the problems and what knowledge and skills he does not have. One of the results of the early dependency on a consultant, particularly if the first interventions are seen as helpful or if his reputation is good, is to transfer the expertise of the consultant in a particular field to others in which his competence to help just is not there.

Concerning motivations, one of the fundamental choices that the consultant must make in intervening in any system is when to be an advocate and when to be a methodologist. The values of the consultant and the values of the system and their congruence or incongruence come together around this point. The choice of whether to work with the client, whether to try to influence the client toward the consultant's value system, or whether to take an active or passive role is a function of the decision that is made concerning advocacy vs. methodology.

This is not an absolute decision that, once made at the beginning of a relationship, holds firm throughout a change effort. Rather, it is a choice that is made daily around the multitude of interventions throughout a change effort. The choice is not always the same. It is helpful to the relationship and to the change effort if the results of the choice are known to the client as well as to the consultant.

Determining the Intermediate Change
Strategy and Goals

Once change problems and change goals are defined, it is important to look at intermediate objectives if enough positive tension and energy toward change are to be maintained. For example, let us suppose that a change goal is to have all of the work teams in an organization consciously looking at their own functioning and systematically setting work priorities and improvement priorities on a regular basis. An intermediate goal might be to have developed within the various divisions or sections of the organization at least one team per unit by a certain time. These *intermediate* change goals provide a target and a measuring point en route to a larger change objective.

One other set of diagnostic questions concerns looking at the subsystems again in terms of:

1. Readiness of each system to be influenced by the consultant and/or entry client.
2. Accessibility of each of the subsystems to the consultant or entry client.
3. Linkage of each of the subsystems to the total system or organization.

To return to the earlier illustration concerning a management development program, let us suppose that the personnel director was highly vulnerable to influence by the consultant and highly accessible to the consultant but had low linkage to the organization, and that the president was much less vulnerable to influence by the consultant and the entry client, here the training manager. Then the question would be who should sign the announcement of the program to line management. The correct answer is not necessarily the president with his higher linkage nor the personnel man with his accessibility and commitment. The point is that weighing these three variables helps the consultant and client to make an operational decision based on data. Whether one uses this model or some other, the concept of systematic analysis of a change problem helps develop realistic, practical, and attainable strategy and goals.

INTERVENTION STRATEGIES
IN LARGE SYSTEMS

The kinds of conditions in organizations that tend to need large system interventions will now be examined.

Change in the Relationships
of the Organization to the Environment

The number and complexity of outside demands on organization leaders are increasing at a rapid pace. Environmental organizations, minorities, youth, governments, and consumers exert strong demands on the organization's effort and require organization leaders to focus on creative adaptation to these pressures. The autonomy of organizations is fast becoming a myth. Organization leaders are increasingly recognizing that the institutions they manage are truly *open* systems. Improvement strategies based on looking at the internal structure, decision making, or intergroup relationships exclusively are an incomplete method of organization diagnosis and change strategy. A more relevant method for today's environment is to start by examining how the organization and its key subsystems relate to the different environments with which the organization interfaces. One can then determine what kinds of organization structures, procedures and practices will allow each of the units in the organization to optimize the interface with its different environment. Having identified these, management can turn its energy toward the problems of integration (of standards, rewards, communications systems, etc.) which are consequences of the multiple interfaces.

The concept of differentiation and integration has been developed by Paul Lawrence and Jay Lorsch.[2] In essence, their theory states that within any organization there are very different types of environments and very different types of interfaces with a relatively volatile environment: the market. The production department, on the other hand, interfaces with a relatively stable environment: the technology of production. The kind of organization structure, rewards, work schedules and skills necessary to perform optimally in these two departments is very different. From a definition of what is appropriate for each of these departments, one can organize an ideal, independent structure. Only then can one look at the problems of interface and communication.

Clark, Krone and McWhinney[3] have developed a technology called "Open Systems Planning" which, when used as an intervention, helps the management of an organization to systematically sharpen its mission goals; to look objectively at its present response pattern to demands; to project the likely demand system if no pro-active actions are taken by the organization leadership; to project an "ideal" demand system; to define what activities and behavior would have to be developed for the desired state to exist; and finally to analyze the cost effectiveness of undertaking these activities. Such a planning method serves several purposes:

1. It forces systematic thinking.
2. It forces people to think from outside-in (environment to organization).
3. It forces empathy with other parts of the environment.
4. It forces the facing of today's realities.
5. It forces a systematic plan for priorities in the medium-term future.

This is one example of large system intervention dealing with the organization and its environment. Another type of intervention is a survey of organization structure, work, attitudes and environmental requirements. From this an optimum organization design is developed.

There is an increasing demand for assistance in helping organization leaders with these macro-organization issues. Much current change agent training almost ignores this market need. Major changes in training are called for if OD specialists are to stay organizationally relevant.

[2]See Lawrence and Lorsch [4].
[3]See Krone [3].

Change in Managerial Strategy

Another change program involving behavioral science oriented interventions is a change in the *style* of managing the human resources of the organization. This can occur when top management is changing their assumptions and/or values about people and their motivations. It can occur as a result of new inputs from the environment, such as the loss of a number of key executives or difficulty in recruiting top young people. It can occur as females in the organization demand equal treatment or as the government requires new employment practices. Whatever the causes, once such a change is planned, help is likely to be needed in:

1. Working with the top leaders.
2. Assessing middle management attitudes.
3. Unfreezing old attitudes.
4. Developing credibility down the line.
5. Dealing with interfacing organizations, unions, regulatory agencies, etc.

Help can be provided in organization diagnosis, job design, goal setting, team building, and planning. Style changes particularly need considerable time and patience since perspective is essential and is often lost by the client. Both internal and outside consultants can provide significant leadership in providing perspectives to operating management. Some of the questions about key managers that need answers in planning a change in managerial strategy are:

1. To what degree does the top management encourage influence from other parts of the organization?
2. How do they manage conflict?
3. To what degree do they locate decision making based on where information is located rather than on hierarchical roles?
4. How do they handle the rewards that they control?
5. What kind of feedback systems do they have for getting information about the state of things?

Change in the Organization Structures

One key aspect of healthy and effective organization is that the structures, the formal ways that work is organized, follow and relate to the actual work to be done. In many organizations the structure relates to the authority system: who reports to whom. Most organizations are designed to simplify the structure in order to get clear reporting lines which define the power relationships.

As work becomes more complex, it becomes impossible in any large system to have *one* organization structure that is relevant to all of the kinds of work to be done. The basic organization chart rarely describes the way even the basic work gets done. More and more organization leaders recognize and endorse the reality that organizations actually operate through a variety of structures. In addition to the permanent organization chart, there are project organizations, task forces, and other temporary systems.

To clarify this concept, we examine a case where a firmly fixed organizational structure was a major resistance to getting the required work done. In this particular consumer-based organization there was a marketing organization that was primarily concerned with competing in the market, and a technical subsystem that was primarily concerned with getting packages designed with high quality. Market demands required that the organization get some sample packages of new products into supermarkets as sales promotions. The "rules of the game" were that for a package to be produced it had to go through a very thorough preparation including design and considerable field testing. These standards had been developed for products which were marketed extensively in markets where the company had a very high share. The problem developed around a market in which the company had a very low share and was competing desperately with a number of other strong companies. Because of the overall company rules about packages, the marketing people were unable to get the promotion packages into the stores on time. The result was the loss of an even greater share of the market. The frustration was tremendous and was felt right up to the president.

Within the marketing organization there was a very bright, technically oriented, skilled, abrasive entrepreneurial person, who kept very heavy pressure on the package technical people. He was convinced the he could produce the packages himself within a matter of weeks as opposed to the months that the technical people required. Because of his abrasiveness he produced much tension within the technical department and the tensions between the two departments also increased. At one point the heads of the two departments were on a very "cool" basis. The president of the company was quite concerned at the loss of markets. He had attempted to do something earlier about the situation by giving the marketing entrepreneur a little back room shop in which he could prove his assertions of being able to produce a package in a short time. The man did produce them, but when he took them to the technical people for reproduction, they called up all the traditional ground rules and policies to demonstrate that the package would not work and could not be used.

The client, here the president, had diagnosed the problem as one of noncooperation between departments and particularly between individuals. Based on this diagnosis he asked for some consultative help with the interpersonal problem between the marketing entrepreneur and the people in the technical department. He also thought that an intergroup intervention might be appropriate to increase collaboration between the groups.

The consultant's diagnosis was that although either of these interventions was possible and might, in fact, produce some temporary change in the sense of lowering the heat in the situation, there was little possibility of either event producing more packages. Rather, the change problem was one of an inappropriate structure for managing work.

The consultant suggested that the leaders of marketing and technical development together develop a flow chart of the steps involved in moving from an idea to a finished promotion package. Then they were to isolate those items which clearly fitted within the organization structure, such as the last few steps in the process which were handled by the buying and production department. The remaining steps, it was suggested, needed to be managed by a *temporary* organization created for just that purpose. The consultant proposed that for each new promotion a temporary management organization be set up consisting of one person from packaging, one from marketing, one from purchasing, and one from manufacturing. This organization would have, as its charter, the management of the flow of that product from idea to manufacturing. They would analyze the problem, set a timetable, set the resource requirements and control the flow of work. The resources that they needed were back in the permanent structures, of which they were also members. This task force would report weekly and jointly to the heads of both the technical and marketing departments. The president would withdraw from the problem.

The intervention produced the targeted result: promotion packages became available in one-fifth of the time previously required. The interpersonal difficulties remained for some time but gradually decreased as people were forced to collaborate in getting the job done.

Change in the Ways Work Is Done

This condition is one where there is a special effort to improve the meaningfulness as well as the efficiency of work. Job enrichment programs, work analysis programs, and development of criteria for effectiveness can all be included here. To give an example, an intervention might be to work with a management group helping them examine their recent meeting agendas in order to improve the allocation of work tasks. Specifically, one can get them to make an initial list of those activities and functions that absolutely have to be done by that group functioning as a group. Next, a list can be made of things that are not being done but need to be. A third list can be made of those things that the group is now doing that could be done, even if not so well, by either the same people wearing their functional or other hats, or by other people. Experience has shown that the second two lists tend to balance each other and tend to represent somewhere around 25-30 percent of the total work of such a group. Based on this analysis a replan of work can emerge. It can have significant effects on both attitudes and behavior. The output of such an activity by a group at the top means that work gets reallocated to the next level, and thus a domino effect is set in motion which can result in significant change.

Another illustration concerns an organization-wide change effort to improve both the way work is done and the management of the work. The total staff of this very large organization was about forty thousand people. During a six month period, the total organization met in their work teams with the task of developing the criteria against which that team wanted the performance of their work unit to be measured. Then they located their current performance against those criteria and projected their performance at a date about six months in the future against the same criteria. These criteria and projections were checked with senior management committees in each subsystem. If approved they became the work plan and basis for performance appraisal for that group.

With this one intervention the top management distributed the responsibility for managing the work to the people who were doing the work throughout the organization. The results of this program were a significant increase in productivity, significant cost reductions, and a significant change in attitudes and feelings of ownership among large numbers of employees, many of whom were previously quite dissatisfied with the state of things. Given this participative mode, it is most unlikely that any future management could successfully return to over-centralized control. Much latent energy was released and continues to be used by people all over the organization who feel responsible and appreciated for *their* management of *their* work.

Change in the Reward System

One significant organization problem concerns making the reward system consistent with the work. How often we see organizations in which someone in a staff department spends 90 percent of his time in assisting some line department; yet for his annual review his performance is evaluated solely by the head of this staff department, probably on 10 percent of his work. One result of this is that any smart person behaves in ways that please the individual who most influences his career and other rewards rather than those with whom he is working. Inappropriate reward systems do much to sabotage effective work as well as organization health.

An example of an intervention in this area follows. The vice president of one of the major groups in a very large company was concerned about the lack of motivation by his division general managers toward working with him on planning for the future of the business as a whole. He was equally concerned that the managers were not fully developing their own subordinates. In his opinion, this was blocking the managers' promotions. The vice president had spoken of these concerns many times. His staff had agreed that it was important to change, but their behavior was heavily directed toward maintaining the old priorities: meeting short-term profit goals. This group existed in an organization where the reward system was very clear. The chief executives in any sub-enterprise were accountable for their short-term profits. This was their most important assignment. Division managers knew that if they did not participate actively in future business planning, or if they did not invest energy in the development of subordinates, they would incur the group vice president's displeasure. They also knew, however, that if they did not meet their short-term profit objectives, they probably would not be around. The company had an executive incentive plan in which considerable amounts of bonus money were available to people in the upper ranks for good performance. In trying to find a method for changing his division manager's priorities, the group vice president looked, with consultant help, at the reward system. As a result of this he called his colleagues together and told them, "I thought you'd like to know that in determining your bonus at the next review, I will be using the following formula. You are still 100 percent accountable for your short-term profit goals, but that represents 60 percent of the bonus. Another 25 percent will be my evaluation of your performance as members of this top management planning team. The other 15 percent will be your discernible efforts toward the development of your subordinates." Executive behavior changed dramatically. The reality of the reward system and the desired state were now consistent.

We have examined briefly several types of organization phenomena which need large system oriented interventions. We will now look at initial interventions and examine some of the choices facing the intervenor.

Early Interventions

There are a number of choices about where to intervene. Several are listed here with the objective of creating a map of possibilities. The list includes:

1. The top team or the top of a system.
2. A pilot project which can have a linkage to the larger system.
3. Ready subsystems: those whose leaders and members are known to be ready for a change.
4. Hurting systems. This is one class of ready system where the environment has caused some acute discomfort in a generally unready system.
5. The rewards system.
6. Experiments: a series of experiments on new ways of organizing or new ways of handling communications.
7. Educational interventions: training programs, outside courses, etc.
8. An organization-wide confrontation meeting, bringing together a variety of parts of the organization, to examine the state of affairs and to make first step plans for improvement.[4]
9. The creation of a critical mass.

The last concept requires some elaboration. It is most difficult for a stable organization to change itself, that is, for the regular structures of the organization to be used for change. Temporary systems are frequently created to accomplish this. As an example, in one very large system, a country, there were a number of agencies involved in training and development for organization leaders. The government provided grants to the agencies for training activities. These grants also provided funds to support the agency staffs for other purposes. Because of this condition each agency was developing programs for the same small clientele. Each agency kept innovations secret from its competitors.

In an attempt to move this competitive state toward a more collaborative one, a small group of people developed a "nonorganization" called the Association for Commercial and Industrial Education. It was a luncheon club. Its rules were the opposite of an ordinary organization's. It could make no group decisions, it distributed no minutes, no one was allowed to take anyone else to lunch, there were no dues, and there were no officers or hierarchy.

In this context it was possible for individuals from the various competing agencies to sit down and talk together about matters of mutual interest. After a couple of years it even became possible to develop a national organization development training project in the form of a four week course which was attended by top line managers and personnel people from all the major economic and social institutions in the country. Only this nonorganization could sponsor such a program. From this program a great many other linkages were developed. Today

---

[4]For one view of this, see Beckhard [2].

there is an entire professional association of collaborating change agents with bases in a variety of institutions, but with the capacity to collaborate around larger national problems.

MAINTAINING CHANGE

To maintain change in a large system it is necessary to have conscious procedures and commitment. Organization change will not be maintained simply because there has been early success. There are a number of interventions which are possible, and many are necessary if a change is to be maintained. Many organizations are living with the effects of successful short-term change results which have not been maintained.

Perhaps the most important single requirement for continued change is a continued feedback and information system that lets people in the organization know the system status in relation to the desired stages. Some feedback systems that are used fairly frequently are:

1. Periodic team meetings to review a team's functioniong and what its next goal priorities should be.
2. Organization sensing meetings in which the top of an organization meets, on a systematic planned basis, with a sample of employees from a variety of different organizational centers in order to keep apprised of the state of the system.
3. Periodic meetings between interdependent units of an organization.
4. Renewal conferences. For example, one company has an annual five-year planning meeting with its top management. Three weeks prior to that meeting the same management group and their wives go to a retreat for two or three days to take a look at themselves, their personal and company priorities, the new forces in the environment, what they need to keep in mind in their upcoming planning, and what has happened in the way they work and in their relationships that needs review before the planning meeting.
5. Performance review on a systematic, goal-directed basis.
6. Periodic visits from outside consultants to keep the organization leaders thinking about the organization's renewal.

There are other possible techniques but this list includes the most commonly used methods of maintaining a change effort in a complex organization.

SUMMARY

In order to help organizations improve their operational effectiveness and system health, we have examined:

1. A model for determining early organization interventions.
2. Some choices of change strategies.
3. Some choices of early interventions.
4. Some choices of strategies for maintaining change.

The focus of this article has been on what the third party, facilitator, consultant, etc., can do as either a consultant, expert, trainer, or coach in helping organization leaders diagnose their own system and plan strategies for development toward a better state. This focus includes process intervention but is not exclusively that. It also includes the skills of system diagnosis, of determining change strategies, or understanding the relationship of organizations to external environments, and of understanding such organization processes and power, reward systems, organizational decision making, information systems, structural designs and planning.

It is the author's experience that the demand for assistance in organizational interventions and large system organization change is increasing at a very fast rate, certainly faster than the growth of resources to meet the demand. As the world shrinks, as there are more multinational organizations, as the interface between government and the private sector and the social sector become more blurred and more overlapping, large system interventions and the technology and skill available to facilitate these will be in increasingly greater demand.

REFERENCES

1. Beckhard, R. *Organization Development: Strategies and Models.* Reading, Mass.: Addison-Wesley, 1969.
2. Beckhard, R. "The Confrontation Meeting." *Harvard Business Review,* March–April 1967.
3. Krone, C. "Open Systems Redesign." In *Theory and Method in Organization Development: An Evolutionary Process,* edited by John Adams. Rosslyn, Va.: NTL Institute, 1974.
4. Lawrence, P. R., and Lorsch, J. W. *Organization and Environment: Managing Differentiation and Integration.* Boston: Harvard Business School, Division of Research, 1967.

MANAGING THE HUMAN SIDE OF CHANGE

Rosabeth Moss Kanter

This is a time of historically unprecedented change for most corporations. The auto and steel industries are in turmoil because of the effects of foreign competition. Financial services are undergoing a revolution. Telecommunications companies are facing profound and dramatic changes because of the breakup of AT&T and greater competition from newly organized long-distance carriers. Health care organizations are under pressure to cut costs and improve services in the face of government regulation and the growth of for-profit hospital chains.

Change, and the need to manage it well, has always been with us. Business

Source: Reprinted from *Managing Change—The Human Dimension,* Goodmeasure, Inc., 1984 with permission of the author and publisher.

life is punctuated by necessary and expected changes: the introduction of new toothpastes, regular store remodelings, changes in information systems, reorganizations of the office staff, announcements of new benefits programs, radical rethinking of the fall product line, or a progression of new senior vice-presidents.

But as common as change is, the people who work in an organization may still not like it. Each of those "routine" changes can be accompanied by tension, stress, squabbling, sabotage, turnover, subtle undermining, behind-the-scenes footdragging, work slowdowns, needless political battles, and a drain on money and time—in short, symptoms of that ever-present bugaboo resistance to change.

If even small and expected changes can be the occasion for decrease in organizational effectiveness, imagine the potential for disaster when organizations try to make big changes, such as developing a new corporate culture, restructuring the business to become more competitive, divesting losing operations and closing facilities, reshuffling product divisions to give them a market orientation, or moving into new sales channels.

Because the pace of change has speeded up, mastering change is increasingly a part of every manager's job. All managers need to know how to guide people through change so that they emerge at the other end with an effective organization. One important key is being able to analyze the reasons people resist change. Pinpointing the source of the resistance makes it possible to see what needs to be done to avoid resistance, or convert it into commitment to change.

As a consulting firm, Goodmeasure has worked with the change-related problems of over a hundred major organizations. We have distilled a list of the ten most common reasons managers encounter resistance to change, and tactics for dealing with each.

1. LOSS OF CONTROL

How people greet a change has to do with whether they feel in control of it or not. Change is exciting when it is done *by us*, threatening when it is done *to us*.

Most people want and need to feel in control of the event around them. Indeed, behind the rise of participative management today is the notion that "ownership" counts in getting commitment to actions, that if people have a chance to participate in decisions, they feel better about them. Even involvement in details is better than noninvolvement. And the more choices that are left to people, the better they feel about the changes. If all actions are imposed upon them from outside, however, they are more likely to resist.

Thus, the more choices we can give people the better they'll feel about the change. But when they feel out of control and powerless, they are likely not only to feel stress, but also to behave in defensive, territorial ways. I proposed in my 1977 *Men and Women of the Corporation* that, in organizations at least, it is *powerlessness* that "corrupts," not power. When people feel powerless, they behave in petty, territorial ways. They become rules-minded, and they are over-controlling, because they're trying to grab hold of some little piece of the world that they *do* control and then overmanage it to death. (One way to reassert control is to resist everyone else's new ideas.) People do funny things when they feel out of control, but giving people chances for involvement can help them feel more committed to the change in question.

2. EXCESS UNCERTAINTY

A second reason people resist change is what I call the "Walking Off A Cliff Blindfolded Problem"—too much uncertainty. Simply not knowing enough about what the next step is going to be or feel like makes comfort impossible. If people don't know where the next step is going to take them, whether it is the organizational equivalent of off a cliff or under a train, change seems dangerous. Then they resist change, because they reason, "It's safer to stay with the devil you know than to commit yourself to the devil you don't."

Managers who do not share enough information with their employees about exactly what is happening at every step of a change process, and about what they anticipate happening next, and about when more information will be coming, make a mistake, because they're likely to meet with a great deal of resistance. Information counts in building commitment to a change, especially step-by-step scenarios with timetables and milestones. Dividing a big change into a number of small steps can help make it seem less risky and threatening. People can focus on one step at a time, but not a leap off the cliff; they know what to do next.

Change requires faith that the new way will indeed be the right way. If the leaders themselves do not appear convinced, then the rest of the people will not budge. Another key to resolving the discomfort of uncertainty is for leaders to demonstrate their commitment to change. Leaders have to be the first over the cliff if they want the people they manage to follow suit. Information, coupled with the leaders' actions to make change seem safer, can convert resistance to commitment.

3. SURPRISE, SURPRISE!

A third reason people resist change is the surprise factor. People are easily shocked by decisions or requests suddenly sprung on them without groundwork or preparation. Their first response to something totally new and unexpected, that they have not had time to prepare for mentally, is resistance.

Companies frequently make this mistake when introducing organizational changes. They wait until all decisions are made, and then spring them on an unsuspecting population. One chemical company that has had to reorganize and frequently lay people off is particularly prone to this error. A manager might come into work one day to find on her desk a list of people she is supposed to inform, immediately, that their jobs are changing or being eliminated. Consequently, that manager starts to wonder whether she is on somebody *else's* list, and she feels so upset by the surprise that her commitment to the organization is reduced. The question, "Why couldn't they trust me enough to even hint that this might happen?" is a legitimate one.

676

Decisions for change can be such a shock that there is no time to assimilate or absorb them, or see what might be good about those changes. All we can do is feel threatened and resist—defend against the new way or undermine it.

Thus, it is important to not only provide employees with information to build a commitment to change, but also to arrange the *timing* of the information's release. Give people advance notice, a warning, and a chance to adjust their thinking.

4. THE "DIFFERENCE" EFFECT

A fourth reason people resist change is the effect of "difference"—the fact that change requires people to become conscious of, and to question, familiar routines and habits.

A great deal of work in organizations is simply habitual. In fact, most of us could not function very well in life if we were not engaged in a high proportion of "mindless" habitual activities—like turning right when you walk down the corridor to work, or handling certain forms, or attending certain meetings. Imagine what it would be like if, every day you went to work, your office was in an entirely different place and the furniture was rearranged. You would stumble around, have trouble finding things, feel uncomfortable, and need to expend an additional amount of physical and emotional energy. This would be exhausting and fatiguing. Indeed, rapidly growing high-technology companies often present people with an approximation of this new-office-every-day nightmare, because the addition of new people and new tasks is ubiquitous, while established routines and habitual procedures are minimal. The overwork syndrome and "burn-out" phenomenon are accordingly common in the industry.

One analogy comes from my work on the introduction of a person who is "different" (an "O") in a group formerly made up of only one kind of person (the "X's"), the theme of Goodmeasure's production, *A Tale of "O."* When a group of X's has been accustomed to doing things a certain way, to having habits and modes of conversation and jokes that are unquestioned, they are threatened by the presence of a person who seems to require operating in a different way. The X's are likely to resist the introduction of the O, because the difference effect makes them start feeling self-conscious, requires that they question even the habitual things that they do, and demands that they think about behavior that used to be taken for granted. The extra effort required to "reprogram" the routines is what causes resistance to the change.

Thus, an important goal in managing change is to minimize or reduce the number of "differences" introduced by the change, leaving as many habits and routines as possible in place. Sometimes managers think they should be doing just the opposite—changing everything else they can think of to symbolize that the core change is really happening. But commitment to change is more likely to occur when the change is not presented as a wild difference but rather as continuous with tradition. Roger Smith, the chairman of General Motors, launched what I consider one of the most revolutionary periods of change in the company's history by invoking not revolution, but tradition: "I'm going to take this company back to the way Alfred Sloan intended it to be managed."

Not only do many people need or prefer familiar routines, they also like familiar surroundings. Maintaining some familiar sights and sounds, the things that make people feel comfortable and at home, is very important in getting employees' commitment to a change.

5. LOSS OF FACE

If accepting a change means admitting that the way things were done in the past was wrong, people are certain to resist. Nobody likes losing face or feeling embarassed in front of their peers. But sometimes making a commitment to a new procedure, product, or program carries with it the implicit assumption that the "old ways" must have been wrong, thereby putting all the adherents of the "old ways" in the uncomfortable position of either looking stupid for their past actions or being forced to defend them—and thereby arguing against any change.

The great sociologist Erving Goffman showed that people would go to great lengths to save face, even engaging in actions contrary to their long-term interest to avoid embarassment.

I have seen a number of new chief executives introduce future strategies in ways that "put down" the preceding strategies, thus making automatic enemies of the members of the group that had formulated and executed them. The rhetoric of their speeches implies that the new way gains strength only in contrast to the failures and flaws of the old way—a kind of Maoist "cultural revolution" mentally in business. "The way we've been managing is terrible," one CEO says routinely. He thus makes it hard for people who lived the old ways to shed them for the new, because to do so is to admit they must have been "terrible" before. While Mao got such confessions, businesses do not.

Instead, commitment to change is ensured when past actions are put in perspective—as the apparently right thing to do then, but now times are different. This way people do not lose face for changing; just the opposite. They look strong and flexible. They have been honored for what they accomplished under the old conditions, even if it is now time to change.

6. CONCERNS ABOUT FUTURE COMPETENCE

Sometimes people resist change because of personal concerns about their future ability to be effective after the change: Can I do it? How will I do it? Will I make it under the new conditions? Do I have the skills to operate in a new way? These concerns may not be expressed out loud, but they can result in finding many reasons why change should be avoided.

In local telephone companies, employees have been told for years that they would be promoted for one set of reasons, and the workers had developed one set of skills and competencies. It is very threatening for many employees to be told that, all of a sudden, the new world demands a new set of competencies, a new set of more market-oriented entrepreneurial skills. Nobody likes to look inadequate. And nobody, especially people who have been around a long time, wants to feel that he or she has to "start over again" in order to feel competent in the organization.

It is essential, when managing a change, to make sure that people *do* feel competent, that there is sufficient education and training available so that people understand what is happening and know that they can master it—that they *can* indeed do what is needed. Positive reinforcement is even more important in managing change than it is in managing routine situations.

In addition to education and training, people also need a chance to practice the new skills or actions without feeling that they are being judged or that they are going to look foolish to their colleagues and peers. They need a chance to get comfortable with new routines or new ways of operating without feeling stupid because they have questions to ask. Unfortunately, many corporations I know have spent a lot of time making executives and managers feel stupid if they have questions; they're the ones that are supposed to have the *answers*.

We have to be sensitive enough to the management of change to make sure that nobody feels stupid, that everyone can ask questions, and that everybody has a chance to be a learner, to come to feel competent in the new ways.

7. RIPPLE EFFECTS

People may resist change for reasons connected to their own activities. Change does sometimes disrupt other kinds of plans or projects, or even personal and family activities that have nothing to do with the job, and anticipation of those disruptions causes resistance to change.

Changes inevitably send ripples beyond their intended impact. The ripples may also negate promises the organization has made. Plans or activities seemingly unrelated to the core of the change can be very important to people. Effective "change masters" are sensitive to the ripples changes cause. They look for the ripples and introduce the change with *flexibility* so that, for example, people who have children can finish out the school year before relocating, or managers who want to finish a pet project can do so, or departments can go through a transition period rather than facing an abrupt change. That kind of sensitivity helps get people on board and makes them feel committed, rather than resistant, to the change.

8. MORE WORK

One reasonable source of resistance to change is that change is simply *more work*. The effort it takes to manage things under routine circumstances needs to be multiplied when things are changing. Change requires more energy, more time, and greater mental preoccupation.

Members of project teams creating innovation put in a great deal of overtime on their own, because of the demands—and the hire—of creating something new. During the breakup of the Bell System, many managers worked 60 or 70 hour weeks during the process, not seeing their families, simply because of the work involved in moving such a large system from one state to another. And the pattern is repeated in corporation after corporation.

Change does require above-and-beyond effort. It cannot be done automatically, it cannot be done without extra effort, and it takes time. There is ample reason to resist change, if people do not want to put in the effort. They need support and compensation for the extra work of change in order to move from resistance to commitment.

Managers have options for providing that support. They can make sure that families are informed and understanding about the period of extra effort. They can make sure that people are given credit for the effort they are putting in and rewarded for the fact that they are working harder than ever before—rewards ranging from cash bonuses to special trips or celebrations. They can recognize that the extra effort is voluntary and not take it for granted, but thank people by providing recognition, as well as the additional support or facilities or comfort they need. While an employee is working harder, it certainly helps to know that your boss is acknowledging that extra effort and time.

9. PAST RESENTMENTS

The ninth reason people resist change is negative, but it is a reality of organizational life—those cobwebs of the past that get in the way of the future. Anyone who has ever had a gripe against the organization is likely to resist the organization telling them that they now have to do something new.

The conspiracy of silence, that uneasy truce possible as long as everything remains the same and people can avoid confrontations, is broken when you ask for change. Unresolved grievances from the past rise up to entangle and hamper the change effort. One new plant manager at Honeywell was surprised by resistance to a quality-of-work-life program, which he thought the workers would like because of the direct benefits to them. Then he discovered that the workers were still angry at management for failing to get them a quiet air-conditioning system despite years of complaints about summer noise levels in the factory. Until he listened to them and responded to their grievance, he could not get their commitment to his change plans.

Sweeping away the cobwebs of the past is sometimes a necessity for overcoming resistance to change. As long as they remain aggrieved, people will not want to go along with something *we* want. Going forward can thus mean first going back—listening to past resentments and repairing past rifts.

10. SOMETIMES THE THREAT IS REAL

The last reason people resist change is, in many ways, the most reasonable of all: *Sometimes the threat posed by the change is a real one.*

Sometimes a change does create winners and losers. Sometimes people do lose status, clout, or comfort because of the change. It would be naive to imagine otherwise. In fact, managing change well means recognizing its political realities.

The important thing here is to avoid pretense and false promises. If some people *are* going to lose something, they should hear about it early, rather than worrying about it constantly and infecting others with their anxiety or antagonism. And if some people are going to be let go or moved elsewhere, it is more humane to do it fast.

We all know the relief that people feel, even people who are being told the worst, at finally knowing that the thing they have feared is true. Now they can go ahead and plan their life. Thus, if some people are threatened by change because of the realities of their situations, managers should not pretend this is not so. Instead, they should make a clean break or a clean cut—as the first step in change, rather than leaving it to the end.

Of course, we all lose something in change, even the winners. Even those of us who are exhilarated about the opportunity it represents, or who are choosing to participate in a new era that we think is going to be better for our careers, more produtive and technologically exciting, as many of the changes in American corporations promise to be.

Change is never entirely negative; it is also a tremendous opportunity. But even in that opportunity there is some small loss. It can be a loss of the past, a loss of routines, comforts, and traditions that were important, maybe a loss of relationships that became very close over time. Things will not, in fact, be the same any more.

Thus, we all need a chance to let go of the past, to "mourn" it. Rituals of parting help us say goodbye to the people we have been close to, rather than just letting those relationships slip away. "Memorial services," "eulogies," or events to honor the past help us let go. Unfortunately, those kinds of ceremonies and rituals are not legitimate in some companies. Instead, people are in one state, and the next day they have to move to another state without any acknowledgement of the loss that is involved. But things like goodbye parties or file-burning ceremonies or tacking up the company's history on bulletin boards are not just frills or luxuries; they are rituals that make it easier for people to move into the future because their loss is acknowledged and dealt with.

Resistance to change is not irrational; it stems from good and understandable concerns. Managers who can analyze the sources of resistance are in the best position to invent the solutions to it—and to manage change smoothly and effectively.

There may be no skill more important for the challenging times ahead.

RULES OF THUMB FOR CHANGE AGENTS

Herbert A. Shepard

The following aphorisms are not so much bits of advice (although they are stated that way) as things to think about when you are being a change agent, a consultant, an organization or community development practitioner—or when you are just being yourself trying to bring about something that involves other people.

RULE I: STAY ALIVE

This rule counsels against self-sacrifice on behalf of a cause that you do not wish to be your last.

Two exceptionally talented doctoral students came to the conclusion that the routines they had to go through to get their degrees were absurd, and decided they would be untrue to themselves to conform to an absurd system. That sort

Source: Reprinted by permission of the publisher and author from the *OD Practitioner,* December 1984. Organization Development Network, Portland, Oregon.

of reasoning is almost always self-destructive. Besides, their noble gesture in quitting would be unlikely to have any impact whatever on the system they were taking a stand against.

This is not to say that one should never take a stand, or a survival risk. But such risks should be taken as part of a purposeful strategy of change and appropriately timed and targeted. When they are taken under such circumstances, one is very much alive.

But Rule I is much more than a survival rule. The rule means that you should let your whole being be involved in the undertaking. Since most of us have never been in touch with our whole beings, it means a lot of putting together of parts that have been divided, of using internal communications channels that have been closed or were never opened.

Staying alive means loving yourself. Self-disparagement leads to the suppression of potentials, to a win-lose formulation of the world, and to wasting life in defensive maneuvering.

Staying alive means staying in touch with your purpose. It means using your skills, your emotions, your labels and positions, rather than being used by them. It means not being trapped in other people's games. It means turning yourself on and off, rather than being dependent on the situation. It means choosing with a view to the consequences as well as the impulse. It means going with the flow even while swimming against it. It means living in several worlds without being swallowed up in any. It means seeing dilemmas as opportunities for creativity. It means greeting absurdity with laughter while trying to unscramble it. It means capturing the moment in the light of the future. It means seeing the environment through the eyes of your purpose.

RULE II: START WHERE THE SYSTEM IS

This is such ancient wisdom that one might expect its meaning had been fully explored and apprehended. Yet in practice the rule—and the system—are often violated.

The rule implies that one should begin by diagnosing the system. But systems do not necessarily *like* being diagnosed. Even the *term* "diagnosis" may be offensive. And the system may be even less ready for someone who calls himself or herself a "change agent." It is easy for the practitioner to forget that the use of jargon which prevents laymen from understanding the professional mysteries is a hostile act.

Starting where the system is can be called the Empathy Rule. To communicate effectively, to obtain a basis for building sound strategy, the change agent needs to understand how the client sees himself and his situation, and needs to understand the culture of the system. Establishing the required rapport does not mean that the change agent who wants to work in a traditional industrial setting should refrain from growing a beard. It does mean that, if he has a beard, the beard is likely to determine where the client is when they first meet, and the client's curiosity needs to be dealt with. Similarly, the rule does not mean that a female change agent in a male organization should try to act like one of the boys, or that a young change agent should try to act like a senior executive. One thing it does mean is that sometimes where the client is, is wondering where the change agent is.

Rarely is the client in any one place at any one time. That is, s/he may be ready to pursue any of several paths. The task is to walk together on the most promising path.

Even unwitting or accidental violations of the empathy rule can destroy the situation. I lost a client through two violations in one morning. The client group spent a consulting day at my home. They arrived early in the morning, before I had my empathy on. The senior member, seeing a picture of my son in the living-room said, "What do you do with boys with long hair?" I replied thoughtlessly, "I think he's handsome that way." The small chasm thus created between my client and me was widened and deepened later that morning when one of the family tortoises walked through the butter dish.

Sometimes starting where the client is, which sounds both ethically and technically virtuous, can lead to some ethically puzzling situations. Robert Frost* described a situation in which a consultant was so empathic with a king who was unfit to rule that the king discovered his own unfitness and had himself shot, whereupon the consultant became king.

Empathy permits the development of a mutual attachment between client and consultant. The resulting relationship may be one in which their creativities are joined, a mutual growth relationship. But it can also become one in which the client becomes dependent and is manipulated by the consultant. The ethical issues are not associated with starting where the system is, but with how one moves with it.

RULE III: NEVER WORK UPHILL

This is a comprehensive rule, and a number of other rules are corollaries or examples of it. It is an appeal for an organic rather than a mechanistic approach to change, for a collaborative approach to change, for building strength and building on strength. It has a number of implications that bear on the choices the change agent makes about how to use him/herself, and it says something about life.

Corollary 1: Don't Build Hills As You Go

This corollary cautions against working in a way that builds resistance to movement in the direction you have chosen as desirable. For example, a program which has a favorable effect on one portion of a population may have the opposite effect on other portions of the population. Perhaps the commonest error of this kind has been in the employment of T-group training in organizations: turning on the participants and turning off the people who didn't attend, in one easy lesson.

---

*Robert Frost, "How Hard It Is To Keep From Being King When It's in You and in The Situation", *In The Clearing*, pp. 74–84. (New York: Holt, Rinehart and Winston, 1962).

Corollary 2: Work in the Most Promising Arena

The physician-patient relationship is often regarded as analogous to the consultant-client relationship. The results for system change of this analogy can be unfortunate. For example, the organization development consultant is likely to be greeted with delight by executives who see in his specialty the solution to a hopeless situation in an outlying plant. Some organization development consultants have disappeared for years because of the irresistability of such challenges. Others have whiled away their time trying to counteract the Peter Principle by shoring up incompetent managers.

Corollary 3: Build Resources

Don't do anything alone that could be accomplished more easily or more certainly by a team. Don Quixote is not the only change agent whose effectiveness was handicapped by ignoring this rule. The change agent's task is an heroic one, but the need to be a hero does not facilitate team building. As a result, many change agents lose effectiveness by becoming spread too thin. Effectiveness can be enhanced by investing in the development of partners.

Corollary 4: Don't Over-organize

The democratic ideology and theories of participative management that many change agents possess can sometimes interfere with common sense. A year or two ago I offered a course to be taught by graduate students. The course was over-subscribed. It seemed that a data-based process for deciding whom to admit would be desirable, and that participation of the graduate students in the decision would also be desirable. So I sought data from the candidates about themselves, and xeroxed their responses for the graduate students. Then the graduate students and I held a series of meetings. Then the candidates were informed of the decision. In this way we wasted a great deal of time and everyone felt a little worse than if we had used an arbitrary decision rule.

Corollary 5: Don't Argue If You Can't Win

Win-lose strategies are to be avoided because they deepen conflict instead of resolving it. But the change agent should build her/his support constituency as large and deep and strong as possible so that s/he can continue to risk.

Corollary 6: Play God a Little

If the change agent doesn't make the critical value decisions, someone else will be happy to do so. Will a given situation contribute to your fulfillment? Are you creating a better world for yourself and others, or are you keeping a system in operation that should be allowed to die? For example, the public education system is a mess. Does that mean that the change agent is morally obligated to try to improve it, destroy it, or develop a substitute for it? No, not even if he or she knows how. But the change agent does need a value perspective for making choices like that.

RULE IV: INNOVATION REQUIRES A GOOD IDEA, INITIATIVE AND A FEW FRIENDS

Little can be accomplished alone, and the effects of social and cultural forces on individual perception are so distorting that the change agent needs a partner, if only to maintain perspective and purpose.

The quality of the partner is as important as the quality of the idea. Like the change agent, partners must be relatively autonomous people. Persons who are authority-oriented—who need to rebel or need to submit—are not reliable partners: the rebels take the wrong risks and the good soldiers don't take any. And rarely do they command the respect and trust from others that is needed if an innovation is to be supported.

The partners need not be numerous. For example, the engineering staff of a chemical company designed a new process plant using edge-of-the-art technology. The design departed radically from the experience of top management, and they were about to reject it. The engineering chief suggested that the design be reviewed by a distinguished engineering professor. The principal designers were in fact former students of the professor. For this reason he accepted the assignment, charged the company a large fee for reviewing the design (which he did not trouble to examine) and told the management that it was brilliantly conceived and executed. By this means the engineers not only implemented their innovations, but also grew in the esteem of their management.

A change agent experienced in the Washington environment reports that he knows of only one case of successful interdepartmental collaboration in mutually designing, funding and managing a joint project. It was accomplished through the collaboration of himself and three similarly-minded young men, one from each of four agencies. They were friends, and met weekly for lunch. they conceived the project, and planned strategies for implementing it. Each person undertook to interest and influence the relevant key people in his own agency. The four served one another as consultants and helper in influencing opinion and bringing the decision-makers together.

An alternative statement of Rule IV is as follows: Find the people who are ready and able to work, introduce them to one another, and work with them. Perhaps because many change agents have been trained in the helping professions, perhaps because we have all been trained to think bureaucratically, concepts like organization position, representatives or need are likely to guide the change agent's selection of those he or she works with.

A more powerful beginning can sometimes be made by finding those persons in the system whose values are congruent with those of the change agent, who possess vitality and imagination, who are willing to work overtime, and who are eager to learn. Such people are usually glad to have someone like the change agent join in getting something important accomplished, and a careful search is likely to turn up quite a few. In fact, there may be enough of them to accomplish general system change, if they can team up in appropriate ways.

In building such teamwork the change agent's abilities will be fully challenged, as he joins them in establishing conditions for trust and creativity; dealing with their anxieties about being seen as subversive; enhancing their leadership, consulting, problem-solving, diagnosing and innovating skills; and developing appropriate group norms and policies.

RULE V: LOAD EXPERIMENTS FOR SUCCESS

This sounds like counsel to avoid risk taking. But the decision to experiment always entails risk. After that decision has been made, take all precautions.

The rule also sounds scientifically immoral. But whether an experiment produces the expected results depends upon the experimenter's depth of insight into the conditions and processes involved. Of course, what is experimental is what is new to the system; it may or may not be new to the change agent.

Build an umbrella over the experiment. A chemical process plant which was to be shut down because of the inefficiency of its operations undertook a union-management cooperation project to improve efficiency, which involved a modified form of profit-sharing. Such plans were contrary to company policy, but the regional vice president was interested in the experiment, and successfully conceal-ed it from his associates. The experiment was successful; the plant became pro-fitable. But in this case, the umbrella turned out not to be big enough. The plant was shut down anyway.

Use the Hawthorne effect. Even poorly conceived experiments are often made to succeed when the participants feel ownership. And conversely, one of the obstacles to the spread of useful innovations is that the groups to which they are offered do not feel ownership of them.

For example, if the change agent hopes to use experience-based learning as part of his/her strategy, the first persons to be invited should be those who con-sistently turn all their experiences into constructive learning. Similarly, in introduc-ing team development processes into a system, begin with the best functioning team.

Maintain voluntarism. This is not easy to do in systems where invitations are understood to be commands, but nothing vital can be built on such motives as duty, obedience, security-seeking or responsiveness to social pressure.

RULE VI: LIGHT MANY FIRES

Not only does a large, monolithic development or change program have high visi-bility and other qualities of a good target, it also tends to prevent subsystems from feeling ownership of, and consequent commitment to the program.

The meaning of this rule is more orderly than the random prescription—

light many fires—suggests. Any part of a system is the way it is partly because of the way the rest of the system is. To work towards change in one subsystem is to become one more determinant of its performance. Not only is the change agent working uphill, but as soon as he turns his back, other forces in the system will press the subsystem back towards its previous performance mode.

If many interdependent subsystems are catalyzed, and the change agent brings them together to facilitate one another's efforts, the entire system can begin to move.

Understanding patterns of interdependency among subsystems can lead to a strategy of fire-setting. For example, in public school systems, it requires collaboration among politicians, administrators, teachers, parents and students to bring about significant innovation, and active opposition on the part of only one of these groups to prevent it. In parochial school systems, on the other hand, collaboration between the administration and the church can provide a powerful impetus for change in the other groups.

RULE VII: KEEP AN OPTIMISTIC BIAS

Our society grinds along with much polarization and cruelty, and even the helping professions compose their world of grim problems to be "worked through." The change agent is usually flooded with the destructive aspects of the situations he enters. People in most systems are impressed by one another's weaknesses, and stereotype each other with such incompetencies as they can discover.

This rule does not advise ignoring destructive forces. But its positive prescription is that the change agent be especially alert to the constructive forces which are often masked and suppressed in a problem-oriented, envious culture.

People have as great an innate capacity for joy as for resentment, but resentment causes them to overlook opportunities for joy. In a workshop for married couples, a husband and wife were discussing their sexual problem and how hard they were working to solve it. They were not making much progress, since they didn't realize that sex is not a problem, but an opportunity.

Individuals and groups locked in destructive kinds of conflict focus on their differences. The change agent's job is to help them discover and build on their commonalities, so that they will have a foundation of respect and trust which will permit them to use their differences as a source of creativity. The unhappy partners focus on past hurts, and continue to destroy the present and future with them. The change agent's job is to help them change the present so that they will have a new past on which to create a better future.

RULE VIII: CAPTURE THE MOMENT

A good sense of relevance and timing is often treated as though it were a "gift" or "intuition" rather than something that can be learned, something spontaneous rather than something planned. The opposite is nearer the truth. One is more likely to "capture the moment" when everything one has learned is readily available.

Some years ago my wife and I were having a very destructive fight. Our nine-year-old daughter decided to intervene. She put her arms around her mother and asked: "What does Daddy do that bugs you?" She was an attentive audience for the next few minutes while my wife told her, ending in tears. She then put her arms around me: "What does Mommy do that bugs you?", and listened attentively to my response, which also ended in tears. She then went to the record player and put on a favorite love song ("If Ever I Should Leave You"), and left us alone to make up.

The elements of my daughter's intervention had all been learned. They were available to her, and she combined them in a way that could make the moment better.

Perhaps it's our training in linear cause-and-effect thinking and the neglect of our capacities for imagery that makes us so often unable to see the multiple potential of the moment. Entering the situation "blank" is not the answer. One needs to have as many frameworks for seeing and strategies for acting available as possible. But it's not enough to involve only one's head in the situation; one's heart has to get involved too. Cornelia Otis Skinner once said that the first law of the stage is to love your audience. You can love your audience only if you love yourself. If you have relatively full access to your organized experience, to yourself and to the situation, you will capture the moment more often.